The
Blindfold's Eyes

The *B*lindfold's Eyes

My Journey from Torture to Truth

Sister Dianna Ortiz
with Patricia Davis

ORBIS BOOKS
Maryknoll, New York 10545

Founded in 1970, Orbis Books endeavors to publish works that enlighten the mind, nourish the spirit, and challenge the conscience. The publishing arm of the Maryknoll Fathers & Brothers, Orbis seeks to explore the global dimensions of the Christian faith and mission, to invite dialogue with diverse cultures and religious traditions, and to serve the cause of reconciliation and peace. The books published reflect the views of their authors and do not represent the official position of the Maryknoll Society. To learn more about Maryknoll and Orbis Books, please visit our website at www.maryknoll.org.

For additional information on this story and the subject of torture and human rights, see the author's website, www.torture-free-world.org.

Library of Congress Cataloging-in-Publication Data

Ortiz, Dianna.
     The blindfold's eyes : my journey from torture to truth / Dianna Ortiz
with Patricia Davis.
          p.   cm.
     Includes bibliographical references (p.   ).
     ISBN 1-57075-435-7
     1. Ortiz, Dianna. 2. Nuns – Guatemala – Biography. 3. Nuns – United
States – Biography.   I. Davis, Patricia.   II. Title.
BX4705.O7183 A3 2002
272'.9'092–dc21

                                                                      2002008965

For my Woman Friend

CONTENTS

PART III

PREFACE

IN NOVEMBER 1989, while working as a missionary in Guatemala, I was abducted by security forces and taken to a secret torture center in the capital city. So I entered a world from which few return. This book is the result of a promise I made: *I will never forget you. I will tell the world what I have seen and heard.* I spoke to the dead and dying — people not lucky enough to have politicians and journalists flooding the phone lines, outraged about their "disappearance." Outrage in Guatemala in 1989 was a luxury too often reserved for foreigners. Guatemala's president at the time admitted that the security forces carried out almost sixty disappearances a month that year for political reasons; people who were considered threats to the status quo were abducted and tortured at a rate of nearly two a day. The president acknowledged that the majority of the victims were women. After "disappearing," people almost always ended up dead.

But I was different. I was an American. And on that November day in 1989, I escaped with my life. I've tried to honor my promise in the years that have passed, speaking out in various ways. I've filed lawsuits, I've given interviews, I've testified in depth before investigators of six different agencies, and I've held vigils. But this is the first time I've dared to write a book. Although for more than a decade people have been telling me I should write my story, I simply couldn't. I wasn't ready emotionally. Even now, the process of reviewing my life and examining how the torture changed it has been wrenching.

As well as pain, my old friend fear has shadowed me through each stage of this book. Every time I have spoken publicly about what happened to me in that secret prison in Guatemala, I have relived the experience. During the writing process, I have felt more in control — I haven't traveled into those memories and relived them. But the risks in writing are greater — the words are on the page forever. Every answer I gave to the torturers was wrong; they tortured me more. And I learned that my words — even the truth — can betray me.

I'm not alone in that knowledge. As Adrienne Rich, in "North American Time," observes:

I am writing this in a time
when everything we write
will be used against us
or against those we love...
where the context is never given
though you try to explain, over and over.[1]

"Words are found responsible," she says. "All we can do is choose them or choose to remain silent." I don't have the right to be silent. For some reason I survived. I have to let the people who were being tortured beside me know that I haven't forgotten them. And as long as I am alive, I have to use my life to work against the practice of torture. Although I would like to be in the classroom, teaching children, I hope I am making the world safer for them by teaching people about what torture is and what it does.

Maybe I survived simply because I am a U.S. citizen. But because of that very privilege, I have a huge responsibility. The U.S. government funded, trained, and equipped the Guatemalan death squads — my torturers themselves. The United States was the Guatemalan army's partner in a covert war against a small opposition force — a war the United Nations would later declare genocidal. I am answerable for what my country has done and is doing and is likely to do, as the world's only "superpower." I have a responsibility to be vigilant and to speak out.

I am but one of millions worldwide who has ascended from the torture chamber. In that place of unspeakable evil, again I was lucky. I found kindness and community. Another woman reached out to me. She told me to be strong.

I would like with this book to reach over differences in experiences, to reach out and tell whoever might read my words to be strong. A black blindfold holds every wave length in the spectrum of light — holds it and keeps it pressed against the head, as if to say, *Don't forget. Even if you can't see the light, it's there.*

ACKNOWLEDGMENTS

I can't possibly thank everyone whose kindness, love, and generosity have led me to this place in my life and the book that has resulted. But I want to mention my family, who have my greatest thanks for loving me back to life (I love you infinitely!).

I am also deeply grateful to Patricia Davis, whose talent as a writer and poet and whose generosity of time have made this book possible. More than words on paper, she gave me the most precious of all gifts, her lasting friendship. From the moment we began working on this project, she dared to journey with me into the past — a past filled with horror and pain. With compassion, Patricia listened, and when all seemed dark, she helped me to see that underneath the blindfold of darkness and fear there was still veiled light and hope. Quite simply, without Patricia, there would be no book.

I owe a deep debt of gratitude to Sister Alice Zachmann for the long sabbatical while the book was in progress, endless encouragement and support, and unconditional, infinite, healing love. I am also grateful to Mary Fabri, for always being there; to Xepel and Malin, for their faithful commitment to the oppressed peoples of the world; to Vianney, for the countless rides, well-timed snacks, ever-present support, flowers, jokes, and the willingness to help in any way at any time — in short, for being a real friend.

To Robert Ellsberg, all my thanks and admiration. More than an editor, he is a friend and an advocate and his selflessness and dedication to the message of this book have helped restore my faith in men. Production coordinator Catherine Costello and copy editor Hank Schlau rounded out the wonderful, supportive Orbis team.

I am grateful to our agent, David Lubell, for his unbelievable patience, good temper, faith, encouragement, and understanding; to the Mount Saint Joseph Ursulines for supporting me, praying for me and the Guatemalan people, and reintroducing me to Angela and the Ursuline way of life; and to Harold Nelson, for being willing to do any kind of research, giving good advice, being a good listener, a good talker, and a wise, loyal, reliable friend. Joe and Marie also have provided constant, never-failing witness and friendship. I am grateful to Ann Butwell for reading draft after draft, making encouraging remarks and helpful suggestions, and always being available for advice and backrubs. To Jennifer Harbury, many thanks for everything. The members of the Assisi Community have been instrumental and have my gratitude and respect for their witness for truth and justice.

This book would not have been possible without the help and friendship of Naomi Periant, who read various drafts with the sensitivity of a poet, the eye of a novelist, and the dedication and support of a good friend; poets Henry Taylor and Myra Sklarew, at American University, who were kind, caring, and supportive before, during, and after this process; Shelley Summerlin-Long and Ryan Moore, who volunteered countless hours of mind-numbing research, reading, tabbing, and ordering thousands of pages of declassified documents; and Alex and Meredith, for excellent research and constant support and friendship.

Without the Marjorie Kovler Center, I wouldn't be here today. My lawyers, Paul, Shawn, Michele, Anna, and Margaret, were there for me during difficult times. Pat, Juanita, Dennis, and Pat Ashe also have my gratitude, for opening their home to survivors of torture when we had nowhere else to go. I would like to thank Ana C., *mi hermana*, wise healer, and the following survivors for all the healing that knowing them has brought me: Monica, Lourdes, Orlando, Kifa, Munawar, Aisha, Ani, Fekadu, Yanira, Mary, Rigo, Otto and Eloisa, Ileana, Martin, Emmy, Carlos A., Adriana, Kyaw, Julio, Catherine, Leny, Blanca, Maria Luisa and Jorge, Aidatu, Charles, Fahima, Htun, Alisa, Carlos M., Julia, Imbrahima, Gloria, Neris and Jorge, Win, Marta, Richard, Sey Naomie, Elizabeth, Dave, Rosa Pu, Hugo, Mr. Ban, Lisel, Jaime, Darija, Lori, Dr. Mahari, Marine, Kadir, Mehdi and Leyla Zana. I can't mention the names of everyone. From each of you, I draw strength and hope for a better tomorrow. Remember, You're not alone!

I also want to mention Miguel Solís, Ani Pachen, Digna Ochoa, and those who were in the building with me: your spirit lives on. I will forever carry you in my heart.

Lastly, I thank my GOD for always being there, even when I doubted her presence.

Part I

In a dark time, the eye begins to see....

— Theodore Roethke,
"In a Dark Time"

Chapter One

THE DARK

THE MAN WITH THE RAMBO T-SHIRT and the gun and grenade in his jacket grabs my arm. The dark cloth the men tied over my eyes after putting me in the car has left me blind. But I know this man's grip, and as he sinks his fingers into my flesh, he starts to hum — the same song he hummed as he pushed me through the hole in the wall behind the convent and forced me to walk before him along the river. The air outside the car is cold, musty, and there's a tangy, metallic odor I can't identify. The floor when I step out feels like smooth concrete. The men's boots clap across it as we walk, then a door opens. Echoes of sounds I cannot make out shiver in the air. A moist palm grabs my wrist and guides my hand onto something cold. I jerk back. But the hand is on my fist again, prying my fingers open. A slender cylinder is beneath my fingers.

"Escaleras," says a voice. A staircase. My hand is around a banister.

I take a deep breath, and I reach out my foot. I'm descending.

At the bottom of the stairs, the men stop me. I hear the turn of a knob and feel a rush of air. The door shuts behind us.

"Where are you taking me?" I am asking for the third time, but still they are silent.

At the bottom of the stairs, the man releases his grip. The Guate-man, I name him — short for the Guatemala City man. On the sidewalk in Guatemala City a few months ago he took me by the arm, hard, and forced me to walk with him. "Are you a student or a teacher?" he asked. "We know who you are. We know where you live." He even knew my name.

He's speaking to the Policeman now. I can't understand what they're saying. They walk off together and I become aware of other voices. I hear men laughing. Then a man and a woman screaming.

By tilting my head up, I manage to glimpse from beneath my blindfold a pair of dirty, scuffed boots. They belong to the campesino — the dark-skinned man with the matted hair and a bad eye. I can hear him breathing beside me. The other two have left me with him. I can't help but feel a kinship with him, maybe because he's Mayan, like the children I've

3

been teaching in the mountain village of San Miguel, or maybe because, standing next to the Guate-man in the garden this morning, he looked young and slight. He wasn't the one pointing the gun at me and demanding that I go with them. He, too, seemed to be following the Guate-man's orders: he had to run ahead and flag down a bus when we came to the end of the path along the river. And I noticed he didn't have a gun. Alone with him I can pray. Please, God, let this be a dream.

THE CONCRETE FLOOR here is rough and footsteps scrape toward me and I know I'm awake. I hear the rasp of heavy breathing.

A HAND GRABS MY WRIST. The Policeman. I can see the stained blue cuff of his sleeve. He leads me, and we walk what seems a long way. The other men are with us. I can hear their boots echo. The screams are loud now and ricochet off the walls. The skin pulls taut on my face and my hands. Keys jangle, and a lock turns before me. "Welcome to your palace." The Policeman laughs.

I begin to lose control of my knees. "Please, if you let me go, it will be like this never happened. I won't tell anyone."

The Policeman shoves me across the threshold. Someone takes my arm and guides me to a chair. "Sit," he tells me. Through the crack between my face and the blindfold I see a brown hand with chewed nails on my wrist. I obey.

The Policeman's voice is behind me. "José," he says to the campesino. "You're her bodyguard."

The Policeman and the Guate-man leave, slamming the door behind them. The silence that follows shatters my ears. Even the screams have stopped. What seems an eternity passes.

Then I hear José's soft, country lilt beside me.

"Don't be afraid. You should rest. You have a long day ahead of you. I'm going to remove your blindfold. Keep your eyes closed, and don't turn around." I feel his knuckles against my head. "Now I am going to leave you for a while."

I want to beg him not to go, I want to throw myself at his feet. No, I will not let him know how scared I am. I have to think positively and seem to be strong and in control. But I beg. "Please don't turn off the light."

"I have been given orders to keep you in the dark."

And with that, night falls, the door scrapes shut, and locks. The room is pitch black and the silence is white. Panic builds inside me.

I become aware of a buzzing. A fly. It has come to comfort me. It sits on my leg, my head. It buzzes around my face and stays on my hand as I stand up and grope my way through the dark. I pad my palms along the damp stone wall. The stone changes to metal, and I feel a knob. I try to twist the knob both ways. It won't turn. I continue my walk. All is silent except for the fly, whose buzz is as steady as breath.

Drunk with blindness and the thick air, I wobble into the center of the room and collide with a metal desk. I tug the handles — two drawers, both locked. Exhausted, I feel for my chair and fall back into its arms.

A rescuer on a sturdy white horse gallops into the night before me. He leaps through the wall, a Mayan with a bad eye, and sweeps me off the hard chair. Would that be too much to ask, God, when I've devoted my life to you? Or simply a voice at my ear: "I'm sorry, Madre, we made a mistake. You are free to go." Or a holy spark of human mercy in the breast of one of these men. "Madre, you are so young. Whatever you did in San Miguel you did with good intentions. Remember us in your prayers." And then I would emerge into the light and go back to the garden with its scent of dewy grass and wet leaves.

A SCREAM hangs in the air.

"GOD, I DON'T WANT TO DIE," I tell the silence that follows. This morning, before going out to the garden, I prayed with Sister Darleen. I asked for guidance on whether to stay in Guatemala, in spite of the death threats I'd been getting. The military was on a rampage. Students, unionists, priests, nuns, teachers — anyone working for change was viewed as a threat and targeted for repression. I closed my eyes and let the Bible fall open where it would. Then I handed it to Darleen, who read: "Thereupon, Nebuzaradan and the officials and the nobles of Babylon had Jeremiah taken out of the quarters of the guard and entrusted to Gedaliah, son of Ahikam, son of Shaphan, to be brought home. And so he remained among the people."

From that last sentence, I made my decision. I would stay with the people of San Miguel, not cede to fear and flee because I had the passport and the means, luxuries the villagers would always lack. God's will had seemed clear. The Good Shepherd didn't lead his sheep into traps, but took them safely through the valley of death. I shouldn't be afraid.

Jesus didn't have that experience, though. In the Garden of Gethsemani, waiting for the soldiers, he prayed that the cup would be taken from him. It wasn't, and as I start to remember all his followers who died horrible deaths, too, I remember that Jesus prayed a second time in the Garden: *If this cup cannot pass without my drinking from it, let Your will be done.* Chill bumps rise on my back.

I shouldn't be praying for my life. I should have faith in God's will, whatever that might be. I should be praying for the people screaming.

"Your will be done," I say aloud. Like a reward for adopting the right attitude, a hopeful thought strikes me. The people screaming must be Guatemalans. I'm an American.

FOOTSTEPS APPROACH and a key clinks in the door. "Keep your eyes closed. I am going to blindfold you again." It is José. If they were going to kill me, they wouldn't care if I saw their faces.

"MADRE DIANNA." José's voice is in front of me. A chair scrapes on the floor and then creaks with his weight. "Madre, I can save you. I have nothing against you." His voice is soft.

God has answered my prayers. I knew it would be José, the quiet campesino, who would save me.

"They tell me you are a nun. Is that true?" He continues before I can answer. "I go to church every Sunday and read the Holy Bible every day. Since you are a nun, surely you must know if God forgives people for the sins they have committed."

He sighs through my silence and raps on the metal chair. "I don't like my work. But I have a wife. I have children. You understand? Do you know what it's like to see your children go to bed hungry and hear them wake up, throwing up worms? Sometimes we live at the expense of others." He pauses.

"I am going to tell you a story about a village that used to be." He makes a harsh, forced sound he must mean as a laugh. "We were fighting the subversion, you know, up north in the Quiché. The colonel said a village was helping the guerrillas, supplying them with food and troops."

He draws his breath in. "So we gathered all the villagers together in the church. We told them we needed to have a meeting. They all came to the center of the town, and I ordered all the boys between seven and twelve years old to assemble on my right. I gave them each a can of gasoline. I told them to pour it over everything in the village."

The air seems thicker. I start to breathe through my mouth.

"A little boy held onto his mother's skirt and refused to move, and an old man came forward. He said, 'Let me take the boy's place. I'll do it.'

I was the commanding officer. I couldn't allow exceptions. I went over and slammed them both in the head with my rifle butt. The boy's head broke open like a ripe watermelon and his mother shrieked. I said, 'Get to it!' and no one dared disobey. The villagers watched as their sons and grandsons and brothers doused their homes and cornfields.

" 'Cheer up!' I shouted at them. 'Like the sweet little priests, we are only sprinkling your homes and cornfields and animals with Holy Water!' " He laughs again, a hoarse, tight laugh that dies in his throat.

"We took the women to the chapel. I hate to tell you what we did to them."

Tears press against the insides of my eyelids.

"Old women, young girls, very young. Pregnant women." His chair creaks again and for a moment I feel that he is next to me, his breath hot on my skin.

But his voice resumes from its position a few feet away. "Then we brought everyone into the chapel, locked the door, bolted the windows, and set the church on fire. The blaze spread across the entire town."

He stops. Even the fly is quiet. Why is he telling me this?

"We burned the animals, even, the dogs and the donkeys. What I cannot forget are the screams. And the children. The children were crying, 'Mama!' "

I hear a sob. A second later his hands are on my thighs, clinging, his head is on my knees, I feel his tears seeping through my blue jeans. I stiffen against his weight.

"I can still smell it — their flesh burning. It was almost like the stench of burned rubber."

I can smell the charred bodies. I can hear the screams, just like the screams that have echoed through my cell. I feel, behind the dark of my blindfold, that I am in that village, watching.

"I did not want to do it. I have nothing against you, Madre. Can you forgive me? I am your friend. . . . You must forgive me!"

The sudden volume, the desperation, the authority in his voice — I start to shake all over.

"Don't you understand? I had no choice! Please." His voice is soft again, wheedling. "Forgive me, Madre. If you, a nun, can forgive me, maybe God, too, can forgive me."

He wants to buy my forgiveness. If I sell my forgiveness for my freedom . . . If I buy my freedom, forgiving him for what he did to others . . . I don't have the right to do that. He shouldn't be trying to buy it, and I'm not the right person to ask. He wants his actions condoned — his past actions and maybe his current work, too. He will have to ask forgiveness from God and from the people who still writhe and scream in his soul.

I remain quiet. José rests on my knees for a moment, then drags himself up. I feel his stare.

"I am sorry, Madre. I could have saved you. If you had forgiven me, I could have saved you." He scuffs across the concrete and the door slams shut.

Chapter Two

COMING HOME

"YOU'RE HOME NOW, DIANNA," the woman beside me says, nudging me out of my daze. "You're safe." I keep my eyes on the black shapes growing larger outside my window as the plane dips down for the descent. This could be Guatemala — the dark mountains and, below them, lights like swollen stars, constellations burning on the ground.

The woman has been crying since Miami, where she picked up a newspaper as we changed flights. She peels out a section to put into her bag.

Out of the corner of my eye I watch her, leaning my cheek against the curve of the window, letting the cool plastic soothe the bruise. I read the headline, "U.S. Nun Released." I want to tell her it's not true. I wasn't released — I escaped. But it hurts my jaw to talk. Anyway, is it even her business? I barely even know her name. Sister Fran. That's it. I study her tall, slim figure, the flowery skirt, the lined, tanned face. She has referred in the past few hours to San Miguel. She has talked about visiting me there and has asked about the children I taught. I remember nothing before the last forty-eight hours, nothing before the glint of a gun in the morning light and the Guate-man's voice behind me. "Hola, mi Amor. We have some things to discuss."

All I have told any of the other women — the members of my community, I guess — is what they could already see for themselves. I was abducted. They told me they knew that much. Sister Darleen — the only one whose name I remembered — said she found my shawl hanging from the bushes at the back of the retreat center garden. She and a lawyer from the Guatemalan archbishop's office wrote up a statement in Spanish as I relayed the bare minimum of what happened to me, sitting on the bed at the Maryknoll House. Darleen, Fran, and a few of the other sisters saw the cigarette burns on my back, so they know what happened while I was detained — at least that part of it. The statement also, I think, says I was "abused in my dignity as a woman." But no one ever needs to know anything else.

9

I have been experimenting with different ways to sit. When we were over the Gulf of Mexico and the clouds relaxed their grip on the blue, I began to sleep. I must have slumped into the seat — I awoke to fire on my back. So now I have stayed awake, listening not so much to Fran's words as to the modulations of her voice, studying her sharp profile occasionally, the honey tones of her hair, and the dark liner that forms a path above her lashes.

We wait for the other passengers to get off. I have told her not to touch me, and when she lifts her fingers to my elbow to help me stand, she draws her hand back. She's learning. I am not who I seem.

Standing in the aisle, I wrap the strap of my small print bag around my hand. I can't carry it over my shoulder, but around my hand the strap is painless. My wrists are scraped from the rope.

Fran motions for me to stay and starts to walk the other way. "You and Sister Elaine are going out the back way to avoid the press," she says. "Don't worry, Dianna. Going out that way, ya'll won't see any reporters. I'll deal with them. They're a mixed blessing. You probably owe your life to them, really. If the news of your disappearance hadn't been spread so far and wide, you might never have been released."

She catches sight of my face.

"I mean, you might have been disappeared for longer. Longer than twenty-four hours."

Breathe, Dianna. Reporters. Have they gotten the videotape? A man my torturers referred to as "Alejandro" and the *jefe* threatened to release the tape to the press if I didn't "forgive" my torturers. It was a tape the torturers made of me during the most awful moments. And I didn't "forgive" them. I didn't and don't.

Another woman has joined me in the aisle. Tired of memorizing faces, I just notice that she, too, has blond hair. We exit the plane, and the bitter chill shocks me. This is not Guatemala. The sign on the building in front of us says Albuquerque International Airport. I start to veer toward the door of the building, but she stops me. "This way. We're going to see your mom and dad." Mom and Dad. Only the words are familiar. No images come to my mind.

She approaches a police car parked on the runway, puts our suitcases in the trunk, and holds the door open for me.

Adrenaline shoots through my muscles. This time I'll run. But I just stand there, frozen. "Come on, Dianna. It's to avoid the reporters. It's just airport security."

When he turns toward me, the man in front is not the heavy-jowled policeman whose pitted face hung like the moon over my nightmare in Guatemala.

I get in the car and grip the cold metal handle of the door. This time there is no blindfold. This time I have some control. In spite of my bravado, doubt begins to gnaw at the edges of my mind and fear leaves my hands so cold that I lift them to my face and breathe on them when no one is looking.

"Who are you? Where are you taking me?"

The blond woman smiles uneasily and tucks her hair behind her ear. "You've been through a lot, Dianna. I know things are a little cloudy right now. He's the airport security officer. I'm Sister Elaine. I'm your friend."

I'm your friend. That's what José said.

The police car pulls to a halt, and the blond woman ushers me into a small blue Chevrolet. Sister Fran is waiting in the car, along with yet another woman. I soon lose track of the turns to the left and right. I only want to close my eyes, raw from lack of sleep. But I stare at the passing streetlights and try to capture the conversation. None of the words stays in my head long enough for the sense to be clear.

After what seems hours, the car finally slows and then stops in front of a well-lit church. The large cross on top of the building casts a shadow that bends across the sidewalk. Suddenly, I feel almost safe. Thankful for the half-light, I put the palm of my hand on the seat beneath me as I get out. I feel only smooth, dry leather. Good. No one will have to know anything.

The women lead me into an adobe house, through a foyer that smells like fresh bread and lemon cleaner and on into a sitting room, where Fran invites me to make myself at home in a tweed chair. The TV is quiet and dark, but the room is so bright that the pulse pounds in my eyes.

A buzzer jolts me out of my daze, then footsteps ring on the concrete, then they are here, a human herd. A small woman with red, curly hair stands in front, twisting a ring on her finger, and a short man with dark eyes, dark skin, and wavy black hair, streaked in places with gray, clings to her arm. A young man and woman hover behind the couple.

The woman in front falls onto me. "Mi hijita," she chokes — "my daughter" — and breaks into sobs, pressing her fingers into the wounds on my back. I clamber to my feet. Then the man closes in on me. As I try to back up, the seat of the chair hits me just above the knees, and he throws his thick arms around me. A familiar smell on his breath. Cigarettes. I feel the stings again in my back, all over my shoulder blades. I smell my flesh burning. The young man and woman bend toward us and stretch out their hands. Behind them is yet another young woman, stretching out her arms. I am trapped.

Suddenly I am in the corner of the room, watching myself curled under the stack of bodies. These people must be your family, I tell myself. Keep your mouth shut. Pretend to know them.

But why don't I know them? Could they be impostors? Has this been staged by the torturers? Have I finally gone crazy?

If you have, no one must know.

I am back in their arms then, and something inside me is curling up slowly, like paper lit at the edges. Someone's tears are on my cheek.

"My Nana," the red-haired woman says. She smells like green apples, her cheek against my neck. She switches to Spanish. "You've come back."

"Come on, Nana," one of the younger women says, sweeping her palm across the ridge of her cheekbone. "Let's go home."

I COMB THE ROOM for details. On the refrigerator are pictures a young child has made — kernels of corn glued onto red paper cut in the shape of a rose, a snowman made out of popcorn beneath a sky of paper snowflakes. "Amber" is scrawled in big unsteady letters at the bottom of the pages. I trace the white lace tablecloth with the tips of my fingers as I study the walls. Near a calendar, a small white crucifix hangs among wallpaper lilies. I have kept my toes curled in my tennis shoes for the past three days, I realize, as I feel them finally go slack. Since I escaped, everyone's eyes have been on me, full of questions — the papal nuncio, the lawyer from the archbishop's office, the U.S. ambassador, the nuns and friends I am supposed to know. But these people are busy with dinner and seem to think I belong here as much as the table or the chairs.

"Barbara, has Amber eaten? I can make her a tortilla." The small red-haired woman — my mother — is washing jalapeño peppers at the sink.

"She had some macaroni earlier, but she might eat something now," the young woman answers, pulling her long dark curls in front of her shoulder with one hand.

AT DINNER, I choke down a bite of tortilla with salsa. Barbara, Mom, Dad, and Amber, who must be Barbara's child, I guess, from the way Barbara watches over her and tells her to drink her milk, talk among themselves, with only furtive glances at me. Barbara starts to clear the dishes, and I get up to help, relieved to have something to do. As I take his plate, Dad pushes back from the table and reaches for a pack of cigarettes on the counter behind him. He pulls one out and puts it to his lips. A match swishes into flame, then an orange glow burns through the smoke. It moves back and forth from his mouth like a breath.

A HAND is on my shoulder. "Nana." Barbara is standing beside me. "You look exhausted. You need to rest." Barbara guides me down the hall.

"Let me put something on that cut," she says, examining the side of my face. She leaves me in a bedroom and returns with a tube of medicine. Her fingers brush my cheekbone and I wince. "No. I'll do it. Later."

"All right. You do your face. But let me take care of your back."

She wants me to take off my shirt. "Come on, lift up your arms and I'll pull."

I can only look at the floor. I keep my hands folded before me.

"Come on, this will help you. You don't have to take off your shirt, then. Just lift it up. Or if you want, get a towel."

I peer around the corner into the adjoining bathroom. A large pink towel hangs from the shower rod. I go in and shut the door, then emerge with it wrapped around me. "I'm OK. They didn't do anything to me."

She starts first on my upper shoulders. To calm myself as the burns reignite I stare at the photos on the dresser. There's one that must have been me, a young girl in a black and white habit, smiling with excitement. I feel the tears come, scalding the open cut on my cheek.

I start to adjust the towel and it falls to my waist. Barbara gasps. She has seen them — all of the burns. She sits down on the bed. "Oh, my God, Nana. Oh, my God. What have they done to you?" She is crying.

I sit down beside her on the bed and clench my fists, looking at the little half moons my nails leave imprinted in my skin.

Barbara finally wipes her face and says we have to continue with the medicine.

"Just close your eyes and put it all over," I tell her. "Don't look."

"I'm afraid I'll hurt you that way. How about if I look away most of the time and just glance to get my bearings?"

"No."

"Dianna, come on. It's nothing to be ashamed of. What they did to you is not your fault. Hey, I'm trying to help you. I'm your sister, remember? Your favorite older sister. Hey — best friend?" She smiles and puts her fingertips, warm and sticky with ointment, on my hand.

I pull my hand away.

Chapter Three

THE AMERICAN

I REMEMBER LITTLE OF MY LIFE before the age of thirty-one, when I was tortured. Now and then, as I heal, random memories return. Those glimpses, which I could count on my fingers, are all I have of my childhood, my studies at the convent, my early years as a teacher in Kentucky, and my two years in Guatemala. But by talking to people who knew me, I've managed to reconstruct a picture of who I was.

Before I was tortured, pulling away from anyone, especially a member of my family, was something I rarely did. My life centered on being connected to others. In my early years as a nun, I was reprimanded, in fact, for being too close to my family: my religious family was supposed to come first once I had made my final vows. But my parents and sisters and I continued to call and write each other often, and my mother sent care packages as usual, heavy with jars of salsa and other Mexican food unobtainable in Maple Mount, Kentucky, a tiny, rural community a couple of hours' drive from the Indiana border. I had lived there since I was seventeen, bearing homesickness and culture shock with the support of my family and my friends at the convent, like Alicia, who took me to her family's home for the holidays when I couldn't afford to fly to New Mexico. I toughed it out because I was sure of my vocation.

According to my family, I received my calling early on. My dad when I was little went around the dinner table, asking each of us what we wanted to do, and I piped up that I wanted to be a nun. I was six years old. From that day on, my family tells me, I was resolute. According to Barbara, in junior high and high school, other girls would tease me, crossing themselves when I walked by. When junior year came, and other students at my public school were talking about careers and colleges, I went to visit a sister I had seen at church who was the principal of the local Catholic school. She happened to be an Ursuline, and the Ursuline mother house, or U.S. headquarters, happened to be in Kentucky. I asked her how I could become a nun, and she invited me to visit Mount St. Joseph, the convent in Maple Mount. I went to the girls' school there for my senior year, then on to Brescia, a Catholic college in nearby Owensboro, where I received an education degree.

My junior year in college, I requested to make temporary vows. I was devout and eager. But by all counts, I was also naive. And I was sent out instead to gain more life experience. I lived with a few older sisters in a nearby town, talking to them at night about their lives and working by day in a daycare center. In working with the children I discovered that teaching was my passion.

Unfortunately, I had a certain brand of religious naïveté that my year of teaching didn't resolve. A companion of mine, Sister Larraine, told me that every time I got in the car, she would insist that I put my seat belt on, and I would refuse, with an argument that drove her mad: "Jesus will take care of me." For my feast day I chose the feast of the Good Shepherd, Jesus as a careful and conscientious tender of the flock.

I suppose when I went to San Miguel, I felt called to emulate the Good Shepherd, tending to the needs of the villagers. Meanwhile, I assumed I was under His care.

I've been told I was interested in missionary work from the very beginning of my time at Mount St. Joseph (or "the Mount," as we called our convent and mother house). I talked to Luisa, an older sister who had worked in Chile, and I visited the mission there before the Ursulines closed it. Working in another culture drew me, perhaps because as a Hispanic I believed that every culture had its own richness and wisdom. I also welcomed the opportunity to learn more about the Hispanic culture, including the Spanish language. My parents, who were both Mexican immigrants, spoke Spanish to each other at times but spoke English to us to make sure we would learn it. As a consequence, like many Chicanas, I could understand some Spanish, but I never learned to speak it. I wanted above all to work with the poor. We were given instruction in all aspects of the Church's work and all current theological interpretations. Liberation theology — the idea that the Church should be involved in helping the oppressed and the poor move toward justice and equality — especially piqued my interest. During a meeting with the parents of kindergartners I was teaching in Kentucky, I showed a film on poverty in the Third World, and I had my five-year-olds writing letters on human rights issues to President Reagan. My nickname there was "the radical teacher."

My nicknames at Mount St. Joseph had nothing to do with politics. The other sisters affectionately called me The Prima Donna and Lady Di. The sisters teased me for my modesty. And I was persnickety about little things. I kept my clothes perfectly ironed, I held my pinkies out when I ate (my pinkies just stick out naturally), and I made a fuss each week when we had to take the laundry from the infirmary, which housed around a hundred elderly and ill sisters, to the big washing machines across the grounds. Week after week, I would pick the sheets up by the very corners, hold them as far away from myself as possible, and say, "Oo yuck, oo yuck, oo yuck. Yuck, yuck, yuck." The other sisters were more stoic.

FROM LETTERS I WROTE while I was in Guatemala, I know how much I longed to stay connected to my friends in Kentucky, and especially to Nancy, my spiritual director:

September 19, 1987

Hola Nancy!

Como está usted? Yo soy muy perfectamente! Well, dear, what do you think of my Spanish thus far? Yes, I'm doing well but also experiencing homesickness. Nancy, we finally arrived in Guatemala City. Maureen and I left Texas on Monday evening and arrived in Mexico City the next afternoon and immediately caught a bus to Guatemala. So far, our trip has taken us 44 ½ hours. Although the journey has been long and tiresome, I have met many interesting people and I'm also becoming more courageous when it comes to speaking the Spanish language. On our journey to Guatemala I met several men and women and we tried to converse with each other. At one point, the air conditioner on the bus was not working and the heat was simply unbearable. I asked one of the fellows a question in Spanish. In my mind I was asking him if he was finding the heat unbearable. Little did I realize that I asked him if he had the "hots." Nancy, I'm sure you can imagine how embarrassed I was.... If that wasn't bad enough, I walked into the men's bathroom. I'm learning to let go of my pride and perfection; and in the midst of that, I'm learning how to *laugh*, really *laugh* at myself.

Since we have been in Guatemala City, Maureen and I have been working on getting our visas. This process is *so* complicated. Anyhow, I managed to get my *foto* (photograph) and find my way back to Casa Benito on my own! I excitedly said to the others: "otra victoria" (another victory). The victories are small but treasured. Nancy, it's strange. The faces of the many children that I have taught flash through my mind as I quietly ponder the beauty of these small victories. Jesus is so good!

Several Franciscan sisters from Maureen's community are visiting us this weekend. They are stationed in El Salvador. It's been great to meet lots of missionaries. Perhaps seeing them together is what causes me to experience a little bit of homesickness. I do *miss* you and all our sisters, but I'm more convinced that God is calling me to live with the Guatemalan people in a lifestyle consistent with their mode of life. I eagerly await the day when we arrive in San Miguel Acatán.

I have heard numerous stories of the political situation in Guatemala, some not so pleasant. A three-year-old child was killed several weeks ago and that really hit the core of my very being. It's hard to understand why an innocent child's life is destroyed. One can see the fear in the eyes of the people. Nancy, I wonder if this fear will ever cease to exist? It's very important that fear does not control the person, but how can that be when fear permeates the lives of innocent victims? I'm finding myself asking too many questions. Someone told me to be extremely careful not to ask these questions to the wrong people. Who are the wrong people? Life sure can be complicated and can often appear to be bleak. Many of the people are faith-filled and believe that every aspect of life in Guatemala will improve in time. As they so beautifully say, "God is alive and walking with us on our journey of faith."

Take good care of yourself and know that you are often in my thoughts and prayers!

Cariño,
Lady Di

I also wanted to connect with the people of San Miguel. That process was a slow one. The people were careful and mistrustful. Mimi, an Ursuline who had worked in Chile before moving on to San Miguel, told me Chileans wear their feelings on their sleeves — they tell you exactly what is going on — whereas the Migueleños would tell a story about some horrible event and give you the impression that it happened a long time ago. Then you'd find out that it happened the year before. The people in San Miguel, who were almost completely indigenous, had no reason to be open. For five hundred years they had been betrayed by the visiting foreigners.

According to Mimi and other sisters, when I first arrived in San Miguel, the people there told me, "Everyone who has come here has left us."

They were referring to missionary priests of the Maryknoll order, who had started a clinic, a furniture and rug-making cooperative, and a school there in the 1940s. Although the clinic and a bit of the cooperative were still functioning four decades later, the school had closed in the mid-1970s, with the spiraling violence of the civil war. Churches were closing all over the Guatemalan countryside at the height of the war. Priests and other religious workers were hunted down and assassinated by the army, which saw them as communist sympathizers and allies of the guerrillas because of their work among the poor. A few years later, as soon as conditions allowed, two members of the School Sisters of Notre Dame traveled to San Miguel to teach the children and run the clinic. The nuns realized that the people of San Miguel desperately needed help. The literacy rate in the village was one in ten. Nearly 80 percent of the children under five were malnourished, and one of every ten infants died. In those respects, San Miguel was a typical Mayan village. The sisters stayed for several years, but in 1980, one had to leave to have surgery, and the other took a leave also, to avoid the danger of remaining unaccompanied in the village. By the time they were ready to return, the fighting was too intense. They never went back.

"You're not going to abandon us, too, are you?" the villagers asked me. "No," I said. "I will never leave you."

February 8, 1988

Dear Nancy,

I've been in San Miguel for two months and much has happened during this short period.

Upon entering the town of San Miguel, one is surrounded and of course greeted by women and men, and yes, numerous children who are as lively as squirrels. Some speak Spanish but the main language is a dialect K'anjobal. There are presently more women than men, many widows and women whose husbands or sons have had to leave the country. Those who remained in San Miguel have survived the bombings, massacres, and harassment from both the military and the guerrillas.

The children of San Miguel are precious. I started meeting with a group of youngsters (ages nine to twelve) on a regular basis. It's like teaching five grades at one time. I had sixteen students on the first day and since then the enrollment has doubled. Basically, we are concentrating on learning skills needed prior to first grade, e.g., recognizing letters, sounds, numbers, cutting, writing, etc. Mind you, most of the instruction is done in Spanish. Sometimes the language is a barrier for the children. Most of them speak K'anjobal, but I have one twelve-year-old boy who understands Spanish fairly well so he translates for me. Starting on Saturday, I'll have a helper on a regular basis. Her name is Elena and she's a gem! She speaks both Spanish and K'anjobal so she'll be able to translate for me. Nevertheless, I'm trying to memorize a few phrases in their language. I've been practicing the following phrases: Today we are going to learn to recognize the letter B (Ja tinanik hoj cu cui jun letra spi B). The next phrase is much more difficult than the above: Today I'm going to read you a story in Spanish, then Elena will translate it in K'anjobal (Tinanik hoj baa leer an jun historia yin castilla y ix Elena hoj ix yin ha ti bejo). Now Nancy, let me hear you repeat that phrase! That's what I call a tongue twister!

I'm really not focusing my attention on learning K'anjobal. I think learning Spanish is a challenge in itself. Working with the youngsters is of greater importance. Today I think more about what I can learn from the children and the people of San Miguel, and less of what I think I can teach them or offer them. They open my eyes to the riches that they have to offer in spite of their youth, in spite of their circumstances!

One of our major concerns in San Miguel is the return of Guatemalan refugees who fled their homeland during the violence and who now reside in refugee camps in Mexico. Many of them want to return to their homeland but are reluctant. The reasons for this reluctance are very clear. Thirty years of military rule has left that Guatemalan countryside in shambles. Despite earnest assurances by the Cerezo government, the refugees' safety is still very much in doubt. We, the people of San Miguel, and the Church on the diocesan level are trying to formulate a plan in which we can reach out to our brothers and sisters.

Living in the midst of a people who have suffered tremendously and who continue to be victimized by the powerful is causing me to have a conversion of heart — many of my so-called precious values are not as important as they were in the past. I don't understand the mystery of this conversion. But I do know that it is one way of being in solidarity with the poor and oppressed of our world.

As far as community is concerned, I would have to say that we have an ideal setting. At times I marvel at the wisdom that Mimi and Darleen have developed through the years. Maureen and I have lots to learn from them and they in turn have lots to learn from our youthful spirits and ideas.

We usually start off our day by praying together. We reflect on the daily readings or whatever comes to our minds/hearts. Nancy,

I feel like I'm really learning how to pray! If that makes any sense at all...

We work with two priests, Efraín and David. They are responsible for six parishes plus all the neighboring *aldeas*. They have their hands full!!

Nancy, it seems like I have said enough for the time being. Know that I think of you daily and keep you in my prayers. Also, I'm still praying that you will be able to visit us sometime. Take care and may you continue to draw strength and trust from the One that wills us to live in peace!

You are loved —
Ki'laa
Dianna

It seemed that everyone in San Miguel Acatán had a relative, friend, or acquaintance who had been disappeared or murdered. From 1979 to 1981, seven massacres took place in the area. People in San Miguel told this story: the military came in and said to several women, "Make tortillas for us. If you don't, you'll be killed." So the women made tortillas for the army. Then the guerrillas came in and cut the women's heads off. I wanted to do anything I could to help the people rebuild their lives.

In spite of my nicknames at the Mount and my reputation for being easily grossed out, in San Miguel nothing was too hard for me. Mimi, Maureen, and Darleen said I was in my honeymoon period. Darleen wrote letters home complaining that the mattresses were as hard as boards when we slept at houses of parishioners in neighboring villages. I raved about everything except the head lice. Once I got over the disgust, though, I realized I had shared in what the villagers experienced regularly, and I had been blessed with one more link to them.

No wonder I was happy. I was doing exactly what I wanted. Fran remembers visiting my classroom and finding sixty kids who had been in public school all day still working as hard as they could. Some of the children were at the blackboard, some were in a corner with clay, some were at their seats doing puzzles I had made. One girl was sitting by herself, reading a book. Fran went over to her to hear her read. The girl straightened her back, blushed with pride, and read.

When my torturers interrogated me, they showed me photographs of myself during my first week in San Miguel. I realized then that I'd been under surveillance since my arrival two years earlier. Mimi, Darleen, and Maureen, I'm sure, were also photographed and monitored. All of us were considered possible subversives. Although in 1986 a civilian president had been elected in Guatemala, following decades of military rule, the army was still firmly in control, and the Church was still suspect. At the Second Vatican Council (1962–65) and the meeting of the Latin American bishops in Medellín, Colombia, in 1968, the Church made a commitment to work toward social justice on behalf of the excluded, poor, and underprivileged. The Guatemalan army, accordingly, "considered Catholics to be allies of the guerrillas," as Guatemala's truth commission would find years later, "and therefore part of the internal enemy, subject to persecution, death, or expulsion."[1] The bishops in Guatemala, in spite of the risks, spoke out on behalf of the poor. In 1988, they issued a joint pastoral letter criticizing the unjust distribution of land, an act which exposed them to more attacks and suspicion: land reform was one of the chief aims of the guerrillas' struggle. But the Church in Guatemala knew that conditions had to change. Ninety percent of the population lived in poverty, over half in extreme poverty. Although more than 65 percent of the population was Mayan, a wealthy minority of European descent ruled the country in a system of virtual apartheid. Two percent of the population owned two-thirds of the land.

Religious workers not only came into the range of the army's counterinsurgency strategy by trying to improve the lives of the poor; they also helped strengthen Mayan cultural and community ties, since the Catholic Church was often the social center of Mayan villages. In the army's view, Mayans were natural allies of the guerrillas, and the Mayan people, their cultural identity, and whatever helped them maintain it should be wiped out.[2]

I had no idea that teaching the children to write in K'anjobal could be seen as subversive. And then there are the musings about the human rights situation that I included in my letters home. I didn't know mail was routinely opened and read; Guatemala was no longer ruled by a military dictator. Even if I had known that mail was inspected by military intelligence officers, I wouldn't have thought that reporting the latest human rights violations would get me into any trouble.

Tuesday morning, June 6, 1988

Dear Nancy,

I'm writing this letter at four-thirty in the morning. Thirty minutes ago we had what they call a "guerrilla scare." *Bombas* were set off and whistles were blown to call all the men from town and our neighboring *aldeas* to gather at once in the main square. Mimi says this is probably the work of the commanders and there are no guerrillas in the area. Another scheme created by the commanders to exert their power.

I'm looking out my window as I'm writing this note. Although it's dark, I can clearly see men with sticks in their hands. Dogs barking and mules braying, and in the far distance a crying child can be heard.

Right now a group of men are headed toward the river. It's difficult to say how many men make up the group. Spoken words can be heard; due to the distance and the sound of the wind, I am unable to decipher what is being said. What are the thoughts and feelings that are going through the minds of the people?

Since the *golpe* — the military attempt to overthrow the present Cerezo government, which occurred a month ago — our pueblo has been permeated with a gigantic cloud of fear! So many rumors are floating around and the tension is so thick that it could be cut with a knife. After this guerrilla scare, the people will be even more frightened.

Nancy, please tell me why the poor are constant victims of oppression. Why is it that God permits oppressive people and structures to manipulate the poor and keep them from knowing true liberation? I know God should not be held responsible for the wrongdoings or actions of the world — but why can't God intervene and do something? So many questions and few answers. How difficult it is to be a people of faith in times of darkness — in times of oppression. Life is indeed a living hope of promise and pain! I'm going to end this note now. Simply had the desire to talk to and with you — this letter is the closest means of communication. Let us pray for each other, that God will teach us, the poor, and those who are constant victims of oppression how to be people of faith in times of darkness!

Hope you are doing well and are enjoying your summer vacation.

Adios
Dianna

The next year brought only new questions. In January, I began receiving death threats.

January 29, 1989

Dear Nancy,

During the past several weeks I have found myself attending courses, community meetings, visiting *aldeas,* and praying with people who are sick and some who believe they are being possessed by

demons. In addition, we have one crisis after another, e.g. boys rob-
bing girls; men beating their wives; problems with alcohol; people
going North, and the list goes on. There must be a full moon out or
something in the air that's bringing to birth all of the above. These
past few weeks have been overwhelming.

Just today, the *zona militar* sent orders to the *comandantes* to
proceed with their annual round-up — where they force young men
between the ages 18–25 into military service. Unfortunately, areas
where poor and indigenous people live are the prime target for these
round-ups. Several young boys who are quite active were taken by
force — but later released! Maureen and I went to talk to the *jefe*
(the man in charge) about this ordeal. According to the Guatemalan
law, they do not have the right to force young boys (who have not
reached the prime age of 18) into military service; nor do they have
the right to come to the pueblo and just pull young boys off the street.

I must be learning to become more assertive; I'm not so sure if
this is good or bad. I asked the *jefe* if these round-ups were done in
all the pueblos. He was reluctant to give me a direct answer and said
it was a common practice. I proceeded to ask him if this procedure
was a common practice in Ladino communities. He didn't respond
to my question and became *bravo* (angry). In case you're interested,
Ladinos would not put up with this type of treatment. Because they
are more educated they know the law and are able to stand up for
their rights. Nancy, it's so disgusting, our people are so afraid to stand
up for their rights and are once again being taken advantage of. No
one seems to do anything — a few complain but the majority quietly
sit back and allow the system to oppress them. This sounds terrible
for me to say, it's like the road is being paved for more oppression!
I suppose it's much easier for me to be critical of the system and to
express my views than it would be for an indigenous of Guatemala.
Since I am a "gringa" I'm supposedly safe. Who knows?

Nancy, I would like to share something with you — I received an
anonymous letter stating, "You are going to die in this country —
return to your country." (It was written in Spanish.) I received this
note a short time after Mimi left to the States for her home visit.
I shared this note with Efraín (our priest) and the others — We
think it might be the *comandante*, or someone playing a joke. Dear
old Jiménez, the sacristan, thinks it was written by someone who
is trying to protect me. He seems to have such a positive attitude
towards life in general. I wouldn't mind having such an attitude.

Back to the note, I haven't allowed it to upset me nor interfere with my work. In fact, I had forgotten all about it, that is, until today. This morning's encounter with the round-ups has sort of made me feel uneasy. I do not fear for my life; I just don't want to bring harm to our people. Perhaps I better learn to keep my opinions to myself. Please don't worry about me.

Blessings of peace
Dianna

Attempts to intimidate us were nothing new. As Mimi recalls:

There was this guy in the town who was always accusing the Church of being communist and subversive. He was with the military, working for them. Before you started getting the threats, the bishop got an anonymous letter about us, saying we were having undercover meetings with the guerrillas in the parish. I feel sure there were either guerrillas or guerrilla sympathizers in the area, just like there were military spies. We had youth meetings, music meetings, and catechetical meetings, which were open to the public. We never discussed what side anyone was for because that wasn't the topic of the meetings, and besides, anyone with guerrilla connections or sympathies would have been secretive about them. We could have met with people who were guerrillas — and we wouldn't have known it.

But now, I was being singled out. And it didn't make sense. Maureen had returned to the United States for health reasons, leaving only three of us, and Mimi and Darleen were older, more experienced, and much more outspoken than I was. They worked with the teenagers and adults and were teaching them about human rights and their rights under Guatemalan law. I was only working with the children, teaching basic literacy. Mimi and Darleen had had many more run-ins with the mayor and the military than I'd ever had. They were the more logical targets. But things were changing in Guatemala, including the army's strategy. The human rights situation had to appear to be improving. The guerrilla umbrella organization, known as the Guatemalan National Revolutionary Unity (URNG), had won international support for a negotiated settlement to the civil war. Oscar Arias, the president of Costa Rica, was interested in helping the URNG and the army reach a peace accord to end the war, which had lasted nearly thirty years, and the URNG had also approached the United Nations about mediating a possible dialogue. The space for the government to avoid peace negotiations was closing, and the government realized that it would have to fight a political and public relations battle on the international stage.

The Guatemalan army, as a consequence, changed its tactics. With the government under an international spotlight, "selective violence" became its new modus operandi. Mimi and Darleen and I were confused about why I was targeted — we had no inkling that the army had devised a new strategy. But the U.S. ambassador to Guatemala, Thomas Stroock, explained the strategy in a later declassified analysis he sent to Secretary of State James Baker:

> That the victims are generally unknown in wider society means a more muted reaction both locally and abroad; it makes the question "why?" more difficult to answer and many nonpolitical explanations, e.g., common crime, can plausibly be put forward to explain the victimization of a relatively anonymous person. While the victims are not figures of wide renown, they are well known within the small groups comprising the left. The bolt-from-the-blue strike against one of their members causes a ripple of terror to go through those groups ("He wasn't even the most important one in our group; if they are willing to get him, nobody is safe!") forcing many members into hiding or exile or at least into abandoning whatever immediate project the group had.[3]

Under the old schema, Mimi or Darleen would have been the more likely target. I might have stayed on in San Miguel if Mimi or Darleen had been abducted, reasoning that I was safe, since my work was only with children. But by targeting me, the army wiped out the whole missionary program.

April 11, 1989

Dear Nancy,

Thanks so much for your letter. As usual, it was good to hear from you. Once again, thanks for bringing joy into my life.

Nancy, I'm getting along fairly well. But since my last letter to you, I have received two other anonymous letters! The person who is writing these letters is evidently trying to convey the same message — "do not walk alone, someone wants to rape/kill you." I've been so busy during this month that I haven't had time to let the notes upset me! Life goes on.

The people in our pueblo and *aldeas* have started to burn their land, which indicates that planting season is just around the corner. The rainy season will be our constant companion for the next four months!

Since pastoral work is slow during the rainy season, I'm planning to study Spanish for three weeks in the city. There is a language school in Guatemala City that concentrates both on improving one's Spanish skills and increasing one's awareness of the political situation in Guatemala. Living in a remote area like San Miguel, one has the tendency to forget that life, with all its joys and pains, exists elsewhere. The name of the school is the Oscar Romero Institute. To allow students to learn more about the culture and struggles of the indigenous, the Romero Institute arranges for room and board with members of the Mutual Support Group (GAM, an organization for family members of people who have been "disappeared"), or others who are working for social change. "Si Dios quiere y la Virgen" [If God and the Virgin wish it], I will come to experience and to know the reality of the Guatemalan people on a deeper level!

We talked about the threats with Efraín. He pointed out that foreigners simply were not being attacked anymore, as they had been in the early 1980s. But after I got the third threat, Mimi, Darleen, and I went to Huehuetenango to talk to the bishop.

He agreed that the threats were probably nothing to take too seriously. Someone in San Miguel might be mad at me for some reason and trying to get even. But the bishop did say we should be careful, keep track of each other's whereabouts, and not go anywhere alone.

In Guatemala City, where I went to study Spanish, I had to go places alone. But I learned more about how to live with the threats. The school where I was studying, which was committed to helping students understand the social situation of Guatemala, had arranged for me to stay with Miguel Solís and Rosa Pu, members of GAM. By staying with them, I was able to learn more about the political situation in Guatemala and also able to afford them some protection, since foreign witnesses, at least in theory, could not be killed without consequences. GAM members were receiving threats regularly for marching and lobbying to demand that the army reveal what had become of their loved ones. "You took them alive!" they would shout, walking down the main avenue to the National Palace. "We want them back alive!" The previous year GAM had begun a campaign to discover clandestine cemeteries, where victims of army massacres were buried. So far in 1989, a GAM member had gone into exile after being abducted, and the GAM office had been strafed with machine-gun fire.

Miguel was a small, gentle Mayan who had several brothers who had been disappeared, kidnapped by army death squads. Like many GAM members, Miguel regularly received death threats. I looked to Miguel for guidance. He instructed me in the fine points of Spanish and in the practical and political realities of life in Guatemala, and he educated me through the courage I witnessed as he walked out the door alone and faced each dangerous day.

As THE DAYS PASSED, the danger grew. The civilian government was becoming increasingly militarized. The minister of the interior had resigned in May, after the army had attempted a coup, and as a result of army pressure, he was replaced by a general. The civilian chief of police, meanwhile, was replaced by an army colonel who was a former member of military intelligence.

Then, in June, a national teachers strike exploded, and at the end of the month, workers in the electric company, the post office, and the public health sector joined in. In mid-July employees of various other government and private concerns joined the strike. Passing by the demonstrating teachers one day in July, I stopped to talk with a few women I knew who were members of GAM. A couple of days later, as I was on my way to class in the morning, I had the sensation that I was being followed. I crossed the street. Behind me I heard a voice: "Dianna!" It was a man's voice.

I looked back and didn't see anyone I knew. I kept walking.

Half a block later, my arm was grabbed by a man with a mustache. I couldn't get away. It was my first encounter with the man whose grip I would come to know.

MIMI REMEMBERS how she reacted when I told her how he grabbed me: "When you got accosted on the street in Guatemala City, we knew it wasn't just San Miguel. It was somebody who could control your movements anywhere. I said, 'OK, you've got to go right now. Right now.' And you didn't like the idea. But, finally, you went. You just didn't feel like it was right to leave. You had a commitment to the people. And you said, 'They can't run away.' I remember saying, 'Dianna, they do run away. Most of them *have* run away. They can and they do.' But you just felt like going home was totally against your commitment to those people."

AT THE END OF JULY, I returned to the Mount, on the condition that I would just go away for a while, until things settled down. By September the strikes had ended, and it seemed that, at least in that respect, things in Guatemala were settling down.

In August, however, the GAM office was destroyed by a bomb. Luckily, no one was injured. But ten student leaders were abducted and disappeared that month, and grenades were thrown at the house of Peace Brigades International, a group of people from all over the world who accompanied Guatemalan human rights activists and others at risk of attack. After August, the violence increased.

But that didn't matter. I had promised I wouldn't leave, and I'd seen Miguel and many other Guatemalan friends live and work through the danger. As an American citizen I had some protection.

Larraine, the sister I argued with each time I refused to buckle up, has told me we had a conversation my last day at the Mount. I told her about several of the recent atrocities in Guatemala. "You said you were afraid," Larraine remembers, "but you said you had to believe that God would protect you."

The leadership council — the major superior and other nuns elected to office — knew about the threats I'd been getting, but they respected my right to decide for myself what I felt called to do.

I went back.

Mimi feels there were signs we should have picked up on, even before I got to Guatemala. "Somebody canceled your reservations back to Guatemala. You got to Miami and you weren't on the list; the reservation had been canceled by somebody else — they didn't know from where. I think it was basically the army's way of saying, 'We know you're coming back.' You and I had been in contact over the phone about the fact that you were coming back."[4]

I arrived in San Miguel in the middle of September. Within little more than a month, another threat came. At that point I was frightened; I could no longer hide or deny it. Darleen and I heard about a Bible workshop in Antigua, a picturesque tourist mecca near Guatemala City. The workshop would be held in a walled convent filled with English-speaking foreigners like ourselves. We figured we couldn't be much safer. There I would have some time to rest and think about what to do.

We were spending a few days in Guatemala City before the course started, staying at a house for missionaries, when a threat was slipped through the mail slot. This time the words were not handwritten but cut out from a newspaper and glued to a piece of stationery:

> Eliminate Diana
>
> raped   disappeared
>
> murdered   decapitated
>
> leave the country

Darleen and I met up with Mimi and went to talk again with the bishop of Huehuetenango, missing the first few days of our Bible workshop. While we were in San Miguel, meeting up with Mimi, another threat came for me. Only four days had passed since I'd received the threat in Guatemala City.

"The bishop advised you to leave," Mimi remembers. "Everybody advised you at that time to go. But the bishop said if you didn't go, you'd have to make the threats public." Publicity could afford a measure of protection. Since everyone would know that I'd been threatened, anything that happened to me couldn't so easily be explained away as a simple case of common crime.

But I thought about my parents' learning of the death threats. If I publicized the threats and they heard about them, I might as well go home because they would beg me to — or if they didn't beg, they would silently suffer. They had already lost one child, my brother Brian, who was killed by a rubber bullet a policeman shot at his heart, thinking he was one of the Hispanics participating in a riot.

I decided to keep quiet about the threats, at least until I had made up my mind about staying or going. If I stayed, I knew I would have to make the threats public. But out of respect for the people of San Miguel, I wanted to tell them about the threats before the news came out in the papers or on the radio. Even though the threats were addressed to me, I believed they were attempts to intimidate the whole community. And I didn't want to be part of that plan. I didn't want to share the threats with the community unless I had to. If I were going to leave, I didn't want to say anything about being threatened.

The retreat center was a place I could untangle my thoughts and pray for discernment. Someone had evidently found out I was in Guatemala City, but I didn't think anyone would know about my stay at an obscure convent retreat center in the small town of Antigua.

Once again, we underestimated the eavesdropping capabilities of the Guatemalan government. Father Dan Jensen, of the Maryknoll order, was organizing the course and remembers how the arrangements were made:

> I received a personal visit from Sister Clare McGowan, who was a psychologist (I believe). She wanted to know if I could, despite the

late date, receive two more applicants for the renewal program, Sister Dianna Ortiz, O.S.U., and Sister Darleen Chmielewski. Since time was short, rather than use the postal system, I sent a telegram to their address in San Miguel, in which I said in Spanish that they had both been accepted, despite the late date, and that we would be expecting them on the twelfth of October at the Posada de Belén in Antigua. I heard nothing more from them. The date of the opening of the renewal program arrived, and Dianna and Darleen did not show up. I figured that they had changed their minds, and so we began the course. Then two days later, Darleen and Dianna arrived. They seemed flustered and asked if they might be able to take part in the program. They had not received my telegram at their home in San Miguel Acatán. It wasn't until later that we realized the nonarrival of the telegram was significant.

It had been intercepted, of course. That's how the army knew where I was. Accordingly, a letter was waiting for me at the Posada de Belén.

"Salga del Pais," it said. Leave the country. The convent secretary, not knowing of anyone by my name who was there for the renewal course, threw the note away. When she heard that I was missing, she remembered the note, fished it out of the wastebasket, and gave it to Darleen.

FATHER DAN JENSEN remembers that Darleen and I had two requests, for security reasons: that we be allowed to share a double room and that our room not be in the front of the building. Father Jensen had already assigned us each a room in the front of the building, facing a tiny park. "Darleen explained that Dianna was nervous about people who might be in the park," Father Jensen recalls. He agreed to move us to one room, facing the inside patio.

Father Jensen's immediate impression of me was that I was "a rather fragile person who weighed about ninety pounds." He noticed that my Spanish was limited and that I "seemed extremely shy and hesitant." He says I spoke with a "little girl voice" and seemed vulnerable. Darleen, he remembers, was "a strong woman, a take-charge person, sure of herself and outspoken."

MARY MATHIAS, who was the Major Superior of my order, has told me I called her long distance from Guatemala to talk about the decision I had to make. She asked me if I was afraid, and I admitted that I was. She suggested that perhaps I wouldn't be able to carry out my work effectively, given the fear I was experiencing. I pointed out that in every retreat I had ever been on with her, she spoke of how we had to pick up our crosses and carry them and walk the road Jesus walked, in spite of hardships and fear. I told her that she was the one who had given me the courage to return to Guatemala and continue my mission. Mathias was silent.

Years later she admitted that she felt I was holding her responsible for my decision. I think, in reality, I was asking for clarification: Isn't this the difficult road I'm supposed to walk? Wouldn't it be antithetical to my life as a Christian to refuse to walk it?

FATHER JENSEN says I seemed to lack energy and need a lot of sleep, and my participation in classes was sporadic. I would absent myself from classes and meals to rest and to pray. On occasion I would mention that I was afraid of "the men in the park." Father Jensen "put that down to a sense of paranoia coming from the threats [I'd] received in San Miguel." I consulted with Father Jensen twice about whether I should stay in Guatemala, knowing that he himself had received threats in Guatemala in 1981 and 1982. "On both occasions I cautioned you to take the threats very seriously," he recounts. "But I also told you that you were the only one who could make the ultimate decision to stay or to leave Guatemala. I told you that if you were to leave the country, it would be a decision with which you would have to live for the rest of your life."

I'VE HAD TO LIVE with my decision to stay and all its consequences, on myself, my family, and my friends. Nothing would ever be the same again. I would never again so easily reach out to another person or let another person reach out to me.

THE FIRST PERSON who tried to "help" me after my torture was an American. I can barely remember him without slipping back into that moment.

I'm curled up on the cement floor, blindfolded. The men are about to rape me again. "Hey, Alejandro! Come and have some fun!" one of them calls.

I recognize the name. They've mentioned it before. They said Alejandro was their boss. "Shit!" a new voice responds, in perfect, unaccented American English. Then he switches to Spanish, which he speaks with a marked American accent. "You idiots! Leave her alone. She's a North American, and it's all over the news." Alejandro removes my blindfold. He is tall and fair-skinned.

"Are you an American?" I ask him in English.

"Why do you want to know?" He understands me but insists on answering in Spanish.

"Bring her clothes!" he calls. He helps me on with my T-shirt and sweatshirt and tells José to go for water. José returns with a plastic pan of water and a rag. I take a sip. Alejandro tries to wipe my face. I jerk away from him and wipe it myself. I clean my hands. I notice José has changed clothes. He is wearing a clean blue denim shirt, just like Alejandro's.

"Come on, let's get out of here." Alejandro leads me down the long hallway. "I'm sorry. I'm so sorry. It was a mistake," he says. "You must forgive them. They had the wrong person. They thought you were Verónica Ortiz Hernández."

His hair is brown, curly, and dark, darker than his beard and his eyebrows. I begin to suspect he's wearing a wig. He has on large, dark glasses.

"What will happen to the other people in the building?"

"Don't concern yourself with them." He takes me up the stairs. There are two landings. We go through a door and into a garage.

In the garage there is space for about fifteen cars. He motions me into a gray Suzuki jeep. I notice that it has a wavy black horizontal stripe on the outside, near the door, and it's in good shape, almost new. A rabbit's foot hangs from the rear-view mirror. "I'll take you to a friend at the U.S. embassy who can help you leave the country."

As we pull out of the garage, light dazzles my eyes. I make out a couple of open iron gates. We go through them and turn right onto a main road with large buildings. My attention is on Alejandro — whether I can trust him. He's told me to forget about the other people in the building. The torturers said he was their boss and they obeyed him. He told them to leave me alone. They did. He ordered the Guate-man and the Policeman out of the room. They left. He told José to bring me my clothes and some water. José did as he was told. Alejandro knows I've seen the torturers' faces — and his face too. He's taking me to kill me.

A tape of classical music is playing. It stops, and he turns it over. On his left finger, a wide, gold wedding band gleams in the light.

The sun is low. It's twilight or early morning, I guess. I sit forward to protect my back. My burns are throbbing.

"Look, you have to forgive those guys, Dianita. They made a mistake."

"They didn't make a mistake. The death threats were addressed to me, Madre Dianna, not to Verónica Ortiz."

"We tried to warn you with the threats, to prevent this, but you wouldn't leave."

"I stayed because I have a commitment to the people."

"I have a commitment to the people, too — to liberate them from communism."

"Your commitment is different because you don't respect human life."

All this time I've been speaking Spanish. He's been responding in Spanish, with grammar worse than mine, beginner mistakes, like using a feminine article with a masculine noun.

But now he switches to English. "Well, you know, we have the photos of you, and the videos. Those could be embarrassing."

My breath stops. He is American and the torturers have told him about what I did — what they filmed me doing. Now he's threatening me — with blackmail. Does that mean he won't kill me? Or will he change his mind, even if I promise to keep quiet? Is he just playing with me?

I look around. The traffic has picked up now. I catch sight of a sign: Zone 5. There is only one place in Guatemala with zone signs, and that's the capital. I'm in Zone 5 of Guatemala City.

Up ahead is a red light. Alejandro slows, and soon we're at a dead standstill. I open my door and I jump.

Then I run as fast as my legs will take me. I can't see him when I look back. After several blocks, while I'm glancing over my shoulder, I nearly collide with an indigenous woman.

"You're the one!" she says. "Sister Dianna!" She must recognize me from the news.

"I escaped! I'm running!"

She takes me by the arm, quickly, looking around. "Come with me. You'll be safe." She guides me into a little house, and sits me at a table. She disappears for a minute and soon comes back with chamomile tea and a plate of beans and tortillas. I'm not hungry or thirsty. My body is numb. My tears are the only living part of me. They keep spurting and coursing and burning. The woman has a statue of the Virgin of Guadalupe, with several candles before it. She tells me to rest and pray. I continue to sit. I sip some tea. But praying is out of the question.

She brings some water to wipe my face. As she brings the cloth up to my cheek, I jerk away, remembering Alejandro.

"It's OK, now, I'm not going to hurt you."

I let her wipe off the scrape.

She tells me again to rest, but all I can think about is getting my passport and leaving Guatemala before Alejandro and the others catch up with me. My passport is at a travel agency in Zone 1. Hayter's Travel, near the Plaza Central. Darleen and I left our passports there, locked in the manager's desk, before going on retreat at the Posada de Belén. If we had to leave the country quickly, we reasoned, the travel agent would have our passport numbers already and could make our flight arrangements quickly. We could pick up our passports with our tickets.

"I have to get to Zone 1 to get my passport," I tell the woman.

She tells me what bus to take to Zone 1, and she gives me the change I need. She walks with me to the door of her house, looks carefully out, and points me to the bus stop. "Don't tell anyone anything about me," she says.

I understand. To give any details that could allow the authorities or army to find her would put her in danger. The rules were simple in Guatemala and after decades of dictatorships, everybody knew them. She helped someone they had wanted to kill. They would punish her for that.

The bus comes almost as soon as I leave her house. I ask the driver to tell me when we get to the stop near Hayter's Travel. The driver knows the place, and I get off at the right stop. Once inside the travel agency, I ask to use the phone, and I get in touch with Darleen. Before long, a group of people I don't recognize comes to pick me up — several women and a man in a jeep. After we've gone for a while in silence, one of the women asks, "Were you raped?"

"No." I just want to leave the country. I don't want any complications.

THE NEXT THREE DAYS were a blur. They took me to the Maryknoll House, where, according to Darleen, I bathed every hour or so. Between baths, I lay on my stomach on the bed.

Guatemalan police officers were at the door downstairs. We were in a room at the back of the house, so I didn't know that the police had come to interview me. The Maryknoll priests sent them away, refusing to be intimidated. The police didn't have a warrant. The police chief, accompanied by his agency's public relations director, vowed to return with a warrant. Luckily, I was spared those details and others that the priests were discussing — how easily a grenade could be lobbed over the low wall around the house, for example. Already the phone lines had been cut.

They decided to move me to the Vatican embassy, where the papal nuncio lived. Officially, once we were on that property, we were not in Guatemala, and the police had no jurisdiction. The building had good security, too. At the nuncio's, I was looked after well. My clothes were washed (no one thought not to wash them, especially since I wasn't being clear about all that had happened). The nuncio prepared a special meal for us. And within three days, I was home.

IN NEW MEXICO, I went through photographs with my six-year-old niece. I pretended I was testing her — "Hey, Stephanie, do you know who this is?" She told me the names and relationships of everyone in the family. I memorized them. A neighbor, meanwhile, called and told my mother that a suspicious-looking man had been driving slowly by our house and photographing it. Sister Fran was staying with us for a while, helping my family and me through what must have been a crisis — my family seeing me so beaten up and changed, the local press wanting interviews, occasional strange phone calls. The strange phone calls and the photographer weren't mentioned to me. Neither were the clicks that the sisters at the Mount had begun hearing within twelve hours of my abduction whenever they used the phone. Afraid the phones were tapped, they now conversed circumspectly with Fran about anything to do with me. I was oblivious to the danger the sisters perceived in New Mexico and at the Mount. And they were kind enough to let me drift off into my own numb world.

BUT ONE DAY when barely a week had passed, Mary Mathias called and told me I needed to get my back examined. From the statement I'd released, the community was aware of the people I'd heard screaming in the building, the people who were left behind. The sisters felt compelled to act — to protest the tactics of the Guatemalan government, at the very least, and perhaps to prosecute. My back was evidence. Two doctors in Guatemala had already looked at my back, but they sneaked into the papal nuncio's residence. They were terrified to be mentioned by name, much less to participate as witnesses in a suit against the Guatemalan security forces.

"Dr. Gutiérrez won't hurt you," my mother told me, watching my hands shake as I buttoned my coat. She turned to Fran, who was going with me to his office. "He's good. He's been our family doctor for years."

I TIE ON A GOWN. When Dr. Gutiérrez pulls it open to look at my back, I feel the torturers' eyes on me again. He looks and looks. My ears wait for the rasp of a match.

He finishes, finally, and wants to examine other parts of my body for burns: chest, stomach, legs?

I can't allow it. I refuse.

Dr. Gutiérrez writes up the statement the community needs for legal purposes, saying that he found 111 second-degree circular burns on my back.

"THAT SHOULD BE SOMETHING the White House is interested in seeing investigated," Kentucky Congressman Carroll Hubbard tells reporters. But the White House has not even made a statement of concern about my abduction and torture. The White House has made no public reference to it at all. So the sisters have hired a lawyer, and I have to go back to the Mount to provide more information about what happened to me during those twenty-four hours.[5]

l feel almost comfortable with my family now, and I don't want to leave. But I pack my suitcase, hoping that at the Mount, I will remember people and be, once again, a person with a past.

I DON'T RECOGNIZE the driveway that leads to the mother house or the pastures and buildings we pass on either side. The Victorian guesthouse Mimi and Darleen and I are staying in is as foreign to me as my parents' house, although people expect me to know where things are. After we settle in, we go to the dining room for dinner, and everyone stands and applauds. I'm baffled, overwhelmed. If these holy women knew what I had done in that basement prison, they wouldn't let me near them, much less applaud.

Dozens of women come and throw their arms around me. Some choke on sobs. They tell me how worried they were. They ask me how I am.

My voice knots in my chest. I don't know who they are.

Chapter Four

THE RULES OF THE GAME

They've taken my sweatshirt off and are explaining the rules. "We're going to ask you some questions. If you give an answer we like, we'll let you smoke. If we don't like the answer, we'll burn you."

"The rules are unfair," I venture.

They burn me.

They ask me my name, age, and place of residence. The anticipation is worse than the burns — wondering if this answer is good enough. But for every answer I give, they burn me. Every time I am silent they burn me. They ask me the same questions again and again. My throat becomes raw from screaming.

They remove my blindfold. Someone holds my head so I can't turn around. It takes my eyes a little while to adjust to the light. They show me some pictures. The first is of me in San Miguel during the festival two years earlier. The army was in town during the feast, I remember. A soldier asked me to dance and Mimi came to my rescue. "We're nuns," she said. "We don't dance."

"Do you know who this is in the picture?" they ask.

"It's me."

They burn me.

"And who's this?"

This one was taken in the village of Yalaj during Lent of 1988. I wasn't there often, but I remember that when I was there the army was also there. "Me."

They burn me.

The next picture is one of me at the teacher's demonstration in Guatemala City. Again they question me. I identify myself. They burn me. The one after that is of me with a group of people from the Bible course, visiting the ruins in Capuchino. It must have been taken just a couple of days before I was kidnapped. It's so useless to tell them it's me. Why don't I just stay silent? Either way I'll get burned. But still I answer. And am burned.

Then they show me a photo of an indigenous man holding a gun. "Who's this?" I don't know him and I tell them so.

They burn me.

They show me a photo of an indigenous woman holding a gun. "This is you,"

37

they insist. She bears no resemblance to me. She's an indigenous woman with long hair. "It isn't. It's not me."

They burn me.

JUST GET IT DOWN on paper, I tell myself — this the last time I will ever have to remember. With the help of Paul Soreff, the community's lawyer, I write a fifteen-page affidavit. The Guatemalan government and the U.S. State Department have claimed for the past two months that with no direct statement from me, no first-person affidavit, they cannot investigate. It takes about ten meetings with Paul, sitting in his little office where many refugees have told their stories of persecution and fear, seeking help with political asylum cases.

Paul questions me gently. If I can't answer, he waits, letting Mimi and Darleen comfort me. When I tell him we can start again, he pushes his wire-rimmed glasses up on his nose, strokes his beard for a moment, and tries to find an even gentler way to ask the same question. But each time I remember what happened, I smell the torturers, hear their laughter, feel their hands. Once I have to run out the room and vomit. Finally, with Mimi and Darleen's support and Paul's help, I finish the affidavit, and Paul makes sure that Guatemalan government and U.S. embassy officials receive it by January 1990.

SEVERAL WEEKS LATER, newspapers arrive from Guatemala with information about my case, and Mimi and I sit down to read them. On the front page of one is an article headlined, "What Happened to Diana Ortiz Was Self-Kidnapping."

My ears start ringing. According to General Carlos Morales, the minister of the interior, "What happened to Diana Ortiz was a self-kidnapping and in no moment did police authorities have anything to do with this incident, and for this reason the government has closed the case."[1]

"How could I have kidnapped myself? What does that even mean?" I explode finally. I'm angry, truly angry, for the first time since the torture. I've shut the anger away because when I expressed anger with the torturers, they punished me. Now it floods me.

"Don't let it get to you, Dianna, it's the typical stuff," Mimi says. "Like remember, three bodies are found on the side of the road and the government says the men killed each other? How can three men kill each other?"

Even Mimi, the person I'm closest to, doesn't know that I remember next to nothing about Guatemala. Sometimes when she's looking away I study her dark, shoulder-length hair, her soft, dark eyes and long eyelashes and try to remember her. "What you need to do, Dianna, is get better," she continues. "Get strong so you can fight back."

For a few days I am resolute. I write:

> The memories of the woman and man being tortured with me continue to haunt me. How many times I have yearned to close my ears to the oppressed people of Guatemala, to forget forever the persecuted and the agonies of the tortured. It's not feasible to forget. My experience has marked me for life and the sufferings of the Guatemalan people have become my sufferings.... In reality, they have become OUR SUFFERINGS.
>
> During the past week, I have seen a dramatic change in myself, particularly in wanting to denounce the hideous injustices that are a daily practice of the Guatemalan government.
>
> I think God and the cries of the thousands of oppressed people of Guatemala are awakening within me this sleeping silence and are breathing courage within me, a courage that is allowing me to take control of my life and that is allowing me to free myself from the fear that seeks to paralyze me and to silence me.

Brave words. But I also remember the Policeman's words: *"If you live to tell about this, if you somehow manage to survive, no one will believe you."*

IN MARCH, Paul and Sister Fran lead a religious delegation to Guatemala City to push for a full investigation of my case. I consider going along. But the Guatemala desk officer at the State Department, Deborah McCarthy, says the U.S. embassy won't be able to guarantee my safety or keep the Guatemalan police from detaining me for questioning. So Fran and Paul go without me, inviting two prominent religious leaders to join them: Marie Dennis, the Maryknoll Justice and Peace Office's associate for Latin America, and Father Joe Nangle, justice and peace director of the Conference of Major Superiors of Men's Institutes.

MIMI, DARLEEN, AND I spend that spring in Mexico; I've decided I'm fine and should go back to missionary work, this time with Guatemalan refugees who have fled across the border. I plan to forget what happened to me in Guatemala. But the people, the language, and the fact that we can see the mountain of San Miguel in the distance on a clear day are reminders — unpleasant ones — of November 2. The Guatemalan army has been known to cross the border.

Forgetting the case is impossible, too. Fran and Paul visit us in Mexico on their return from Guatemala to report on all that happened there.

We meet in a restaurant in Mexico City, and Paul whips out a newspaper and holds it up for us to see. A large picture of the delegation is on the front page, beneath the headline, "Church Demands Investigation."

"We made our point." Paul is beaming, eager to fill us in on all the details. "President Cerezo agreed to form an independent commission to investigate your case, Dianna. What that means is, first of all, we can get to the truth. The government may not have the power or desire to investigate, but the commission will. It will include Archbishop Penados, the vice minister of the judiciary, a human rights official yet to be decided, and myself. Second, you won't have to go before a Guatemalan court to prosecute, so you won't have to be up on the witness stand."

Me, on the witness stand, talking about what they did to me? I'd never even imagined it. I had no idea that I might have been asked to do that. I would have refused. When I was working with Paul on my affidavit, he said the case would never be tried in court. He'd sounded sure about the commission. But it must have been touch and go for a while.

Paul thumps the edge of the table with his fingers. "It's good news."

I return his smile. Maybe the commission can prove I'm telling the truth.

Paul passes on more good news. President Cerezo read my affidavit avidly when they met with him, as though he'd never seen it before. Then he said he had no reason not to believe me. The police, he said, had concluded my case was a "self-kidnapping" because they couldn't find anyone to support my version of events and they "couldn't come up with any motive for this having been done." That night, when he was interviewed on television, Cerezo stated again that he had no reason not to believe me.

President Cerezo's attitude took the delegation by surprise. A few days after my abduction, Cerezo had made a statement to the Guatemalan press acknowledging that I was abducted, although he had refused to admit that state security forces were involved: "This was an act perpetrated by extra-governmental groups not under the control of the authorities." By January, though, Cerezo had aligned his story more closely with the army's. He told Americas Watch my case was invented to embarrass the Guatemalan government at the February meeting of the United Nations Human Rights Commission. Now, Cerezo suddenly said he had no quarrels with "my version of events."

The delegation also met with Defense Minister General Héctor Gramajo and Minister of the Interior General Carlos Morales. Both had told the press in November that my abduction was a hoax. In January Defense Minister Gramajo told an Americas Watch investigator that I wasn't abducted but had sneaked out to meet a lesbian lover. The gash on my face resulted from a lovers' spat. As for the cigarette burns, he said he didn't believe they existed. Gramajo called my accusations "a big injustice" to Guatemala and its security forces. Americas Watch considered Gramajo's version "to be pure invention and indicative of the extraordinary lengths the military leadership will go to deflect exposure of its secret practices."[2]

Paul confronted Gramajo with the statements he had made, and Gramajo took them back. Paul got him to put his retraction in writing: "This note serves to confirm our conclusions in our talk today that in reference to the case of Sister Diana Mae Ortiz, specifically in reference to my impression that her motives for leaving the hotel she was in were due to matters related to amorous deception, I agree with you that the evidence in the hands of investigators are not conclusive to support this impression, much less to affirm practices of sexual deviation (lesbianism)."

Gramajo continued to insist, however, that my abduction was a "self-kidnapping."

Morales wasn't familiar with my affidavit — he didn't seem to have read it — but he also continued to maintain that I had staged my own kidnapping, although he refused to give any evidence to support his claim. His position was that the investigation was closed, and if we wanted further action, we would have to go to court.

"FROM AMBASSADOR STROOCK," Paul tells me, pulling some letters out of his briefcase and putting them on the table before us. "Before I tell you about our meeting with him, I want you to get an idea of the dialogue we've been having."

I glance through the pages, and stop at this sentence: "Sister Diana's refusal to be interviewed or to give any direct information to investigators from any agency has seriously complicated efforts to find the criminals and solve the crime."

"Paul, I just wrote a fifteen-page affidavit. The ambassador was saying they couldn't investigate because they didn't have a first-person statement. Now they have it. And now they're saying they can't investigate because I won't be interviewed?"

Paul sighs.

I keep reading. The investigation, according to Stroock, has also been hampered by a "lack of any evidence that could be used in court."

But the evidence includes the T-shirt I was wearing, which the men burned me in for a while before removing; two separate doctors' findings, since one of the Guatemalan doctors was now willing to allow his name to be used; and the six threatening notes I received. Anyway, we don't plan to pursue the case in court but before the investigative commission.

ANOTHER PARAGRAPH catches my eye: "Had we been able to retrace [Sister Ortiz's] itinerary in the hours or even days immediately following her reappearance, we might have been able to effect the rescue of the persons being held. The indifference to the fate of those undergoing torture is inconsistent with the January 3rd affidavit's reference to a 'commitment to a suffering people.'"[3]

"Murderer," the Policeman hisses again in my ear. "Now more people are dead because of you."

I SINK MY TEETH into my lip to keep it steady and try to reason with the Policeman's voice. There was no way I could have retraced my "itinerary" or, as Stroock asked, made a "map backtracking [my] route from the point of [my] arrival in Zone 5 to the location at which the affidavit indicates [I] was held." My affidavit didn't indicate any location at which I was held. I had no idea where I was held. I wouldn't know the place I was held until I saw it and every cell in my body remembered it. And Stroock had met with me himself the day I escaped. He didn't ask me a single question about the place I was detained.

Stroock in the letter also asked for information about the indigenous woman who helped me after I escaped from Alejandro. "Please ask Sister Diana to provide her name and address."

"He wants her name and address so he can give it to the Guatemalan army," I tell Paul. "And then she can 'disappear.'" The woman asked me to forget her name and where she lived, and I have buried that information under a rock in my mind.

"And then, about Alejandro," Paul begins.

My heart speeds up at the mention of the name.

"I wrote to Stroock and the State Department asking for photographs of U.S. citizens in Guatemala so we could try to identify him. Deborah McCarthy, the desk officer, said that was too broad a pool of people, so I narrowed it down."

"And?"

"This was the ambassador's response." He points to a paper:

You saw fit to make a specific reference to Americans assigned to "the embassy, the military, or to any police training programs." As the personal representative of the President of the United States, directly responsible for the supervision and coordination of all United States Government personnel and activities in Guatemala, I find the insinuation that U.S. Government personnel in Guatemala are involved in any kind of human rights violations against anyone to be insulting, absurd, and ridiculous. The fact that this allegation is couched in the most cowardly and indirect form of innuendo makes it no less reprehensible.

This charge constitutes a scurrilous smear on the good names of the fine Americans who serve their country in this mission and brings sadness and consternation to them and their families. In my opinion, it is an offense against the 8th commandment. It raises the most serious questions about the credibility, sincerity, and motives of those who conceived and are attempting to spread it.[4]

"When we met with him, he was even angrier about it," Paul tells us. "He berated us for accusing U.S. embassy personnel of being involved in your torture. I explained that you never said Alejandro was an embassy employee, just a man who said he had a friend at the embassy. But the ambassador said that even the statement that a man with *ties* to the embassy was involved was an 'insult to every mission employee.' He asked me if I would write a public statement saying that we were not trying to impugn any mission employee. So I said I would."

According to Paul, the meeting was tense from start to finish. It began with a twenty-minute tongue-lashing, where the ambassador read from prepared notes, criticizing the Ursuline order for not cooperating with the embassy, not trusting the embassy, and making outrageous statements in the press about the embassy's lack of a statement of outrage on the case.

For a statement of outrage, the ambassador said the delegation members should read the State Department's 1989 human rights report (which mentions my case but expresses not the slightest bit of outrage). He also mentioned his remarks at the Rotary Club, in which he criticized the Guatemalan government for ongoing human rights abuses (but did not mention my case at all). Finally, Stroock argued that he was presented with affidavits on both sides of the case — the "witnesses'" affidavits and mine — and he did not know whom to believe.

I stop Paul right there to ask him what witnesses Stroock means. Paul takes a deep breath, straightens his glasses, and starts to update me on the police investigation. "It's been closed," he says. "It was closed in March. The police concluded that no kidnapping occurred. The State Department and embassy seem to be accepting the police version. Even back in February Deborah McCarthy wrote me that 'two people saw Sr. Ortiz at or leaving the retreat house by herself.' " Paul didn't need to tell me what was missing from that sentence. It was the word the embassy and State Department officials were always using when they spoke about my case: "allegedly."

Paul pulls Deborah McCarthy's letter out of his file and holds it out for me to read. "Subsequent to Sr. Ortiz's departure," McCarthy wrote, "the police interviewed all the drivers of the inter-city buses in Antigua. None remembered having seen Sr. Ortiz board a bus."[5]

I suppose McCarthy was using data Ambassador Stroock had sent her. From cables that have since been declassified, I know that in a document sent to the State Department, dated November 1989, Stroock insisted that there was some new information: the police had interviewed "all the drivers." But that "information" is never reflected in any police report; we received copies of all of them. What the November 13, 1989, police report actually says is that "several" bus drivers were interviewed.

The police's initial findings, reported in the Guatemalan press, stated that no signs of a struggle were found. "Initially," said the press report, "the authorities are saying it's a 'plot' of several religious leaders and Diana Ortiz to hurt the prestige of the Guatemalan government." According to the newspaper account, the police were claiming that, while no signs of a struggle were found on the first day of the investigation, on the following day, November 3, a watch, a Bible, and shawl were found in the garden, "which someone had placed there intentionally to make the abduction seem more real."[6] The police later dropped this contention, after learning that Darleen had reported finding my shawl to embassy officials on November 2.

Paul and Fran talked through the police reports with me. I didn't see how Stroock could believe the police — they were not known for their honesty. And I found it strange that Stroock could be so convinced by the "witnesses" for the police. In early November, the police said they had interviewed all Posada de Belén employees, and none of the employees had seen anything. They claimed to have only one witness, who was a glue-sniffing vagrant and petty thief. By February the police claimed to have two witnesses, one of whom was supposedly a Posada de Belén employee, who supposedly was interviewed by police on November 2. He told the police he had seen me walking alone in the garden with my Bible. The police, in the analysis section of the report, added to his testimony; they insisted that I was walking toward the bushes and seemed to be looking for a way out of the garden. In the November police report, the first witness, who identified himself as Carlos Ajtum Asturias, stated that on November 2, at 8:30 a.m., he was walking along a little street next to the banks of the Río Pensativo, when "he saw that in the bushes a young woman with the same physical characteristics as the disappeared was trying to exit and that she went toward the street that leads to the exit of this city, with the destination of the capital city." In a statement only days later, Ajtum said that "as he was returning to his home around 8:00 he realized that among the bushes which are located in the back of the Posada de Belén, a young woman with the same characteristics as Diana Ortiz was emerging. He only observed her from behind because she was already looking for the road to the capital city, where the buses pass."

If he only saw me from behind, how could he know my age, eye color, or skin tone? The "witness" also was mistaken about some of the clothes I was wearing. He said I was wearing white leather sandals, when in fact I was wearing white tennis shoes. Darleen in her description to the police the day I was abducted made the same mistake — she said I was wearing white leather sandals. Darleen also omitted the length of my hair in her description. She said only that it was curly and coffee-colored. The "witness" described me in Darleen's exact words, saying my hair was curly and coffee-colored. But he took a guess about the length. He said my hair was long. I'd had it cut short when I started getting the death threats. Mimi had laughed — "Yeah, that's really going to throw them off, Dianna. They'll never recognize you now." If nothing else, the haircut should have proved that the "witness" was lying and that the police had fed him Darleen's description. That, in turn, should have raised the question of motive: Why would the police have provided him Darleen's description? Could they have concocted this witness to cover up a crime the military or one of their own had committed? But the U.S. embassy and State Department seemed blind to that possibility.

I just kept wondering why Stroock didn't believe me and asking myself what I could have done differently, how I could have been a better kidnap victim.

EMBASSY POLITICAL AFFAIRS OFFICER Lew Anselem was at the embassy meeting with Paul, Fran, Marie, and Joe. "He had a statue of two nuns on his desk," Fran told us. "And you know what he said? 'These are my do-gooder lesbians.' Later, during the meeting, Anselem sat back in his chair. He said, 'I'm tired of all these lesbian nuns coming down to Guatemala.'"

"What did the ambassador do?" Mimi asked Fran.
"Nothing. Just sat there. The meeting went on."

THE RELIGIOUS DELEGATION had gone to Guatemala, not only to push my case forward, but to support and thank the Church leaders who had defended me from the Guatemalan government's attacks, at great risk to themselves. The repression against Church leaders had intensified steadily in 1989. Sister Patricia Denny, an American Maryknoll nun, was forced to leave the country in October after receiving serious threats and escaping an abduction attempt by armed men. Bishop Quezada Toruño, a well-respected Church official, said army officers were visiting rural priests to gather information about them and their parishioners and noted that the army was trying to control religious activity. Archbishop Próspero Penados del Barrio and others in the Archbishop's Human Rights Office were receiving repeated death threats. In spite of these pressures, Church leaders went out on a limb for me. In November, Archbishop Penados had made a televised statement about my abduction and torture — "This attack cannot be seen but as a direct attack on the Catholic Church to force the Catholic Church to be silent and impede its denunciation of the crimes that occur in Guatemala." The Guatemalan Conference of Religious (CONFREGUA) took out a full-page paid advertisement defending me against Guatemalan officials' claims that the abduction was a hoax.

Stroock downplayed the persecution. Not to do so would have allowed a context for my abduction. In a note to the secretary of state he acknowledged, "The issue of Church/State relations has begun to draw the attention of foreign and local human rights groups." But he dismissed the statements Penados had made about Church persecution, calling them unsubstantiated. "We have no evidence that the government of Guatemala or the military have mounted a systematic campaign of attacks on the Catholic Church and its personnel," he wrote. In regard to the news from Quezada Toruño that the army was collecting information on priests and parishioners, the embassy's comment was, "The surveys are run by the army's civic affairs units, which carry out development projects in the countryside; they collect such information to know their operational areas better and to be able to plan appropriate projects."[7]

In March, Archbishop Penados risked his life for me again when Minister of the Interior General Morales said the police had concluded their investigation and found that the abduction was a self-kidnapping, a hoax. Penados told reporters the general's statements were false, and the paper ran an article headlined, "The Minister of the Interior Lies." Archbishop

Penados said the security forces "are covering the facts of her torture with an unwelcome smoke screen to make people believe they investigate things."[8]

At the end of the delegation's visit, the archbishop offered his office for a press conference, and Archbishop Penados and Auxiliary Bishop Juan Gerardi were present for it, openly supporting the delegation's conclusions. Around thirty journalists attended, including some from wire services such as UPI and AP.

The worsening human rights situation in Guatemala and the surge of violence against foreigners were now a focus of international attention. My case was one of the first against foreigners, but in December, a month after I was attacked, the office of the International Committee of the Red Cross had been bombed, and the second secretary of the Nicaraguan embassy was assassinated. Three volunteers with Peace Brigades International, including an American, Meredith Larson, were attacked by knife-wielding men one block from their office in Guatemala City, and two were seriously wounded. The motive of the attack was clearly political; the men made no attempt to rob the women, and the Peace Brigades office had received several telephoned threats before the grenade attack on the office in August.

In January, after prominent Salvadoran politician Héctor Oqueli was murdered in Guatemala, a U.S. congressional letter signed by eighty members of the House decried the increasing level of violence in Guatemala in general and the rise in violent attacks on foreigners in particular, mentioning my case and Meredith Larson's among others. An April article in the *Los Angeles Times* noted:

> According to figures supplied by the human rights office of the Guatemalan Congress, fifty-four people were killed in politically related incidents in the first two months of the year; fifty-two others were kidnapped.... [T]here have been 100,000 deaths and 40,000 disappearances. These numbers far exceed the totals in Argentina and El Salvador, where political violence has been more widely publicized.... "The victims," one European diplomat said, "are almost always people whose views or activities are aimed at helping others to free themselves of restraints placed by those who hold political or economic power. Even a doctor who tries to improve the health of babies is seen as attacking the established order...." The situation is expected to get worse. Diplomats and human rights figures say that both the radical right and the military, trying to take

advantage of uncertainty brought on by elections later this year, will seek to create such instability that the army will be forced to take over.[9]

For the U.S. and Guatemalan governments, the situation was a public relations disaster. A declassified U.S. State Department analysis probably written in 1987 states the issue bluntly:

> Our ability to provide military aid and higher levels of economic assistance to democratic Guatemala will depend in large part on our ability to persuade skeptics in Congress and the media that improvements are in fact taking place.... A few highly publicized disappearances or killings of GAM members or others could easily undermine our efforts in Congress to assist Guatemala economically and militarily.[10]

In retrospect, it seems the embassy and the Guatemalan administration were badly in need of good PR, and promising to form a commission to do a serious investigation of my case was an easy way to get it.

The embassy was eager to claim credit for the commission. Paul had asked Stroock to make a public statement saying that the embassy believed me; journalists were telling Paul the embassy seemed not to believe me. Stroock wrote a letter to Paul, saying:

> Both this Mission and the undersigned, personally, are very pleased that — at your insistence — the President of the Republic of Guatemala has agreed to appoint a public commission to investigate the case of Sister Diana Ortiz. This is a very positive step; it indicates the seriousness with which the government of Guatemala views the charges made by Sister Diana. Further, it evidences a desire to find out the truth and resolve the situation.
>
> We support and applaud this action of the Guatemalan authorities and are pleased to think that our efforts on Sister Diana's behalf may have helped to move this matter forward.
>
> As you know, I personally visited with Sister Diana immediately after the incident in early November. I know, from my own personal observation, that she was seriously beaten and mistreated. She suffered a horrible, traumatic experience. As a fellow human being and the father of four daughters, I have suffered and prayed for her.
>
> No one in this Mission has any reason to disbelieve the sworn affidavit given by Sister Diana. However, as you know, important information is missing from her narrative. It is our opinion that,

with Sister Diana's cooperation, the additional facts and information needed to solve the crime can be brought to light. The Guatemalan Commission then should do everything in its power to bring a just resolution to this case.[11]

Stroock told Paul he could use the letter publicly but declined to say publicly himself that the embassy believed me. We were all so excited about the delegation's achievements. We were all so naive.

I decide to go back to Kentucky to get well so that I can participate in the case. Living in fear of the Guatemalan army, only fifty miles from the border, and struggling with regular nightmares and flashbacks, I've helped no one — not the refugees, not myself. Before I leave Mexico, Mimi mentions that some of the sisters at the Mount have been helped by inpatient stays at Our Lady of Peace, a psychiatric hospital in Louisville run by the Sisters of Charity. She's being diplomatic. I know she wants me to consider that maybe it's time for me to get some help.

She has a point. I'm not getting any better by pretending to be the Sister Dianna everyone used to know, with the mere addition of some cigarette burns on my back.

But it's hard to stop pretending. It's become a habit.

On good friday, the sisters at the Mount gather in the chapel to commemorate the fourteen Stations of the Cross.

I sit close to the front and stare at a large wooden cross that has a purple velvet cloth draped around it. I remember that when I was abducted, I was wearing a purple shawl given to me by one of the women in San Miguel.

The first station is announced. We stand and a reflection is read: then we kneel to recite, "We adore you, Oh Christ, and we praise you." I move my lips and stand and kneel, but only to fit in, to keep from arousing suspicion. I don't understand why we are adoring an act of torture, lingering on each detail, as if in the torture itself there were some kind of glamour.

There has been talk this week about Jesus' resurrection. His body died but his spirit continued to live. I wonder if the whole story is a hoax, a fabrication. How could he have kept his spirit alive? My chest aches with wanting to believe it.

The pew is hard. When we sit my tailbone throbs. The Policeman kicked me there.

Jesus meets his mother. We are supposed to be reflecting on Mary's pain as she saw her son mistreated — the helplessness she must have felt. Instead I see my mother, as I saw her when José left me in the dark, before the interrogation started. I traveled in my mind or with my spirit and found her in her bedroom, lying on her side, facing the wall. Again, I see her that way. She is sobbing. Barbara and my sister Michelle sit with her, weeping. I sit on the bed beside her and run my fingers through her short, red hair, as she has always done with me. Mom, it's OK, I'm here. I'm with you. She keeps sobbing. She doesn't hear me. My dad is in the kitchen, trying to be strong. But I can see the pain in his eyes. I reach out to take his hand. My hand slips right through his, as if I were a ghost, already dead. I wander into the boys' room. J. R., Josh, and Nick are sitting on the floor, speechless and still. The only sound in the house is my mother sobbing.

Veronica wipes the face of Jesus. I tremble hearing the name. *This is you, Verónica Ortiz Hernández.* She wiped the sweat and blood that poured off Jesus' face. I remember Alejandro bringing the wet cloth near my face.

Jesus is stripped of his garments. I am not reflecting, but remembering when and how each piece of my clothing was removed.

Jesus is nailed to the cross. I see blood spouting from his hand, flecking the head of the iron spike, spotting soldiers' knuckles. It takes several blows before the spike sinks through the web of his flesh. I watch each spike driven in. People are standing around. They can't look away. They feel horror but stand and watch in silence or mutter a few words of praise about his courage. His side is pierced with a spear — he is tortured, slowly murdered. The onlookers acquiesce.

The thought hits me like lightning: like them, I'm a silent witness, too. I thought I could get away with the affidavit as my only testimony and then begin life anew, forgetting what I'd seen and heard in that basement prison. And my tentative plan to get strong and fight back — my excuse for returning to Kentucky — was that just another way of running from Guatemala and my mission to help the people? As for the hospital stay I was thinking about — Would I take that step so that I could be more involved in the case, so that I could help prosecute? Or did I just want a break?

God, let me resurrect. Guide me out of this paralysis. Help me act to stop the torture.

Chapter Five

OUR LADY OF PEACE

THE DOOR OPENS before I can answer the knock. A man is in my room. I struggle to push myself up straighter on the bed, move the pillows and put my back against the wall. He tells me his name is Dr. Snodgrass. With a few brisk strides he reaches the far side of my bed, where he seats himself in a wooden chair, the only piece of furniture in the room besides the bed and a bureau. His back is to the window. He's blocking part of the light. I would much rather be able to look out at the parking lot and keep track of the cars pulling up. But I make myself give him a smile.

He flips his notepad to a clean page, wraps his long fingers around a pen, and asks what has brought me to Our Lady of Peace.

No notes, I want to say. They could fall into the wrong hands. But I say nothing. He would ask me which hands and how the notes could fall into them. And he would know what a tenuous line I walk between a world that seems vaguely familiar, a world that everyone else thinks is real, and the world I know, in which nothing that seems is, in which nothing can be trusted. I fix my eyes on his shoes to hide my fear. I'm good at it. This was my tactic when the Guate-man and the Policeman interrogated me: eyes down, mouth shut.

The Guate-man had a notebook and a pen, too. He wrote down my answers. And in that room, too, there was a wooden chair.

Like the Guate-man, Dr. Snodgrass is tall and fit-looking, in his thirties. He, too, has a mustache; the whiskers hang down in an orderly, uniform way. His forearms look well-scrubbed under their fringe of brown hair, and they are muscular, veiny. Another similarity: Dr. Snodgrass is meticulous about his looks. His short-sleeved, light-green dress shirt is perfectly pressed, and it goes with his dark-green pants and brown shoes. Even his straight-backed posture in the chair suggests a kind of rigid order, an attention to appearance you could expect of someone in the military — or someone who has something to hide.

I should know. I myself am hiding beneath a squeaky-clean facade. Before bed I showered, then again in the wee hours of the morning, and again before breakfast. When I smell the rancid odors and feel the hands on me and when I remember what my own hands have done, the shower is my refuge. I try to scrub and steam myself clean.

Because of the notepad, I say nothing. Nevertheless, Dr. Snodgrass scribbles something down. Then he sits back.

"Sister Dianna, one thing that comes to my mind is that you're thin. Very thin. How do you feel about that?"[1]

I have no idea what to say. I keep my eyes fixed on the carpet beneath his feet.

"You told the nurse you've had a twenty-pound drop in your weight. We need to keep an eye on that. The good news is, it's nothing that can't be treated. One has to learn how to eat responsibly again. Do you think you can do that?"

The Policeman's sleeve, I can see it from under my blindfold, his hands on my wrist. He yanks me up off the floor. A single stroke of a far-off saw. No. A zipper. On my cheek, against the open wound his fist left, a clammy touch. A pulse.

I RAISE MY HAND to my cheekbone to quell the throbbing. Dr. Snodgrass's sharp brown eyes follow my hand.

He clears his throat. "The sisters tell me you were beaten and burned. If you'd like to discuss that" — he gestures with a hand — "or if there's anything else you'd like to tell me, feel free. This is a safe place."

I look up quickly at Dr. Snodgrass to see if he's telling the truth. His eyes express nothing. Maybe he's only a surface, perfectly groomed — skin with nothing beneath it. I half expect him to evaporate when I blink. But he's still there, waiting for me to speak.

But I myself am no longer present, not really. The part of me that feels and thinks is watching from a corner near the ceiling and from that safe vantage point observes this woman sitting on the bed, bent over a pillow she has under her crossed arms. She twists her crucifix ring around on her finger. It has gotten too big.

He shifts in the chair.

"It just . . . takes me a while to feel comfortable," she stammers.

"Well, take your time. I'm not going anywhere." But after a few minutes he looks at his watch, tucks his pen in his breast pocket, and rises to his feet. He says he'll be back tomorrow and shuts the door behind him.

Was he real, a human being, I wonder when he has gone — or was evil using his body as a mask? I banish this thought. Although Dr. Snodgrass had seemed two-dimensional, like a paper cut-out, everyone else seems that way too at the hospital, myself included. I am a body without feelings, a shell the animal has abandoned.

THE SMELL OF FOOD has the power to tug me back into my skin, at least momentarily. The scent, though faint, falls around me like a warm blanket, and my blood wakes up a bit during the trip down the hall from the ward to the cafeteria. I notice everything I missed when Sister Mary Mathias helped me check in this afternoon: the black and white marble floor of the hallway sports little suns here and there where the lights on the ceiling reflect off the stone. Paintings of landscapes are hung along the cream-colored walls. It's a beautiful hallway, especially compared to the ward, where the TV room and the meeting room are carpeted in a light gray shade and the furniture is covered with a rough tweed.

I MISSED THE ARTISTIC DETAILS, but I did give special attention to the foyer when Mary Mathias and I entered the building earlier in the day. Although the hospital had looked safe enough from the outside — large, modern-looking buildings of dark-red brick and darkened windows, fortress-like atop a hill in a neighborhood of large houses and winding streets — exteriors can be deceiving. And when you've been abducted from a walled convent you pay special attention to buildings and entrances. I scanned the corners behind the potted palms and the niches behind the big peach-colored chairs before I entered the building. I might have taken some comfort in the fact that all the doors to the wards were locked and only the hospital staff had keys — no one could get in without an escort. But no one could get out, either, and being locked in a building is not something I relish.

THE CAFETERIA is my favorite room because it isn't locked. The wooden doors that swing into the cafeteria from the hallway have windows of thick glass molded into a criss-cross pattern, which reveals only colors and forms. I can eat without being spied on by outsiders. If the danger comes from within, I can escape, dash into the hall and out through the foyer. The white linoleum floor under the buffet is spotless, the gray and green carpet under the tables equally clean. The smell of tomato sauce, meat loaf, and cornbread laces the air. The salad bar, topped by fake sunflowers and ferns, contains things I have a chance at eating: yogurt, baked potatoes, cottage cheese — soft things.

IN THE NEXT ROOM, I hear people laughing and talking. Suddenly, I envy them. I unwrap my baked potato and hold it for a moment in my cold hands, and the envy that gnaws at my chest becomes a flutter, a butterfly laughing with its wings. This place must have helped them. It will help me.

This hope spurs me to take part in group activities, such as the morning check-in, where we gather in a circle in the TV room and talk briefly about how we are doing. I just say, "I'm Dianna. I'm doing OK." But I take the participation in group events a step further a few days later when a short, stout woman with curly, brown hair announces at dinner that a volleyball game is planned for that evening. Angie is her name. She plucks at her staff shirt, a baggy, blue blouse with turquoise and purple designs. "It's first floor against the second floor," she says. She raises her fist and gives the air a couple of punches. "Go first floor!"

"All right!" several people cheer.

"It will be a lot of fun. I hope everyone will join in."

I want to be normal and laugh and cheer, so I follow Angie across the driveway and down a slope to the gym. In the gym it's cold and I shiver for a moment: entering cold buildings reminds me of that day nearly six months ago in Guatemala. But the wood floor sparkles, and in a corner are some tables with bowls of popcorn and pitchers of lemonade. I remind myself this is not Guatemala, and the shivering stops.

A stocky young man called Dan appoints himself the unofficial captain of our team. As he points people to their positions, I notice his arms, large and hard and veiny, and his chest muscles bulging against his thin white T-shirt. He motions me to a position by the net and saunters to his place behind me, stretching out his biceps. We haven't even started to play and sweat is already trickling down the side of his round face. His lips are drawn to a pucker of concentration and he trains his blue eyes on the other side of the court, as if daring the ball to disobey him.

For Dan, the game seems a matter of life and death. He dashes around, slides onto a knee now and then (which I'm amazed he can do in his tight jeans), swears, calls out the score, and directs the other members of the team. He leaves me alone until I let a high ball sail over my head, expecting Dan to get it. I'm afraid to run backward, since I might fall into someone.

"Hit the ball," he whines.

I turn around.

Dan has taken a few steps toward me and is scowling. I can smell his sweat. My legs start to tremble. I give him what I hope is a dirty look, to hide my fear. Could he be the Guate-man in disguise? I try to concentrate

on the game instead of examining this thought — but he has the Guate-
man's muscles, his short hair, and the same military strut. And he gives
orders, takes charge. But it's his smell that's exactly the same, the acrid,
heavy odor of sweat. I try to concentrate on the game instead of wondering
what's behind the facade of his body and whether the Devil can inhabit
anyone. I try to concentrate on the game instead of wondering whether
my torturers and the Devil were one and the same.

Another ball slaps the ground behind me.

"Hit the ball!!" This time the order is a howl.

Something in me snaps. "Who are you? Who are you to order me
around!" I have wheeled around to face him and am shouting. "Why do
you think you have the right to tell me what to do?" I continue yelling
after losing track of my words.

His face is two inches from mine; suddenly, his hands are on my
shoulders, shaking me, his sweat drips onto my cheeks.

This is what I imagine. What he actually did I don't know because I
have bolted out the door and am running up a hill. My breath rips at my
chest. I look back. No one has followed. I allow myself to collapse under
a tree and sob into the soft new grass. I turn my head and let the blades
ripple with my breath. Through the grass I catch sight of tennis shoes,
pant legs, bright white in the dusk, coming toward me up the hill. White
slacks, a nurse's outfit, a tall, blond woman.

"Sister Dianna."

She squats down beside me and puts a hand on my back. At her touch
I pull myself up.

"It's all right. My name's Helen. Angie told me about what happened
and asked me to see how you're doing. I want you to know it's OK to be
angry. You told Dan what you felt and that's good. That's what it's about."
She tucks a strand of blond hair behind her ear. "You OK?"

"I don't think so." She's trying to comfort me, but I need information,
not comfort. I need to know what's happening to me. I had no way of
knowing I was going to start yelling and no way to keep myself in check.
I just did it. If I can't control what comes out of my mouth, I'm in worse
trouble than I thought. "Helen, I can't even play a simple game without
losing control. What's wrong with me?"

Helen offers no explanations but walks me slowly back to my room.
"Let's see if we can arrange something special for you that will help you
relax." She closes my door.

I won't let them inject me. I won't lose control of myself. I won't get
into a state where they can get me talking without my knowing it. I finger

the straw cross I have brought with me, carefully wrapped in tissue. I am told it was a gift from one of the women I knew in San Miguel.

A few minutes later, Angie knocks. Her face dimples up in a smile and she hands me a hospital gown. I know what this is for. She's smiling to reassure me. But the gown is so I can't escape. Once they have taken my clothes I'm helpless.

"Upstairs," she says.

In the elevator, I regret not bringing the cross with me. I'm being transferred. The first floor, where I've been, is for people "not a danger to themselves or others." The second floor is like the first, and the third floor is for those who are dangerous. The elevator rises, and the orange light migrates through the three, stops on the four. The fourth floor I've never even heard of. It must be for people who are unfit for any kind of communal activity.

"I just don't want to be by myself," I tell Angie. The doors open.

"I'll stay with you," she answers, and leads me to the end of a hallway. She slides a key into the last door, opens it, and motions me in. The room is steamy.

"Go ahead and change. I'll stay right here and turn my back. The whirlpool's in the corner."

Sunk up to my neck in warmth, I watch my gown rise and undulate on the bubbles. I move so a jet caresses the back of my neck, just where my hair begins. The water is cleansing me; it is pushing me back into existence, back into my self. My blood throbs. I draw my head under the surface and listen to the faint beat of the water. I gulp the air when I let myself up.

Angie has her back turned, assuming I'm half-clothed, and to keep me company she is talking, telling a story about how she baked a cake for her aunt's birthday and used something in a Tupperware container that she thought was sugar. It was dishwashing powder. Angie bows her head to cover her eyes with a hand. When she flicks her hair back from her face and smooths it with her hand, I can still hear the smile in her voice. "But Aunt Mary, she ate it, you know."

A laugh bubbles up inside me. Warmth finds its way into my bones, and for an instant, I am completely inside my body, completely present. Tears of gratitude slide down my cheeks — gratitude for Helen and Angie, and for this gift, this warmth.

This is the first of many whirlpools, a secret between Angie and me. A bit of the warmth stays in my blood, surges up each time I see Angie or Helen. Helen always smiles and asks me how I'm doing as she goes about her rounds. When Angie and I meet, often she winks and points upward. "Eight o'clock OK tonight?" — and again, the warmth tumbles through me. After less than two weeks at the hospital, I realize I'm starting to shake the chill of the dank clandestine cell.

Maybe because he sees I'm stronger, Dr. Snodgrass becomes more insistent about my progress in therapy. Up to now, I've offered little information. Maybe I've said something about the lovely grounds, the nice selection of food, my physical discomfort (abdominal cramps, nausea, that sort of thing). But he makes it clear that today is no day for small talk. "You haven't gone back to volleyball," he says, to open the session. He clears his throat.

"No," I answer. I'm starting to sweat. We haven't discussed the volleyball incident.

He begins to twirl his pen. The light blue cuff of his long-sleeved shirt rivets me. What's the difference between his wrist and the wrist of the Policeman? I finally pull my eyes off his sleeve to steal a look at his face.

He is sitting back in his chair, his left hand cupping his chin, two fingers pressed against his lips.

"You've been here more than a week now, Sister, and have had some time to get acclimated. We have you down for group therapy, and, indeed, I think you would benefit."

A hot current of fear runs from the soles of my feet to my chest.

"I'm not sure I'm very good at being with people."

He combs his mustache with a few fingers for a moment. "Well, maybe you could use some practice."

What if I lose control again? What if I hurt someone? I want to ask but I don't. He doesn't know what I'm capable of. He thinks I'm a sweet little nun. I pick at a thread on my jumper.

"Your weight is continuing to drop and the nurses tell me you hardly eat anything. I've also heard you have trouble keeping food down. Do you typically vomit after meals?"

"Yes. I...I don't mean to. I have parasites and I'm taking some medication. I don't know if that's what's upsetting my stomach."

"I think we need to look deeper than that. Are you sure you're not making yourself vomit?"

Could I be making myself do it? My body seems to vomit on its own. In fact, lately I don't seem to be able to make my body do anything; it seems to have been wrested from my control. I yelled at Dan without meaning to; and before that, before coming here, my body was changing, my breasts were hardening and growing. I was pregnant and there was nothing I could do about it except the one thing I did and I'm not going to tell Dr. Snodgrass about that. I can't trust him. I can't trust any man.

I also can't think of a clear answer to his question so I say something like, "If I'm making myself vomit, I don't mean to."

"Well, let's see what happens if you make an effort, a real effort, not to vomit after your meals. But first you need to try to eat enough. Then we need to try to do something to help you keep your food down."

Wire my jaws together after meals? Tie them shut?

"Would it help you to be with other people after you eat, for example? Maybe you could spend some time in the TV room socializing after meals and stay away from the bathroom until your food settles."

I let out my breath, grateful for these harmless suggestions. "I wonder if one of the nurses could lock my bathroom door and that way I couldn't throw up?"

Dr. Snodgrass is pleased with my idea. As he stands to leave, he looks at me as if to say, "You're the type of person who'll make progress here."

I think how little he knows of me. My cheek begins to throb. I could tell him if I dared. I could stop him, say Wait, listen.

Open your mouth, they tell me. Fingernails dig into my gums. Hands pry my teeth apart, open my jaws so wide my mouth rips at the corners. It is on my tongue, the thing that pulsed at my cheek. It is on my tongue. It tastes of urine, it vomits into my throat. I gag, I can't breathe. I try to spit out the slime. Someone wipes my mouth and my face with a rag that smells like wine.

DR. SNODGRASS might finally have something worthwhile to write down in his notebook, the single word that begins the blank page I've become: whore.

At the next session, I tell Dr. Snodgrass I have gotten a typewriter from the nurses so that I can get some thoughts down on paper. At night, between showers, I type away, listening to my Walkman to keep at bay the screams I hear if I listen too hard to silence. Since I can't sleep I may as well make use of my time. The writing is painful, but it's like making a cross above a snakebite wound. The poison needs a place to come out. Dr. Snodgrass must want to respect my privacy. He never asks to see anything I've written, even though when we are meeting and I shift positions on the bed, the papers crinkle beneath the mattress.

UNDER THE MATTRESS, among other things, are my thoughts about Miguel. José had asked me about him. The other two had left me alone with José after interrogating and burning me and after all three had done worse things to me. But José's soft voice, his soothing Mayan accent, his country lilt added weight to his words: "I'm not going to hurt you. Just tell me everything you know and then I'll pass the information on to them. I promise I won't let them hurt you. Trust me."

Although I was blindfolded, I knew he was genuinely concerned about me — I could tell from his voice. He wanted to avoid any more brutality. That's what I told myself. It only shows that when a person is so desperate and feeling so alone, she is willing to latch onto anything or anyone that can keep her alive and quiet her fear. I told José what I knew. I figured it was nothing the army didn't already know. Rosa and Miguel had told me they were under surveillance by the army.

José asked me if I had lived with Rosa and Luis Miguel Solís and I admitted that I had. He wanted me to tell him more about them. I told him that they had family members who were disappeared, that they were active in GAM, and that Miguel was active in the group CONDEG, the organization for people in Guatemala displaced by the war. José said they had someone inside CONDEG who was reporting to them on Miguel's activities. I didn't tell José anything that he and the others didn't already know. I really believed I would be released, and I had already decided that the first thing I would do would be to warn Rosa and Miguel, and let them know CONDEG had been infiltrated. I was going to tell them to be careful. I wasn't released, and I wasn't able to warn them. I was fleeing for my life. But because I failed to warn them, I felt I had put Rosa and Miguel's lives in jeopardy. This is what I was writing about. I would learn later that Miguel was disappeared. They came for him. I have never been able to clear from my head the voices that tell me I am responsible.

To COMMUNICATE with Dr. Snodgrass and relieve some of the pressure building inside me, all these memories and thoughts I can't voice, I turn to art. The weather outside is gray and I am in the arts and crafts room by myself. Inside I am gray, too, numb as a cloud. I sit at the wooden table with a piece of paper before me, and before I know it I am sketching myself from behind, the broad plane of my back, my shoulder blades. I need a match, and I go to the TV to ask one of the patients who smokes. Returning with the pack of matches, I strike one, let it burn, and blow it out. Then I hold the hot tip to the paper, again and again. Small black marks appear. I make scores of little black burns on my back.

When I meet next with Dr. Snodgrass, I hand him the drawing. He is silent. I don't know what to say, either. I tuck the drawing back behind my bed. What is there to say? This happened to me. He already knows that.

I'm not sure any response of his could help me, anyway. Most of the time I don't understand what he's saying. I'm afraid to ask him to explain what he means. I'm afraid he'll think I am crazy. And I've heard what happens to crazy people. So, if I don't understand, I just let him keep talking.

"Have you been socializing with the other patients?" Dr. Snodgrass asks me.

"Some."

"Have you been making an effort to mingle?"

"I go to the TV room after every meal."

"And that's helping you not to vomit?"

"A little bit."

I do go to the TV room after meals and sit with other patients. I don't often talk. I don't look at them. I don't know their names. But I listen. It was in the TV room that I heard what happens to crazy people. A woman and a man were talking, standing in the hall behind me. The man told the woman he wasn't being allowed grounds privileges, and he felt locked up. His therapist was afraid his urge to drink would overpower him and he would find his way to a bar.

The woman said, "You think being locked in here's bad! My husband decided I was crazy and they locked me up in the state institution. They treated us worse than animals. Don't ever let anyone think you're crazy. They'll put you away. They gave me shock treatment."

It was at that moment, two weeks into my hospital stay, that I decided at all costs to seem normal. Now I force myself to smile when the nurses are around. I sit in the TV room as instructed and busy myself with crafts, flipping through magazines and cutting out pictures to make collages. But I can't stop throwing up. Because my bathroom door is now locked after meals, it works out better for me to be in the TV room, since I can sneak into the common bathroom down the hall. I carry a small can of air freshener in my sleeve so no one will suspect that I haven't mastered the art of keeping my food down.

Looking good is a hallmark of mental health, of caring for oneself. But I can't stand the remarks, even when they're made by the female nurses and patients — "You look great today. What a pretty outfit." Avoiding mirrors is nothing new — I'm afraid of the eyes I will see staring back — but now I abandon my long skirts for jeans. I stop using my tinted Chapstick. I stop wearing earrings and painting my nails. The Policeman also found me attractive. I'd rather not look pretty. I'd rather not look like a woman.

I keep up my routine of acting normal, and I let Dr. Snodgrass talk because if I stopped him and asked him to explain — if I told him I didn't remember much of the English language — he would ask if I had learned Spanish first as a child and if we had spoken it in the home. And I would have to say, "No, English is my native language and I don't remember the meanings of simple words. They sound familiar, I even find myself using them, but I don't know what they mean." And even if he didn't lock me away, the torturers would be proved right; they had told me that if I managed to get out alive, people would think I was crazy.

When my memory was wiped away, chunks of my vocabulary went with it. Trauma does that sometimes. I know that now, but then I didn't. I felt like a foreigner in my own country. My mother tongue, the only language that really resonated with me, was a language of images. My only real vocabulary was composed of the only vivid memories I had: being burned, being raped, being tortured. The language of that world was real to me, and in the same way that experiences are processed through language, all my experiences were filtered through those memories. The language of this world, in which some things are harmless, in which words are used to connect one person to another, for communication, not for degradation, this language was foreign and new. My tongue remembered it, but my mind couldn't take it in or make sense of it.

In spite of the language barrier, my world of dissociation and fear — the bubble in which I am encapsulated — begins to break in the hospital. It starts with group therapy. A nurses' aide opens my door and peers into my room. "Dianna, it's time for group!" My head is throbbing and my stomach hurts. The little lunch I was able to eat went straight through me. All I want to do is lay my head on a pillow and dream this nightmare away.

But I trudge to the room at the end of the hall. The aide is watching me. She has me under surveillance. I must keep this thought to myself — it's probably crazy. I turn the corner into the room, then draw back. When I turn around to tell the aide I don't want to be here, that I've changed my mind, she's disappeared.

The chairs are arranged in a circle. I study the room, already half-full of men and women conversing, laughing. A few people interrupt their conversation and welcome me with smiles. I spot an empty chair between two women. One is biting her fingernails, her face half-hidden by matted hair. The other stares vacantly at the carpet, arms crossed, hands clasping her waist. The thought of sitting next to a man repulses me.

I sit down, draw my knees up against my chest, and rest my head on them. I run my fingers in circles over my temples to try to stop the throbbing. I take some deep breaths.

When I raise my head, across from me is Dan. Our eyes lock. This is the first time I've seen him since the volleyball incident. I had no idea he'd be in the group. I feel tricked. It's a set up, I've been pitted against him for the entertainment of the patients, maybe even the staff; after all this is a boring place. Maybe they want to see us interact to gauge my level of dangerousness or lunacy, to verify whether I am consistently a banshee. Or maybe they just want to see us patch things up. But they tricked me. I want to leave the room but I can't move.

I won't let him stare me down. I meet his eyes and I begin to shake, not with fear but with rage. In his blue eyes, a glint of fear, unease. Am I imagining this? Is he afraid of me? Does he recognize the evil I've tried to hide? I've let it show now, twice with him, on the volleyball court and in the fierce look. I look away, at the same time he does.

The therapist is a woman I haven't seen before, nicely dressed in a green business suit. Her hair is short and blond and gold earrings jangle as she talks. She welcomes us and introduces me to the group as the new member. I squirm. She reveals nothing about me, other than my name. I wonder what she knows? We go around the circle. Each person has ten minutes to talk. I make a decision not to speak, other than to "check in" as some of the patients are doing. I'll say I'm fine, I'm glad to be in the group, I'm working on eating issues.

A woman talks about her visit with her husband and children over the weekend. A man speaks of his urge to have a drink. I barely listen. I can barely breathe. I'm that angry. It's Dan's turn to talk. He clears his throat, rubs the palms of his hands together, and sets one of his legs going in a nervous bounce. I contemplate my shoes. I realize these are the tennis shoes I was wearing when I was abducted. I make a mental note to throw them away. My thoughts can't wander for long. Dan is talking to me.

"I know I upset you the other day. I can get a little competitive some-times and forget a game's a game. I told you to hit the ball because you weren't hitting it. It was meant as friendly advice. And I guess I'd like to know why you got so furious about it."

Tears start to stream down my cheeks. I'm crying in front of a group of strangers. I've lost control again. Before I can stop myself, these words come out of my mouth — "When you ordered me to hit the ball, I heard the voices of my torturers. And I hated them because they raped me." I begin to sob, lost in my thoughts. Someone jangles change in a pocket.

"*Heads, I go first, tails — you go.*"

A coin slapped on skin. "*Heads. She's mine.*"

They're gambling for my clothes. No, not my clothes. My body.

Dianna, pull yourself together, the sun is dancing on the floorboards by your bed, lighting the wood, the white curtain at the window is breathing with the breeze, the children are waiting in the classroom, this is your siesta, you've overslept.

The Policeman drags me up by the hair, as if pulling a mound of weeds from the earth. How he would delight in removing the skin from my head, peeling it off with his knife as if he were peeling an orange.

"*Take your blue jeans and underpants off.*"

Does he really believe he only has to ask and I'll submit to his every demand? If he wants me that bad, he's going to have to fight me.

"*I told you, take your clothes off.*"

Come on, Dianna, don't give up. Fight. Be strategic, the way women are supposed to be in these situations. I begin to tremble and ask God to forgive me for what I am going to do. Taking a deep breath, I command my hands to touch the Policeman's body, to prostitute themselves for my survival. They tremble with shame as they rest on his hips. My throat constricts with nausea when the Policeman's body starts to relax, when he says, "*Very good. Now you want to cooperate.*" *He calls out to José and the Guate-man,* "*Hey, she wants me.*"

Don't feel. Don't think. I pull my body closer to the Policeman, I feel his sex harden and grow.

Then, I step quickly away and throw my knee with all my strength at his groin. A hand wrenches my knee away before it can hit. How can he have known? Can he read my mind? Another hand grabs my hair.

Pain pounds through my knee. My scalp feels like it's on fire. I clamp my mouth shut. I won't let him know he's hurt me. And no matter what, no tears. They can take my flesh apart but my tears are mine. His breath is heavier now, shallower, faster. It is the only sound in the room.

If he attacks you now, there's no one to blame but yourself. It's your fault, a voice in my head whimpers.

Trembling, I gasp, "*Forgive me, please. Give me another chance. Please.*" *My words echo in the darkness. A fist rams into my stomach. I fall to the floor.*

"*It's a bad dream,*" *I hear myself say. And if it's not, God will get me out of this alive, untouched. Right, Dianna. He's had hours to get you out. If he exists.*

The Policeman is on top of me, tearing at my jeans. I fight to lift him off me. He smells of alcohol, cigarettes, body odor, and a hint of orange. My Spanish is broken, my lips tight — "*You're hurting me.*"

He laughs.

"Don't. Please don't. You're only doing this because you've had too much to drink." People don't hurt each other like this for no reason. They can't.

His actions roughen, he runs his hands over my body as if he were plowing soil.

"Please God stop him."

"I want to see your pretty face," the Policeman says and snags the blindfold down.

He slides his tongue across my eyelids, my nose, and my cheeks, leaving a slug-like trail of spit.

"Open your eyes."

I fight to keep my eyes closed but he pries them open and grunts.

What I see sends a jolt of horror through me. Flesh scarred as if by acid. Satan picks masks that please him. The eyes dead, like buttons. The lips pulled back in a yellow grin.

"You'll enjoy this, my little virgin."

The Policeman yanks my jeans and underwear off, throws my legs apart. Then he slices every nerve in me apart.

God, stop, stop.

He sighs with satisfaction, whispers into my ear: "Gracias."

"Your God," he says, pulling himself up, "is dead."

And the Guate-man and José take their turns on me. Each thrust pushes the Policeman's words deeper.

I curl up, watch my body jerk in spasms, dried blood, cigarette burns, bite marks on my breasts, and on the floor the last of who I was, a deep red stain.

Chapter Six

THE SECOND ABDUCTION

ALL I SAID was that I was raped. But when I lifted my head off my knees and looked around the room, everyone was wiping their eyes. My eyes met Dan's. His eyes were glassy with tears.

I saw clearly then that I'd been wrong. These people are not the torturers, I realized. I don't need to fear them. Someone passed down a box of Kleenex. I wiped my face and passed the box back to one of the women beside me. After putting it aside, she took my hand.

I WENT BACK to playing volleyball. No one ever yelled at me again. "Nice ball, Dianna!" my teammates called whenever the opportunity arose.

I decided to take part in other group activities, and two weeks later a nurse with small, blood-shot eyes told me I'd be getting out soon.

None of the patients cared for her — they called her the Bulldog. This must be her idea of a joke, I thought, making fun of how wrecked I am.

"Well, you're better," she insisted. "You've been here a month, and there comes a time when if you wallow you get worse."

She was misinformed. I wasn't leaving. I was well enough to start healing at the hospital but not nearly well enough to leave.

Remembering how wrong I had been about Dan made me braver with Dr. Snodgrass. He may not show his feelings, I thought, but he has them. According to what other patients had told me, he was a good therapist. If he played his cards close to his chest, it wasn't that he had anything to hide. It was just part of his job.

It was odd, though. He never referred to my torture as torture. He called it "abuse." And he had put me into classes to learn how to deal with stress and become more assertive. In assertiveness training, we role-played, telling other patients when our feelings were hurt and asking for what we needed — "I could really use a hug right now. I feel hurt when you don't ask how my day was."

65

I DREW SEVERAL MORE SELF-PORTRAITS. In one, I was clutching my chest and screaming. In another, I was throwing my head back and screaming, crying for help.

Why can't I just *tell* him that I'm having nightmares — that, whenever night falls, I feel their eyes, I smell their bodies, the Policeman, the Guateman, José. They're watching for their chance.

I asked myself that every morning, but I didn't find an answer. I just continued to keep watch at night. The parking lot that my bedroom window looked onto was so well lit that I could see faces clearly. If I drifted into sleep, the smallest noise woke me up. That, no doubt, was a blessing. A car door slamming, a night bird's warble pulled me back out of the secret prison.

TELLING DR. SNODGRASS about what actually happened in Guatemala — not about my nightmares and fears now — was challenge enough. I wanted to tell him about the pit.

I drew a tangle of limbs and heads. I drew myself from behind, naked, suspended above the bodies by the wrists. I couldn't draw the lime that frosted the dark hair of the corpses. I couldn't draw how it felt to have rats land on me as they were dropped from above, their claws on my head, in my hair. I couldn't draw the feel of bodies twitching under my bare feet — women, children, men, some decapitated, some moaning still, all caked with blood and swarming with flies and rats. I don't remember Dr. Snodgrass's response to my drawing or to what I said. I guess he just couldn't take it in. In the medical records he says I described being "thrown into a 'pit' with other alleged dead bodies."

I hung over them until I passed out. Arms. Heads. Why would he write "other," since I was not dead? Why "alleged"?

But I wanted desperately to believe in him and his ability to help me get better, so I tried not to find fault with anything he said or didn't say.

And I was getting better.

"ANGIE, I'VE GOT SOMETHING, I've got a fish!" Only a few minutes had passed since we had trekked down the grassy hill to the lake and baited our hooks with bread.

"Shh," someone said.

"Reel it in!" Angie came to stand beside me in case I needed help, but I wound the reel and up out of the lake came a silver, gem-like fish. It flipped around on the line, opening its gills wide.

Angie lifted it off the hook. "We throw them all back in."

A stream of pink ran from a corner of its mouth.

I took the fish by the tail and tossed it out over the gray water. It sailed for an instant and splashed down.

I would never fish now, but I loved it then. It was the first activity I loved after returning from Guatemala. I don't know if it was Angie's ridiculous stories, our laughter rippling over the water, each fish's fight to live, or the way each one got to tumble back, after a near-death interlude, into its world and go on.

On the way back from the lake, I noticed the treetops were green, and half-grown leaves were waving in the breeze. Near the driveway I spotted a patch of flowers I must have passed for weeks. Daffodils, Angie said. Beads of dew glinted on the yellow cups. I stopped to sniff. Sniffing was my excuse. I was standing still for a moment to let the sunlight fall through me.

SEVERAL TIMES A DAY I had to drink Ensure, a protein substance that tasted like chalk. I put on a little weight, and I wanted to believe Dr. Snodgrass and the nurses when they said I was making progress. I wanted to believe that every smile I flashed the treatment team was real. I would have preferred to be well.

But the real me — not the Dianna who was agreeably pinpointing strengths and weaknesses in self-assessment groups — the real me knew I was dying. I made a collage with clocks ticking, and pasted words around the edges: "Time is running out." I brought into therapy a self-portrait I'd made: my head barely above the surface, I am sinking into a sea of blood and reaching up with one hand to a sky raining more blood. The whole scene is enclosed within a vase. Why a vase? Dr. Snodgrass didn't ask. Maybe I felt people looked at me as they would look at a vase — a graceful-looking, decorative thing — and they couldn't see inside, where I was drowning in a storm and sea of blood. There was a small hole at the top of the vase, too small for a rescue team, perhaps, and maybe even too small for a rope. But the hospital was my chance to get help. I had to try.

I drew another portrait, this time of myself in profile. My belly is puffed out. Inside it is a spiral, mirrored by a spiral in my head. Disordered words come from my mouth — *change, freedom* — which hang in the air, along with some images: a jagged boundary that's been stepped across; a tombstone with my name on it.

Dr. Snodgrass must have questioned me about the drawing — "What's in your belly here?" Or maybe I blurted out what I had done when I found the torturers' seed developing in me. Sometimes I wondered whether the seed the torturers left really was destroyed; I wondered whether it would grow again in me and choke the last of who I was. That was another reason I barely ate. I couldn't nurture it. Anyway, I remember asking him, "Am I like them — am I like the torturers — because I did that?"

"No," he answered.

I wanted to weep with gratitude.

AT THE NEXT SESSION his attitude toward me hadn't changed. He didn't seem afraid of me or revolted by me. He looked at me in the same way as before, as if he were studying me, trying to understand. He accepted me.

But I didn't have long to enjoy that acceptance. He told me that I was better. "In a couple of weeks," he said, "you'll be ready to leave."

I thought of how I could answer: "But Dr. Snodgrass, this place has felt safe. If I seem better, that's the reason. Out there, who will be waiting for me? I'm still taking four showers a day. I haven't told you anything about all the nightmares I've been having — I haven't even had the courage to share them with you yet." Instead I said just a few words. "I'm . . . afraid to go. I don't know if I'm ready."

He suggested that I was afraid of exerting control over my own life.

I said nothing.

I STOPPED making such an effort to eat. I stopped trying to mingle. I stopped going to activities. When Dr. Snodgrass and I met again, he didn't understand that I was trying to tell him, once again, that I wasn't ready to go. "Perhaps you're withdrawing, Dianna," he said, "because you're afraid of improving."

THERE WAS NOTHING TO DO. I'd had my treatment, the community had paid a large sum of money, and it was time to move on. You're a survivor, Dianna, I told myself. You're tough. You can handle whatever comes your way.

IN ART THERAPY my hands knew better. They drew another self-portrait. My body, this time, was a male body, the body of the Guate-man. My head was an open can with worms writhing out of it.

I showed Dr. Snodgrass the drawing and told him I had opened a can of worms by talking about the rape and the pit and the choice I had made — and instead of being able to keep everything contained, now the worms were spilling out.

He still thought I was ready to go. He said he would see me in six weeks and after that we would meet once a month.

Six weeks? I wasn't going to say anything. I was tough.

He would refer me to a new counselor, whose office was closer to the Mount, for weekly visits, he said.

I didn't like the idea of a new counselor. I had just made a huge investment in Dr. Snodgrass by revealing my secrets to him. But I had my pride. I wasn't going to beg. And when the moment came I packed my bags stoically and gave Angie and Helen stiff hugs. It was the best I could do. If I'd hugged them any other way, I would have cried.

SHORTLY AFTER I GOT BACK to the Mount, my mother, my sister Barbara, and her daughter, Amber, came to visit. A sister named Kim brought her five-year-old nephew, Dustin, to play with Amber. After breakfast we watched them chase each other up and down the driveway on tricycles Kim had brought. They shrieked and hollered and raced. Along with my mother, Barbara, and Kim, I found myself smiling.

ONE DAY we went to the pool, left over from the time when the Mount had a girls academy. I wore a long T-shirt over my swimsuit, which gaped open around my legs. The shirt covered the bad fit, as well as the burn scars.

I slid out of my shorts, and before anyone could see much of me, I splashed on in. My T-shirt billowed up, the cold set me trembling, but I didn't care. It was as if I were off in a corner, watching myself stand in the water, then step slowly forward. Amber swam up to Kim and wrapped her arms around Kim's neck, and Kim swam her around while Amber slapped her feet on the water like a beaver flapping its tail. I held the cement lip of the pool and watched. Amber called out to Mom, "Gama, Gama, it's cold!"

Barbara inched her way down the steps and let out a squeal when the water rose over her waist.

"Hurry, Mommy," Amber called. But Barbara was tiptoeing still, folding her arms up like wings to keep them dry.

"Chicken! Bak-bak-bak-bak!"

Barbara seconds later was covering her head to protect it from the deluge of Amber's splashes. Listening to Barbara's shouts and Amber's cackles, the heaviness lifted off me and drifted away. My mother sat in a chair, watching.

"Mom, you doing OK?" Barbara kept asking that. "Sure you don't want to come in? It's waa-rrmm...."

Mom smiled even more and waved away the possibility. When she thought we were no longer watching, her mouth relaxed. Her eyes looked swollen around the rims.

I GAVE BARB a ride on the four-wheeler Kim had taught me to drive. But mostly during that week, I spent time alone. I was afraid that when Mom and Barb and Amber touched me, which they often did, the slug trail left on me would spread to their skin. You can't get it off. Even when you can't see it, it's there.

MOM YEARS LATER told me, "I thought maybe you blamed me for what had happened. I thought to myself that my *hijita* was angry with me because I had given birth to her, brought her into this world."

BARBARA SAID SEVERAL TIMES that she loved me. Amber hugged me a lot. I would be stiff as a tree stump, but when she pulled away, there was no disappointment in her face. Kim, who worked with deaf people, taught Amber to sign "I love you." Amber kept giving me those signs all week.

Mom, Barbara, and Amber were flying back to New Mexico out of Louisville, and Kim offered to drive them to the airport. At the gate, Mom pulled me into a tight hug and kissed my check. "You take care of yourself, Nana." Tears were streaming down her face. I kept my own tears in. Barbara was also crying and fingering her rosary, maybe because she was afraid to fly. Barbara and Amber both hugged me.

"You sure you're OK?" Mom asked. Her tears had left welts on her face. I had seen her with those marks several times during the week.

I looked quickly away. "I'll be fine. I'm all right. Please don't worry." *Don't leave. I need you.* I forced a smile to cover those thoughts and waved them out of the gate, then stood watching at the window until their plane was high in the sky.

IT WAS AT THE MOUNT that I cried, in the shower and the bath where no one could hear me above the water. I cried before going to sleep. I got a scab under my right eye from crying. Most of the time I slept. I woke up for lunch and slept again in the afternoon. Then I'd go for a walk in the park, sit by the lake, and cry there too. My journal was my confidante:

> I'm told that the Mount is my home and that the sisters are my family. Why can't I recognize people? Why do I feel like a stranger in a foreign land? Many of the sisters give the impression that they

know me. Are they being sincere or, like my torturers, are they trying to play with my mind?

I am walking silently with Mary Mathias down the driveway toward the shadowed expanse of the park, where the trees will shield me from other people's eyes and the wind in the leaves from other people's ears. I've asked Mathias if I could have a word with her outside. I have to know if I really can be part of this community. We reach a picnic table and sit at it side by side. To keep my hands from shaking I tuck them under my crossed arms. A fly lands on the chipped green paint of the table. *Don't hurt it,* I think. Mathias shoos it away.

"What I wanted to talk to you about, Mathias...," I begin. "At Peace I started to talk about some of the things that happened. And I...I wanted to share with you..."

"All right."

The leaves are waving in the breeze. A robin drags his shadow across us. Fear has made every detail sharp: Mathias's gray skirt and simple white blouse, her white hands folded neatly in her lap.

"One of the things..."

I can't meet her eyes. Unless I please her, I'm not safe because she's in charge — just like my torturers were. And what I'm going to reveal will not please her. If she feels I'm not worthy to be in the community, she'll ask me to leave. Sister Dianna will cease to exist. I'll be left with them, the torturers, what they made me.

"Go ahead," Mathias says.

The words tumble out in a squeak. "I'm not sure I deserve to be a nun."

"Why is that?"

"Because" — I stammer between sharp sighs — "I — I w-was... rr-raped."

"That's not a surprise, Dianna." Her voice is gentle. "We thought something like that might have happened. Of course, we didn't want to ask you, we wanted to let you bring it up when you felt the time was right. But that doesn't mean you don't deserve to be a sister. It wasn't your fault."

I look up to meet her gray eyes. Behind her large, black-framed glasses, they are softer than I've ever seen them.

"It wasn't?"

"No."

"Sometimes I wonder... if I fought hard enough."

"You didn't ask to be tortured and raped."

"I feel like I contaminate people. The other sisters..." I don't find the nerve to tell her what I've noticed, how when I enter a room conversations stop; when I put my tray down on a table everyone at the table falls silent. The sisters must sense the evil in me.

"This may surprise you, Dianna, but some of the other sisters are struggling with the same issues. Some of the sisters have had very difficult pasts, including sexual abuse. Don't feel like you're alone with this. Because you're not. We're all here for you."

My hands have stopped shaking. I put them on the table before me. "Thank you, Mathias." She squeezes my hand. Then she stands up, turns to me, and enfolds me in her arms.

WE WALK BACK in silence, our shadows falling on the asphalt before us, nearly life-sized in the afternoon light. Relief is flooding through me. I can trust her. As for the thought that creeps into my mind — What would she think if she knew about the rest? Would she still let me stay? — I turn my face to the sun and let the thought melt away. Someday I'll tell her, maybe. But for now, I have to savor the moment and the green, tender bud that has started to open inside me.

KIM AND I drove around nearly every day on the four-wheeler to see the fields covered with corn and the big round bales of hay, the green tobacco and the Queen Ann's lace. In spite of those diversions, it soon became clear that what had been pushing open inside me was not a green bud. It was not even the can of worms I had drawn for Dr. Snodgrass. It was more like a barrel of cobras. The flashbacks were coming almost nonstop. A squirrel, a trip down the stairs, or a bad dream set them off: I woke up and I was in a flashback. I had started dreaming about the Woman. In dreams, I relived every instant.

My torturers take me down the hall to another room and leave me there. The walls and floor of the room are spattered with blood. In the middle of the room is a cot and something or someone is lying on it under a blood-stained sheet. I find a corner, put my arms around my knees and weep. Whatever is under the sheet is alive — I can hear raspy breathing, and the sheet is moving almost imperceptibly up and down with the breaths. I steel myself, walk toward the cot, take a corner of the sheet and slowly peel it back.

A woman. She opens her eyes, and they are light brown in the black and blue of her face. Her teeth appear in the crack of her swollen lips. She is trying to smile.

I catch a sob in my throat and gently take her hand. Her breasts have been cut and maggots are crawling in them.

She squeezes my hand as if to say everything is going to be all right. With tears in her eyes, she asks me my name. I tell her my name.

She tells me hers, or tries to. I can't understand and it's so hard for her to talk that I don't want to ask her to repeat it. She says, "Dianna, be strong. They will try to break you." For what seems like hours, we hold on to each other.

The Policeman, the Guate-man, and José burst into the room. José is holding a video camera. "So you've met," says the Policeman. "Now are you ready to talk? If you aren't, this will happen to you." He gestures toward the Woman.

I notice that he's holding a machete. He walks over to me, holds the machete out. And thinking the time has finally come, at last they're going to kill me or let me kill myself, I take it. Then he gets behind me, traps my hands under his, and forces me to stab the Woman, again and again. The blood is splattering everywhere. My cries are lost in the cries of the Woman.

I woke up to blood covering my hands. It was on my face, too, and smeared along the stucco walls. I kept a pan and a sponge under the bed to clean up. And if the sisters saw this? Would they believe I struck out at the wall in my nightmares and skinned my hands? Or would the blood be evidence against me?

I wrote God notes in my journal:

God, I don't know who to turn to. I don't even believe in you but yet I talk to you. I feel so raw that I want to die. The memories of the torture are so vivid and are gnawing at me. I don't want to remember the details of this nightmare. Please, God, take away these memories. Please.

From my window I could see the Madonna room in the building across the courtyard. There were a lot of paintings of Mary in the room, but my favorite hung on the wall not far from the grand piano. I would sit before that painting in the afternoons, surrounded by dozens of depictions of the Mother of God and her Son. But in that painting, she had no baby. She was alone, and there was pain in her face. Sometimes I thought there were tears welling in her eyes, but that was when they were rising in mine and making her blurry. Her eyes reminded me of the Woman's. Mary seemed to say with her eyes, "It will be all right. Be strong." After bad dreams I peered out my window. She was there, on the other side of the dark yard.

I SUPPOSE that was why I didn't move my bed away from the wall, into the middle of the room where I wouldn't hurt my hands. I wanted to be able to look out, not only at the Madonna room but at the courtyard, as soon as I heard the slightest sound. The Mount wasn't a safe place. The torturers knew where to find me. They had a knack for getting into convents, and this one didn't even have a wall.

Nightly, the Policeman was on top of me. I fought to lift him off and for a second, I did. Only then I found the Guate-man in his place. After another battle, José. I wrote about these encounters, but I told no one:

> Last night the Guate-man, the Policeman, and José tried to enter my room. They had the dogs with them. I heard the growling. I have to find a way to hide from them because sooner or later they're going to break the door down and the torture will start all over. If I told anyone this, they would say it was only a dream. To me it was so real.

I pulled a chair in front of my door and lodged the back of it beneath the knob. At least it would make noise scraping across the floor.

At meals the sisters stared at my puffy, scraped hands. No one asked about them. But Anne Rita, an older sister I often sat with, one day took them in her hands after we'd finished eating and wordlessly tried to massage them. I tried not to wince. While her touch hurt my hands, it was a balm to my spirit. She wasn't afraid of me.

AFTER THE MEAL, she often reached into her pocket and pulled out a peppermint candy, pressing it into my hand. I treasured those candies, for the thought, the gesture, and the clean taste. Another sister gave me a pair of cotton gloves, simply saying, "I thought these might help." I tore my hands through them, and in the morning when I woke up, the cotton was stuck to the wounds. I wasn't thinking very clearly then. Only later would I think to stack pillows around the walls.

Eventually, going to meals became impossible. The dining room was half-underground, and I started having flashbacks going down the stairs — once again, I was going down to the basement prison.

IT WAS SO HARD to make the call, to start all over with someone new, but Dr. Snodgrass had given me Dr. Walker's number, and I knew I needed help. She gave me an appointment, without further ado, but approaching her office I was surprised to see the sign: Family Crisis Center. My family's fine, I thought.

Dr. Walker, a tall, blond woman, took my hand and welcomed me. Her breath smelled like smoke. Her office, a dark room with brown leather furniture, also smelled like cigarette smoke. I sat on the edge of a big chair. Droplets of sweat started rolling down my back.

"How are you?" she asked.

"Fine."

She told me she was married and had two small children. "What about your family?"

"I come from a large Hispanic family. I have a father, a mother, two sisters, four brothers, five nephews, and four nieces. My mom's name is Amby. My dad's name is Pilar. The names of my nieces and nephews are J. R., Nick, Rick, Isaac, Stephanie, Veronica, Melanie, and Amber." I recited the information in a robot voice. I could barely breathe. The talk stayed focused on my family. We never got to why I had sought her out. My impression was that Dr. Snodgrass had told her nothing. But it didn't matter because we finished our "introductory" session early and I got out into the gray afternoon, gasping lung fulls of damp air. I was never going back.

I needed a long scrub in the bath. I needed to wash my hair. I gathered the Ajax and bleach — soaking in them was a trick I had learned to feel cleaner. Laying out my things in the communal bathroom at the end of the hall, I encountered a sister.

"Didn't you take a shower this morning?"

I stared at her.

"We're trying to conserve water, you know." She smiled tightly.

I don't know if she was teasing or if we really were supposed to conserve water. I felt a little guilty — here I was again, doing something wrong — but I washed my hair three times anyway, and soaked in the tub for a couple of hours. Even so, the smell of smoke persisted.

PAUL VISITED the Mount in late May to give the Leadership Council an update on the case. Congress, he said, was pressuring the administration for a total suspension of military aid. He pulled out of his briefcase a copy of the foreign aid bill recently passed in the House of Representatives. "Look," Paul said, putting it down in the middle of the table, "the House bill bans the sale of lethal arms to Guatemala and limits future military aid."

I could tell Paul was excited, but I wasn't sure what any of this information had to do with my case.

He scanned the bill for a moment, then read aloud, "Of particular concern to the Committee is the case of Ursuline Sister Diana Ortiz, a United

States citizen who was abducted and tortured in November 1989 and who has implicated Guatemalan security forces in her sworn testimony. The Committee is pleased that President Cerezo has recently decided to form a special commission to investigate this case. However, progress on this case will be a factor in timely receipt of any foreign military financing or economic support funds."

Paul stopped for a moment and looked around. "So even if Ambassador Stroock doesn't feel Dianna's case is one the Guatemalan government has to solve, Congress does."

My brain felt dull from lack of food and sleep. "Paul, can you explain a little more about what that means?"

"Unless the Guatemalan government makes progress on your case, the Guatemalan army might not get any money from the U.S."

"Money? But Paul, why are they getting money to begin with?" I put my head in my hands. I was just too stupid to get this.

I WOULD HAVE APPRECIATED the bill more if I'd known that the State Department had tried repeatedly to get my name removed from it and that members of the House had insisted on including my case. I would learn that only later, when documents were declassified. Among the documents was this memo from Desk Officer Deborah McCarthy, informing a colleague about the foreign aid bill:

> The addition will be a new condition calling on the GOG [Government of Guatemala] to show demonstrable progress on the investigation of cases of human rights abuse and politically motivated crime to include Blake/Davis, the San Carlos University students, Oqueli, Meredith Larson, and Diana Ortiz. I . . . indicated that the list was the same we had been pressing the GOG on with the exception of Ortiz. That case, I pointed out, has been hindered only by Sr. Ortiz's continued stalling on providing key information needed.[1]

The State Department, I would learn from another document, also opposed the idea of a special commission to investigate my case. A cable drafted by McCarthy and signed by Secretary of State James Baker tells officials at the U.S. embassy, "We are very skeptical about the proposal for a special commission and do not think we should pursue it actively with the G.O.G. [Government of Guatemala]." The embassy is "requested to inform the appropriate G.O.G. officials of the request for the special commission but not to pursue the idea."[2] Stroock in his letter to Paul said he was pleased to think the embassy may have helped with the commission;

but, probably because the embassy didn't help, the commission was never appointed, formed, or called together.

EVEN THOUGH the details of U.S. foreign policy didn't make perfect sense to me, at least I recognized Paul. I looked forward to his visits.

ONE DAY a sister I didn't recognize appeared at my door with a bottle marked "Holy Water." "It's from Rome," she told me. "It was blessed by the Pope. It will help you heal. It might also help you sleep. If you sprinkle it on yourself and all around your bed at night it should keep the nightmares away."

I thanked her, but I wondered if she'd seen the torturers and was trying to get rid of them. I pictured the holy water sizzling when it hit my skin. I imagined myself melting. I'd been careful, avoiding Mass as much as possible. If I went to Mass, I would have to stay in the pew, conspicuous, while everyone else went to Communion. Lord, I am not worthy to receive you.

I left the holy water untouched.

I ALSO RECEIVED a gift from Sister Rita, who was the principal of the kindergarten where I had taught before going to Guatemala. It was a small, hard-cover Bible in Spanish — the Latin American version. I was delighted to get it, but I never opened it. I went into a cloth store once when I was in town and bought a black cotton bandanna, which I wrapped around the Bible, then knotted.

Bound, gagged, and blindfolded. That's how I kept my Bible. I was just so afraid that if it fell open, I would find words of judgment and reproach. I would hear God — a God I believed in just enough to fear — telling me I was evil.

I'M IN BED, listening to my Walkman, having missed breakfast one Saturday, when Sister Joyce comes to visit. She has brought me homemade bread and jam and a large pink rose, which she puts in a vase on the nightstand next to my bed. The fragrance fills up the room.

"This rose reminds me so much of you — beautiful and pure."

I look into her hazel eyes. She seems to mean it. Is there still something human and pure in me?

She sits on the edge of my bed. "You had a hard night, didn't you? Your eyes are swollen."

If I speak tears will come.

She pulls a sheet of paper out of her purse. "I wrote a poem for you. I don't know if you want it or if you'll like it."

I take it from her and unfold it. "Thank you, Joyce. That means a lot." After reading it, I keep my eyes on the paper.

"Dianna, I didn't want to be harsh, but I needed to share my feelings. You're part of this community. You don't live in a vacuum, you know, and your behavior impacts on all of us. A lot of the sisters are angry. They feel hurt."

I pull my knees to my chest and wrap my arms around them. "What have I done to hurt anyone?" She must know.

"Now don't get all worked up over this." Her voice is soft again. Like José's. She reaches out to touch my arm. I don't let her.

"Look, it's just that a lot of the sisters feel like you've shut them out. And it doesn't seem fair. If you knew how we prayed for you. We called everyone under the sun. We did everything we possibly, possibly could."

Her voice wavers. "We thought you'd never come back. For a lot of us, that was the worst night of our lives. And then we thought we had you back. But you're not back."

I can't look up. I know she's near tears. "Like you and I, Dianna, we were friends, we used to talk all the time, we used to share everything — and now you act like I don't exist. I mean, you're so secretive, like you don't even trust me."

"Joyce . . ."

She's running a finger under her eyes.

"You don't understand what happened." I'm fighting to keep control of my voice.

"Dianna, I do understand. I understand all too well." She flips her chestnut hair back. "Maybe you're not aware of this, but sexual abuse did not begin and end with you. There are a lot of Guatemalas here. And while there's a time to grieve, there's a time to get over it. And I don't see you doing that. A lot of the sisters don't think you're making an effort. They think you're feeling sorry for yourself. And it's painful for them. They see you like this and you remind them of what they've been through, and a lot of them don't want to remember."

"I'm trying to get better. It's not that easy."

"OK, I know, but what I'm saying is you're not the only one who's been affected. The community went through hell thinking you were dead and then you come back and you walk around like you're on another planet. And yeah, people feel hurt. And angry." Joyce stops and looks out the window for a moment. "The thing is, Dianna, you made a choice to go back to that country . . ."

"Guatemala." I don't like the way she spat the words out. That country.

"Right. You were getting death threats and we were all telling you not to go. But you went. You chose to go. No one else is responsible for that. If it's anyone's fault what happened to you there, it's yours."

"Please leave. Leave me alone."

The bed creaks as she stands and I hear the door slam. My hands are shaking. I've been so careful to keep them to myself and still I've hurt people. I invited the torturers in — I chose to go back to Guatemala. Now they continue their work through me, spreading pain.

I run down the hall to the bathroom, grab the toilet with both hands, and try to heave them up. I can't. I get into the shower, hoping the water will drown out the words in my head, their words: *You're one of us. You'll never be free.* As the water slaps the tiles it sounds like their laughter.

When I return to my room, the rose is still there and so are the torturers. I can feel them. I take the rose out of the vase and remove the petals one by one, crumple them in my fingers, and throw them away.

YEARS LATER I would understand that some of the sisters were reacting to my torture and the loss it brought them, not to an evil in me. The psalm in the lectionary for November 2, 1989, was Psalm 30. That night, waiting for news about me, the sisters prayed it:

> I praise you, Lord, because
> you have saved me
> and kept my enemies from
> gloating over me.
> I cried to you for help, O Lord my God,
> and you healed me;
> you kept me from the grave.
> I was on my way to the depths below
> but you restored my life.
>
> Sing praise to the Lord,
> all his faithful people!
> Remember what the Holy One has done
> and give him thanks!
> His anger lasts only a moment,
> his goodness for a lifetime.
> Tears may flow in the night
> but joy comes in the morning. . . .

That prayer may have seemed prophetic. The next morning I was alive. But it wasn't that simple. The sisters who had been my friends before November 2 had to grieve losing the friend they'd known and went through all the stages, denial and anger included. One sister has told me, "It was like you were a different Dianna, and I didn't have a chance to grieve the loss of the old one, and I was at a loss as to how to relate to the new one."

When the sisters learned I'd lost my recollection of all those years, they could understand why I treated them as strangers, but in some ways this information gave them more to grieve. All that we'd shared was lost on me. Alicia, for example — one of my first and closest friends at the Mount — had often invited me to her family's house for the holidays, and her family treated me as another daughter. When her father died, I apparently shared with her a beautiful dream I'd had about him, which helped her through that time. When Alicia found out that I no longer had any memory of her father, she mourned the loss of him again. He'd been annihilated from my mind; it was as if, for me, he had never existed.

Also, seeing me after I returned from Guatemala, the sisters had to face the evidence of what humans can do to one another, what God allows them to do. A few of the sisters found their faith shaken.

Torture is calculated to destroy trust and the ability to communicate; in an atmosphere of mistrust and silence, organizing becomes impossible. Predictably, one of the ripple effects of my torture was that communication broke down. I had lost my sense of trust, so I confided in almost no one. Many of the sisters, meanwhile, didn't trust themselves with me — they were afraid they would say something that would upset me. Some of the sisters — including Nancy, my old friend and spiritual director — thought I needed space and wanted to respect my privacy. If I wanted to talk to them, they reasoned, I would seek them out. Others found it too painful to interact with me. Either they couldn't bear to see how unlike my old self I was, or I reminded them of pain they had suffered and wanted to forget. Many just didn't know what to say.

ONE DAY I was sitting on a bench under an enormous sugar maple. I had my eyes closed, and I was listening to the birds. From time to time I opened my eyes to see the leaves, the blue sky through them, and, now and then, a flash of red wings. I was forcing myself to be aware of all the beauty I'd missed in recent weeks.

"Hi, Dianna."

I opened my eyes. One of these sisters I was supposed to know was standing above me. She sat down.

"How are you doing?"

Before I could think of an answer, she asked, "Are you eating? You just keep losing weight. How much do you weigh now?" How much do *you* weigh? I wanted to ask. But she couldn't help being overweight. Her weight was none of my business, and mine was none of hers.

After a pause, she continued. "You do know that... the Catholic Church prohibits suicide." She was having trouble getting the words out, and I would have felt sorry for her discomfort, maybe even touched by her concern, if I hadn't been so angry.

She'd hit a nerve. I fantasized about suicide day and night. It would just put my body in step with my spirit. I'd made no particular plans, but I'd clung to this dream of a dark hole where I could curl up and close my eyes. She wanted to take that from me.

I stood up in silence and stalked down to the rose garden. To be fair, she'd taken nothing from me; she'd only pointed out what I wished I could forget: suicide wasn't an option.

Before I had taken lives, I had begged to die. It was after I'd been raped the first time. I was still curled up, sobbing, when I heard the Guate-man telling José to bring him a bottle of wine. I knew then that it wasn't over. As he stood over me with a bottle in his hand, our eyes met.

"Please, just kill me. Please."

He didn't say a word. He poured the wine all over me. Then they brought in the dogs.

I PLEADED AGAIN hours later. I was in a courtyard. Next to me was the open pit. I could hardly remain standing. José was holding me up. I heard a gun shot. I thought the next shot was intended for me. Under my breath I thanked God.

"Are you going to kill me?" I asked José. He gave me a sad look and shook his head.

"Stop asking questions."

"You can kill me. Please."

Just then the Policeman approached. He asked José what we were talking about. I couldn't make out José's words.

Then the Policeman turned to me. "Tell me what you were saying to him."

I ignored him and lowered my head. He grabbed hold of my hair and put his face next to mine. "When I speak to you, you look me in the eye. What were you and José talking about?"

I didn't respond.

"I'm going to ask you one more time. What were you saying to José?"

I didn't want to make him angrier because I knew he would take it out on me.

"I asked José if you were going to kill me."

The Policeman waited for me to continue.

"Then I asked José to kill me."

The Policeman let out a loud laugh. "I say when you die." Then he raped me again.

NEXT TO THE ROSE GARDEN was the cemetery, the final resting place of all the sisters in the order. If I chose to kill myself now, I realized, gazing at the headstones, I would have no guarantee that it wasn't at the Policeman's prompting. He lives inside me, comes to me in dreams. Maybe he's tempting me.

The Church prohibition isn't the hindrance — I've already broken so many of those. It's knowing that I'll be in hell and there waiting for me will be the Policeman, José, the Guate-man. The torture will start all over, and it will be eternal. I could beg and beg to die but even that escape would be closed.

I have to stay alive.

Finally, only one more day remained until my appointment with Dr. Snodgrass. Mimi was arriving from Mexico on the same day. Good things come in pairs, I thought.

I braved the steps to dinner to load up on coffee. I had to stay awake all night. I couldn't go to see Dr. Snodgrass with swollen, bruised hands. I was supposed to be better. To disguise my weight loss, I would wear my blue jean jumper with a pullover sweater. Skin-colored makeup under my eyes would hide the dark circles.

But as I paged through my journal, thinking about how the last six weeks had gone, I realized I would have to tell Dr. Snodgrass I was worse. I needed him to help me. Maybe I could ask him to prescribe some pills that would help me feel better, sleep better. Maybe I would explain why I couldn't eat. If I could bear the shame of telling him, we could move on to other things, maybe the loss of memory.

I lay back against my pillow, relieved to know that finally I would be able to confide in someone, and sleep overcame me.

I WAS BACK in the secret prison, naked and trembling in a corner of the cell. I had returned to propose a deal: if the torturers would leave me alone, I would call off the investigation.

The torturers conversed among themselves. Smoke rings floated up to the ceiling. Then the Policeman began to laugh. "What an idiot," he said. "Can't she see that the people who are helping her are really us?"

I woke up thinking that even if the flashbacks ceased, even if the torturers got out of my dreams, they inhabited the people around me, the people I turned to for help. That's what the Policeman had said.

I was no longer eager to see Dr. Snodgrass.

KIM AND I are waiting in the reception room, paging through magazines. I can't focus on anything, not even the pictures. I'm working on breathing slowly. I hear footsteps in the other room. My eyes meet Kim's and she gives me a smile. I read her look — It's OK.

The door opens. Dr. Snodgrass is as crisply dressed as ever.

"Hello, Dianna! Come on in."

The greeting is warm enough.

He points to a straight-backed chair opposite his desk. I suppose that means I'm to sit in it. He goes behind his desk and takes his seat. Then he actually gives me a smile. I remember the torturers' smile, a smile of approval. *Very good. Now you want to cooperate.* I drop my eyes to hide my nervousness. I feel his eyes on me, hear his soft breathing.

At last he asks, "So, how are you?"

I can't let him see my eyes — he might see the torturers, he might notice their presence has grown. "Not very well." I want to stop there; the words are so hard to get out. "I'm having a lot of nightmares. And the memories . . . they're so awful now, so vivid. And I don't know how — to talk to anyone, to tell them what I'm dealing with. I feel so alone. I want to disappear."

"Perhaps you're feeling sorry for yourself."

Nothing comes out of my mouth when I open it. It's that feeling of being punched in the stomach — no air is available. I've started shaking. I won't let him see me cry. I stand up and walk out.

"Let's go," I mouth to Kim. She puts down her magazine, eyes wide with surprise.

We sit in the car for a moment before I can talk. "He thinks I'm feeling sorry for myself, Kim. That's why I'm worse."

"Why would he say that? That's absurd! I'm sure it will get cleared up.

It'll be OK." Kim reaches into the glove compartment and hands me a Kleenex.

"I'm not ever going to see him again. Kim, he doesn't understand! I needed him to help me!"

"Mimi's going to be here in a few minutes. She might know how to find someone else. She might have some ideas."

At least Mimi is coming. And at least I stood up for myself. I couldn't speak, but by walking out I told him he was wrong. I refused to subject myself to that kind of treatment. I took care of myself.

Mimi arrives, jumps out of her car and holds her arms out, beaming. I get out of the car and fall into her embrace. We hug for a long time. I don't even want to pull away.

We get into Mimi's car, and I tell her what happened.

"Dianna, why don't you come home with me," she says, "maybe stay a couple of nights? Mom's got plenty of room. That way we could spend some time together, I can tell you all about Mexico, and you can catch me up on all that's happened at the Mount."

I long to go. Mimi's family is like my own. Her mother is so lively, and her eleven sisters and brothers and their children would be in and out. To be surrounded by that warmth would be wonderful. Then I remember that Mimi's father died only a few months ago. She was at his funeral when I was abducted, and she never got a chance to grieve with her family. I tell Mimi I'd better go back to the Mount. We drive on in silence.

Since it's already late, Mimi, Kim, and I stay at our friend Bill's in Louisville instead of driving back to the Mount. The next morning, Mimi and I hug goodbye.

I know when I get back to the Mount I'll have to talk with Mary Mathias, tell her Snodgrass is not the right doctor for me, and ask for her help in finding another. I feel gritty from the car ride and my bones are aching from stress. As soon as we arrive at the Mount, I get my things together to take a shower. Before leaving my room, I hear a tap at the door.

It's Mathias. "Can you come to my office, Dianna, when you have a moment? I'd like to talk to you."

What a relief. She's saved me the difficulty of asking for some of her time. She says it can wait until after my shower, and I stand under the hot spray, trying to wash off every breath Snodgrass breathed, every word, every look, every drop of Snodgrass.

Mathias's door is open. She and another council member, a friend of Mimi's named Suzanne, are sitting on the couch. Their faces are white.

I pull my lips up in a smile and say hello.

Mathias jumps to her feet. "Come in, Dianna. I asked Suzanne to be here."

I sit down on a couch across from them.

"Dr. Snodgrass called today. He told us what happened." Her voice is shaky.

A silence falls. Suzanne is biting at a hangnail.

My underarms are getting slick. Why doesn't Mathias continue? Was it that rude of me to walk out?

"Dr. Snodgrass said — his exact words were, 'I'm bound in conscience to let the community know that I consider Dianna suicidal.'"

"What?"

"He's afraid you're a threat to yourself. He wants you in a safe place. We know what you're dealing with, Dianna. He told us about the abortion." She clears her throat. "We've made the decision to readmit you to Our Lady of Peace. All the arrangements have been made."

This isn't happening.

"Dr. Snodgrass thinks it's the best thing, Dianna. He can help you. You have to give him a chance."

My throat closes up. I participate in packing my bags, and as we start off down the driveway I notice for the first time the American flag flapping above a building, right at the convent's heart. The torturers were in front of me the whole time, wearing the masks of friends. I can almost hear them laughing.

Chapter Seven

THE SECOND WOMAN

MIMI WAS WAITING at the door to the hospital when we pulled up. My memory of that afternoon is dim, but Mimi remembers it vividly and has filled me in:

> There was *nothing* I could do. Mathias and Rita kept saying, "You don't know, Mimi, you don't know." I guess they assumed that you hadn't told me about the abortion. I said, "I know what we're talking about. Let me take her home. We'll watch her day and night. Nothing will happen. My family even offered."
>
> But there was no way to convince them that this was not the best thing for you. In all the other cases where Peace has intervened with any of the sisters, it's been good for them. This was something just totally out of anybody's knowledge, but Mathias really honest to God thought that was the best thing for you and was really fearful that you would take your life.
>
> You had this death grip on my arm and wouldn't let go, so they let me go up with you. There were two or three women moaning or screaming down the hall. It sounded like a bunch of people. There were no frills. We got to the room and you just collapsed. You said, "I'm not going to think about it." I said, "Dianna, you have got to fake it. You've been here before, you know what the rules are, and you've got to fake it and get out of here."

It was good advice, but I was in another world. To this day I have no memory of Mimi's presence at the hospital, no recollection that she accompanied me upstairs. I was back in the clandestine prison. My first memory of that hospital stay — the second abduction, Mimi and I call it now — is watching myself crouched in a corner, screaming, flinging my head against the wall. Then I crawled into bed and pulled the covers over my head. The sheets were soft and white. But even in that light, domed world, the torturers spoke. *No one gives a damn about you.* I tried to reason this voice into silence. In the park Mathias had told me it wasn't my fault.

86

She had hugged me. But she was talking about the rape, and the abortion was another matter. It was my choice. She knows what I'm capable of now. I tried to keep myself locked up at the Mount. I tried to keep the filth inside me a secret, I tried to quarantine myself, but I was found out. They've rejected me now. They have me locked me up on the floor for those who are dangerous.

But if I were completely evil, why would I be concerned about the people in Guatemala, Rosa and Miguel, my family, Mimi and Darleen? Is there any way to convince the community that a part of me is not all bad?

I hoped I'd be back in my room at the Mount, just waking up from a bad dream, and peered out from under the covers.

It smelled like cigarettes. Smoke was creeping in under the door. The room was eerily clean. Perhaps the Guate-man and the Policeman have disguised my cell — added a bed with a light above it, and a window and a bathroom. But they forgot to take care of the chair. There it is, the wooden chair. They want to make me believe I am safe, that I am in a hospital — a place where people are cured, not injured. They want me to trust again and reveal information they can use to destroy me. Rita, Mathias, and Suzanne — my whole community, perhaps — conspired with them. And, like that day eight months ago in Guatemala, I didn't resist. I went like a lamb to slaughter.

Within me, I heard the Woman's voice. *Be strong. You still have Mimi.* I had forgotten Mimi, but the Woman remembered.

THE FIRST PERSON I noticed in the hospital was a woman pacing the hall outside my room. I nearly mistook her for the angel of death. Her black clothes flowed out behind her. She was thin and oddly beautiful, with black hair that fell in front of her shoulders. She looked up for a second as she passed my door. Our eyes met. Her lips crinkled up in what seemed a try at a smile. She moved on, but her look stayed with me. Blue eyes, sleepless half-moons beneath them.

For a moment I hoped that she was the angel of death. I feared hell — the eternal reenactment of my torture. But at least when I was being tortured my body was in shock, and the physical pain blocked some of the psychological pain. In hell, anyway, I would hope for nothing.

The footsteps stopped outside my door. She'd come for me. A knock (as if I had a choice in the matter). The door opened.

It was only a nurse. That's what I thought at first, anyway. She dumped a pill into her hand and held it out to me, hissing. Then I knew she was an instrument of the torturers.

"Sister, I know you're upset," the nurse said. "I have something that will help you sleep." Too hoarse to respond, I turned to the wall.

"If you have second thoughts, Sister, just come to the nurses' station."

I'm not imagining it. She's hissing. Have a bite of this apple. Try that line, it worked for you once. Nothing held out can be trusted.

EVEN IF IT BROUGHT ME PEACE I wouldn't take the pill. I need to be awake. I'll lie here awake, perfectly lucid, and plan my escape.

THE NEXT MORNING, sunlight cut itself into squares on the wall and fell across the salmon-colored carpet. The furnishings hadn't vanished.

Perhaps this was no more than a hospital, and the nurses well-meaning Sisters of Charity. Even so, they couldn't help me. I had been through the Adult Treatment Program before and had been offered before, as the brochure on my bureau advertised, "the opportunity to learn valuable interpersonal skills, such as the ability to relate better with others, to meet new challenges with a renewed sense of self-reliance, and a healthy capacity to cope with everyday problems."

A shower, some careful grooming to set me apart from the other inmates, and I was walking out.

I have this unrealistic way of hoping.

Barely interrupting my step — which I hoped matched my tone in being both casually light and authoritative at once — I told the hallway nurse, "I'm going out for a walk."

When she didn't answer, I looked back. She glanced up for a moment, smiled, and continued filling bottles with pills. "Sorry. The only place you're going is breakfast."

I begged. She scolded me. And when she turned her back, I ran to the door. Of course, the knob didn't turn. I shouted, "Let me out!" and pounded on the door for a long time before sinking down on the floor.

A crowd of patients gathered above me. A Kleenex wafted down. Ashamed to be making a scene, I barely looked up but managed to catch sight of the person who dropped it, a red-haired woman with a trembling hand. "I know just how you feel," she said throatily, before the nurse sent them all back to their rooms.

Angie walked through the door and found me crouched next to it. She wiped my tears and stroked my hair and convinced me to go to breakfast.

But now she had a notebook, like Dr. Snodgrass. Her job was to record what I ate. I ate nothing. I was watching the angel of death. Angie was telling me how thin I'd become, how if I wanted any privileges I had to eat, and so on. I interrupted her to tell her I wasn't suicidal and I didn't belong here and to ask the name of the woman in black. Clarissa, Angie answered, and went on with her cajoling.

We had our own dining room on the third floor. I was sure that for those who died, there was a third-floor cemetery as well. The dining room here was eerily quiet. The only noise was the occasional scrape of a fork on a plate, a pot or pan clanging, and people chewing bacon or toast. Grits, eggs, muffins — the patients were eating it all, staring at nothing.

Everyone seemed to have been drugged or flogged into compliance — maybe even surgically altered. I wondered momentarily if they were the people I had heard screaming in the building in Guatemala, people who'd been tortured and broken. They had that look.

But Clarissa was building a pyramid on her plate, tearing a biscuit into tiny pieces and stacking them up. When the structure was balanced, she carefully lowered her hand and squashed it flat.

Next she reached for her orange, rolled it palm to palm for a while, and hurled it across the room into the garbage. A perfect shot. No one even noticed. Clarissa must have felt me watching. She turned around.

I smiled.

BEFORE LEAVING the dining room we had to line up, single file. I couldn't imagine why, although I tried. Was forming a line one of the "everyday problems" we had failed to solve? Were we being given another chance to meet this challenge? Or was it that we would trample each other in our excitement to get back to our rooms? It didn't make sense. The reason for the line became clearer when I realized how drugged the other patients were. They could amble out and still smack into the walls.

Trying to line up, people kept tipping backward and stepping on the toes of the ones in line behind them, who then lost their balance, sending the wave of instability on. Clarissa started to laugh. She was at the end, just behind me, and everyone turned to look at her. This set off a true catastrophe. People didn't tip. They fell into each other. They caught each other. Clarissa laughed even harder. Eventually everyone laughed, and laughing, they fell to the floor and had no strength to get up. The aide finally gave up — even she was smiling a little — and opened the door.

"GOOD MORNING." Dr. Snodgrass was heading for the chair with a blank legal pad tucked under his arm. His sat down somberly and drew a pen from his pocket. He could look at my back. I turned to face the wall and hugged the pillow to my chest. I pictured myself spitting in his face, wrapping myself around his neck like a snake. In the silence that followed his greeting, sleep overtook me. When I woke up, he was gone.

I dreamed of a large, white-gloved hand, moving toward my mouth to extract something, or to force something down my throat. Behind the glove, Dr. Snodgrass. I woke up screaming, found the telephone, and called Mimi.

"You can't leave me here, Mimi," I told her.

Mimi was silent. "Dianna, listen," she said at last. "I don't know if I can get you out of there."

"But . . ."

"I've tried and I'll keep trying. How many times have I called Dr. Snodgrass? At least half a dozen. He won't take my calls. I've talked to Mathias time and again and so has Carolina, the woman from church who was tortured in El Salvador. We've explained that the hospital is the worst place for you — that being locked up and listening to people scream and being under the control of someone who's betrayed you will only bring back the torture. There is nothing I can say that will make her think I know anything that comes close to what Dr. Snodgrass knows. She's listening to him."

"Mimi . . . don't leave me here. I can't stay here. I can't be here alone. Will you visit me?"

Mimi was silent for a long time before she spoke. "I want to, Dianna, but you don't have privileges. Not until you 'cooperate.' Like I said, I'll keep trying, but I'm afraid that playing the game may be your only way out."

I was furious with Mimi. I had tried cooperating the first time. I had confided in Dr. Snodgrass, and my compliance was turned against me. My only safety lay in refusing to play the game, in silence. Anyway, if I "cooperated," I would have to accept Dr. Snodgrass's assessment of me — that I was suicidal, that I belonged in the hospital, that he was right. I would have to betray myself.

I was furious with Mimi because she couldn't get me out. I felt bitter and abandoned and black inside.

It was a mood I couldn't maintain. Gratitude ate at the edges of it. I began receiving gifts.

The first was a basket of candy bars, anonymously left on my bed. Since what I ate was my choice, my only choice, and it was probably some kind of trap anyway, I tossed it into the trash. But then I remembered the red-haired woman who had dropped me the Kleenex. She had also given me countless quarters for the phone. I'd had to beg, since I'd arrived with no money, but she had put me at ease. She was in the TV lounge when I first approached her, looking at a newspaper that was upside down on her lap.

She pressed a quarter into my hand, and with slurred speech she told me her name was Susan. "If you need more, just let me know." I was touched that even in her state she was noticing and tending to the needs of other people. Perhaps I should have saved the candy bars for her. Angie, too, had left me things, some hard candy and a stack of quarters on a little smiley face note. I put the candy into my mouth, not sure if the warmth starting to flow through my veins was only a rush of sugar.

But Clarissa gave me the greatest gift: a way out.

She was in the TV room, which would have been where I met the Woman, if this were the clandestine prison — a big room off a long hall. Clarissa was reading a book and grasping her pony tail in one hand, holding it forward over her shoulder.

I sat on the other end of the couch and pretended to watch TV. She was so elegant in her tiny black warm-ups and matching black running shoes. She must have realized that I was glancing over from time to time to try to get a glimpse of what she was reading.

"Do you like Plath?" she asked, putting the book on the coffee table so I could see the cover.

"What?"

"Sylvia Plath?"

"I don't know her."

"She's great. You can look through if you want."

I moved closer, picked up the book, and paged through. "What does she write about?"

"Death."

"Oh."

"Other things too. She's got this one poem about all the suicide attempts she's made and how she always manages to survive them."

I put the book back down on the table. "I saw you with the orange."

Clarissa returned the book to her lap and looked away. Then she turned back and studied me. "Do you have hunger pangs?"

"What?"

"Do you have hunger pangs?"

I didn't answer. I wasn't sure what pangs were.

"How much do you weigh?"

"I don't know."

"Right."

She was quiet for a moment. Then she surprised me. She took a shoe off. "I've got something to show you." She lifted out the double insoles and put them on the table. "Look inside."

I didn't really want to touch what she'd been running on for months, but Clarissa intrigued me. I didn't want to hurt her feelings. So I grasped the top one around the edges and peeled it back. In the white coffin her insoles made were two razor blades.

She picked one up and held it out. I wasn't sure if she was showing or offering it. If I wanted it, I would have to take it by the sharp side. I wanted it. I reached out. She pulled it away for an instant, then relented and held it before me again. She kept the blade still while I carefully closed my fingers around it.

"Thank you." I held it in my palm, turned it to catch the light, then took my shoe off and tucked it under the sole. I've got a secret, I remember thinking. Clarissa and I have a secret together.

That night, I took the razor blade out of my shoe and went into the bathroom, where no one would disturb me. I crouched against the wall, holding the blade in front of me. Maybe death will just be a long sleep, I thought. Maybe a short period of rest, anyway, before the trial begins, where God will be the judge, and the Woman, the people in the pit, the thing I destroyed, and the torturers will be witnesses against me. "She did this," the torturers will say, gesturing toward the Woman. "She could have resisted but she gave in." I will try to explain that I tried to resist, but all of us will know that I should have been stronger. Miguel will be there, branded with wounds, mutilated. He will be there to speak of my omission to warn him. The people in the building will testify. If I could have provided more information, they might have been rescued. *You should have been stronger. Murderer.*

Razor blade, no. Not yet. I put it back in my shoe.

EVEN IF IT WAS FEAR that prevented me from taking my life, having the means to die and choosing not to gave me strength. With the razor blade I was no longer the victim of the torturers' decision to let me live. I was no longer the victim of the sisters' decision to hospitalize me or of Snodgrass's assessment that I was suicidal. I had control over whether I would live or die. And I was defining myself by choosing to live.

CLARISSA WASN'T AT LUNCH. I knocked at her door. "Clarissa, time for *Love Boat!* She had told me she didn't like to miss it, even if they were all reruns. I liked the program, too, and if they were reruns, I didn't remember. One good thing about memory loss. Not seeing her anywhere in the halls or common rooms, I asked a nurse about her. She told me Clarissa had improved. She'd been moved to the first floor.

Mimi and now Clarissa. My only friend here is gone. She'll be able to go for runs on the grounds, be out in the sun, even have visitors. And all the while she carries a razor blade in her shoe.

Once the anger had passed, I realized Clarissa had given me another gift. It was clear to me by then that no one was going to rescue me. If I was going to get out, I was going to have to get myself out. The only way was to play the game. During the interrogation in Guatemala, no answer I gave was right. Here I knew what the right answers were. I just thought I couldn't give them without betraying myself. But Clarissa had shown me that playing the game didn't mean total surrender.

As children when they tell a lie cross their fingers to signal their faithfulness to the truth, I kept the razor blade in my shoe as a sign of my loyalty to myself — a symbol of defiance and of my respect for myself, my own life. And I began to "cooperate."

Dr. Snodgrass was surprised when he made his daily visit. "Good morning, Dr. Snodgrass," I said, before he could get a word out. I asked him how he was doing. Settling into the chair, he gave me a quick, uncertain look and muttered, "Fine."

I was facing him, sitting up on the bed with the pillow behind me. "I'm fine, too." I plastered a smile on my face.

"Your mood seems better."

"Yes. I've been thinking a lot about what you said, Dr. Snodgrass, last week when we met in your office." I had rehearsed this silently all morning and the words tumbled out. "You were right. I was feeling sorry for myself. And all this not eating, not talking — this has been one big temper tantrum. I'm finished now. I'm ready to get better."

He smiled, smug, complacent, gratified. His pen flew across the page.

I was feeling pretty smug, too, in spite of the rage kicking around in my rib cage. He pretended he could help me. If deception was the game, two could play it.

ANGIE WAS ASTONISHED when I loaded up my plate at lunch: mashed potatoes, Jell-O, crackers, yogurt. She gave me a smile and squeezed my arm. She, too, had something to write. And I ate. The mashed potatoes were warm and fluffy, sweet and salty, buttered. The yogurt creamy, with bits of peaches. If nothing else, my body was relieved. I started to feel better.

And within a day I got transferred. In the hall with my suitcase I read the sign on the door to the stairs: "Staff, use caution when opening door. Patients from third floor will attempt to elope down stairwell." I got taken down on the elevator.

Once on the first floor I found Clarissa's room. She let me in, smiling, pulling on her bony hands. Light poured through the window and illuminated the bureau, where in neat rows she had laid out a hairbrush, lipsticks, a nail file, all her books, pencils, and pens, six packets of Saltines, and six packs of breadsticks.

"Welcome to the first floor. So you've graduated. Sit down," she said and swept her arm toward the bed. I was relieved she didn't point to the wooden chair. She had her hair up in a bun, and when she spoke, I saw all the sinews in her jaw. She sat beside me on the bed, brushed back little wisps of hair, and folded her hands in her lap. As usual, she was covered in black — a long skirt and a long-sleeved shirt. Even her socks were black. "How was your trip?"

"Great. I've been dreaming of walking out that door for days. Seems like years. I finally just fibbed and told Dr. Snodgrass I was ready to get better."

"You aren't?"

"I am, but it's not possible here."

"You might surprise yourself. Sometimes you get better in spite of it all. I should know. This is my fifth time here."

"Do you think it's helping you?"

"This time it is. I'm finally confronting the root causes. Yep, after my third suicide attempt and years of anorexia and making myself throw up" — she rolled her eyes — "I'm finally dealing with the real issues."

"Good."

"Well, it's hard, but if you don't do it, you wreck your life, even more than you've already wrecked it."

AT BREAKFAST, the dining room was filled with light and the clatter of voices. Clarissa was quiet. She reached for the salt, and her sleeve rode up. Three bright cuts marred the white skin of her wrist. I quickly lowered my eyes. I didn't know if she knew I had seen. I didn't know whether to say anything. This must be how the sisters felt when they saw my hands. As we took our trays back, I said, "Be gentle with yourself."

She dropped her eyes and didn't answer.

I CONTINUED with my plan of resistance. I pretended to take the antidepressant Dr. Snodgrass had prescribed. The nurse's hand as she held the pill out didn't look human. I was sure that if I grasped the right place on her wrist, I could peel that white, manicured nurse hand off like a glove and beneath would be the callused, blood-crusty hand of the Policeman.

Every morning, I made a show of taking the pill. Then I spit it out in a tissue.

Dr. SNODGRASS was beginning to suspect he'd diagnosed me wrong during my first visit, when he'd noted in my records that he thought I had a "long history of an eating disorder" that predated the "abuse." By the end of my second stay, he'd changed the diagnosis to "atypical eating disorder" and added "rule out" — which I've learned means he decided I had an unusual type of eating disorder and had been looking for evidence of it, but as yet had found none.

I wish he had just told me he had no experience treating torture survivors and would read up on the subject or refer me elsewhere.

BECAUSE I WAS RIDING the exercise bike, as required by the "target heart-rate program" Dr. Snodgrass had placed me in, and because I was talking to him and doing artwork, I soon got visitor privileges. Mimi, her sister Ottie, Kim and Luisa (a sister who had worked in Chile), and our friend Bill came to see me regularly. They would bring Chinese food and we'd have picnics in a small room at the end of the ward, where we'd push some tables together. (If we wanted to take the food into the main part of the ward, where the bedrooms were, all the boxes and bags would have to be inspected.) I would always invite Clarissa to eat with us. Sometimes she'd come to enjoy the company — she didn't get many visitors — but she would never eat.

I ALWAYS had to get out of my room after Snodgrass had been in it. Clarissa always welcomed me. We'd sit on the floor with our backs against the bed. Often we'd talk about clothes, looking through magazines and smelling the fragrance pages. After about a week of this, I asked her why she always wore black. Because it was her favorite color, she answered, and it made her look thinner. "I would have made a good nun in the olden days, huh?"

"Maybe, Clarissa. A better nun than I make."

I told her, finally, about why I was there, and a little of what happened in Guatemala. I had to talk about it. I told her why I despised Snodgrass, how he betrayed my confidence. I told her about the abortion.

She put the magazine down. "I had one, too. I remember it every year. Now that I have children, it especially hurts. But I just couldn't have had a baby back then."

"You have children?"

"Yeah, two little boys and a little girl. They're great." She smiles for a moment, then wraps her arms around herself. "I don't see them much. My ex-husband got custody. They said I was unstable — which I guess I was."

"Do you think maybe someday you could get them back?"

"Maybe. One thing I've learned is that I don't really want to die. If I did, I would have pulled it off by now. It's not like it's rocket science." She's quiet for a time, staring over her knees, which she's drawn up under her chin. Then she turns her head sideways to me. "Anyway, Dianna, if I'd been in your shoes, I would have done what you did. And I don't think the nuns saw the torturers in you. I don't see them in you. I think they just don't understand. Not everyone is going to understand you."

"No, they don't understand. And neither does Dr. Snodgrass. I feel so dishonest when I talk to him and so . . . alone. And the real problem is that here I'm pretending to be making a miraculous recovery so I can get out, but when I get out, where will I go? I dread going back to the Mount. I can't go back there. I don't know who to turn to." I'm in serious danger of crying. I really don't want to cry in front of Clarissa. She never cries in front of me.

As if she knew that I was struggling to keep my composure, she stood and looked out the window. She started reciting something.

"I have no need for friendship, friendship causes pain," were the words that stayed with me.

"No one's there for you when you really need them," she concluded. "Don't turn to anyone, if you ask me." She perched on the window seat, drawing her shoulders up and turning sideways so all I saw in the darkening light was the outline of her straight nose, thin lips, and bony little chin. She reminded me of a raven.

"But Clarissa," I finally said, "I thought we were friends. You're the only friend I have here."

After a minute she came back and sat on the bed. "We are friends. It's just tempting sometimes to live by the words of that song. Every time you trust someone you risk getting hurt. But you have people you can trust, Dianna. I'm your friend. And Mimi's your friend. She's here all the time. So you're not so alone. Hang on to Mimi. I wish I had a friend like her. She's the real thing."

"I think you're the real thing, too."

"I hope so."

"Of course."

An awkward silence fell. To break it, I asked what she had been doing in art therapy. She fished under the bed and pulled out a piece of paper, then turned on the lamp. She had painted hands reaching out, with deep red cuts in each wrist. Under the image she had written "Self-Portrait."

You're more than your wounds. That's what I should have said, but I'm not sure I understood it myself. I just thanked her for letting me see.

"Clarissa," I said as she put the drawing away. "Do you think the reason your suicide attempts haven't succeeded is that somewhere, deep down, you know that there's goodness in you — you know that you deserve to live?"

"No." She was sitting on the bed above me, now, staring straight ahead with her arms wrapped around her knees. "I stay alive for my children. I don't want them to have a suicide as a mother. And I want to see them grow up. Although when they get older, they'll probably be embarrassed by me. There's no way to keep this from them. All they have to do is look at my wrists — if their father hasn't told them already. You know, sometimes I think about how I've wrecked my life and how much easier it would be just to end the suspense, to be able to put all the questions to rest, like, How badly have I wrecked it? Will I ever get my children back? Will I end up destroying myself? Will I end up destroying them? It would just be easier to kill myself and get it over with than to live with the fear."

"But you don't do it."

"No, I don't. I haven't yet."

"And as many times as you try it, you keep coming back here and trying to get better. Maybe your children will someday realize that they're lucky to have you for a mother. They can learn a lot from you."

She looked at me quickly. "Like what?"

"Like how to fight. How not to give up."

"Dianna, I have a confession to make." She picked at the pieces of lint on her skirt.

"But I'm not a priest."

She ignored my try at a joke. "You know the razor blade?"

I pointed to my foot. "I still have it snuggled inside my shoe."

"I gave it to you because I hated you."

"But Clarissa! Why did you hate me? What did I do?"

"Oh, it was nothing you did. You were skinnier than me."

She got up and walked over to the bureau, opened a drawer and pulled something out. "I have something else for you now." With it hidden between her hands she came back to the bed.

She lay it down on the bed and waited for me to lift the cloth it was wrapped in.

I pulled back a corner. Something gleamed. I looked at Clarissa.

She was smiling.

Another corner, and light shot off a bracelet, made up of tiny plastic shapes of all different colors.

"I thought it was like our friendship. It's beautiful, isn't it? Unique."

"It is." I slipped it over my wrist.

THAT NIGHT AT DINNER Clarissa gave me a copy of the Simon and Garfunkle song she liked, about being a rock and having no need for friendship. I carried it around for years because it expressed what I often felt or tried to convince myself to feel so that I could remain protected. It would take me more years still to appreciate the irony: Clarissa lettered out this song for me about being an island, and she was my first bridge back.

WHEN CLARISSA was able to go outside, she started bringing me rocks. Perhaps it was the exercise program, or maybe the stress of pretending to be well, but I was not gaining weight very fast. I couldn't even go out in the sun yet. One of the conditions for my final release was a minimum weight of a hundred pounds. Susan and a few other patients with grounds privileges joined Clarissa in sneaking me stones. I hid them in my bureau between weigh-ins, sometimes bringing them out to hold them. It felt good to close my fist around them, as if I were holding on to the truth I had to hide — Dr. Snodgrass wasn't helping me and couldn't help me, and the only way I could get better was to get out of the hospital. Some of the other patients understood this, and the rocks represented that understanding. They meant I was not alone.

I FINALLY GOT GROUNDS and even off-grounds privileges. I went to the TV room to tell Clarissa. She smiled and seemed happy for me. But beneath that smile was a bigger smile. Her eyes were gleaming.

"Dianna, I've got good news, too! I'll meet you in your room — give me fifteen minutes!"

Her children must be coming, I thought.

She tapped a happy rhythm on the door a few minutes later and walked in. Too alive with joy to sit, she shifted from side to side and tapped the back of one hand in the palm of the other. "So can you guess what the news is? I'm getting out! I'm going home!

"When?"

"Today! And I talked to my ex and he said the children have been asking for me and want to see me and we might even be able to set it up for this weekend! God, I've got so much to do! I want to get my hair trimmed and find something with color to wear so I don't look like a witch and clean the house and get them some presents — What's wrong? Why are you looking like that?"

"Like what?"

"Like you swallowed something you shouldn't have. You're not happy for me."

"No, I am. I'm really happy for you, Clarissa. I'm very happy. Congratulations."

"I'm going to see them! I've got so much to do." She was counting off on her fingers: "I've got to pack, make calls, sign forms — I'll talk to you later!"

She was already at the door, with her hand on the knob.

"I'll miss you, Clarissa."

She careened back to the bed and gave me a half-hug, so unexpected that I didn't even have time to stand. This was the first time we'd touched. "I'll miss you too," she said, and was gone.

I DIDN'T WANT to be alone. Some patients were painting at a card table in the TV room. I also didn't want to talk, so I took a seat on the window ledge and looked out at the powder-blue sky. Two clouds were merging, forming a face. The eyes in it widened as the clouds split apart. The mouth gaped open.

"Dianna."

Only a few minutes had passed, but Clarissa was beside me, her eyes swollen and red. She handed me a piece of paper. "Here's my address."

"Clarissa, what happened?"

"My ex — he called. He decided he won't let me see them. He said" — she waved a hand in front of her, as if chasing his words away, but all the same she struggled to say them — "he said he has to think about what's best for the children long-term, not what they want right now. I'm too negative. That's what he said. And my 'energy' could hurt them. I threatened to call my lawyer and he said don't push it. He might consider fixing it so I can't see them at all." She started to shake. "If that happens..."

Clarissa's chin was trembling, her nose was running. "If that happens, I don't know what the point is. If I can't be their mother, what would it matter whether I die?"

"Clarissa, hang in there." I grabbed her arm. "You'll get to see them. You have that right. They need you."

"I called my shrink."

"And?"

"And now she has to see me before they let me out. She didn't like the way I sounded. But she can't see me until tomorrow, so I'm stuck here! God, I should just..." A sob cut her voice. She practically ran from the room.

In her own room, she was sobbing. I could hear her through the door. "Clarissa."

"Go away! I'm sorry, Dianna, I need to be alone."

"All right. I'm sorry.... Clarissa, just don't give up."

I TOLD MYSELF that I wanted to respect her privacy. But I knew I should have insisted. I should have kept knocking until she let me in. I should have gone in anyway and laid my hand on her shoulder or just sat beside her. That's what I would have wanted if I had been her. I was afraid I would see her etching her pain into her skin with the razor blade. I was afraid of seeing blood.

After dinner, I knocked again. This time she didn't answer. I left after hanging a bag with an apple and crackers on her door and pacing the hall for a while.

IN THE MORNING Clarissa's room had been emptied. I was told she'd been discharged and seemed in pretty good spirits. That meant nothing, I wanted to tell the nurse. Anyone could fake their way into being released.

Mimi and I were planning to go to the arboretum, but all I could think about was whether Clarissa was alive or dead.

"Look, she's probably fine," Mimi said. "And if she isn't, it's not your fault."

"But it is my fault. I should have told someone what she said, before they could release her. I should have told them she had a razor blade. But I didn't want to betray her." Was that the real reason, or was it simple cowardice?

We convinced a nurse to call her. I just wanted to hear her voice. The phone rang and rang. "No one," the nurse said. "She must not be home."

At the time I hadn't read the statistics. I didn't know how common it was for people to kill themselves after being released from a hospital. I didn't know that someone who had made previous attempts was much more at risk. I tried to tell myself that since she hadn't killed herself yet, she wouldn't do it.

Mimi agreed to drive to her house. We searched for the street on the map and found ourselves driving into neighborhoods with ever-bigger houses and yards. The house with the number on the mailbox matching the one Clarissa gave me was a huge, red-brick colonial with a tennis court in back.

"Mimi, will you come to the door with me?"

Mimi rang the bell about ten times. No one answered. We sat in the car for maybe an hour, listening to the birds, not knowing what else to do.

A black sports car roared up behind us. Clarissa jumped out. She was carrying shopping bags. "You! What are you doing here?"

I got out of the car and stared down at my feet, feeling the blood pool in my cheeks.

"It's great to see you!" she said. "Hey, Mimi!"

I'm sure Clarissa must have told us how the situation with her children turned out, but I don't remember. I probably wanted to believe that it was irrelevant, that she would have chosen to live regardless, even if she were going to be considered forever dangerous to the ones she loved.

She showed us a dress she had bought. It wasn't just black, if I remember right, but had gold in it, too, and some turquoise. Before Mimi and I left, Clarissa and I embraced. I could feel the blades of her shoulders as she breathed. Beneath my hands, they dipped and rose again like wings.

Chapter Eight

BREAKING OUT

FINALLY THE SCALES hit one hundred pounds. Walking down the marble
steps in the foyer, opening the glass door, I made a vow: I will never let
anyone take control of my life again. Coming out onto the driveway, into
the air scented with just-mown grass, my body hummed, nearly weightless.
I was walking out through my own will and wiles and the solidarity of
others. I had rocks in my pockets as keepsakes. And I didn't hurt anyone.
No one died.

Mimi took me to Wendy's to celebrate my freedom and a new life. I
didn't have to go back to the Mount. Mimi and I would be living in Owensboro, a small town about fifteen miles from the Mount, distinguished by
the largest number of fast food restaurants per capita anywhere. I would be
working in the library of Brescia College, where a decade earlier I earned
my degree in early childhood education. Mimi had found some tutoring
jobs that would leave her enough time to visit me frequently. The Council, which had set up the library job, had also arranged for me to live in
a community with several other sisters. Mimi would have to find her own
place. A couple of the sisters were people I had lived with before I went
to Guatemala. I didn't remember them. But Kim, Clarissa, and Mimi had
taught me that I could have friendships, and I was looking forward to
living in a community, working, and being a normal sister.

While I was relieved not to be back at the Mount, I was troubled about
my relationships with the sisters there. I felt betrayed by the Council, but
the rift with the community at the Mount went beyond that. Even before
I was packed off to the hospital, Joyce was telling me people thought I was
feeling sorry for myself. She said the mere sight of me caused some of the
sisters pain.

I had been in my own world, I realized, and had hurt other people
because of it. I would apologize.

Dear Sisters,

*It is with great difficulty that I write this letter. Yet I feel the need to
share with you one fragment of my life's journey....*

I am most hopeful that each of you knows in your heart that the two years that I spent in San Miguel Acatán, Guatemala, were perhaps the most invigorating and faith-filled years of my life. In such a short time, I grew to love, to respect, and to empathize with an oppressed but hope-filled people. With the help of the indigenous people, Mimi, and Darleen, and each of you in your own unique way, I know what it means to live justice! During [my stay in Kentucky last summer] I discerned my call to be of service to the people of Guatemala. I truly believed God was calling me to accompany the Migueleños on their journey towards Resurrection. On September 18, I excitedly returned "home" [to San Miguel]. I was and continue to be grateful to Sister Mary Mathias and the present council for respecting my decision to return to Guatemala. And by no means do I regret my decision to accompany my sisters and brothers of Guatemala in their struggle towards liberation!

In the next paragraph I dropped in some information that I hoped would help the sisters understand me: I mentioned that I was raped and that the memories of the rape and torture kept me from believing in myself and life. Then I continued:

My way of coping with this . . . struggle often leaves me feeling drained and hopeless and gazing at an unknown destination with so many unanswered questions: Will the pain ever subside? How does one gather courage to once again face life with confidence? Will innocent people continue to suffer? Is promoting the kingdom of justice a hopeless cause? So many questions and so few answers . . . I yearn to crawl under a rock and hide from what I sometimes consider to be my greatest enemy — reality. It is your love and gentle, yet challenging, encouragement that give me the courage to keep the storm of injustice from leaving its legacy. This same encouragement that is a light within me . . . enabling me to believe that in the middle of winter there is within me an invincible summer!

The sharing of this fragment of my life's journey is by no means intended to be a sob story or a plea for sympathy! Rather, it is my way of thanking each of you for your support. I realize at times I appear to be distant, insensitive, and unappreciative of the countless ways in which so many of you have reached out to me and continue to reach out to me. My intense feelings of shame, filth, fear, humiliation, anger, etc., often leave me feeling unworthy of acceptance and love. And the last thing I would want to do is "contaminate" any of you with this ugliness that is so much a part of me. I apologize if I have in any way inflicted pain upon you, whether it be my remarks or insensitivity. I reiterate that your presence and support

*continue to affirm my shaky belief that someday the KINGDOM OF
JUSTICE WILL PREVAIL!*

I was owning my past, taking responsibility for my decision to go to San
Miguel and for my behavior since returning. What I couldn't own was the
present. In fact, I didn't feel loved and encouraged by the community, and
it wasn't the community that was showing me the light of the invincible
summer within me. I was the one insisting on that. I told myself that I
had gotten so much better.

AT THE LIBRARY I didn't have to interact much with people, and the
people I did interact with were patient, kind, and soft-spoken. One of my
jobs was to catalog books on the computer. I had never used a computer,
and I could barely recall the basics from day to day. I'm surprised I didn't
delete all the files. The library was a clean, well-lighted place with whole
walls of windows, and I was kept busy. When there was no other work, my
supervisors had me decorate the bulletin board. It was odd to be drawing
something positive. It was hard. But I could do it because I was well.

I told myself that each morning as I walked the two blocks to Brescia
and each afternoon as I walked home. I could do whatever I needed to
do. When squirrels leaped out of the bushes and darted across the road, I
paused and breathed hard for a moment, then walked on. I still scanned
the sidewalks daily for any signs of the Guate-man, the Policeman, José,
or Alejandro. I was now on public property, not in a convent tucked away
among farms. They would have every right to walk down the street. When
dogs barked, my breath came faster than my footsteps, and I didn't dare
look behind me. Dogs were used in my torture in a way that was too horrible
to share with anyone. Even now I don't talk about that part of the torture.

WORSE THAN THE WALK to work was the trek to the Rape Crisis Center,
another four blocks away. I had to see a counselor there, according to
the terms of my release from the hospital. I'm sure the counselor meant
well. Maybe she was trying to explain that I wasn't treating myself with
compassion; but all I remember are the words she said on my third visit —
"Don't you see? You're just like the torturers."

That session was my last. I didn't need to see her anyway. I could get
along without any help from anyone.

But she'd poked a hole in my confidence. She'd seen through me. She
knew. I was like the torturers, and it was inevitable: I was going to hurt
someone else.

I withdrew. Instead of going to meals, I stayed in my room. I barely spoke to the sisters in the house. Mimi was the only person I talked to. I needed her so badly that I wouldn't even allow myself to consider the possibility that I would hurt her.

THE SISTERS in the house concluded that Mimi was the problem. If she weren't around so much, I might make an effort to bond with other people. She was blocking my recovery. A Council member told Mimi that the sisters in my house would like her to stay away from me.

Mimi just pretended that no one ever passed the message along and kept coming by. Her attitude was, "It's an Ursuline house and I'm an Ursuline." "Besides," she tells me now, "if I weren't taking you out for Wendy's hamburgers you would have starved to death. That's how I gained all this danged weight. I'd say here, eat this, this is good. And you'd look at it and I'd eat it."

According to Mimi, I was losing a lot of weight and having flashbacks. A counselor who was head of the psychology department at Brescia says I came to see her regularly, at times distraught after something had triggered a memory. I don't remember any of that. I told myself I was doing well, and I must have made myself believe it. I had little choice. I wasn't going back to the hospital. At the mere thought of Dr. Snodgrass, my head throbbed.

AS THE SUMMER came to an end, I received information that Rosa, Miguel's widow, was in danger. She had been abducted and temporarily detained, apparently by men linked to the army. I had answered the torturers' questions about her, and I hadn't warned her — just as I hadn't warned Miguel.

I signed some papers to sponsor her for a visa so that she could come to the United States. I don't remember feeling anything. I don't think I was letting myself feel at that point.

ON NOVEMBER 2, the first anniversary of my abduction, the sisters in my house organized a gathering after work. It was a small gathering, which was what I wanted — just my four housemates and Mimi, Luisa, Kim, and Suzanne. I wasn't quite comfortable with Suzanne yet. The memory of how she and Mathias had forced me into the hospital had never left me. But she was a good friend of Mimi's, and she was making a special effort to be nice to me, I could tell. Maybe she regretted the role she'd had to play that day as a Council member.

Our plan for the evening was to play board games and card games and keep our minds occupied with pleasant thoughts. But the sisters at the Mount sent me a dozen blood-red roses, which reminded me of the occasion. Flowers, as if I were dead? Or a rose for the survival of each month? I was confused and unsettled by the gesture but touched, anyway, that the sisters had remembered the date.

THE SAME WEEK Paul called me. *Prime Time Live* wanted an interview with me, he said. "It would be Diane Sawyer. You know, she's from Kentucky. She's very good."

"I don't know."

"Dianna, I know it would be very hard for you. And this may not be the time, so use your own judgment. Dr. Snodgrass has already weighed in, and he thinks it's not a good idea."

"Why?"

"He thinks you're not strong enough, is what he said, not ready yet."

He's not even my therapist anymore. What gives him the right to weigh in? Why was he asked before I was asked? Once again, Snodgrass was the expert. He knew more about me than I knew about myself. Again, people were making decisions for me, as if I didn't exist, as if I were dead. I remembered the vow I made — no one was ever going to take control of my life again — and I decided to do the interview.

The producer seemed very gentle and sensitive, and she agreed to some ground rules. They would give me the questions in writing beforehand, and no follow-up questions would be allowed. I could take a break or stop the interview whenever I wanted. I could have Paul, the Brescia counselor, and Mimi in the room.

I WAS TERRIFIED. Proving Dr. Snodgrass wrong was no longer sufficient incentive. But since the Good Friday service seven months earlier, I'd known I had to do more than file an affidavit. I had prayed then for the opportunity to act, to speak, and now I had it. The U.S. and Guatemalan governments had used my silence as an excuse to push aside what happened to me. They say there are holes in my story, I thought. Well, now I'll fill them in.

Prime Time Live was interested because Guatemala was now a story. In June, Michael DeVine, an American, was killed in Guatemala, decapitated with a machete. His murder got a lot of attention and the U.S. State Department finally announced a cut-off of military aid. But what about all the Guatemalans who had been killed? What about the hundreds of thousands? Miguel? The Woman?

I owed it to them to speak for them.

I prepared for a couple of weeks, reading through my statements and going over the questions. I began to think about acknowledging what had happened to the Woman. It seemed only right to tell about her suffering. I couldn't remain silent about her and not be an accomplice in covering up torture.

The interview was at the Mount, in the Madonna room. There I would have the Woman with me. I had felt her with me anyway in those weeks. I had felt her breath as I breathed.

MIMI STAYED WITH ME in the guesthouse the night before, guarding me from nightmares. I was still uncomfortable there, but I hoped that after the interview the community would understand what had happened, why I still wasn't the old Dianna.

THE POLICEMAN'S VOICE came to me as I walked across the grounds.

I am holding the Woman's hand. The Policeman gestures with the machete. "No one cares about her. No one is looking for her. Just like no one is looking for you. Yeah, I still have fun with her. And if you survive, no one will care about you. No one will believe you."

I REACHED BENEATH MY COAT and held between my fingers the sweater Mimi taught me to knit during her late-night visits, patiently taking the yarn from me when I made a mistake, fixing it, and handing it back almost perfect. I was wearing it as a testament to the life I'd remade and to Mimi's caring. The Policeman was wrong. Mimi cared. Mimi believed me. Also my mother. Barbara. My dad. There was a long list.

TRAINED ON THE SPOT where I would sit were two eyes, inhuman. Glass. The eyes of the torturers. The eyes that watched me thrust the knife in. The eyes that knew the filth on my soul. Alejandro's threat flashed through me: We have the videotapes and photos.

I hadn't allowed myself to remember. Now I knew that might be the price of the interview. I would have to speak about the Woman now, tell the story my way, say I was forced, before Alejandro could leak the film to the press. The torturers could have edited it, distorted it; they could have filmed from an angle that made the stabbing seem my choice. Even if the film showed the Policeman's hands on top of mine, a torturer was behind the camera. It would be his image of me that the world would see, me as what he'd made me, me as he chose to portray me.

As soon as I sat down the cameras peered into me, searching. Diane Sawyer was giving me a warm smile. "I've made a mistake," I wanted to say. "I can't do this." The woman in the painting said with her eyes, "Be strong for us, for those who didn't survive."

Recounting what happened — calling up the memories, putting them into words, I felt the burns, I felt my skin tear. My cheekbone throbbed. My tailbone ached. I felt the rough hands, smelled the blood. I heard the Woman screaming.

I remember so little of the interview, other than the pain. I've learned that it lasted five hours, and ten times I collapsed, sobbing. According to Mimi, when my feelings got too intense I went out into the hall. I carried with me a picture of some women we had known in San Miguel, and in the hall I would take the picture out and look at it. Then I would pull myself together and go back in.

After the interview, I asked Mimi if I had said anything about the Woman.

"What woman? No."

"Mimi, what did I say?"

"You talked about the pit. And the burns and the rapes."

I went to bed and wept. I had abandoned the Woman again; I had failed her. The torturers were still in control. Through the fear they'd put into me I had hurt her again.

After a while, I was aware that I could still feel her presence. She had not abandoned me.

A few days after the interview, a phone call came into the library. It was for me, but I wasn't there, and the person who answered the phone asked if she could take a message. The caller, a woman whose native language seemed to be Spanish, said, "Tell Sister Dianna to stop talking about Guatemala or else."

The call was reported to the Owensboro police. According to the report the police submitted to the FBI, I was in the room when officers came to discuss the incident but "did not make any statements and appeared very withdrawn."

I must have pulled so far into myself. I remember nothing about being in a room with Owensboro police officers. I wiped the whole incident from my mind, including the call. I guess I just couldn't live with the fear.

Classifying the call as a "terrorist threat," a misdemeanor under Kentucky law, the police limited their investigation to "spot checks" on the house, meaning a police car drove by at certain intervals.

Mimi remembers seeing a police car drive slowly by my house several times a week, and the spot checks are mentioned in declassified FBI documents. I refused to notice the police car. I was living in a LaLa land of deep denial, where I was a sister like any other.

But the sense that I was in danger must have sunk in.

I AM IN MY ROOM in the afternoon when the back door opens. Keys rattle. Then a long pause, silence. I don't hear the door shut. Footsteps cross the living room, so heavy I can hear them on the carpet. Again, silence. Moving quietly, carefully, I crawl under the bed. My breathing is loud, and I stifle it, putting my hand over my mouth. Across the dining room, into the kitchen. A drawer opens. The swish of water. Another drawer. Whistling. The Policeman and the Guate-man whistled. The footsteps approach, through the dining room, the living room. The back of my hand is wet with tears. The back door opens and closes. It's a ruse. He has his knife, now, is hiding in the house, waiting for me to think it's safe.

MY BODY took over for me: I fell asleep. When I awoke the house was still and my fear was gone. I crawled out from under the bed, dusted myself off, and noticed that the room was still bright with the afternoon sun. I sat for a few moments in its warmth before a larger, colder fear ripped through me. I had realized it, finally: I was worse than ever. A year earlier I wouldn't have cowered under the bed in the middle of the day, trembling and crying, falling asleep or passing out from hyperventilation, whichever it was, because a housemate had come in for lunch.

Now that the wall of denial had fallen, I lived in terror. Flashbacks were no longer triggered only by surprises, sudden dogs, or squirrels. Walking into the office that I'd worked in every day for months I had a flashback looking at the desk. It was big and metal, like the desk in that basement prison. Feelings began to overtake me. The most potent was rage. Rage at the Council, at many of the sisters, at Dr. Snodgrass, at the Policeman, José, the Guate-man, the Guatemalan government, the U.S. government, and the God I used to believe in, the God I prayed to during that time when I was "disappeared," the God who let me suffer then and now. The God who let the Woman suffer, who let children be thrown half-dead into an open grave, who let defenseless people be tortured and slaughtered. The only people I had seen as angry as I was were the torturers. I remember how rage distorted the Policeman's face. He left his seeds inside me, and yet another abomination had sprouted, was winding around me, choking me, taking over. What if I mistook some innocent person for one of the torturers, as happened with my housemate, whose footsteps and whistling had me convinced when I was under the bed? My judgment was impaired. The desk in the library, though not identical to the desk in Guatemala, for a moment was the same desk to me. What if I attacked someone in uniform who looked momentarily like the Policeman, or some strong, dark-haired man my eyes rendered as the Guate-man? I was dangerous.

People in Guatemala were also at risk. I could start to talk; I could tell more about the indigenous woman who helped me after I escaped; I could talk about people in San Miguel.

Loose talk would be bad. Paul was encouraging me to meet with State Department officials. He explained that if I didn't do the interview, the State Department and embassy would say that I was not cooperating with the investigation and that I didn't want justice, only publicity. It would give them an excuse to do nothing. She talked to *Prime Time*, they would say, why can't she talk to us? The question itself suggested that I had ulterior motives and something to hide.

The question was easy to answer. For one thing, Alejandro didn't tell me he had a friend at *Prime Time Live*. His friend was at the embassy. The State Department gives orders to the embassy. I could only wonder if the embassy gave orders to Alejandro, who gave orders to my torturers — if the State Department was the ultimate boss of the men who took my life away. I didn't think I could talk to those people, especially when I was feeling so out of control.

"It's the only way we can move forward with the case," Paul told me.

How could I say no? If the Guatemalan security forces could do what they did to me, a North American nun whose case had caused international uproar in Congress and the press, if they could do this to me and get away with it, they would know they could do anything to anyone. More people would suffer. Talking, I could kill people. Remaining silent, I could kill people.

I told Paul I would think about it, and I started carrying my razor blade with me in a matchbox and sleeping with it under my pillow. If the courage found me in the middle of the night, I could do it quickly, before I lost my resolve. If the torturers found me, I would do it before they could take me again.

IN THE MIDST of this turmoil, Darleen called to pass along a message from Sister Alice Zachmann, the director of the Guatemala Human Rights Commission, in Washington, D.C. From the commission's publications, I had found out about Miguel's disappearance and the ongoing atrocities in Guatemala. I was afraid Darleen had bad news. But the news was good. Alice had told her about a treatment center where Central Americans who were tortured were getting help. The director of the Marjorie Kovler Center was a Guatemalan. The center was in Chicago, but I would be able to stay at Su Casa, a Catholic Worker house specifically for torture survivors, run by two Sisters of Mercy and a Christian Brother. About a dozen torture survivors lived in the house, Darleen said, all from Central America.

I asked Darleen for the number of the Kovler Center and dialed it more than a dozen times, hanging up before Mario González, the director, could answer. When I finally summoned the nerve to let him pick up, his voice was soft, the lilt particular to Guatemalans pulling the ends of his sentences up, even in English.

I told him I didn't trust people, and he said that was just what the torturers had wanted — torture was designed to break down trust.

He used the word "torture." I was so relieved.

We talked for a long time. "Mario," I said finally, "I feel like I'm out of control. I feel crazy."

"Are you crazy?"

I took time to think. "No," I said, "I'm not."

"Well, I don't think you are, either, because if you were we couldn't be having this conversation."

I laughed, half crying, and heard him laugh.

"You're normal, Dianna, for a torture survivor. Everything you're feeling is a normal reaction to an abnormal social situation, the situation of torture."

He told me he thought the Kovler Center could help me, and I believed him. There was a problem, though, and I didn't know how to bring it up. Some sisters had already remarked on the amount of money the community had spent on me. One told me, "The community paid for Mimi and Fran to bring you back from Guatemala. Then we covered your expenses to and from Mexico. Then all the legal fees. Then your time at Our Lady of Peace." I couldn't ask the community for anything more.

Mario, as if he'd guessed what I was thinking, told me I didn't have to worry about expenses. Everyone who worked at Kovler volunteered their services.

I CALLED PAUL and told him I would talk to the State Department, but after that, in January, I was going to the Kovler Center in Chicago and I didn't want to be contacted there. I just wanted to heal.

First I had some business to take care of in New Mexico. Mimi and the counselor from Brescia went with me. After supper my first night there, we called everyone but the children into the living room — Mom, Dad, Barbara, and her husband, Abel; my other sister, Michelle (Shell for short), and her husband, Richard; my brother Ron and his wife, Ida; and my brother John. I told them I was interviewed by *Prime Time Live*. Then I stared at the rug. I heard Mimi clear her throat. Maybe she was trying to encourage me. "I . . . I told Diane Sawyer a lot of things about what happened, and the interview is going to be broadcast in the spring. I wanted to let you know what I told her before it came out on TV."

"I don't think it's such a good idea to have all that coming out on television." I didn't dare look up to see who was talking. I heard the person turn to Mimi — "It's just going to cause her more pain." I let Mimi answer. I was busy imagining what they might say about the rape and how I would answer. You shouldn't have let them do that to you — didn't you fight? You shouldn't have gone back to Guatemala. It was your choice to go back to that country. If anyone is to blame for what happened, it's you.

I couldn't bear to tell them. I handed out copies of my affidavit. A minute went by; paper rustled as they turned the pages. Then Mom started wailing.

Beside her on the couch, my dad put his arms around her. "She's still alive," he said. "Stop doing that. She's still here." He knew what we all knew. Latin women wail that way when someone has died.

My mother's wails finally broke into sobs.

The others were still reading. Paper crinkled. Barbara let out a scream, a sound so like the Woman made.

I was hurting them. "Do something," I told Mimi.

"Sons of bitches!" Abel cursed. "I'll kill them."

"Listen, y'all, Abel, that reaction you're having, now you understand why Dianna has to fight this," Mimi said. "This cannot just happen and no one do anything about it. That's why she has to make it public, so they can't just get away with it."

Little by little, the sobs subsided, Abel fell silent, and everyone stood to circle around me in a hug. "We love you, Nana." *It wasn't your fault*, I heard in those words, those touches.

"So how are we going to fight it, what's the plan?" someone asked.

I wished they hadn't said "we." I saw my mother, pallid, red-eyed, and

I wished I were an I alone, an island, no community, no family. Then no one else would get hurt.

Mimi told them about the meeting with the State Department next month and my plan to go to Kovler. "Dianna needs to get strong to fight back. And she needs to fight back to get strong, to get her life back."

After a silence, my dad spoke up. "We'll support you in whatever you decide to do, Nana. God will be with us."

"It's not just about you, it's about the other people in the building, isn't it?" Shell asked, stroking my hair.

I nodded, and Shell circled me tighter in her arms. "Then do it, Nana. Fight."

"I think what matters right now is what's best for Dianna." My mother's voice was uneven and hard. "This is just going to keep hurting her."

FRAN AND PAUL were in Guatemala, trying to move the case along. Guatemalan Attorney General Acisclo Valladares was blocking the formation of the independent commission to investigate the case, questioning the president's authority to appoint it.

The president wasn't putting up much of a fight. He wouldn't meet with Paul and Fran and would be out of office soon anyway. At least Paul could bring to the ambassador the good news about my upcoming meeting with State Department officials.

Only a few months earlier, Stroock had complained to Paul in a letter:

I am very concerned that, as we approach the first anniversary of the crime suffered by Sr. Diana, very little to no progress has been made in seeing that justice is done. The more time goes by, the more difficult the task.

My staff and I continue to wait for the information requested at the beginning of the year and to have Sr. Diana speak directly with trained investigators. Without this information and the cooperation of Sr. Diana, it will be very tough if not impossible to bring the perpetrators of the crime against her to justice. In addition, Sr. Diana's affidavit reports that other people were being tortured at the same site and time as she: We would like to help find this place of illegal incarceration and torture, shut it down, and bring those operating it before the courts.[1]

Stroock should have rejoiced at the news of my meeting — he could finally shut down this clandestine prison. Instead, as we learned years later when documents were declassified, he panicked, cabling the State Department the following message:

> Embassy understands there is a possibility a representative of ARA/ CEN [Andean Regional Affairs/Central America] will meet with Amcit [American Citizen] Sr. Diana Ortiz either next week or early next year. Embassy wishes to state its strong objection to such a meeting. We see the proposed meeting as a lawyer's stunt meant to blunt our criticism of Sr. Diana's year-long refusal to talk to the appropriate USG investigations, e.g., the FBI.[2]

The State Department responded:

> For the past year we have consistently told Paul Soreff that there are key aspects of Sister Diana's account that need to be clarified and that at some point she should make herself available for a full accounting of what happened. If we do not follow up on Sister Diana's offer to talk about the events, our refusal could be misconstrued to mean we are washing our hands of the case which is not our intention.... We feel more at risk, from a public relations point of view, in refusing to meet with her than in doing so.[3]

Stroock replied,

> We believe that the "up side" of meeting Sr. Ortiz under these conditions is only a short-term PR gain. The "down" side is that if the Department meets with her, pressure from all sorts of people and groups will build on the Department to act on the information she provides; she of course, will be free from any legal responsibility for any possible misstatements.
>
> We remain concerned that we are going to get cooked on this one unless we follow the FBI line, i.e., the case is closed until she cooperates with the USG agency that has the responsibility. Until then, we believe there isn't much more we should do.[4]

In January, Deborah McCarthy and her colleague Bonnie Paige came to the Mount. Stroock had been overruled. I'm not sure how excited McCarthy was about the trip. Paul had asked specifically for her, saying I would only talk to a woman. "SHE HAS RISEN FROM THE DEAD!"[5] McCarthy wrote in an internal memo referring to me. She went on, "I guess my great reputation of a sweet, well-bred, compassionate Catholic has spread far and wide.... This is my fate in life: last December I flew down to baby-sit the only witness to the Jesuit murder. This winter it is Kentucky and a kidnapped nun. What next?" But she did think the State Department should meet with me to show that they were still working on the case. She also understood my fear and mistrust and sent me photos of herself and Bonnie Paige, along with some personal information. Paige was the mother of a young child, whom she was holding in the photo. McCarthy was in a restaurant in her photo, pushed back from the table and smiling, looking toward someone on her left. She was pretty—blond, young. But as far as I was concerned they were the enemy.

I WASN'T VERY NICE to them. I sat down across from them and met their chitchat with a cold stare. After the interview, a sister who had been in the meeting asked Mimi why I had to be so rude to those ladies. I was supposed to sit down and have a pleasant chat and smile and compliment them, I suppose, then tell them it was a pleasure talking with them. Well, it wasn't. I relived the torture again for the second time in two months.

No questions were sent to me in advance, but I did impose some rules. I told McCarthy and Paige that they couldn't look at my face, they had to look down. And they did. Mimi checked. I basically read them my affidavit. That way I knew I was revealing only the information I wanted to reveal and nothing that would endanger anyone else. I didn't understand what information they could gain from the meeting that they didn't already have, but I must have answered some questions, too, because after the meeting McCarthy wrote this memo to Phil Taylor, the chargé d'affaires at the U.S. embassy:

> Basically I believe something horrendous happened, she was questioned and tortured and probably raped. But she is not telling the whole story as to what she may have been involved in or on all the details of how she was picked up and released. She looks like a little girl but she is very articulate and strong in her own way. The order was delightful. I think even they are getting frustrated with her. I think we have enough to go on and suggested to Soreff that they hire an investigator. We got many details on the location and Alejandro. He may have been an American.[6]

One of the women, in the notes she took during the meeting, wrote, "Is it possible that someone fr mission rescued her? Nick Ricciuti says it could have happened."[7] Later, Bonnie Paige wrote Deborah McCarthy the following memo: "Have you talked to Phil [Taylor] on secure [phone]? Please let me know. Nick Ricciuti, my office director, wants to talk directly to Phil on secure if you haven't been able to convince him to take our theory seriously."[8]

Nick Ricciuti — Bonnie Paige's boss — was the head of Consular Emergency Services for U.S. citizens abroad and would know better than anyone how embassies might operate when an American disappeared. He had also been consular general at the U.S. embassy in El Salvador during some of the worst years of the dirty war there. And he found McCarthy and Paige's theory entirely plausible: Alejandro was an American from the U.S. embassy ("fr mission") who had taken me out of the secret prison. Perhaps Stroock had argued so desperately against a meeting between me and State Department representatives to prevent just such thoughts.

Part II

Speak, bear witness....
    Between the hammer strokes
        the heart survives

    like the tongue
        that between the teeth
            and in spite of everything

        goes on praising.

—Ranier Maria Rilke,
    The Duino Elegies

Chapter Nine

SU CASA

SILENCE WOULD NOT STALK ME at this old house in Chicago — not as it had in Owensboro, at the hospital, and at the Mount, where in the quiet of night I had almost heard again the screams of the man and the Woman. Voices wafted up from the street, buses rumbled by, and all the way down the hall, radios were playing, even though it was nearly midnight. My new housemates were as sleepless as I was.

The only person I'd met so far seemed familiar — not her alabaster face or the dark hair pinned up off her neck, but the way she hunched, as if trying to hide. Coming out of the cold night into the dimly lit house, we had descended a long stairway to the basement, where the kitchen was, and she was there wiping the counter. I couldn't take my eyes off her. She didn't see us. She just rubbed and rubbed at the counter, as if willing it to reflect a different face than the one she bent above it. She raised her head after a while and glanced toward the pantry doorway, where I was standing. Our eyes met. She was afraid, I could see it. She was taking my measure. Looking into the white light of her fear, I seemed to be seeing myself in a mirror.

Mimi and Suzanne, who had driven us up from Kentucky, were in the pantry fixing snacks. The volunteer who was showing us around finally led us on into the kitchen and introduced us to Dolores.

"Hola" was all Dolores said. And she went back to wiping the counter.

THE JANGLE OF MELODIES from my neighbors' rooms had almost lulled me to sleep when a woman called my name. "I am Eloisa," she said in Spanish. "Can I come in?"

I scooted up onto the pillow, drew my knees to my chest, and said yes. *Sí.*

A large woman with dark hair hanging down her back bounced to my side and folded her arms around me. "Bienvenida," she said.

The last time I remembered hearing that word it came from the Policeman: "Bienvenida a su palacio."

119

Pulling out of the hug, she seated herself in the chair across from me. The lamp beside her revealed fine wrinkles in her forehead. She told me she was from Guatemala, from the capital. And she smiled.

I tried to smile back.

But she had dropped her eyes to her lap, and when she raised them they were full of something she wanted to say. As she began to speak, I felt my soul floating up like a soap bubble to the corner of the ceiling, where I could rest, safe, and look down. She was like José. Her story was a sad one — in her case about the reasons she had to leave Guatemala — and she confessed something she had done that she wasn't proud of but had felt to be necessary. I could only wonder why she was telling this to me, a stranger. Was she going to ask me for forgiveness, like he had?

"I know a little of what happened to you in Guatemala, what we heard from the news," she finished. "I just wanted you to know that there are people who understand. There are people who have suffered, too." She stood up and gently touched the hand I held against my mouth. I let her take it.

"If you want to talk sometime, I am here," she said. "You can confide in me." She kissed my forehead and gave my hand a squeeze. "We have suffered," she said, "but, Dianna, we are alive. Never forget that."

LATER PAT AND JUANITA, the sisters who ran the house, came to ask if I had everything I needed. Juanita recalls that I was curled up on my bed, in a corner. When she knocked I turned toward the door. "You had such a frightened look," she remembers. "Your eyes darted back and forth. I realized how traumatized you were. And I thought, 'Oh, dear God, give me strength so we can handle this.'"

She was right, I was afraid. I was remembering that I was alive. That meant there was something the torturers could still take from me.

I set my coffee on the table beside Eloisa, who reached over and squeezed my hand. She knew that within an hour I would be having my first meeting at the Kovler Center. "A hug for Dianna!" she called. Two children ran into the kitchen and pressed themselves against my legs.

I couldn't help smiling. They trusted me enough to press their little bodies as close as they could get. If I were completely evil, they would have sensed it and stayed away.

One of the little girls was Eloisa's child, the other Raúl's youngest daughter. Raúl was fixing toast for her and his three-year-old son, Marcos. While Raúl poured coffee, his older daughter, Celia, spread the toast with mayonnaise and poured the young ones their orange juice. Celia was seven and her childhood was over. I could see that in the way she carried herself, as if her small body were meant for work, and in the way her round, dark eyes kept watch.

Raúl had been a rural Protestant catechist in Guatemala, educating people and distributing food. When his work became too dangerous, he left for Mexico, then went on to Texas, where he was in a program to go to Canada. He planned to bring his wife and children to Canada once he got settled. But while he waited, his wife was disappeared. He started back to Guatemala to get his children and was arrested on the way. In the Mexican prison where he was detained, he was beaten, tortured, and starved until he was close to death. A man in the cell adjacent to his, whom he never saw, kept telling him, "Don't give up. You have to make it. You have children." One day his neighbor said, "I'm going to be leaving. I'll get someone to come and get you out." Soon, a Franciscan missionary came and got him released. Before leaving, Raúl asked the guards where the man in the cell next to him had gone. The guards told him there was no man — that cell had always been empty. Raúl believed the Lord had been speaking to him. He went to Guatemala, got his children, and swam back across the Rio Grande into Texas with his three children clinging to his back.

It was pat, the older of the sisters, who drove me to my appointment at Kovler. Pat was gray-haired, slim, and energetic and had worked as a missionary under the repressive regime in Peru. Mimi accompanied us, and while I was grateful for her support, I was too tense to do anything but stare out the window at the frozen lake and the joggers beside it, chasing their clouds of breath.

Too soon we were parking beside an enormous white building. The Kovler Center, Pat told us, occupied just a few offices on one of the floors. The building inside was run down and dingy — worlds apart from Dr. Snodgrass's plush waiting room. The Kovler Center, I would learn, was the idea of an Argentine doctor who worked in a Chicago emergency room, where she saw Latin American patients terrified of the bright lights, the instruments, and the table. She realized they were torture survivors — like herself — and she knew a center like Kovler was needed.

DR. ANTONIO MARTÍNEZ offered me tea and we sat down in his office. I had a good feeling about him. He had nice teeth, warm, brown eyes, and fuzzy thinning hair. "It is hard to be here, yes?" he said. "It will get easier. But, Dianna, I have to be honest with you: you are going to feel worse before you feel better."

I didn't believe him. I couldn't feel worse.

BEFORE OUR NEXT MEETING was over I knew he was right. I felt worse.

"What would you like to talk about?" he asked, and a long silence followed.

I didn't know whether to trust him. After our first meeting I'd been so sure of him. Antonio had agreed not to take notes about me then and had put his notebook away. I had almost laughed when he asked, respectfully, if meeting again on Wednesday would be convenient for me — as if I were in Chicago for any reason other than to meet with him. Emerging into the hallway, where Mimi was waiting, I had told her, "I'm in the right place."

But now it was Wednesday and I'd had a few days to think. People can seem nice at first. Maybe I was swayed, the first time, by the crinkles around the edges of his eyes, his deep smile lines. Maybe his Puerto Rican heritage influenced me, the fact that, like my father, he was a naturalized citizen, a Hispanic, and spoke English with that accent. I resolved not to walk into another trap.

I had my affidavit in my backpack, figuring I could give it to him if I decided to trust him that much. I stared at the floor, trying to make a decision, and felt his eyes on my face.

"Please don't look at me!" I hadn't meant to sound that harsh. I hadn't meant to say anything.

"I did not want to make you uncomfortable," he answered. "What can we do to put you at ease?"

"What?"

"How can I help you feel safer?"

"Why don't you face the wall?"

He stood up, turned his chair to the wall and sat back down. "Is that better?"

"Yes." I listened to his breathing. I sniffled. Keeping his head turned away, he pushed a box of Kleenex toward me across the desk.

We sat in a long silence.

After a while I asked if we could stop, and he walked me back to the waiting room. I couldn't stop my tears. And he saw me with them.

He said something to Pat that I couldn't hear, then told me he'd see me next week. I couldn't look at him. He had seen me cry. And asking him to face the wall — he knew how weak I was, how frightened, how crazy.

As MIMI AND PAT and I walked down the stairs to the dining room I could hear the clatter of Spanish conversation and plates being served. But when we entered the room, everyone became quiet. Sister Juanita, a soft-featured woman who was warm and open with her emotions, came over and wordlessly gave me a hug. Eloisa put her arm around my shoulder and patted me on the back. The silence continued through dinner. We understand that you are in pain, the silence said. I glanced up once at Dolores. The fear was gone from her eyes.

I HAD MANY MORE silent sessions with Antonio, staring at the bald spot on the back of his head. From time to time he would ask if I was OK. I would say yes and we would let silence fill the space between us again. The first week of my forced stay in the hospital, when I had refused to talk to Dr. Snodgrass, the tension in my chest and the tension between us had grown. Finally I was forced to talk. It was my only way out. Between Antonio and me as the moments passed a bond formed. He showed me that there would be no punishment for "not cooperating," for not playing the game. I was the one who set the agenda, who drew up the rules. He cooperated with me.

I started bringing my Woman friend with me. In the silence, I went back to the room where she was, took her by the hand, brought her out of that building. I imagined her sitting by my side. No, I willed her to be there, and I tried to put myself in her situation. I tried to envision what it must have been like to have another person — me — bring harm to her. Maybe it was selfish on my part, but I wanted her to hear from me what had happened. What she must have suffered before we met I'm sure was horrible. And after I left, if she was alive, maybe they continued torturing her. Or maybe she was thrown into the pit with all the others. I don't know.

I didn't ask her to repeat her name. I have anguished so much over this. If only I had, I could have tried to find her family. I could have told them about the daughter, the mother, the sister they had been separated from. I could have helped put closure to her life on earth. When she told me her name, I couldn't understand what she said. I didn't want to exhaust her, to drain her of the little strength she had. I thought she would need that strength for a later time.

Bringing her to therapy was my way of conveying to her that not knowing her name didn't keep me from remembering her and all she had suffered. She was and continues to be part of me. Sometimes I imagined that this bright light was calling her, waiting for her, and she was like a lost soul in limbo. She held back and turned away from it. Like me, she needed healing. Maybe she, too, had been forced to do things and what she had seen and been forced to do kept her from walking toward the light, from allowing it to embrace her. I wanted to say to her, Whatever happened, it was not your fault. Leave your burden behind with me. Go and rest. Be at peace.

Mimi went back to Owensboro to quit her jobs. Pat and Juanita had offered to let her help out at Su Casa. Her Spanish was fluent, and she could drive. She could be useful. I was relieved. I did what I could to mingle, meeting the other guests in the kitchen at night where they, like me, drank coffee. Pat and Juanita seemed accepting of me — they hadn't said anything about all the showers I was taking or the meals I missed. But basically I was afraid. I wanted Mimi to stay, but I also wanted her to have her life. "Mimi, don't you want to go back to Mexico, or maybe to Chile again?" I asked. "You don't need to stay here for me. I'm OK."

"Dianna, even when I was in Mexico, I wasn't really in Mexico. If I'm going to worry about you I'd rather have you right here in front of me, where I can see you're doing all right. What, are you trying to get rid of me?" She gave her big smile.

Eloisa was the first person I really got to know. She always had something to teach me. She was tossing withered peppers into the trash can, sorting through the weekly box of vegetables we got from an organization that distributed food to shelters for the homeless. I started on the fruit. On top, with large gray spots on the sides, were peaches. I got brown goo on my hand picking one up. I started to pitch it into the garbage.

"No!" Eloisa cried. She took the peach from me, rinsed it, and carefully sliced around the rot. "Those are still good. We can use them for shakes or fruit salad."

She was right. The piece she handed me was firm and sweet.

Dolores was a shy person, like me. The first conversation we had was about a Venezuelan soap opera. "She plays two characters, this woman, one who is evil and one who is good." Nearly every guest in the house was glued to the set. Dolores summarized the ins and outs of the plot. Slowly, as time passed, she did the same for her own life.

We were alone in the kitchen one night, the same place I had first seen her, the light leaping off her black hair, which hung now down her back. I was making coffee and she was boiling water for tea, and as we sank into our chairs with our respective brews, she said she was tired. She had to get up at five o'clock in the morning to be at work on time, and getting up early didn't agree with her.

"It's not your cup of tea." I smiled, hoping my little play on words would work in Spanish.

She looked at her cup for a minute, then at me. After a moment's hesitation she began to drink the tea anyway, and I could see it was no time to explain that my remark, in English, made sense. She was far away. I watched her steep her tea, lifting the bag in and out, holding the string between her chapped fingers. "I left them in Honduras, you know, my children, with my mother and sisters. Two daughters and a son. That is why I am working so hard, to send them money."

She cleaned a home for disabled children. She didn't mind the work, but getting up early and going out to wait for the bus in the dark was scary. Our neighborhood was known for drugs and crime, and some of the guests at Su Casa had been mugged.

In Honduras, she told me, she had been an accountant for the government. Her husband had worked for the courts but was fired when a new administration came in. He was trying to claim some money the government owed him, and the government resented his efforts. He was followed and threatened by armed men.

"I could see him some nights, when he could sneak home, but most of the time he was in hiding. Then he stopped coming. And these men came to the house and asked me where he was. More than once. They threatened me."

DOLORES WAS QUIET for a while, staring into her cup. In the silence I poured myself another cup of coffee, imagining what she hadn't said. "You have to tell us everything you know or we start on your children. Then your sisters. Then your mother. We know where they are. Or maybe we take you." One of the men probably touched her under the chin with mock tenderness. "A real man would come to rescue his wife." Or maybe they did more to her than she was going to say.

So Dolores left.

When I sat down before her again she wiped her face with the palms of her hands. "I do not know where he is. He always hides with his friends when he is in danger. Probably he is hiding. When I get political asylum I am going to bring them here, my husband and children."

DOLORES WAS A FEW YEARS younger than I, and as time passed and we spent more evenings together in the kitchen, I began to feel she was my sister. We would work on each other's hair sometimes. She even trusted me to give her a trim and a perm with a kit we had found among the bags of donated clothes. Dolores had a few bad hair days after that.

Sometimes a priest came to Su Casa to say Mass. I remember the first time. I had been in Chicago for about a month. We were gathered in a circle in the living room, all twenty of us who lived there, including guests and staff. Raúl led the music, strumming his guitar. No one went to Communion but Sister Juanita, Sister Pat, and Pat's brother Dennis, a Christian Brother. The rest of us stood with our heads bowed. I wondered if the other guests, like me, felt unworthy. I hurt for them, if so, and at the same time I was relieved. I didn't feel so sinful, so out of place as Communion was given. No need here to move my lips as if I were praying. The prayers were few and simple and many people remained silent instead of participating.

From a discussion of a Gospel reading, I knew a number of the guests didn't quite believe in God. The priest had invited us to reflect on the passage where Jesus asked his disciples, "Who do people say the Son of God is?" and "Who do you say I am?"

The room had become very quiet. It was quiet for a long time. One of the men said at last, "I do not know God. I do not know who God is. My God died when I was put in prison and beaten." I think it was Eloisa's husband, Otto, who spoke, or maybe Rigo from Honduras, or possibly Luis, from El Salvador. They had all been beaten. I just stood there with my mouth open, feeling like I was the one who had spoken.

Raúl answered, "I do not know God, either, but he is somewhere. I know this because he has watched over my family. He has led us here."

Sister Juanita cleared her throat. I was worried about what she might say to the first person who spoke. She, after all, was a nun, and someone had just said God was dead.

Her voice was gentle. She turned toward the person who had spoken first. "Sometimes," she said, "sometimes our life experiences change our image of God." She said this in Spanish, a language she was just learning. She was reaching across the divide, not only of language but of experience — she herself had not been tortured. I don't know how her words affected the person who had spoken, but for me they opened up a world of possibility.

She didn't say directly — No, God has not died. That would only have started an argument. But she suggested that the idea one had of God could die, the conception, while God could still exist. One could learn to see God another way.

I knew my old God had died, the God who was strong, powerful, a protector. The Good Shepherd was no longer someone I believed in. If I were to see God in a new way, based on my experiences, God would have to be helpless, broken, tortured, but still alive and able to love. In the corner of the room on a cross hung Jesus, whose resurrection I had questioned during Easter services at the Mount. How could he still survive? I had asked. How could he have risen?

From Antonio I was learning about the goals of torture, that torture was a strategy, something people studied, that the torturers wanted me to see myself and the world in a way that would render me powerless. I was starting to question some of the things the torturers had said to me about myself. It was an act of resistance to question. I was not letting them define me. Then why let them define God? Wasn't it an act of resistance to refuse to believe that God was dead, to reject the world they had tried to make me believe in? Maybe my absence of belief in God was another blindfold the torturers had tied on, one I could now take off.

I UNWRAPPED MY BIBLE one Sunday afternoon, unknotting the black cloth. I was learning that no one was going to reprimand me or toss me out of Su Casa for doubting, and without the pressure to believe I felt freer. At the Mount I always worried about that. Maybe I shouldn't have, but I was well aware that God was the center of a nun's life and that I didn't believe in God. I felt panicky about it. The only shred of my identity I had left was that I was Sister Dianna. That was the only link I had to being a member of a community, to belonging anywhere. And it was centered on a lie. I was in a community of nonbelievers now, of doubters, and I was free to question and explore.

ANTONIO, MEANWHILE, helped me understand that I indeed had a community. He had played by the rules I set in therapy and had never pressured me, and he had earned my trust. I let him read my affidavit, and I told him about my feelings of dirtiness. I told him I felt guilty.

"It is not a surprise that you feel that way," he said. "Many survivors feel that way, feel they could have done something more, something different.

I don't believe you are dirty. I don't believe that you are contaminating me. I haven't heard from the guests at Su Casa that they feel you are contaminating them. I have heard that they care about you. And the children, they love you."

Those words are ingrained in my mind, almost as deep as the torturers' words. Maybe deeper.

As FOR MY OTHER COMMUNITY, the Ursulines, the ties seemed to be snapping. Antonio had recommended that I try a medication called Halcyon, to help me sleep. I trusted him enough to try a drug he recommended, but the problem was the expense. Normally I didn't need money. I paid no rent. Food and clothes were provided. But now I did need it and I would have to call the sisters and ask. I was scared. That one sister's remark about all the money the community had already spent on me gnawed at me. But I was learning to ask for what I needed — we were encouraged to do that in therapy and at Su Casa. People can't read your mind. You have certain needs as a survivor and you have to make those known. The torture has left you with the fear that whatever you ask for will be denied, that your very need will be used against you. You are not back there in the torture chamber. You have to be brave and ask. Besides, this was a different sister, not the one who had made the comment.

I was embarrassed to say I was going to be taking medication. I just said I needed some money.

There was a pause. Then her voice: "Dianna, I really don't think it's right of you to ask the community for any more money."

LATER, PAT AND JUANITA waited as I struggled to tell them about the conversation. Then they explained that Mercy Hospital would donate the medication.

Not long after that, Pat asked me to a staff meeting. I walked down the hall with my lower lip between my teeth, biting down to steady my nerves. But Pat didn't look stern. She asked me to sit down, then invited me to join the staff part-time. I would work as a liaison between the guests and the staff, interpreting for the Spanish-speaking guests, teaching English as a foreign language, and supervising the children and helping them with their homework.

I said yes, blinking back tears of gratitude for their trust in me. Years later I learned that other staff members weren't paid. Pat and Juanita gave me a stipend so that I could have some pocket money.

I TOOK THE MEDICATION for a few months and I got some sleep, but because the nightmares that came with the sleep were so intense, I eventually opted to go off it. Antonio supported my decision, fortunately.

He suggested another change, as well. "I think you would feel more comfortable being able to talk also with a woman therapist," he said. "What do you think?"

His suggestion surprised me, but I felt relieved. He and I both knew there were issues I wouldn't discuss with a man.

That session, in spite of my relief, was especially hard. Maybe it was the fact that I had finally been offered a woman therapist, that someone was looking out for my needs, that I was being understood and listened to, even though I'd said nothing about wanting a woman therapist. I felt so vulnerable after the hour was up, like a husk had been stripped away.

THE LONG RIDE BACK to Su Casa with Pat was painful. We sat in silence, my feet on the seat, my legs folded up before me. I felt naked.

Sleet tapped on the car roof. The windshield wipers creaked back and forth. Against the glass, ice crystals were coming to life and streaming down the windshield, as if they'd been freed. How scary, I thought, to slide like that, to careen out of control, to give way again to the earth's pull.

AT A GAS STATION where Pat stopped, a police car pulled up behind us, and the policeman got out. Even though this man was an African American, above his light-blue shirt I kept getting glimpses of the pock-scarred face of the Policeman. I jumped out of the car, ran into the gas station office, and hid there until the police car pulled out.

He would tell the Guate-man where I was living now, and they would come for me. I wondered if the seed he had planted in me — the seed of hatred and rage, the seed that grew into my participation in the incident with the Woman and my choice about the pregnancy — I wondered if that seed had spread, if, like a plant germinating, the very evil within me had caused the Policeman to spring up behind us.

At Su Casa, when we got out of the car, I was shaking. My fingertips were bleeding, where I had bitten the nails down. I wondered if the Policeman would tell everyone, all these people who had treated me so warmly, what I had done to the Woman.

Welcome to reality. You thought you could escape. The Policeman's voice. My shoulders ached. My cheekbone and fingertips throbbed. On the mirror next to my bed was a picture of a quetzal, Guatemala's national bird. A Guatemalan sister had sent it to me, thanking me for caring about all the quetzals who were in captivity. She meant people, Guatemalans, but couldn't say so in a letter. The picture and her thoughtfulness weren't enough. The nightmare was starting again. I let my eyes wander down to the Bible on the dresser.

Please, God, I prayed, I need you to tell me I am not all evil. I wanted to let the Bible fall open to any page God chose, but I was afraid of words of condemnation. There were words like that in the Bible. I knew from praying with the sisters at the Mount, reading the Breviary. Finally, I dared. I closed my eyes and let the pages part.

The Bible fell open to the Parable of the Sower. As he was scattering the seeds, some fell along the path and the birds came and ate them up. Some fell on rocky places, where the seeds had little soil. Plants sprang up quickly because the soil was shallow; but so were the roots and when the sun came up the plants were scorched and withered. Other seeds fell among the thorns, which grew up and choked the plants. Still others fell on good soil and bore grain.

As I understood the parable, the torturers, like the birds, had tried to take God from me. They had filled me with weeds and stones and a burning rage, but there was still good soil in me, soil where goodness could grow.

AFTER THAT, I began to ask, "How do I put my life back together, God? How do I live with what's happened?"

The Bible kept falling open to the Miracle of the Loaves and Fishes.

I kept slamming the Bible shut in disgust. God's idea of a joke, I guess. Go get a snack, Dianna.

AT OUR NEXT MEETING, Antonio introduced me to Mary Fabri. I spent the hour looking at her long, dark hair. Eventually, I would learn about her work counseling terminally ill patients and their families at the county hospital — even about her love for good margaritas. In that first session I just looked and listened, hearing her gentleness even through the sharp, flattened vowels of her Chicago accent.

In a report she wrote the next year for legal purposes, Mary said:

The first meeting between Sister Dianna and myself was in April of 1991. She was dressed neatly and simply. Her demeanor was quiet and withdrawn. She requested that we sit in such a manner that she could view me from the side rather than face-to-face. She apologized for this and explained that direct eye contact was too difficult. She spoke softly and her affect was sad and frightened throughout the session. At times she was tearful.

She tearfully admitted to transient suicidal ideation but reported that she had no intent or plan. She stated that she just wished she could "go to bed and never wake up." This feeling, although less frequent, still arises in response to stressful situations.

Although her cognitive processes appeared intact, Sister Dianna had and continues to have profound gaps in memory. This includes simple premorbid information, such as her date of birth, and other more recent details, such as dates outlining her return to and events in the United States after her kidnapping and torture. These memory difficulties persist, consistent with the diagnostic criteria for post-traumatic stress disorder.

As the session neared completion Mary asked, "How are you doing?"

"Not well. Scared."

"Of what?"

"Going back to Su Casa. The car ride. I don't know how to explain this, but it's hard to be in an enclosed space with someone else for forty-five minutes after this. I feel so exposed."

"What if we met at Su Casa?" Mary asked softly. "Would that be better for you?"

I wished she had been facing me, so I could nod. My voice came out ragged, as if it had squeezed through a barbed wire fence in my throat.

As a staff member, I had some structure built into my life and had to interact with people other than Mimi. I had to get out of my room, where I used to sit for hours with a dictionary, relearning simple words. "Slow as a turtle," someone had said. What was a turtle? But teaching English to our Spanish-speaking guests reminded me that I did have mastery of my mother tongue. Words here and there were missing, but not the kinds of words you use every day, which is what they needed to know. And spending time with the children was a blessing. In the afternoons I baby-sat Raúl's youngest child, Marcos. "I want to be like Dennis," he'd say — he revered Pat's brother — and he would toddle across the room, stiff-legged, sticking his belly out as far as it would go.

After dinner, the children would perform little plays or dance to a boom box to show us their latest disco moves. It was irresistible. No matter what we were dealing with in therapy or our lives, everyone, down to the last person, laughed. If there was an unspoken rule at Su Casa, it was try to celebrate whatever you can. Birthday parties, saints' days, even minor holidays were cause for a party. Celebrating was hard for me, but I was learning that sometimes you can pretend to feel something and end up feeling it. *Pretend,* after all, also means *try.*

I was both trying and pretending. I was making it down to dinner more often, and with the other guests I thanked God for the food and for the others standing around the table hand in hand. We asked God to help the homeless and the needy of the city, and to end the blessing we sang a song in Spanish that began with the vow *Alabaré* — I will praise. Looking around I saw people who had suffered every bit as much as I had, if not more, people who also questioned God's existence, and they were praising and thanking God and asking God's blessing on those less fortunate. Just in case. I went along with it. I sang. Because I wanted to believe.

EASTER WAS A CHALLENGE. I still didn't believe completely in resurrection, not Christ's, not my own. I was still sealed up in a dark cave. Some days, when I felt better, it was more like a translucent bubble. But I was separated from others, walled in, numb and half-dead. I had never completely walked out of that prison. I'd brought it with me. But the Easter story was a challenge to go on believing, in spite of not seeing any prospects for living, to risk hoping that one day I could break out.

I READ AS MUCH as I could about the life of Jesus. Time and again, he had been labeled and misunderstood by those in authority — and even by those who were his friends. Jesus also was tortured, and he cried out on the cross, "My God, my God, why have you forsaken me?" When I thought about the Son of God saying those words I was comforted. Jesus acknowledged his aloneness, his estrangement from God and the human family. I suppose he became absorbed in himself. For a moment he forgot about the other two men who were being crucified. He forgot about the hungry, the poor, and the oppressed. When I was first taken down to the basement of that building in Guatemala I asked myself the same question — Why had God abandoned me? I prayed for my deliverance first, then remembered to ask God to help the people whose screams were ringing through the room. And I was a nun, a woman who had committed herself to God's people, to service. Scripture was allowing me to see that human weakness doesn't make one wholly evil. God can exist in the midst of it.

I BEGAN TO LOOK for the God in the human and found God in Otto, as he let Eloisa sob on his shoulder after a phone call from their daughter in

Guatemala, who was despairing of ever seeing them again. When Eloisa quieted down, Otto wiped the tears from her eyelashes with his fingers. I saw God in Brother Dennis when he was on his way out the door to teach a college class and Marcos burst in from the yard, grabbed Dennis's pants, and pulled him toward the kitchen. "Brader Dennis, I wan — wa."

Instead of telling Marcos to ask someone else or saying "I don't understand you," Brother Dennis let himself be tugged along, filled a glass of water for Marcos, and left him with an affectionate pat, never checking to see the grimy little hand print on his pants. I saw God in Raúl, when he played the guitar and got everyone to sing along. I saw God in the volunteers from the synagogue who prepared a meal for us once a month and sat down with us to eat. God, I saw, was not a shepherd watching over us, his sheep. This was a God of the same species. I began to consider that we were made in God's image and that everyone — except the Guate-man and the Policeman, who I still equated with the Devil — contained the seed of divine goodness, even the people in the State Department, even Ambassador Stroock. I loosened my grip on the real world. I let my list of enemies shrink.

In June, when *Prime Time Live* aired, everyone gathered to support me — all the guests in the house, the staff, Mary and Antonio, Mimi, and Darleen, who came from California just to be there with us. The State Department, meanwhile, had made its own preparations for the broadcast. Four months after the women from the State Department took my description of Alejandro and concluded that he could have been an American, Deborah McCarthy sent this message to a State Department colleague:

ORTIZ CASE: VERY IMPORTANT: We need to close the loop on the issue of the "North American" named by Ortiz as being involved in the case. In a letter to Soreff (copy attached) we said that upon receiving a fuller description of the man, we would be happy to inquire as to whether he was known to anyone in the Embassy. This was an effort to respond to his request to have photos and names of all Americans in Guatemala, including Embassy personnel. We now have a fuller description, both that given to Bonnie Paige and I (e-mailed to Embassy as part of our notes) and in the new affidavit. We will send cable asking embassy to follow up. The EMBASSY IS VERY SENSITIVE ON THIS ISSUE but it is an issue we will have to respond to publicly when the show airs.[1]

I dreaded watching the *Prime Time Live* segment, but I wanted to find out what I had said, if I'd mentioned anything I shouldn't have. A bit of Mimi's interview came at the beginning of the show. She was asked about the reasons I was targeted. She said, "The message it's sending to the Church is pretty clear: Don't help the indigenous. Don't help the poor."[2]

There was footage of the garden I was taken from, the dirt road the Guate-man and José led me down, the drawings I had made in the hospital of the pit and of my back. I heard myself telling about what I felt in the pit: I felt myself walking on heads, I felt bodies jerking. I heard myself telling that I was raped and that my breasts, as well as my back, were burned.

I started to smell the alcohol, the cigarettes. To center myself I looked at Otto. Although his eyes were on the screen, they were vacant. He seemed to have drifted off, perhaps to thoughts of Eloisa's rape or to memories of his own beatings when he was "disappeared" after supporting unionists.

Raúl's face was twisted up, and he was shaking his head. I knew he was wondering if the army had done the same things to his wife that I was describing. I had put them all back in their prisons of memory. I could only hurt people.

I left the room. Mary came and sat with me in my room for a couple of hours. She says I lay on my bed, facing the wall in a fetal position, and told her I felt evil. Eventually, I fell asleep and Mary left. Mimi stayed with me during the night, and Mary came back the next day for our session. I was in the same position. I didn't want to talk. She just sat with me.

I WAS IN A SUPPORT GROUP BY THEN for Guatemalans who had suffered trauma. They had invited me to join, overlooking the fact that I was an American, a citizen of the country that had given rise to their suffering, overthrowing a democratically elected government in 1954 through a CIA-sponsored coup and then supporting decades of military dictatorships. To them, I was not an American. I was one of them. After *Prime Time Live* aired, Adriana, a woman I knew from the group, wanted to talk about the broadcast. She thought that maybe the bodies of her two young daughters were in the pit I'd described. They had disappeared with other family members during an army raid on the house. When Adriana had arrived, the soldiers were hosing down the floor.

I didn't know what to tell her. I was just sorry that I had given Adriana another possible ending to the story, one that would haunt her.

The Guatemalans thanked me for doing the interview and speaking about what was happening in their country. They knew I had spoken for all of us. I appreciated their comments, but I was sorry for the damage the truth could do.

THE NEXT TIME Mary and I talked, I asked her what she remembered of the broadcast. I had missed a lot. *Prime Time Live* had interviewed officials in Guatemala, Mary told me. I asked Mary what they had said — I both wanted to know and didn't. She told me that former Defense Minister General Héctor Gramajo was asked about his allegations that a lesbian love affair was the cause of my disappearance. "I never said lesbian," General Gramajo insisted. Diane Sawyer showed him several sources quoting him: a *New York Times* article said Gramajo "claimed the abduction was a staged ending to a lesbian love affair"; a *Boston Globe* article quoted him calling me a "leftist and a lesbian."

"You did say lesbian," Diane Sawyer insisted. With a sheepish smile, as though he'd been caught at a school boy prank, Gramajo repeated, "A love affair."

Sawyer passed along to him questions I had raised: "How could I have inflicted burns on my own back? How could I have raped myself? How could I have tortured myself over and over?"

Gramajo was no longer smiling. "This is outrageous, this is outrageous, I'm sorry if those things happened."

"But you believe this was a love tryst? Torture? Bruises? Burns?"

"I said that but then I signed a letter to the Roman Catholic Church." The letter was the one Joe, Marie, Paul, and Fran had gotten him to write a year earlier, in which he had said there was no evidence that any love affair was at issue.

MARY GAVE ME the basics. It would take ten years before I could watch the video myself and catch all the details. But the basics were enough.

SAWYER INTERVIEWED Minister of Government General Morales. She asked him about the rumor that I had staged my own abduction to cover up a lesbian tryst. General Morales said he was told this by some people in the U.S. embassy.

Sawyer noted that, according to sources in Washington and Guatemala, Lew Anselem said I was a lesbian. "A member of the ambassador's staff, Human Rights Officer Lew Anselem, started spreading rumors about her, and pretty vicious rumors at that. Several sources told us that Anselem had told them that Sister Ortiz was a lesbian. And before long Guatemalan officials were saying similar things in public." No embassy officials would talk to Sawyer about the rumors or about Alejandro.

Knowing what I know about the video now, I'm glad I didn't see it all when I was at Su Casa. There was some footage from a massacre: in December 1990 thirteen unarmed civilians, including women and children, were gunned down as they peacefully protested outside an army base in Santiago Atitlán, calling for an end to army violence against their community. In the first five months of 1991, more than five hundred people throughout Guatemala were disappeared, and in September of the previous year, a Guatemalan anthropologist had been stabbed to death on the street. I wouldn't have had the strength to see the indigenous women rocking back and forth, wailing over the bodies of their loved ones, to see Myrna Mack, lying in a pool of blood on the street, or to see General Gramajo's round, heavy-jowled face, his tiny beady eyes, his smirk as he lied.

It was hard enough to hear this secondhand from Mary. I knew already that the embassy didn't believe me. I knew the Guatemalan government had said I was a lesbian. I knew that Lew Anselem had made some derogatory comments about lesbian nuns and about me to a congressional aide. I didn't know that "some people in the embassy" had told the Guatemalan minister of government — the official in charge of investigating my case — that my abduction was only a hoax, a cover for some illicit affair. So this was what the embassy, which ever vowed its seriousness in getting to the truth, was doing on my case.

MY TRUST IN EVERYONE was shaken again, including my trust in God. Why would God allow the goodness to be scorched or choked out of people? And if evil could conquer good in a person, when would it overtake me?

I became intent on gardening. We didn't have a garden, but I made one in the courtyard behind the house, and I watched carefully for weeds. Sometimes it was difficult to distinguish them from the things I had planted.

Before our sessions I took Mary out to show her what was growing. As the weather warmed, I suggested having our sessions outside, on the steps leading down to the courtyard. She sat on the middle step. I considered. I could sit next to her, or a step in front of her, or a step behind her. I sat down beside her. Later on I set out lawn chairs, side by side. As the summer progressed I turned them by tiny degrees until finally Mary and I faced each other.

I wasn't afraid of her by then. But I was afraid she would see the torturers in my eyes. "You're going to think I'm crazy," I said. "But they live inside me."

Her face showed no surprise. "It makes sense that you feel that way. Do you want to hear how I see things?" She waited for me to say yes. "We all have personal space and psychological space," she continued. "In torture those personal boundaries are totally broken down."

What she said sounded right. Even the barrier of my skin was broken. Cigarettes and fists did that. Words broke the membrane of my beliefs.

"It makes sense that you feel the torturers have seeped inside you," Mary said. "And we can talk about ways to release that negative energy." She gave me some tactics other than showers. I started burning sage, a Native American tradition to dispel evil spirits. Eventually I tried various kinds of alternative healing techniques under Mary's supervision, from Raike to treatments by a Shaman. I felt they worked. The therapy also worked. Mary was compassionate. She supported me, and she never judged me. She permitted me to be myself, and I grew to trust her completely. I could tell her anything.

When I told her I not only felt the torturers inside me but sometimes next to me, as well, in the room, she still didn't think I was crazy. "You were tortured, and torture happens," she said. "There are torturers in the world. So in a way you're right. They're out there. That negativity you feel is part of reality, a part that we all have to acknowledge. If we don't acknowledge it, we can't do anything to stop it. And if we don't acknowledge that all of us, under the right circumstances, have the capacity to be torturers, we can be led down that path."

Mary believed in fighting the evil without and within. She became my ally.

MIMI WENT BACK TO CHILE, realizing that I was in good hands. She had given me the strength and support I needed to settle in. I was doing well. I was busier than ever and stretching myself into new tasks. Julio had arrived. He was a young Mayan, twenty-three years old, with broad cheekbones, luminous brown eyes, and a beautiful toothy smile. He arrived with his friend Pedro not long after being released from a Guatemalan hospital, where he had spent six months in a coma. Julio had refused to join his town's civil patrol, a supposedly voluntary organization of civilians who were armed and took orders from the military. As a result, he was picked up by the army, taken to a military base, and tortured for a month. He wasn't released. He was left for dead on a roadside a hundred miles away from his home. His throat was slit and his belly cut open. Volunteer firemen found his body and took it to the morgue, where a heartbeat was discovered. When he regained consciousness, emerging from the coma, he was unable to utter a word. He finally managed to gain enough control over his hand to write his name. That's how his family was contacted.

He was still having trouble speaking. When Julio would try to speak to people at Su Casa about what had happened to him, he would simply say, "Julio... torture," and lift his shirt to show some of the scars. His father, who came to Su Casa later, was asked to speak at a university in Chicago. He kept repeating, "I am Joaquín Chualcu Ben, the father of Julio Chualcu Ben. My son was tortured." I was asked to translate, and Joaquín kept repeating the same thing, ten times at least. After the third or fourth time I asked, "Do you want me to say that again?" And yes, he wanted me to repeat it. Some of the people in the audience later told me I should have said something else. "How could I have said something else?" I answered. I was translating for him, and this is what he wanted said. And no one left that room without knowing his name and his son's name, and without knowing that his son was tortured.

There was a man on staff, but Julio and Pedro felt comfortable with me, and they wanted me to show them things. So it fell to me to show them how to use the toilet. They had never seen a toilet. In the countryside, you use bushes. I took them into the bathroom and stood before the toilet with them and tried to explain what it was for. They didn't understand. Finally I reached under the cabinet for some liquid soap, the kind that comes out of a hole in the top of the bottle. I held it down near my crotch and aimed it into the bowl. At last they erupted in laughter — Oh, you urinate into this thing.

JULIO AND HIS FATHER worked in the garden with me. It was physical and spiritual therapy. We got seeds for a type of Mayan squash and planted the vegetables with mounds of dirt around them, as they do in Guatemala. Julio needed to practice moving. His right side was very stiff. In the sun I could see even more clearly the enormous scar on the left side of his head. I think it was from a machete. Working the earth with Julio, sharing excitement over things that were growing, was one of my happiest times.

Almost all my memories of Su Casa are good ones, but I know I wasn't really doing that well. Mary's assessment of me, written after I had spent a year there, makes that clear:

> Every aspect of Sister Dianna Ortiz's functioning has been impacted by her experience of torture. She describes, accurately, torture as

the destruction of personality. Certain aspects of daily living are extremely difficult for Sister Dianna. These include making direct eye contact; shaking hands and receiving other expressions of warmth; seeing uniformed individuals; entering long hallways and descending stairways; and smelling cigarette smoke and alcohol. Each of these stimuli resemble an aspect of her torture and can precipitate at the mild end an intrusive recollection and at the extreme end an actual sense of reliving the torture. Her efforts to avoid these activities and situations impair her daily functioning, as well as her relationships with other people.

Although Sister Dianna describes herself as overreacting to events which symbolize an aspect of her torture, overall she has a diminished responsiveness to the external world. This is psychically protective emotional numbing. Sister Dianna describes it as "being in a bubble," seeing the world around her but not experiencing it. She feels detached from others and unable to express emotions.

This lack of emotional investment in daily activities includes not only interactions with the external world but also Sister Dianna's relationship with herself. Her self-image and self-esteem has been damaged by the torture experience. Sister Dianna describes a profound sense that the evilness of the torture has infiltrated her being. An increased sense of arousal and hypervigilance persists for Sister Dianna. She has difficulty falling asleep and remaining asleep, and reports significant numbers of nightmares. Her ability to concentrate has been impaired. She has difficulty completing tasks and even describes having difficulty reading for pleasure. . . .

Sister Dianna is profoundly aware of the limitations that she brings to interpersonal relationships as a result of her torture experience. Although there is a wish to be more involved and freely express her feelings, it is marred by her fear of loss of control. For example, as she experiences anger, she anticipates that rage will be unleashed and potentially cause harm, whether emotional or physical. In addition, the expression of her feelings also leaves her feeling exposed and vulnerable to others. These two aspects of control and vulnerability result in ambivalence towards the expression of her feelings. At times Sister Dianna admits to preferring her "bubble" where she feels nothing, yet this promotes the feelings of isolation and results in the feelings of being a "nonperson." This predicament is directly a result of the strategic torture process which dismantles an individ-

ual's personality and leaves one with the task of rebuilding a sense
of trust, not only in others, but in oneself.

None of us at Su Casa felt entirely safe, and healing in that environment
was difficult. Activities in Chicago to support human rights or raise awareness about Guatemala's poor had been infiltrated; "participants" would
show up with the trademark dark glasses and military strut of the members
of the Guatemalan intelligence services. Residents at Su Casa sometimes
received anonymous threats by phone or mail, especially before their political asylum hearings, where they would have to talk about the abuses
they had endured at the hands of the Guatemalan army. Oftentimes the
phone rang, and on the other end of the line was dead silence. Pat wore a
whistle around her neck for just those occasions. Someone was interested
in monitoring our activities at Su Casa, that was clear enough. One day
Juanita was talking on the phone and Pat, to make her get off and attend to another task, was walking back and forth in front of one of those
motion-sensitive toy dogs that barks when you pass by it. A while later the
phone rang. Pat picked up and heard a click, then Juanita's conversation
in full, with the dog barking in the background.

IN THE MIDST of these kinds of events, Paul called and asked me to consider
returning to Guatemala to press my case through the judicial system. In
my dreams I played out my options. I either sat by and watched others
being tortured, or I risked torture myself to save them. Little did I know
those dreams were prophecy.

*The Woman is crying for help. I am paralyzed with fear. I sit in the corner
and weep. She walks up to me and embraces me. Together we weep, paralyzed,
sitting there watching as they torture and rape other women and children.*

"I HEAR THE CRIES of the Guatemalan people twenty-four hours a day,"
I wrote in my journal, "as if their cries are coming from a clandestine
grave site. I must never forget that I had so many people to fight for my
life — my family, my Ursuline family, my church family, the international
community, etc., but what about the people of Guatemala? Who will speak
on their behalf?"

*Please forgive me! José cries out. My Woman Friend is coming toward me. She
vanishes. I have her, the Policeman says. If you want to save her, you have to
come to me first.*

THROWING OUT THE IDEA of the independent commission, the new administration in Guatemala had assigned a special prosecutor to my case, the first in Guatemala's history, and the court system was now our only option. The prosecutor had offered at one point to let me send him answers to his questions in writing, and Paul had invited him to come to the United States to interview me, but we had heard nothing more from him. Paul wanted me to consider going to Guatemala to speak with him and to formally file suit in a higher court.

Paul explained that I wouldn't have to give my testimony to the court there. The court had my testimony already because we had filed it with a judge in Kentucky, in compliance with a formal request sent by the court through diplomatic channels, a process known as "letters rogatory." But I might have to answer a few questions, Paul said, and do something called a "judicial reconstruction," which would involve going back to the scene of the crime, the garden of the Posada de Belén.

I HAD SOME MISGIVINGS about the trip to Guatemala, but Julio confirmed my decision to go. One morning I was working with him in the ESL classroom, teaching him English phrases and helping him relearn and practice Spanish ones. After a few minutes he asked if I were sad.

"Yes," I told him. "Dianna está triste." I told him I had had nightmares.

He repeated the word several times, practicing, and nodded. He knew what it meant. Then he walked over to the map and pointed to Guatemala. "Tortura," he said.

I nodded.

He nodded, too. He let his eyes wander over the map for a while, then pointed to Peru. "Tortura?"

"Yes," I told him.

He pointed to Colombia. "Tortura?"

I nodded.

He scanned the map again and pointed to China. "Tortura?"

"Yes. I think so." I went over to the map and pointed to some other countries: Honduras, El Salvador, South Africa, and Russia. "Aquí también. Tortura."

Julio shook his head. I had never before seen him angry, but his voice was hard and loud. "No. Dianna habla. No tortura. Dianna habla." Dianna speak, he was saying. Dianna must speak out against it.

AT CHRISTMASTIME, our celebration was one of mixed traditions. Everyone got a few useful items wrapped up in Christmas paper, and sometimes the guests would shed tears, overwhelmed. Presents weren't a given in their culture. In the nights preceding Christmas, we observed the Latin American tradition of the *posadas,* or the inns. The children played the part of Mary and Joseph and their guiding angels, reenacting the search for shelter in Bethlehem as Mary neared the end of her pregnancy. Adults played the parts of the innkeepers. Approaching the first two innkeepers, the children sang a plea for lodging and were turned away with a harsh chant — "If you do not stop bothering me, I will hit you with a stick." The third innkeeper let them stay in the stable, since the inn was full.

Daniel, a man who had arrived from Guatemala several months before, was sitting at the kitchen table, holding his head in his hands. He said the *posadas* made him feel sad. Just Daniel and I were in the kitchen — everyone else was upstairs — and in the late-night quiet I asked him to tell me why. He turned his face to me and ran his hand up and down the pink burn scars covering one side of it. He had been burned in a factory fire. Doctors at the hospital where he was treated advised him to get plastic surgery on his neck, chest, and face. When he tried to get the factory owner to cover the cost of the surgery, the owner fired him.

Daniel pulled out his wallet, flipped it open, and showed me a photo. "That's my wife, Marisol." She was young and slim. "And that's Silvia, she is five years old. And this is our baby, Jacqueline." She seemed about two and had rounded cheeks.

He put the wallet back in his pocket. "My friends told me that I was asking for problems, but I kept fighting for my rights. These men, tough guys, started following me. I did not want my family to be in danger because of me." He paused for a moment. "I am going to bring them here when I get asylum."

It was the same story so many of the guests told — Dolores, Rigo, Luis, Otto, Eloisa, all were petitioning for asylum, which only a tiny percentage of Central American applicants obtained. Many were turned away before they could even apply. Daniel, after journeying through the Mexican desert, was picked up by U.S. border police who told him he would be sent back to Guatemala the next day. He was taken to a detention center, which was better than the desert. He had a place to lay his head, and he had food. A nonprofit organization that provided legal services to refugees told him he could apply for asylum and helped send him to Su Casa.

"So you found refuge," I said.

"Yes, but the *posadas* still make me sad. I do not know how Eloisa did it," Daniel said, staring down at the table top, keeping his head turned away from me to hide the scars. "She had three children with her. That they are still alive is a miracle. The border police were much kinder to me than my own friend. They gave me a place to stay. My best friend, he turned me away. My house was being watched and I was afraid for myself and my family. I needed a place to stay while I got ready to go. I asked my friend if I could stay with him, just for a few days. He said no. I spent the night in an alley behind a broken car and left to come here the next day."

AFTER HEARING STORIES of the folks at Su Casa, I had some perspective on my own feeling of being a refugee in the United States. While I felt estranged and lost, I had not left my family on the other side of an international border. I felt like a person with no identity, but at least I could work. The others at Su Casa had to beg for a green card. I didn't have to struggle with a totally unfamiliar language, and I had a college degree. Many of them, as they tried to cope with their past, were also trying to support children, find work, get legal status, and master the language. Some were not privileged to have had an education at all. Eloisa couldn't read or write, even in Spanish. If she wanted to work, someone would have to go with her to fill out the forms. Others at Su Casa were highly educated but couldn't work in their areas of specialty because our country didn't recognize their credentials.

The first times I watched the *posadas* were also hard for me, although the children were cute, and I helped them wrap up in sheets. Unlike Daniel, I had no memories of being turned away from a haven. I simply knew no haven was safe.

The convent retreat center I was abducted from, the Posada de Belén, translates into English as the Inn of Bethlehem. As the children playing Mary and Joseph were invited into the stable, I could not help but think about myself, the Inn of Bethlehem where no new life came forth, only death. The other guests sang the song of praise for the shelter Mary and Joseph had found. Did they really think Mary and Joseph were safe or that they themselves were safe? I knew they didn't. They lived with the fear of being deported. Even Su Casa was only a brief refuge. With time they would be expected to find work and move out. Mary and Joseph themselves had to leave the stable and flee in the night to Egypt, threatened with political violence against their child. Yet the guests celebrated. I came to understand that, although all shelters are temporary, maybe some last long enough for birth, or rebirth.

Some of the adults put on blindfolds and whacked at the Christmas piñata, but mostly just the children played. The blindfold, the stick, and the smacking sound made the game hard for most of the adults. I tried to take the sting out of watching by asking what the game symbolized. One of the Guatemalans, Otto, I think, said the piñata tradition reflects our journey through life: we try to find the good things and work hard to get them. Raúl's version was different. The piñata symbolizes the Devil. You have to hit him hard enough to make him let go of all the good things he has stolen.

Chapter Ten

BACK TO THE GARDEN

THE PLANE'S SHADOW slid along the Guatemalan earth, vanishing now and then in ravines but always reappearing beneath us, waiting for us to close the distance, to fly back down into it and be whole. Like my old self, I hoped. All we would have to do was touch down in Guatemala, and I would step back into the person the sisters at the Mount missed, the Dianna with a past, with memories of childhood.

I was going home. We would spend Holy Week in Guatemala — the place where my body and spirit had parted. If Jesus could rise, break out of that tomb of darkness and still live, maybe that was a journey we were all supposed to make, not after life, but here on earth — a journey from darkness to light, from numb half-life to full consciousness.

I would prove to the torturers that I was still alive and they hadn't knocked the fight out of me. Maybe it would weaken their resolve to see how ineffectual they had been and they would give up. There were others lucky enough to survive torture — Otto, Julio, and Eloisa were just a few — but not all were lucky enough to leave Guatemala, and those who did still had family there. They couldn't easily go public with what had been done to them, and they certainly couldn't demand justice. The security forces had made the mistake of torturing an American and letting her live, and I would prosecute, hold the Guatemalan army accountable for the first time in history for the crime of torture.

That was a kind of resurrection in itself. If they took my past, they didn't take my voice or my will.

I squeezed Mary's arm. Look! A volcano stemmed up in the distance. She, Sister Mary Agnes, and Father Mike LaDoux, who were all new to this journey, peered out the windows. "Mimi, we're almost there," I called across the aisle, not because she didn't know that but because I had to call it out. Fran and Paul sat in front of us, reading. They had made this flight too many times to look and only two months earlier had come to make arrangements for our trip. Sister Mary Agnes, a Council member, was along to report back to the community and to lend support and authority to our group. Father Mike was there to provide support and whatever clout a priest could add to our cause. Shawn, a young lawyer working with the Center for Human Rights Legal Action, was helping Paul with my case and, unlike Paul, was fluent in Spanish. We were ready.

I shuffled through the newspaper clippings Paul had given me, reminding myself that in spite of my excitement I needed to be realistic. The special prosecutor seemed none too friendly. After Paul and Fran had come down to make the arrangements, foreboding articles began appearing in the Guatemalan press. "Linares, the first special prosecutor in Guatemala, said he has never been able to speak with Ortiz," read one, "and the event occurred such a long time ago that gathering evidence is becoming more difficult all the time. 'Many people are now controlling what Ortiz says and does, especially the Council of Ursuline nuns,' Linares said. 'Perhaps they are trying to hide something. After two and a half years,' he said, 'she is offering to come to Guatemala and we hope that she helps us now, although much of the evidence has vanished. In any case, she must prove the veracity of the incidents of threat, kidnapping, rape, and torture, and in no way permit her lawyer, Paul Soreff, to try to make a political image of a case that should be strictly judicial. We have carried out many investigations, but because of the lack of cooperation of Sister Ortiz in the past, this case is practically stalled,' he added."[1] A Reuters article was headlined, "Guatemalan Prosecutor Calls on U.S. Nun to Back Rape Charges" — as if he didn't know we were already planning on returning to Guatemala to prosecute.[2]

Paul had fired off a letter to Ambassador Stroock: "We are extremely saddened and concerned to hear that the individual that we had been led to believe would conduct a thorough and impartial investigation into this case is taking a public stance questioning Sr. Dianna's cooperation and veracity, before he has even met her (especially given his persistent refusal to interview her)."

But the articles kept coming out. As we circled above the airport, I tried to brush off a sinking feeling. The truth cannot be denied indefinitely, I told myself. It has its own force.

IF AMBASSADOR STROOCK'S ATTITUDE toward the case had been published in the paper, my resolve would have broken up like a cloud. Unlike Linares, he was secretive; the cables containing his opinions would remain classified for several more years. After Paul and Fran left Guatemala in February, Stroock had written the secretary of state: "The Ortiz delegation has modified its former antagonistic approach to the embassy. There was no mention of previous accusations of USG [United States Government] involvement in whatever happened to Ortiz November 2–3, 1989. It remains to be seen, however, if Ortiz actually comes to Guatemala, and, if so, what will result from her interview with Linares. Tune in next week for the next episode of what has become, most unfortunately, a sitcom instead of a serious attempt to discover the truth."[3]

If I had been able to read Stroock's memo, as I was able to read Linares's remarks, I would have wondered who Stroock thought the actors were and what was funny. If he realized that no serious attempt was being made by the Guatemalan government to discover the truth, Stroock should have been concerned — he had said, repeatedly, that discovering the truth in my case was an embassy priority. He should have leaned on the Guatemalan government to get the job done. At the very least, he should have told us about the "sitcom" and saved us the trip.

UNFORTUNATELY, I was staying at Ambassador Stroock's house. The idea repelled me, but my lawyers and the Ursuline community thought it was the best, if not the only, option. They were concerned for my safety, and the embassy had offered to let us stay there, conduct all our meetings there, and provide transportation and an escort everywhere we went. I wanted to go to San Miguel, but the embassy wasn't up for it. At any rate, I was afraid of endangering the people there by my presence.

If we had known how Stroock was using his offer of protection and hospitality, we would have stayed away. In a cable to the State Department he said, "Ortiz is now due to arrive in Guatemala next month to testify and will, for her protection and ease of mind, stay at my residence — a development unthinkable at the outset of this case when our officers were accused either of having taken part in her alleged torture or trying to cover it up."[4] According to Stroock, our acceptance of his invitation meant we no longer believed the embassy was guilty of anything.

WE FLEW DOWN into our shadow, and several people clapped. When everyone else was off the plane, embassy officers boarded to inform us that they had planned to get our passports stamped while we waited in a lounge area, sequestered from the press, but the media had squeezed into that room and were waiting for us. The officers suggested that we leave by a side door. I refused. The embassy was trying to silence me. I wanted the Guatemalan people to know why I was there.

We walked out of the gate and I was pinned against the wall, blinded.

Cameras snapped like jaws. I crouched down behind Mimi and Mary, but still the eyes found me, exposed me.

"Did you hear that, Dianna? They said they were for you, not against you. That reporter said they had to cover this story so that impunity could end."

I TRIED to take it in. These people are regular people, I told myself. They are not the torturers. I repeated those sentences like a mantra during the following week, in various situations, many in which the mantra didn't fit.

SOME THINGS I remember with absolute clarity, but many of the common-place details escaped me. Perhaps it's best if Mary Agnes tells part of the story. She was paying attention to details, writing an account for the Ursuline community:

> The group was driven in a bullet-proof van to the Ambassador's resi-
> dence, where they were greeted by Ambassador Thomas Stroock and
> his wife, Marta. Dianna, Mary, and Mary Agnes were shown to their
> rooms on the second floor. The others were taken to the Camino Real
> Hotel in downtown Guatemala.

We were tired from traveling but had a full day ahead. We had to coordinate strategy with our Guatemalan lawyers from the Archbishop's Human Rights Office, and we were meeting with them that afternoon at the Maryknoll House. On the way, through the thick glass windows of the van, I saw soldiers with submachine guns patrolling the streets, buses oozing black fumes. I wasn't feeling at home. During the meeting, I kept looking around for something familiar, but I didn't remember anything about the Maryknoll House. I had spent time there the morning I escaped, but it seemed to me that I'd never been there before. That worried me more than my court appearance, which was a mere formality. I began to suspect that I wouldn't recognize anything in Guatemala, that this home would be as strange to me as the United States, as strange as the self I'd left here.

My Guatemalan lawyers, Ronnie and Edgar, were intent on the case. The stakes were high. Lawyers working on cases against the army had been known to show up riddled with bullets or dead from convenient "accidents." The Archbishop's Human Rights Office, where Ronnie and Edgar worked, had already received a number of death threats. Ronnie and Edgar were helping with the case because they knew the Guatemalan court system, and we had to have lawyers licensed to practice in Guatemala. We were counting on the high profile of my case to protect them; as long as my case received international attention, the army couldn't harm them without consequences. You could see the tension in their faces, and sometimes a paper they were holding would tremble.

AFTER THE MEETING, Father Mike said Mass, and I took Communion. Lord I am not worthy to receive you, I said — the same words that had haunted me for years; but for the first time I heard and believed the second part of the phrase: but only say the word and I shall be healed. God would make me worthy to partake of the grace and strength Communion conferred. God would, perhaps, forgive me for the choice I made regarding the pregnancy, for not being strong enough to resist the force of the Policeman, for not warning Miguel. I was actively fighting the torturers now, and that made the separation between myself and them more clear. I was on the side of the good, the same side as God, and on the side of the people. God represented truth and that was why I was there.

When I took Communion, I felt strength flow into me, as if I had been reunited with God.

DINNER WAS AT Ambassador Stroock's house. If not for the account that Sister Mary Agnes wrote, I would have no idea that Stroock's wife was at the long dining room table with us, along with Deputy Chief of Mission Phil Taylor and his wife and Consul General Sue Patterson. Stroock was talking about his term coming to an end and life back at his ranch in Wyoming, and I listened only long enough to know it was chit chat, that the order of the night was to wear a mask. Then I withdrew. I played with my forks, which were lined up according to height. They reminded me of a children's story I'd read to Marcos. A big fork, a medium fork, and a baby fork. One was supposed to be just right. I didn't know which. I had never had more than one fork. The elegant china threw back the outlines of my head, but my face had disappeared into shadow. In the mirror of this opulence I didn't exist. This is what Goldilocks might have felt like if the bears had invited her to stay for dinner, ignoring the broken chair, the dirty spoons, the porridge she'd marred — their smiles dripping with honey. They were biding their time, setting some kind of trap. Fran and Mary Agnes were the only ones willing to banter. At my end of the table, where Mary sat, silence hung thick. I couldn't eat. I excused myself.

WE SPENT THE NEXT DAY meeting with our lawyers and Church officials, including Bishop Juan Gerardi and members of the Conference of Guatemalan Religious (CONFREGUA), the group of religious leaders that, at peril to themselves, had placed ads defending me. At the meeting, CON-FREGUA leaders discussed the 1991 stabbing of anthropologist Myrna Mack, another case they were involved in denouncing. The police investigator, who posited that her murder was a political killing, not an incident of common crime, was a little too honest. He was shot to death after identifying a member of military intelligence as a suspect.

CONFREGUA was also involved in the case of Brother Moíses Cisneros, a Marist monk who was the principal of a Marist school. In a speech to the parents of the students attending his school, he had said, "For you, the poorest, the most needy, the Marist school exists. You are the first who have the right to be registered here. . . . You, the poorest, are the preferred in the Marist school." A month later, he was stabbed to death in his office.

CONFREGUA HAD A DINNER for us. The room was full of Guatemalan religious leaders. They wanted me to speak, but I couldn't. I was overcome by emotion — they had stood up and applauded when we entered the room — and I got Mimi to speak for me, thanking them for their courage and support. Efraín and David, the priests I had worked with in San Miguel, had traveled down from the village to see us. Everyone kept telling me how important it was to push my case through the judicial system, to expose the brutality committed by the state, to demand accountability and be the voice for those who had none.

MIMI AND I were up way before sunrise. I laid out my clothes, along with the necklace I would wear, loaned to me by the Argentine doctor who founded the Kovler Center. She had made it in prison. In the shower I prayed for strength, closing my eyes, feeling the hot steam rise around me. God, you are the Truth — speak through me. I asked the Woman to lend me strength and be with me in the courtroom, to let me speak for both of us.

Sister Mary Agnes recorded the details of that morning:

April 7: Very early on Tuesday morning (6:40) the van and the hotel group arrived at the residence to take Dianna to court. No time for breakfast. They were going very early to try to avoid the press. The van was permitted to drive into the basement garage of the court house and the group crunched up on one elevator and were taken up to the court room. The press were there waiting and stayed around for several hours.

Sister Dianna was whisked into the court room as soon as Judge Leticia Secaira arrived.

The judge, the court reporter, and Special Prosecutor Fernando Linares all introduced themselves. Linares was middle-aged, with short, black hair still bearing comb marks. He held his head high on his stiff neck. He reminded me of the Guate-man. A cold chill traveled through me as he shook my hand.

Shawn and I were instructed to sit on a small, hard couch. This was like no courtroom I had imagined. A large desk stood opposite the couch, on the other side of the room. The judge seated herself behind it and shuffled papers until a photographer appeared. She invited him in and, to my surprise, she walked across the room, positioned herself on the couch next to Shawn and me and looked at his camera. I tried to stand up to get out of the photo. Stay, I was told. We had our picture taken.

I caught Mary's eye. She looked worried, but tried to give me a reassuring smile. Mary and Antonio had gone to great trouble to submit to the court in advance a report detailing how interviews and judicial proceedings could affect survivors of torture and what could be done to make the experience less traumatic. The report made no mention of cameras, but I didn't like being ordered to stay and have my picture taken. The report made clear that, for survivors of torture, being ordered around and having no say in how the proceedings unfolded paralleled the dynamics of the torture:

> Torture survivors, like rape victims, . . . must prove that the event actually occurred, that they are innocent of some yet unidentified wrongdoing, and that they are of deserving character. The legal system is experienced, not as an advocate for victims, but as an adversary. This experience complements the tactic of torturers of telling the victims, overtly or by inference, that no one will listen to them, believe them, or care about what happened to them. This is a way of increasing the likelihood of later silence. The torturers' tactics are reexperienced and reinforced when survivors are in a situation in which their story is not believed.
>
> Torture destroys an individual's sense of personal control. Tactics include spontaneous shining of a flashlight in a victim's face, intermittent awakening for observation, tying victims' hands so that they cannot use them to cover their face, around-the-clock scrutiny, and intrusive face-to-face interrogation. Staring also undermines the survivor's sense of control. . . . The torture survivor has frequent loss

of composure while being interviewed. These displays of emotion are ... accompanied by intense feelings of vulnerability and defenselessness. The survivor has a need to recompose and control such displays as much as is permissible by the questioning process.... The survivor needs an available network of support to counteract the impersonal and unsupportive treatment by investigating agencies. The therapist's presence at questionings can be an important source of emotional support for the survivor.

What Mary and Antonio didn't note was that, unlike in the case of rape victims, the government in a case of torture is often the investigator, the prosecutor, and the accused. And government officials involved in a case of torture represent not only authority (which is difficult in itself for us, since we were ordered around helplessly) but the very authority that betrayed us.

IF SHE HAD READ the report, the judge wasn't swayed. She said that the report, as well as a psychological evaluation of me that Mary had submitted, were inadmissible because they were on the wrong kind of paper. I don't know whether Linares had read Mary and Antonio's report. If he had, he drew on it for ideas, and if he hadn't, he made lucky guesses. The first thing he did was object to Mary's presence. The judge asked her to leave. He objected to the presence of everyone in our delegation except myself and one Guatemalan lawyer.

Edgar, the lawyer who stayed, suggested that Shawn act as interpreter. He knew that if Shawn left, he and I would be facing the Guatemala army alone, with no international legal presence. The judge appointed Shawn to act as interpreter, but Linares again objected, saying an interpreter had been chosen already. He went to his office and he returned with a woman who, as we later learned, would pass on information to U.S. embassy officials.[5] Edgar kept arguing for Shawn. "There is nothing illegal about having someone here to verify the interpreter's work," he suggested. "Shawn could do that." The judge let Shawn stay.

Next she pulled out a sheaf of papers. "Unfortunately," she said, holding up my affidavit, "the court in Kentucky before which you swore this testimony was not competent to receive it."

The Guatemalan government had issued "letters rogatory," requesting that I make a sworn statement before the appropriate U.S. authorities. I had done that over a year ago. I didn't understand why the judge was saying that the court in Kentucky wasn't competent.

"Also," she continued, "it is not on the right kind of paper. You will have to swear your testimony today, before this court."

Well, OK, I thought, I can do that. I swear to tell the truth, the whole truth, and nothing but the truth and it's right there on that piece of paper. That's what I did in Kentucky, when I swore the testimony in response to the letters rogatory.

Shawn was pale. "Dianna, she says the affidavit is invalid," Shawn whispered. "She won't accept it."

"Shawn, what does that mean? I have to tell the whole thing again?"

"Yes."

A humming began in my ears. I would have to testify. If I said no I would be letting people down, giving in. See, she's not cooperating, the authorities would say. She's not telling the truth. She has something to hide.

IF I COULD GO BACK to that moment, knowing what I know now, I would have walked out of the courtroom and called a press conference. I would have told the media that the court was refusing to accept my affidavit, although the U.S. Department of Justice (DOJ) and the embassy of Guatemala had processed and approved it. I would have mentioned that the affidavit arrived in Guatemala a year and a half after I swore it before the court because the Guatemalan embassy in Washington sat on it for months. I would have said the Guatemalan judiciary was obstructing justice, trying to wriggle out of its obligations by saying the affidavit was on incorrect paper, a detail the Guatemalan embassy should have noticed. I would have offered to have it retyped on correct paper. I would have challenged the media to ask the court why the Kentucky federal court was found incompetent to receive testimony pursuant to a letter rogatory when the Justice Department and the embassy of Guatemala and the Guatemalan foreign ministry had apparently found otherwise.

Instead I let myself be interrogated, just as I walked with the Guate-man and José out of that garden without screaming. If you scream, the Guate-man had said, we'll hurt your friends. This time silence could hurt them.

LINARES KEPT GETTING very close to me and staring at me. Shawn had told him I couldn't bear to be stared at, but he didn't stop doing it. He barked questions out, interrogation style, and used words that made his disbelief apparent — words like *alleged* torture, *supposed* abduction. He was calling me a liar, indirectly.

I was trembling and couldn't get warm. I rubbed my throbbing cheek.

My tailbone ached. I was waiting for the break — wasn't there usually a break? — but the questions went on. They were asked in Spanish and translated to English, the language I preferred to testify in. I responded in English, the interpreter rendered the answer in Spanish, and the court secretary typed the response into the record. Then he read the answer back in Spanish, which was translated for me into English so that I could make sure the answer was the one I had given. Then the next question was asked. The repetitions of my answers were like the echoes in that cold building — I had to hear my answer as I said it, then three times more.

As in the interviews with Diane Sawyer and the State Department officers, while I told what happened, I was feeling the physical pain of it. But this time the present vanished. The Guate-man, José, the Policeman were coming toward me. I smelled the alcohol on their breaths, felt the cold cement against my bare skin. I screamed, "No, stop!" I held my arms out, struck at them and cried as I began to feel the blows and the burns.

The judge called Mary. We went into the bathroom and she tried to put me back together. Then I had to go back in. I felt exposed, naked, ashamed. I knew I had lost track of reality, lost track of what I was saying, talked to people who weren't there. The judge and Linares probably thought I was talking to myself. They probably thought I was crazy. I could barely get my feet to take me across the threshold, but I thought of the Woman, of all the women, of the people in the pit and I went. As I entered the courtroom, the officials were laughing and chatting.

I screamed myself hoarse, and no one rescued me. The torturers were coming alive in Shawn and Edgar, as well as in Linares and the judge. As if they were at a play, everyone watched but no one lifted a finger. I expected Edgar or Shawn to stop the proceedings and say this was way too much for me, I was having flashbacks. But their attitude seemed to be that I was OK, I would get over it in a few minutes. Each of those minutes I was feeling the burns of the cigarettes. I was feeling raped. I hoped they would stop and say we needed to find a way to do this that was less revictimizing to me. No one at any point asked me what my needs were. I would have said I needed Mary with me, I needed the right to have breaks any time, I needed statements rather than questions — for example, Let's talk about this part of your experience, tell us what you remember — and I needed not to be stared at. But it was clear that what I needed didn't matter, and I knew protesting was useless. I was afraid I would be accused of complaining and feeling sorry for myself. I kept hearing the Policeman's voice: *Nobody cares about you. No one is going to rescue you. Where are your friends now? Where is your God?*

Those are the same thoughts I had before the Policeman even voiced them for me, the same ideas that came to me when I was first left in that dark room. Where was everyone? How could they have let this happen? How could God have let this happen? How could I have let this happen? I had walked back into the torture chamber. I heard the torturers' laughter. Estúpida!

The judge and Linares seemed tired and impatient, but they were the ones prolonging the session with myriad questions and delays. It occurred to me that they were trying to see how much I could take, waiting for me to break so that they could say I stopped the process. I wouldn't stop it, I wouldn't break. I answered their questions.

Finally, my flashbacks were so intense and numerous that the judge and Linares let Mary stay and sent Shawn out. Mary purposely kept me in the room. She wanted the court to have to see the flashbacks instead of shuttling me out the door. Mary remembers that Linares, during the flashbacks, joked with the court interpreter.

At the end of the court session, twelve hours later, Edgar and Shawn encouraged me to object to Linares's tactics formally and for the record. By then the damage was done. I was beaten down. I felt abandoned, and I felt the lawyers had betrayed me.

THAT NIGHT, I couldn't eat. I vomited and lay on the bed, my body aching. Well, they can't say I didn't cooperate, I thought. Tomorrow is the reconstruction. But at least I won't be in court for twelve hours, answering questions.

I wondered if I had done as Jesus would have done. I thought of Jesus at his trial, how he refused to proclaim his innocence or speak much in his own defense. He was turning the other cheek. More than that. He was handing his body over to be crucified. He had challenged the institutions that trampled on the lives of the poor, those who were treated unjustly by the rich, those who were thrust off to the margins of society. That's why he landed up in such trouble. Was it not his obligation, there before Pilate, to speak out, to continue to defend the truth and the rights of the poor, and to hold accountable those who violated their rights?

If Jesus wasn't obligated to speak, was I? Couldn't I quietly, in good conscience, accept the official characterization of me as a liar, my story as a hoax, when Jesus himself did that? My brain was trying to look out for me. It wanted me to give in. But I knew the analogy wasn't apt. Jesus, after his torture, walked as a nobody with his disciples. They didn't understand him or believe him when he identified himself. They thought he was dead.

That was more like my situation. He had to open his hands and side to Thomas and stand the pain of being examined. That was the cost of being believed, of spreading the message.

THE NEXT MORNING, at the Posada de Belén, I was told to begin the reconstruction by sitting on the stone I had sat on the morning I was abducted. As soon as I entered the garden and saw the stone and the trellis arching above it, I had a flashback. Nothing had changed, it seemed. And if I took my place, sat down on the stone, the action would begin, the events of my torture would play out inexorably. I did the things requested. I found the stone and sat on it. I relived the moment, as required, playing again on my Walkman the "Cry of Ramah" tape I had been listening to at the time.

Next I had to find the hole in the wall the men led me out of the garden through. A new wall had been built behind it and reinforced with bits of broken glass cemented into the top, and I had to climb up and look over it, at the old wall. I found the spot and felt triumph and righteous anger well up in my chest. No one seemed impressed. And the journey wasn't over. Mary Agnes, in her report, wrote about that long morning:

> Retracing her "walk to Calvary" was exceedingly painful for Dianna. Many times she would sit and sob before she could go any farther.

Mary, who was next to me during the proceedings, picked me up when I fell and held me when I couldn't support myself anymore. She wiped my face with tissues.

WE UNDERTOOK the next leg of the reconstruction, walking alongside the river to the main road where the buses passed. Linares stopped at a stand to buy a pack of potato chips. He began crunching away, then looked at me and smirked. "Want one?" he asked.

I have a clear recollection of this incident and of the image that popped into my head in response: a vision of myself smashing the bag of chips in his face.

The walk along the river was hot and dusty. Court officials were knocking on the doors of the houses alongside the little footpath, asking if anyone had seen me being kidnapped two and a half years before. Apparently the police hadn't yet asked and court officials felt this was the time, with an entourage of TV cameras behind them. Very few people answered the door and those who did said no. "See, we just can't find anyone to corroborate your story," Linares said.

Just then the bus rumbled over the bridge on its regular run. It was all too real and Dianna suffered flashbacks.

José flags the bus down. The Guate-man opens his jacket to show me a grenade. If you try anything, innocent people will die. José gets on first, then I get on, with the Guate-man behind me. The Guate-man takes the last seat, the one directly behind the driver. The driver lets me sit on a container next to him that looks like a large white jar. Every now and then the Guate-man puts his hand on my shoulder, reminding me. A sticker of the Virgin of Guadalupe watches from the front window.

MARY KNEW TO WAIT until my breathing slowed or until she saw a pause in the movements of my eyes. Then she could say something to orient me and I might be able to hear her. But because I was flailing and screaming, Mary was pressured by the others in the van to intervene. "Paul or Linares or someone said 'Do something — stop this!'" She ignored her better judgment, said my name and touched my arm. I gouged her with my fingernails. A while later I asked, "Who are you? Where are you taking me?" The embassy driver identified himself.

Mimi said, "It's Mimi, Dianna. It's OK. I'm here."

"How do I know you're not working for the torturers?" I shouted. "How do I know you weren't all sent by them?"

It was about fifty minutes before she was able to resume the trip in the van, this time accompanied by the court officials.

I was supposed to identify the little lane where the police car was waiting. Mary said, "You don't have to do it, Dianna. We can stop this now."

I said, "No, I can do it. I can recognize it. Let's just get it over with."

They drove on the bus route back to Guatemala and Mixco. As mysterious as it may sound Dianna was able to recognize the area where they took her off the bus, crossed four lanes of traffic, and led her into this secluded area where the police car awaited her. We parked and walked around the tall bank of earth to the hidden lane.

The Guate-man is pressing hard on my arm. I try to twist away but he clamps down harder and shoves me into the car. "I see your trip was successful," the driver says, turning half-around. It's the Policeman. He sneers. The motor turns over. José pulls the dark blindfold out of his backpack.

It was a long time before she could regain her composure. The judge called closure for the day.

Dr. [Mary] Fabri wanted to stop the whole process before it destroyed Dianna. The Guatemalan lawyers came up to the hotel room and discussed the implications. Stopping now meant (1) the court would close the case and declare she had made it all up; (2) the Catholic Church in Guatemala would suffer in many ways because they had supported her; (3) the lives of the four lawyers would be in grave danger. At this Dianna uncurled from her fetal position and said, "I will go on!" It was at such a poignant moment as this that one was acutely aware of the power of the prayers of the community — no other force could have given her such strength — God was truly bearing her up.

At 8:00 p.m. we once again met with CONFREGUA to discuss the wisdom of continuing the campaign. The papal nuncio found out we were meeting and called the Maryknoll House to invite himself. The superiors told us this case and the paid ads were the only voice Guatemalans had. If any Guatemalans spoke out they would die. Their only hope of letting the world know how bad things were for the poor in Guatemala was for us to continue the ads and the efforts to keep the world's attention on their plight.

After the meeting with CONFREGUA we went back to the hotel to plan. I could barely focus. It was Wednesday night, and I hadn't eaten since Sunday. Whenever I tried to eat, I vomited. I even vomited when I drank. I huddled on the bed while the lawyers discussed the statement I was preparing to give at a press conference the next morning. I had done what I could with it and they were touching it up.

My lawyers had told me before not to mention the American who gave orders to my torturers. "If you do," they said, "we won't get any help from the embassy." And everyone knew that if the embassy didn't set up meetings with Guatemalan government officials, getting the meetings was impossible. On this trip, we had been totally dependent on the embassy for security. It was hard to picture pursuing the case without the embassy's help. In the written statement we prepared to pass out to the press, I made no mention of Alejandro.

After the press conference, I would go to the courthouse and resume the judicial reconstruction. I had to try to identify the location where I was tortured and the area where I escaped from Alejandro's jeep. Then there were photos of police officers to look through.

It's possible that I had made a start already in identifying the building where I was tortured. During one of our drives, we passed a colossal building, castle-like and walled. I tensed up and squeezed Mimi's arm. I went into a cocoon, Mimi says. The tops of my thighs found my chest and I sat there, curled up, breathing fast. When we got by it I said, "I feel like we've gone past a really evil place." I don't remember that incident well, but Mimi and Mary were struck by my reaction and found out that the building was the Politécnica, an old military academy where people were known to have been tortured.

> *April 9:* We met at 6:30 Thursday morning for breakfast at the hotel to plan the last day. Mimi went to court at 8:00 a.m. to give her testimony. Sister Mary Agnes accompanied her. Sister Dianna went to meet with Archbishop Penados, who called to say he was back. But his receptionist mixed things up and they did not get to meet. At 9:00, eighty to ninety media people showed up for the press conference. Dianna read her statement although she broke down a few times. The dreaded time for question/answers came . . . once again prayer empowered her and she spoke her answers in a strong, clear voice.

I began my press statement with a verse of a poem by Guatemalan poet Julia Esquivel:

> There is something here within us
> which doesn't let us sleep,
> which doesn't let us rest,
> which doesn't stop pounding deep inside. . . .
> What keeps us from sleeping
> is that they have threatened us with
> Resurrection!

The *New York Times,* the *Washington Post,* and the *London Times* covered the conference. Networks that broadcast throughout Latin America also were there, and in Guatemala my statement was aired in full on TV. I made it through my statement, saying the things I needed to say:

> In January of 1989, when I first began to receive written threats, I knew that I could return to the United States and leave my fears and the dangers behind. But there was something about the indigenous people of San Miguel Acatán that kept me from fleeing. I felt at one with them; they had become part of me and I had become part of them. Their suffering had become my suffering.

My commitment to a suffering people has grown to include more than the people of San Miguel Acatán. It includes all Guatemalans who have suffered any abuse of their basic human rights and their dignity as human beings created in the image of God, whether they reside in Guatemala, in refugee camps in Mexico, or in the United States or Canada, seeking political asylum and simply trying to survive. I return to Guatemala for you. I pursue the investigation of my abduction, interrogation, and torture not just for myself but for all of you who have been tortured or disappeared or forced to flee your homeland . . . and for all of you who carry in your hearts the pain of the hideous crimes that your loved ones have suffered and continue to suffer.

Likewise, I pursue the investigation for all of those who dedicate their lives to justice and all the people who risk their lives in promoting the Gospel of justice and peace. I pursue the investigation because the truth of your oppression must become known to the rest of the world, and because the torturers and assassins must be stopped!

Accompany us on this vigil,

> and you will know what it is to dream.
> You will know how marvelous it is
> to live threatened with Resurrection . . .
> to dream awake,
> to keep watch asleep,
> to live while dying and
> to know oneself already resurrected!

Weeks earlier, when I'd written the talk, I had believed those words. I was dead again now. I didn't trust Paul and Shawn, who sent me off to what Fran and Mary Agnes kept calling my Calvary. They all watched, silent and complicit witnesses. I didn't trust my Guatemalan lawyers, who, as I saw it, did nothing to protect me and were putting the burden of their safety on my back. I was back in the torture chamber the night they laid it all out for me: if you don't talk, innocent people will die. Now are you ready to cooperate? I didn't trust in my own goodness. I could kill with a shake of my head. Mimi and Mary I could perhaps trust; but who knew? Appearances couldn't be trusted and neither could my judgment.

A number of reporters approached me after I spoke. Paul kept them at bay — I had to go on to court and didn't have the energy or time to give interviews. But in the hall a couple of reporters passed and quickly slipped me pieces of paper. I read them on the way to the court. One was a poem of encouragement, and I knew that the reporter meant the words for himself, as well. He was the one running the real risk. I would be flying back to the United States the next day, but he would be here, playing a dangerous game with words. Which one would tip the balance and get him on a death list? Even giving me the poem was a risk. I carried in black and white a sentiment the army would consider subversive: respect for the truth.

The other note said "Sea fuerte." Be strong. I was sure that the Woman was speaking through him.

> At 11:30 Dianna returned to the courtroom and came out at 5:30. Something had happened to Señor Linares — he was much more human. They decided to end this session. They said she could have her forensic medical exam in the States — and at a later time could return to identify pictures at the national police office and point out the building where she was tortured. They realized Dianna had given her all and could do no more at this point.

In fact, I could go on. I was saying I wanted to go on. I wanted to look at the photographs of police officers at the police headquarters. I wanted to finish the judicial reconstruction. I offered to submit to a medical exam to prove I had scars on my back. Let's just get it over with, that was my attitude. I've come this far. Let's go all the way. But the court canceled the judicial reconstruction, saying the reconstruction of the day of my escape would have to be done on a day with similar weather and time of sunrise. The court would have to consult the governmental department responsible for keeping records on the weather patterns. As for the medical exam, the judge said it wasn't possible due to the late hour and a scheduled holiday the following day. It was also too late, she said, to look at photographs at the police headquarters. When we asked about doing it the next day, we were told that a parade would prevent access. According to an account Shawn wrote up, "The judge indicated that Sister Dianna's testimony provided the court with ample information to take further steps to investigate her case, including calling additional witnesses who could provide additional information.... The judge also indicated that she would be sending further 'letters rogatory' to the U.S. Federal District Court in Kentucky to receive any additional testimony or medical examinations needed for the case to proceed. She did not explain why the court would be any more 'competent' to accept this request than it had in the prior instance."

I was frustrated. One thing seemed clear: the court had shut the proceedings down.

PERHAPS THE COURT had never intended to carry out all the proceedings and had counted on my inability to go on, my "lack of cooperation." Maybe the Guatemalan government, by ending the court session, hoped to give international media interest a chance to subside. In my press statement I had criticized the minister of defense and the minister of the interior for slandering me; I had criticized President Serrano for refusing to permit the formation of the independent investigative commission that President Cerezo had appointed; and I had blasted Linares for refusing to interview me in the United States, for saying I hadn't cooperated, and for adopting a partial attitude in favor of my torturers. I stated that the Guatemalan government had never fully investigated my case and the only significant action the Attorney General's Office had taken was to appoint the special prosecutor.

The news coverage was very positive. "Lawyers representing the Ursuline Sisters have accused authorities of blocking the investigation to cover up official complicity, while international human rights groups have cited the case as an example of the Government's unwillingness to prosecute crimes involving the security forces," the *New York Times* reported.[6] Although I had not mentioned the American in my statement, we'd handed out my affidavit to the press, which contained the information about Alejandro, and the *New York Times* reporter included that information, ending the article on this note: "The next day, the statement said, a man with what Sister Diana described as a North American accent apologized for her treatment and took her from the warehouse."

BY THE LAST DAY of our trip, I was hating Guatemala. I asked if we could go to an area where there were ordinary people, like the people I had worked with. Nothing had snapped me back into the self I had inhabited before I was taken out of the garden. Maybe nothing would. But one part of that self that had stayed with me and that I didn't want to lose was my love of the Guatemalan people. We visited the city garbage dump, where the poorest lived, scraping together an existence from the discarded things they could save. Smoke hung in the air from garbage burning in a pit. Shacks made from cardboard boxes swayed with the wind. Raw sewage flowed through ditches.

Above us I heard wings. Black birds bigger than any I'd ever seen were gliding in circles and descending to perch on hills of garbage. I thought of the birds of the Bible that ate the seeds of the Lord's word before they could root. But beneath the birds children were playing, people were living and working as a community, getting by as best they could. A priest from Kentucky was helping to build a church. Women were teaching in a makeshift school. There was a kind of intangible truth in that, a goodness the birds couldn't steal.

Chapter Eleven

THE EMBASSY'S CROSS

THE MOON MUST HAVE BEEN nearly full, since it was almost Easter, and I imagine our shadows lay down beneath us on the driveway as we waited for the basement door to be opened. It was a few hours past midnight, and there was probably one of those predawn breezes that carries the scent of wet leaves. Maybe the garden, where Julio had been digging, mixed into the wind a scent of soil and mint. It's hard to know. All I remember is waiting for the door to open and wanting to lie down. Juanita rang the bell again. After a minute the door was pulled open and a long, dark hallway was before us. The shadows made it look like a tunnel.

Juanita and Pat caught me as I collapsed, screaming. After a while I could hear them. They told me I was home.

The Policeman's hand was not on my wrist. We were not coming back from the room where the Woman was. I was not naked. Her blood was not running down my arms. They told me I was home.

But I didn't recognize the wide oak stairwell, the room they said was mine, with a postcard stuck in a corner of the mirror, a cracked pottery bowl on the dresser. Juanita already knew how lost I was, and I didn't try to hide it. When Pat had come to pick us up at the airport, I had turned away from her embrace and had barely mumbled a greeting. I just didn't remember her. So when Juanita asked me if I wanted to take a shower, I answered honestly, "Yes, but I don't know where that is."

"I'll get your things together and take you there." She led me down the hall and handed me a towel, a bucket of shampoos, and a pair of checked pajamas. These belonged to someone else, another self I had left behind in the prison. Juanita slept on a mattress on the floor beside me, and I lay awake with the lamp on until a gray light filled the room and it was safe enough to sleep.

Someone is holding a glass out. I could barely ask for the water. Thirst dried the word up, but he understood. The light is behind him, his face in shadow. The rim is warm. The liquid is warm. I gag, spit it out, try to wipe it from my lips

with my bare arm, but it has invaded my throat, seeped into my tongue. He is
laughing.

"DIANNA, you need to try to drink this." A small man with dark hair and
glasses and a long, wiry mustache was next to me.

"Dianna, this is David, my husband." Mary Fabri was beside him. "He's
a doctor."

"I can't drink."

"Try, Dianna." Mary took the glass from him and held it out.

Her eyes were full of concern, and I remembered her wiping my face
and holding me up. I took the glass from her and tried a couple of times
to get it to my lips. I gagged.

Later in the morning I had visitors. People with Guatemalan accents —
a couple of men, a woman, some children. Another woman with pretty
eyes. They all looked worried when they saw me, but still they smiled.
One of the women tried to touch my shoulder. I pulled away.

"I don't remember them, Juanita," I told her when they had gone. "I'm
supposed to know them, aren't I? Tell me their names."

"The man with the chipped tooth is Otto. The larger woman was Eloisa,
and the young, slender one is Dolores."

THROUGHOUT THE DAY, in the quiet between songs on my Walkman, I
heard the Policeman hiss: "Eres una loca. Estúpida. La mataste." *You killed*
her. I told Pat I needed more noise and she brought in a TV to drown
out the torturers' voices. Mimi stacked pillows against the walls and the
window so I wouldn't hurt myself and switched off with Juanita and Pat,
guarding me at night. If I went from a nightmare into a flashback, Mimi,
Juanita, or Pat would talk to me, telling me where I was until I came back
to the present.

I COULD HEAR the aquarium in the hallway and I imagined myself as a
tropical fish, suspended in a different element, separated from the world
by a glass wall — able to see out but untouchable. Unable to harm or
be harmed. My words mere bubbles, breaking on the divide between my
world and theirs.

THAT'S HOW it should have been in court, I thought: the words I blurted
in my flashbacks should have vanished on the frontier between past and
present. I don't know what I said.

I WASN'T SURE if I was dreaming. Someone was talking about the hospital, getting me in before my kidneys blew out. I opened my eyes. Juanita, Mimi, and Pat were talking with Mary and David in a corner of the room.

"Don't send me to the hospital." I was trying to yell but my voice was barely audible. I pictured Our Lady of Peace, the locked gray door at the end of the hall, Dr. Snodgrass, whose face kept fading into the Guate-man's. "Don't send me there. Please, Juanita, Mary. Mimi, don't let them."

Mary came over to me after a moment and took my hand. "We're not sending you anywhere. You're staying right here with us."

David came back with an IV and gently put it in my arm while Mary talked to me. "You don't have to do anything now," Mary said, "just rest and recover. And try to drink this." She left a glass on the bedside table, and it was still there the next day, when she brought me more. Finally I took the risk. I drank it. It was some kind of herbal tonic, Mary had said. It tasted awful, but it was cool and nothing like urine.

IN A MATTER OF DAYS, according to Juanita, I was calling the other guests by name — I'd either relearned their names or regained the memories; I'm not sure which. But at some point all my memories of Su Casa did come back. And meanwhile Eloisa made it easy. "Dianna, soy Eloisa!" She always announced herself and pushed the door open with her hip to bring me oatmeal with sugar and milk. Dolores brought me slices of avocado and warm tortillas. Eloisa would talk about her children or herself or something random, but Dolores and I would exchange shy smiles and I would swallow over the knotted fist in my throat while she sat and made half-hearted small talk. Dolores felt hurt at the way I was acting. She knew I had forgotten her. Shame hung in my chest, shame about hurting her and having been so weak in Guatemala, so quickly broken. Shame about needing like this, being dependent. It was more than my pride. It didn't feel safe. Needing anyone was a set up for betrayal.

As the guests at Su Casa were taking care of me I thought about the Woman, wishing I could have helped her, nurtured her back to health. And the ones moaning in the pit, I wished I could have pulled them out and cared for them, kept their life within their bodies. I suppose I'd had a secret hope that going to Guatemala and speaking about the people in the pit would undo their deaths. I would prophesy, like Ezekiel in the valley of bones, and they would be clothed with life. My trip was a rescue mission and I had failed. They were dead. I couldn't even talk about the Woman. I couldn't do her the honor of acknowledgment. And when I talked about the pit Linares and the judge didn't believe me — it was clear from their questions. Where was the honor in that for the people who died in that building? Their grave had been spat on, and I was the agent of that dishonor.

I should have died back there in Guatemala, I thought. I survived the first time, while others died, and the second time I survived too, walking out, leaving the dead.

I DIDN'T WANT TO EAT, but I was afraid I would be sent to the hospital if I didn't. I choked the food down and kept it down, and after a week David took the IV out.

I had lost fifteen pounds but was no longer dehydrated. Mary visited every day. She said what Juanita and Pat and Mimi were saying — that I had been strong and gone the distance and made a difference in Guatemala and I should be proud, not ashamed. I wasn't convinced. I had lost control of myself. Even over the noise of my Walkman and the TV and the birds singing in the trees outside I heard the Policeman saying, "No one will ever believe you. They will think you are crazy."

And now I had proved it, losing control of myself in the courtroom, in the van, in front of the cameras at the Posada de Belén. I had meant to show that one can survive torture. I had meant to wrest away some of the army's power over the people, diminish the terror. Instead I had been an advertisement for the army's power, like the bodies left on the roadside with the eyes burned out. I had shown what torture can do. I'd worked for them again, been their instrument, just as I had taken the machete, only to find my hands trapped. They would always trick me, use my will against me.

I had hurt the sisters at the Mount the first time I returned from Guatemala. I had hurt my family later, telling them about the rape. Now I had hurt people once again, terrorizing the Guatemalans with my obvious lingering trauma and making my close friends sad. Mary looked tense and dismal. She had drunk in the evil I carried. Juanita's eyes were puffy. I remembered that she had lupus. She should be resting instead of waiting on me. And Mimi should be back in Chile, not sitting here with me, trying to be cheerful. I had taken her away from her life. I had taken the life out of all of them.

AFTER A WEEK OR SO, I was strong enough to get up. I did what I had to do — helped cook or clean — but whenever I could I stayed in bed. I kept thinking about my lawyer Shawn and the hug she had given me after my

twelve hours in court, as if she cared. I wanted to believe her. Maybe she
was waiting for me to tell her when I'd had enough and couldn't go on.
But I just remembered how she and Edgar watched while I was burned
again. I thought about Paul, too, his suggestion that I drop the accusation
about Alejandro. Either he didn't believe me or the torturers had gotten
to him. Maybe he was working for them.

Out my window I could see a ruined church. It had all been one complex once; Franciscan Friars had worshiped in the church and lived at Su
Casa. I had walked through the narrow passageway that connected the
two from a door leading off a landing in our stairwell. The tall gothic
windows of the church were boarded up from the inside but light beamed
through in places. Wooden benches, ornately carved, served as pews. Even
in the dusty light I could tell the church had been beautiful.

From my bed I kept my eye on it. Homeless people slept in there, we
were told. We had to keep the door to the passageway bolted. I wondered
if the torturers had taken up residence, if they were responsible for the
liquor bottles that littered the yard. Would anyone protect me from them
if they decided to come for me? I doubted it. No one had protected me
in Guatemala when the torturers had shown up in the form of Linares,
the judge, and my lawyers. I didn't even protect myself. A friend who has
heard me speak of the trip had a dream: I was nailed to the shut door of
the courthouse, and there, in public, I was being raped. I hadn't thought
of it that way, but I think that's what it felt like. And once again, I didn't
fight hard enough. I betrayed myself.

When I wasn't staring out the window I stared at the wall. Like the
floor it was wood and the light glowed gently off it. A whorl in the dark
wood seemed to form the face of a cherub, or maybe a dolphin, arching.
I dreamed once that I was sinking, moving toward a light flooding the
underwater world, and a dolphin took me to an island where I rested in
the sand. Remembering the dream, I took comfort in the wooden image.
Then it changed. I saw the Policeman's face.

Is this what the rest of my life will be like — if I look at something and
think it's beautiful is it going to change? The torturers were invincible.
They had fooled me at the Mount, when I was sent to the hospital, and
in Guatemala again, and now they were in my room. I couldn't decide
which was real, the smiling cherub or the ghoulish leer. The smell of Pine
Sol came from the hallway bathroom, strong enough to keep the torturers'
odor of liquor and smoke away. The blankets piled on top of me kept out
the cold, and I wrapped the sheets around me like a shroud. The weight
made my body ache, but I didn't mind. I let them push me down. The

Earth Mother was saying go ahead, come, I'll catch you. I no longer cared whether it was a trick. The torturers appeared here on earth in so many disguises. At least once in hell I'd know not to trust.

THAT'S WHAT MY MIND was saying; my body was struggling to heal. Andrea, a massage therapist who volunteered at Kovler, came several times during those first weeks. I kept my clothes on but let her touch my shoulders and my feet. Nearly every day Juanita took me to sit in a whirlpool that a priest named Father Jerry had in his bathtub. Sometimes Father Jerry cooked for me, and I was relaxed enough after the whirlpool to eat.

Faced with my body's willfulness, my mind must have intensified its tactics. I guess this is too painful to remember — somewhere my memory put a moratorium on pain — but when I talked to Juanita and Pat years later as I was piecing together the odds and ends of my time at Su Casa, Juanita's face reddened and her voice broke. "If I talk about this, I'm going to cry," she said. "When you came back from Guatemala you were very bad and we almost lost you. You called me in and said, 'I want to show you something.' You had a suicide letter. It was a letter to your family. It said that you couldn't face this anymore, it had to stop." Tears were running down Juanita's cheeks. "You felt that you didn't have a life, that this wasn't living."

I asked Juanita more about her reaction, sorry that I had caused her such pain. She said:

> I was surprised that the letter was to your family. You hadn't talked to them for almost a year. You agonized over it, but when they would call, you'd say, "I can't talk to them. I don't know them."
>
> And I thought, This will be the first communication that they will get from you.
>
> You said you couldn't go through this anymore, you were very tired, and you hoped they would understand. You just couldn't go on.
>
> I kept my composure, but it was really hard. I said, "It would really make me and many people here sad if that happened to you, but I don't know your pain and I can't say you don't have a right to do it. And we're here for you." But I was nervous after that. Pat and I took turns accompanying you at night for about eight weeks after that trip.
>
> I showed the letter to Mary, and you talked to Mary about the letter, too. You had a battle going on. You said, "I have a right to die," and you felt that Mary should help you do it. You were furious

with her for refusing to help you. You didn't even want to meet with her because each time you had the same conversation.

I guess I thought Mary should understand how raw I was and have compassion. The flashbacks that had stopped for nearly a year were back, and I'm sure I was doubting that I would ever be free of them. Also, I apparently felt alone with the burden of the case. I had gone to Guatemala as a voice for the voiceless, and that was now my sole reason for living. But it was a constant reminder of the deaths of the people I had left behind in that clandestine prison. Mary, nonetheless, wouldn't be persuaded.

While Mary was trying to pull me back together, the American embassy also was working to repair the damage my visit had done. Consul General Sue Patterson was helping Linares's investigator, Carl West, track down information about Clara McGowan, the Maryknoll sister who had arranged for Darleen and me to go to the retreat at the Posada de Belén. Patterson had heard that McGowan was a psychiatrist, and she and West were trying to establish that I needed a psychiatrist before I was ever abducted. Patterson, who had heard that McGowan lived in Belize, wrote to her counterpart, Rudi Boone, the consul general at the embassy in Belize: "One of our crosses to bear is the case of Sister Diana Ortiz. Big political problem for Guatemala because everybody believes a nun more than they do the Guatemalan army.... Let me know what you can learn. I write this informally because we have to be so careful so as not to be accused by Sister Diana or her lawyers of being partial or disbelieving."[1]

AMBASSADOR STROOCK was busy with my case, too, that spring, passing along to the secretary of state the opinions of Guatemalan government officials. In an interview several years later with *CNN Presents,* Stroock provided a context for his comments:

> *CNN reporter:* Let me go back to her refusal to cooperate or to talk to embassy officials [after escaping]. Given the fact that she believes there was some American connection, wouldn't it stand to reason that she would be suspicious of people in official capacities?

> *Stroock:* No, I really don't understand. You have to believe that the United — to do that you'd have to believe that the United States government is involved in a huge conspiracy in Central America to take away people's rights.

> *CNN reporter:* Given the long-standing ties between the United States government and the Guatemalan military and the Gua-

temalan government, extending back to a 1954 coup, is it so unreasonable that she would be suspicious?

Stroock: Yes, I think it's totally unreasonable because what you're saying therefore is that the United States embassy is going to take the side of the Guatemalans, and the official representatives of the people of the United States are going to support Guatemalans over Americans. And that's an outrageous suggestion as far as I'm concerned.[2]

But Stroock's April 1992 reports to the secretary of state contained these comments:

Due to the inconsistencies in the information Ortiz has provided it is impossible to draw any conclusions as to who might have committed the acts. Both Special Prosecutor Linares and Judge Leticia Secaira have doubts about her version.... Linares is also puzzled about why her torturers would not have resorted to stronger, more effective methods of torture if the cigarette burns were not achieving results. He thinks the torturers exhibited unaccustomed patience. When asked about his future plans, Linares indicated he will not resign for now. However he may resign prior to Sister Dianna's next trip to Guatemala, as he feels his continued presence might provide wind to the sails of the GOG detractors. He said, "This is all a big show, and I am not the best actor."[3]

The investigation and court proceedings *were* a big show — Linares himself admitted it — and Linares *was* an actor in that show, not someone really trying to prosecute my case or achieve justice. Stroock passed these comments along to the State Department without any expression of concern about a miscarriage of justice in the case of a U.S. citizen.

Instead of finding out how to press for justice, rather than a "show," Stroock in the same cable went on to outline for the secretary of state the ways my case could be closed:

The CG [consul general] asked how, assuming the GOG is not able to identify the perpetrators, could the GOG finalize the case once it had gotten all possible information from Sister Diana and pursued all leads. Linares said that there is a little-used way to close a judicial case called "sobreseimiento." The concept is roughly equivalent in U.S. terms to "quashing." It is used when the accused person dies prior to sentencing, when there is insufficient evidence to support the facts, or when there is a lack of evidence that a felony was ever committed. Depending on what happens, this may be the route the GOG follows. In this case, the Attorney General's Office would have to request the judge to close the case based on the inconsistencies and lack of proof. This written request could be published and publicized, and be considered the final report of the case.

The ambassador in the same cable reported on the meetings embassy officials had been having with the judge to learn about the testimony I had given and what her opinions were — even though the ambassador himself would be giving testimony in my case, and the question of the involvement of an American connected to the embassy was still an issue in the court case.

On April 23, Judge Secaira visited the embassy at our request and met with the charge and CG. She too has serious doubts about the veracity of Sister Diana's story. Secaira reported that in the courtroom when Ortiz was asked a question she did not know how to answer (such as "about how many bodies were in the pit into which you were thrown?"), she broke down and cried and then requested a recess during which time she went into the bathroom with her therapist. Upon returning to the proceedings Ortiz provided the answer. Throughout the proceedings Ortiz appeared to be parroting information provided by others. . . . In addition, her attorney asked both the judge and special prosecutor Linares not to look at Sister Dianna as it made her too nervous, a request with which they could not comply.

I think it's just as well that I didn't have access to these secret documents back then. I had my razor blade under my pillow, as always, and was just a hair away from using it. But first I wanted Mary's sanction. I wanted her to tell me I had a right to end my pain. Instead, she said that if I ended my life I would be allowing the torturers to control me. I would be completing their attempt to silence me. I still felt I didn't have the right to be alive. So many others weren't, and I couldn't bring them back. But Mary had thrown a wrench in my plans with her comment; now I remembered the Policeman's remark: "Bien, ahora quieres colaborar." Good, now you want to cooperate. And I couldn't do it.

SOMEHOW MY MOTHER ended up visiting. I had exiled myself from my family, not wanting to hurt them anymore, but I'm sure cutting off contact with them was more painful for them than anything else I could have done. Nonetheless, my mother came.

The weather was warm and we spent a lot of time in the garden. I showed her what I was growing and she gave me helpful tips. She fit in at Su Casa, speaking Spanish, cooking Mexican food, and making herself useful. And so I had a family again, two families really, including Su Casa.

Meanwhile, my family at Su Casa was growing. Danila, a guest from El Salvador, had a baby and asked me to be the godmother. I was flattered and thrilled, and I got to lavish on JenJen all the attention I would have shown to the baby I didn't have.

But our extended family — all those relatives waiting to be brought to the United States once the conditions were right — shrank by one. One morning, as I emerged into the hall after my shower, Dolores was standing by her door, mesmerized. "Don't you smell it?" she asked, without looking at me.

"What?"

"My husband's cologne. Can't you smell it?"

I couldn't.

THE NEXT DAY I heard her sobbing after a phone call. Dolores allowed me to come in when I knocked on her door — she didn't let many people in when she was upset — and she sat up, moved to the edge of the bed, and put her feet on the floor. Even though I was closer to her than any of the other guests at Su Casa, she wouldn't lie on the bed and sob in my presence. She pressed a Kleenex against her lips and let the tears flood her cheeks in silence. After a long while she spoke. "He was shot." Her husband had been in prison for over a year, she explained, and after he was released, when he was walking away from the prison, he was shot in the back. "When he visited me yesterday, he was asking me to help him. He was warning me. I didn't understand."

I suggested that maybe his spirit had come to visit her after he was dead, to tell her he loved her and had not forgotten her.

She couldn't see it. She was to blame, that was all she knew. She didn't protect him. To make matters worse, she couldn't go to the funeral because she was afraid she would be detained.

I was afraid for her, too. I thought she might be killed if she went back to Honduras. And, since her asylum case was still pending, she might not ever get back into the United States. Not going to the funeral meant no chance for closure, no chance to grieve with her close friends and relatives, no chance to see her children. She would also be adding to the suspicion among some of her relatives that she had run off to the States to be with another man.

I hugged her, took her hand, patted her shoulder.

She received my shows of affection stiffly.

I wanted her to know she wasn't alone, but I couldn't imagine what she was going through, separated from her children and mother and sisters, knowing the man she loved was dead. That night I dreamed she was out in the ocean, and I was in a rowboat. I saw her, but she wasn't calling out for help. I had a life jacket on and she was going down, and I threw her the life jacket and she said, "No, don't give it to me." I said, "Put it on." I also threw her the lifeline, and it went in every direction, but not to her. She just kept floating farther away and I just kept throwing the donut. Eventually she did take hold of it, but she didn't have the strength to hold on to it. She let go of it, and then I woke up. I initially thought it meant she was going to die. What I came to understand was that a part of herself was going under and couldn't be saved. She was sadder after that, permanently sadder.

BUT I COULDN'T spend all the time I wanted with Dolores. I had to face the question of the case again. We were supposed to go back to Guatemala in a matter of months to finish the reconstruction, and I had to decide whether continuing was worth it.

Mimi had already gone back to Chile. "It's all talk," she'd said, packing up. "There won't be a second trip because the court's not going to do anything. They don't have any interest in calling you back. If they were serious about the case they would have let you finish everything the first time."

But Paul and Shawn had more faith in the judicial process and were soon back in Guatemala City pursuing leads for the next phase of the reconstruction, when I would have to identify the place I was tortured. Shawn had her baby with her and she posed with him on her hip while Paul snapped pictures of them outside the Politécnica. The pictures weren't really of them, of course — Shawn and her baby were nearly out of every frame in the roll Paul shot. He got the building from every angle. Once back in the United States, he sent the photos to Juanita, and she called me into the conference room, shut the doors, and opened the envelope.

Two pictures was all it took. I ran from the room and threw up. Looking at the rest of the roll, my eyes were convinced of what my body knew. The Politécnica was the place.

Knowing I could go back and identify the site of my torture, I felt I had some ammunition, ammunition for the truth. I was furious with the embassy for the letters they were sending to my supporters and with Linares for the remarks he continued to make to the press, now questioning my mental health. All I could do was rant and plan to go back. I would lead them to the place. Everything would be just as I said.

MARY SUGGESTED A PLAN. If I decided to go back, I should wait until I was fully ready and use the trip as an opportunity to exert my will and reclaim control. Mary knew I felt victimized by the proceedings. We had been caught off guard by the court's requirements, and we had all been too passive. Going back, we would know what to expect, and we could be prepared. If going through the court proceedings mirrored the situation of the torture, perhaps asserting myself and having a team of people with me to support me would be a chance to revisit that day in the secret prison, not as a passive, helpless victim, alone, abandoned, and betrayed, but as a forceful person with a community of people fighting beside me.

AMBASSADOR STROOCK had offered to testify, so, contrary to Mimi's prediction, the court proceedings were moving on. As the ambassador put it to the legal adviser at the State Department in a May memo, "We believe that it is clearly in our interest to do (and be seen to be doing) all possible to clear up this case."[4]

The secretary of state wrote back, granting Stroock permission to testify and outlining the parameters of his testimony — "Ambassador Stroock's deposition will be limited to those questions which Judge Secaira provides to the Embassy prior to the deposition."[5] The State Department would also review the questions before the ambassador's appearance in court. Secretary of State Baker also sent a cable to Stroock saying, "Department reiterates its request to review the proposed answers before the ambassador's deposition."[6] Ambassador Stroock was urged to keep with him a copy of the limited waiver of diplomatic immunity note, stating that he would answer only the questions he had seen in advance.

The judge did as the State Department asked, and the ambassador forwarded to the secretary of state the list of questions, along with his proposed answers, all of which have now been declassified:

Does the embassy have any knowledge of whether a U.S. citizen named "Alejandro" collaborated with the security forces of the Government of Guatemala in November of 1989? The Embassy has not been able to identify "Alejandro," nor do we know if any U.S. citizen of that name and description collaborated with Guatemalan security forces. We polled every employee of this embassy, both U.S. citizens and Guatemalans, to see if any had such knowledge, and none did.[7]

Under oath, however, Stroock changed his answer from the one he proposed to the State Department to a one-sentence statement about not knowing the name "Alejandro": "No one in the embassy knows that name, nor do I personally."[8]

What worries me about that permutation of his answer is that I might have been mistaken about the American's name. After all, I was blindfolded. All I heard was someone — the Guate-man, I think — call out, "Hey, Alejandro! Come and have some fun." I was focused on trying to curl into a ball, trying to defend myself from being raped. Then I heard, "Shit!" I assumed that the man who had cursed in perfect American English was Alejandro, answering the invitation. But what if the American had someone else beside him named Alejandro, someone who had led him to me and disappeared before my blindfold was removed? I cannot swear that the American's name or code name was Alejandro; I may have made a blind assumption.

STROOCK ENDED THE LIST of questions and answers he sent to the State Department with this remark: "Comment: We cannot get into any trouble if we stick with the facts of what we know and what we did. We are firmly on the side of truth, justice, mom, and home-cooked apple-pie."[9]

I KNEW the ambassador's statement wouldn't be helpful to me, but I was hoping it would be outweighed by the testimonies of Darleen, Archbishop Penados, the female attorney who had written my first statement in Spanish, and the dermatologist who had examined me in Guatemala the day I escaped. If I had known for sure that the judicial process was "all a big show" I would have told them all not to bother. Darleen had been uprooted from Guatemala because of me and was living in California, trying to make a new life for herself. I knew it would awaken memories for her to go back, that she had been traumatized when I was disappeared, and that the case was dragging her back into that trauma. I felt responsible. But in order to speak out and obtain the truth, I had to hurt someone. That was the pattern. If I had known what a farce the whole proceeding was, I wouldn't have wanted the Guatemalans involved to endanger their lives by testifying. The court, however, had subpoenaed them, based on my testimony, and I'd been told that if we dropped the case, my Guatemalan lawyers' lives would be in danger. And all those people I was speaking for and demanding justice for would be abandoned. So the doctor, the woman lawyer from the archbishop's office, and the archbishop went bravely forward and told the court what they knew.

After they testified, Stroock sent the following summary to the secretary of state: "The court has achieved no new information on the 24 hour period when Diana was missing." He recounted Linares's opinion that "none of the recent testimonies has provided useful new information, including that of Darleen. Linares termed the 24 hour period a mystery." He said the court wanted to interview the indigenous woman who helped me and would take depositions from former Defense Minister Gramajo, former Interior Minister Carlos Morales Villatoro, and former Maryknoll priest Maurice Healy. "Linares does not expect any breakthroughs on the case," he concluded.[10]

WHILE DARLEEN TESTIFIED, Fran, Paul, and Shawn met with Stroock, protesting the remarks he had made in his letters to my supporters about my activities during our April trip. Stroock reported on his response to them in a cable to the secretary of state:

> The ambassador stood by his written comments. He pointed out the case has failed to move precisely because both sides seem more interested in generating publicity and engaging in debates via press conferences and paid advertisements than in pursuing an active and thorough investigation. We underlined that nearly three years after the reported November 2–3, 1989, kidnapping and abuse of Ortiz, "we are no closer today than we were then to solving this case and getting to the truth."
>
> Comment: As we have done for the past nearly three years, we will keep pressing all sides to move this case forward and seek a resolution ASAP. We will also keep pressing on all the need to confine activities to the judicial process: despite all the admitted shortcomings in the Guatemalan legal system, it is only in the Guatemalan courts that the case can be resolved.[11]

At the end of the declassified cable is a handwritten note from one embassy or State Department employee to another: "KS-Mitchell should fill you in on the bad history of this case — it will continue to plague us. RSJ"

At least that part of the document was true.

MEANWHILE, someone was sending messages to me. Juanita and Pat picked up the mail and handed me an envelope addressed to me, but my name was made up of cut-out letters, just like the final threats in Guatemala City. I refused to open the envelope. I asked Juanita to do it. Inside was a threat. Neither Juanita nor I remember the exact message — I forgot all about the incident, and only discovered it again going through write-ups of interviews the FBI did with Juanita years later. Juanita remembers that the threat was aimed at getting me to shut up. Another letter, similar to the first, arrived a few weeks later. I must have been frightened, so frightened that, as I had with the phone calls at the Mount, I blocked the letters out. If agents of the Guatemalan government were trying to terrorize me into silence, they didn't count on a denial mechanism so honed that it wiped out their words, as if they had never spent hours paging through magazines, looking for a z to write my last name, as if they had never meticulously cut out the letters and glued them on the page. At least they learned what it's like to put forth an effort, deliver a message, and have it be futile. They got a small taste of my court experience in Guatemala.

UNDETERRED, I continued talking to Sister Alice Zachmann about the possibility of traveling to Washington, D.C., to speak at a conference on torture in Guatemala. Alice wanted me to give the keynote address. After a number of phone calls back and forth, I said I couldn't make a firm commitment to speaking. Hundreds of people were expected, and I had never faced such a large crowd. I would have to see how I felt when I got there.

I RODE DOWN TO D.C. with Pat, Juanita, and Dennis. During the drive I looked over my talk. I was worried about how I would sound. I was afraid people would think I was crazy.

THE CONFERENCE WAS HELD in the auditorium of Catholic University, and the place was packed. It was Friday night, and everyone had come to hear the keynote speaker. I scanned the audience, saw no one from the Mount, and felt something between disappointment and relief. The people who were here looked serious and well educated, though, and according to biographical information in the program, nearly all the speakers were professionals. Many could list initials after their names: M.D., Ph.D., Psy.D. On official documents I followed my name with O.S.U., Order of Saint Ursula. I tried to console myself with those initials but couldn't quite believe they gave me the right to speak.

I was relieved to find no mention of my name in the program. Alice had left a space open for me to speak if I wanted to, but she had set it up so that I had no obligation.

I DON'T REMEMBER when I first met Alice. She became so important to me that it seems I've always known her. Maybe we spoke at some point during the reception or found a moment to talk during a meal. I was intrigued with her, I do remember that, and I'm sure I asked her questions about how her ministry evolved. Being from a southern, rural, conservative community, I knew few politically active nuns other than Pat and Juanita, who had chained themselves to nuclear reactors and participated in dozens of protests and all kinds of social justice work before beginning Su Casa. Alice's focus was on ending human rights abuses in Guatemala, and I felt a debt of gratitude to her before I had even met her. The information she had passed on about Kovler had been vital to me. I'd also heard that she had mobilized her networks and worked for my release on that November day.

She was gentle, with a quick smile. She gave anyone she was talking to, no matter who they were, her full attention and was savvy but down-to-earth at the same time. She had started the commission in 1982, during the worst of the massacres. After a trip to Guatemala, she had intended to move there to become a missionary. She had felt so comfortable with the people and had been so moved by their simplicity and courage and the horrific poverty they endured — perhaps because she had known terror and poverty herself in Minnesota, where everyone in her town had spoken German until the United States entered World War II, and they feared they would be put in concentration camps. People in Guatemala asked Alice to put aside her plans for missionary work there. They wanted her to be a reverse missionary — to go to Washington and tell the people of the United States about the holocaust that was unfolding in Guatemala. Little information was getting out in the news. Alice left her work as a teacher and school principal and with no money and not one contact in Washington, she moved to D.C. and opened an office in a room at Catholic University. Eventually, the office had grown. The small staff conducted a campaign against torture, bringing people from Guatemala to speak in universities across the United States, lobbied Congress, and now were putting on this international conference. Alice was already at the age when most people retire, and she was a bundle of dry wit and energy.

THE KEYNOTE SPEAKER at the conference was Allan Nairn, a reporter who had written for the *New York Times*, the *Washington Post*, the *New Repub-*

lic, and the *New Yorker.* He had covered events in Guatemala for many years and had witnessed a massacre in Dili, Indonesia. Allan and another reporter, Amy Goodman, had placed themselves in the front of the crowd as soldiers began firing on East Timorese demonstrators. Allan and Amy shouted that they were journalists, hoping that the soldiers would realize the international press was there and act with more moderation. Instead the soldiers beat both Amy and Allan with rifle butts, fracturing Allan's skull.

In his first sentence Allan said, "Over the years people like you have tried to publicize what is happening in Guatemala and to change the criminal complicity of the U.S. government in the mass killing and torture there."

The hair on the back of my neck stood up. This was the first person I had heard speak of the U.S. government's complicity in torture in Guatemala. Alice, sitting at the end of our row, was nodding slightly, her mouth set. Hardly anyone in the audience looked shocked.

"The tragedy in Guatemala," Allan went on, "is repeated in country after country. Last year in East Timor I had an experience similar to what many thousands of Guatemalans have suffered. I am alive to tell about it mainly because I am a U.S. citizen."

I wondered if he, too, suffered the shame of having been saved. As he continued speaking, I realized how important it was that he was alive. As an American, he understood our system of government, had the freedom to speak, and was able to press for change.

Allan began telling us about his experience and what it allowed him to understand about Guatemala:

> During the chaos of that terrible event in East Timor, I thought of the massacre at Santiago Atitlán in December 1990. In the middle of the night, soldiers had broken into a house and beaten a man — nothing especially remarkable in Guatemala. That night, however, as word about the incident went around, something happened in the town. People snapped. And, as the Timorese did in Dili, the residents of Santiago Atitlán spontaneously poured out of their homes in the middle of the night. The mayor and mayor-elect were there. Unarmed, the people marched to the plaza and then to the military garrison to beg the military commander to stop the torture and repression. As the crowd approached the base in Santiago Atitlán, the military fired on them with U.S.-made M-16s, the same weapon used by the Indonesian troops in East Timor. The guns used in Santiago

Atitlán had been part of a shipment of sixteen thousand M-16s sent from the United States in 1989 as a result of a deal negotiated by Democrats in Congress.

I knew about the massacre in Santiago Atitlán. That had actually made the news. I didn't know the guns used to kill the people — including a thirteen-year-old child — had been sent to the army by my own government. Something crumbled inside me, a wall I was hardly aware of that stood between me and the truth. Some of that flimsy wall I built myself — I didn't want to believe my government had betrayed me. I didn't want to believe I lived in a country that had overseen my torture. The wall had allowed me to stay at the embassy during my trip to Guatemala. To sit at the table with the U.S. ambassador. To leave the mention of the American out of my statement to the press. I had even hoped at times that he'd been no more than a hallucination. Allan spoke and the wall crashed down. Tears came down my face, tears of anger and sadness and also of relief — I wasn't crazy. I didn't imagine Alejandro.

But where did it end? With the wall down I felt afraid. The Guate-man had a pistol, not an M-16, but I found myself wondering if it, too, had come from the United States.

Allan continued:

Over the years I've talked to many torturers in Guatemala, El Salvador, and elsewhere — soldiers who describe how they cut off people's fingers, tore out their tongues, or administered electric shock. While a few of these people were crazed or psychotic, most came across as relatively normal in other aspects of their lives. The fact is, the number of true psychotic killers in Guatemala is not large enough to stock an army. They wouldn't stock even an intelligence unit. However, to impose systematic terror on a country, the leaders must pressure normal people into acting in this demented, inhuman way. And the frightening thing is that it works.

José, before collapsing in tears on my knees, told me his family was hungry. He said, "*Sometimes we live at the expense of others.*"

Allan explained:

Torture is not rooted in the culture or society of a country. If, over the years, the U.S. had adopted different policies toward Guatemala, there would be no need for this conference. Torture as a systematic policy in Guatemala is something that appeared at a moment you can mark on the calendar. It is something that is traceable to a policy decision made in Washington — and then other policy decisions made to reaffirm the first one.

From 1944 to 1954, Guatemala had democratic reformist governments that began to move the country out of a semi-feudal system, give basic legal rights to peasants, develop a health care system, and make Guatemala a modern capitalist society. Threatened by these changes, the United Fruit Company labeled the reforms "communist" and asked the U.S. Central Intelligence Agency to stop them. The CIA sent down a counter-intelligence team headed by David Atlee Phillips, who later wrote about the experience.

From Arbenz's government files and those of other public organizations, the Phillips team compiled the "black book of Guatemalan communism," a list of more than seventy thousand people who belonged to labor unions, left-wing or reformist political parties, student organizations, professional leagues, etc. The Guatemalan military death squads used the black book to compile their death lists. Phillips referred to this information as "intelligence pearls that could be fondled for years." For decades, people returning to Guatemala from exile for occasions such as funerals would be abducted minutes after passing through the airport. Their bodies would be found on the side of a road. Their names were still in the CIA-complied "black book of Guatemalan communists."

In the early 1960s, when the CIA used Guatemala as a staging ground for the Bay of Pigs invasion, cadets from the Politécnica revolted.

The Politécnica. I was tortured at the seedbed of the revolution I was accused of supporting.

The CIA flew bombing missions in Guatemala to quell the revolt. When some ex-cadets and others formed the first strong guerrilla movement in the country, the U.S. military attaché in Guatemala, Colonel John Webber, organized an operation called the Mano Blanca. Working with the self-described "party of organized violence" and the Guatemalan military hierarchy, Webber put together a program in which Mano Blanca members were licensed to kill peasants who were guerrillas or "potential guerrilla supporters."

During this operation, they killed approximately 180 guerrillas and 10,000 "potential guerrillas." They compiled death lists with pictures drawn from several sources, including passport and police files. These lists were dropped from military planes and scattered through Guatemala City and the countryside. Some are still around. Many on the lists were hunted down, killed, and then photographed — some with their amputated genitals stuffed into their mouths. Leaflets with the photographs were circulated to show what happens when someone defies the army.

General Arana, a leader of Mano Blanca and military attaché in Washington, was made president. In his inaugural address he declared, "Those who do not obey the law will be broken in two." During the next few years, after the guerrilla movement was essentially crushed, between twenty and forty thousand civilians disappeared. In addition to armed insurgents, targets included anyone organizing or showing signs of independent thought, people from the Church, and those becoming active in labor.

In the late 1970s, the U.S. stopped sending military aid to Guatemala, but the White House national security adviser negotiated with Israel to send field rifles, transport planes, and submachine guns. A myth about U.S. policy says that in 1977, when the United States cut off aid to Guatemala, the military there went wild and the U.S. had no leverage to control them. The truth is that the U.S. covertly sold specialized military equipment to the Guatemalan military — more than thirty-five million dollars worth of tanks and laser-aimed rifle sights. In addition, the U.S. gave its blessing to Israel, which was supplying Guatemala with the large hardware items.

When Rios Montt came to power, he sent the army sweeping through the northwest highlands, decimating village after village. Soldiers told me how they would pull people out of the crowds at random. One soldier demonstrated how they used a rope around the neck as a tourniquet: "With this, we would make people tell the truth." The soldiers would ask, "Who here is against the army, is critical of the government, is close to the Church, gives food to the guerrillas?" If a person failed to spit out names, they would simply strangle him or her and move on to the next person.

The army destroyed 662 rural villages, including hamlets, during this period. It was no secret. The Guatemalan Bishops Conference issued a pastoral letter saying the assassinations were becoming genocide. The conservative newspaper El Gráfico listed more than five hundred massacre victims and described a massacre in which babies were decapitated and pregnant women's wombs were slit open.

Amid this holocaust, what did the United States have to say! United States Ambassador Chapin said, "The massacres have stopped.

Guatemala has come out of the darkness and into the light." After meeting with Rios Montt in Guatemala, President Reagan said Rios Montt was getting a "bum rap" on human rights. When Rios Montt was asked about the Guatemalan army's scorched-earth policy, he replied, "It is not true.... We have a policy of scorched communists."

After Rios Montt, the abductions and assassinations were more selective because what they considered the guerrillas' rural base of support had been almost totally obliterated. During this period, the Mutual Support Group (GAM) was born. Relatives of the disappeared, led mainly by women, held vigils in front of the National Palace, asking the whereabouts of their loved ones. President Mejía Victores said, "This is becoming intolerable. It is a threat to peaceful Guatemalans." When GAM leader Héctor Gómez, known as a particularly effective orator, left the GAM meeting during Holy Week of 1985, he was abducted at a bus stop. His body, with the tongue torn out, was found the next day. At his funeral another GAM leader, Rosario Godoy, gave a speech blaming the army for Gómez's death. A few days later Godoy, her brother, and her infant son were abducted. Their bodies were found in a ravine. She had been raped and mutilated, and her baby's fingernails had been torn out.

At a news conference, when I asked General Mejía how the Godoys died, he took a drag of a cigarette and responded, "They died in a traffic accident." I said, "If they died in a traffic accident, how were the baby's fingernails torn out?" He replied, "That is disinformation." This in spite of a photograph taken of the baby's body at the wake. How did the U.S. government respond? In response to a letter from Amnesty International, Elliot Abrams, then assistant secretary of state for human rights, said that no evidence indicates that the Godoys did not die in a traffic accident.

The Guatemalan military began to realize they would have problems restoring open U.S. military aid to Guatemala as long as one military regime succeeded another. Drawing foreign investment and tourism would also be difficult. So in 1982 the military leaders made plans to seat a civilian president, but with the army retaining power. In 1985 a presidential election was held.

Only weeks before Cerezo took office, the outgoing Mejía passed a total amnesty for members of the military for any crimes they might have committed. When members of the Christian Democratic Party asked Cerezo to repeal that amnesty, he refused. Cerezo did promise that if the killings and disappearances continued, he would denounce them. The army, however, sent Cerezo a message to ensure that this would not happen.

Beatriz Barrios was a school teacher who twice had been abducted by the army but escaped because she had relatives in the army. In fear for her life, she asked the Canadian Consulate for asylum in Canada. Until she was to leave the country, she stayed with friends at night because she was afraid. The night before her scheduled departure, she ordered a cab to take her to the airport for her early morning flight. She never made it to the airport. Her body was found the next morning with machete marks across the chest and her amputated hands lying on her body along with a note that said "Faltan más" — more to come. This occurred just a few days after Cerezo's election.

She was abducted in a taxi, I realized, not in the usual SUV with tinted windows. When the Guatemalan government says I couldn't have been abducted on a bus because the security forces don't use buses, maybe I should bring up the case of Beatriz Barrios; even though they don't use taxis either, as a rule, in each case they do whatever makes the most sense. And she wasn't going to step into a Land Cruiser with tinted windows. In my case, since I never went out at night and since praying in the garden in the morning was the only time I was ever out alone — according to Darleen, it was something I had a habit of doing — the torturers knew they had to abduct me in daylight hours. Stuffing an American nun into a vehicle with tinted windows — a "death-squad vehicle," as they were known — in broad daylight in a tourist center full of foreigners could raise some eyebrows. Having me get onto a bus in front of a man whose gun and grenade were in his pocket didn't look so suspicious.

I turned my attention again to Allan.

Assassinations, torture, and disappearances actually worsened during Cerezo's administration. However, with a civilian as president, Democrats in the U.S. Congress could say that things had changed in Guatemala. They restored U.S. military aid, such as the shipment of the M-16s. The U.S. sent the National Guard and Reserve units to teach maneuvers to the Guatemalan military and Green Berets to work with the Kaibiles, the self-described "messengers of death."

The United States has maintained an extensive military relationship with Guatemala, but much of it is off the books, in the sense that it is not covered under a foreign aid bill and does not go through the appropriations process. Under the guise of fighting drugs, the U.S. government openly sends down helicopters and U.S. pilots, even though the Drug Enforcement Agency admits that the main drug traffickers are the Guatemalan generals themselves.

With the new administration in Washington, a change in U.S. policy is possible.

It was a year of hope — Pat and Juanita had talked about it on the way down in the car. Although none of us wanted to be unrealistic, Clinton had just been elected, and it seemed that, for once, things in Latin America could change. Allan reminded us that the Democrats in Congress had not had a clean record:

> Although the new administration will include Democrats who, over the years, have supported the Guatemalan military, they will be challenged to justify their policies. After all, Guatemala, like East Timor, is not an area of high strategic interest to the United States, as are the Middle East with its oil, South Africa with its mineral reserves, and Europe with the massive U.S. troop commitment.
>
> More than three hundred U.S. corporations make money from cheap Guatemalan labor resulting from the country's crippled labor unions; but that money is a tiny fraction of the total income of U.S. multinationals. With sufficient grassroots pressure, every aspect of U.S. aid to the military could be cut off — including the so-called war on drugs, government and commercial arms sales, economic support funds, and various covert CIA programs and Pentagon projects in Guatemala.

This was the first mention I had heard of covert CIA programs. Generally, when I mentioned the American who gave orders to my torturers, people looked either shocked or doubtful. But here was a well-known journalist, telling me, for the first time, that what I had been saying made sense: the CIA had various covert programs in Guatemala. So perhaps the man I'd always thought of as Alejandro was with the CIA.

> The reign of terror in Guatemala continues. Citizens there realize that efforts to change the situation can still result in a bullet in the head or the disappearance of a loved one. In spite of this, and after decades of terror, Guatemalans continue to oppose the repression. One question remains: How will the Guatemalan government continue to respond? I think that depends largely on what the U.S. government does. A complete withdrawal of support would tell Guatemala that no longer will we prop up its military. In effect, that means we are throwing in our lot with the people — the

Church, unions, human rights groups, and peasants. I believe that
state terrorism in Guatemala would disappear in a matter of months.

The answer to torture in Guatemala lies in Washington, D.C. The
roots lie in policy decisions made largely without the knowledge of
the U.S. public, thanks to the media, which often either distort or
fail to cover the situation. Guatemalans are putting their lives on
the line to change the situation in their country. But they cannot
change U.S. policy. Only we can do that.

Rising to my feet I realized how much lighter I felt. I was no longer
alone with a secret few people believed and with the burden of guilt and
responsibility that knowledge entailed. Everyone in the room — around
five hundred people — understood the involvement of the United States
with Guatemala's torturers. Their applause was a promise to change it.

Time to speak had been left open for me after lunch. I was still vacillat-
ing. I had none of the dulling exhaustion that had steadied me through
the press conference in Guatemala. My intestines knotted when I even
thought about speaking. There was a stage and a podium and graduated
rows of seats. I had heard that some of the Guatemalans speaking at the
conference had been accused of terrorism and criticized by the president
for staining their country's image. In a newspaper article included in the
program, President Serrano said, "The army does not torture," and he
vowed to put an end to such accusations. That was tantamount to a
death threat, yet here they were, speaking. I felt a twinge of shame.

But I believed firmly in the right of survivors to protect themselves in
whatever way necessary from situations that recalled the torture. And I
knew that with rows upon rows of eyes on me I would feel naked, exposed,
and unsafe. I had worn jeans, knowing that I probably wouldn't speak. I
don't have to talk, I told myself. No one can make me. I'm in control here.

The words of the next speaker coaxed me out of my mulish and fearful
frame of mind. Vitalino Simolox, an indigenous Protestant pastor working
with rural communities in Guatemala, said, "Torture is an institutionalized
practice in Guatemala, but there is little known about it because the
majority of those who have been tortured are killed. Only very infrequently
do we have access to survivors' testimonies."

I uncrossed my arms. Maybe I had something important to offer.

However infrequent his access to survivors' testimonies, Vitalino understood torture. "Torture breaks human beings in the most intimate ways,"
he said, "shattering one's sense of self." While this was hardly news to

me, I was astonished that someone outside my Chicago circle understood so well the devastation of torture. It shouldn't have been so surprising. The effects of torture are the same all over the world. But Chicago was the only place where I had found people who understood them, and even there, sometimes, people seemed to forget. Julio and his father were being pressured to give talks around town at churches and schools. They were being encouraged to file charges against the army. Julio, it seemed, was viewed by some as a case or a political tool, when in fact he was a human being who needed to be loved and healed, not objectified once again.

Vitalino had established his credibility with me, so I believed him when he said, "What most hurts torturers is when their victims speak out about their hope and denounce what they have suffered."

If he was right, some torturers were hurting. Another survivor was speaking, a young woman about my age whom I had met once at Su Casa, where she had stayed overnight as she passed through Chicago. Carmen Valenzuela was a Guatemalan doctor who had been kidnapped and tortured three months after I was. I could see fear in her eyes, and as she began speaking, I could hear it in her halting voice:

> Two days ago Guatemalan Defense Minister José García Samayoa was quoted in Guatemala's major newspapers as saying that torture does not exist in Guatemala. I am living proof that General García is wrong. I was kidnapped from a women's softball game by members of the Guatemalan military. They detained me for eight days in a military installation located on La Reforma Avenue in the heart of Guatemala City.

This would be important information. Carmen, I would learn later, was detained at the same place I was.

> Army officials tortured me — brutally beating me and slowly puncturing my legs with wires. During my ordeal they kept my hands cuffed and my head hooded. I felt as if I was going to suffocate. This technique, called "the hood," consisted of tightening a plastic bag around my neck to force me to talk. They also might have broken one of my ribs with their fists or their feet; I don't know.
>
> I was released thanks to an intense national and international campaign that pressured the government. But my release was conditioned on my agreeing to give an "official story" to the media and police about my kidnapping. I was told to state that I had been kidnapped by criminals seeking a ransom. They said that unless I agreed

to tell the "official story," my family — which is still in Guatemala — would suffer the consequences. Upon my release my captors made me promise to contact them every two weeks so they could monitor my activities and my "contacts" for an undetermined period of time. Under those circumstances, my life has never been the same. They said to me when they released me, "Your suffering, Doctor, has just begun."

Carmen and the torturers both knew what so many others struggled to understand — surviving torture is worse than the torture:

The magnitude of the social conflict in my country is so great that the government has undertaken a campaign of terror unprecedented in Latin America in order to preserve its hold on power. It uses torture as its principal tool to keep the population silent and passive in the face of a dehumanizing social system. During my detention my captors explained the "need" for torture in Guatemala. One of them said to me, "Do you believe, Doctor, that President Cerezo himself doesn't have a security force that does all these things in order to 'maintain stability'? What we do might be construed as illegal, but we do it precisely in order to control those who are outside the law."

It has taken me more than two years to speak out about my experience. This is mainly because I have felt guilty — guilty for still being alive; guilty because they didn't rape me and stopped torturing me after four days when I started to "collaborate"; guilty because I caused my family and friends suffering; guilty because I was released even though those responsible for kidnapping and secretly detaining Guatemala's many victims rarely release their prisoners; and guilty because some of my relatives, and many of my professors, classmates, and friends, who weren't as "well connected" as I was, were killed, and I did nothing to help them because I was afraid. I also feel guilty because I would like to be in Guatemala, doing something to help prevent the torture and abuse of others. But I am too terrorized to consider going back.

The fear is overwhelming. I am extremely afraid for my family in Guatemala. I believe the threat issued by my abductors before they released me — that any statement revealing the truth will result in reprisals against my loved ones — was real. I am also nervous about my family's reaction to my public statements. I am sure they will think I should have consulted them before speaking out. I simply do not have the right to jeopardize their lives. But I can no longer be silent. The mental anguish is overwhelming.

Carmen was in a more helpless and dangerous position than I was. I could go back to Guatemala, at least for short periods; my family was safe from physical harm; and as a U.S. citizen, I could demonstrate, lobby, and vote in elections here, three things Allan Nairn mentioned as pivotal to changing the situation in Guatemala. I began to wonder why I wasn't doing those things instead of gardening and teaching English. Carmen's personality was different from mine; she was an extrovert, a go-getter. She had played on Guatemala's national softball team and been elected president of the Guatemalan Women's Medical Association when she was only thirty. But as she continued speaking I realized how similar the impact of torture was on our lives:

> From the time of my torture, I have been confused and ambiguous about decisions in my life: where to live, what to study, what to wear, what to eat. My life, which used to have very well-defined interests and goals, became a total mess. And I was unable to communicate my feelings because I was embarrassed to speak bad English.
>
> Try to imagine yourself in my situation. I was a physician, university professor, and respected scholar. I had finished graduate studies and was appointed to numerous positions in professional and women's organizations. Suddenly I was forced to abandon everything. I was forced to live in exile and start from scratch. I had to seek immigrant status, apply for a scholarship, prove through tests that I can be a scientist, and look for a job in order to subsist.
>
> But not everything has been negative. I still feel that I was a lucky survivor. I feel fortunate to have had options, and I feel that if I am still alive it is because — as my mother says — I have something important to do.

What was it I had to do? I refused to think about it; it was too overwhelming, and I was having enough trouble just staying in my chair.

My body seemed to know already that I was going to speak. That, at least, was one thing I could do.

HUNDREDS OF PAIRS of eyes were on me. I'd told Juanita, Mary, and Pat to look at the floor. At least I knew some people weren't looking at me. I could look at them and that made me feel safe.

"What I would like to share with you this afternoon," I began, "is based not only on my personal experience of torture but on the experiences of other survivors of torture. I stand here before you, not as an individual, but as one with them."

Mary, Antonio, and Mario knew nothing about the friend I was going to introduce. But they had told me over and over that it was OK to feel whatever I was feeling and think whatever I was thinking — that I wasn't crazy. So I continued: "On behalf of other survivors of torture, I have the honor of introducing to you a rather unique friend, a friend who is a frequent visitor of ours, a friend who journeys with us wherever we go, a friend who comforts us in our darkest moments." I held up beside my face the razor blade Clarissa had given me:

> Perhaps for some of you it's beyond your comprehension how anyone in their right mind could consider a razor blade a friend. With a little help from our friend, we know that we can put to rest the violent memories of torture that have been embedded within us. With the help of our friend, we can say goodbye to yesterday. When we are feeling most alone, haunted by the memories of the past and with no hope, we sometimes reach the conclusion that the only way to escape from the web of this nightmare is through death.
>
> But we do have a choice: to participate in the torturer's ultimate goal, which is to destroy life, or to embrace life. Destroying our own lives would grant the torturers the satisfaction of knowing that their mission to destroy and silence us was accomplished.
>
> Our friend, who may represent the destruction of life, speaks to our conscience, reminding us that torture continues to exist. At this very minute someone is being tortured. Someone is being interrogated. Someone is being forced to participate in the torture of another human being. Our friend reminds us that death is everywhere. We are resigned to dying. But before that, we must make known the ugly truth about torture. This unique friend of ours refuses to allow us to run away and hide, confronts us with raw experiences of pain, calls upon us to abolish torture in our world.
>
> We believe the spirits of our tortured sisters and brothers who have gone before us dwell within us, giving us the strength to hold firm to our convictions of justice for all people and to bear witness to the heinous atrocities committed by oppressive governments like Guatemala's.

I had come to this position after Dolores's husband was killed. Remembering the peaceful, half-smile on Dolores's face as she smelled her husband's cologne and sensed his presence, I was sure he wasn't communicating urgency. He had come to tell her he was moving on. I began to believe that, just as Dolores had mistaken her husband's message, perhaps I had misinterpreted the flashbacks and dreams and memories I so often had of the Woman and the people in the pit. I had taken them, on some level, as rebukes: Don't go on into the future. We weren't able to live. Why should you? But maybe the memories, dreams, and flashbacks were the only means those souls had of telling me they were with me. I remembered the note the Guatemalan journalist had written: "Sea fuerte." The Woman had found another way to speak to me, and I felt her presence more strongly, as if she were not only beside me but within me, vying for space with the torturers. The spirits of the people tossed into the pit I believe came back with me, too. By returning to Guatemala I had opened myself up to those spirits and allowed them to find refuge in me. I understood, now, that I was not a voice for the voiceless, but a voice with them. And with them I spoke:

> We're here to say to all the Rios Montts and all the Gramajos of the world, No matter how many times you have slashed our throats and thrown our bodies into ravines to be eaten by vultures, no matter how many times you have beaten and burned us with cigarettes, no matter how many times you have humiliated us in every conceivable way, we are alive.

Chapter Twelve

INTO THE OTHERWORLD

"THROUGH THE HOLLOW TRUNK of a tree you descend into the Otherworld, the place of your journey." Soft drumbeats began. Journeying was a Native American tradition, and Mary, Juanita, and I were incorporating it into the measures we were taking to strengthen ourselves for our next trip. Going down to Guatemala, we always said. Descending. That was an other world, too, and I had made a decision to go.

Mary said the court proceedings could be therapeutic the second time around. We would set limits with the lawyers and with the judge. I would not lose all my memories of people at Su Casa, she assured me — not permanently — and I not would not go crazy or kill myself on returning. She would be right beside me the whole time.

But there were things she couldn't help with. Paul was going to ask for the identity of the officer in charge of the Politécnica in November 1989. Even if the government denied knowledge of who tortured me, the officer in charge of that military installation would be in the army's records. And, as the officer in charge, he would be responsible for what was happening in his building and should be called to answer questions before the court. Was I getting too close now? This time, would Alejandro release the videotape of my crime against the Woman? To silence me, he might prefer to use a bullet. No amount of preparation on our part could control what Alejandro, the Guatemalan torturers, or others in the Guatemalan army might do.

In spite of the limitations of the exercise, it wasn't my place to deny Mary and Juanita this journeying experience; and if they felt I needed to be part of it so that we could bond more before going down to Guatemala, I was at least going to try it out. We were lying on the floor with our eyes closed in a room where a friend of Mary's practiced different kinds of alternative healing. I was shivering, in spite of the blanket she had laid over me, because she had described the Otherworld as the "lower world" that appears through "an opening in the earth." It sounded like hell, and I knew the torturers would be waiting. But I didn't object. Mary and Juanita had already spoken about why we needed to "journey": Mary said that the last time we'd gone to Guatemala we hadn't been prepared, and the corners of Juanita's eyes had reddened when she'd spoken up to add that the trip had taken a toll on everyone and everyone had felt isolated. What I was feeling was too complicated to articulate. I didn't know how to draw the line between my responsibilities to the Guatemalans, dead and alive, and my responsibilities to my family. I would probably survive the trip. Even so, during my week in Guatemala, my mother — no, my entire family — would relive the trauma of the night I was missing. No doubt they had during our last trip, too. But now that I had contact with my family again, I was all too aware of their suffering. Aside from hurting my family, I could hurt Guatemalans if I was too weak or disoriented to carry out all the proceedings just as I should. In a flashback I could reveal details about the indigenous woman who helped me, facts I'd locked away from my conscious mind. I could also become too tired and too traumatized to go on. According to our plan, we would stop the proceedings if that happened. That was the whole point — not to be revictimized. But then the case might be closed, and my Guatemalan lawyers, left without the publicity that involvement in an international case afforded, might suffer retaliation. And if the proceedings ended prematurely because I stopped them, we wouldn't be able to take my case to the OAS. The torturers would walk free. I would be giving them that right.

I was already beginning to feel dangerous again.

"IN THE OTHERWORLD, which you will glimpse at the end of a long tunnel, you will find the animal that accompanies you on life's journeys, the animal that gives you power."

The rhythm of the drumbeats was soothing, matching the rhythm of my heart, and I started to relax. I imagined the tree and saw myself enter the trunk's hollow. Inside was a hole in the earth. I gazed in. A delicate scent rose from the opening. I leaned forward to try to see and started falling. Soft white sand buffered my landing. I was on an island, surrounded by a turquoise sea. The fragrance that had drawn me was the tang of salt air. I sat for what seemed hours in the sun, with the foam from broken waves lacing around my shins.

A dolphin wound through the waves and rested in the foam beside me. Her skin would feel like satin, I knew. I wanted to run my hand across it, but I was afraid my touch would wound her. I looked away and waited for her to leave. Out of the corner of my eye I saw her trying to get my attention, thumping her fins on the wet sand. A mound of sand was forming beside her fins as she thumped. Finally I turned to look. She was building a sand castle. I was astonished, then moved. Then I went cold. It wasn't a castle. It was the Politécnica.

I smashed it with my hand.

MIAMI, where we met up with Paul's legal adviser Frank, as well as with Mimi, Fran, and Ted Keating, the head of the Conference of Major Superiors of Men, was our first stop on our way to Guatemala. The sand was white, the ocean the same bluish green as the sea in my imagined journey. Mimi walked on one side of me, catching up on community news with Fran. Juanita and Mary walked behind me, talking with Andrea, my massage therapist, and trying to prepare her for the trip. Andrea had decided only a few weeks before to come to Guatemala with us and had missed out on the "journeying," meditating, praying, and chanting that Mary, Juanita, and I had been doing together.

I trusted Andrea completely, but I had learned only a few facts about her in the year she'd been giving me massages. She was in her thirties and was married, with a daughter and a little son named Erik. Like Mary, Andrea often volunteered at the Kovler Center. She and Mary could both be making tons of money with pleasant clients who would talk about their boyfriends or children or gardens. Instead, they were choosing to involve themselves for no money at all in the gullies of torture survivors' anguish. I realized how much they were giving up, in general, and in particular, for me, by going on this trip.

Andrea, like the torturers, used touch to bring about change. But her mission was to heal, not destroy. I was hoping that getting massages from her in Guatemala would remind me that my body belonged to me, not to the torturers, and that I didn't cause pain to everyone who came close enough to touch me.

Andrea kept a journal on the trip. In Guatemala she kept her difficulties to herself, or anyway, kept them from me. In her journal she wrote, "I feel deeply the responsibility I have right now to reserve the space we have created for Dianna's grief and pain. My own will wait." Even while we were still in Miami, Andrea noted, "Painful, difficult memories of the last trip are surfacing for almost everyone. The tension between Paul and Mary is palpable. Makes me tense."

Mary would never tell me so, but I knew she was dreading this trip. I think she felt more pressure than the first time, since she had assured me that we could do things differently and possibly make the trip therapeutic.

Her realization that she had to be vigilant and take more control — or encourage me to — may have been the source of the tension between her and Paul.

I tried to ignore the tension and pain I felt I was the cause of and remember the dolphin and the rest of my imaginative journey.

After squashing the dolphin's sand Politécnica, I drew my legs up and placed my head on my knees, exhausted. Cold water rained down on my head and I heard a gurgled bleat. The dolphin was splashing me, laughing. So I waded up to my waste in the sea and splashed back. We played like that for a while. Then the dolphin motioned with her head toward the deep ocean. I refused — I couldn't swim.

"Don't be afraid," she said. She came and offered me her fin. I took it and we swam far out and floated for a while on the water. Then she wanted to swim to the bottom of the sea.

She wanted to take me under. I didn't want to go. I found myself tensing as the water rose over my ears. The dolphin placed herself more firmly beneath me, turned her head, and said, "No one can hurt you here. You're safe with me." I stared into her eyes and realized she was the same dolphin I had dreamed about. I hugged her, and we swam to the sandy ocean floor. There was nothing scary down there. There was nothing but peace.

After our deep dive to the ocean floor, the dolphin and I walked on the beach. I know it sounds strange. Dolphins don't walk. Dolphins cannot survive out of water. This dolphin could negotiate both elements. In the murky underwater she could see. She could go beneath the surface, find nourishment, and carry herself back up.

We stopped near a large palm tree, and some women were there, sitting in a circle. As I strained to make out their words, I heard the rapid drum beat used to call us back. The dolphin took my hand and turned around. "But I'm not ready to leave," I said. I wanted to see the women's faces. I followed the dolphin, turning around once more to look at the women. But the women were gone.

ANDREA'S JOURNAL has given me some insight into what happened during our trip and what she experienced:

> *Saturday Night, Miami:* Watched Dianna battle out the editing difficulties in her statement to the press with Paul, Frank, and Shawn. She's feisty! I was feeling *great* to be part of the team, but also tense, nervous — pounding headache.

If the feelings of anger and betrayal that I harbored toward Shawn and Paul — irrational as they may perhaps have been — had any advantage, it was that they made me more willing to fight for myself and stand up for what I believed in and wanted. I was trying to set a tone: what I say goes. But it was so much more complicated than that. My case was much bigger than me. It involved many more people and had implications for many more people than myself. Was it really my right to make decisions based on my needs?

Sunday Afternoon — El Camino Real Hotel: Our entrance into the country was smooth. Before we knew it we were in the bullet-proof van, escorted by the assistant U.S. ambassador and Mike, a serious, suited, six-foot-tall American assigned as our armed guard for the week. The hotel we will call home feels like any large, nice hotel in the U.S.

Although the hotel was better than the ambassador's residence, the plush lobby was a shock after the simplicity of Su Casa and the pollution and grime of Guatemala City. We had three adjoining rooms with two double beds in each. Paul and Ted Keating shared the farthest room from us. Andrea, Fran, and Shawn were in the middle room, and in the last room, Juanita and Mary shared a bed, while Mimi slept with me. We designated our room as a "safe" place, meaning we would have no meetings related to the case there. We proceeded to cleanse the room of negative energy, lighting sage and carrying the smoking herb into every corner. Juanita followed with a rattle and a drum, pounding the evil spirits out.

Paul was worried about our secret service man, Mike, who was stationed outside our door, and the Guatemalan man hanging out around the corner — a short man with dark sunglasses, tan polyester pants, and a white button-up shirt. He was so much a type that he may as well have worn a badge that said "G-2."

"What are they going to think you're smoking?" Paul demanded as the rituals went on in our room.

"I don't care what they think," Mary answered. We kept smudging and rattling and drumming.

On the dresser we made an altar — a place where we grouped things that were special to us. Everyone put something on it — everyone except Paul, who wasn't quite at home with our rituals. Poor Paul. I think he thought we had lost it.

Sunday Evening: Dianna held her first press conference to announce her arrival and her itinerary. I was awed by the crowd of press that came to this on a Sunday evening.

I remember feeling relaxed and confident as I announced our plans for the week and explained the reasons not all the procedures were carried out on our last trip. I was glad to be able to correct Linares's and Stroock's disinformation (which was remarkably similar in content — what Stroock wrote in his letters to Congress Linares echoed in statements to the Guatemalan press). Linares had resigned, since we had protested and requested a new prosecutor, and Stroock was back on his ranch in Wyoming. Good riddance, I thought.

I made a point of setting some limits with the press — the first part of the plan Mary and I had talked through to keep me more grounded this time around. "I ask that while I am here, you respect the fact that I will not always be available to respond to you. . . . I ask that you not pressure me." I talked about how the legal system treats survivors of rape and torture and said that while I would provide all the relevant information I could, I would not allow myself to be revictimized.

MEETING NEXT with our Guatemalan lawyers, we explained our plan to them. Fernando, a young lawyer who had participated in the conference on torture in D.C. and had been threatened for it, was on the case now. He and Edgar were gentle and understanding as we explained that we would have to regulate the pace of the events so that they wouldn't overwhelm me, and they seemed willing to negotiate with the judge whatever scheduling changes I needed. Edgar, like Fernando, was running serious risks for his work. After my first trip to Guatemala, Edgar's mother was called by someone who, without identifying himself, told her that Edgar had died in an accident. Edgar, who was in Miami at the time, got a call minutes later at his hotel. He should call his mother, he was told. With this routine, the anonymous caller was able to let Edgar know that, even in Miami, he was being tracked. His mother's whereabouts also were known, and Edgar and his mother both were given to understand that Edgar's life was in danger. To top it off, Edgar had to listen to his mother's concern and pain, minutes after she thought he had died. It was an effective reminder of the costs of his work:

The Guatemalan lawyers are very formal with Dianna, *very* respectful. They say they want to demonstrate commitment to the judge by agreeing to meet early, 9–9:30 a.m. Dianna agreed. They spent a long time establishing the need to set limits with the judge — to take a small part every day. (This trip is also about finishing the processing of everyone's grief and horror of last time.)

Edgar asked Dianna what her objectives are for the case: Dianna said justice, not revenge, for her and for others, especially others in the prison she was in. To identify the place and the people who did it and hold them accountable.

The next morning I lay in bed, gathering my strength. I would see a lot of uniforms at the National Police headquarters, where I would spend the day looking at photos and trying to identify the Policeman.

Juanita, Mary, Andrea, and Mimi were carrying out the morning meditation. Someone began tapping on the drum, and I found myself remembering my second and final journey to the island of the dolphin.

THE TUNNEL that led to the Otherworld now was strung with lights. The dolphin, I knew, had put them there, sensing my fear of the dark. As before, I landed on the beach, but this time the dolphin was waiting for me. "This isn't where I'm supposed to be," I told her. "I'm supposed to be with the women." I looked around the island for the palm tree where their circle had been.

The dolphin tried to pull me into the water. I dug my heels into the sand. She splashed me. "No, I don't want to play," I told her. "Don't you understand? I have to be with the women." The dolphin scooped up sand in her fins and poured it over my feet. The sand was warm, and my muscles began to relax. "You have a long journey ahead," she said. "You need to learn how to take care of yourself, to let go of your fear, to play."

"You don't understand," I sputtered and lowered my eyes to keep her from seeing the anger in them.

"I understand everything about you. I know about your feelings of despair. I know you want to be free of the torturers and erase the past. You're afraid to trust other people and even yourself. We're here to help you, to give you strength."

"Who's we?"

I looked up to find I was sitting alongside the other women now, and the circle had grown. Some of the women were so familiar, with their broad cheekbones and dark hair. I knew I should remember their names, but I didn't. Mimi was in the middle of the circle, adding wood to the fire. Darleen was going around, pouring some kind of drink into the women's cups. Mary and Juanita were there for a moment, but they disappeared. Then Darleen and Mimi also vanished.

Next to me was my Woman Friend. She reached out and took my hand. Our hands locked, as they had in that basement room, and again she smiled.

I tried to find words.

"There's nothing to explain," she said. "You did what any of us would have done under those circumstances. You fought and you're still fighting. You're fighting for all of us."

The other women in the circle, like my Woman Friend, had black and blue marks on their bodies and their skin was rent and hung from open gashes. Dry blood was caked on their thighs and lips. The faces of some of the women were completely disfigured. But they didn't seem to be in any pain. I realized then that the external appearance was inconsequential.

They each came up to me in turn, took my hand, and offered me a drink from their cups. This ritual completed, we sat around the circle, and although no words passed between us, we knew each other's thoughts.

My body started trembling and my cheekbone began to throb, as it does when I sense evil. I turned to see the Policeman and the Guate-man approaching. I couldn't see José. Fear made my breath short.

My Woman Friend took my right hand. A child took my left. Blood oozed from the sockets that had held her eyes, but a smile spread over her face. All the other women also locked hands. The Policeman tried but couldn't break through the circle. The Guate-man took a turn, too, and failed. They stormed away, and the Policeman turned to shout, "Volveremos!" — We will return!

We were too strong for them. That had to be auspicious. During the second journey I was connected with the women, and the sense of solidarity and connectedness was so great that the torturers couldn't break it. Maybe this time, Guatemalan authorities and anyone else acting on the torturers' behalf wouldn't be able to break me.

WE HAD BREAKFAST with several members of the Guatemalan Religious Conference (CONFREGUA) and the new papal nuncio. I couldn't eat, but it was nice to be with them, exchange hugs, and feel their support. I didn't talk much, and I barely followed the nuncio's analysis of the political situation in Guatemala. High-level leaders of the army and the Church were having discussions moderated by the president. That was as much as I got. Maybe that was as much as I wanted to hear. If Church leaders felt so threatened that they were having to meet with the army, in the president's presence, I wasn't so sure I wanted to know about it. Archbishop Penados, when he'd spoken about my abduction three years earlier, had attributed it to just such tensions.

And I needed to be calm, not fearful. Mary and Shawn would be at my side at all times. The new judge, Leticia Lam, was far more understanding than the one we'd had on the previous trip. She was already the fifth judge on the case. The judge we'd had on the previous trip had resigned after reporting anonymous threats. According to articles in the Guatemalan press, she said she thought they were coming from Supreme Court President Juan José Rodil Peralta.[1] I didn't doubt that the Guatemalan military was ultimately behind the threats she and Edgar had received. I wondered if the Guate-man himself had called.

I ran my fingers across the silver dolphin Mary had given me to wear around my neck and touched the soft wood of the cross Raúl had made me. Before he went into exile, before his wife was disappeared, and before he was tortured in a Mexican prison, he had faced difficult situations in Guatemala. One day in group he told us about the people whose town served as a base for his itinerant preaching and education work. He distributed food there as part of his ministry. Raúl arrived on the bus as usual one day, got off with his provisions as usual, and found that everyone in the village had been slaughtered by the army. On another occasion, he switched seats with a man, riding the bus from one town to another. The bus was stopped en route by armed men who boarded it and wordlessly shot to death the man in the seat Raúl had originally taken. The bullet, Raúl knew, was meant for him. He had lost family members, too. Shortly after arriving at Su Casa, Raúl received news that his father had been killed and dismembered by the army. His sister was killed a few weeks later. He got the news just before Christmas and told no one at Su Casa until Christmas night. He didn't want to spoil the day's celebrations.

Raúl had shaped the cross from dark wood. Another person might have taken the cross as a sign of hope, evidence that Raúl could still believe and create and give after all he'd been through. But since November 1989, I have never seen a cross as anything other than an instrument of torture. So I wore it as a symbol of the torture Raúl and other Guatemalans had suffered. "La llevaré," I told him. The Spanish verb *llevar* means both "to wear" and "to carry." I hoped I could keep my promise.

I GLANCED DOWN and saw the morning paper next to my chair, at Paul's feet. I scanned the headlines. None of them read, "La Monja Dianna es Asasina." Alejandro was biding his time. "Sister Dianna Will Not Be

Revictimized":[2] that was the headline in the paper that Monday morning. I imagined the Guate-man, the Policeman, and Alejandro reading it. Would they be provoked into testing my claim?

PIGEONS FORAGING on the sidewalk flapped out of our way, but the police headquarters remained solidly in front of us. We would have to go in. "The sun's already warm," Shawn said and took off her jacket. I was starting to shiver.

Inside it was even colder. Our footsteps rang on the stone floor and our voices echoed. I seemed to see the Policeman's round, acne-scarred face above every uniform we passed. I had to look closely and shake the dolphin, which had a tiny bell inside that called me back to what was real: I hadn't seen him yet. But I wondered if he was around the next corner, or somewhere in the building, watching. Hey, I'm strong. That's what I wanted my body to say. You didn't win. I held my head up high, but my eyes might have given me away. I wasn't going to stop checking every corner, every movement.

MARY, SHAWN, AND I were shown into a large room lined with file cabinets. "You can start wherever you want," an official told us. We stood there, stunned, with no idea where to find the photos of employees in 1989. Finally one of the officers who was escorting us through the building went to a file cabinet and pulled open a drawer. We looked inside. Employment cards with small black-and-white photos in a corner were stacked upright in the drawer — thousands of cards. I knew there was no way the photograph of the Policeman would be left in the files for me to find. But I started in. I had to carry out all the procedures the court in Guatemala required, exhausting all legal remedies within the country, before I could pursue my case before the Organization of American States.

When my vision blurred from the strain and my brain became numb from concentrating, I stretched my legs and rested my eyes by walking down the hall to the bathroom. On one of these trips I met in the ladies' room a female officer. Seeing me, she peered under the doors of the stalls, and finding no feet there, she threw her arms around me. She said, "Thank you, Sister Dianna, for what you are doing."

My chin rubbed against the fabric of her uniform, a fabric my skin knew. Feeling her arms on my back, I tried not to panic. The external appearance is inconsequential, I reminded myself. Beneath the uniform is a person. When she pulled away I saw kindness and honesty in her face.

Maybe someone like her, who wanted change, had put the Policeman's picture in the file for me to find. I looked with renewed vigor, but two drawers and several thousand photos later I realized I would have to settle for finding photos of officers who resembled the Policeman in some way. "He had hair like this," I told the judge. "The shape of his face was like this." I went through about ten photos with her, trying to give a picture of what he looked like. We finally left, hoping to have more luck the next day developing sketches of the torturers with a forensic artist.

> *Tuesday:* Again, the morning papers cover Dianna's story on the front page. Since one of the main goals of this effort is to educate this society about the torture in its midst and to create an open, public dialogue about military/government involvement in torture, we feel immensely satisfied with the press response to Dianna's case. This, despite their crazy claims and outrageous inaccuracies. Today the papers report that she identified ten policemen who tortured her, which is absurd!

The sketch artist we met our second day at the police headquarters wasn't wearing a uniform and couldn't have been more than twenty-four. When I showed him the photos that matched some aspect of the Policeman's features, he studied them carefully, and a crease formed between his brows. Seeing the Policeman's face, even on paper, could send me into a flashback. I was nervous. But the artist's youth, his seriousness, and the plain clothes he wore all helped me to trust him and feel comfortable, and I was glad to have a chance to rest as his pencil whispered across the pad on his lap. After about an hour, he blew some eraser dust off the sketch, touched something up, and nodded slowly. He passed it across the table.

Fred Flintstone minus some hair stared back.

Shawn started to snicker. I trapped my laugh with my hand. One of the Guatemalan lawyers hissed to the official in charge, "Did you get this guy off the street?"

The artist blushed.

I don't remember what I thought of the results of the other sketches because I could barely look — I was afraid I would burst out laughing. From a declassified document, however, I know it wasn't just our overwrought nerves that made the lawyers and me either laugh or sigh at the artist's attempts. Consular General Sue Patterson surveyed the sketch of Alejandro with the judge. Both thought it looked like Fidel Castro.[3]

Later that afternoon, I had to select hairlines, eyes, noses, and mouths from a box and create "composite" pictures of the torturers. The only problem was that the kit was imported from the United States, and all the features were for Caucasians, Asians, or African Americans. I did my best. "The nose isn't right," I said, putting together a composite of José. "It's a Mayan nose, not an African American nose." In Mary's words, "It was an exercise in absurdity."

As WE BROKE FOR LUNCH, it started to rain, and with the rain came bad news. I had to have a medical exam. The court had the record of the exam performed by my family physician, Dr. Gutiérrez, about a week after the torture. But I had to provide more proof.

It's hard to explain why the scars provoked such shame, and why they still do. Each scar is like a thumbprint to me. As an artist who works with clay leaves fingerprints in the finished piece — or as the aboriginal artists of Australia sign their rock art with a hand print — the torturers, leaving scars, declared that they made me, remade me. They owned me. My own skin declared that I was inextricably bound up with them. One of them held the cigarette to his mouth to light it. One of them, the Guate-man, I think, moved the cigarette toward my back and pressed it against my skin, and my back like parchment carries that tale of their mouths and hands and brains. I'm still trying to learn the lesson about disregarding the external.

We HAD TO WAIT forty minutes for the judge in the court's basement garage. From all I've seen and heard, I understand that judges and lawyers in Guatemala, no matter how well intentioned, often become paralyzed with fear and hopelessness. They arrive late. They forget or inexplicably neglect to do important things. By comparison to many, our judge was phenomenal. Two of her brothers had been killed in the violence, and she, I believe, was trying her hardest.

Nonetheless, the garage was dark and damp and I was afraid. I held on to my dolphin and pictured warm sand on my feet. It didn't work. My feet were freezing. I had to be able to get through the examination of my back. If I could do that much, maybe the court would be lenient about the rest of the exam, the gynecological part. I didn't know if I could go through with that. Mary and Shawn would be with me to support me. I needed their support. But I couldn't imagine having that sort of exam with them standing there. The judge might also insist on attending. What proof of rape a doctor could find at this late date was beyond me — maybe some scarring. I didn't know what those exams could reveal, but I was terrified that the doctor would find evidence of the choice I had made. Sister Dianna Is an Assassin. The headline flashed before me again. If the doctor found such evidence, the government would have another tool to convince me to drop the case.

The judge finally arrived, and we drove until the tall buildings and little businesses vanished, and farther still. When at last we turned down a driveway, someone said, "Look at all the ads for cheap funerals." If there's one thing that's a bad omen when you go to the doctor's office, it would have to be multiple signs for funerals. Of course, the ads made sense given where we were going: the doctor's office was in the city morgue. But I still considered the signs bad omens. I told myself as we pulled up to the building, "The court wants me to see a particular doctor. This is where he works. There is nothing more to it." But my gut knew we were driving into a deserted place under a darkening sky. Anything could happen. I remembered the heightened tensions between the Church and the army. Maybe they would want to make an example of me once again. This, for example, could happen: I go into the doctor's office. Mary and Shawn are forbidden to enter. It's just me and Judge Lam. The doctor arrives, takes us through a door in the back, maybe through another door, and there, waiting, are the Guate-man and the Policeman. They take us back to a basement prison. They torture the judge. They force me to stab her. They torture me again and kill me this time, or maybe have someone else do to me what I did to the Woman. To those waiting in the van, the doctor would say that I went to change into my gown and that was the last he saw of me. The judge said she was going to look for me, then she, too, vanished. Perhaps the judge had felt sorry for me, having to undergo so many procedures, and wanted to hide me. Perhaps we had run away. Perhaps I had something to hide. Another hoax the Church was perpetrating on the army.

MARY, MIMI, SHAWN, JUDGE LAM, AND I climbed out of the van. My legs were unsteady. I had no idea what to expect. I had never been into a morgue. I was dreading what I would find inside. Dianna, I told myself, the Woman died long ago. There is no way she could have survived. So often I'd hoped she hadn't died that I had almost persuaded myself she was still alive and still could be rescued.

But one wrong move on my part and the torturers would kill her. Maybe that wrong move was returning to Guatemala a second time. Maybe they had killed her and left her for me to find. Maybe that was why the medical exam was taking place in a morgue.

An official at the door told Mimi she couldn't come in. Only Mary, Shawn, and the judge could go into the morgue/exam with me. I curled my toes against the sole of my shoe. My razor blade was in there. I don't know if I was keeping it with me as a sign of strength and resistance or as a possible out in case I got taken again.

We were led to a large room. I was shocked at how well lit it was. It smelled of chemicals, not of urine and blood. The floor and walls were spotless. But the differences ended there. As soon as I stepped into the room I felt alone, unprotected. The circle of women was breaking. The room was freezing. Our footsteps and voices echoed. "Hang on, don't give in," I told myself.

In the middle of the room was a table — not a padded examination table that normal doctors have, but a metal table. It reminded me of the cot the Woman lay on. I was so afraid I would blink and be back there — the walls splattered with feces and blood, the Woman there in front of me. Don't go through with this, a voice inside was telling me. But I listened to a stronger voice: I have to because this is something they're holding against me.

A man in a white coat walked in, carrying a clipboard. He washed his hands. My mind projected a scene: he turns toward us, peels off his face, which is no more than a mask. It's the Policeman. He has a machete.

I stood between him and the table. The light shone out from behind him. He was walking toward me. Darkness spilled out of him. It slid along on the ground before him. His shadow reached and consumed me. I turned away and saw his shadow or my own fall across the cot like a knife.

THAT WAS THE LAST THING I knew. According to Mary, "The doctor apologized that he had to do this. He asked you to undress. You started screaming, backed into a corner, and crouched down, screaming and crying — 'No! Stop!' The doctor said, 'I can't do this,' and he left. They left me in the room with you to get you oriented. It took a while."

FOR ANDREA and the others in the van the wait was hard:

> Mary, Shawn, and the judge accompanied Dianna into the building. Mimi tried to go in with them, but was turned back, and returned to the van in tears. That's when I really began to feel the horror of that place, of this whole case. In the van we all waited in silence. I felt like I was sitting by as someone I loved was being raped. The wait was agonizing, and I had a hard time controlling my fear, my horror, my tears. Finally she came out sobbing, more broken than I've seen her. Shawn's face was grim and set and she shook her head to Paul, communicating no

success. Dianna had a flashback when the doctor approached her, so the exam never happened.

I assumed I had gone through with it.

Back in Dianna's room, we all sat in silence until finally Dianna asked Shawn what had happened. Again, my tears flowed, and I so much wanted to break down and just cry & cry. I fought it back and urged Mimi to let me give her a massage. It helped me to recompose! We all realized what a mistake it was to give in on our most important guideline of the trip — only one event per day.

The evening got better as we all gathered to eat and laugh with Brother Gregorio, an American who has lived in the Guatemalan highlands for eleven years, enduring flying bullets, nearby massacres, and constant military threats. But we were all left with a sense of ominous clouds on the horizon — tomorrow's reconstruction. Is it really worth it to risk these terrifying flashbacks when the results are so questionably important? We all weighed the consequences and ultimately looked to Dianna for the answer.

Wednesday: The judicial reconstruction. Dianna has been given one final opportunity to say no, but she has said yes. She will go ahead.

We asked Ted to say Mass in our room in the morning. I knew I would need the strength it could provide. During the reconstruction at the Posada de Belén, with the garden, the opening in the wall, the path that the torturers led me down, the places where we got on the bus and into the police car, I relived the abduction. It took all day to reconstruct, although the abduction itself probably lasted only an hour. Now we'd move on to the torture. The morgue had represented to me a piece of the torture, the part with the Woman. But the Politécnica, which I would have to identify, represented that and everything else that happened during those twenty-four hours. Unlike the metal table, it was more than a symbol or a trigger for memory. It was the actual place.

But I was going ahead with the reconstruction. If I couldn't manage to present my body as evidence yet again and if the sworn accounts of Darleen, Mimi, the archbishop, and the doctors who examined my back in Guatemala and New Mexico weren't proof that I was tortured, that basement itself would be proof. The new prosecutor and new judge — both of whom seemed much better and more fair-minded than the last — could go in and find the garage, the door, the steps leading down to the basement, the long hallway with the rough cement floor, the water cooler I'd mentioned, the room with metal filing cabinets I had noticed before leaving with Alejandro, the room with the metal desk that I was kept in, the cement slab that covered the pit of bodies in the courtyard. I was afraid of the pain — of reliving in flashbacks every step of the torture. But I wasn't going to miss my chance to prove that the torture occurred.

ABOUT THE RECONSTRUCTION I remember few details. Shawn let me wear her jacket because I was cold. Andrea rode in the other car, and she must have been writing in her journal the whole time:

> — It's hot, and we *wait*. This time, because Mary is sick, Dianna seemed so distraught/scared/hurting in the a.m. Though an interview with two reporters from Telemundo, the Spanish language station from Miami, seemed to enliven her tremendously. She gets more frail and looks so frightened going into these hard days. Her breakfast consisted of mineral water with a slice of lime. She finds it almost impossible to keep food down.
>
> The van and a fleet of press vehicles met outside the court where Juanita, Mimi, & I went w/Paul in Edgar's car, Ted & Fran split into cars with press people, and we took off like bats out of hell for Mixco — the embassy driver drove like a *madman* all day long. Somewhere, twenty minutes later, on a hillside, the caravan turned around and re-traced slowly, under an underpass which Juanita said she last year identified as the place where she was taken off a bus and put into a police car. Dianna got out at one point and was crying. And down the road a way, *Mary* got out to go behind a building — to throw up! The press was mostly respectful and kept a distance, but how embarrassing.
>
> The caravan continued at break neck speed, back into the city, to locations behind and around the Instituto Politécnica — that horrid building that looks like Erik's castle all grown up.
>
> Now we've stopped 2 blocks from where we think she was detained — she's probably having a flashback.

As an eyelid peels back to reveal an eye, the faces of Mary, Shawn, and the judge peel off. The Guate-man, José, and the Policeman await. From beneath the van the police car emerges. We are going back to the basement. Su Casa, Mary, Juanita — all of it was a dream. I slept while the torturers drove me around. I've woken up. I never escaped.

Top:
Dianna with children in San Miguel.

Above:
Dianna with Mimi and "Pixane."

Right:
Children of San Miguel in a Christmas procession

Above:
At the 1993 reconstruction of her abduction in Guatemala, Dianna with Judge Leticia Lam.

Right:
Dianna and Judge Lam.

Below:
Judge Lam, Mary Fabri, Dianna, her lawyer Shawn, and Mimi.

WHEN WE STOPPED AGAIN, someone said, "Well, here we are." But I wouldn't look up from the ring on my finger. I could feel the evil. It made my cheekbone burn.

Someone asked if I felt like getting out. There was no way I was getting out of the van. That would be the first step to being in that building again. I put my left hand up to my cheekbone, and I could smell on my wrist the perfume my mother had given me. Sweet Honesty, it was called. Every day I had worn it as a kind of invisible charm, a way of staying in the present when the smells of cigarettes and body odor invaded and a way of keeping the recent past — my mother — with me. With my right hand I held the cross Raúl had made.

Someone asked me if I wanted to go on record identifying this as the place.

If I even looked at it, everything I had accomplished or pieced back together in my life was going to crumble — the memories I'd built up in the last three years, my love for my family, God. I kept smelling my wrist and holding Raúl's gift. And I raised my eyes. There it was: gray, massive, grotesque. The building seemed to vibrate. Maybe I was trembling. Chills went up and down me. My mouth tasted bitter.

I remembered the passage from the Acts of the Apostles that describes Peter's release from prison. The chains snap, the doors swing open. As we sat there, I stared at the building and wished with all my strength to see people walking up out of the basement, out the door. The Woman.

That didn't happen.

WE DROVE around the block, looking at the building from all angles. We saw what looked like a parking garage, maybe the one Alejandro had led me to. Then the judge got out and talked with the soldiers standing at the gate. They were armed with submachine guns. They wouldn't let her through. She asked if she could take some photographs, just from the outside.

The soldiers said no.

I wondered if the Guate-man and the Policeman were peering out through the window slats, observing us. They were probably just going on, doing their work. Why wouldn't they? They didn't have to let anyone in, not even a judge. I could point out the building but I couldn't save anyone.

I DID GO ON RECORD. That was the place I was kept. And as we drove away I was still whole. And Mary was still Mary; Shawn was still Shawn; and the brave judge was still the brave judge. Reality hadn't betrayed me.

When we stopped at the next place, I got out and my legs held me. That was when I realized that the women of the circle were with me still, the women I carried inside me — or the women who carried me. I was able to face that building only because the people who died there had given me the strength.

> From there we went to the Banco de Guatemala, where we could finally get out of the car and be close to Dianna. She looked very good, and as we returned to our cars, Shawn gave the word — she's doing *great.* Hooray! Back in the car, on the way to the next and last stop on the reconstruction, Juanita, Mimi, and I all held on to each other and let some of the tears come. Then I could feel how completely scared I had been — now that it could be balanced by VICTORY!!! Next stop, travel agency where we all waited downstairs while Dianna and the officials went up.

According to Mimi, one of the Guatemalan lawyers pointed out to her and Andrea which of the bystanders looked like a G-2 agent. He was wearing dark glasses, standing on the stairs. Apparently, his job was either to keep watch over the group or intimidate us. But Mimi, who finally had somewhere to direct all the anger that had built up in her over the years, let all her rage out through her eyes, glaring until he eased away.

THAT NIGHT CONFREGUA had a reception for us. As Andrea noted in her journal, the CONFREGUA members broke into applause when I entered the room. I couldn't take in that detail myself at the time, not only because was I tired, but because I knew I didn't deserve it. They deserved the applause. They were risking their lives by supporting me, and they were risking their lives every day by doing their work. Photographs of religious people who had been killed working for human rights were hung around the walls, along with roses and baby's breath. I didn't take in too much more through my ears or my eyes. I was taking in through my heart the support of the people there and feeling, finally, a flicker of joy. I saw them, in spite of the darkness they lived with, celebrating a moment of being together. I started to realize that I could celebrate, too, maybe even under the eyes of the martyrs, without feeling guilty. Yes, I survived while others died, I realized, and perhaps I don't have the right to live. But what the CONFREGUA people showed me is that, for those of us who are living, maybe being able to have fun and enjoy life is the ultimate act of defiance before an authority that survives on terror.

Thursday: While we sit in morning meditation Dianna has a nightmare while she is attempting to nap. Of course, all the most awful memories have again surfaced in her.

Last night Shawn and I were interviewed by a reporter and were able to focus in on the treatment of Guatemalan refugees and post-traumatic stress disorder. Guatemalans are almost in *complete denial* as a culture about the trauma of torture — they don't understand why Dianna as a religious woman has not yet recovered from something they "take in stride." (What toll, we ask, in abuse of children, wives, alcohol, drugs?) To some extent this society has been effectively silenced. And it certainly points to how "psychologized" is *our* culture!

A quick breakfast. Then, to the court to FINISH.

Linares left three hundred questions for me to answer. These were the kinds of questions Linares wanted the judge to ask: "When you were being burned, did you protest?" Luckily, the judge ruled that 85 percent of the questions were obstructive, repetitive, or irrelevant. I answered the ones that remained.

The judge, as we understood it, agreed that we could continue to work at composite drawings in the United States. According to Andrea's journal, she also said that the medical exam could be conducted by a U.S. forensic doctor.

After court is over, 1:30 or so, in the van, Dianna is triumphant. "We're done," she declares, and we all clap and cheer.

I was kidding myself. The worst part of the day was before us. We were meeting with Rosa, the woman in the family I had stayed with that summer in Guatemala City — Miguel's widow. That was why I'd had the nightmare. Sometimes alone in my room at Su Casa I would think about Rosa and what she lived with on a daily basis. I thought about her children, now fatherless. And I asked myself a question I still ask: Why had I remained silent?

I don't remember exactly how or when I learned about Miguel's disappearance. I only remember knowing and agonizing about it during my first hospital stay. Receiving the news must be another event I've blocked. And the fact that the torturers asked me about Miguel and Rosa, was that something I'd remembered all along — something I perhaps just didn't want to think about, since I had answered — or something I recalled only when I learned of Miguel's disappearance? I didn't say anything to anyone, not to Miguel or Rosa, not to Paul, who could have warned them on his trips to Guatemala, not to Mimi, who could have helped me decide what to do. After Miguel's disappearance, I didn't warn Rosa that the torturers had asked about her. And then she had been abducted, too, and detained for a few days. That was over a year and a half ago now. Rosa had tried to remain in Guatemala, but things had gotten worse, so the staff at Su Casa were helping to bring her to the United States. I was sponsoring her for a visa, and we were meeting with her to iron out the details of her trip.

When we got to the CONFREGUA office, she was already there, in the small sitting room. She was staring at the floor. When she saw us she got up and embraced me. In her woven skirt with its colorful Quiché pattern, her long, dark ponytail dancing, she could have been any stranger, simply another Mayan woman who'd come to the city to live. I didn't recognize her. But how closely we were linked. She was pressed against me, and I could smell the sorrow in her breath. I breathed it in. It belonged to me, too.

"Como estás, Dianna?" she asked.

All I could do was nod, to indicate that I was OK.

The confidence, energy, hope, and all the strength and solidarity I felt from my imagined circle of Mayan women were flaking away like cheap paint. The grain underneath would be exposed and in it Rosa and everyone else would see, not leaping dolphins, but the face of the Policeman.

I held the dolphin Mary gave me, letting the metal warm in the palm of my hand, letting the warmth travel through me.

Rosa took a gulp of the coffee we were offered. It was steaming hot, but she didn't seem to notice. She clasped her dark, weathered hands together tightly and told the story of her search for Miguel.

I couldn't listen.

Some of the words found their way in. *Amenazas.* Threats. Fear for her children.

The room was closing like a coffin. My shoulder blade strained against its joint. I drove my nails into my hands and pressed my teeth together, about to blurt out, "It's my fault that Miguel disappeared!" I wanted to confess, to give the poison a way out, to be, if possible, forgiven, and if not, justly punished. But I wanted even more to protect myself, the life I had, the friends and love I had found. So, like the Guatemalan government, I kept quiet about my role.

I hugged Rosa goodbye, when the time came, and told her I'd see her in Chicago. She patted me on the back and turned around to say goodbye to Mary, Mimi, and Juanita, and I looked toward the door, planning to make a beeline for it.

There, leaning against the doorjamb, was a woman who I assumed was waiting for Rosa. She was dressed in a turquoise top with bright embroidered flowers and a skirt of traditional indigenous cloth that had faded from washing. On her feet she wore black plastic sandals, which I remembered from San Miguel. The women there wore them because they were good for the mud. They didn't slip, like tennis shoes, and were easily washed. Regaining a memory of San Miguel brought a smile to my face.

The woman didn't return my smile, but she responded by walking across the room and taking my hand. She was shorter than me, and I bent down when I saw that she wanted to put her mouth to my ear and whisper. Pressing her fingers gently into my hand, almost massaging it, she thanked me for what I was doing. She kept hold of my hand. She had more to say.

"My son, Victor, they took him. He was lost for a long time, but we found his remains. The only thing that was left to me were some pieces of his bones."

She pulled away for a moment and I could see tears glistening on her face. With her free hand she pressed a small object into my palm. "I want to give you one."

I turned my hand over and opened it. A small white bone with a tiny hole in it lay in my palm. It looked like a vertebra, or part of one, but was smooth. It sounds corny, maybe even sick — part of someone's body who was probably tortured to death brought me peace. But it was true. A peace or energy — maybe simple gratitude — was flowing through me.

WHEN WE GOT BACK to the hotel I turned on the hot water in the bathroom sink and let it run until I couldn't see myself in the mirror, until I couldn't even see my hands in front of my face. Shrouded in steam I crouched against the wall and sobbed. I didn't feel worthy of the woman's gift. I knew that Rosa and Miguel were in danger even before I was tortured. What I told the torturers was common knowledge — the groups they belonged to, that sort of thing. But did I say something that I don't remember? Did I know something about them that I don't remember knowing? Did I say something that would make it easier for them to disappear Miguel, reveal something about his habits, the places he went? I was being burned. I wasn't thinking clearly.

But there is no excuse for the way I forgot them when I got back to the States. I should have at least written a letter to Rosa and Miguel telling them to be careful. Their safety shouldn't have been pushed to the back of my mind. It should have come first. Rosa even now doesn't know that I answered questions about them. I'm afraid she'll blame me for what happened. All I can say is that I tried to be careful. I felt that their questions were a trap — they were asking me things they already knew to check whether I was telling the truth. After the torture, I was effectively silenced. The torturers had severed my connections, quashed my will to do anything. And I will spend the rest of my life trying to come to terms with the effects of my silence on Rosa and Miguel.

I doubt that I shared with anyone on the trip what was going through my mind. I know I didn't talk to Andrea about Rosa and Miguel and how I had failed them. She was aware of some of the difficulties surrounding the case and some of the pressures we were still facing in Guatemala, and she felt in my body that I couldn't let her healing touch in.

Thursday Night: The complexities of this scene here are immense: the case is influenced by the Church/military conflict here — the seeming incompetence and/or fear being exhibited by the Guatemalan lawyers — the fears of the judge. The antiquated judicial system — the crazy, inaccurate sensationalism of the press.

The last 2–3 nights were made especially crazy by the need to give time to press interviews. Phones ringing constantly, much pressure to respond to Guatemalan & U.S. press people.

As for Dianna, her capacity to receive is waning. The tension she is holding just will not let go. Sometimes her feet are the only part of her body I can touch. Other times I can soothe her neck with calming oils. Finally, I gave some good work to Juanita and Mary, who fell into bed. Then *I* fell into bed, after ½ of Fran's beer and some stretches for my poor back.

On Friday, I dressed quickly, already thinking about the trip home that afternoon. After the press conference, we'd stop by the archeological museum and the crafts market before we caught our plane. I thought about things I could bring back for people at Su Casa (I hadn't forgotten them!). I didn't bother to spray perfume on my wrist. After the morgue and the Politécnica, the press conference would be a piece of cake. I practiced my statement several times nonetheless, knowing the effect the clicks and flashes of cameras could have. Sometimes the flashes blinded me. Sometimes it was only my nerves or my tears that made the words blur together.

We didn't know how much media to expect. Because of the tension between the Church and the army, we couldn't ask the archbishop's office for help. Paul had instead asked the embassy to send out our press release.

I didn't care too much how much press we got. The words of my statement themselves were enough to relish. Whoever showed up, I would get to say:

I have provided the courts and the government with sufficient evidence. The military has failed to provide the names of the commanding officers, civil patrol leaders, and officials of the G-2 in Huehuetenango in the area where I was working, and during the reconstruction of the events, the military refused to allow the court permission to photograph the military installation where I was held. It is up to the court and Public Ministry and the government to follow through on my case to reach a resolution. I hope that they will proceed effectively and without additional delay. If they do not, the case will be pursued in the Inter-American Commission on Human Rights, given that I have exhausted all recourse within the country.

Mimi walked with me down to the hotel conference room where reporters were gathering, setting up their cameras and settling in their chairs. I arranged my papers, adjusted the microphone, and felt a dull thud begin in my cheekbone. I smelled Alejandro's cologne. Mimi asked me afterward if I had seen the G-2 agents, if that was why I had suddenly become so tense. They didn't even register. My cheekbone didn't burn, and my tailbone didn't ache when the little men with dark glasses followed us around and tried to be menacing. They simply weren't evil enough. What set my jaw throbbing was the presence I felt in that room of power mixed with pure evil. I had felt it before, with the Guate-man and with Alejandro. I scanned the crowd. None of the men holding notebooks and tape recorders and meeting my gaze expectantly resembled either one of them. But my body knew: one of them was near, just outside the door, maybe in the next room.

I picked up the first page of my statement and it shook so much that I had to put it down again and lean over close to see it. I thought about going back to the room, where our sage and all our talismans were — where I could lock the door. Shawn could report on the week's events. My fingers closed around the cross Raúl had given me, the dolphin from Mary, and the piece of bone that had formed part of Victor's body. Touching it reminded me of his mother. And then I thought of Rosa and Miguel, of obligations I hadn't fulfilled, and of the damage silence can do. And I started to read.

Much of what I talked about was revictimization and the after-effects of torture. I wanted anyone who had been tortured to know that the guilt and the shame and the rage, the feelings of being dirty and crazy, were normal and could diminish with time. I wonder if I was trying to convince myself as much as anyone else.

I had a message to deliver to the Guate-man and Alejandro, as well, a tacit one implicit in the fact that I was standing up and speaking: "I'm back and I'm strong. You're not going to beat me. You failed." I had to insist on that, even though it was hard to hold my head up, to find space in my throat for words. The evil in the room was a stone drawing me under. I was gasping for breath and breaking into sobs because the evil wasn't just out there; I wore it around my neck, the invisible weight of Miguel, the Woman, and the child whose life I had ended. But I managed to finish, remembering the dolphin arching above the water, feeling the Woman's hand on mine and the touch of the child with no eyes.

Chapter Thirteen

A LEAVE OF ABSENCE

THE PORCELAIN CUP was warm against my cheek, drawing the ache out. Mimi sat across from me in the living room at Su Casa, the small one for the staff, which Mimi was part of again at least until she felt I had "life-giving plans for the future," as she put it. I don't know if someone told her how close I'd come to having plans of another kind after the trip to Guatemala the year before. I was much better this time, but Mimi wasn't taking any chances. She's always felt she almost lost me once because she was away — that if she'd been in Guatemala, she could have prevented the abduction somehow. Now she'd postponed her return to Chile, and every morning we drank coffee together and talked about our plans for the day and beyond. Sometimes we just listened to the bird calls coming through the window and watched the flashes of color in the trees. The view from my place on the couch was good. Through the window I could see the remains of the old church, which had been torn down after being deemed an unsafe refuge for the homeless who sought shelter in it. The Guate-man, the Policeman, José, and Alejandro would have nowhere now to hide. All of beauty that could be salvaged had been removed, and all that remained were piles of stones that were bleaching in the sun.

I remembered the church in its last days, how it would tremble when buses rolled past — the same way my hands trembled lately as I cleaned the house, gardened, laid out coloring books for the children, held my tea. How long would it be before the darkness inside me broke loose — before the walls I hid it behind caved in? The time was coming. I could feel it.

So I wanted to go on a cruise ship. I showed Mimi the brochure: "Jobs at Sea." The white, cursive letters hung above a cerulean swimming pool glimmering in the center of a ship. I could nearly smell the chlorine, a smell like bleach, and the clean salt air and the geraniums that hung around an awning and dotted the rail. They would smell the way the earth smelled

217

after a rain. "See, they have child-care jobs, I could take care of the plants, and I could clean. It would be so different from Su Casa."

Mimi knew what I meant. I wouldn't be with other survivors, listening to their stories, living their pain. Nothing would remind me of my own ordeal. I would stand by the rail and stare out at the fuzzy seam of the horizon. The spray on my forehead would cleanse me, the breeze would run its fingers through my hair, and at night the waves would lap at the ship and lull me to sleep.

In therapy with Mary, I had focused on my feelings of guilt. But no matter how much I talked about those feelings and no matter how much Mary said I wasn't to blame for anything, I knew that I was. I wasn't suicidal — Mimi needn't have worried — but as I lay awake at night, listening to buses rumble by on the street, watching headlights flash on the wall and vanish, I knew I had to find something to live for, something that justified my life. With the case more or less over as far as my participation went, I no longer would have the opportunity to be a voice for the Guatemalan people, a survivor fighting on the side of right. That identity had allowed me to stand myself. Now I had to give it up, and who was I? Miguel was still dead. The Woman, too. And the growing seed whose life I had ended was dead.

On the ship I could grieve. No one would know me. No one would tell me just to turn it all over to God. No one would have to worry about deportation, green cards, the safety of family members, and I wouldn't feel by comparison so fortunate that grieving for myself seemed wrong. The passengers would be people on vacation, people who were happy, who were living the life I might have had. And it would be OK for me to feel all the rage at what had been taken and cry as much as I needed and let the sun bake out of me whatever the tears couldn't release.

Maybe the beauty around me would find its way inside me. Maybe floating countryless I would find myself, and find myself to be something other than Sister Dianna, assassin, fraud.

"Mimi, I need to ask you something," I said, after she'd looked through the pamphlet.

"Shoot."

"Do . . . do nuns go on cruises?"

"Well, I don't know. They could. You'd be working. And you might have some time to think."

Her answer worried me a little. I was afraid of thinking. As long as I was preparing for trips to Guatemala, I had focused mainly on what I was going to tell the court and how I was going to get through the proceedings. My secrets — the questions I had answered about Miguel, what happened to the Woman, the choice I had made — were thoughts I had pushed aside. But as long as they were assailing me — and they were, now that the case was over — I might as well be on a cruise ship.

In truth, I was hoping Mimi would say, "No, nuns and cruise ships don't mix." That answer would give me an excuse for the second move I was thinking of making. "Mimi, if I went," I ventured, "I wouldn't go as a nun."

"What?"

"I'm thinking of leaving the community."

"Dianna, why?" She put her cup down and searched my face.

I dropped my eyes. "I don't feel worthy to be an Ursuline."

"You're worthy. Of course you're worthy."

Her answer baffled me. She knew about the things I had done. What I had done with the pregnancy — the Church considered that murder. And I couldn't look down at my hands without thinking of them splattered with blood. I was living in a state of mortal sin. What that meant was that whatever torture I might get from here on out — even for all eternity — I deserved.

There was the sacrament of confession, but I didn't believe in it. Whenever I went to Mass, I dreaded the Lord's Prayer — "Forgive us our trespasses as we forgive those who trespass against us." I wanted desperately to be forgiven, but I couldn't forgive my torturers. I didn't understand how I could forgive them without condoning what they had done to me and to other people. So what right did I have to forgiveness?

After a few moments of silence, broken by nothing but the shrieks of a blue jay, Mimi suggested a leave of absence. She explained that I would still be an Ursuline, but the leave would be a way of claiming an exemption from some of the expectations and traditions. I would only be bound by the vows.

That was fine with me. I was comfortable with a simple lifestyle, so the vow of poverty was no hardship. As for the vow of chastity, I would never let anyone touch me. Obedience was the only vow I didn't like: the first memory I had of obeying was remaining silent in the garden when the Guate-man told me not to scream. I've always regretted following that order.

"But the leave of absence would take the pressure off you," Mimi argued, "and give you time to learn about what the vow of obedience really means, what living as an Ursuline means."

I turned it over in my mind. Lying in bed at night, I kept remembering the circle of indigenous women that Mimi and Darleen had formed part of on the island of the dolphin — and how they had vanished. I wondered if that was a premonition.

FINALLY ONE MORNING during our break in the staff room I brought it up. "Mimi, my friends who are Ursulines are so important to me — you, Luisa, Kim." A tree near the window beside me was reflected in my cup. I turned the cup in my hands, but the tree with the window and the blue sky never moved. "If I took a leave — if I decided not to be a nun...I don't want to lose you."

I heard Mimi take a couple of steps to cross the room, and I felt her sink in beside me on the couch. "Dianna."

I looked up at her.

She put her hand on top of mine. "I don't care if you're an Ursuline or not, Dianna. You'll always be my sister."

"Nana, why are you doing this?" Barbara was sitting beside me on the bed I must have slept in throughout my childhood and the bed she must have sat on numerous times before to question and counsel me. Out of the corner of my eye I could see the hand she held out, palm up, as if to receive my answer. The bed creaked, and the mango, vanilla, coconut smell of her hair, freshly washed, was stronger now than the fragrance of coffee and bacon that lingered from breakfast. She must be leaning toward me, I realized, trying to see my face. But I just wanted her to watch my hand. Then she could add her name beneath, on the line designated for the witness. Her name was simple, Barbara Murietta, with no "Sister" in front of it. I could have a name like that.

But I didn't seem to be able to get the pen down to the page. Everyone, like Barbara, would question what I was doing. Even I questioned it. That's why I couldn't afford to meet Barbara's eyes. If she saw the loose threads in my resolve and tugged at one, even gently, my decision would unravel. And I would lose control. I would cry.

One of those loose threads was fear. I was afraid that some of the sisters at the Mount might say, "Ingrate. Once the case is over and we've spent all this money on her recovery, once she's well enough not to need us, she moves on." Guatemalan and U.S. officials might start rumors that I was suspended from the order for sexual activities or that I was leaving because I wanted the freedom to have love affairs at will. Another snag in the weave of my plan was my own pride, my defiance. If word of my leave got to the Guate-man and the Policeman, they would feel smug, knowing they had destroyed my faith, at least the kind of faith I once had, a calling. I didn't want to give them that satisfaction. Most of all, I wanted to avoid the pain of admitting, even to myself, that the Policeman had taken my faith. But he had and it hadn't come back. If I looked for that calling, I might find that it was gone forever. I was running that risk and a greater one: If I admitted that I lacked the commitment now to serve God as a nun, the evil the torturers planted in me might have nothing to contain it. Staring out the window morning after morning at the piles of stones that had been the church, I realized "Sister" was the shelter I took refuge in, a shaky structure that no longer served. I envisioned darkness invading the daylight as I tore that structure down and spreading, inking the sun out.

The bed creaked again. I tried to think of an answer for Barbara. I gave her the only short one I had. "I don't feel worthy to be an Ursuline." The long answer was that I hated myself, I hated life. I was bitter toward God, the torturers, my community, and the lawyers. Yes, the lawyers again. They were not at all convinced that the case would move forward in Guatemala. I had heard them say that before, but I had clung to the belief that the information I provided would persuade the court to continue to investigate, that the torturers would be found and held accountable. Believing that was the only way I could get myself through the proceedings. I suppose I'd also hoped someone would come forward and confirm what I was saying. I even hoped that person would be José. I was still waiting for him to rescue me.

Now I finally understood. I remembered what I had done with the Policeman, running my hands down his hips. I had believed I could prevent him from hurting me if I played his game. Now I felt that I had prostituted myself, not to one person, but to an entire oppressive institution that was interested not in truth but in protecting those responsible.

I couldn't really fault my lawyers for my naïveté, my refusal to believe their warnings. I tried to remind myself that, even if we didn't obtain justice in Guatemala, at least more people were aware of the dirty secrets of the Guatemalan army. Still, I was bitter. And I was afraid that hatred and bitterness would consume me. Mimi described me as gentle and understanding — she reminded me about the children when they came knocking at the door in the morning in San Miguel. I always would stop and be friendly with them, even if I had work to do. Or if they brought me rocks, no matter how ugly, I was grateful. But I didn't know that person. That person was dead. I had hoped to resurrect her with my trips to Guatemala, but she was buried and I was a person full of hardness and without any memory of my faith, of why I had become a nun.

I didn't believe in the God the sisters invoked, the God who was aware of the fall of every sparrow. As a nun I was supposed to turn my life over to God. I couldn't do it, not again. Before I had gone out into the garden at the Posada de Belén, when I was praying with Darleen, I had put my life in the hands of God. When the Bible fell open to Jeremiah, I felt God was directing me to stay in Guatemala. And following that God, I had lived a parody of the Christian ideal: I had died to my old self and been reborn, not in Christ, but in the image of the torturers. Fear no evil, we are told. But I trusted in the Shepherd and was led into a trap.

I remembered praying in that dark room: God, I have given my life to you. Get me out of here. Is that too much to ask? Maybe God had gotten me out of there. Sometimes I thought so. But by then I didn't know if I was still a lamb. I didn't know who I belonged to. I had made a kill. Maybe I was a wolf in a fleecy wrap, the mantle of holy sisterhood, sent back to lure the sheep into the wilderness, one by one.

BUT IF I WERE the torturers' instrument, as I feared, every action I took — the leave of absence included — might be just one more way to hurt my community and my family. The leave would certainly confuse people and open the door to misinterpretations. But going on as I had, I had also caused pain, and I was likely to cause more.

I couldn't clear up the confusion. I couldn't tell Barbara and my parents that nuns don't carry in their souls a hatred, a rage so deep they could kill if given the chance. Often I imagined myself back in the basement of the Politécnica. But this time, there was a gun on top of the desk, a gun the Policeman or Guate-man left there. I reach for it, I have the gun now, aimed at their hearts. They are begging me to spare them. The Policeman is on his knees, saying, "Please, please." There is a part of me that wants to listen. But I say, "No. This is from me. This is from the Woman. This is from my family and my friends in the community. This is from every person you hurt." And I unload the gun into them, bullet by bullet.

Time after time I had sinned in my thoughts. The paper in my lap seemed like a confession, something the torturers had written up that I had to admit to. Guilt rolled through me like a black wave. I signed the form.

MY MOM AND DAD when they asked about my decision got the same answer I gave everyone else: I wasn't worthy to be an Ursuline. They didn't press me for explanations. But Barbara has told me that after I left New Mexico, my mother said, "They must have done something worse to Nana, something she hasn't told us."

Pat and Juanita were growing smaller. When I could no longer see them out the train window, I sat down and massaged my neck.

Now I've done it, I thought. I've made my choice, and there's no going back.

Juanita had said, "You're always welcome at Su Casa. You know you can come back anytime." Dolores had asked several times, "Are you sure this is what you want to do?" She was probably just trying to encourage me to talk about my decision. Or maybe she didn't want me to leave. But I read into her question a doubt about my ability to handle the outside world. I would prove her wrong, her and anyone else who didn't think I could survive on my own. No matter how my decision turned out, I wouldn't go back. I had my pride.

A voice at my shoulder made me jump. I turned to see a man in a uniform staring at me. My mouth dried out.

"Ticket?" he said.

I rooted through my backpack, my hands shaking. *Stay calm, Dianna. You have your ticket.* I gave it to him and he left, but every so often he strutted down the aisle and panic knocked at my chest. I was afraid of having a flashback. But at Kovler I had learned ways to ground myself, and I practiced them. I counted my fingers several times, then counted the wrinkles on the backs of my fingers. Closing my eyes I tried to recall the pattern of creases on each. Memorizing my fingers was a way of making them mine. So was using lotion. So often I would check my hands for roughness, calluses, growth, any signs that they were becoming the hands of the Policeman or the Guate-man. I was even afraid that the wrinkles could harden into ridges like crocodiles have, into scales, the reptilian evil I carried in them finally drawn to the surface. I painted my fingernails to exert my will and have my hands reflect it.

When my nails had dried and the sun was sinking behind wheat fields I pulled out my book of crossword puzzles. I didn't even read the clues. I wrote my own messages in, finding words that intersected:

```
                        H
W H Y D I D I L E A V E S U C A S A
H             L         C         D
A             P         A         V
T                       R         E
A       P E T R I F I E D         N
M                       D         T
I                                 U
D                                 R
O                   E S C A P E   E
I       S
N       T             B
G E T O F F T H E T R A I N
        P             C
                      A
                      L
                      M
```

It got dark before I could finish. I knew I wasn't ready to leave Su Casa. I was still afraid of the dark. I was afraid to get up and go to the bathroom, so I wouldn't let myself drink anything. I should have waited until I was better, I thought, until I could handle cigarette smoke and the smell of liquor and men I didn't know walking around half-dressed. Then I could have gone on the cruise ship.

Instead, I was going to a place where I wouldn't have to face those things. I was going to the West Coast to be a consultant at another treatment center for survivors of torture. It was small, just starting up, and Julio and his family would be there, along with a family from San Miguel. If I had flashbacks, people there would understand. If I asked people not to smoke, they would know why. And I had a unique gift to offer. Anyone could take care of plants and children, but not many people understood survivors of torture firsthand. Also, I knew that if I'd waited to leave Su Casa — waited until the dark and smoke didn't scare me — I might have waited forever.

The cruise ship was tempting, but when I imagined myself alone with my rage and grief, feeling it, finally, I saw myself losing control, screaming, going wild. I couldn't do that around total strangers. There would be consequences.

I was so afraid of my anger. There was a point during the torture where I lost control and screamed out in anger and was punished with something so horrible I can't even say it. I imagined the people on the ship tossing me overboard or having me committed at the first port we came to. And deep down, I still didn't believe I had the right to grieve and feel rage, and I wanted to distract myself again with other people's pain. It was so much less scary than my own.

WITHIN A FEW WEEKS I knew I had made a mistake. At Su Casa I had learned to reclaim my voice, but at the new treatment center my voice didn't seem to matter. I didn't agree with the authoritarian manner in which the program was run, but because it was run in that way, no one wanted to hear what I had to say about it. I wanted to help people who hadn't been tortured understand those who had, but I found myself in a situation similar to the torture — my words were useless. Furthermore, I was told that since I was at the center as a staff member and not to receive treatment, I had no right to have feelings.

I told myself to grow up and deal with it. This was the real world. And I was afraid to discuss the situation with Mary. She might say I had made a mistake, that I'd left Chicago before I was ready. But finally, out of desperation, I gave in and called her.

"What?!" she said. "You don't have to put up with that kind of treatment!"

I was relieved to hear that the "outside world" could be better, and I started planning my next move. In the privacy of my room, I combed the newspaper ads. I was willing to do just about anything.

As luck had it, in a nearby shopping mall a nanny agency was conducting interviews. I sneaked out. That is, I tried to sneak out. Julio's thirteen-year-old sister, Juanita, saw me leaving and wanted to come with me. She needed a mother in this strange new world and sought her in me, sticking to me like glue whenever she could find me. "You are my American mother," she said, trying out her English. "I go with you."

I had no good excuse prepared. I just told her I had something I had to do alone.

At the interview I was much smoother. I amazed myself. I sat down face-to-face with a strange woman and answered questions. No flashbacks, no tears, no fumbling for words, just answers like a normal person. I mentioned nothing about my torture. I had been a teacher in Kentucky and a missionary in Guatemala, I said, and I had a degree in early childhood education. "You're going to be in great demand," the interviewer told me. "A lot of mothers are going to want you to take care of their babies."

I was stunned. Not only was I coherent and "normal"; she must have seen a part of me that was gentle and nurturing. I held on to her words and replayed them again and again in my mind.

A COUPLE OF WEEKS LATER in the mail was an offer for a job in New York, taking care of a baby adopted from Mexico. One of my tasks would be to speak Spanish to the child. I pictured holding the baby, feeding her, changing her, talking and singing to her in Spanish. And I knew I would have to say no. Taking care of an infant, I would consider the child mine: the child I didn't have. It would be a bad situation for everyone.

WHAT I WANTED more than anything was to go back to Guatemala. I stayed at the treatment center, tantalized by the promise that soon they would open a center in Guatemala. My plan was then to transfer there. I told myself I had a number of friends in the U.S. Congress now and the army wouldn't dare do anything to hurt me. Besides, the situation in Guatemala would soon be different. Ramiro de León Carpio, the former human rights ombudsman, was now Guatemala's president. He was elected by Congress after President Serrano declared an "auto-coup," dissolved Congress and the judiciary, and was forced to resign, under national and international pressure. De León needed time to get settled, the Guatemalans at the center told me. He had only been in office for about six months. He needed more time. Then things would change.

A LETTER caused my plan to disintegrate. It was from Paul. In September, he told me, General Gramajo had spoken on a panel in Washington, D.C., about civil control over Latin America's militaries. The conference was sponsored by the Woodrow Wilson Center, and the room was packed with scholars, journalists, and Latin American military officers. When the time for questions came, Paul stood up and reminded Gramajo that he had been sued under the Alien Torts Act and had failed to appear before a federal court to face charges that, as defense minister, he was ultimately responsible for my torture. The moderator tried to call on someone else, but Paul walked up on the stage and handed Gramajo a summons requiring him to show up the next day and declare his assets, since he would no doubt be found guilty by default. Gramajo never went to my lawyer's office, of course, but he was red in the face and speechless, and the media that was present to report on the progress of Latin American militaries and their respect for civil rule focused instead on the case against Gramajo.

How powerful I felt. If the Guatemalan court system was a waste of time, at least in the United States Gramajo could be held accountable and if not actually forced to pay me or the other victims, at least embarrassed publicly. It was a small victory. Very small, I began to realize. Maybe too small for the cost involved: now he and his friends in the military would be enraged with me. Now I didn't dare dream of a life in Guatemala.

I no longer lay awake in bed, calculating how many more months it might take to set up the treatment center, what season I would arrive in, what I would pack. But Paul and I decided that in January I should go to Guatemala for a week. Mary, Juanita, Andrea, and Mimi wouldn't accompany me this time. I wanted to prove I didn't need them. Only Fran and Paul would be with me. They were making one final trip to check on any progress in the case before turning all resources toward the OAS case. This time, as a follow-up legal procedure, I would be asked to identify, once again, the Politécnica, but not from the safety of the van. I would have to go inside.

We stayed at the fancy hotel again, arriving on a Sunday. Paul had told embassy officials that he didn't think an escort from the airport or a bulletproof van with an embassy driver would be necessary this time, given the lower profile of the case and the improved conditions in Guatemala. Conditions had actually worsened, though, and we ended up with a van. On December 10, International Human Rights Day, GAM leader Mario Polanco had been abducted, brutally beaten with a baseball bat, and left naked, unconscious, and bleeding on the side of a road — a message to the international community from the army: That's what we think of your Human Rights Day. The month we had chosen to return, January 1994, ended up being the bloodiest month in Guatemala since 1991. According to the Archbishop's Human Rights Office, forty-six people were assassinated that month for political reasons. Twenty more people were attacked, ten were abducted, and three were tortured.

We spent the first part of the week in meetings. The Human Rights Ombudsman's Office was our first stop. We wanted to know if the investigation of my case had progressed any since our last trip. To our surprise, the judge who presided during my first trip to Guatemala — the one who told embassy officials that I was parroting Mary, who must be giving me the answers during our breaks — was now working in the Human Rights Ombudsman's Office. That was only the first bit of bad news. The second was that my entire case file had disappeared.

The new ombudsman, Mario García Laguardia, said, "A number of files that were here before are gone now." He shrugged, indicating his helplessness. Someone on the previous staff had cleaned out the cabinets, it seemed.

MEETING WITH JUDICIAL OFFICIALS, we learned that the court had done nothing since I had been in Guatemala the previous year. No sketches had been circulated, no police officers had been called to testify, and no answers had been given by the military to our questions about the army officers in relevant positions of command at the time of my abduction. Judge Lam had done all she could. Only a month after I had identified the Politécnica as the place I was detained and finished the reconstruction, Acting Ambassador John F. Keane met with Supreme Court President Juan José Rodil Peralta to find out what would be needed to close my case. In Washington, too, officials were making Judge Lam's job difficult. The judge had asked the U.S. embassy for the names of all U.S. government employees working with the Guatemalan security forces in October and November of 1989. The embassy turned to the State Department for guidance on how to respond. The answer, Keane asserted, would have to meet the "objective of putting to rest the issue of whether someone connected to the embassy was somehow involved in the alleged kidnapping of Sister Diana [sic]."[1] A dozen notes were written between embassy and State Department officials debating how to answer. The State Department finally advised the embassy to respond that it was "unclear the kinds of cooperation to which the [judge's] note refers." The response acknowledged that "Embassy officials had contact with personnel from a wide range of agencies and entities of the Government of the Republic of Guatemala, including the security forces, in the course of their official duties," but invoked a semantic argument, claiming that none were "assigned" to the Guatemalan security forces during the period in question. "The GOG is well aware which U.S. personnel work with units of its police and armed forces," the response noted. The State Department, in effect, was telling Judge Lam to find out the names of those U.S. employees from the Guatemalan government.

IN SPITE OF THESE OBSTACLES, we forged ahead. On Wednesday morning, Fran and Paul and I met my Guatemalan lawyers, Ronnie and Edgar, as well as a young American interpreter named Karen, Judge Lam, and the helpful U.S. embassy consular officer, Chuck Keil, outside the Guardia de Honor, a military institution just behind the Politécnica. At the Guardia de Honor I went through the motions: I suppose I entered the building and looked around. But my focus was on the Politécnica.

Common sense told me the army would have left no evidence at the Politécnica of anything I had described — not of the stairwell, the metal door at the bottom, the desk, the file cabinets, or the pit. Logic told me time had passed. But that building and that day, November 2, 1989, were intertwined in my mind forever. Maybe the building represented that place inside of me where time hadn't passed, where I kept waiting to do that day over, to undo it, to make it not have happened.

I had this fantasy: I would walk in with my lawyers, with the judge; I would go down the stairs; I would find them there, still torturing the Woman. "There they are!" I would say. We would stop them. I would save the Woman and myself.

That may be the real reason I agreed to do the identification again when it was clear that the case in Guatemala was going nowhere. Paul had talked to me about the importance of doing everything possible with a view to our case before the OAS. But the legal ins and outs didn't really interest me anymore. This was a battle I had to fight; I had to prove that I could walk back in and retrace my steps.

SOLDIERS WERE WATCHING from the guard towers and their eyes and bits of their faces showed through the windows in the turrets. We went through the side entrance. Every bit of my body was listening for the screams. As we got closer an odor thickened the air. I don't think anyone else was aware of it. It was the smell of the pit.

I was walking back into that day. The ground would give way beneath me; I would be back in that basement with no judge, no team of lawyers. This time the torturers would end it as they'd meant to. It was my own death I was smelling.

I remembered when the rage had found its way out, I had shouted, and the Policeman was preparing a punishment that filled me with a fear so intense. What he did to me is too humiliating to recount; putting words to it would only rekindle the shame that engulfed me as I stood at the door of that building with my legal team and felt every instant of that punishment. My skin, my nerve endings remembered it.

And I ran.

"THE URSULINE lost control and fled through the gate that opens onto Second Avenue, between First and Second Avenue in Zone 10," a reporter wrote. "Those accompanying her went in pursuit of the nun and after reaching her took her to the hotel."[2]

The rest of the proceeding took place without me. The judge entered the building and examined the rooms she was shown by military officials. Since the year before, when she'd been turned away, the army must have had time to seal up a stairway.[3] She found no sign of a basement.

AT OUR PRESS CONFERENCE the next day I gave vent to some of the rage I had held within me for so long, stating that Guatemala was "a country whose democracy is defined by the military." I reiterated my certainty that the Politécnica was where I was held and said my case was one more example of how the Guatemalan government pantomimed the administration of justice. I ended with a promise to the people of Guatemala and the Guatemalan army:

> Although I may not physically be present in Guatemala, I will continue to struggle for your liberation and your justice! And I say *loud and clear* to the individuals responsible for these acts of disappearances, kidnappings, assassinations, and torture that I will remain a piercing thorn in your side until justice is done!

Well, I had committed myself.

BUT I FOUND MYSELF on a plane a few weeks later, headed for New York, where my work would have nothing to do with Guatemala, torture, or refugees. I was tired, and I needed something that would bring me back to life. Children would do that. I loved working with children. In New York I would live with Kim in a community of other sisters and take care of children whose mothers were in prison.

BREAKING THE NEWS to Julio, Joaquin, and Julio's sister Juanita hadn't been easy. I knocked on the door of the room the family shared and said I had something to tell them. Julio and Joaquin sat down on a bed to listen. As Juanita and I sat across from them on another bed, Juanita took my hand. Her hand was hot and sweaty. I tried to pull away but she tightened her grip.

"I want to tell you that I'm leaving," I said.

"Vacation? To visit your family?" Joaquín asked me in Spanish.

"Fa-mi-li-a." The corners of Julio's mouth lifted.

"No. I'm going to stay in New York with a friend."

"When will you come back?" Juanita asked. In her brown eyes I saw her fear.

"I'm — I'm not coming back."

JUANITA LET GO of my hand. Her dark hair fell in front of her face and her shoulders started to shake. She had lost her brother, in a way, and she had lost her family as she knew it. She didn't need to lose anyone else.

Julio took Joaquín's hand and said something to him in Cakchiquel. Joaquín answered, Juanita chimed in, and then Julio turned to me and said in Spanish, "No. Dianna stay here. No a-ban-don-a."

I pushed my feelings away with words. "Julio, I have to leave. I'm not doing any good here. I'll always carry you in my heart."

Juanita turned to me. "Don't go. We need you here."

Joaquín asked me to stay until they left for Guatemala. But I knew that if I waited, even a couple of months, I might be too depressed to go anywhere.

"I can't do it. I can't stay. I'm not happy here. I'm very, very sad."

"Triste. Dianna triste," Julio said. He nodded. He understood.

Juanita cried again when we hugged goodbye. Julio's and Joaquín's eyes were full, like mine. I didn't cry until the plane was rising up into clouds so thin they were barely distinguishable from the air, just wisps of thickness that gathered and disappeared as if they had never existed.

I told Kim that I was only staying for several months while I figured things out. I enjoyed getting the two kids in my charge ready for school and helping them with their homework. Stephan, a little African American boy, sat on my lap, squeezed my cheeks, and kissed me on the nose. Danny, an Italian boy, told me about what he would do with his mother when she got out of prison. And I had time to read *Newsweek*, *Glamour*, *People*, *National Geographic*, and the *New York Times* and piece back together my knowledge of the world. But I kept trying to think of ways to get back to Guatemala or to work somehow for change there.

As if fate were testing my resolve, I got a phone call from a woman named Jennifer Harbury. Her voice was hoarse and tired but enthusiastic as she told me about a group she was forming, a coalition of U.S. citizens who had been attacked in Guatemala or lost relatives to the political violence there.

Jennifer was one of the ones who had lost a relative. Her husband, a Guatemalan guerrilla commandant, had disappeared in a battle two years earlier. Jennifer believed he'd been captured by the army. A young man who had fought under her husband and had been captured himself had seen him at a military base, being tortured. Jennifer hoped that by joining together we could exert pressure on U.S. government officials to adopt policies that might lead to change in Guatemala, as well as lobby for action and information on our own cases.

Another coalition member Jennifer mentioned was Meredith Larson, who was stabbed at the end of 1989 while working as an escort for human rights activists in Guatemala. Jennifer and Meredith were contacting other people they knew of and working to expand the group. "So, do you think you might be interested in joining?" Jennifer asked.

"It sounds like a way to be a thorn in the army's side." I was going to tell Jennifer I had promised no less in my last press conference but as soon as I got the first sentence out her laugh came through, high and startled, and ended in a low chuckle.

"Yeah, we'll stick it to them all right." Then her voice was serious again, hoarse and gravelly with fatigue. She told me that the prisoner who had seen her husband, Everardo, being tortured had seen thirty-five other captured guerrilla combatants in secret detention. They were being held and tortured by the army as part of a new program aimed at turning them into permanent army informants. Santiago, the witness, had been in detention for two years before he managed to escape and get the news out about the secret program.

"There's a good chance they're still alive," Jennifer said. "The whole point of the program is to keep them alive so they can be useful to the army. And what I'm asking is that the army comply with international humanitarian law and its commitments under international treaties: present the prisoners, hold them in a public place where they can be monitored by the Red Cross and human rights groups, and give them a fair trial. But don't torture them. Do you think that's something you can be part of?"

"Yes, Jennifer," I said. "You can count on me."

ABOUT A MONTH LATER, I received an information package. Meredith and Jennifer were organizing a congressional briefing. We would each tell what had happened to us and ask Congress to pressure the Guatemalan army in specific ways. We were going to ask, for example, that Congress cut off Guatemala's military and economic aid until the human rights situation improved. They wanted to know if I would participate.

I called Meredith and told her I needed time to think about it. Pushing my case through the court system in Guatemala, I was hardly a threat to the army. I'd learned that much: if judges and lawyers were not intimidated, eliminated, or bought, the system itself was so inefficient that the military was guaranteed impunity. Gouging a hole in the army's coffers was another matter. And publicly joining with a guerrilla commandant's wife as we made those demands could open me up to accusations that I really was affiliated with the guerrillas and had a political agenda. The torturers would feel justified in having interrogated me and applied measures to force answers from me. After all, they could tell themselves, I was a subversive.

Those who doubted I was tortured in the first place would be able to say that the torture story, like the congressional briefing, was a stunt to get a cut-off of aid to the Guatemalan military. If I had asked the lawyers whether I should join in the coalition's efforts, they probably would have said no. I wondered if it was worth the risk of participating — if I really had anything to say in a briefing that other coalition members couldn't say as well or better. But I remembered my promise to the Guatemalan army — that I, personally, would be a thorn in their sides — and I remembered that people, including Jennifer's husband, were being tortured. I called Meredith back, and as I told her I'd be there, I felt a swell of defiance and strength.

JENNIFER WAS AT THE GATE to meet me, along with Alice, the director of the Guatemala Human Rights Commission. The commission, or GHRC, as it was known, was the only group in Washington that was willing to support Jennifer in whatever way possible. Other organizations were afraid of being associated with the case of a guerrilla. Alice looked no older than when I had seen her a couple of years earlier, at the conference on torture. Someone had told me she was nearly seventy, but she looked no older than fifty. Jennifer looked younger than I'd thought she would be. I'd expected gray hair and a lined face to match the tiredness in her voice. But her hair was sandy brown with streaks of blond where the sun had bleached it, and her face was smooth and young. I felt silly in my skirt. I thought that since I was going to Washington I had better look professional. Jennifer was wearing jeans, beat up pumps, and a tattered black coat. But she didn't seem to notice what I had on. Her large green eyes shone, and she wrapped her arms around me in a light hug. "I'm so glad to finally meet you," she said. Alice hugged me, too, and the chill I had felt on the plane disappeared.

I stayed at the Assisi community, where Jennifer was living, along with about fifteen other people. The members of the community had chosen to live a simple lifestyle, in an old row house in a low-income neighborhood, and all had some connection to peace and justice issues or Latin America. I knew of some of the people who lived there. Father Joe Nangle, another community member, had visited me at Our Lady of Peace to tell me about the trip he and Marie Dennis had made to Guatemala in the beginning of 1990 to press for an investigation of my case. I was glad I would finally get to talk to Joe and Marie, but I was also tired and nervous about the upcoming events, and I didn't want to socialize.

EARLY THE NEXT MORNING we turned into the driveway of an old two-story stucco house not far from the Assisi community. "This is it," Alice said. Her car rattled after she turned the engine off. "That's its death rattle," she said, patting the dashboard.

A huge strip of Guatemalan cloth hanging on the wall above the landing was the only thing to look at as we walked up the creaky flight of stairs to Alice's second-floor office. In white letters that nearly glowed in the dim light of the stairwell the banner spelled out a message: "For a People's Right to Live." I guessed that was Alice's mission statement.

The GHRC office was clean, and sunlight poured through the large windows. Jennifer was in the other room making last-minute photocopies. Alice was washing out mugs in the bathroom so we could have coffee when a woman in her forties with shoulder-length brown hair and a delicate, sensitive face came up the stairs. She introduced herself shyly as Trish and wandered around, looking at the photos. Randy was the next coalition member to come. He may have been about the same age and was dark-haired and clean-cut. He looked like a responsible businessman. A blond woman bounced up the stairs behind him and threw her arms around me, introducing herself as Meredith. Then she began bustling around the office, taking papers from Jennifer and thwacking them on the table to straighten the edges. She was in her late twenties, with flushed cheeks and piercing blue eyes. Josh also was young and extroverted like Meredith. Tall and lanky, with curly blond hair, he shook my hand and gave me a broad smile.

Jennifer sat down and rattled words off so quickly that I looked around to see if other people were staring at her without following, the way I was. No, they understood her, and when they spoke it was with the same vocabulary and intensity. Maybe I had been living with Spanish speakers too long. Or perhaps I just didn't fit among these people. When they introduced themselves, I learned that Trish was a professor. Randy had an important job with the Federal Deposit Insurance Corporation. I already knew that Jennifer was a lawyer with a Harvard degree — I had read that in her testimony, which came in the packet Meredith had sent me. Meredith was working in an AIDS prevention program in San Francisco and was applying to graduate schools in public health, and Josh was in law school in Michigan. I was the only one who had no second degree, no plans to get one, and no idea about the legislative process.

But as soon as the conversation turned to our own cases, the differences in our backgrounds no longer concerned me. We all had pain in common and the loneliness of being U.S. citizens and knowing what we knew — that our country was largely responsible for what we and the Guatemalan people were suffering. And when Jennifer asked toward the end of the meeting who would assume leadership as the coalition chair, I felt comfortable enough to volunteer, if someone else would agree to be co-chair. Meredith took the job on.

AFTER THE MEETING, Meredith, Jennifer, and I had dinner at a restaurant down the street. Jennifer looked at her shoulders as we sat down and raked them quickly with her fingers, clearing off the fallen hairs. "I need protein," she said. "My hair's been falling out like this ever since he disappeared."

"Your hair's been falling out for two years?" Meredith asked.

"Well, there was a break in there," Jennifer said, opening her menu and ignoring it. "He disappeared in March and after a couple of months we thought there was no way he was still alive. The way it always happened was the army would torture prisoners for a few weeks and then kill them. That's why there have been no prisoners of war in Guatemala in more than thirty years of conflict. Just to be sure, we tried to have the grave exhumed where the army said he was buried. I went as an international observer, since no member of the URNG (the Guatemalan National Revolutionary Unity, the guerrilla umbrella organization) could go into the country to make sure the forensic report wasn't falsified. Besides, I was the only one who would recognize his teeth. I took some friends from Texas — lawyers, a politician. Just as we're getting down to the body bag, Attorney General Acisclo Valladares comes running up and orders the exhumation to be stopped. We told him we had permission from the human rights procurator. He said it didn't matter. He gave a series of bad reasons why we couldn't see who was in the grave. He was red in the face, panting. He had flown by helicopter from Guatemala City to get there in time."

"What was it that he didn't want you to see?" Meredith asked.

"Everardo wasn't in the grave," Jennifer answered. "We finally got an exhumation last summer and it was a young *compa* who was tied at the ankles, shot, strangled, and beaten to death. Meanwhile they had Everardo under torture. None of us thought he could still be alive. When the exhumation was canceled, we figured whether he was in the grave or not, he was dead. So from May to Christmas I grieved for him and tried to go on with my life. I went back to Texas, started working again on the book I was writing when I met him, went for long runs. Then we found out from

Santiago that during those whole seven months that I was running and writing and thinking he was dead Everardo was under torture. I'll never give up on him again."

Jennifer was quiet for a moment, looking at the menu before her without seeming to see it. "It's a long shot," she said after a while, "but I think there's a chance we can save him."

She looked from me to Meredith, and I realized that by "we" she meant us.

I asked how the embassy had been.

"Great until a couple of months ago, when Ambassador McAfee sent a letter asking for my case to be removed from the congressional resolution on Guatemala."

"You're kidding!" Meredith said, leaning forward on the table.

"No, she wrote a letter to Congresswoman Morella's aide. She said there was no evidence he was ever captured. There's plenty of evidence and she knows it. McAfee was really good until now. I mean, this could get him killed. It's a clear message to the army that the U.S. doesn't care what they do with him when they're finished with him." She took a long drink of coffee, hiding her eyes behind a curtain of steam.

"Your case was included, Dianna."

I was surprised. McAfee had asked for Jennifer's husband's case to be removed, but not mine. How strange. Maybe the U.S. embassy was now willing to take my case seriously. What a change from the embassy under Stroock.

"Why do you think Everardo might still be alive, Jennifer?" Meredith asked the question gently.

"The information he has."

"And if he's given it already?"

"He hasn't. If he'd talked, the entire command structure of his faction, known as the Revolutionary Organization of the People in Arms (ORPA), would have gone down. When someone's captured, normally all the safe houses are changed right away. But Gaspar, as a way to honor Everardo, didn't even change the safe houses."

Gaspar. He was the head *comandante* of ORPA. I knew that from reading the commission's *Human Rights Updates*.

"Everardo was Gaspar's closest friend. Gaspar said, 'Everardo doesn't even talk as it is. If they make him mad, he sure won't talk.' If all goes according to plan, the army will find that it's more trouble to keep Everardo and more costly to kill him than to present him or just let him go. I've been meeting with the defense minister and unofficially negotiating. I told him that if the army managed to find Everardo, in the jungle or something, I wouldn't ask any questions. I'd thank the army publicly for helping me find him. As a show of good faith, I even offered to stay for six months in a military prison, where they'd know I couldn't blast them for human rights abuses. I'd let bygones be bygones. Just so they give him back. The defense minister was very interested all of sudden. He said, 'You're a very intelligent young woman' and offered me another cup of coffee. I think he's trying to work it out with the rest of the army. It would be a big PR coup for the army."

Our food came, and we tried to turn the conversation to lighter topics. I was nervous about my manners — Meredith and Jennifer were the kind of people who would know which forks to use at a fancy dinner.

But Jennifer gave me a smile and started talking about her time in the mountains interviewing combatants for her book, eating roots cooked over a fire, and bathing in a stream.

I could guess that the campfire etiquette among campesinos wasn't too strict. I started to feel at home.

THE BRIEFING ROOM must have intimidated me — the raised platform, our names placed in front of our seats on a long, curved table, a silver pitcher of water, and row after row of well-dressed, sophisticated-looking people who stared back at us, read, or worked at something in their laps, as if every moment of their time were precious. But what I remember is pain, not fear. Trish carried it in every muscle of her face. Her teenage daughter was in the audience, and Trish's pain was mirrored in her face until Trish looked up at her. Then her daughter managed a little smile of encouragement.

We were speaking in chronological order, so Trish went first. Her sister, Ann Kerndt, was killed in 1976. After her sophomore year in college, she was volunteering for the summer in an agriculture project in the Guatemalan highlands. Because the roads were so bad in the mountains, people got around when they could by plane. An American Maryknoll priest, Father Bill Woods, had his pilot's license and a small plane, and he was transporting a group of people that included Ann to a neighboring province. His plane crashed midway.

Trish went through the facts without flinching; her voice betrayed only a slight edge of outrage when she told how her family was lied to by the Guatemalan government. Bad weather was responsible for the crash, the government said. But Trish's family found weather records for that day. It was perfect weather for flying. Then Guatemalan officials claimed the plane had exploded and burned, but witnesses at the crash site attested that none of the wreckage and none of the bodies showed any signs of having been burned. The information about the fire was quickly deleted from the official government account of the crash. The next explanation the government put forth was that engine failure had caused the crash. But the engine was thoroughly examined by the National Transportation Safety Board and found to be in working order at the time of the crash.

In the years following the crash, the U.S. State Department ignored requests for further investigations from congressional allies of Trish's family and the families of the four other Americans killed when the plane went down. But the families learned on their own that Father Woods had received numerous death threats, and just before the crash, the U.S. ambassador had told him his name was on an official army death list. Several witnesses came forward and said they saw Guatemalan military snipers shoot the plane down.

Randy's brother, Nicolas Blake, was a young journalist in Guatemala who was working on a story about the country's civil war. Along with his young photographer, he was executed in 1985 by members of the Civil Defense Patrol in Huehuetenango.

I spoke next. The aqua carpet stretched out across the room like a calm sea beyond the black and white of the page I held before me. I read, trying not to think about what the words meant, thinking instead of the people beside me, how we made a curve there on the dais, as if we were part of a circle.

Meredith told about walking with two coworkers back to the house where they all lived in Guatemala. It was night already, and they had met her at the bus stop to walk home with her because members of the house had been receiving telephoned death threats and a few months earlier a grenade had been thrown and had damaged part of the house. Meredith was a spunky twenty-three-year-old at the time, so when two men rushed out of the shadows with knives drawn, Meredith put her arms in front of her chest, as she'd learned to do in a self-defense class. The assailant's knife opened a gash in her arm instead of her heart. Meredith and her companions threw their valuables down and yelled at the men to take them, but the men had no interest in their money. They fled back into the night, after stabbing Meredith a couple of more times and wounding the other two human rights workers less severely.

Meredith stopped talking for a moment. Her cheeks were flushed and she kept her eyes on the table before her. With the fingertips of her right hand, she absently traced over the long scar that ran down from her left shoulder to her elbow. She seemed unaware that she was providing a visual aid to her testimony with a gesture that had become habitual.

She took a deep breath, wiped her eyes, and went on. The embassy doctor attended to Meredith and she was transferred to a hospital in the United States to be checked for nerve damage to her arm. The following spring, when Ambassador Stroock was recalled to Washington to show the seriousness of the U.S. commitment to human rights, the State Department mentioned Meredith's case as one the Guatemalan government would have to resolve. But Ambassador Stroock told a visiting delegation in Guatemala that the attack wasn't politically motivated; it was a case of Latin American men getting excited over North American women.

In 1990, Josh was working with homeless children in an organization that gave them housing and took care of their basic needs. As he was standing on the sidewalk in Guatemala City, a man in plain clothes grabbed him, held a gun to his head, and dragged him toward an unmarked car. Police officers intervened and asked the man for ID. Josh's assailant produced military identification. The officers let him go, beat a street youth who was with Josh, and attacked Josh's coworker. Then they put Josh into their patrol car, drove him around for an hour, and threatened him.

Jennifer gave the final testimony, holding up a photo of Everardo. He had black hair, full lips, and intense black eyes. The photo seemed almost alive, and Jennifer held it the entire time she spoke. She explained that Santiago had told her the Guatemalan army was trying an experiment that had worked in Argentina: using physical and psychological torture to break certain valuable prisoners and redirect their sympathies so that they would work permanently for the army. The prisoners were taken out in handcuffs to identify their fallen comrades and reveal the locations of weapons caches and other information. After months of torture and reeducation, they were given an army uniform and a salary. On some, this tactic worked. Not on Santiago. He pretended to have been broken. He joked with the officers, all the while learning their names, ranks, and nicknames. After a couple of years of being a model worker but giving old or rather useless information, he asked to visit his uncle in a nearby town for Christmas. He was given a pass to leave and he fled to Mexico, where he went straight to a human rights organization to report the entire operation.

Santiago saw Everardo tied to a table at the military base two months after Everardo disappeared. An officer was pointing a gun into his mouth and telling him he'd better talk. Two months later, Santiago was sent to another base on a mission, and there he saw Everardo again. His right leg and arm were in a cast. Some kind of drug was being administered from a tank beside the table. Everardo's face and body were grotesquely swollen, and his speech was slurred. Jennifer was sure the army would keep Everardo alive as long as possible. A *comandante* with seventeen years of experience in the mountains, he would be a treasure trove of information, and as long as the peace talks were underway he was valuable as a negotiating chip. Besides Santiago's testimony, the army had left a paper trail. After Everardo disappeared, the URNG leadership requested a description of the body the army said it found after the battle and buried in the cemetery. The army sent the guerrilla leadership a perfect description of Everardo, feature by feature down to the centimeter, including the type of underwear he was wearing. With the description, the army had proved that they had him. And Jennifer had proved that he wasn't in the grave. "I'm not asking that he be exempted from the law," Jennifer finished. "Obviously, he was breaking the law. He was a guerrilla combatant, a revolutionary. I am only asking that the Guatemalan government abide by the Geneva Conventions and international humanitarian law, which make it illegal to secretly detain and torture prisoners of war. This is a test case. Is the Guatemalan government serious about the peace talks? Does it plan to adhere to the human rights accord it just signed with the URNG two months ago? Is the international community — the United States, which is playing a key role as a facilitator in the talks — going to stand by and let the government sign pieces of paper and call that progress toward peace when one of the highest-ranking guerrilla *comandantes* is in a secret army detention center being tortured, when in the past two months alone, human rights violations have skyrocketed? If the army can get away with secretly detaining and torturing the husband of a U.S. citizen, in spite of eye-witness testimony and other evidence, protective orders by the Organization of American States, and condemnation by international human rights organizations, the army will know they can get away with anything. And they will be right."

Jennifer spoke for us all when she asked members of Congress to suspend aid to Guatemala's military until human rights reforms were carried out and to cancel a U.S. National Guard training program that paired U.S. reserves with Guatemalan army soldiers in ventures such as road building. We also asked Congress to withhold economic support funds until the Guatemalan government respected labor rights — many union organizers were still being harassed or killed. Also, we wanted the civil defense patrols abolished; they were supposed to be voluntary organizations, but Julio's resistance to participating was only one example of the brutality that followed such refusals. We demanded, too, that the Guatemalan government recognize communities who had fled into hiding during the massacres of the 1980s as civilian populations instead of continuing to bomb those communities, and that political prisoners and prisoners of war be released or presented to the courts for fair trials. Finally, we demanded that all files containing information about victims of politically motivated disappearances or assassinations be released to family members and human rights organizations, that the rights of returning refugees be fully recognized and respected, and that impunity be brought to an end.

BACK AT THE OFFICE, Alice, Jennifer, and I discussed the briefing after the other coalition members had left. The briefing had gone over well, and we talked about the coalition's potential for growth: at least twenty-six U.S. citizens had been killed in Guatemala since 1976 in circumstances pointing to the Guatemalan army.

I talked about my work in New York and how I was searching for something that would put me in closer touch with Guatemala. Alice crossed her arms, cleared her throat, and tilted her head to the side. "Would you ever consider working here?"

I was flattered. But listening to the children in Queens speak longingly of their mothers and watching Trish and her daughter interact at the briefing, I wanted more than anything to be with my family.

AFTER LEAVING WASHINGTON, I said goodbye to Kim and the children in New York, packed up, and went to New Mexico. I spent my days talking with my mom, playing Scrabble with her, and helping her cook, visiting with Barbara, who had the summers off from teaching, getting to know Shell again, and playing with my nieces and my little brother. Nights we sat around the table long after dinner and talked and joked and listened to my dad play the accordion.

I thought about getting a teaching job there in Grants, or a job gardening or landscaping. I also thought about the job at the commission. Alice said the offer was good whenever I wanted to take it. The job at Alice's office sounded tempting. I wanted to see how she carried out her faith, how she meshed being a nun and working for human rights. She seemed to get a lot done, and I had a feeling that if I were in Washington, I could also make things happen. But that job would mean leaving my family. And I was actually, for the first time I remembered, having fun.

Every now and then there was an entire day when I forgot about what had happened. On one of those days my mom, Barbara, my nieces Amber and Stephanie, and I were having a "girls' day out" in Albuquerque. We did that sometimes — we'd window shop, eat lunch, and see a movie. Sometimes we would link arms or all join hands walking down the sidewalk. The touch of my family no longer threatened me. I craved that touch.

On this particular day, I was having a great time. I wasn't even feeling guilty for doing nothing useful, for living, for enjoying myself. We were in the shopping mall. Mom and my nieces went off in one direction and Barbara and I went in another to look at different things before meeting up later. Barbara and I decided to do something wild, something that would remind us of one another, wherever we were. We each had pierced ears — piercing a baby girl's ears is part of the Hispanic culture, a rite of initiation into the culture and the role of the female. Now that I have a niece with a pierced belly button, what Barbara and I did seems tame, but at the time we felt so radical: we got our ears double-pierced.

I suppose the second piercing was another rite, a mark of my passage back into my family. Each time I put an extra earring in, I think of Barbara and that day, the exhilaration and the sting of the gun and the closeness it forged between us.

WE BOTH KNEW I'd be leaving soon. I knew it somewhere deep down, but I hadn't come to grips with it yet. I had made a promise to the Guatemalans, who were still being butchered. Part of me never wanted to think about torture or human rights violations again. That part wanted to eat my mama's cooking and just be. That part had its way for a couple of months and I would have given into it a while longer.

But I got a package in the mail, a brown envelope that looked like any I might get from Meredith or someone at the Mount. The only thing missing was a return address. I thought maybe Luisa had been rushed — she often sent me flowers from her garden in Kentucky. By the time they arrived, the petals were dried and the stems were rotted with mold where she had wrapped them in foil with water. These flowers were worse than usual, I thought, reaching inside and turning my nose away from the stench. But my hand closed around another envelope, a white one, with something bulky inside.

Denial is amazing. There in my family's house I thought I was safe, so I opened the envelope and pulled out what was inside: a dead rodent, stiff and cold, wrapped in a Guatemalan flag.

For a few minutes I was back in the pit with the claws in my hair. I ran to the bathroom and vomited, then stood under a hot shower where

I could sob without being heard. I wondered for a moment if someone was playing a sick joke. But I was pretty sure the source was more sinister than that. The rage I had squelched for so long burbled to the surface. I refuse to stay in that prison, I thought, that pit, that dark hole of fear and despair. They want war, I'll give them war.

I got out, dressed, and threw the critter away — whether it was a mouse or a baby rat I'm still not sure. Then I called Alice and told her to expect me.

Chapter Fourteen

EVERARDO

THE AIR IN WASHINGTON was thick. Between the branches of trees and the walls of buildings hung something like despair, trapped ideas, ambitions held and let go of. In spite of the wide, tree-lined streets and neighborhoods that changed, wealthy to poor from one block to the next, the heaviness pressed down all over the city. It was something I had noticed since arriving. Maybe it was only the heat that hung in the leaves' umbrella, the pressure of that blurry world that rose up off the street and wanted to keep on rising.

That's what I finally decided, sitting next to Jennifer on the Assisi house steps. We were eating ice cream, and her free hand fluttered as she talked, like a bird testing out the ways it could move. The afternoon shadows stretched out on the lawn and fell across the neighbor's plastic ducks, caught in mid-waddle in a bed of ivy.

Jennifer chewed her cone in quick little bites and leaned back on her elbows in the sunlight. "Hope springs eternal," she said. It was one of her favorite sayings.

Beside her, I almost believed it. There was a grim smile on her face and a kind of steel in her posture, in spite of what she'd just told me: the defense minister had stopped negotiating. On her last trips to Guatemala he wouldn't even meet with her, and no one else in the army would, either. Ambassador McAfee had admitted asking for her case to be removed from the congressional resolution, saying she didn't believe in holding development hostage to an individual case. When Jennifer pointed out that she hadn't asked for other individual cases to be removed, McAfee said, "Well, you have to admit, Jennifer, this case *is* different — he *was* a combatant." Jennifer pointed out that the law didn't recognize any such distinction. McAfee was silent.

"She said I had misunderstood the minister of defense — he had never negotiated. She looked weird, pasty and teary-eyed, like she was going to cry, and she was saying I had no reason to believe Everardo might still be alive. She said, 'Well, he's been gone for such a long time now, Jennifer, and you know how the army is.' "

But beside Jennifer, I could believe that despair was only heat — which, after all, was only a form of energy. Because even now, when she was quiet and staring straight ahead, I could see she had a plan. "I've told the army before," she said at last, "we're all chained by the neck. If he goes down, I go down, and I take them down with me."

I wasn't exactly sure what she meant, but her defiance gave me strength. "Keep your hope alive, Jennifer," I answered.

JENNIFER HAD NO IDEA of her influence on me, or if she did she didn't let on. "You're getting so much stronger every day," she'd tell me every so often as we drank tea together in the dining room or washed dishes after dinner. "I see such a change in you from a few months ago. It's like you're blooming."

Her words were what made me stronger. I clung to them and pictured myself a tall, strong sunflower, standing straight up and opening.

OUR TRIPS TO THE CORNER STORE for ice cream became a daily ritual. I found out later that Jennifer didn't like ice cream; she ate it the way she did most things, absently. But I was glad to see her give herself time to sit. There on the shade-dappled steps, she let her mind slide into the past, and she told me stories about her time with Everardo. I guess she allowed herself that luxury because she was eating the ice cream with a view to the future. It was part of a plan to get him out.

Jennifer explained that Everardo loved her solely for who she was inside, in spite of her looks. Many American men Jennifer had come across saw her big green eyes, her blondish hair, her big chest, and little else. Jennifer had a perfect score on her math SAT, but the men she served cocktails to during a college waitressing job added up the check for her, as if she couldn't. Everardo, on the other hand, understood Jennifer at once.

He cooked her tamales and left them for her breakfast, disappearing before she arrived, or quietly sat beside her at dinner, as if that just happened to be where he found room. When Jennifer had been in the mountains only a few weeks, collecting stories for her book, one of the women told her it was obvious that she and Everardo were interested in one another. She said Jennifer should encourage him; she was an older woman, after all, forty to Everardo's thirty-four. And Everardo needed encouraging. He had already lost two wives, Jennifer explained. The first was shot down before his eyes. The second was disappeared.

To complicate matters, he thought Jennifer might be a CIA plant.

"And you know, he thought I was kind of weird-looking. Like my eyes — he'd never seen anything like them. He told me that finally, once we had gotten together. I thought I was going to get a compliment. But he said they reminded him of a bird of prey."

Jennifer laughed. That was the best thing about the stories. And I liked learning about Everardo. In some ways I could relate to him. He wasn't going to trust just anyone. He wasn't going to become instantly close to someone who might be pulling the wool over his eyes or someone he might end up loving, then losing. He wondered, like me, where the reality lay.

I knew, of course, that Jennifer wasn't CIA. It was the URNG I was worried about. Sometimes I wondered if her ties were closer than she admitted and if she was just using me to push her objectives along. All I could do was continue to get to know her. So the afternoons on the porch and the stories continued.

"We went to a carnival once in Mexico City," she told me. "Everardo had never been to one before. We came across one of those booths with rifles, one of those target shoots. He looks up at the stuffed animal prizes hanging above and says, 'You like those things?'

"I said, 'Yeah. Sure.'

"So he crouches down, spreads his feet apart, and lowers his head, like he's avoiding a hail of bullets.

"I'm looking around thinking, oh, no, he's supposed to be underground in Mexico. You know, he was working on the indigenous position for the peace talks and I was supposed to make sure he was safe. And he's not looking like the average guy at the rifle booth. But it was the only way he knew how to shoot. He hit every little duckie, needless to say, and then handed me this huge teddy bear."

I loved to see her happy, even for a moment, in memory's grip.

"Once we were lying in bed. It was a quiet moment, we were just lying there and Everardo reached up and pinched my nose — an affectionate kind of pinch. I kept a straight face and went 'quack!'

"His eyes got huge. He tried it again, slowly, almost like he was afraid to see what would happen.

"So I quacked again.

"He lay there a minute, staring. Then he just busted out laughing. He never knew what he'd get with me. But that was all right," Jennifer said with a smile. "You know?" She flipped her hair out of her eyes. "He was game for life with this creature he'd ended up with — whatever it was."

I FOUND MYSELF WONDERING, like Everardo, just what kind of creature Jennifer was. She said she was an atheist, but I had never seen anyone so giving, so devoted to doing the right thing, so focused on other people. She saw that I was shy and uncomfortable with nearly everyone in the house, and took it upon herself to help me feel at ease. "It's OK," she would tell me. "These are really good people. You can trust them." She gave me little summaries of my housemates, picking out elements of our lives that were similar. Brother Vianney had been a health promoter in Bolivia, she told me, where many of his friends and coworkers had been disappeared and killed by the army. When Vianney came back to the United States, he tried to talk about the violence he'd seen and the loss he'd experienced. The brothers in his order didn't really want to listen — at least not in the way that Vianney needed them to listen. He had a breakdown and was hospitalized and put on such high doses of drugs that he barely knew where he was. He was using his knowledge of mental illness now to help the homeless of D.C. He counseled them, helped them with day to day tasks, and took them on spiritual retreats. John and Ann, a lively young couple, had lived in El Salvador. Ann conducted travel seminars there, and John had been a musician for church-related events. Because of health problems, both came back before they were ready, and they were having some trouble readjusting to life in the United States and finding the way that they could be most useful.

I saw Jennifer take time to talk with Vianney in the morning and after supper, and she scheduled breakfast with him at a nearby greasy spoon, even when the circles under her eyes were dark purple. She noticed before anyone else in the house when I was having a bad day, and she made time to talk to me and offered me her bubble baths and face creams, the only luxuries she permitted herself. Once she slipped off the silver ring on her finger. "Here, want to wear this for a while?" She put it on the table beside me.

I picked it up and looked at it closely for the first time. The ring appeared to be a silver twist, but it was an arching dolphin. This is a sign, I thought. Jennifer is the dolphin on my journey. She had led me to a circle of people, many of them wounded, and she was inviting me to reach out and take their hands. The dolphin of my reverie was playful, confident, invulnerable. Jennifer could seem that way.

But after the funny stories the sad ones came. She stared blankly at her bare feet and didn't even try to finish eating. Her ice cream lay melting in the ivy. She'd wanted to have a baby. She and Everardo had tried for six months. Finally, she found herself pregnant. But when the news came that he had disappeared, she lost the baby.

She brushed some imaginary dust off her jeans. My eyes filled with tears. I couldn't help thinking that the soldiers had taken two lives, not one, because I didn't think she'd get Everardo back. Jennifer saw my eyes and blinked hard to keep her own tears in. I had felt the depth of her wounds, and I no longer questioned whether she was a guerrilla plant, telling carefully concocted stories for propaganda purposes. Sometimes it's easier to believe you're being hoodwinked — a barrier of doubt and mistrust are protective. You don't have to do anything. You don't have to feel the other person's pain. From then on out, everything that hurt Jennifer hurt me.

WE BECAME LIKE SISTERS. I talked to her about my secret wishes — things I wouldn't have told anyone else, not even Barbara or Michelle. I thought they might be too conservative to understand, and besides, I didn't trust the phone or the mail. I thought no one but Mimi would understand, and she was far away in Chile. So I told Jennifer that I, too, had a secret wish to be a mother, to have another chance.

She didn't judge me for the choice I made when I found myself pregnant, and she didn't judge my desire for a baby. She said it was a natural desire for a woman to have. She didn't seem to think it mattered that I was a woman who, at least technically, was still a nun. Bodies, she explained, don't understand such distinctions. I still had the feelings of a woman. She talked to me about artificial insemination, just so I would know there were options, ways to have a baby without ever going near a man. She answered all my questions. And she told me she thought I'd be a good mother.

I looked forward to the stories on the porch and to all the intimacies we shared, and I felt I knew Everardo, that I had seen him through Jennifer's eyes. But I wondered if he would ever be the same, if he would ever reach out to touch another person so easily or be capable of play and laughter — if I should show Jennifer his future through my eyes. The torturers had me for twenty-four hours and I had begged to die. I still kept my razor blade nearby, under a seashell on my dresser. I was still sure sometimes that dying back there would have been preferable to this afterlife. And what I thought as the ice cream ran in quick tears down Jennifer's cone and the sunlight gleamed off her thinning hair, what I thought and would never say, was that if he was lucky Everardo would already be dead. That meant he would be lying, perhaps, in a mass grave, thrown away like a piece of trash, like he didn't matter, like nothing he ever did mattered. But at least the torture would be over. I knew what they had done to me in twenty-four hours. They would have had him for two and a half years.

THEY'D HAD ME for twenty-four hours and I still struggled. Organizing Coalition Missing materials, a tiny task I'd been hired to do, drained my strength. By two o'clock, sometimes even by noon, I had to leave. Alice gamely took me home, day after day, without raising an eyebrow. "You'll get used to the work," she said. "It takes a while."

On every page of every report were police officers, bodies. I had planned to forget about my case. I had done all I could, and pursuing justice through the OAS simply involved waiting while my lawyers carried out the paper work. I had meant to focus, not on what happened to me, but on the broader issue of Guatemala and what I could do to help. But I couldn't read the reports of unidentified bodies found on the roadside without smelling the stench of the pit and seeing the limbs, the caked blood on the skin. When I read about the marks of torture I heard the screams that echoed in the basement.

Alice and the other staff member, Patricia, who translated the human rights reports sent from Guatemala, seemed to have put a wall between their feelings and the atrocities. Patricia focused on finding the right words. She asked us to help her choose between phrases like "a unionist was beaten to death" and "a unionist was found dead of blunt force trauma to the head." What sounded most like English, most normal? Alice, the interns, and I were supposed to proofread the *Update* before it went out and pinpoint anything that sounded awkward. The staff was almost obsessed with perfection, as if by reporting the horrors in the most irreproachable way they could somehow right them. After a few weeks I begged off from proofreading. The artifice of words couldn't protect me. The words simply drew me in to the other side of the Politécnica's stones and left me there with the screams.

I discovered my own way of coping. When the *Update* was finished, I took it to my office, which overlooked the leafy treetops. The sunlight fell onto my desk, onto the page, dazzling me. I lit a candle. Then I carefully cut out the names of the disappeared and tortured and placed them in a large glass jar which I kept hidden under my desk. I remembered the names, held them in my head. Those people, at least, were not anonymous. They were not forgotten.

I think I was so focused on capturing names because I hadn't gotten the Woman's. But the names curled around each other as they mounted up. I couldn't remember them all, and I couldn't see them all. The jar was filling, becoming a mass grave of names, a pit.

Each name needed its own space. I started a notebook, gluing one name onto one page at night when everyone was sleeping. When I had worked my way through the *Updates,* I closed the notebook. The cover thudded shut, like the lid of a coffin. And more people just kept dying.

I suspended my rescue attempts with the scissors. But still I tried to save the names from the cold pages of a report, from oblivion, from silence. It occurred to me that I could call the State Department's new desk officer, Peg Willingham, every day — it was a local call — and ask for updates on each case. I said the names of the assassinated and disappeared aloud. With each call she had to repeat the same thing: there were no updates. I was hoping that, out of the tedium of this litany if nothing else, she would find some new information.

I was never at a loss for cases. Between May and July, a GAM member had been stabbed, two campesino leaders had been shot to death, and another human rights leader had been killed by a military commissioner. The fifteen-year-old son of a labor union leader was shot and stabbed to death as he walked down the street, and a unionist was abducted with a friend in Guatemala City. Their bodies were found two days later, with numerous stab wounds and marks where they'd been strangled with barbed wire. Another labor leader was in a coma after being shot six times. Several students involved in progressive causes were shot by police officers, and a newspaper reporter was abducted, beaten, and interrogated. In only twelve weeks, forty people had been tortured and seventy-four assassinated. Although Guatemala was moving toward a peace treaty with the help of six countries, including the United States, acting as facilitators and many more watching the process and promising money when the accord was signed, the army was getting away with murder.

Alice explained that the army was getting rid of the opposition before the United Nations Verification Mission arrived. The UN mission, which would consist of hundreds of observers, would monitor the human rights situation and report on violations of the accords already signed. Until then, apparently, it was open season.

As ALICE WAS DRIVING me home one day, I asked her how she could keep working when the situation was so bad and whatever we did seemed so useless. She worked from eight in the morning until suppertime, then from eight in the evening until midnight, every night of the week. Instead of taking a salary from the budget, she lived on the $500 a month her family and friends sent. I couldn't see what good it was doing.

She looked over once, quickly. Her eyes were clear gray and her words when she spoke were those of a woman who knew a childhood of long winters, with average temperatures of twenty below, crushing poverty, and the fear that her ancestry and her mother tongue would mark her as a traitor. They were sensible, German American, Minnesota words: "Well, you don't know how much worse it might be if we wouldn't be doing the work."

STILL, I ASKED MYSELF if I was in the right place. Was I only revictimizing myself, subjecting myself, though a few steps removed, to the helplessness of watching other people be tortured? Was the idea that we could help only a cruel illusion? I pictured the sisters in my community clucking and saying I should move on with my life, that I was obsessed with Guatemala and what happened to me. I felt guilty sometimes. Teaching children was what I had been trained to do and the Ursulines were a teaching order. Every day that I went to the GHRC office was a reminder that I wasn't living as an Ursuline. It was a reminder of my rift with God.

BUT ALICE WAS SURE that what she was doing was God's work. She had so much confidence in her judgment. Also a member of a teaching order, the School Sisters of Notre Dame, Alice had been a first-grade teacher and a school principal for decades before moving into human rights work. A glass plaque on her desk that said "Jesus" and the cross she wore around her neck were the only overt indications of her faith, but when she had a decision to make she became quiet and drew into herself. Then she would move ahead with confidence. "The thing is, Dianna, we're teaching people about Guatemala," Alice told me once. "And you can't say that's not education. It's something that no one else is doing. The schools aren't doing it and the newspapers sure aren't doing it."

I still had my doubts — not about Alice's intentions but about the ability of some of our pupils to be educated. They were members of Congress, immigration judges, INS officials, and State Department officials, as well as the general public. Someone had to try, I guess, but there was also such a thing as being realistic.

Yet didn't Jesus himself ask us to have the faith of a child? Maybe practicing faith and hope on a religious level gave Alice an advantage in human rights work — she learned to believe in her own efforts and hope that conditions would change in Guatemala.

PARADOXICALLY, what gave me hope was a paper I came across in a file one day, a list with names of the dead. "Religious Killed or Disappeared in Guatemala since 1976," it said at the top. Beneath the heading were twenty-six names. Thirty-six religious workers had been killed in Guatemala — in fewer than twenty years. I had no idea so many had died. I stared at the list for a long time. Most of the dead were Guatemalans. Others were Spanish, Belgian, French, and American. Words I had heard for years from U.S. embassy personnel went through my mind: *Why would anyone attack an American nun? What would they possibly have to gain?* — as if it had never happened before. And here in Alice's files was proof that in the nine years before my abduction and torture, three other U.S. missionaries had been killed. All the circumstances suggested the army.

Attacks on internationals and religious alike seemed to have ended during the mid- to late 1980s. That's why the bishop of Huehuetenango advised me not to worry too much about the threatening letters; it wasn't the early 1980s, he said, and foreigners weren't being attacked. But in 1989, the army's campaign against the Church, as well as against internationals, resumed. And by attacking me, the army was efficient. It hit two targets at once.

Scholar Angela delli Sante, in *Nightmare or Reality: Guatemala in the 1980s*, describes the scene well:

> As a result of [the Church's] persistent criticism of government corruption, as well as of almost all government policies, including military spending, in conjunction with its growing support for the grass roots movement, the poor, the National Dialogue, and peace talks with the URNG, repression against the Catholic hierarchy, clergy, nuns, and catechists was greatly intensified in 1989. For example, during the entire second half of the year, the archbishop was to receive constant threats, warning him to give up his involvement in the problems of the country or face death, while in April, two Guatemalan priests were attacked, robbed, and beaten up. Furthermore, in October, sister Patricia Denny, a U.S. nun, was threatened and told to leave the country or face death.... [I]n November, Rolando Lam, a member of the Archdiocesan Lay Committee, was assassinated.... Moreover, during the very last month of the year, the parochial house of Santa Cruz Comitancillo was raided, and the priest and General Vicar of the diocese of San Marcos, Father José Maria Carrera, was threatened. Not of lesser importance are the cat-

echists, many of whom suffered diverse forms of repression, including kidnappings and disappearances throughout the entire year.

Besides transgressions against individuals, the army apparently tried to intimidate the Catholic congregation as a whole, by attempting to interfere with freedom of religion. Two things strongly suggest this. First, in an unprecedented act, they sent out questionnaires to certain parishes, asking parishioners to express their views about the priests, the Church, the armed forces, etc., and second, they instructed the PACs [civil defense patrols] in some communities to pressure Catholics into refraining from participating in Catholic meetings, discussions, and religious services.[1]

The poverty I saw in San Miguel had made me angry. I know from my letters that I'd begun, for the first time, to question. I no longer believed that the way the world was was right. It was unjust. Did the army intercept my letters? Or did God intercept my doubts? Which one decided to punish me?

Or was the torture, in fact, not about me? At Kovler the therapists had tried to teach us that torture was political, not personal, that we were attacked as part of a strategy involving the broader society. I never understood. It seemed personal when it was my own skin that was burned, my own memories that were obliterated. Seeing the list, I understood, finally, that the Guatemalan army may not have had any personal issue with me, Dianna Ortiz. It was the "Sister" in front of my name that had made me a target — like the Sister and Father and Brother in front of all these other names. The attack on me was actually an attack on the Church.

I wish I could have understood sooner. The torturers' words had interfered. They kept telling me I had to be questioned because I was the woman in the photo, who they said was Verónica Ortiz Hernández, a guerrilla. Alejandro, too, said they had made a mistake and confused me with her. I couldn't quite believe that; I looked nothing like the woman in the photo, and the torturers knew I was a U.S. nun living in San Miguel Acatán. But still I had trouble untangling all the threads. When people like Mimi said I was abducted because I worked with the Church, I would find myself thinking, "No, I was abducted because the torturers confused me with somebody else." Then I would remember why that couldn't be true, and I would end up thinking, again, "Why me? I wasn't involved in anything concerning the guerrillas." Now I could finally see the answer clearly. Representing the Church was subversive enough.

Yet all the millions of monks and nuns, laypeople and priests in the Maryknoll order and Christian Brothers, who had endured the losses of so many, continued believing in and working for God. They must have found a way to forgive God, or a way to exonerate God. I couldn't forgive my torturers, but if they and God were not one and the same — were not, somehow, linked, by complicity if nothing else — I mean, God could have stepped in when I begged and pleaded, and inaction *is* complicity; but if God were separate and blameless, trustworthy and worthy of reverence or forgiveness, then there was hope.

THE ASSISI HOUSE was a "faith community," which means the ideals and activities of the house were centered on principles of faith. Each morning at dawn the community prayed together, and once a week, before the house meeting, Joe said Mass. At Assisi, unlike at Su Casa, everyone went to Communion. I didn't go. In Guatemala I absolutely needed it for strength, and I made an exception for myself, but I knew well enough that somewhere in the Bible was the instruction not to bring any hard feelings or resentments to the altar. And since those Guatemala trips I had hardened. If I did take Communion, could God's grace even find its way, I wondered, past the stalactites of bitterness in my chest?

At Su Casa, we'd all struggled to get through the day, with no energy or belief left over. Although each day lived was a statement, an act of resistance to the torturers simply because it was lived, at the Assisi community people were embracing life and working to resist the culture of selfishness, imperialism, domination, and violence — the culture that in many cases had given rise to regimes that tortured. They had faith in themselves, in their work, in their lives, and in God (with the exception of Jennifer — and it was clear to me that, although she didn't believe in God, God believed in her and was working through her).

I felt so inferior to everyone else. I woke up when the sun was already shining in the window at full strength and the odors of coffee and toast were rising up the stairwell. When I went downstairs I would avoid meeting anyone's eyes. The last thing I wanted to see was reproach. I'd slept through prayers again.

One night at the house meeting I summoned the nerve to explain my absences. Until I heard Marie's alarm clock and stirring in the house, I couldn't sleep, but as soon as the room lightened and people were awake I felt safe enough to drift off.

I expected an uncomfortable silence in response to my explanation, strained, polite mumblings, perhaps some coughing or surreptitious hand-wringing as people wondered what they had gotten themselves into by letting such a nutcase move in. Instead, a chorus of voices assured me that being at prayers was something people did for themselves if they found it helpful, not something that was required or even expected. "There are all kinds of ways of praying," John said. "What we do, the work we do every day, is prayer."

THAT THOUGHT gave me a new kind of freedom. Getting up and going to the office didn't have to be something that confirmed my alienation from God and my community but could be instead something that joined me to both. I began to search for God, not only in people, but in the actions I took throughout the day. If work was a form of prayer, it was a way of encountering God. The religious life that I had chosen so long ago and that I thought I would have to leave behind — the life I thought the torturers had taken — didn't seem so irreconcilable anymore with my experience in Guatemala, which had brought me to the work I was doing now.

As for doubts, Joe, Marie, and Vianney, who seemed so holy and full of faith, doubted God at times, too, I learned. And as far as obsessions went, Marie, Jennifer, and Alice all were said to be obsessed with their work. But if they knew about such criticisms, they ignored them, and the majority of people who spoke about them said they had vision and commitment. Things had so many dimensions. The world wasn't so flat and predetermined. There were so many possibilities. I had so many choices, even of ways to see.

JOE PICKED ME UP one day from work just as the leaves started turning. As I ducked into the car I was dazzled by the carmine leaves of a maple tree. "Joe, look how beautiful that tree is!" I said, jumping back out.

He looked. Then, settling himself back and starting the car, he said, "Now I know you're better. I've never heard you say something is beautiful. Your eyes are dancing."

I had seen the beauty of the spring foliage during my first stay at the hospital. But pointing out something beautiful to someone else was new, and I had done it spontaneously. Joe could have answered, "How interesting that you find beauty in something that's dying. What does that say about you?" Or "It does nothing for me. Anyway, in a few weeks it'll be gone." I was showing him a treasure I'd discovered, and if he had told me it was junk when I had so recently decided it was treasure, when I'd so recently decided to scoop it up and hold it — I and it would have been crushed. But Joe said, yes, that's treasure, how good that you see it.

Although it was afternoon and the sun was sinking and the days growing shorter, the leaves were keeping the sun's colors — the pink of dawn, the gold of day, and the red of sunset — and would hold them through the night. I, too, was starting to hold summer light.

LATE AT NIGHT, early in the morning, I found myself thinking, "Hang on, Everardo. Be strong. Jennifer's fighting for you. She's trying to get you out."

I began pestering Peg about Everardo's case. Her response was the one Jennifer had heard from everyone else in the U.S. government: "We're continuing to raise the case at the highest levels."

"How about doing more than raising the case? Since when has raising a case ever saved a life in Guatemala?" Living with Jennifer, I knew all the comebacks.

Peg spluttered for a moment. By the next day she would have some kind of answer. But by the next day my heart would pound even faster as I dialed her number. In spite of what I told myself about Everardo being better off dead, his suffering over, I wanted him to come out of that prison. If anyone could bring him back to who he'd been before through love and determination alone, it was Jennifer.

I wanted him to teach me all about herbs. I was growing basil and cilantro in the back garden. I pictured him gently hollowing out a space in the earth for seeds of new plants I had never seen. (Even though he was a *comandante* I knew he was gentle. Jennifer didn't have to tell me so specifically. She had sketched him out for me and he had taken on life.)

He was proud and stubborn, too. We had that in common. When he was a child, he lived in a shack with a dirt floor, like all the other workers on the cotton plantation. From the time he was big enough to be useful, he was in the fields. When his father was away, his aunt was supposed to feed him, but she beat and insulted him first. So he quit asking for food and tolerated the hunger. By the time he was in his teens he realized that nothing lay before him but long, backbreaking days and unending poverty. He ran off to the mountains and met up with the guerrillas. Gaspar taught him to read and write. The hunger and harsh conditions continued there, but there he had hope and self-respect.

I pictured talking to him across the table. I'd ask him about the ancient Mayan civilization, and I'd tell him of my love and respect for the culture and my concern about the poverty. I'd acknowledge how the Church I belonged to had oppressed the Mayans in previous centuries when missionaries imposed the Catholic faith. I would tell him I understood why he had taken up arms, even though I didn't think I could ever do that. Maybe I would elaborate and tell him that if I had had a gun in that clandestine prison I would have used it — but that I could never take up arms now. I would kill myself if I picked up a gun. And violence wasn't the best way. But no, I'd probably just tell him I understood, and I'd watch him eat and watch Jennifer beside him, her eyes filled with light.

THE OPPRESSIVENESS I explained away as the Washington weather didn't diminish as the mornings became brisker and the grass and leaves whitened with frost. If I hadn't been steeped in denial, I might have attributed the heavy air to the held breaths of hundreds of thousands of people keeping secrets. Within about twenty square miles were the CIA, NSA, FBI, DEA, DIA, Pentagon, and State Department. But I'd forgotten about them. Washington for me meant Sister Alice and human rights work. That was the only way I could live there. Luckily, no one ever told me that Washington was a nerve center of Guatemalan intelligence operations, that Guatemalan agents who specialized in keeping tabs on U.S. human rights activists were based there, and that I was living in the very mouth of the beast. Within a year that beast would begin to bite. But even after a few months I heard the first low growl.

It came in the form of a hello. I was finishing my walk, fixing in my mind the sloping green lawns and the gardens with roses bending under their own weight. Bringing those images back into the office made the work easier. The yard next to the office had just been cut, and mown grass lay in clumped rows. I stepped onto the stairs that led up to the office and breathed deeply, filling my lungs with the sweet scent.

"Hola, Dianna." The voice was a man's, a Latino man's. He had come out of nowhere. How else could it be? It would be the Guate-man. He would have a gun. Everything would start over. I didn't want to turn around. This world would be taken from me.

His hair was short and dark. But his forehead wasn't high, and his lower lip wasn't thick beneath a long, uneven mustache. He wasn't the Guate-man. And he didn't have a gun.

But he curled his lips into a gloating smile. I stared at the ovals of dark plastic that hid his eyes. I understood his smile: the army could feed out the leash, let me run a bit, give me the illusion of freedom, but at any moment jerk the chain back and cut off my breath.

He was right. My breath wasn't coming. But I forced myself to stare a bit longer at the darkness in front of his eyes, willing my own eyes to betray nothing. I wanted him to believe he hadn't scared me. I wanted him to know that I wasn't afraid to look out and see the world as it was — the brilliance of the sunlight — and I was no longer afraid to show what was in my eyes.

Then I turned and climbed the stairs, trying not to run, trying to be dignified. But I was listening for his footsteps behind me, waiting for his hand on my arm.

The worst the G-2 could do to me here, I consoled myself after reaching the safety of my office, was to say "Hola" and smile. It would take more than that to get me to stop working.

I HAD PROVED TO MYSELF that I could look people in the eye — not only normal people, but G-2 Guatemalan army people. If only he hadn't been wearing sunglasses. If he'd had to meet my gaze, could he have done it? Could anyone who had been involved in torture and murder look into the eyes of a survivor coldly, without remorse?

I jumped at the chance to find out. When Alice mentioned she'd been invited by the State Department to address a group of Guatemalan army officers, I told her I wanted to go. I wanted to make them look me in the eye. I wanted them to squirm.

ALICE CALLED the State Department contact and asked if she could bring along another staff member.

"Yes, of course," the State Department contact answered. When Alice gave her my name, the State Department officer's voice became strained, polite but slightly frantic. "What might Sister Dianna be planning to say?"

Alice explained, "She just wants to listen."

I WORE THE BUTTON Alice had sent me years ago that said, "Torture in Guatemala: Make It Stop," and sat at the front of a large room at Georgetown University, staring down at the heads of row upon row of uniformed men. Alice gave her talk on human rights, and at the end of it an officer raised his hand.

"You have said that in Guatemala there is torture. How do you know that this is true?"

"Well, Sister Dianna Ortiz is sitting right here," Alice said.

All the eyes turned to me.

They were seeing what I had done to the Woman, that I was like they were, an example of a torturer, not of someone who was tortured. I wanted to hold my hands before my face. But I forced myself to look back, straight into their eyes, and told myself what I had told Alejandro: we're not the same because you don't value human life.

Everyone was silent for what seemed a long while, then the officers began clearing their throats and shifting in their chairs.

Alice dismissed them with an awkward remark of thanks, but I continued to stare. They slinked past me, one by one, out the door. One officer stopped in front of me, and I dropped my eyes to my hands. I had gone too far, I was now in for it. I braced for a punch, an insult, warm saliva trickling down my skin.

"I am sorry for what happened to you," he said. "We are trying to improve the past. We are trying to reform."

I almost wanted to raise my eyes; he sounded sincere. But no doubt I would see hatred in his face, a leer, sarcasm, and realize I'd been tricked. It was one of their tactics. José, too, had sounded sincere, had asked for forgiveness, sanction. And what was I supposed to say, "That's OK"?

"I am sorry," he said again. And after a moment he left.

Now I wish I had dared to look him in the eye. That was the real test — not to look in the eyes of those who wished me ill or didn't believe me. Defiance was so much easier than trust, so much easier than hope, so much easier than daring to see in the eyes of the enemy the humanity that could link us.

IN SPITE OF MY ANTICS, the G-2 man's "greeting" had affected me more than I wanted to admit. When I heard his voice, the world I'd come to believe in since escaping almost vanished. It's hard to explain. It was as if the torturers had given me a few years to dream a sweet dream of freedom, just to be cruel, just to have the sadistic pleasure of seeing my face when I woke up again. They didn't take me back. My life went on, but not my belief in life. I found it harder to hope. If hope was a bird, it was back in its cage. The torturers were too powerful and this life too uncertain.

I TRY TO TALK to Everardo. But I picture him getting out and not knowing who Jennifer is. I picture him containing nothing more than what the torturers have poured into him. What if they've destroyed him and hand him back as a cruel joke, an example of their power — if for the rest of his life he tries to move forward against the pull of the torture that has made him untouchable, blind — and if he just keeps snapping back into his past, into the bowl of his head, the only world they left him?

"If I were in your situation, Everardo, I'd try to find a way to get myself killed, even if it meant aggravating the torturers. If you have that way out, take it."

Why did I say that to Everardo? I wonder later. I've been telling Jennifer to keep her hope alive. And I'm telling Everardo to get himself killed.

I DON'T REMEMBER how Jennifer told us of her plan. Neither does anyone else. I suppose no one wants to remember. But I have the letter she wrote us just before she started her last-ditch effort to save Everardo's life:

October 6, 1994

Dear GHRC and Assisi House Friends —

I want to start by sending you all a big hug with much love and thanks for your great support and kindness for me throughout this saga. I will never forget.

I am writing to put down all of my thoughts on medical intervention, etc., during the hunger strike. I want to make my decisions clear, but so much depends on how the army and the international community responds that it is hard to make clear-cut decisions in advance. However, I've thought it over carefully and this is what I think is best for me:

(1) If, prior to 20 days, I should lose consciousness or suffer renal failure, etc., I consent to hospitalization. (Shorter than 20 days will have little impact — so I am willing to go to a hospital.)

(2) At the end of 20 days, I will have had plenty of time to evaluate and will make a clear decision as to whether or not I want medical intervention at a later date or not.

(3) I accept all advice from friends about the situation and my own status, but reserve the final decision as my own to make — barring the circumstances in #1 above. If I choose *no intervention* at the 20-day mark, please let the decision stand. I realize that I will later lose reasoning abilities — but this will only be part of the process I have chosen. I take *full* responsibility.

Love and Abrazos —
Jennifer

The army would have to give Everardo or his body back or Jennifer might die. I wanted to scream this at the house meeting the night before her hunger strike started. The community members were joking, laughing — talking about other issues — cooks for the week and who would do the shopping. I wanted to shout at them that we only had twenty days, think about it, and what if even then the army couldn't give Jennifer what she was asking for? What if Everardo was dead and his body had been burned or thrown into the sea? What if Jennifer was getting herself into a situation she couldn't get out of?

But I was new, and these people had been activists for years. Maybe that's why they weren't afraid — because they had so much experience that they knew things would work out all right. But Marie was pale and quiet, and her lips were set in a straight line. A chill went through me. I pulled my sweater tighter and crossed my arms, but still I was starting to shake.

Jennifer began her hunger strike in Guatemala the next day, faxing up an announcement which we sent out all over the United States. Patricia, who knew Jennifer well, was faxed a power of attorney. Shaking and hoarse, she could barely speak. "She's going to die, Dianna. She won't give up. When we were in Guatemala over the summer we were talking about that movie *Thelma and Louise*. You know the part where Thelma says, 'Let's not get caught. Drive, Louise'?"

I hadn't seen the movie, but I nodded.

"She says, 'Drive, Louise,' because they're surrounded by police and their only choice is to surrender or to drive over the edge of the Grand Canyon. So they go roaring over the cliff. Jennifer said, 'That's the way to do it. You don't surrender. You die.'"

WITHIN THE FIRST WEEK we had faxed and called everyone on a long list of friends, some of them Jennifer's, some of them ours. And by the end of that first week we knew that many of the groups and people we had counted as friends were turning their backs. Either they were afraid of being too closely associated with Jennifer because her husband was a guerrilla or they disagreed with the measures she wanted the United States to take to pressure the Guatemalan government on her case. Important groups in New York and in Washington, especially, clung to their own agendas regarding policy and pressure points. That Jennifer's life was at stake, as well as Everardo's, was inconsequential. Yes, they had met her. Yes, they had promised to help in whatever way they could. But they wouldn't be pressured by a hunger strike.

I knew what the real problem was. I had heard it articulated at a meeting during one of my first weeks in Washington. A leader of one of the groups had said Jennifer was a plant from her husband's URNG faction and was trying to control policy in Washington. I was the only one from GHRC present, and I should have spoken up in her defense. But I was shy and afraid and I kept my mouth shut. Or was that back when I wasn't sure of

Jennifer myself? I felt like Judas. Maybe all this indifference, which could cost Jennifer's life, owed, in part, to my silence. I vowed never to let my fear stand in the way of defending her again.

At least she wasn't alone in Guatemala. People from all over the United States were taking turns going to Guatemala to be with her, affording her some protection and attending to her needs as best they could. Human Rights Watch and the National Lawyers Guild were organizing delegations to Guatemala, and outside of Washington Jennifer had the support of many individuals and groups. Calls and faxes poured into the State Department, the Guatemalan embassy, and the White House. The State Department's fax machines, we heard, were completely tied up.

What Peg Willingham said as Jennifer's condition worsened was, "Well, Jennifer has chosen to be in that weakened state."

She has chosen the slurred speech, the eyelid drooping from nerve damage? She has chosen it or the United States has driven her to it by refusing to do anything to help Everardo? Now I wasn't the only one calling every day, peppering Peg with questions. We heard that the State Department had to put in a special line to deal with the volume of calls. Poor Peg. I guess I was the first flake of snow in the avalanche she was standing under.

We worked sixteen-hour days, often sleeping in the office at night in case some emergency arose. Even if it didn't, there was always more to do, another fax to read, another phone message to jot down, another contact to make. This must be a tiny taste of what Jennifer has dealt with these two years, I realized. Any moment of rest could cost the life of the person you were trying to save — and, as you worked, so could any mistake, misstatement, misjudgment, missed chance.

For Jennifer, though, the situation was much more complicated. Not only every moment that she did nothing, but every step she took — every bit of publicity, every bit of pressure on the army — was a step that could get Everardo killed. As the publicity and pressure increased, the army could kill him to retaliate or to begin covering the evidence of such a highly publicized crime. "You know that when you start looking for them, that's when they kill them," a human rights official in Guatemala had told Jennifer the year before, just to make sure she understood the way the army operated.

"I know," Jennifer had responded. "I just can't bear to think of him under torture. And I have to try."

I LEARNED FROM SANTIAGO, the witness who saw Everardo, that not everyone is affected by torture in the same way. When he came into the office,

I was shocked to see that he was barely more than twenty. He had the dark skin of the Mam indigenous, the kind of down-turned nose you could see portrayed in the art of the ancient Maya, long eyelashes, clear, dark, intelligent eyes, and a quiet, dignified manner. He was extremely polite to everyone. Even to visitors who spoke no Spanish, he communicated respect — standing, nodding, smiling, and shaking hands. He was in Washington to testify before the Inter-American Commission of the OAS. While he waited for his OAS hearing to be scheduled, he managed to find ways to help around the office, taking on photocopying jobs to free up people's time for other things, sending faxes, weeding the garden, cleaning the yard.

But his time could be spent in more valuable ways. When we called State Department officials to ask them to act on Jennifer's case, they invariably said the same thing: "We have no independent evidence of clandestine detention in Guatemala. If we had a witness, it would be different." The answer infuriated me. If there was no clandestine detention, where did they think torture happened? In a public place, where people were free to leave? Or did they also deny that torture occurred?

We called the same officials back. "The witness is right here," we told them, "and he wants to meet with you." We made appointments for Santiago with Peg Willingham and various other State Department and congressional representatives. I knew the meeting with Peg would be difficult, and I wanted Santiago to have a survivor with him, someone who understood how it felt not to be believed. No one had believed him yet. Jennifer had sent his testimony out a year and a half earlier, but U.S. officials had ignored or dismissed it.

ALICE DROPPED US OFF at the door of the monolithic, gray building. I was terrified. Only a few months ago I had been afraid to appear before Congress with Jennifer — well-spoken, middle-class, ivy-educated Jennifer — because she was the wife of a guerrilla. Now I was in the State Department, the institution Stroock had worked for, with an indigenous guerrilla combatant.

After handing over our identification and receiving a badge in exchange, we waited for Peg to escort us up to her office. I recognized her before she introduced herself. She looked as I thought she might — short hair, of a brownish color, glasses, and pointy blue shoes. We walked down the long, white hallway, and her work identity badge bobbed against her chest like an external heartbeat.

I remembered the cigarette game, how the torturers insisted on who I was, who I wasn't. I wasn't going to wear any badge the State Department gave me, especially one that said Visitor. I wasn't at the State Department to visit. I was there to make something happen. I held the badge in my hand.

Peg sat crisply down at her desk and motioned to a couple of chairs on the other side. "So tell me what you know about the Bámaca case."

"I will." Santiago was sitting up very straight. He looked like a Mayan prince.

I pressed my forearms against my stomach to keep it from nervous rumbling, but Santiago clearly wasn't frightened by Peg or her manner.

"I will tell you about Comandante Everardo, but first I am going to tell you a little about the history of the guerrillas, what the movement is and how it began."

I was stunned. But walking in and telling Peg he'd talk about what he liked — and of all subjects to choose the one least palatable to the U.S. government — was nothing, I suppose, compared to what Santiago had already done and what was still left for him to do: name the officers who tortured and detained him and many others. Then, instead of asking for political asylum, he would go back to his life in Mexico. I knew he planned eventually to return to Guatemala and he planned to live there, even after implicating the highest levels of the army in dozens of cases of secret detention and torture. He was in love and planned to settle down when the war was over with a woman who'd fought by his side. That was Santiago, even after months of brutal physical torture and years of psychological torture. A thought crept into my mind as Santiago began his measured, dignified discourse. Everardo, getting out, might be able to live and love. He might be OK.

People were fighting for the rights of the destitute Mayan majority, Santiago said. The struggle had really been going on for five hundred years, since the Spanish conquest.

Peg began twirling her pen. No doubt she thought Santiago was spewing propaganda — Marxist, Maoist, or at the very least terrorist propaganda.

But Santiago went on. His faction, known as the Revolutionary Organization of the People in Arms (ORPA), was led by a city-bred intellectual of European descent, Gaspar Ilóm. Gaspar was the son of Miguel Ángel Asturias, who had won the Nobel Prize for Literature. An educated, privileged, upper-middle-class young man, Gaspar could have had a comfortable life, but he put all his inheritance into the armed revolution and went off into the mountains, where he encountered Everardo, who became the fourth member of Gaspar's group. Gaspar taught him to read and write.

Santiago fought under Everardo and knew him well. When he saw Everardo in the base in San Marcos, Santiago recognized him instantly. He saw Everardo chained to a table, being interrogated by an officer who was shoving a gun barrel into his mouth and screaming at him, "How do you want to die?"

Later, Santiago was sent in to demoralize him, to tell him the revolution was over and he may as well give up and tell everything. Everardo had already heard it from other guerrillas, people he'd once fought with who had snapped after five months of brutalization. Santiago entered the room and didn't say a word. Everardo looked into his eyes. He could see that Santiago, in spite of his army uniform, hadn't been broken. Then he spoke: "Tell the *compañeros* I'm here. Get word out that I've been captured."

"I can't get out," Santiago whispered. "I'm watched too closely."

SANTIAGO'S EYES ROLLED BACK. He rubbed at them.

I didn't know if the eye movement was the start of a flashback. I'd seen him struggling with his eyes from time to time in the office, and on the days he rubbed them most he'd go home with a migraine. I wished I had an aspirin or something to give him. Finally, after a few hard blinks, he folded his hands in his lap again and stared at them.

"I just couldn't get out. They would have killed me if I had tried to escape sooner than I did. And then I couldn't have gotten the word out about him at all. I thought about it all the time. One hour I'd have one plan. The next hour I'd have another plan. But none of them would have worked. I had to wait."

Santiago was wrestling with his guilt. I had heard so many survivors of torture go over and over a choice they had made. No matter how logical and obvious it was that they had made the best choice or taken the only course of action open to them — sometimes there were no choices — they still felt that they could have done something different, and no amount of reasoning took that feeling away. I knew that from experience. I hoped Peg wouldn't notice how Santiago was struggling and try to exploit his guilt, as Stroock had done in my case, telling Paul that if I had remembered the location of the clandestine prison, some of the people I heard screaming could have been saved.

No. Peg was looking at her watch.

Santiago saw Everardo being put into a helicopter, which he heard was bound for Guatemala City. A short while later, an officer gathered all the prisoners together and announced that Everardo had tried to escape, once he was in the capital, and had been shot to death. He watched their faces closely to see who reacted. Santiago kept his face like a stone.

He next saw Everardo when he was asked to take a typewriter into a room. He was on a different base now from the one where he'd first seen Everardo, and he believed Everardo was dead, so he was shocked to open the door and find Everardo lying on a cot, his body swollen to twice its normal size. Colonel Julio Alpírez, along with several other officers and a doctor, was bent over him, and a tank of some kind of gas was next to the bed. Everardo's arm and leg were in a cast. He was speaking in a strange voice, babbling, as if he were drugged. Santiago took in the scene in about three seconds, which was all the time he had before he was ordered out and threatened with death if he ever revealed what he had seen.

Five months more of careful obedience and Santiago escaped. "So that is what I know of Comandante Everardo," he finished. "The last time I saw him was in July of 1992. The officers wanted us to think he was dead so we wouldn't talk, but he was alive and they wanted to keep him alive. For that reason a doctor was present. I was a prisoner for two years and I would have remained one much longer if I hadn't escaped. I am sure some of the people I was captured with are still there, with the army. And so I believe that Comandante Everardo is very possibly still alive. He was the most valuable prisoner of all."

Peg's eyes were hard. Nothing Santiago had said had changed anything.

After a few words I didn't bother to hear she led us out, past the people wandering the endless halls with their names hung around their necks.

In the warm fall sunlight we perched on the curb, waiting for Alice, watching a mockingbird dive and flit and stake out the top of a bush as a stage for his repertoire. Finally I said to Santiago, "I'm not sure Peg was really listening."

He smiled and readjusted his feet.

"It makes me mad that you had to go through that. For nothing."

"No, you say what you've got to say. Some people will hear it, others won't. But if you let those who won't make you bitter or angry, the anger only eats at you. That kind of anger only hurts you. To have anger about something that you can do something about, that's different. Because then it drives you, gives you courage."

JENNIFER KNEW HOW to use her anger. She was never self-destructive or irrational. Her emotions didn't work that way, and neither did her brain. Jennifer had a New Englander's self-control. She unleashed her anger as coldly and carefully as a terrorist setting loose a cluster of deadly germs. She was engaged in biological warfare. The target was the Guatemalan government, but the site of the attack was her own body.

A fax arrived from her, which I read to Santiago:

Saturday, Day 5
October 15, 1994

Dear Friends,
   [Ambassador] Marilyn McAfee came by and told me she was very concerned and had spoken again with Enríquez. She still opposes any kind of economic sanctions, saying she is an "evolutionist" and believes in slow change.

How slow does she want it to be? I wondered. How many people had to die in the meantime? I looked at Santiago. He was looking at the table, listening, waiting for me to go on:

What she doesn't seem to understand is THE key role of the army is to prevent any change or evolution. Change will only be possible when the army is out of power and can no longer control the institutions in the country.

"Well, yes, that is true," Santiago said.

I appreciate her efforts to protect me. I just wish she would try to protect Everardo. He needs it more than I do.
   Archbishop Penados came out in the rain to see me yesterday. He was very sweet and told me to come to the human rights office Monday.
                                        Love to all — Abrazos
                                                       Jennifer

"Archbishop Penados is a good man," I told Santiago, remembering the way he had risked his life for me. Then I looked down and saw the P.S.:

Someone just walked by and whispered that Everardo has been seen alive.

Santiago looked up and smiled ever so slightly. "Vaya," he said. Wow.
   I tried not to feel anything.

A FEW DAYS LATER we got an early morning fax. The previous night a car had screeched into the plaza, stopping next to Jennifer and her group. Someone riding in the back thrust a large gun out the window. Some thought it was a rifle. Others said it was a machine gun. After a few seconds the car sped off. Jennifer wrote:

> They didn't shoot and clearly feel they cannot. But we are in good communication with each other, even though there have been no formal messages.

I hoped there would be no formal messages, if by those she meant bullets.

> Marilyn McAfee came out again to ask about my health and safety. She continues to insist that all institutions like courts and police must be strengthened. But cash won't strengthen them until the army no longer controls them. A judge in fear of his life cannot rule correctly.

I thought of my case, of how Judge Secaira said she had gotten death threats, of how Judge Lam had suddenly been transferred off the case, supposedly because of the new penal code. The judges, too, were at the mercy of the army.

Jennifer mentioned that UPI, AP, and Reuters had all written articles and that the *San Francisco Chronicle*, *Miami Herald,* and *Christian Science Monitor* had interviewed her.

This was news. When we'd talked to someone at the *Washington Post* about Jennifer he'd replied, "Central America isn't even on our radar screen." But the press was finally taking an interest, and Jennifer seemed happy about it.

> Why do I always get my photo taken when I look my absolute worst?

Only Jennifer could find a laugh in the situation. Nine days with no food, her clothes ballooning, her cheeks sunken in — and she jokes about it like it's a bad hair day.

The next paragraphs were serious:

> Many people have asked me why I am taking this drastic step. It's really simple. Time is up for Everardo. He is still useful for his military information and as a negotiating chip in the peace talks. The army still has to negotiate the issue of what their role will be after the cease fire and they need him until then, but not for much longer. I calculate I have until Christmas to get him out alive....
>
> So I am, unhappily, down to this. I will not let them keep Everardo. If the army shoots him, with the clear evidence that exists, plus the outcry from the international community, who will they kill in the future? They

are testing us. I will do what I can to make them give on this case. Everardo is not someone I can bear to lose.

In that last sentence I heard something Jennifer may or may not have intended. I heard that she would prefer to die than lose Everardo. She would stay there and starve to death.

MY SUSPICIONS were confirmed in the next fax:

I will not allow him to be secretly detained and brutally tortured for 2 and ½ years, then assassinated in some dark corner as if he were garbage. Quite literally, that will happen over my *dead* body. I'd rather die.

That letter was dated Day 19. Our time was up, and Jennifer had made her decision.

Chapter Fifteen

STARVING NEXT TO THE PALACE

MARIE WOULD BE GOING DOWN TO GUATEMALA on the morning flight, and I had a seat beside her. It was nearly dawn. My last few hours to back out. The birds in the magnolia tree outside my window had begun to sing. I sat down on my bed and took off my shoes. My backpack on the floor beside them was stuffed and ready to go. I had been in the office all night, making photocopies of Coalition Missing materials to take with us, gathering up letters and newsclippings I thought Jennifer might like to see, making lists of contact numbers in Guatemala and in Washington in case something happened while we were down there. The house creaked a couple of times, stretching. Marie would be up soon.

I knew I belonged on the plane beside her. While I had lived in the office for weeks, eating peanut butter and crackers and whatever else I could find in the cupboard near the coffee maker, I had the sense that nothing I had done had been very useful. Organizing the Coalition Missing delegation seemed to take me so long. And the religious delegation I'd been trying to organize fell through. The bishop of Detroit, Thomas Gumbleton, was willing to go to Guatemala, and Joe and Marie, of course, but another bishop we asked would have nothing to do with Jennifer's hunger strike. He said it was tantamount to suicide, which, as a representative of the Church, he couldn't condone.

I was speechless, unfortunately. I'd assumed he would understand that if people would support her, she wouldn't die — and since she wanted that support, she didn't even have the intent to commit suicide. But I felt I'd been slapped in the face when I heard him say no and accuse Jennifer of immorality. "You should be proud to be associated with her," I muttered, after hanging up the phone.

The other bishops we asked couldn't participate for various reasons. Since the point of the delegation was to demonstrate the Church's support by having high-level representatives talk to the media and Guatemalan government officials, the presence of only one bishop would just raise questions: Why not more? Doesn't the Church support her? So Joe, Marie, and Bishop Gumbleton decided to attend meetings in Guatemala with members of Coalition Missing and pressure the government quietly instead of publicly.

PEOPLE FROM GUATEMALA had been calling, telling us Jennifer could barely walk. Josh, Meredith, Trish, and her brother Peter, who was a doctor, were going to Guatemala as members of Coalition Missing. They would support Jennifer and create pressure by meeting with government officials and having as much contact as possible with the press. I had more ability to draw the press than anyone else in the group — Guatemalan reporters knew me from all my trips back. But the delegation would be in Guatemala on November 2. Most years on that date I shut myself in my room. The Policeman, the Guate-man, José, and Alejandro always came back on that day. I had my tactics, my rituals to fight them. I lit candles to combat their odors and played music to drown out their voices. They always tried to take me back with them. I distracted myself by reading, working crossword puzzles, repotting plants, but the memories always assailed me. They were stored in my body, it seemed, and on that day my body or mind or whatever it was fired them off, one after another. To erase the geographical distance at a time when the psychological distance nearly vanished seemed impossible. It had been almost a year since I'd had a flashback. I was hoping I would never have another. In Washington, even if I smelled and heard and remembered the torturers, I would have a chance of realizing I wasn't actually back in that prison. In Guatemala, with cameras whirring and flashing, hearing my name shouted by strangers in Spanish, smelling the smells of the Guatemalan streets, seeing the uniforms of the Guatemalan police, knowing that the torturers really could come and get me — that would be a setup for a flashback. This time there would be no bullet-proof van, courtesy of the embassy. There would be no armed embassy security guard accompanying us at all times. If I was honest with myself, I had more to worry about than flashbacks. I would be lucky if I just *thought* I was being taken back to that prison.

LIKE MY TORTURERS, the Guatemalan government switched back and forth between accusations, no matter how inconsistent and self-contradictory they were. First the defense minister had accused me of the usual — I was a guerrilla, a subversive. Then, perhaps prompted by the U.S. embassy, Guatemalan government officials switched to the assertion that I was a lesbian involved in a romantic tryst, which explained my absence on November 2–3. Things went badly, which explained my burns (or was it a sadomasochistic relationship?). Later, in light of the public flashbacks, it was more convenient to term me crazy, no longer calculating and sneaky, as I would have to be if I were a guerrilla or a nun getting out of the convent for sex (but there were plenty of women in the convent!). Now, I guessed, it would once again be convenient for the army to call me a guerrilla. Folding clothes into my suitcase, I remembered how the Policeman had hissed, "Eres una guerrilla, una subversiva." I'd play into the army's hands, proclaiming publicly that I was in Guatemala to support the wife of a guerrilla commandant. *You're a guerrilla. See, I was right.* It would make the Policeman so happy. And if the Policeman was right about that, what else was he right about? That I was stupid, useless, a whore, a murderer? That I killed the Woman?

But only a couple of months earlier I had let fear control me when I could have defended Jennifer — and I had made a vow in the wake of that Washington meeting. I wouldn't let her down again.

Jennifer was sitting in a lawn chair, surrounded by a crowd of Guatemalans who were listening as she spoke to someone. She was talking as she always did, using her hands, stopping to listen, nodding. My legs felt weak, and I looked at Marie and saw my relief reflected in her smile. Jennifer was looking OK. My slowness in organizing the delegation, my helplessness as far as making the Church hierarchy act, whatever bumbling, stupid things I had done in the office hadn't killed her. Not yet.

There must have been fifteen people around her, standing under the hot sun, reading the banners she had laid on the ground, listening. Some looked as if they were waiting to talk to her. A couple held flowers to add to the collection of bouquets at each of the banners' corners. The Guatemalan people were with her. Jennifer had said that in her letters, but it was different to see it, to see the respect and caring, to watch the interchanges. It meant so much to me after the betrayals in Washington. The Guatemalan people were giving her strength, holding her up.

We stood at the edge of the crowd and waited while Jennifer finished her conversation. When she caught sight of us, her face softened into a smile, and she held out her arms. Under my hands I felt the ridge of her spine and the blades of her shoulders. Her hair, poking out beneath her denim hat, brushed my face, and I felt in it the nights and days in the rain and the sun — a stiff paint brush texture on my cheek. One of her eyes was half covered by her eyelid. When she moved over to embrace Marie, sweeping her frayed hair back with one hand, her eyelid twitched. The skin was drawn tight across her face, and every bone in her hand showed.

She invited us to sit down. We spread our sweaters over the hot pavement and sat next to her, facing the National Palace, an enormous, gray building housing the president, the G-2, and other army offices. Among the lush palm trees and well-tended beds of flowers stood soldiers in camouflage with submachine guns. They were all looking our way.

Jennifer's nose was peeling. But she asked us about our trip in her usual, rapid-fire way, as if she were impervious to the sun, her drooping eye, her dropping weight. When I commented on how good she looked, she said the army had sent a doctor to examine her, and he had said she was in excellent shape. The army couldn't drag her away and force her into a hospital until she was near death, she told us — there was a law that permitted the prevention of suicide. Until then, they just had to put up with her.

I thought about how ironic it was. When they captured Everardo, the army soldiers thought he was just another Guatemalan. Nothing could happen to them — they could do whatever they liked with him. That's the way it was. That's the way it had always been. They had no idea that the woman who loved him was a U.S. citizen who also happened to be a brilliant lawyer. And, just to make the nightmare complete, she happened on top of it all to be amazingly strong — "a bionic woman," as their own medical doctor had proclaimed her.

The army had met its match. In her first meeting with the defense minister a year earlier, Jennifer had told him that if he met her demands and complied with the law, she wouldn't have to cause an international scandal. He looked at her as if to ask, "You? What could you do?" Maybe he even thought she was kind of cute, with her gutsy little threat to the head of the most brutal army in the Western Hemisphere. She was hearing reports now that he was losing it. The man who had always had a smooth answer ready for journalists and diplomats, who came across as moderate and reasonable and forward-looking, could only froth at the mouth and fly into diatribes when the subject of her case came up. That's what her reporter friends were telling her, anyway. The army's attempts to frighten her and wear her down, meanwhile, only energized her. That was probably what was driving the defense minister mad. But not long after the incident with the gunman in the car, when Jennifer left the square to talk to her lawyers, an angry crowd formed around her two observers, screaming and holding up tape recorders and asking if they were connected to the subversives. That was Jennifer's only vulnerable spot, the fact that the army could hurt her friends, and the army seemed to know it. *You may not care what happens to you, but you can't protect your friends from us.* That was the message. *Watch your step.*

But Jennifer already had a great victory on her side, and she was dying to tell us about it. "Guess what?" she asked. "*Sixty Minutes* is doing the story. The full story." Mike Wallace was going to cover not only Jennifer's story, but Guatemala and the atrocities that were occurring day after day. We gave each other awkward high fives — it wasn't a gesture we'd had a lot of practice at, not yet. The UN mission hadn't begun to operate, so *Sixty Minutes* would be invaluable as a check on the army's campaign of terror. The show might expose the horrors as well as hundreds of observers could, and the information would certainly get out to a broader audience. The show would reach millions of people — people who had the power to demand trade sanctions and urge a cut-off of joint army training programs, study scholarships for officers in the United States, and other tax-funded perks. With such high-level publicity about the army's atrocities, the Guatemalan military would need a PR coup badly after the show aired. Maybe turning Everardo and the other prisoners over would be the only way the army could save face — and preserve its privileged relationship with the United States.

The best news of all was that maybe it wasn't too late. Jennifer counted off three different people who had seen Everardo alive after Santiago had. They had approached her fearfully, whispering what they knew when the crowd had dwindled down. One was the girlfriend of a soldier who had seen him on a military base. Another person had seen him being taken through a town.

Hope shone through Jennifer's eyes and hit a place inside of me that was clear, like a mirror, and smooth and could give the light back.

Toward evening, when Joe and Bishop Gumbleton had arrived, Jennifer's voice was weak, but she swigged her electrolyte mix, cleared her throat, and said, "I figure I can stay out here a couple more weeks, maybe longer." She looked at each of us in turn. She wanted us to understand. There would be pressure, and it would mount. But would it mount fast enough to outpace her body's decline? What she was telling us was that she was going to gamble on it.

We went to the Maryknoll House that night, to comfortable beds with warm blankets, and I could only think of Jennifer, lying out on the cement, yards away from the soldiers. She'd had a recurring dream ever since Everardo disappeared. Just as she was drifting into sleep his voice would come to her. "I'm cold. I'm cold." She couldn't figure out what he meant, where he was. He could be lying on a metal table without a blanket, as he was when Santiago first saw him, his hands and feet chained down. They'd kept Santiago like that for months, too. He could be in the grave. He could be in the National Palace, which was known to have basement rooms used for torture and secret detention. They could be lying yards away from each other, solid granite walls and soldiers armed with machine guns between them. There was no way to know.

I was supposed to be thinking about another question, one I had to answer by morning. Mike Wallace wanted to interview Meredith and me. I was prepared for the Coalition Missing press conference. We would all stand shoulder to shoulder and read into the cameras statements about the rights of prisoners of war, the necessity of presenting Everardo. But looking into a camera and talking about my own case, alone, was another matter. I wasn't prepared.

Mike Wallace seemed nice, though. When Jennifer had introduced us in the plaza, I realized he reminded me of my Grandpa Joe. He had the same gentle manner, the same gentle eyes. I could hardly believe he was a reporter. Many reporters I'd met tended to bark and shove. But he had a warm smile and a soft handshake, and something about him led me to believe I could trust him. I told him an interview would be hard for me because cameras were used in my torture, something I'd never told any reporter. He looked startled, but luckily, he was tactful. He didn't ask me what I was doing as the torturers filmed me. He just told me to take some time to reconsider.

As the night wore on, I reconsidered without coming to any conclusion. An image kept floating before me: the women of the GAM, keeping vigil near Jennifer, facing the National Palace. Sitting in chairs in front of the palace wasn't a typical form of protest for GAM. But there they were, several women accompanying Jennifer and demanding the return of their own loved ones. To be anywhere near Jennifer and to treat her as more than a curiosity — to ally themselves publicly with her — was practically suicidal. People with GAM were always accused of being guerrillas. They could be accused of knowing her, of having contacts with her or her husband. In the history of Guatemala, only Jennifer had been able to demand the return of a guerrilla commandant and that was only because she was a U.S. citizen. And here the GAM women were, demanding, implicitly, the return of Everardo. They might pay with their lives. Nineth, the leader of GAM, was there. Ever since she'd begun her search for her husband nearly a decade earlier, she had received calls regularly, sometimes in the middle of the night, sometimes during the day. The daytime calls could be the scariest. "Come pick your daughter up at school," she was told once, "all the pieces of her." Mario, her *compañero*, was there, less than a year after he had been beaten into unconsciousness. Other GAM women, who carried years of suffering in their faces, sat under the hot sun — just sat, silently, defiantly, even if it cost them their lives.

I wondered if Mike Wallace would interview them or at least have the camera pan across their faces — and why it took an American like Jennifer to bring the media to a place where stories of courage were being lived out every day. A reporter might argue that for an American audience the story of the GAM women was just too foreign, too hard for people to understand, whereas Jennifer, as an American, was someone the audience could relate to — they could identify with her, look at her and picture themselves in the same situation. That's the tragedy of U.S. foreign policy. Not enough Americans suffer the consequences of it. And foreigners, those whose lives are touched or devastated by decisions our government makes, can't vote. Too often they can't even tell their stories to anyone who will listen.

That was all the more reason I should agree to the interview. But I remembered part of a letter Meredith had sent me months before. I had read it over so many times I'd practically memorized the words:

> I got off the phone with you his morning and cried. I cried because of the pain you have gone through, the pain I have gone through, and that of many others who unfortunately share similar experiences. I cried also because of the tremendous anger I have about all this. And because I was glad — glad that finally four years later the two of us have connected.
>
> Our struggle is twinfold — yes, for social justice and peace, particularly in Guatemala, but also for peace within ourselves, which includes when, where, and how we want to share our stories.

I knew Meredith would support me if I decided not to be interviewed. Finally I started to relax, feeling my shoulders loosen. It would be good to see her. She was coming in on an early plane, and I had only a few more minutes to lie in bed and wait for the sky to lighten.

AFTER WE SETTLED HER IN at the Maryknoll House, Meredith listened to my reasons, sitting quietly on the bed while I sifted through my feelings. She was a good listener. This was her first trip back to Guatemala since she was stabbed, just a month after I was abducted, and she had her own trauma and thoughts to deal with. But she gave me her full attention. She said she understood that I was barely keeping my head above water, that I was fragile, that it was almost the beginning of November and I was afraid of a flashback.

"But what if you look at the *Sixty Minutes* interview as a chance to take the camera, which the torturers used as a weapon against you, and turn it back on them?" she asked. "What if you use it as a tool to help Jennifer and the Guatemalan people, to show what's happening here and who is responsible? You can take your power back."

At Meredith's words, I felt a door swing open within me. I could be filmed with another woman friend, supporting her instead of hurting her. I could denounce the true torturers, the Guatemalan army. Millions of people would hear me.

Meredith's eyes when I looked up were the deep blue of an October sky. She was like Jennifer and Santiago, smart, insightful, feisty. She was inviting me to be like they were — to have the guts to outsmart the army, to use their own tactics against them. She was throwing me a rope. I could take it and find my way, hand over hand, out of the dark prison that had started to enclose me again. I hesitated, and in the long silence some words of Santiago's came back to me: "We can't let our fear and shame paralyze us and keep us from doing what we need to do." He was talking about how he'd decided to testify, but in some part of my mind I knew his words applied to me. Shame and fear were the driving forces behind my desire not to be interviewed. And I would be risking so little compared to the GAM members, who were risking their lives. The videotape could be released, but I wouldn't die. My pride would suffer. I was ashamed of not being stronger and afraid of what people would think of me. I didn't know how I would face my family and my community. But all the names I had freed up from silence and white space, cutting the *Updates* and calling Peg, found their way into my mind. If by speaking I could help save one life, then I would speak. Lives were far more important than my pride.

AT HER FIRST GLIMPSE of Jennifer, Meredith burst into sobs and covered her face.

"Meredith, it's OK." I touched her wrist.

She moved her hands away and sobbed onto my shoulder.

"Meredith," I said after a minute, "we have to be strong for Jennifer. She needs us."

Her sobs quieted. "I know," she said. "I know. She just looks so awful."

"She's OK. Really. She's doing well."

Meredith took a deep breath and wiped her eyes carefully — we would have the *Sixty Minutes* interview soon — and by the time we reached the center of the plaza, the pink blotches on her face had faded. The Guatemalan media had found us, so reaching the center of the plaza took a while. Cameras flashed and reporters crowded in. I stayed behind Meredith's shoulder, and she fended the questions off, explaining that we would have a press conference the following morning after Josh got in. Josh had narrowly escaped an abduction attempt by an armed man in plain clothes, just a year after I'd been abducted. A uniformed policeman had intervened, and seeing the man's military identification, he let the gunman go. Then the policeman and another officer drove Josh around in their car for an hour and threatened him. The parallels to my case were obvious: he was a U.S. citizen who was only working with children but was targeted for abduction by someone armed and wearing plain clothes; and the police, if not involved in the abduction itself, allowed impunity to the military. Meredith explained who Josh was, to placate the reporters, but she would say no more. She looked tough and resolute, like a human rights advocate with a plan. I hoped I could look that way by the time our press conference came around. We would all have to exude confidence to make the Guatemalan government believe we could pull strings in D.C. to get its funding cut and its trade privileges revoked if Jennifer's demands weren't met. In other words, none of us could look, for any reason, scared.

Unfortunately, I was scared, and the Guatemalan press was part of the reason. A headline in the daily paper proclaimed that, according to the army spokesperson, I was "La Portavoz de las Guerrillas." My Spanish was so rudimentary I didn't know what *portavoz* meant, and I had to ask Joe. "Voice carrier — spokesperson," he said.

I was the spokesperson of the guerrillas.

At first, I had laughed. Even when I spoke English I stumbled and used words I hoped existed but too often found out were my own inventions. To think that the guerrillas would ask me to go to Guatemala to speak on their behalf in Spanish was ludicrous. And why would the guerrillas choose as their spokesperson someone who, according to the army, badly needed a psychiatrist?

Soon enough, fear replaced the laughter, settling in beneath my rib cage. The charge was a veiled threat: the army had created the conditions to justify violence against me. The guerrilla excuse had allowed the army to murder two hundred thousand people already, with total impunity. As long as they could say that someone was a guerrilla, the security forces could do what they liked. And the U.S. government, by failing to act on

Everardo's case because "after all, he was a combatant," was proving the army right.

I hadn't mustered the confident look yet when *Sixty Minutes* filmed us. Watching the tape of the broadcast now, I realize how afraid I was, almost choking for breath between words. I didn't once let my eyes meet the camera — the sight of the camera trained on me could send me spinning into the past. I spoke slowly, but I spoke, breaking the torturers' hold. I said only a few sentences — that I was abducted, tortured, and raped — but with those sentences, I hoped I spoke for the Woman and the others who died in that prison, for the thousands of others. I hoped I carried their voices.

WHEN JOSH ARRIVED, smiling broadly under his mop of curly blond hair, we moved to the Spring Hotel. The place had musty rooms but a friendly, trustworthy staff and a big, sunny courtyard where we could sit and talk. There we prepared for our next undertaking — a meeting with the U.S. ambassador. We reminded each other that no matter what assurances McAfee gave us of her interest, she had asked for Jennifer's case to be removed from the congressional resolution. She had also strongly implied that Jennifer should give up hope. Jennifer's theory was that she knew something she wasn't telling or she had orders to simply try to shut the case down because it was a hindrance to the peace process. The United States wanted to conclude the peace negotiations as quickly as possible so that Guatemala could be brought into a NAFTA-like accord that would encompass all of Central America. In light of the recent sightings of Everardo, it seemed more likely that the ambassador was simply trying to hush the case up so that the peace talks could be concluded. But it was a dangerous position for the embassy to take — dangerous for Everardo and for all of Guatemala. If the ambassador allowed the Guatemalan army to sign a peace accord, ignoring the secret detention of a high-ranking guerrilla commandant, if she let the Truth Commission investigate the case as one of the tragic abuses of the past, the precedent would be set: the accords could be broken with impunity. And if Everardo was still alive, she was giving the army a green light to kill him.

I WAS GLAD TO HAVE Josh, Meredith, Joe, and Marie with me as the officer at the passport check punched the iron gate open and we proceeded up the steps toward the familiar eyesore of a building, gray concrete dotted with bright orange tiles. We were surprised to find six people in McAfee's office already, sitting stiffly on the soft, white furniture with notepads on their laps — the political affairs officer, the human rights officer, the consular officer, and several other people whose titles I didn't get. We looked around nervously. We were outnumbered by embassy staff. The ambassador greeted us warmly and invited us to be seated. She introduced her staff, then resettled herself in her armchair, tucked her white-blond hair behind her ears, and told us she was very concerned about Jennifer.

I watched her face closely. I saw no indication of dishonesty. She did seem concerned, and there was a tension in the air you could almost hear, a kind of static. She seemed to be giving a speech she'd rehearsed. Her clothes flowed perfectly from her slender limbs in a bloom of wrinkle-free, peach-colored silk. Her matching fingernails shone in the light, resting on the arms of the chair when they weren't involved with her hair. She was still talking about her concern for Jennifer's health when a wave of anger crashed over me. I wanted to ask her why she didn't do something for Everardo if she was so concerned. But she had worked sincerely on my case, unlike any other ambassador. She had arranged meetings with Guatemalan government officials for me earlier in the year; she had invited me to meet with her in her home and removed her large poodles from the waiting room when she saw that I was afraid of them. In more recent months, she had responded with concern to my letters about the lack of progress in my case. I decided it was best to keep my anger to myself.

A State Department officer, Richard Nuccio, had been in the country meeting with top-level Guatemalan government officials, McAfee was telling us. As a result of his meetings the Guatemalan government was willing to appoint a special investigative commission to look into the whereabouts of Jennifer's husband. The commission would work with UN observers and would interview witnesses at the site of the battle where Everardo disappeared. It would be a very thorough investigation. She scanned our faces.

Jennifer had told us all about "Nuccio's brilliant idea." She had gotten her hopes up when she heard Nuccio was coming to Guatemala, but when she learned his proposal was that the Guatemalan government form an investigative commission, she was furious. Joe, Marie, Meredith, and Josh repeated her arguments to McAfee, telling her the case had already been investigated by the UN and the OAS. Everardo was clearly captured by the army, and Santiago had named ten of the officers involved and given the exact locations where he was held. The army needed to produce Everardo or his body. After that, a special prosecutor could investigate all he wanted to determine the criminal responsibilities. But until then, any investigation was an attempt to stall for time and to appease Jennifer and the U.S. public.

An uncomfortable silence followed, broken only by the noise of each member of the embassy staff scrawling notes. McAfee was looking at her lap. Joe asked, "Have you been able to learn anything about what might have happened to Jennifer's husband?"

McAfee leaned forward, her pale green eyes full of sincerity. "If I knew anything, I would tell you."

The calendar flipped to November, the month the old Dianna died and the new, evil Dianna was born — the birth date of my murderous self.

But it was five years later, and I was sitting beside Jennifer, holding her hand. When she looked at me there was love in her eyes and I felt it bound from me back to her. And I realized they hadn't ruined me, the torturers. They hadn't broken me. I could still love, and I could still fight. Here I was on their doorstep, doing both. Facing the National Palace, shaking hands with the Guatemalans who approached us and said they were tired of their silence and didn't care anymore if army spies were watching, talking quietly with Meredith, Joe, Josh, Jennifer, Marie, Nineth, Mario, and Bishop Gumbleton, all of us bound by love and resolve, I found a way to understand that the date and place of my torture and rebirth represented more than evil. The Politécnica was a burial place. Unlike the members of GAM, at least I knew where the Woman had died. At least I had a place to mourn. At least I knew where the bodies of those moaning in the pit lay.

But the Politécnica was more than that, too. It was the place where I had reached out to the Woman — reached across my fear to uncover her face — and the place where she reached out to me across her pain, asking my name, telling me to be strong. It was the place where I took her hand, where we held on to each other. Yes, other things happened. But those acts of ours, those reaches, those were the acts we willed, and no one could ever take them away. Perhaps they lent some measure of sanctity to that blood-stained room. They were something to remember and honor.

MARIE, JOE, MEREDITH, AND BISHOP GUMBLETON were with me. I had brought my camera, and as a way of feeling powerful, I used it as we circled the building in the weak morning sunlight. The soldiers in the turrets, on the roof, and by the main door saw me. And photographing a military installation was illegal. But they decided, for some reason, to let it go, and I went on, taking shot after shot, wondering, on this anniversary, if I could capture something that might show up as evil or something that might be holy.

When my film ran out, we moved closer. As we approached, chills tumbled up and down my spine. It was probably my own pulse that made the gray castle seem to grow and shrink, almost imperceptibly, like a live thing, but the place seemed to throb with evil and I began to tremble. Memories were returning. The scarlet blood stain on the gray cement floor after I was raped. Even the floor stained with my blood. The floor, too, had participated.

We were close enough to touch the wall. That's what we had come to do. It wasn't enough to stand on the sidewalk. To pray for the people who'd died in that building and for those who might at that moment be smelling their own skin sear or feeling the skin of their cheeks raked off by fists, we had to be touching the rocks that kept them from us. For me, to be prayer, it had to be that kind of reach — across my pain, through my fear. We, the living, the ones who were not being tortured, had to stand as close as possible to the dead, to the ones within those walls, no matter what that took.

Meredith has told me I sobbed in the taxi on the way back. Marie, who was sitting in the front with me, comforted me. I don't remember that. But I remember what I prayed as we stood with our hands against the wall. I remember the way the stones felt. The sun hadn't risen enough yet to warm them, but they weren't cool, either. They were just about as warm as our skin. They had been painted to make them gray. Green was visible underneath, and beneath that, rusty red. I called on God and on Saint Michael the Archangel and on all the angels to be there inside the walls. I asked them to sprinkle handfuls of angel dust on the eyes of the torturers so that they could see what they were doing, how they were hurting their brothers and sisters. *Let them see. Melt the evil and rancor in their hearts.*

I may have been praying for myself, too, without even knowing it, for the part of me that never came out from behind those walls, and for the part that was born there, the new part which I kept detained and secret and walled in. Perhaps I was praying to God to melt the evil and rancor in my heart, too.

I REMEMBER a casual conversation I had in the plaza with a Guatemalan human rights worker. "What do you do when you're not working?" he asked. "What do you do for fun?"

I just looked at him. Finally I mentioned gardening.

"What else?"

Alice, director of the Guatemala Human Rights Commission.

Coalition Missing press conference in Guatemala City, Fall 1994.
Holding banner are Jennifer Harbury (with a picture of Everardo), Dianna,
Meredith Larson, and Josh Zinner.

*Dianna,
Marie Dennis, and
Bishop Thomas
Gumbleton with
Jennifer Harbury
during her hunger
strike in
Guatemala City.*

Below:
The Politécnica.

Father Joe Nangle, Marie, Meredith, and Bishop Gumbleton praying at the wall of the Politécnica.

I collect the names of the disappeared. No, I couldn't say that. "I read," I said at last.

"What kinds of things do you like to read?" he asked.

"The Bible. Books about Latin America, human rights."

"You're so serious. You should have some fun."

A lash of anger whipped through me. How could I have fun when people were being tortured, when people were dying, when I should have died? Mary and others at Kovler might call it survivor guilt, but whatever they wanted to name it, the fact was that I escaped with my life when others didn't, and I knew things about torture that most people didn't, and that put an enormous burden on me. *So don't talk to me about having fun.*

It wasn't much of a life, but then again it was a life that I could bear to lose. So if they came for me again, I was halfway ready.

"You know, the torturers have won if they keep you from living your life," he said. I don't remember his face, probably because I was looking at the ground, but I remember his tone. It was gentle. "If they keep us from living, really living, they've won."

AS THE MEDIA COVERAGE of Jennifer's case intensified, the Guatemalan government honed its harassment tactics. While we were having our meetings at government offices — and not coincidentally, the day after our press conference — several Guatemalan officials approached Jennifer in the plaza and began firing questions at her, which they said she was under legal obligation to answer. Jennifer asked to undergo the interrogatories, as they were called, in a place that was more private and out of the midday sun. Meanwhile she contacted her Guatemalan lawyer. The officials took Jennifer into a nearby building, but when her lawyer arrived, they barred her from the room. They questioned Jennifer for three hours on her relationship to the guerrilla movement, perhaps hoping that in her weakened condition, without a lawyer, and speaking a language that wasn't her own, she might make a statement that could be used against her. Or maybe they were hoping that in that hot room, deprived of water and forced to speak for three hours, she would faint. She didn't do either one.

So at the end of the meeting, government officials popped a surprise: they told her they believed Everardo was buried in a town five hours from the capital, and the body would be brought out of the grave the next morning.

Jennifer stayed up all night preparing, lining up forensic specialists, calling her lawyers, gathering together international observers, arranging rides, notifying the press. All these measures would be helpful if the government tried to perpetrate a fraud and pass off another cadaver as Ev-erardo's. Jennifer got herself ready to look closely at another set of teeth in another decaying head. She set off at 4:00 a.m. and made the arduous trip to the town, only to be told once there that the exhumation had been post-poned for her convenience. But she was allowed to see the judicial records in the morgue before returning to Guatemala City, and she learned that two bodies had been buried in the grave. Both were URNG combatants who had been killed ten days before Everardo even disappeared. Jennifer would still have to go through with the exhumation within the next few days, though, once it had been rescheduled. She would have to stand for hours as partially decayed bodies were brought up out of the earth and skulls were held before her. If she passed out, the government could rush her to a hospital and hook her up to an IV. That would end the hunger strike and her chance for answers. But she had no choice. For all she knew, the army's plan was to switch the bodies and place Everardo's in the grave as a means of meeting her demands and giving back his remains.

After the canceled exhumation, we saw her in the plaza. She didn't even notice we were there. She stared off into space.

JENNIFER MADE IT THROUGH the rescheduled exhumation, and there were no surprises — in the grave were the URNG combatants killed before Everardo disappeared. I was back at the office in Washington when I found out she was placed at the head of a death list sent to the Guatemalan media. The army must have been frustrated that she hadn't passed out, even while standing in the hot sun all day and bending over corpses.

The Guatemalan army and the U.S. government would soon have more to lament. *Sixty Minutes* had dug up some information that was never supposed to get out to Jennifer or the U.S. public. Alice, Patricia, and I had settled in front of the TV at the house of Jennifer's lawyer, Jose, to see how the *Sixty Minutes* piece turned out. About halfway through, the revelation came: the U.S. embassy, which for years had claimed to know nothing of Everardo's disappearance, had information from intelligence sources stating that Everardo had been captured by the Guatemalan army. The documents had been in State Department files for a year and a half.

I remembered Peg Willingham's words and Ambassador McAfee's words and the responses we had received to so many letters we'd written: "We have no independent confirmation of clandestine detention in Guatemala. We have no more information about what could have happened to him. If I knew anything I would tell you."

Betrayal was an old wound and the scab burst. But this time more was being violated than my honor, my right to justice. U.S. government officials let Everardo be tortured while they lied. They were going to let Jennifer die while they lied.

THE PIECE RUN by *Sixty Minutes* got Jennifer a meeting with some high-level White House officials. Jose went to Guatemala to give Jennifer the news. "I'm going down to bring her back," he told us. "I think she'll come off the hunger strike for a White House meeting." The next day he phoned our office. "Reserve another seat on the flight back," he said. And we knew she was coming home.

Soon a page came through the fax. I skimmed it quickly. It was a press statement from Jennifer. Taking the opportunity offered her, she was calling off the hunger strike to file criminal charges against the military officers seen torturing and detaining Everardo. Then she was going to Washington to meet with White House officials.

One of the military officers she was suing was the Guatemalan minister of defense, for cover-up and complicity in torture and murder. I couldn't believe the Guatemalan army would let her out of the country alive. But the *Sixty Minutes* report had forced the U.S. embassy to support Jennifer's version of events and contradict the army's version. Jennifer now had the U.S. government on her side, however unwilling the U.S. government was to be there. Ambassador McAfee called Jennifer into the embassy shortly after her press conference. She informed Jennifer that she had issued a démarche, or a formal diplomatic statement, to Guatemalan president Ramiro de León Carpio. The démarche said that the U.S. had information that Everardo was captured by the army and was lightly wounded at the time of his capture but that his injuries were not life-threatening.

Jennifer and Jose peppered the ambassador with questions — where the information came from, who had captured him, what happened next.

She didn't answer their questions, Jose told us, giving us an account of their meeting in a phone call afterward. She just kept saying there was no information to indicate that he was alive for more than a few weeks beyond the time he was captured. "Is there information to indicate that he is dead?" Jennifer asked. Santiago had seen him four months after his capture, and then there were the more recent reports of sightings. "Do you have any documentation stating that he's dead?"

"No," the ambassador answered. "We have no further information."

The démarche asked the president to investigate the army's involvement in Everardo's capture and secret detention. This was an improvement — the investigation the ambassador had touted earlier was aimed at resolving his mysterious disappearance. Oddly, though, while she explained the contents of the démarche several times, the ambassador wouldn't give Jennifer or Jose a copy of it.

BUT JENNIFER WAS ALIVE, and she was getting out of the country safely. I tried to fight my own dark mood. A group from the Assisi house and the office met her at the airport with bouquets of flowers and a huge welcome home banner Santiago had helped us write in Mam. Her red blazer hung off her shoulders, and she seemed to have just enough skin to stretch across the bones of her face. But she was beaming, and she made the rounds, hugging us each in turn.

Then she went to talk to the reporters who had gathered at the gate. The Guatemalan army must be furious, I realized, watching Jennifer before the cameras. Although she had come back without Everardo or his body, a number of unintended positive results had come with her hunger strike. She had exposed the army's brutality internationally; she had proved that the army did capture Everardo and keep him a secret prisoner; and she had probably weakened the army's negotiating position in the peace talks.

I stood off to the side, trying to be inconspicuous. I hope Everardo's dead, I thought. The army would take out its rage on him if he wasn't. Tears came to my eyes and I closed them for a moment. This was a time to be happy. Who was to say he was suffering? But I knew how the army worked. He was suffering if he was alive. And if he wasn't? Well, it had to be a blessing.

Jennifer spread butter across the bread Marie had baked, but she ate it methodically, losing the thread of the conversation now and then and staring vacantly. In spite of regular meals, her face looked as drawn as it had the week before when she'd first arrived in Washington. I wondered where her mind was — back in her White House meeting with Richard Feinstein, Anthony Lake, and Leon Fuerth, where she'd asked for a suspension of joint training programs and scholarships to Guatemalan officers and had received nothing, not even any new information? Reliving a moment of her past with Everardo, on a mountain trail or a sidewalk in Mexico City? Or in an army base, Santa Ana Belén, where Santiago saw Everardo tied to a table?

She would snap back to the present and start chewing again, as if she had been recalled to her mission. Eating, I guessed, was something she was doing for him, just as starving had been. I wondered if she would have preferred to die in the plaza in Guatemala, to dwindle day by day as the light in her eyes had done since her return.

That thought reflected my own wishes. I no longer talked to Everardo or pictured the day he would show me different herbs. I spoke instead to the Woman, and I wrote to her in my journal. What I said to her was similar to what I'd said to Everardo in moments of despair. I encouraged her to cross the divide, to travel into the next world. How clear it is to me now that in talking to both of them, I was speaking to myself.

Why can't you just let go — go on into the next world?

The Woman — rather, what I did to the Woman — had started to haunt me. In spite of caffeine, willpower, and fear, at night I fell back into the room where she lay rasping beneath the sheet, the room where I took the machete. I dreamed about how it sank into her chest. The blood. Our screams.

In some dreams, she was alive and she beckoned.

My mornings and nights are filled with a deep sadness. This sadness is diminishing all traces of hope within me. My old friend has revisited me and once again, she invites me to travel to a faraway place, a place unfettered with memories.

I couldn't hold on to the positive memories, the way I'd reached out to her and taken her hand, not any more, because it didn't keep her alive — it wasn't enough — just as all we had done for Jennifer and for the people of Guatemala wasn't enough. The peace accord wasn't signed in December. The U.S. government had sent the National Guard troops down at the beginning of January to continue the Fuertes Caminos, a joint training program. And Jennifer a short while later announced that she would resume her hunger strike.

She'd stopped too soon, she said. The White House meeting was a red cape she had charged at. White House officials still refused to give her copies of documents underlying their statements about Everardo's capture or take any measures to pressure the Guatemalan government. They just kept saying they had no reason to believe Everardo was alive beyond a few weeks after his capture.

Less than four months had passed since Jennifer had starved for thirty-two days. She could blow a kidney out in the first week. At least she would be in Washington this time, since her objective now was to make the U.S. government tell what it knew. I tried to support Jennifer instead of arguing with her. More than once I had heard her say, "I thought he was dead

before. I gave up on him. I can't give up on him again. People said they'd
seen him recently. But you know what the ambassador said about that?
'Jennifer, people think they've seen Elvis, too.' They just want me to go
away and forget about him, and I won't do it."

I knew the hunger strike was a matter of principle for Jennifer this
time, as much as a matter of strategy. And I suspected that, with things
for Everardo looking so bleak, she would now almost welcome death.

Jennifer asked us to help her organize a rally on March 12, to mark the
third anniversary of Everardo's capture and the beginning of her hunger
strike in front of the White House. Her mother and I worked together on a
T-shirt with a map of Guatemala on the front, including statistics of all the
dead and disappeared. On the back was a drawing that Jennifer's mother,
an artist, made from a photograph of Everardo, aging him according to
the time that had passed. "Where is Everardo?" we wrote. "Ask the White
House."

IN GUATEMALA the situation was as bad as ever. The UN observers had
arrived, finally. But, as if to show that their presence didn't matter, those
responsible for the violence went on a killing spree. Between February 20
and February 22, twenty-two people were found dead, with signs of torture. By the end of February, the year's death toll included six university
students, who had been abducted and found with signs of torture or shot
at point-blank range on the street. A unionist had also been abducted,
and two journalists had been shot to death. Several human rights workers, too, were abducted and tortured, beaten in their offices, or shot and
wounded.

> *February 28, 1995:* Meredith, I don't know what's happening to me.
> Lately I've been under a lot of stress. I feel as if I'm standing on the
> edge of the world and looking nowhere. My urge to disappear is so
> intense. How I yearn to live a normal life — one of inner peace.

I told Meredith about my hearing before the Inter-American Commission of the OAS. I had to demonstrate that I'd been abducted and tortured
and that obtaining justice in Guatemala was impossible. Paul and Shawn
had kept careful records of the Guatemalan government's evasions and
delays, and a young lawyer based in Washington, Michele Arington, had
taken over my case with help from Jennifer's lawyer, Jose, and another
local lawyer named Anna Gallagher. During the hearing I managed to
stay grounded and avoid flashbacks, and the lawyers did a good job, but
the experience took its toll.

The OAS representatives were extremely respectful and supportive. Naturally, the Guatemalan representatives were total jerks. They read a detailed report that highlighted the government's persistent work on my case.

Meredith would get a kick out of that. She'd accompanied me to a meeting with Attorney General Ramsés Cuestas in Guatemala during Jennifer's hunger strike there. In that meeting, in the presence of the new good and helpful embassy Consular General Chuck Keil, Cuestas promised to send me a monthly report about the government's actions on my case. He'd sent only one report, which was a summary of the case — no more had followed in the three months since the meeting. Meredith and I took a particular dislike to Cuestas. He looked like Humpty Dumpty — a round torso and, ballooning above his tie, a perfectly round face. He wasn't scary to look at, but his cartoonish appearance was deceptive. The meeting with him was one of the most traumatic parts of the trip for me. As the meeting began, I told him I was concerned that Linares had said that my case should be dismissed for lack of evidence, and I mentioned that I had written President de León Carpio and Ambassador McAfee to insist that the information I had given the courts be pursued. Cuestas, in response, attacked. He dispensed with the usual accusations that I hadn't cooperated with investigators and that my testimony was inconsistent. He had a more powerful weapon, and he seemed to know it was powerful enough to be used alone: "Why didn't you have a gynecological exam?"

He'd knifed me with his first sentence. As if he knew what I had done with the life growing inside me. I pushed at the space between the ribs in my chest. I told myself there was no way he could know anything. I tried to keep my voice strong and explained that in New Mexico a doctor examined my back, and even that exam was like being tortured and violated again. I wasn't going to let anyone touch me further than that.

That was true. Dr. Gutiérrez had wanted to examine and treat the burns I had on other parts of my body — and I had them all over. I wouldn't let him.

There was evidence of the torture,[1] Cuestas admitted, but not of the sexual abuse, and that was by far the most serious act committed.

I started shaking. "The rapes were very, very painful. I still remember them. But what really gets to me is having to see other people tortured and not being able to do anything to help them. That is the worst nightmare I have lived for five years, and it's something that is still continually happening today and I can't just sit back and not do anything!"

My voice broke and I caught some tears on my fingertips. Meredith reached over and touched my hand. Without thinking I yanked my hand away.

"I think the case is very strong," Cuestas said after a pause, "apart from this issue of the sexual abuse."

Meredith lit into Cuestas. She told him she'd worked on a hotline for victims of sexual abuse and not to undergo an exam was the norm after being raped because of the retraumatization involved. She added that the rape was not the worst of my experience — it was the overall pattern of torture that had caused me the most suffering and the rape was just a part of that. Cuestas repeated that, although it was too late now for an exam to do any good, a doctor's certificate would have been the best manner of proof.

I wanted Meredith to know it wasn't just Cuestas now. The Guatemalan government, before the OAS, had adopted the same line of attack.

> Much to my dismay, Meredith, the Guatemalan representatives continue to focus on the rape issue and to insist that I be required to have a gynecological exam. The issue has upset me immensely. Oh, Meredith — how much more can I put up with this crap? Is it worth it? By subjecting myself to this form of treatment, will our Guatemalan sisters and brothers be less prone to having their human rights violated?

I was still afraid that, somehow, a gynecological exam could reveal the choice I had made. Was that why the Guatemalan government was insisting on it? Government officials had harassed me with that "requirement" before, during my second trip to Guatemala. But the focus on it, the harping to this extent, was new. I had to ask myself if someone had found something out.

Life at the Assisi community had become difficult, too, because of the choice I had made about the torturers' developing seed. That choice seemed to be following me around and haunting me. I didn't tell Meredith everything that was bothering me, but on the same night I wrote her the letter, I wrote in my journal:

> At last night's community meeting I heard people express their views on a delicate issue. . . . Whenever I am in a state of hopelessness, I tend to misconstrue or distort what is being said. Hearing folks articulate strong views on this delicate issue has left me imbued with shame. There were moments when I actually felt as if I were being judged. Their

words echoed loud and clear...a judgment made on me: GUILTY of another sin committed against humanity. Without a moment's warning, I transform like the torturers into a ghastly and repulsive monster that can bring harm to others.

At this moment I am deliberating whether to remain in the Assisi community. Renting an apartment is one option. Another option is relocating elsewhere...a place where I am not known.... But where would I go?

Instead of confiding these thoughts to Meredith, I turned to issues involving Jennifer. Maybe, without quite realizing it, I was proposing an answer to the question of where I would go. I would starve myself to death.

I spoke with the Guatemalan desk officer at the State Department and voiced my concern for Jennifer's welfare. I asked what the U.S. government was doing to resolve this crisis. Needless to say, the State Department does not know what to do. I did say to Peg that I would not sit back and watch my friend wither away. I hinted that perhaps I would consider doing civil disobedience or that I might fast with Jennifer. She was horrified with the idea that I would consider joining Jennifer on her hunger strike.

Peg responded by saying that the government cared about Jennifer's case. I knew better than to believe her. One State Department official, Richard Nuccio, had already met with human rights groups and tried to dissuade us from supporting Jennifer — the case, he said, could damage the peace talks. But the extent of the U.S. government's dishonesty wouldn't be clear for another few weeks, and it would be a couple of years before this e-mail from Peg to colleague Lee McClenny, dated November 30, 1994, was declassified. The subject was a call from Mike Wallace:

He says that he understands that Jennifer Harbury, now back in Guatemala, will have to add murder to the criminal charges she's filing because the army executed [Everardo]; he adds that CBS has "pretty good information" that he was executed and that "all concerned — and by that I mean State Department and elsewhere — knew about it." He says he doesn't know if Jennifer Harbury knows this, and he "doesn't want to lay it on her" without talking to us first.

What he wants is State Department comment about what we knew and when we knew it, and if we've told JHarbury. We have clear press guidance on that score but I'm sure he wants more than that. Good luck! Peg.

McClenny, responded:

Good brief . . . I mean good grief! I checked quickly with AFW re this, recommending that we stick with the guidance: (1) We do not know whether Bámaca is dead or alive; (2) We have no evidence that he was alive any time more than a few weeks after his capture; and (3) We have always acted on the assumption that he could be alive. If pressed on what we knew and when, the answer is that this is an intelligence matter that we cannot discuss. If pushed harder on this, about all that we can say is that we have consistently done everything we can to assist Ms. Harbury in her search for her husband, including providing her with the pertinent information that we have on this case. We have not tried to conceal anything from her.[2]

Jennifer, meanwhile, was preparing to resume her hunger strike. She did get a call from Lowell Bergman, the *Sixty Minutes* producer, who said he had good information that Everardo was dead. But without being able to see any evidence — documents to that effect, or a body — Jennifer couldn't take a risk. She had to fight for him. Alice said I shouldn't join Jennifer in her fast; if Jennifer wanted to call on us to join in the fast at anytime, she would have to make that call. In the meantime, we had more than enough to do. I knew Alice was right. We were understaffed as it was, and none of us had fully recovered yet from our round-the-clock work in the fall.

I LET SOME of the Assisi members' remarks on the subject of abortion drive away my sense of belonging. I was sure my Ursuline family and my mom, dad, and sisters would react like people at Assisi if they knew about the choice I'd made. But at least I was needed at the office. I plunged into the work.

The weekend of the rally arrived all too soon, and the night before, we were having a party, which meant more work. Jennifer had hired a PR firm, and the owners of it said they thought a party might be a nice way to welcome folks from out of town. They offered us their large, beautiful house, we set everything up; and the party began. In theory, we had a victory to celebrate. The day before, the White House had suddenly announced a change in U.S. policy toward Guatemala. Fuertes Caminos troops would be withdrawn from Guatemala in June, when the training period for the troops already there had ended, and scholarships for military officers to study in the United States would be suspended. They cited several cases that needed to be resolved before the Guatemalan government could count on a resumption of the programs — among them, my case, Jennifer's case, Michael DeVine's case, and Myrna Mack's case. Officials also said the overall human rights situation in Guatemala would have to improve. Richard Feinberg, of the National Security Council, called Jennifer into his office to tell her personally about the policy change. He apparently hoped it would be enough to convince her to cancel her planned hunger strike. She said the measures were too weak — they wouldn't save Everardo's life, and she was going ahead with the strike, as planned.

Nineth, Amílcar, Jennifer's friends from Vermont, a busload of people from Chicago, people from California, people from all over the country came to the house for the party. Laughing, talking, hugging, joking, drinking soda, wine, beer, it was clear they were celebrating. I watched their reflections in the mahogany table. It all seemed surreal. We were in this big, elegant house, having a party, and Jennifer was going to die. I wondered if the PR people had loaned us their house out of pity, understanding that the party might be more than a way to welcome people. Resuming the hunger strike was a mistake, they'd said. Jennifer would get no press. That story had already been done. She would be across from the White House with the other protesters who had been living there day and night for years with no results, with the homeless and the mentally ill. Maybe they understood it as a wake.

I must have been so depressed that I couldn't conceive of any outcome of the hunger strike except Jennifer's death. The rally, in my mind, was a continuation of the send-off we'd begun the night before.

We put up the stage, and behind it, we assembled the wall we'd made as a backdrop. We had painted a rift in the wall where the stones were cracking apart. "Break the Wall of Impunity," we'd written on the stones in big black letters. I liked the idea: the wall that protected the torturers was opening up. It was the same wall that kept the prisoners in. We could pull them all out into the light. The brutal Guatemalan army would have to stand before everyone and explain. And those who were still prisoners of denial, injustice, secrets, and lies could escape. I could escape — there was a crack in the wall I could slip out through.

I distracted myself with these reveries when the day's events became too painful. The rally coincided with the twelfth anniversary of a massacre in the village of Río Negro. We'd invited a survivor of that massacre to speak. He stood in front of the wall and spoke of how his entire village was annihilated. He tried to run and came across women being raped and killed. He returned to where the other children were. He pleaded with a civil patroller who was about to kill his little brother. He watched his little brother's brains dashed out against a rock. He was only about ten himself, and the civil patroller, his brother's killer, took him to his house, where he worked for years as a virtual slave.

The survivor wore dark glasses and a baseball cap as he spoke and was using a false name during his stay in Washington. We knew members of Guatemalan military intelligence were in the crowd watching. They always showed up for events. The survivor knew it too, and he was going back to Guatemala in a matter of days. But he stood there, struggling to tell his story.

Nineth and Amílcar spoke, and I also said something. Glancing up from the page, I saw beyond the stage the white crosses the listeners held aloft. We had hammered them together from two-by-fours, painting on each the name and birth and death dates of each of the 107 children and 70 women killed in the massacre. I seemed to be looking out at a graveyard that wouldn't be still, or an ocean, breaking in silence.

After twelve days on the hunger strike, Jennifer called the office and told us to be at a press conference in front of the Capitol. When we got there, Representative Robert Torricelli, of New Jersey, was speaking. Jennifer sat near the microphone. I could tell from her eyes. They were an empty sea. Everardo was dead.

Jennifer went to the microphone, still holding Everardo's photo. At least he wasn't being tortured anymore, she said. At least she knew that much. But she wanted his body, she wanted to give him a decent burial. And she wanted to see justice done.

Twelve days on the hunger strike had taken fourteen pounds off Jennifer. Instead of resting during the strike, she'd walked the halls of Congress and had meeting after meeting, pleading for information. Finally, State Department Officer Richard Nuccio told all he knew to Congressman Torricelli, who called Jennifer into his office and shared the information with her: U.S. intelligence documents showed not only that Everardo had been captured by the army, but that he was ordered executed by Colonel Julio Alpírez.

We all recognized the name. He was the one Santiago saw bending over the torture table. He was the one in charge.

Colonel Alpírez, Torricelli said, was working for the CIA. The same month that Santiago saw Colonel Alpírez threatening and interrogating Everardo, the CIA paid Alpírez $44,000.

I felt I had stepped into a movie — Jennifer, standing in the new grass behind the Capitol, saying the CIA was involved in killing Everardo. The "real" world was gone, the world where ideas about the CIA and its link to Guatemala were poor judgment, paranoia. I longed for that world suddenly, the safety of it, even if in that world I was wrong.

But that world was the fiction. In the Politécnica I had seen the reality. The United States was up to its neck in torture and murder.

At least he isn't being tortured anymore, Jennifer was saying. I tried to hang on to that thought. I had prayed for his death so many times so that the torture would stop. I'd hoped against hope — Jennifer's hope — that Everardo was dead. But I saw all her grief and I wanted him back for her; I wanted him alive again, under any circumstances, just not to see another part of Jennifer die, just not to see that endless, endless grief that had taken hold of her — her stricken face, the emptiness in her eyes. She reminded me of Dolores, drowning.

My torture taught me despair. Nothing I did or said made the torture stop. All I could hope for was to be destroyed completely. From Santiago I knew that captured guerrillas were used to talk each other into surrender. You've nothing to gain by silence, they would tell their captured comrades. Collaborate with the army. We are defeated. We have lost. They were used as instruments of despair. Had I too been used as an instrument of despair, telling Everardo to give up? Had the torturers released me with that poison so that I would spread it? I had told him survival was too painful after torture. What if the Woman had said that to me? I had allowed the torturers to speak through me. I had been their *portavoz*. If Jennifer ever learned that I had prayed in that manner and worked against her, she would despise me. Even as I was sitting beside her, holding her hand, I was a murderer.

Chapter Sixteen

TORN SECRETS, TORN SKIN

WALKING BENEATH THE CHERRY TREES was a springtime rite in Washington. Even during that chaotic April, with news breaking each day about deeper U.S. involvement in Guatemala, people in the Assisi community planned to go out and see the blossoms. I could never see a cherry tree without thinking of our first president, who, it is said, couldn't tell a lie. I couldn't stand the thought of seeing the trees now, no matter how beautiful, no matter how pink and delicate against the pale dawn sky. Times had changed.

So while my housemates headed for the van, I sat at the dining room table, a cup of coffee in my hand and newspapers from the past few days beside me. The sun, barely risen, peeked into the room. By the time I had finished my coffee, the sun was warming my shoulder and spilling onto the pages, but the chill inside me persisted.

Ever since 1990, when military aid to Guatemala was supposedly cut off, five to seven million dollars a year had been sent through the CIA station to pay for eavesdropping equipment, weapons, and lethal training for the Guatemalan army, I read. Not only the CIA, but the U.S. military was in Guatemala, "assisting the Guatemalan army in an effort to extinguish the opposition."[1]

The Guatemalan army extinguished combatants and noncombatants alike. Working at the GHRC, I knew the statistics. Between 1990 and 1995, 2,165 civilians were murdered for political reasons. Many fewer guerrilla combatants were killed. There were hardly that many in all the guerrilla ranks. The number was kept secret, but I had heard that the entire guerrilla force during that period consisted of somewhere between eight hundred and two thousand people. Did the CIA and the U.S. army make any distinction between armed combatants and civilians, I wondered, or did they, like the Guatemalan army, consider unionists, students, and human rights workers to be fair targets? Was the eavesdropping equipment used to bug civilians' offices and tap their phones? The death squads always seemed to know where to find them and when they were alone. I tried to imagine how eavesdropping equipment could be used against any-one other than civilians. I couldn't. The guerrillas lived in camps in the mountains surrounded by land mines. They had no telephones or offices to bug.

I moved on to another article, about the CIA's activities during the years that I was in Guatemala. The CIA from 1988 to 1991 kept senior Guatemalan officers on its payroll, "giving them sums far in excess of their salaries." Former president Cerezo said the CIA gave the Guatemalan army information about guerrilla movements or contacts in some areas. Cerezo's account of the CIA's activities "contradicts repeated statements from United States embassy officials that the Unites States never was involved with the counter-insurgency campaign." But, the article went on to say, the CIA station chief had twenty CIA officers under him and an annual budget of at least ten million dollars, half of which went to pay Guatemalan informants.[2]

Twenty informants at $250,000? Forty at $125,000? Maybe more informants still, at less remunerative rates?

Cerezo was quoted as saying he "realized during his presidency the over-whelming presence of the CIA in Guatemala," but "he tried to keep some control over his military," demanding "that Guatemalan officers inform us of issues that they handled with the U.S. intelligence agents and that they not undertake any operation with them that was not authorized by the government or by the general staff of the army. This was the official policy — but that doesn't mean that in some cases some officials don't do things that could be considered irregular."

I had to stop for a minute and gaze out the window into the back garden. A calico alley cat was lying on our patio. Beyond her some buttercups were blooming out of the dirt. The world out there was so simple compared to what I was learning. I tried to hang on to the pieces. The CIA was in Guatemala not just gathering information, but ordering operations and paying assets more than they earned in their regular jobs to carry those operations out. Who was really in charge during those years when so many people were murdered, disappeared, tortured? Who had ordered those operations? And my own torture?

I couldn't bear to think about it. I fixed my eyes on the paper again. A couple of paragraphs down, Ambassador Stroock was speaking about the DeVine case. Six weeks after Michael DeVine was killed, he said, it occurred to him to wonder if any CIA assets were involved in DeVine's murder. He asked the CIA station chief, who told Stroock that no assets were involved. The ambassador believed him, the article said.

I got another cup of coffee and an ice pack for my cheek. Did Stroock ask the station chief if any assets were involved in my case? Was it so unimaginable to him that CIA assets could have abducted and tortured me and that their American contact — in light of all the uproar, all the calls to Congress and the press — could have come to get me out? How could it have been so inconceivable when he could imagine CIA assets being involved in human rights abuses against Michael DeVine, another innocent American citizen?

I wasn't the only one outraged by all the breaking news. State Department officials, too, were upset. Marshall Carter, who worked in the Department of Human Rights and Labor, had met with Santiago and had given him a cold reception, insisting that there was no independent evidence of clandestine detention in Guatemala. But on March 30, 1995, Carter wrote to State Department Human Rights Officer John Shattuck:

> I am disturbed by the theme that seems to be developing in the official response to the allegations of CIA connections with Colonel Alpírez, in turn allegedly involved in, if not responsible for, the deaths of Michael DeVine and Efraín Bámaca in Guatemala. Exactly what the CIA knew and when it informed others of what it knew is of course very important.... The larger question in my view, however, is not *when* we know about what the CIA is doing, but rather *what* the CIA is doing. Enormous damage is done to the reputation of the U.S. and its ability to play a credible role in challenging the abuses of other governments by our apparent use of major abusers to provide us with intelligence, implicitly condoning this behavior and its funding by public monies.
>
> Our approach to this should be to press for sharply reining in the agency on operations. Forty years of support for the dirtiest kind of military in Central America has produced neither democracy nor social peace, and the intelligence that may result cannot outweigh the costs. CIA and other intelligence practices must now come under very close scrutiny by a body of wise men of some sort, including perhaps respected former Supreme Court judges or others sensitive to human rights and ethical matters in general.... The price is too high. We compromise our position on human rights. We corrupt our foreign policy. And we corrupt our intelligence as well.... The problem is precisely the principle that we press on other governments: accountability. The single-minded pursuit of information, with virtually unlimited funds, and without rigorous accountability

for methods, has distorted the intelligence function. Foreign misinformation campaigns and counter-intelligence activities could hardly
do more damage to our intelligence capabilities and our international
reputation. Who will call our own agencies to account?[3]

That April the quiet days I had to mull things over were few and far
between. Jennifer had a memorial service for Everardo, although she still
didn't have his body. Her parents and sister came and sat in the front
pew of the church, just as they would have if his body had been nearby.
Jennifer stood most of the time, facing the dozens of people who had
come to grieve. She didn't shed a tear. She couldn't allow herself that
show of emotion publicly. And she couldn't let herself break down. There
was still too much to do. Coalition Missing had press conferences and
congressional briefings, and then Senate hearings would be held, where
Jennifer would have to testify.

ON THE WAY to briefings and interviews, we talked among ourselves,
digesting what we could of the whirlwind happening around us. Why
Ambassador McAfee and the State Department and National Security
Council officials had lied to Jennifer was clear enough: they didn't want
to tell her that they knew Everardo had been captured and killed because
Jennifer would ask, By whom? If they answered honestly, Alpírez's name
would come up. And if the U.S. government accused Alpírez, he could
blow the whistle on the U.S. government and expose the entire covert
CIA operation in Guatemala. All he would have to say: "Guess who was
paying me?"

MY EXPERIENCE in Guatemala and afterward had made me as lifeless and
useless as dead wood. That's how I saw myself then: rotted, weak, not
good for anything. But now my experience had a context. And now I was
on fire. I thought about how, at the lawyers' suggestion, I had kept quiet
about the American during our trips to Guatemala. They said it was the
only way the embassy would help us. But, of course, with the clarity of
hindsight, I knew the embassy couldn't and wouldn't help us with our case
against the Guatemalan army. Anything that proved me credible would
damage the embassy, even if I kept quiet about the American for the rest
of my life; my allegations about him had appeared in the press early on.
In the United States, I had gotten so many blank looks from people in
Congress, friends, and colleagues when I mentioned that the CIA was in
Guatemala — blank, maybe even half-pitying looks — that I sometimes

had begun to doubt myself. People would tell me that maybe Alejandro was a mercenary, that the CIA really had no reason to be in Guatemala. See, the Berlin Wall was down. The Cold War was over.

But I was right. And no one would ever shut me up again.

Now when I told reporters that Alejandro said he was in Guatemala to liberate the people from communism, they rolled their eyes and sighed sympathetically. I was used to seeing eyebrows rise when I merely said he was an American. But now I told them I believed Alejandro must have been working with the CIA, and *Newsweek*, the *Los Angeles Times*, and the *Washington Post* published articles including my account. While I knew publicity could help the Guatemalan people by putting pressure on the army, I was angry to be taken at my word only now, after the brutal murder of my friend's husband, caused by someone working for the CIA.

THERE WERE SMALL VICTORIES to savor, all the same. A federal judge in Boston, ruling on the civil case we had brought against General Héctor Gramajo under the Alien Torts Act, found the former defense minister guilty. Gramajo hadn't even bothered to show up to defend himself. The judge ordered him to pay me $5 million and nine other Guatemalan massacre survivors $42.5 million in reparations for his role in "an indiscriminate campaign of terror against civilians." As head of the armed forces, Gramajo was ultimately responsible for all the human rights violations committed under his command. For that reason, the judge found him guilty in my case.

In the case of the massacre survivors, his responsibility was more direct. As army vice chief of staff under General Efraín Rios Montt, who seized control through a coup, Gramajo designed and supervised the scorched-earth tactics in the early 1980s that killed many thousands of people and wiped more than 660 villages off the map. In a May 1982 editorial, after a massacre in Semihados, a tiny Guatemalan village, the conservative Guatemalan newspaper *El Gráfico* denounced Gramajo's campaign of violence. "Massacres have become the order of the day. There is no respect or mercy shown for grandparents, children, or grandchildren. All were exterminated equally. How is it possible for a human adult to murder in cold blood a baby of less than a year and a half? How is it possible to behead an eight- or nine-year-old child? How is it possible, General?"[4]

Gramajo thought his strategy represented an improvement. In a 1991 article in *International Review*, a Harvard journal, Gramajo described his approach to army maneuvers: "You needn't kill everyone to complete the job.... We instituted Civil Affairs, which provides development for seventy percent of the population, while we kill thirty percent." Gramajo acknowledged that he was personally in charge of and supervised "the thirty-percent aspect of the program."[5]

One of the plaintiffs in the case, at the age of nine, was forced to watch as his father fell victim to the 30 percent solution. Soldiers under Gramajo's command jabbed sewing needles under his fingernails and toenails, burned him with hot irons, forced him to walk over broken glass, then cut pieces of flesh from his chest, arms, and back. At last, they shot him and threw him into a burning pit, where he struggled and twisted for ten minutes before dying.

By the mid-1980s Gramajo had grown more careful about leaving evidence. A Department of Defense document, dated April 1994, discusses the "suspected presence of clandestine cemeteries on a military installation." The DOD report notes that the airbase at Retalhuleu was "reportedly used in the mid-eighties as an operations and interrogation center for the D-2." The D-2 was the Directorate of Intelligence, or central command section of the G-2. "The commander of the theater during this time was former minister of defense General Héctor Alejandro Gramajo Morales." The document goes on:

> Small buildings on the base that have since been destroyed were used as holding cells and interrogation rooms for captured insurgents and suspected collaborators with the insurgents. There were pits dug on the perimeter of the base, now filled with concrete, that were once filled with water and used to hold prisoners. Reportedly, there were cages over the pits and the water level was such that the individuals held within them were forced to hold on to the bars in order to keep their heads above water and avoid drowning.
>
> One technique used to remove insurgents that had been killed during interrogation, and at times, that were still alive but needed to disappear was to throw them out of aircraft over the ocean. IAI-201 Arava's were normally parked at the south end of the runway after midnight, manned only by a pilot and co-pilot. D-2 personnel would drive bound prisoners and bodies out to the waiting aircraft and load them aboard. The pilots were instructed to fly 30 minutes off the coast of Guatemala and then push the prisoners and bodies out of the aircraft. In this way, the D-2 has been able to remove the majority of the evidence showing that the prisoners had been tortured and killed.[6]

I RECEIVED NUMEROUS CALLS from reporters who wanted my response to the judge's ruling. I was pleased, I said; one member of the Guatemalan military had at last been held accountable for the atrocities he had committed. But what about justice for all the other Guatemalans?

GRAMAJO KNEW he had little to fear from the United States, as a conversation passed on in a declassified cable illustrates. During a November 1991 reception, Political Affairs Officer (poloff) Lew Anselem asked Gramajo about the suit we had filed:

> [T]he general said his strategy is to keep insisting with the court that he is just a retired army officer and cannot afford either an attorney or to travel to Boston to appear in court in what is a politically motivated harassment. He expects, nevertheless, a "default judgment" against him but that "since it is a civil suit, not a criminal suit, I can ignore it." Poloff asked if he really does not have an attorney. Gramajo laughed and pointed to a rich Cuban-Guatemalan businessman a couple of yards away, and said, "He's arranged two very good Boston lawyers for me."
>
> Poloff asked about the Sr. Ortiz portion of the law suit. Gramajo said, again trying out his Harvard English, "They are trying to screw [not quite the word used] me [laugh] and you, too. . . . "
>
> He said he talked to congressional staffers recently and "nobody believes that story. When the facts come out it will be seen Ortiz was not harmed by Guatemala security forces. It was probably a boyfriend." He said that earlier in the evening he had talked to Human Rights Ombudsman Ramiro de León Carpio, who would soon issue a report on Ortiz "not favorable to her." On the law suit, we don't know if Gramajo is being a bit too optimistic. Just "ignoring" a civil suit judgment does not strike us as a great tactic. But then, he's got the Boston lawyers, we don't.[7]

Gramajo's plan to lie to the court was of no apparent concern. The cable, signed by Ambassador Stroock, was sent to the secretary of state and the U.S. ambassador to the OAS.

FOUR YEARS LATER, during all the April uproar, the U.S. government seemed to be doing better. After the allegations of a possible U.S. role in the executions of Everardo and DeVine and as the information about U.S. involvement in Guatemalan human rights violations mounted, President Clinton called for an investigation of the cases of a number of U.S.

citizens killed or attacked in Guatemala. He wanted to make sure that no member of any U.S. government agency had been involved in or acted improperly in the violence against Americans.

Human rights organizations quickly began pushing for the extension of the investigation. It was Everardo's case, after all, that had caused the information about Alpírez to be released. The message we were all trying to convey as we fought for Everardo was that no one — American or Guatemalan, ladino or indigenous, suspected guerrilla collaborator or confirmed guerrilla *comandante* — should be tortured. International law forbids it.

We asked the administration to order an investigation into CIA ties with human rights abusers throughout the hemisphere. We also called for an independent human rights expert to take part in the investigation President Clinton had ordered the Intelligence Oversight Board (IOB) to carry out. Finally, we requested the declassification of U.S. government documents on Guatemala.

Our efforts were futile, although we met several times with National Security Advisor Anthony Lake. The investigation would be conducted solely by the IOB, which press reports described as a four-person board composed of Washington lawyers and business executives, and the scope of the investigation would not change.

I tried to feel fortunate with what was being offered. I was one of the lucky ones. My case would be investigated, along with the cases of other U.S. citizens attacked or killed in Guatemala since 1984. But I was also disturbed. It seemed that, to the U.S. government, the Guatemalans didn't matter. The Woman, and what my torturers did to her; the children and women and men in the pit; the people I heard screaming in that building; the Guatemalans whose names I had memorized; and the thousands and thousands who had disappeared before I even knew about Guatemala — all were irrelevant.

Also, in spite of the protests of human rights groups, the board would focus only on the actions of U.S. agency members, not assets, although it was the actions of an asset, Colonel Alpírez, that had caused so much public concern. The issue raised by the public, the press, and human rights groups was the CIA's employment of torturers and murderers. Even in the cases of Americans, however, the involvement of assets apparently wouldn't be the main concern of the investigation. The IOB's charter was to review and report to the president on intelligence activities that might be unlawful or contrary to an executive order or a presidential directive. And paying assets who tortured and murdered wasn't illegal.

What was illegal was purposely concealing assets' involvement in human rights abuses from Congress.

In my case, the IOB would investigate the identity of Alejandro and examine whether any actions he took were illegal. The IOB would examine the embassy's conduct, the CIA's conduct, the State Department's conduct, and the actions and conduct of any other agencies involved. That's what I assumed.

With the help of journalist Allan Nairn, we were already getting some leads on Alejandro's identity. In an article in the *Nation,* Nairn revealed the names of some CIA officers who had been working in Guatemala. One — whose name Nairn said was provided by Guatemalan sources and a former DEA agent named Celerino Castillo — was Randy Capister. Celerino described Capister as a "thin, blond man in his forties."[8]

I tried to imagine Alejandro without the dark wig. He could be blond — his sideburns were light brown, his skin was fair — and the age Celerino had given seemed about right. Nairn's Guatemalan sources said Capister met regularly with Guatemalan army chiefs and was seen in Guatemala just a year earlier. Nairn mentioned that Castillo worked with Capister and had photographs of himself with Capister in the field and at embassy functions.

My lawyer Anna was intrigued. She wrote Capister's name down.

Allan Nairn had uncovered other information, too: Gramajo was on the CIA payroll.

MAYBE THAT EXPLAINED WHY no embassy or State Department official ever publicly rebuked him for his nasty public remarks about me. Maybe he was just following orders. Maybe the CIA was feeding him his lines. General Morales, the minister of the interior, said he heard the lesbian love affair rumor first from the U.S. embassy. Then he repeated it himself. Maybe Morales, too, was on the CIA payroll. I had been doing enough reading to know it wasn't impossible. Colonel Hooker, the former DIA chief for Guatemala, told a *Miami Herald* reporter that "the agency payroll is so large that it incorporates most of the army's top decision makers. . . . I'd hate to think how many guys were on that payroll. It's a perfectly normal thing."[9]

None of them were nice. "They were a mean, rough bunch," a U.S. official was quoted as saying. "The whole concept of human rights was like talking to a stone wall. There was not a single officer who had not been a combat veteran. . . . Their whole meaning in life was to go out and kill people." Allan Nairn, on *The Charlie Rose Show* (March 31), voiced the same opinion: "There are dozens of Guatemalan officers on the CIA payroll who've been involved in thousands of murders."

At that point, I began to wonder about the Guate-man and the Police-man. The Guate-man, I knew, was an officer. He was in charge. He and the Policeman gave orders to José. The Guate-man and the Policeman seemed of equal rank themselves. They had to flip for me.

"There are Americans inside the G-2," Allan said on *Charlie Rose.* I guess Allan had said that at the conference on torture in 1992. But I held on to his words, as if I had never heard them before, as if they made my very existence viable. Liar, the Policeman had called me. "Mentirosa." I had felt like a liar ever since.

"And it's not just the CIA operatives," Allan said. "It's the State Department, the Pentagon, and the White House. This is mass murder. If the American people knew about it, they wouldn't stand for it." Congressman Robert Torricelli, on the same show, added, "The United States government has been deeply involved in death squad activities. Our government had no business being so deeply involved in death squad activities. We made no effort to separate ourselves."

My feelings see-sawed. One minute I felt triumphant — I had been right all along about U.S. involvement in Guatemala — and the next minute, for the same reason, I felt sick. Beneath those two feelings was a low, constant hope. Besides the IOB investigation, Senate hearings would be taking place in Jennifer's and Michael DeVine's cases, and there was some possibility that more Senate hearings would be held for other Coalition Missing members. Meanwhile, Attorney General Janet Reno had ordered the U.S. Attorney's Office to investigate my case and Michael DeVine's case under the Anti-Terrorism Act. If the Department of Justice (DOJ) decided that I had been targeted to affect U.S. policy, the DOJ could prosecute Alejandro and my Guatemalan torturers. The Department of Justice could request their extradition to the United States, where they would be tried. If convicted, the maximum time they could serve would be ten years. It wasn't a lot, but it was much more than they would ever get in Guatemala.

MEANWHILE, THE SENATE INTELLIGENCE COMMITTEE HEARINGS took place. Jennifer; Michael DeVine's widow, Carol DeVine; Secretary of State Warren Christopher; and the acting CIA director testified about U.S. actions in the cases. The State Department position was that officials had told Jennifer for months that Everardo was dead, but she hadn't wanted to accept it. They had done nothing wrong, they said. The CIA insisted that it had committed no crimes, either; the information about Alpírez's possible involvement in both murders should have been passed along to Congress, but somehow it just "slipped under the rug." Closed-door sessions were held where, according to news reports, even less was learned. But sitting in the audience at the hearings, I did manage to get a message to Senator Arlen Specter, who was presiding. I told him my case was one of those involving Americans that should be investigated further. The Senate Intelligence Committee, before wrapping up, promised to hold more hearings.

Coalition Missing was calling for hearings that would include our testimonies and for a full investigation into CIA, Pentagon, and State Department complicity with the Guatemalan military. We also wanted the United States to declassify all government documents related to our cases and to all other human rights cases in Guatemala. At the same time, we pressed for a cut-off of all U.S. aid and support for the Guatemalan military, including the removal of all Guatemalan army officers from the CIA payroll; the revocation of State Department licenses to sell firearms or helicopter parts to Guatemala; the withdrawal of all U.S. troops and CIA advisers from Guatemala; and the revocation of travel visas for Guatemalan officers guilty of human rights abuses.

The only measure that eventually succeeded was the suspension of one visa for one Guatemalan officer (it happened to be Gramajo), and the suspension didn't go through until the fall of that year. Nonetheless, the Guatemalan army was scared and angry, most of all at Jennifer. In addition to whatever she had actually done to hurt the army, she had hurt the army's pride. Cartoon strips featuring Jennifer were appearing in the Guatemalan papers. One depicted Jennifer sitting cozily in an armchair, wearing a housecoat, sipping tea. "Jenny the Huntress" the caption said. Mounted on the wall behind her were the heads of a number of Guatemalan army officers.

ONE OF MY LAWYERS, Anna, worked with me to take advantage of the pressure and interest that were starting to mount. We met with dozens of congressional representatives and aides to ask that hearings be held on my case. Anna had pointed out to me early on that if we managed to get Congress to hold hearings, more attempts would be made to smirch my reputation. "She is ready to handle anything that comes," Anna wrote in her notes.

I suppose I was. I wanted everyone to know the extent of U.S. involvement in Guatemala. Some of the media were presenting Jennifer's case and the DeVine case as evidence that the CIA was a rogue agency, operating alone and out of control. An even more positive slant being put on the situation was that the CIA wasn't out of control at all but simply contained a few agents who had misbehaved by failing to pass along information about Alpírez, one Guatemalan asset who had committed human rights abuses. The real story, of course, was that the U.S. government at the highest levels had authorized a program in which the Guatemalan army — an army of human rights abusers — was paid and equipped to wreak atrocities on an opposition that was primarily unarmed. Because Congress wouldn't fund this army openly, given all its human rights abuses, and because the U.S. public wouldn't embrace the war as a policy objective, the whole maneuver was carried out secretly. That was the outrage.

I wanted Congress to help me learn the full truth in my case, and that truth would support the broader implications of Jennifer's case.

REPRESENTATIVE TORRICELLI was one of the people we hoped to enlist as an ally in our quest for more hearings. He was the one who had saved Jennifer by telling her about Everardo. And he was on the intelligence committee. As I recall, his legislative aide called me and told me Torricelli wanted to set up a meeting.

I was sitting in the waiting room when he came out of his office, and our whole conversation took place there, as he stood and I sat.

I gave him a four-sentence summary of my case and told him I wanted his help in getting further hearings and declassification.

"You say an American was involved," he said. "But your lawyer told the embassy that he thought the man was an Israeli."

My throat closed up.

Torricelli remained looking at me.

My mind ground a thought out: he must be referring to Paul. Anna and Michele aren't in contact with the embassy. I heard the Policeman's voice. *No one will ever believe you.* Liar. *Mentirosa.*

Torricelli was still staring, waiting for an answer.

And I was trapped. "I've always maintained that the man who took me out of the clandestine prison was an American," I said, finally, my voice shaking.

Torricelli stood there for a moment, then said he would do what he could and walked back into his office.

QUESTIONS DOGGED ME down the hall. Was it true that Paul had told the embassy he thought Alejandro was an Israeli, not an American? Why would he betray me like that? Paul had always told me he believed me. How would Torricelli know what Paul had told the embassy? Had Torricelli spoken to Stroock?

Jennifer would have had a perfect answer if something like that had been sprung on her. In less than a second, she would have said — "Paul wasn't acting as my lawyer if he made that remark. He wasn't *representing* me. He was giving his opinion, without my knowledge or consent." I wished I could be more like her. But Jennifer had nerves of steel. I had no nerves. *Estúpida. Idiota.* The syllables fit the rhythm of my feet as I wandered, lost, searching for the elevator.

YEARS LATER, Paul would admit to me that he told Stroock he thought Alejandro was an Israeli. Paul's explanation was that he was giving the embassy a way out so that officials there could help us prosecute the Guatemalan army without feeling accused. Someone, Paul told me, could have Israeli citizenship but could have been brought up in the U.S. and be indistinguishable from any U.S. citizen. And Israel, he noted, was known for its record of aiding the Guatemalan army. He said that he now believes without a doubt that Alejandro was an American.

ANNA AND I had sixteen meetings on the Hill in two months. Some went better than the meeting with Torricelli, but as a rule, members of Congress were more interested in supporting the Torture Victims Relief Act than they were in holding more hearings. The bill would allot funds to torture treatment centers in the U.S. and abroad so that they could help survivors free of charge or on a sliding-scale basis. I was lobbying for the act because I knew that to heal, people needed a place where they could talk freely about what they had witnessed and experienced. Congress liked the idea of treatment centers. Sympathizing with victims was easy. Turning the spotlight on the abusers, especially when it involved looking at our own role in the abuse, our own complicity, was another matter. It didn't involve feeling virtuous. It involved contention, conflict, and possibly making enemies. And Congress just wasn't going there.

IN JUNE, the identities of the CIA station chiefs came out in an article in *The Nation,* and Allan Nairn called on Congress to hold hearings that would include the station chiefs' testimonies. "If Congress is serious about investigating the U.S. role in Guatemala's holocaust," Nairn wrote, "it should call these men to testify — publicly — along with various higher-ups. . . . The point of calling these men would not be to use them as fall guys for Washington's crimes (the policy, after all, has been made by the White House, the State Department, and Congress itself) but rather to illuminate — with first-hand details — how the U.S. terror system works on the ground." To illustrate that the CIA wasn't acting alone, Nairn pointed out that Gramajo said he was introduced to CIA station chief Alfonso Sapia-Bosch (with whom he "did official business") by Ambassador Stroock. For Gramajo, there was no real distinction between the CIA and the rest of the embassy. As Gramajo described the CIA, "It's part of the country team, not separate identities."

Nairn's experience with Congress, however, was similar to our own. "It certainly appears at the moment, though, that Congress does not want such a probe. A senior investigator for the Senate Intelligence Committee says, for example, that he 'hopes' the CIA will 'come to us' if it happens to notice that it has anyone 'suspicious' on its payroll. But he said the committee does not plan to review the full payroll itself."[10]

Not even a check into the behavior of Guatemalan assets. Not even a glance at a piece of paper to see if any names stood out.

We had to face it. We didn't have a chance for more hearings.

My lawyers and I decided that I should go ahead and testify informally before the Senate Intelligence Subcommittee. My testimony, unlike Jennifer's and Carol DeVine's, would be given to several aides, not to the full committee of senators themselves. And the testimony would take place in private, not before a room full of policy makers, members of the public, and members of the press. Open hearings were what we had pushed for because everyone present in the audience is a witness to the testimony, to the questions asked or not asked, and to the promises made. But we scheduled a meeting with the subcommittee and hoped for the best.

I WAS NERVOUS — I would be questioned by a group of Senate aides — but I was also ready. I had been waiting and pleading for this chance.

Father Ted Keating, the head of the Conference of Major Superiors of Men, accompanied my lawyers Anna and Michele and me to the Senate Office Building. He lent a dignified presence to our side of the table, with his black suit, silver hair, and wise, weathered face. He sat beside me. Michele, who was small and blond and barely thirty-one, was at my other side.

A tall, thin man introduced himself as Ed Levine, an aide to Senator Specter. He explained that I should tell them what had happened to me in Guatemala, giving as much detail as I could, and then a period of questions would follow.

I held together well during my testimony. Anger, righteousness, and a budding self-assurance carried me through the hard parts. I didn't even hear the torturers' voices, smell their breaths, or feel their hands.

Ted and Michele gave me little approving smiles as Ed Levine shifted his papers and prepared to move on to the questions.

"In the statement before 1991," Levine said, referring to my 1990 affidavit, "some people say that there are inconsistencies. How should we take them?"

"What inconsistencies?" I challenged him.

"Let me try to recall: (1) how members of the U.S. embassy treated you; (2) the building where you were tortured; (3) the identity of the police car; (4) were you able to remember anything about the bus from Antigua; (5) the riverbed in Antigua."

I KNOW THE PERIOD between a blow and the pain, that moment when you can still think or speak or act. That was my window to answer. "I can't say personally that the ambassador was rude to me when we met. The first delegation that went to Guatemala, however, felt that the embassy was not responsive. The fact that a North American was involved and said that he was going to take me to the American embassy, I believe, made Stroock mad. I believe there has been a cover-up."

I didn't know how to answer the other charges. The "inconsistencies" referred to points that weren't mentioned in that early affidavit — the place where I was tortured, for example. I didn't identify the Politécnica until 1993. How members of the embassy treated me was never in any affidavit. No inconsistency about the dry riverbed was in the affidavit — my torturers led me up the dry riverbed behind the Posada Belén. In my 1990 statement, I mentioned very little about the bus. Was Levine saying that in one part of the affidavit I said I remembered one thing and in another part I said I remembered something else? Where was he getting his information? Had he even read my affidavits? It became clearer and clearer that he hadn't. He had just talked to Stroock, or someone with the same line.

After a short silence, he continued. "With regard to the North American, I am told that there are a lot of Guatemalans who have dual citizenship or are raised in the U.S. and return to Guatemala and that there are many of German ancestry. Are you convinced that it was a North American — or perhaps one of the above?"

"He was a North American."

"On a later trip, did you suggest that someone in the embassy may have been the North American? I was told that you saw someone at the embassy that might have been him."

"That's not accurate."

AT THE TIME, I was baffled. Now, after seeing declassified documents, I realize Levine was referring to the flashback I had in the van on my first trip back, when I gouged Mary with my fingernails. That Stroock knew it was a flashback is clear. In April 1992 he wrote:

> According to ARSO [embassy security officer], upon reaching the highway where she states she was forced in 1989 to board the public bus, Sister Diana had a serious flashback and appeared to be hallucinating that she was actually reexperiencing the kidnapping. When she was calmed, the group proceeded down the highway to where she said she and her kidnappers got off the bus. At this point she slipped into the past again. Screaming and crying, she seemed to think that the embassy driver and the ARSO (who arrived at the post only two weeks ago) were part of the group of kidnappers.[11]

It was a CIA document, which cites Lew Anselem's summary of my case as its source, that twisted my flashback into an identification. "At one of the public presentations made by Ortiz," the document claims, "she allegedly identified a recently arrived embassy security officer and a Guatemalan embassy driver as accomplices in her abduction."[12]

WHEN MICHELE ASKED LEVINE what information he had about this "identification" of a person at the embassy, he answered that during a general conversation with someone, that person (a man) told him that I had made such an identification on a subsequent trip to Guatemala.

Someone (a man) had been giving Levine false information before he had ever heard a word from me.

Before Levine ended the meeting, Anna asked if hearings would be held in which CIA station chiefs and others would be called as witnesses.

Levine said there would be another two or three months of work before a decision was made, but open hearings were a possibility. Another staffer assured us that the staff and Congress wanted to get to the bottom of the matter.

BUT ONLY TWO WEEKS LATER the door had shut. Joe Nangle, Anna, and I met with Levine and another intelligence subcommittee staffer, Patricia Handback, to provide more information on particular points the committee had asked us to clear up. Levine had asked for confirmation that Lew Anselem had said I was a lesbian.

Anna was ready for him. She had managed to get in touch with Miles Lackey, the congressional aide who had spoken with Anselem at a party at the U.S. embassy in December 1990. She shared her notes of her conversation. "Miles felt that Anselem was inappropriate. . . . Miles felt that there was an actual campaign to make people back off, with the lesbian rumors and self-inflicted wounds. He's willing to speak to you. I have his number if you want."

Ed Levine didn't pick up his pen.

Joe recounted Anselem's remark in their 1990 meeting that he was "tired of all these lesbian nuns coming down to Guatemala."

Levine didn't seem impressed. "Rudeness and stinginess on the part of embassy staff," he said, "aren't intelligence problems."

Anna promptly pointed out that when such behavior involves outright lies, it may signal a cover-up.

Levine said that if the intelligence committee discovered a cover-up and found out that Anselem was told to put cold water on the case, then they would talk to him. Otherwise, he said, he didn't consider talking to him relevant.

Levine, at Anna's suggestion, had spoken to Allan Nairn, who had given him some possible leads as to the identity of Alejandro. Stroock had confirmed to Nairn that Randy Capister did, in fact, exist. Anna passed this fact along to Levine.

Levine just shrugged, saying that, nonetheless, he wasn't even sure that Capister existed.

Anna asked Levine if the committee would speak with any witnesses we might find in Guatemala who could offer information about the identity of Alejandro.

"It's possible that members of the committee staff could go to Guatemala to interview them," he said. "Or representatives from the FBI could go, or representatives from the Department of Justice, the Department of Defense, the Department of State, or the CIA."

My hair started to prickle, as if a wind were blowing through the conference room. What sense would it make for the CIA to interview a witness who would have information about a CIA cover-up? I was new to Washington, but even I knew that the whole reason for congressional oversight committees was to oversee, in case there were cover-ups and wrongdoing. That's why we were asking members of this oversight committee to investigate. And he was suggesting that we let the CIA do the investigating themselves.

Levine said he would be reluctant to do the interviewing or have his staff do it because the committee didn't want to be responsible for any disappearances in Guatemala.

His remark struck me. Whenever I mentioned the possibility of witnesses being disappeared if I gave information about them — the woman who helped me after I escaped from Alejandro, for example — I was told not to worry, the U.S. government could guarantee their safety. But even Ed Levine knew better than that. Maybe I could call him as an expert witness.

That was all he was likely to be good for. Even Anna, who was generally more optimistic than I was, agreed. After the meeting, she wrote in a memo, "I got the distinct impression that the committee staff are not interested in the least in pursuing in any serious fashion an investigation of this North American. It seems like this may be a cover-up."

THE INTELLIGENCE OVERSIGHT BOARD (IOB), meanwhile, hadn't even started investigating. The board was supposed to finish its investigation by July, and it was already June. We were told that the IOB was waiting for the inspector general reports from within each agency to be completed. The IOB's report would incorporate that information, we were told, and the report would be out by the end of September.

JENNIFER WASN'T AROUND MUCH that summer, and I had so many feelings but no one I was really comfortable sharing them with. I didn't understand what was happening to me. Jennifer could have told me right away that she had seen the same symptoms in so many of the GAM women she'd stayed with in the mid-1980s: loss of appetite, problems sleeping, paranoia, negative thinking, withdrawal. I was getting deeply depressed. Jennifer, no doubt, would have found a way to tell me what I was experiencing without using the word "depression," which for me was one more label — and I hated labels. She might have told me I was grieving or I was profoundly sad, and that might have helped me feel less crazy. But she was gone, and I felt crazy. And the more crazy I felt, the more I withdrew — I didn't want anyone to know that I was acting again as I had in the months immediately following the torture. Being taken by force to the hospital was something I would never forget.

And the more I withdrew, of course, the more depressed I became. I couldn't even name what was eating at me. I couldn't sort out my feelings.

I'm sure I felt guilty and disgusted with myself, though, for feeling so sad when nothing was really wrong with my life and while Jennifer was in Guatemala, looking for Everardo's body.

The State Department had learned its lesson about withholding information from her and had passed along some intelligence: a report said Everardo was buried behind a military base in southwestern Guatemala. Jennifer was at the base, trying to recover his body. We were sending out her letters home, keeping in touch with the press, putting daily updates on a hotline, and doing whatever we could to help Jennifer. This was her first trip back to Guatemala since she had filed criminal charges against so many officers in the fall. The news about Everardo's death had broken since then; Alpírez's link to it had been documented; and the covert CIA program that supported the army had been curtailed accordingly. Jennifer was afraid she would be arrested as soon as she entered the country. One of our staff members, Patricia, was with her, along with my lawyer, Anna, a high-level Amnesty International delegate, a congressional aide, and a camera team making a documentary.

She had made it out to the military base, but so far, she hadn't been allowed to dig. She had to settle for getting the camera crew to film the pitted, uneven ground behind the base. That way, if anything was moved, she could pinpoint the changes.

For a military base, the place was poorly defended, Jennifer wrote. It was open-sided, consisting of bunk beds and a roof — no walls. Jennifer learned that the base had been used solely as a torture and execution site, and behind it was a mass grave containing anywhere from five hundred to fifteen hundred remains.

As JENNIFER WAS TRYING to have the gravesite excavated, Alice arrived at the office one morning to find the door ripped off its hinges. It was the outer door, the one made of iron.

"Someone must have chained that iron grate up to a truck," Alice said when I arrived. The door lay on the steps that led up to the porch. Alice was still surveying the damage. "After they ripped the outer door off, they must have rammed this door so hard that they broke the lock." She traced her fingers over the dent above the lock. The door was metal, and still they had dented it. The wood of the door frame was split.

"Hooking that grate up to a truck is the only way they could have pulled it off the hinges like that and bent the bars. I just can't believe this." She shook her head. "I didn't leave until midnight last night, and I got here at eight in the morning. They must have been watching, chomping at the bits, waiting for me to leave."

I followed Alice up the stairs. Her purse was on her chair where she'd left it the night before — in plain view, and still full of credit cards and cash. The computers were all there. But a couple of telephones had been ripped out of the wall — the wires lay torn on the floor — and the telephones were missing. The answering machine with updates on Jennifer's case was missing, too. The message was clear enough. The G-2 wanted us to quit helping her.

I BURNED SAGE in the office to try to smoke out the traces of the air they'd exhaled. I cleaned, dusted. And even though I was afraid, I continued my efforts to learn everything I could about who was involved in my abduction and torture, how it had happened, and why. I stayed busy, kept going to all my meetings. But as soon as I got back to the house I went to my room.

I KNEW I WAS STUCK in a deep sadness, and I wanted out. I was trapped in the past as if it were my own skin. As long as I was the only one who seemed to know anything about my torture, my skin, my mind, my past were the only evidence. I embodied the torture.

My skin was as thin as the skin of an onion or a snake. The smallest things hurt me. I wanted to be able to shed the past, to leave it coiled behind me.

I HAD TIME to read the paper again, but I never knew whether to brave it. The news, after all, was unpredictable. In June, the new CIA director, John Deutch, said the CIA would disseminate new guidelines to its officers on how to deal with informants who raised human rights issues. Deutch also said the CIA would produce written regulations and instructions, illustrated by examples, concerning how and when officers and management had to report to Congress.[13] He said he hoped to alter the CIA "culture or mindset" and force changes in "education, training, and procedures" that would improve the agency's profile over a period of years, not weeks or months.[14] But the CIA inspector general's report found very little that needed to be corrected. While the report criticized two successive station chiefs for withholding information from U.S. ambassadors and for withholding some information from superiors at CIA headquarters, it suggested that Alpírez was innocent of Bámaca's and DeVine's murders, finding "serious flaws in CIA reporting in 1991 and 1995 that initially linked" him to those cases. Like acting CIA Director William Studeman at the Senate hearings, the inspector general said the CIA's failure to inform Congress about 1991 intelligence information indicating that Alpírez was present at DeVine's murder was "management inattention," not a decision to deceive. He didn't recommend firing anyone. We weren't allowed to know what else was learned. The report was over two hundred pages long, but the public was given a four-page summary.

Some of the responses to the report were encouraging. An editorial in the *Boston Globe* the next day stated, "The horror of American complicity in this mass murder of indigenous peoples cannot be diluted by any rationale based upon a U.S. security interest."[15]

But by August, officials quoted in the *New York Times* were saying ridiculous things again. "We find ourselves dealing with people who have done things which are illegal and unsavory — organized death-squad activity, state-sponsored terrorism. In order to find out what they are doing we have to recruit them."[16]

It's not like we were stopping them, once we found out. We kept paying them instead of calling them to account, instead of taking them off the payroll, instead of reporting them to the UN or even to our own Congress. We were simply their sponsors and accomplices.

WHEN JENNIFER CAME BACK from Guatemala, she showed me some declassified documents that her lawyer, Jose, had faxed to her there. One said Efraín Bámaca "was captured, interrogated, and killed." It was a DIA document, and at the top of it was the information about where it was sent — to the secretary of state. The date was September 1993.

By the time the State Department received that cable, Jennifer had been begging the embassy and State Department for information for six months. They said they had none, and they continued to say that for another year and a half.

I saw a document, too, that must have gone past Stroock's desk. It was dated March 18, 1992, just six days after Everardo was captured. It reported that Everardo had been captured and was lightly wounded but was being well treated by the army, which "would probably keep the news of his capture secret, or even claim that he was killed, to maximize his intelligence value."[17]

The document details what Everardo told his torturers about how he obtained food for his combatants, how often he communicated with the ORPA command in Mexico, and how troops felt about Gaspar Ilóm. Everything he said, according to URNG sources, was false. But the CIA source wrote, "Commander Everardo continues to cooperate";

and the information was cabled to the U.S. embassy in Guatemala, CIA headquarters, and the White House Situation Room.

Another State Department document released to Jennifer was a chronology that included these events in 1993:

> February: Santiago Cabrera López and Jorge Augusto Recinos (noms de guerre: Carlos and Willy) testify at UN Human Rights Commission in Geneva about seeing Bámaca and 35 other guerrillas in clandestine army detention.

> Mid-May: Unidentified Guatemalan senior officers claim that army holds URNG members in clandestine jails. The officers reportedly believe the accounts of "Willy and Carlos" regarding seeing Bámaca alive. They also claim that there were 340 to 360 former URNG members under military control.[18]

I stared at the document for a while, wondering if the numbers were typographical errors. "No," Jennifer told me, "those are the right numbers." Santiago and the other former prisoner had personally seen thirty-five prisoners who they could name between them, but the total number of captured and secretly detained combatants in the army's program must be in the hundreds, she said.

What did the U.S. government do with that information? I wondered. Did they ask for the locations of these URNG members, these secret prisoners of war? Did they report them to the United Nations? Apparently not, although the United States was a member of the "Group of Friends," six countries who were helping support the peace process, along with the United Nations. The senior army officials would know about their own army programs. Why would the State Department use a word like "claim"? And what ever happened to those POWs? Did the United States let them die when their deaths, like Everardo's, could have been prevented? Did the United States let a war crime take place? Everardo's experience, Santiago's experience, multiplied by 360?

Were they still alive?

By AUGUST, when I received an invitation to speak in Louisville at the annual meeting of the North American Ursulines, I accepted, out of desperation. I had marooned myself, and even though it seemed impossible, I had to start building bridges. I decided I had to be as vulnerable and honest as I could. I had to speak openly about my feelings and about the past. I needed my community to understand me.

In my presentation, I admitted that the torture had left me feeling alienated and estranged from my community. I acknowledged that two of my greatest fears were that I did not deserve to be an Ursuline and that I would contaminate all the other sisters with the evil the torturers had planted within me.

I sensed an immediate connection with the sisters from Mexico after I gave my talk. With the sisters from my own community, I felt an immediate distance. I wanted so badly instead to feel the same connection with them. In openly acknowledging the distance and alienation I felt from the community, I only seemed to have made it worse. It would be years before I would understand that the sisters in my community had their own pain related to what happened to me and their own ways of coping. At the time I took the increased alienation I felt as an indication that I didn't belong in the community.

ON RETURNING TO WASHINGTON, I had no time to consider the question of my religious vocation. The Intelligence Oversight Board wanted to begin investigating my case. The leave of absence my community had granted me was for a year, and that period was over, but the leadership allowed me more time to give the thought I needed to the decision. In the short-term, at the suggestion of my lawyers and the IOB, I spent my time writing up a new affidavit that would include every detail I could possibly remember. Details could only help me, they said. I wanted to take away the torturers' ammunition, I wanted to be free of their hold, and I wanted to do homage to the Woman. Maybe the rest of the U.S. government didn't care about Guatemalans and couldn't bother to focus on them, but I could make at least one Guatemalan part of my testimony, and I had done her a disservice by not including her before. I had been like the U.S. government, in fact. I had omitted her, covered up the brutality she suffered to protect myself. I wrote a new affidavit, putting in everything I remembered and everything that happened in that room with the blood-stained walls. It tore everything out of me to write the affidavit. I didn't use spell check, I didn't check the grammar. I just handed it to Anna and Michele and went home, where I stood under the shower for over an hour, trying to cleanse myself.

BY FALL IT WAS CLEAR that open hearings wouldn't take place. No more hearings would, in spite of Senator Specter's promise — not on Jennifer's case, not on my case, and not on the cases of other members of Coalition

Missing. The IOB report was again delayed. We were told it would be released at the end of the year.

By then the public and the news media would have forgotten about Guatemala. Free of such scrutiny, the U.S. government could more easily squirm around the question of U.S. involvement in atrocities which happened to involve U.S. citizens, not to mention an entire nation of Guatemalan civilians. We were losing the window of opportunity Jennifer had won us at such cost. Among ourselves we speculated that the U.S. government was playing a waiting game. The war, after all, wasn't over yet.

MY LAWYERS were hoping for results from the Department of Justice (DOJ) investigation. I expected it to be another show. My attitude toward life and everything in it was growing more negative by the day. In our first meeting with two investigators from the U.S. Attorney's Office, I asked why, after nearly six years, the DOJ had suddenly decided to investigate my case. The investigators answered that they couldn't investigate my case before because I had refused to cooperate with FBI agents. It's true that I wouldn't be interviewed in 1990, when FBI agents were calling Paul. He kept explaining to them that I wasn't emotionally capable of speaking to anyone, especially men representing the U.S. government. But the FBI, which had, in fact, been conducting investigations in Guatemala, closed my case before even a year had passed. The FBI reopened it in 1991, not to see if I could speak with investigators yet — the FBI didn't even ask — but to get a copy of the testimony I had filed before the court in Kentucky in response to the letters rogatory from the Guatemalan court.

My mistrust of the FBI turned out to be well founded. The FBI was planning to pass anything I said back to the Guatemalan police. According to a January 1990 letter from Assistant Attorney General Carol T. Crawford to Congressman Carroll Hubbard, the FBI had "agreed to lend technical assistance to Guatemalan authorities" conducting an investigation of my abduction. "As part of that process," the FBI was going to "furnish whatever information results [from interviews of witnesses both in the United States and Guatemala] to Guatemalan authorities." A cable sent from one FBI office to another set forth the priorities: "The adverse publicity for the government of Guatemala and the alleged implication of Amembassy Guatemala City in Ortiz's abduction make it imperative to disprove the allegations or conduct investigation to identify those responsible."[19]

Dan Seikaly, the DOJ's chief investigator, did little more to inspire my trust. He said that until I released my new affidavit to him — the one I had prepared for the IOB — the DOJ investigation would be stalled. I clammed up and wanted to leave the room. Tell us everything or you'll get no help from us. That was the embassy's strategy, and that was the torturers' tactic — you haven't told us enough yet. Now the DOJ was following suit.

But I wanted to trust the investigators. Reclaiming people from the torturers — the way I had reclaimed friends I once might have suspected as the torturers disguised — was always a victory. Frank Fountain, a lawyer on the IOB, for example, had treated me with respect. He listened to me instead of dismissing me, and the tiny bit of trust I found myself able to place in him was like a handful of precious sand from a land submerged, flooded, and forgotten but now suddenly visible again.

Dan Seikaly was furious with Fountain. I had given the IOB my most recent affidavit. Seikaly had asked for it, and Frank Fountain, honoring my request that he keep it confidential, had refused to hand it over. Seikaly would have to convince me to share it with him.

In the end I did share it with the DOJ. I decided that my feelings of mistrust toward DOJ officials were based on my experience of torture and had nothing to do with the reality before me. I listened to my lawyers and other people. They had less biased impressions, I decided; my own experience of men in positions of power asking a lot of questions had left me with some strange ideas. Besides, Seikaly promised that only he and one other team member, Michael Tubach, would see the affidavit.

Once I had messengered the affidavit over, I had the sinking certainty that I had fallen into the torturers' hands.

ON SEPTEMBER 29, in spite of the inspector general's recommendations, CIA Director John Deutch fired two senior CIA officers and disciplined eight others. That, anyway, was a small step in the right direction.

THE NEXT DAY, Meredith and I went to the Latin American Scholars Association (LASA) conference, which was being held at a nearby hotel. I was going mainly to support Jennifer, who was speaking on a panel about U.S. relations with Guatemala. I wasn't looking forward to hearing all the guests speak. On the panel with her was Ambassador Stroock. I had no inkling, however, of what was in store.

Meredith, years later, wrote me this letter about the events of that day:

> What happened at the LASA conference and afterward was one
> of the most traumatic events of my life, ranking right up there with
> what happened in Guatemala — not only did I have my own personal

traumatic entanglement with Stroock, but I almost lost you — we almost lost you. If you had left us, Dianna, I would have been so devastated, and I know all of us would have been. It is hard to imagine life without you. In fact, I am crying as I write this.

It's largely scholars and human rights researchers that attend these meetings. But that year, because the LASA conference was being held in D.C., many local human rights activists were planning on attending, and I think many in the human rights community were looking to hold Thomas Stroock accountable for his time in Guatemala and his handling of your case....

In part, Meredith was referring to some of the information that had come out about Stroock's role in the secret U.S. support for the Guatemalan army. Allan Nairn wrote that, as ambassador, Stroock had "supervised the CIA station chief and, according to three of his intelligence colleagues, had access to the asset list." Nairn pointed out that the acting CIA director, William Studeman, had testified to the Senate Intelligence Committee that in Guatemala, as normally, "the chiefs of station coordinate extensively with the ambassador.... The ambassador is authorized to know all that the chief of station knows." Also, Stroock had admitted to the *Casper Star Tribune* (April 16, 1995) that he "knew that covert American [CIA] payments continued to the Guatemalan military" after Michael DeVine's murder and the purported 1990 "cutoff" of military aid. "At least seventy-four arms deals were completed under Stroock," according to Nairn, "in addition to the big M-16 deal, which was completed in the early months of his term, in which the sale of 16,000 Colt rifles were authorized." Nairn said some of those weapons were used in the Santiago Atitlán massacre of December 1990. Also, the elite Kaibil paratroopers, known as the "Messengers of Death," were trained secretly during Stroock's term.[20]

Meredith's letter continued:

We had agreed to meet up just before the panel started.... As we entered the room, Jennifer asked both of us something like, "If he gets out of line talking about his great human rights record in Guatemala, would it be OK if I brought up your cases?" — to illustrate why he wasn't so great, in fact, anything but. Both of us said yes, there was no problem. Frankly, I think many of us were thinking that this event might be cathartic — a lot of us felt angry about all that had been happening vis-à-vis Guatemala, that this was a way of holding Stroock — and the U.S. government — personally and publicly accountable for their actions down there and their actions on your case.

The two of us decided to sit close to the front so that Jennifer could see us, so that we could offer our moral support in a visual way. I think we were in the third row, or something close to that. . . .

Not long after we were seated two men joined us. This was a very strange event. At that point, there were empty seats all around us, but one of them chose to sit right next to me, on my left (the aisle seat) and the other chose to sit right next to you, on your right. I don't remember if they arrived together or not, but they clearly knew each other. And we overheard one of them refer to Stroock as his former boss. They wore dark suits and they looked a lot different from a lot of the other attendees in terms of dress and style. The two of us immediately had the same reaction — we had suddenly been closed in on by some men from State or from the CIA. You scribbled me a private note on your notepad, something like "Look who's joined us" and made some reference to their institutional affiliation. I remember being very annoyed and uncomfortable with the whole situation. But that's probably what they intended when they sat next to us!

The auditorium filled up, and eventually the session began. Frankly, I don't remember much about it, except the debate on stage was lively and at points heated. Then, of course, as was expected — Stroock began to discuss all he had done for human rights in Guatemala. Jennifer cut it short and brought up some contrary examples, including how he had handled our cases.

Stroock got very angry and countered, saying that he had handled our cases well, etc., etc. (This is where my memory gets fuzzy.) Immediately, I felt sick and extremely distressed — in fact, I have a strong memory that I wished I could disappear into thin air.

Jennifer wasn't as traumatized by the exchange as Meredith, and she has also shared her memories of the event with me. According to Jennifer, Stroock said, "I see you out there in the audience, Meredith Larson and Sister Dianna. Sister Dianna, I offered you the services of a doctor, but you didn't want a medical exam, did you, Sister Dianna? Why didn't you want a doctor to examine you? Get up to the microphone and answer."

Stroock had taken the same tack as the Guatemalan government. I had heard the question enough times to know he didn't mean a medical exam by doctors who would examine my back. I had had that exam in Guatemala and in New Mexico and he knew it. He, like the Guatemalan government representatives, meant that I hadn't had a gynecological exam. And why not? Perhaps he, too, knew the answer.

> I looked at you — you looked enraged and had started to shake with anger. Suddenly, you stood right up and bolted from your seat, moving down our row as fast as you could...to the back of the center aisle where there was a microphone for public comments.
>
> I wasn't sure what I was going to do, but as soon as I saw you bolting from your seat I knew that I needed to go after you. I probably arrived a few seconds behind you after you took the mike and I sat right next to you in a center aisle seat at the back that happened to be empty.
>
> You grabbed the mike and with obvious fury stated, "Everything you said, Mr. Stroock, is bullshit!"
>
> I'm pretty certain that then you received immediate applause. I'm not even sure you were aware of the applause because at that point, to me, you had entered a totally different space. It seemed to me as if you had begun reliving the trauma, but in a very acute fashion — and you were very, very angry.... And, as I recall, you got pretty specific..., making sure that he and the public knew that he did *not* do you any good — in fact, the opposite. When you concluded, you received tremendous applause.

As Jennifer remembers it, Stroock kept tearing into me. Every time I managed an answer, he came back with an attack, leaving me to struggle with another charge. To the audience, it was obvious that I was having a flashback. Finally, members of the audience started booing Stroock, and the moderator stopped the exchange.

> You collapsed into tears once back in your seat. I was devastated, seeing how upset you were. I desperately wanted to take you out of there. I think you replied that we should wait until it was done in order to be there for Jennifer, and then we would leave together. Because of my own trauma around the event, I remember practically nothing about the panel. You had entered your own space — highly traumatized — crying, and literally seemed to be elsewhere. I'm not sure how aware you were of me at that point. I so wanted to be able to comfort you, I tried, and you didn't respond to the comfort I was offering. We sat there for what seemed like an eternity until the panel ended.

The room began to empty, and some people, largely women, came up to offer us words of support. Jennifer finally managed to disentangle herself from her panel responsibilities and came quickly to us, and all three of us left immediately. We walked out, then sat next to an alley where no one else was around. I remember us sitting on some steps; you with your face in your hands, still crying. My anguish over this situation had become extremely acute at this point, I felt desperate and extremely frustrated that I wasn't able to provide whatever comfort you needed. I seemed to be trying and failing. Jennifer also tried to comfort you without too much luck either. She looked incredibly worried, and I recall she felt awful. While she had asked our permission to bring up our cases, she certainly hadn't expected things to turn out the way they did. I remember Jennifer remarking to me that she had lost so many friends at that point that it was a miracle she still had you around, that you had made it — and that she treasured you so much as a friend.

We sat outside the hotel for a while trying to comfort you but unfortunately not really being able to make much of a difference. It became clear that things weren't getting any better. The decision was made that she would finish some things up at LASA, we would take care of some things at GHRC, and Jennifer would join us back at home later in the day.

As we entered the house later, after finishing up our work at the office, I asked if I might join you upstairs. I wanted to be there for you, hoping that at some point my support would make a difference. You said no, that you needed to be alone for quite some time, and also that you had phone calls to make. I figured this meant you were going to try to reach Mary, and I was hoping and assuming that you would reach her and that she could provide support to you at this point, when the rest of us were not able to provide what you needed.

I retreated to the couch in the living room, profoundly sad, depressed, and traumatized by everything that had transpired. . . . At some point in the afternoon, I went upstairs and knocked on your door, softly calling your name. There was no response, all I heard was music. At that time, I interpreted the lack of response to be that you did not want company. During our friendship, I have learned that it is very important for your well-being to give you space when you request that space, so I returned downstairs, not wanting to impose on you.

Jennifer returned home at the end of the afternoon, and dinner started. She was very concerned about you and asked how you were doing. I gave a brief update, which was not much — because I hadn't actually been with you. At some point during dinner, Jennifer got a worried look and left the table, heading upstairs toward your room. What I didn't know then and what she told me later was that she heard the shower running for a very short time. She thought this was odd — no one takes such a short shower — and maybe she even suspected what was happening.

Jennifer has told me she had her ear glued to my room. She had hurried home as fast as she could because she knew I wasn't better — she'd heard from Alice that I'd locked myself into one of the rooms at the office and wouldn't open the door or talk to anyone. She heard a brief gush of water just as dinner started and assumed it was the shower. It wasn't. I had turned on the sink full force to stop the blood.

After some while passed, Jennifer came downstairs and said to me, "Meredith, Dianna would like to talk to you. Could you come upstairs?"

I went upstairs with Jennifer and entered your room — you were lying on your bed, looking so, so sad — and you said, "Meredith" and you turned your wrist up toward me.... I started to cry a bit and leaned forward to give you a hug. All I could say was "Dear Dianna. I am so sorry."

It seemed as if you and the torturers had battled for your spirit that afternoon — and that you decided that your only escape was to try to leave us and go to the other side. I am so, so glad that Jennifer found you in time and that we were able to bring you back and keep you here with us. The grief, devastation, and loss all of us would have felt if we had lost you would have been too much to bear.... My sadness, however, deepened significantly — now knowing that you had attempted to take your own life. I fell into a depression after that weekend that lasted for some time to come.

Meredith kept from me for years the effect on her of my attempt. She knew I tended to feel I could only hurt people, and she knew I would just take whatever she told me as more evidence that I was dangerous and needed to kill myself before I hurt more people. Even when she did tell me, I viewed her depression as evidence that the torturers, through me, had reached her too — not as evidence that she loved me. But torturers count on love for the ripple effects of destruction.

BESIDES CUTTING MY WRIST, I had taken the halcyon pills that the psychiatrist had prescribed to me when I was living at Su Casa, along with six Valium pills that a fellow survivor had given me to help me sleep. Jennifer called the Poison Control Center because she saw the empty bottle in my hand, and she found out that what I had taken was serious. The staff on the line threatened to turn Jennifer in if she didn't take me to a hospital. But Jennifer ran that risk for me. She and Marie had already tried to talk me into going to a hospital. They remember that I cried and cried and begged them not to send me to a hospital. I think they knew what being locked in would do to me, and they weren't going to subject me to another round of psychological torture. Jennifer and Marie risked their ease of mind for my own. They called a doctor friend to the house, who examined me, bandaged my wrist, and gave me charcoal tablets to suction out the poison. He slept on the couch, leaving my friends to watch me through the night. They watched to make sure my breathing was steady and had to keep waking me up when I fell asleep. They weren't sure if I was falling asleep the wrong way. "You know, permanently," Jennifer said when I asked her what the wrong way meant.

Meredith recalls:

> The next day, you asked me if I would please change the bandages on your wrist. It seemed to be such a moment of tenderness and sadness between us as I peeled off the bandages. I saw the razorblade cuts in your wrist, the living physical reminder of the torture you had relived the day before and the reminder that we had almost lost you.
>
> I tried to be as gentle as possible, cleaning the wounds and applying gauze and medical tape. I was glad I was able to do this one small thing for you. And it was also a strange, surreal reminder of six years earlier when one of my friends would peel the bandages off my chest and arm every day, clean up the blood, and apply new bandages. It felt as if we hadn't yet escaped the violence. And that's what torture is about — there's not meant to be an escape, there's meant to be a continuing legacy of devastation and trauma in the survivor and in their community.

In my journal I recorded my own account:

Sunday, September 31, 1995

On Friday, I decided to go with Meredith to a session where former Ambassador Stroock, Ambassador Mulet, Helen Mack, and Jennifer Harbury would address the issue of the CIA in Guatemala. My main purpose for going was to offer support to Jennifer. She has been through HELL. I think people tend to forget that her husband was brutally tortured and murdered and that she carries that pain with her. As always, Jennifer presented herself with dignity and courage.

Stroock, on the other hand, was a jerk and criticized a number of people in the audience, including Meredith and myself. Through the years I have gathered the strength to defend myself, the Guatemalan people, and torture survivors, or so I thought. Stroock knew exactly what button to push and he was successful in breaking me. As I approached the microphone he grinned at me, the same smirk I saw on the faces of my torturers.

I became disoriented. His grin brought back the memory of what happened with the Woman. I found myself back in the clandestine cell with my Woman Friend — facing those monsters as they grinned, as they forced me to hurt her. The smells and sounds of that November day began to seep into my being. What I find so disturbing is that I could not respond to what Stroock said. I allowed him to take that power away from me. I lost control. Angry, garbled words fired out of my mouth. I felt as if I were in a war zone — shooting at my enemies. I don't recall what I said. I was seething with anger and couldn't control myself. Not this time. In the past it was the torturers who humiliated me — but this time I followed in their footsteps. I was the one who humiliated myself. I didn't think I could ever face people again. People had seen my weakest side — that part of me that I've tried for years to keep secret. I never wanted anyone to see me in this state. I was so ashamed and at that moment all I wanted to do was die — to undo that scene where I had become like my torturers.

THAT SCENE was something I didn't dare describe, even in my journal. I didn't only seethe with anger. I didn't only babble as I stood at the microphone. I saw myself hurting Stroock, stabbing him. Afterward I heard the torturers say, *"Murderer. You're just like us. You'll always be like us."*

The intense desire to close my eyes journeyed with me back to the office and back to the Assisi community. In my mind I mapped out

very precisely what I would do to free myself from Stroock and all
my torturers. I mapped out in my mind what I would do to end
the psychological torture that I continue to endure at the hands of
both the Guatemalan and the U.S. governments — or perhaps I was
planning to punish myself for all that happened on November 2,
1989.

I swallowed a handful of sleeping pills. I guess I thought that by
taking the pills first, I would become listless and feel no pain as I slit
my wrist. I was wrong. The pain was there — but even worse than
that was the sight of the blood. I wasn't seeing my blood but the
blood that gushed out of your body when the machete was thrust
into you. I tried to make the bleeding stop. . . . I watched as the white
towel soaked it up . . . it was as if this inanimate object was willing
to cleanse me from that which I've kept locked up all these years. I
don't know how to describe this . . . but I suddenly felt this deep urge
to live. I wanted to live — to reclaim that desire to live life as fully
as possible. I knew that I had made another big mistake.

I must have gone into my bedroom after I cut myself because that's
where I was when I heard Jennifer knocking.

"Dianna. Dianna," Jennifer called.

I opened the door.

Part III

Do not fear the truth,
hard as it may appear,
grievously as it may hurt.
It is still right
and you were born for it.

> —Dom Helder Camara,
> "Do Not Fear the Truth"

Chapter Seventeen

FIRE AND SILENCE

JENNIFER'S LAWYER JOSE was targeted in January. A firebomb was thrown at his car while it was parked in his driveway in northeast D.C. The car must have burned quietly for a while before exploding. With a little breeze, the flames easily could have leaped the short distance to his house while he and his family continued to sleep.

The FBI investigated, and a spokeswoman told reporters that the bomb was not the work of amateurs or kids out to vandalize a vehicle but the work of "adults with experience."

"Pros," another agent added.

The firebomb was considered a possible act of international terrorism, and it made international news. Jose explained to reporters that Jennifer was again in Guatemala, trying to get Everardo's body exhumed, if indeed it was buried behind the remote military base, as the intelligence report suggested. The Inter-American Commission also was deciding whether to send Jennifer's case to the Inter-American Court of the OAS in Costa Rica, where the Guatemalan army would face a civil trial and, if she won the case, punitive measures.

That's what Jose said to the press. To us he talked mostly about his garbage cans, which had melted. They were the big, green, plastic kind the city delivers. Getting anything from the District of Columbia was a struggle. "It took ages to get those," he said. "I'll never get them to bring me any more." But if he was trying to laugh the incident off, it wasn't working because he couldn't even get himself to smile. Instead he sounded obsessed, the way I sometimes obsess about the dry skin on my hands when I have fears about bigger things. It was months before I learned that Jose and his wife kept jolting awake at the same time each morning and peering out into the dark, waiting for another explosion. She was Guatemalan and only a few years earlier had lost a sister in the war. She thought she had left the war behind.

THE NIGHT AFTER Jose's car was bombed, our community was shot at. A bullet lodged in the living room wall, and it came from a nine-millimeter handgun. In Guatemala, casings from nine-millimeter handguns are the army's calling card: those types of handguns are issued by the government specifically to the G-2.

I was sure the bullet was another message for Jennifer. The Guatemalan army's threats against her hadn't worked. Letting her know they could hurt her friends was the next logical step.

The shooting was covered in the papers and linked to the bombing of Jose's car: another possible act of international terrorism. The next day a woman named Nancy Soderberg called and asked to speak to me. She said she worked with Anthony Lake at the National Security Council. She knew I was a survivor of torture and she thought that the shooting might have affected me. She wanted to make sure I was all right.

No one from any government office had ever called me to express concern about my fear level. I was so astonished I couldn't even take in who she was. I assumed she was Lake's secretary. She was actually Clinton's deputy assistant for national security affairs.

WE TOOK ADVANTAGE of the administration's helpful attitude. Coalition Missing wrote to Secretary of State Warren Christopher, asking him to cancel the visas of all Guatemalans who were known human rights violators. At least two we knew of were in Washington: Colonel José Luis Fernández Ligorría, who was at the Inter-American Defense College, and General Luis Francisco Ortega Menaldo, who was on the Inter-American Defense Board. Ortega Menaldo was head of the G-2 in 1989, when I was tortured, when twelve university students were disappeared, when cases of torture, especially against Mayans, increased dramatically, and when human rights violations of all kinds reached levels not seen since the early 1980s. Many other violations occurred when he was G-2 chief — and when, according to Allan Nairn's sources, he was also on the CIA payroll. Nevertheless, here he was in Washington, in a prestigious post.

REPRESENTATIVE CONNIE MORELLA wrote on our behalf to Attorney General Janet Reno. She urged Reno to continue investigating until the attacks on Coalition Missing members and Jose had been solved and to make it clear to Guatemalan officials that the United States would not tolerate threats or attacks against its citizens. Morella said the incidents may have been instigated from outside the United States by Guatemalan citizens, constituting acts of international terrorism, adding that "as there are several prominent Guatemalan security and intelligence officials of questionable reputation currently in the United States, serving in diplomatic posts or inter-American organizations, it cannot be ruled out that they may have played some role in these incidents."

FOR NEARLY A YEAR I had hoped to get to the bottom of how the United States was involved in my torture and who the Guatemalan torturers were. I had hoped that, as in Jennifer's case, all the information would come out. But it seemed clearer each day, with the dead-end FBI investigations into the attacks on us, the administration's inaction in response to our requests, and the delay of the IOB report, that the U.S. government, once again, was protecting the Guatemalan army.

Even Frank Fountain, the IOB member who had been kind to me, seemed to be stalling. I had trusted him ever since he'd refused to give my affidavit with the information about the Woman to the Justice Department team, infuriating Seikaly. But now Frank was infuriating me.

I had called to ask him whether the IOB's findings and U.S. government documents would be declassified. I also wanted to know whether the board would release any information to Guatemalan victims if the IOB uncovered the names of people who had violated *their* rights. He skirted both questions.

Then I asked him if there were any new developments or leads in my case, and he said it would be "inappropriate" of him to give me information, since the U.S. District Attorney's Office was conducting an investigation of my case.

I told him that perhaps I needed to take some type of action to get some answers: perhaps a hunger strike or civil disobedience.

Immediately, he said he thought that such actions could be counterproductive. He said the board members were very sympathetic and knew how difficult the investigative process was for me; they certainly didn't want to harm me. He admitted that a thorough investigation wasn't carried out just after I was tortured, and he said the U.S. government was conducting that investigation now. He said a number of times, "Trust me."

Next he asked me if I could provide them with the identity of the woman who assisted me.

I explained to him that I had little or no memory of the woman. Then I asked a rhetorical question, trying to prove a point: "If I provided you with information about the woman, would you guarantee her safety?"

"We could bring her to the States," he answered. He still didn't understand.

"Would you guarantee the safety of her family, her community, and anyone who has had contact with her?"

"The immediate family would be protected," he answered.

I wondered if his concept of protection included automatic political asylum, housing, jobs, and education. I thought maybe I should send him to talk to Ed Levine, the Senate aide, about what happens to witnesses, and then to Su Casa to talk to Dolores and Eloisa about the difficulties of exile.

WHEN ANNA AND I met with Frank a few days later, he immediately pressed again for information about the woman who helped me. I didn't understand. Stroock in a letter to Paul had said it was important for police to talk with the woman in case I had told her "details that I later forgot." Stroock seemed to be anxious to help the police find more "inconsistencies" in my story.

Was that, perhaps, what these investigators also wanted? Or, better yet, a fearful denial from the woman that she had ever even seen me?

I was being paranoid. Why would they want to trap me like that? But what else could they want with her? If those who might prosecute my case just wanted to prove the parts of my story that it was possible to prove — to bolster my credibility — the woman could verify what I had said: that she had seen me running down the street, that she had recognized me from the news and taken me in and given me tea and let me cry and rest for a while, then loaned me money for the bus and told me how to get to Zone 1. But Mimi and Darleen could also prove that I was telling the truth about everything that happened before the abduction, and the two workers at the travel agency could verify that I had arrived there and asked for my passport and made a couple of phone calls.

Anna, in her notes of the meeting, wrote, "F.F. said that if the prosecution is putting together a case, it would be helpful to have an eye-witness to describe Dianna's condition." But that reason made no sense at all. Plenty of people had witnessed my condition — the two workers at the travel agency, at least six people at the Maryknoll House, the papal nuncio, the archbishop, a lawyer from the archbishop's office, two Guatemalan doctors, and Ambassador Stroock. Their accounts coincided. I had an abrasion on my left cheek; my jaw was swollen and bruised; I couldn't sit back against the chair; I had numerous burns on my back; and I was traumatized, fearful, and crying. The woman's life would be endangered, and she could add nothing substantial or useful. I kept her buried deep in my mind.

FRANK URGED US not to expect too much from the IOB investigation. He told us we had to "keep in mind the difficulty in finding information under the circumstances." Anna wrote in her notes, "F.F. was very nervous about possible hunger strikes, etc."

As MUCH AS Frank Fountain annoyed me, pressuring me to reveal information and answering none of my questions in return, he treated me with kindness and I couldn't help but like him, especially when I compared him to DOJ investigator Michael Tubach. Unlike Frank Fountain, who had a rather introverted, mellow nature, Michael Tubach oozed ambition, condescension, and conceit. I could barely sit in the same room with him, and I couldn't imagine telling him in detail about my torture. He was a short man in his early thirties, with fine, blond hair. His shoes were very shiny. He would sit by judgmentally, I could already guess, looking at his watch, as I journeyed back to that prison. I didn't trust him, I couldn't trust him, I couldn't tell my story to him. I appealed to Mary for help.

MARY DID EVERYTHING she could to help, dropping her work to fly to D.C. so that she could meet with Tubach. Anna and I were at the table, too, along with several FBI agents who were working on the case. After a few preliminary questions from Tubach that I had to answer, Mary shifted in her seat and set to work trying to melt the frost that hung on each word exchanged between myself and Tubach.

She told him I had trouble trusting anyone in authority, especially a male who represented the government. My torturers, too, were males representing the government, and they had complete authority over me, which they abused, she said. I believe she may have mentioned a little bit about our experience with the courts in Guatemala and how that only added to my sense that I couldn't trust anyone representing the legal system. She went on to explain that legal jargon isn't always accessible to or affirming of the survivor and that sometimes even the way a phrase is worded can make a difference. "For example," she said, "the way you're asking the questions, the way they're worded, it sounds like you don't believe Dianna."

Tubach was quiet for a long moment. "It doesn't matter," he said finally, "if I believe her."

Mary was stunned. She realized she could do no more. She didn't know how to facilitate communication that would help build trust between us when Tubach's answer implied a lack of trust that was so basic.

I don't remember Tubach's answer myself. I must have tuned it out because letting it sink in would have hurt too much.

Not that what he said was such new information. I knew, deep down, that he didn't believe me. I could see it in the way he looked at me, in his sneer. His condescension, though, only made me more determined to prove that all I was saying was true. I couldn't stand to face the possibility that the investigation would yield nothing. I wanted results too badly.

But something must have sunk in. I must have realized, on some level, that it might be a good idea to go over the heads of everyone on both the IOB and the DOJ team. I wrote to President Clinton.

February 7, 1996

Dear President Clinton:

I am writing to implore your assistance in an urgent matter. It's my understanding that you've been briefed on my case and for that reason I will not bombard you with specifics.

For more than six years I have battled tirelessly to learn the truth of why I and innocent Guatemalans fell victim to inhuman acts committed both by Guatemalan and U.S. citizens. After my release, U.S. officials opted to ignore what had happened to me; instead, in concert with the Guatemalan government, they concealed the truth by orchestrating a smear campaign against me with the intent of ruining my credibility. It was not until last spring's scandal that a sudden interest was awakened in my case and those of countless Guatemalans. But even with all of this, I still, to this day, more than six years later, do not know the truth.

In April of last year, I filed my Freedom of Information Act request to obtain access to U.S. government documents on my case. I find it very disturbing to know that various entities that are conducting an investigation of Guatemala cases — the IOB, the Senate Intelligence Committee, the Justice Department, etc. — all have access to my documents. I, on the other hand, have not received one shred of paper, nor have I been given any substantial information on my case. I am the only one who has nightmares about what happened. Yet I am the only one, it seems, who is not allowed to know.

I would like to share with you how the experience of torture continues to torment me. Like many torture survivors, I dread the arrival of night. . . . I know that if I close my eyes the torturers will return. Awake I fight them. Asleep I am powerless. Recently, unable to fight my body's need for sleep, I closed my eyes. I dreamed my torturers escorted me into a room. . . . The walls were splattered with dried blood. . . . In the middle of the room was a cot-like bed with a blood-stained sheet. My torturers ordered me to peel the sheet back. On the cot lay the unblemished body of a woman. I watched as they marred her body, severed her breasts, charred her skin into round holes with the tips of their cigarettes. The once unblemished face was black and blue, covered with blood, and distorted beyond recognition. The woman cried out for help. I tried to protect her from these monsters. The room became an arena and Alejandro sat in the seat of "honor." Behind him sat an entourage of U.S. officials. With a pipe in his mouth, he watched nonchalantly as a human life was destroyed. I awakened — with a bloody nose and bruises where my flailing hands had pounded against the wall.

You see, Mr. Clinton, I always want out. Out of this nightmare. Out of this past. Out of this room with Alejandro and my Guatemalan torturers. But the nightmare doesn't end when I awake because Alejandro is not just a dream image. He is a pivotal piece of my past and a symbol of the very real and daily fact: He represents six years of U.S. officials who have lied to me, concealed the truth, denied me basic information, and tried to keep me in the darkness.

Why is my government concealing the truth from me, from the Guatemalan people and the American public? Who is this Alejandro, Alejandro who not only was present in the torture chamber but had the authority to give orders to my torturers? Why is my government protecting him? Is national security a higher priority than human life?

Like the Guatemalan people, I want desperately to put the past behind me. I have been very patient for six years. What would you do? God forbid, but what if it happened to your daughter, your wife? What would you tell her? Forget?

Mr. Clinton, you can put these ghosts to rest by ordering a comprehensive and rapid declassification of U.S. government documents pertaining to my case and to *all* human rights violations in Guatemala. Give us the truth and let us rest.

Time is running out for me. If the IOB report does not reveal answers to my search for truth, then I have no other choice than to take strong action. Perhaps hunger strikes or other actions are the only means of obtaining truth in this country. I don't want attention. All I want is peace . . . for myself and for the people of Guatemala.

I sent copies of the letter to Frank Fountain, IOB Chairman Anthony Harrington, National Security Advisor Anthony Lake, and John Shattuck, the assistant secretary of state for human rights, as well as various members of Congress.

Frank Fountain responded first, a couple of hours after I'd faxed him the letter. He said that, from my letter, he understood my two concerns to be declassification and the status of my case. Suddenly he could tell me all sorts of things. What was holding up declassification and the IOB report was my case — the ongoing criminal investigation by the District Attorney's Office. He said the priority of the IOB and the DA's Office was to try to put closure on my case.

A FEW DAYS LATER, Anna learned some information about the investigation from Celerino Castillo, who had worked in Guatemala as a DEA agent. Anna had interviewed him once before for any information he might be able to give us on my case. Now Celerino had a little more to offer us: the DOJ had called a grand jury and had asked him to testify.

Did the DOJ have a suspect, Anna asked Celerino, or was the grand jury called so that the DOJ team could issue subpoenas?

Celerino didn't know.

What was more important to me was whether the entire grand jury had seen my affidavit. I had a feeling Seikaly had lied to me. He and Tubach weren't the only ones working on my case, and I had no doubt that they weren't the only ones who had read my affidavit. From what I understood, at least four FBI officials and another DOJ investigator were also involved. And now, perhaps, a grand jury.

MY PLAN TO GET ANSWERS developed gradually. Late at night I lit candles and, sitting on the floor of my room, I imagined the Woman, Everardo, Miguel, Mimi, and the people in the pit. I thought about Saint Angela, too, the founder of the Ursuline order. I couldn't really picture her, a fifteenth-century Italian woman, but I managed to feel her as a presence, a form of energy. I told Everardo how, even after Jennifer had risked her life and gotten a firestorm of press, things had gone back to normal. It seemed that the CIA and the U.S. government were going to get off the hook. The Guatemalan people would never have the rest of the story, and neither would we. He was a brilliant strategist. What would he do?

I asked Miguel to help me have courage. I'd like to rest. But I escaped and you didn't, and I only escaped because I was an American, a citizen of the same country that helped start your war and supported the army decade after decade. So Miguel, even if I wasn't to blame for your abduction by giving the torturers answers when they asked me about you, I was to blame in a larger sense and I have a wrong to redress. You were an activist. Tell me what to do.

The Woman just held my hand. She let me know that she was with me, whatever I chose to do. And she told me to be strong because if I tried to fight they would try to break me.

The women and children who were in the pit still had blood caked on them, limbs missing, but they were sitting beside me, wise indigenous women, nodding, saying, "Pues, hay que luchar, Dianna, porque tu puedes luchar y nosotros no" (Well, you must keep struggling, Dianna, because you can and we cannot).

Angela gave me strength. She seemed to ask me to look beyond the DOJ and to allow myself the freedom to see a wider range of options than the ones the investigators offered. I felt she was urging me to turn to the sisters, to swallow my pride and overcome my fear and ask for their prayers and advice.

I WROTE TO THE SISTERS and asked them to pray for me. I was scheduled to be interviewed by DOJ investigators. Anna, after a battle with Michael Tubach, had convinced him not to tape the interview but only to take notes. Marie Dennis and Joe Nangle came with us to the meeting to lend support and to even out the numbers. There were four of us now, seven of them.

One FBI agent, Tim O'Neill, wore cowboy boots. Another, a woman named Xanthie, left a better impression on me than anyone else in the group. She had dark hair, but I've blocked her face. I've blocked all their faces. George Calhoun and Bob Chaney were the only DOJ investigators I hadn't met yet. I don't remember George Calhoun at all. Bob Chaney sticks in my mind as a round man with a pot belly and white skin. He seemed used to being in a position of control and knowing all the answers. He reminded me of Tubach in that way.

Dan Seikaly began the meeting by saying he would follow up on any leads or suggestions we made, adding that he expected the investigation to be completed by the end of March.

That's about a month away, I thought. The DOJ team hasn't even interviewed me yet and still they plan to end the investigation in a month. They must not be planning to follow up on any leads or information they get from me.

"Now, we intend to share everything we can within limits," Seikaly went on. "We cannot share the following: classified documents; grand jury material; or confidential law enforcement sources."

He must have noticed that I looked puzzled. "What that means," he said, "is witnesses who give information but don't want their names used.

That is, we won't divulge the identity of the person but we may divulge the information."

"Do you have classified documents in your possession?" I asked.

"I think so."

He *thinks* so? I looked at Anna. And they expect to wrap up the investigation in a month?

"But there's not a great deal of classified documents," he added quickly. "So far I've only seen the kinds of documents that would be routinely classified."

"Are you speaking with 'confidential' witnesses?" I was for once asking questions in the manner they did, and for once I was getting answers.

Then Michael Tubach stepped in. "There are people with whom we have spoken who did not want their names used. The policy of the DOJ is not to provide information relating to an ongoing investigation because we don't want to see our investigation in the press."

He was telling me, I assumed, not to push it, that I was lucky to be getting answers at all. A burning started in my chest.

"Of course, Michael can give you unclassified documents, if you want," Seikaly offered.

As I understood it, since I had filed my Freedom of Information Act request, I had the right to see information the government had about me, including classified information. Yet Seikaly was sitting there, smugly telling me that Tubach could do me the favor of giving me unclassified documents.

"No, I actually can't give you documents from other agencies, including unclassified documents," Tubach said. "I could only give you documents that are in the public domain that may be available in other places."

I understood. He was saying that he could only give me anything that might also be found in a library.

Anna changed the subject. "We hear a grand jury's been called," she said. "Was it called for investigative or indictment purposes? I know you told us before, Michael, that the grand jury was called mostly for investigative purposes, to issue subpoenas."

"I can't comment on whether the grand jury was called for investigative or indictment purposes."

Anna sat back in her chair.

"The Assistant U.S. Attorney's Office will look at and consider all in-formation that you provide that is relevant," Tubach continued. "I've been working on the case full-time for five months. We've interviewed quite a number of witnesses, and interviews are continuing."

"Are you still conducting interviews in Guatemala?" Anna asked.

"It's not clear if we'll question more witnesses in Guatemala."

"What about Randy Capister, the CIA agent — he is a CIA agent, right? Did you interview him?"

"I can't tell you if he's a CIA agent or not — you need to go to the CIA and ask."

"OK, can you confirm that he exists?"

"No, I won't confirm that Capister exists."

"Has any progress been made on determining the identity of the North American?" I asked Tubach.

"I can't talk about it."

"Do you plan to put Dianna before the grand jury?" Anna's voice was sharp now, her Philadelphia accent hard.

"The decision to put Dianna before the grand jury is an investigative decision influenced by Dianna's wishes," Tubach answered.

I tried to listen while he explained what a grand jury was and how it functioned. Anna crossed her arms. No doubt she had learned about grand juries before, in law school.

"A taped interview of Dianna might obviate the need for her to testify before the grand jury," Tubach said, finally answering the question.

I kept my gaze on the shiny wood table, afraid that if I looked up, Tubach would be gloating: he would win, one way or another. See, if I didn't testify before a grand jury, he would tape me.

Anna ignored his answer and whatever reference it might have contained to their drawn-out battle about whether he could tape his interview of me. "Is the DOJ investigation holding up the processing of Dianna's Freedom of Information Act request?" she countered.

"I don't know."

"How is a decision made to investigate a case like Dianna's?"

"I don't know, but you could speak with Jim Reynolds, the head of the Terrorism and Violent Crime Section."

Joe Nangle broke the silence that followed, asking if the principal aim of the investigation was to determine the identity of the North American.

We should have listened carefully, much more carefully to Tubach's answer.

"The DOJ has jurisdiction to prosecute anyone who commits a crime for terrorist purposes. However, no decision has yet been made in Dianna's case that it was committed for terrorist or nonterrorist purposes." Anna was taking notes, but in retrospect I think she should have put a comma after "committed." No decision has been made that a crime was committed — that's what Tubach was saying.

I'm not sure if I caught more than Anna in Tubach's answer. But I knew Tubach was acting like a jerk. Seikaly, too. And I wasn't about to make myself vulnerable in front of those men. When Tubach spread his hands apart, said we were finished, and asked me if I was ready to be interviewed, I said no.

WHILE I ASKED THE SISTERS for prayers, I asked Jennifer, Alice, Anna, Jose, and some of the Guatemala Human Rights Commission board and staff for advice. We got together late one afternoon at the commission, when the midwinter dusk hung outside the windows. Alice made coffee for everyone and I waited nervously while Anna and Jose and Alice caught up on small talk. Jennifer already knew why I had gathered them together. I had told her one night after dinner about Plan A. She had lowered her eyelids and taken a long sip of tea. "Why don't we think about it. You have to do something, you're right about that. Why don't we think about it and maybe talk to Alice, Jose, Anna. See what people think might work."

So here everyone was, sitting down, finally. Alice cleared her throat and said, "Dianna, you want to start? You have something you wanted to ask or tell us about?"

"I'm thinking of going to a foreign country." I chipped at some old nail polish on my fingernails. "And burning my passport."

I could picture the flames bursting through the pages, the mess of plastic melt and ashes — the passport I had longed for during those twenty-four hours six years ago. My ticket out of Guatemala, my ticket to freedom. I wanted to burn it publicly and tell everyone that it had done me no good: my own government held me prisoner to the past, shackled me and all of Guatemala with misinformation and secrecy.

Everyone was looking at me blankly. Alice had gone a shade paler.

"I'm not going to just take this," I said, my voice thickening. "As a citizen of this country, I'm supposed to have rights, but apparently I don't, so maybe I shouldn't be a citizen of this country. Maybe I should go somewhere else."

"Where are you thinking about, Dianna?" Alice asked.

"Anywhere."

"Dianna," Jennifer said, "if you renounce your citizenship, they win in the end. You're no longer a thorn in their side. They've silenced you, and you've allowed yourself to be silenced. What do you think, Alice?"

"I think that's right."

The truth of what they were saying struck me. Both the U.S. and the Guatemalan governments would celebrate their good fortune if I headed for a foreign country, never to return. Well, then, Plan B. That was the real plan, the one that made my stomach queasy, not the fantasy that gave me pleasure to consider. That's why it was so much harder to think about or share with anyone.

"My other idea was doing a vigil outside the White House."

Alice cleared her throat. "How long would this vigil last?" she asked, sitting back and folding her arms.

"I don't know." I kept my eyes on my fingernails, in case anyone saw my fear. As long as they all thought I wasn't afraid, they might not discourage me. And I didn't want to be discouraged. This was what I had come up with, after all those nights of prayer and all those visits with the friends who formed my circle.

No one told me I shouldn't do the vigil. I think they were relieved that I wasn't going into exile. But no one said the vigil was a great idea and would surely produce results. And when the meeting was over the doubt I was hoping to dispel still gnawed at me. As Alice and I gathered up the coffee cups, she said, "Dianna, it will be hard being out there day and night. I don't know if you realize how hard it will be."

"Alice, I've been tortured," I answered. "I can handle it." I took the cups into the bathroom to wash, clanking them down in the sink. Of course I could handle it. Sometimes Alice acted like I needed sheltering from the cruel world under her wing. Well, I had seen the cruel world. Why did everyone think I was so naive?

To BE HONEST, I was hoping I wouldn't have to handle the vigil. I sent a letter announcing the vigil to President Clinton, Anthony Lake, and Frank Fountain. Then I tried not to wonder each time the phone rang if it would be for me, if someone would say, "Sister Dianna, you don't have to go on a vigil day and night to get information in this country." It was an election year — surely the president wanted his administration to look good.

But the days passed, and no phone call came. Two weeks, finally, were all that remained. The time for benevolent voices on the phone had come and gone. I sent out a letter to my friends and human rights contacts, announcing what I was going to do and closing off my last exit.

I scheduled the beginning of the vigil for Palm Sunday, which commemorates the day Jesus journeyed into Jerusalem on a donkey. Jesus had the courage to make that journey to his trial and crucifixion, to do what he believed was right for humanity. My search for the truth was not just for myself but for the people of Guatemala. I hoped that remembering Jesus' courage would give me the strength to do what was right for them, not simply what was most convenient or comfortable for myself.

Starting the vigil on Palm Sunday also reinforced for me the idea that all people are called to carry their cross and walk their journey; and however difficult that journey and however heavy that cross, the journey is toward life, ultimately. Each step is one more step toward life.

The vigil, in some ways, would be the opposite of the clandestine prison, and the miniprisons I used to protect myself would be absent. On the vigil I would be sitting in the open air day and night — I, who so often shut myself in my room. I would be highly visible, even though I was known to say when I was having a hard time, "I just want to disappear." The vigil represented a step out of the prison I carried within.

Beginning the vigil on Palm Sunday, I would have the opportunity to speak out on the situation in Guatemala and frame those thoughts in a faith context. I asked myself how I could do that. I still couldn't say, "Yes, God, I commit my life totally to you." And I felt like a hypocrite for not being able to say that because, after all, I was a nun. But I was beginning to realize that faith involved more than my relationship to God and the Church and the sacraments. It involves our relationship with all the universe, including ourselves. And I was starting to have a kind a faith. I had started to believe in the goodness of nature. Squirrels, for example, no longer seemed evil to me. Nature was no longer suspect, a potential vehicle for the Devil — or the torturers — to work through. I was also starting to have faith in myself. I believed that I could stand up for what was right. Instead of thinking I had done everything wrong on that day six years ago, I realized that when José asked me to forgive him, I hadn't erred. It wasn't that I was hard-hearted. I had refused to let him prey on my fear, bribe and sweet-talk me into betraying my principles as he dangled the promise of freedom before me. I had believed then that God would be with me. And I was starting to believe that maybe God had been with me, giving me the strength to resist temptation and to stay alive. I had a kind of faith. So I dared to start my vigil on a sacred day and derive the strength I could from that day and its symbolism.

I was afraid, though. Things were going well enough. Why kick up dust?

But what good was I doing for myself or the world waiting around and being lied to by government officials, at their mercy for a scrap of truth?

When I called my circle of friends together at night, they seemed to tell me they would be with me, no matter what I chose. If I packed my bags and went to another country or another city, they would still support me. But if I chose to do the vigil, they would be with me out in the park. For the first time, I felt really free to choose instead of being constrained to act, half-resentfully, from a sense of moral obligation.

THE FRIDAY BEFORE THE VIGIL was scheduled, I received a couple of pieces of mail. The first was a white package found at the back door of the Assisi community, on the steps down to the patio. Under my name was my old address at Su Casa, in Chicago. The package had no postage and no postmark. Someone had placed it on the steps, evidently, or had thrown it from the alleyway behind the house. Also missing was a return address.

I refused to touch the package and asked Marie to open it. She took it into the dining room. When she broke the seal, some of the contents spilled out — crumbly dirt and dog or human feces.

A few of my housemates thought the package was an allusion to my remark to Stroock that everything he'd said was bullshit. Perhaps whoever sent it was trying to remind me of that humiliating moment when I'd lost control. Maybe the sender was trying to suggest that everything I was saying now was bullshit. The package may have been intended to accomplish all those aims at once. It even foreshadowed, by design or accident, the second piece of mail I received.

That one had a return address. It came from the desk of Bill Clinton, via breathless messenger, late in the evening. Its contents were less disgusting and less frightening than the morning package but hardly more substantial.

March 29, 1996

Dear Sister Ortiz:

Thank you for your letter bringing your concerns directly to my attention. I deeply regret the suffering you so movingly describe and offer you my sincere sympathy.

I believe you are aware that I have directed the Intelligence Oversight Board (IOB) to conduct a complete review of all intelligence information that may bear on the facts of your case. In parallel with the IOB's review, the Justice Department is also currently investigating your case. The IOB is working as quickly as possible to complete its challenging work while ensuring its review is thorough. The IOB hopes to finish its review in the first half of this year.

Once I have reviewed the IOB's report, I intend to make all appropriate information available to you, the other victims or their families and the public. The IOB will contact you directly to share this information with you.

The experiences you recount are terrible and clearly haunt you still. The IOB's unprecedented review is nearing completion, and I hope its report may help you gain some measure of peace. In the meantime, I know the IOB will continue its dialogue with you on the status of its review.

Sincerely, Bill Clinton

I read it several times. A pointless, last-minute answer was still an answer — but hardly the benevolent voice I'd been waiting for to tell me I could get the truth without facing the dark, the cameras, the park police, the crowds.

I WAS WRAPPED in my electric blanket, with soft lamp light falling around me, my last night of warmth and light. Sister Suzanne was sleeping in the next room. She had come down from Chicago, where she was in graduate school. Knowing she would be beside me during the vigil made me even warmer. I was thinking already of the dark, the cold, the police, the cameras and staring eyes. I could handle it, couldn't I? Jennifer had slept in the rain. She had slept in a garbage bag, on hard cement, while she starved. She had done all that in Guatemala.

But I wasn't Jennifer, and I couldn't be Jennifer. I wasn't that strong. I wondered if I was backing myself into a corner. How long can I stay out there? Will it do any good, or will the U.S. government toy with me and keep me out there until I break and have to surrender in shame? Will the torturers show up?

The night was long and I had many more hours to think. I let my mind turn to the Woman, and finally, I wrote to her.

March 31
   My dear friend, in a few hours the sun will rise and people from the four corners of the world will commemorate the day that Jesus, a man who opted for justice and truth, modestly paraded into Jerusalem. This was the beginning of a journey that would lead him to the cross. Very soon, we too will begin a journey that will lead us on the perilous road to Calvary. Today is the day that we will begin our silent vigil for truth in front of the White House — the truth about our case, and the truth about all our sisters and brothers who have suffered at the hands of death squads supported by the U.S. government. This afternoon I will be holding a press conference at

Lafayette Park and I will make a public statement announcing the silent vigil. I am seriously thinking of removing the lid from my Pandora's box and releasing the dark secret that has kept us silent for more than six years. I want to set you free and give you a decent burial. I want others to know that I wasn't the only person who was tortured on November 2, 1989. You are among the tortured. I seek your permission, my friend, to tell of the horrors that you yourself endured. I seek your permission to tell of the pain that I inflicted on you. Please try to understand that what I am about to do is to free all of us from this prison of darkness. For years, I have reluctantly talked about some of the horrors of the torture that I was subjected to, but I have never had the courage to let others know about your torture.

It was barely light when I went downstairs, but Vianney — the Franciscan Brother who'd been a health promoter in Bolivia and had had many of his friends and coworkers disappeared and killed by the army — was already loading up the car with the sleeping bag, gloves, cooler, and everything else he had taken me to buy in the preceding weeks. Vianney would be making trips back and forth all day, dropping Jennifer, Suzanne, and the others off at the office or the park. The entire community was planning to attend the day's ceremonies, and many had already given up hours of their time helping me to prepare. Joe and Marie had selected scripture readings, and Marie had taken the extra step of selecting prayers and readings for every day of the vigil to follow, for anyone wanting to gather in the afternoons to pray. Ann and John, the young couple who had lived in El Salvador, helped in various ways, John leading us in the songs we had selected for the program. And that was only the beginning. Everyone in the community signed up on the list to accompany me through the days and even the nights of my vigil.

THAT MORNING IN THE OFFICE I made the final changes to my talk and printed it out. My friend Patricia promised to read the part of my statement about the Woman if I broke down and couldn't go on. Even if my voice failed, I would bring her to light. I tried to think of it that way — *dar a luz*, give to light, which in Spanish means to give birth. I would give birth to her again, bring her to light, resurrect her, or at least her memory.

The Policeman's voice, hissing that I was a murderer, I squelched, running off copies of the program for the afternoon. The whirr of the copier drowned out the questions my mind repeated: What will my mom and dad think? Alice was going to fax my statement to the grocery store my brother managed. And my community? Can I still be a nun? Could I possibly be put in jail?

FROM THE CAR I surveyed my new home, the park, while Vianney looked for parking. Vianney stepped on the emergency brake after turning off the motor. The brake creaked, and I grabbed the cross around my neck. I wished I could calm down. To let my knotted muscles loosen, I breathed deeply. I ran my fingers across the smooth bone I wore above the cross. Let me be worthy of this gift, I prayed. A woman's last trace of her son. Let it give me strength to fight for change in Guatemala. Maybe the people in the White House and the Old Executive Office Building, walking to their windows and doors, will see me and somehow sense around me all the others, the dead, the tortured, day after day, and a time will come when they can't stand to look out the windows.

That was my little reverie as I walked across the grass. Then I had no more time for prayers or hopes or fantasies. Reporters from the *New York Times* and the Associated Press were already waiting on a park bench. Some Spanish-language media were present, too. My friends were getting the podium set up, and Mary McGrory, of the *Washington Post,* walked up and introduced herself to me and asked when we were going to start. "In a little while," I answered, thinking she didn't know how long a wait she had if she'd come to hear me speak. I planned to go last. But at least the reporters would hear Craig Powers, who was an aide of Connie Morella's, Carlos Salinas, of Amnesty International, and Meredith, Jennifer, and Lisel, a new Coalition member. Maybe that would satisfy them.

People began to gather, some holding an Amnesty International banner, others holding a banner calling for justice, and still others with one that said something about the CIA. Some arrived chanting in Spanish, bearing elaborate banners they laid down on the ground to display. There were hundreds of people before long, all standing in a huge circle beneath the bare black branches of old trees, and behind them cherry trees and tulip magnolias frothed with bloom and the Washington buildings stood implacable, like stone mausoleums. Carlos was speaking. I could scarcely focus on what he was saying. The sun was soft and the sky a pale cloudy blue. Doves kept flying across it.

Craig Powers was next. He explained that Connie Morella was traveling out of the country but he was there to say for her that the U.S. government owed me any information it had that would help me bring a just resolution to my case.

I don't remember how it happened, whether it was Jose, Jennifer, Patricia, Alice, or all of them combined, but someone managed to convince me that I had to speak next. The press was there, they had come to hear me, and press was important.

Two cameras were right in my face. My hands were shaking as I shuffled my papers. People were applauding already, although I hadn't said anything. Once I told them the truth about myself, their attitude would change. Maybe I'd chosen both options, A and B after all. I was burning my passport to the human race and going into exile on an island where no one could reach me. But I wouldn't be alone there. The Woman and the others in my circle would be with me.

I began.

Today, on Palm Sunday, I begin my silent vigil for truth in front of the White House — the truth about my own case, and the truth about all those Guatemalans who have suffered and died at the hands of the officially sponsored death squads. For those of us who know and love Guatemala, it is painfully clear that our own United States government has been closely linked to these death squads and has a great amount of detailed information about those of us who have survived, as well as those who have perished. We need and demand this information so that we can heal our wounds, bury our dead, and carry on with our lives. We need and demand this information so that we can insist on change, insist that these terrible realities never be repeated.

People ask how long I will be in front of the White House. I can only respond with a question: How long will the U.S. government keep the truth from me? Who is Alejandro, the U.S. citizen present at my torture? He is a pivotal piece of my past and a symbol of the very real and daily fact of my continuing torture — the torture of silence and secrecy. On behalf of all of us I demand that President Clinton declassify all U.S. government information related to human rights abuses in Guatemala, from 1954 to the present, and that the IOB release the full text of its report, not just a summary. I want the full truth about Guatemala.

Now I will maintain my silence, not a silence of complicity and cover-up, but a silence of commemoration for the thousands of known and unknown victims and survivors who have been abducted, tortured, assassinated, and disappeared in Guatemala in the past three decades. I will not be alone on this vigil, for I know that those who have lost their lives or their beloved family members and the thousands who have been tortured will be with me in spirit. A candle will burn day and night as a reminder to President Clinton and his administration that there is a *presence* in the park — a *presence* that represents those victims and survivors whose flame will never die. As President Clinton and his administration sleep peacefully, many of us fight to stay awake — to protect ourselves from the recurring visits from our torturers.

Many of you know my story. What is overlooked is that my experience is a daily occurrence in Guatemala. Six people a week, on average, are killed for political reasons. Two a week are tortured. The total death toll may never be known. The army's counter-insurgency campaign has left an estimated 200,000 dead and another 45,000 disappeared, victims of the dreaded official death squads. This staggering death toll is far higher than that of the dirty wars in Argentina, Chile, and El Salvador. Most of these violations were visited upon the Mayan population. Some 440 Mayan villages were wiped off the map. Hundreds of people vanished. Their mutilated, charred remains are only now beginning to emerge from secret mass graves. The truth, in Guatemala, is beginning to be unearthed. What about in the United States? When will the truth be exhumed?

I cannot forget those who suffered with me and died in that clandestine prison. The memories of what I witnessed and experienced that November day haunt me day and night.

I looked over to Patricia. She was standing nearby and looked ready to take over, but both she and Jose mouthed me encouragement to go on.

Even to this day, I can smell the decomposing of bodies, disposed of in an open pit. I can hear the piercing screams of other people being tortured. I can see the blood gushing out of the Woman's body as I thrust a small machete into her body.

I broke down. As soon as I could, I lifted my head off the podium and stumbled into Anna's arms, then on into Jose's embrace. I stood sobbing against his chest for a couple of minutes. "You did it. You did it," he said. "You're so strong. Now go on. Go on back and finish."

Patricia, who had read the details about what had happened with the Woman, moved away, and I went back to tell how the torture of silence and secrecy continued. I told of the package I'd received, too. "In spite of the memories of humiliation, of the pit, that this form of psychological torture recalled, I stand with the Guatemalan people. I demand the right to heal. I demand the right to know. I demand the right to a resurrection, a future built on truth and justice."

My pulse was so loud in my ears that the ground leaped with it. I sat on the grass next to Suzanne, who pressed me against her. Slowly my trembling stopped and I could listen to Jennifer:

> I myself have now spoken to two Guatemalans. One was a torture victim who was lying on the floor in a secret cell when a North American man walked in and talked to his captors in heavily accented Spanish. The man left after a while but made no attempt to rescue or assist the prisoner.
>
> The second person I spoke with is a member of the security forces in Guatemala. He described being present during torture sessions in which electrical shocks and other methods were used. On more than one occasion very tall North American men would walk in and out of the sessions. Both witnesses told me they would fear for their lives if they were to speak publicly about these matters. They fear the Guatemalan army and they fear the United States.
>
> The documents I've received contain several ominous headings, such as "Clandestine Military Prisons," with all ensuing contents blocked out. Another document refers to clandestine burial grounds for army torture victims. None of this surprises me, for Guatemalans and U.S. citizens have long reported that embassy staffers had critical information about death squad victims and the "disappeared," information that could only be obtained through very close links indeed to the death squads themselves.

Jennifer had told me she had found some witnesses, but I didn't really know what she'd meant. I thought she was talking about her case. She'd found witnesses to help support me, witnesses who'd seen American men walking in and out of torture sessions. I could only imagine what kinds of risks Jennifer had run, hunting such witnesses down, and the risks the witnesses themselves were running by talking to her.

Drumbeats broke my thought, and sage filled my nostrils. Palm fronds were distributed and the leaves rustled against each other, like a whisper of dry bones.

John struck up the chords of a song I'd chosen, "Todavía Cantamos," which expressed the hope of the Argentine people as they waited and prayed to see their disappeared loved ones again. I loved the song because of the defiance of the chorus: "Still we sing, still we pray / still we dream, still we hope... / in spite of the ingenuity of the hatred...." I didn't have all the words by memory, but spotting Jennifer's face in the crowd I realized what a mistake I'd made. Her face was full of pain. "Still we hope to know that it's possible / for the garden to be lighted / with the laughter and song / of those we love so much." We had always sung that song before at all the gatherings where Jennifer was, but now things had changed. There was no hope. I had forgotten.

After all the palm fronds were laid in a pile, after we all swore "never again," I took my candle, lit it, and spread out my tarp next to the sidewalk across from the White House.

Chapter Eighteen

THE VIGIL

It RAINED. I had diarrhea. Nerves did that to me, and the worst wasn't over yet. I had to hear what my family would say. I had to hear what my community would say and what the papers would say. Every half-hour I got someone to walk with me through the park. Darkness pooled on the sidewalk in the intervals between the lamps. Then we had two more blocks to go, down the deserted streets to the Hilton.

Each time the need struck, I told the people sitting with me that I wanted to stretch my legs again. If word got around that I was sick, I was afraid I'd be pressured to go home. I remembered my words to Alice when she'd said the vigil would be hard: "I've been tortured, Alice; I can handle it." And here I was just four hours in, shivering, feverish, and sopping wet. The umbrella, rain jacket, and tarp seemed useless. I stayed as close as I could to my candle.

A police officer had sauntered up just after nightfall. "That candle's a fire hazard," he said. "It could catch the grass on fire!"

I looked up at the pouring rain and the long puddle the water was making at the edge of the sidewalk. The flame was struggling as it was, even though the glass candle holder cupped and partially sheltered it. I said nothing to the officer. I was on a silent vigil.

After a tense silence, he went away, and our candle stayed lit.

But another officer stopped by later. He smiled and said hello. The rain had let up, my shivering had stopped, and I was wrapped in a blanket, still damp but slowly warming. As the policeman continued to stand there, though, a trickle of cold sweat wound slowly between my shoulder blades. His smile didn't matter. My body remembered the uniform. Maybe my body was sensing something else about him, too.

"You gotta watch out for the rats out here," he said. "There are rats all over this park, rats the size of cats that'll snuggle up to you to get warm when you're asleep." That was the only thing he said. Then he ambled away. For the rest of the night, every rustle made me jump. And I knew that no matter how long I was on the vigil, I wouldn't ever sleep.

Dawn finally came. I went home and showered, and came back to the park dressed in warm, dry blue jeans and thick socks.

Sister Suzanne put her arm around me as soon as I walked up. "The Intelligence Oversight Board and Nancy Soderberg want to meet with you."

I heard the excitement in Suzanne's voice. We both hoped, though we didn't dare say it, that another night wouldn't be necessary. Someone had put a couple of articles down on the blanket for me to read, and Suzanne said they were both favorable toward me. Maybe the White House didn't want to risk even the tiniest bit of bad publicity. Whatever the reason, something must have shifted.

Nancy Soderberg had come over earlier to express her concern, Suzanne told me. She had peered at my signs: "Declassify All U.S. Government Documents on Guatemala from 1954 to the Present"; "Who Is Alejandro?" She looked especially hard at the sign a friend made with a cover sheet borrowed from the Justice Department. "Top secret," it said. An edge of the cover sheet was folded back to reveal some lines meant to resemble a government document. "What's that?" Nancy asked, trying for lightness.

Suzanne had also spoken to Mary Mathias that morning.

Remembering that I couldn't talk, I scribbled a quick note. "Did she get the fax Alice sent?" It was yesterday's statement.

"Yeah, she got it."

I wondered if the community was ashamed of me, if they wanted no more to do with me. Suzanne anticipated my questions. "And we're proud of you. The community is behind you all the way."

I snuffed out the glow that was starting to spread through my chest. Those might be Suzanne's feelings, I reminded myself. Suzanne might be protecting me. How could she know the sentiments of everyone in the community? Some of the sisters thought I was enjoying the attention I was getting for having been tortured, wallowing in self-pity, obsessing about what had happened to me in Guatemala. They had told me as much only months after my abduction. They were bound to think I was now taking matters to ridiculous extremes.

And what would they think about my admission that I'd killed a woman?

I couldn't look at Suzanne. I didn't want her to see my doubt, and I didn't want to see anything in her face that would confirm it.

Alice, a few minutes later, came with some flowers and a brick. "This is what we used to do in Minnesota," she said, taking the brick out of her purse and putting it by my feet. "We'd put them in the oven to warm them, then put them in our beds. There. That'll keep your feet warm." Alice also had a plastic bag with a folder of faxes and e-mails from people writing to encourage me. "Well, you won't get bored out here with so much to read. And I talked with your family this morning. They all said they supported you a hundred percent. Your mom and dad said to tell you, 'Mi'jita, we love you.'"

I pulled my umbrella down to hide my face. "Thanks, Alice." Black plastic was all I saw. All I heard was the plunk and ping of the rain. I smelled the sodden dirt and new grass struggling up. And then the scent of green apples came to me, my mother's red curls, her soft voice, her fingers in my hair, Barbara's laugh, and her long, black hair wet and smelling of coconut, mangos, and vanilla. My dad's face, his bear hug. Amber signing me "I love you."

And I knew I was back. They were with me.

Our footsteps echoed on the staircase. The meeting room, luckily, was upstairs. Still, my nerves tightened and I felt weak. My eyes itched with sleeplessness or fever. I was relieved that along with Suzanne, Anna, and Michele, I had brought Jennifer, Lisel, Meredith, Marie, and Maryknoll Father Steve Judd with me. They all had an interest in the IOB report. I figured the IOB should meet with them, too.

We were shown into a pale green room with elaborate molding on the ceiling. Once seated at the vast table, I looked into the faces of the board members. Frank Fountain gave me a small smile. The young, blond woman near him must be Nancy, I realized. She had gray eyes and looked bright, friendly, and relaxed. Anthony Harrington, the IOB president, looked relaxed, too.

I decided the news they had must be good. My stomach lurched with hope.

No one seemed in a hurry to begin, so Meredith, with her usual forthrightness, took hold of the meeting. Meredith was a character. She wasn't even thirty yet, but she opened her notebook to a blank page and asked Anthony Harrington when they expected to release the report.

The investigation was taking longer than anticipated, Harrington answered, because certain efforts were underway that were worthwhile to pursue. These efforts related to more than one of the cases. He said he hesitated to put out a date because a date contributed to frustration.

Not if it's met, I thought.

"We expect that the investigation will be concluded in the first half of the year," he added, polishing his glasses.

Jennifer shifted in her chair. "I go to Guatemala almost every month," she said. "Two people have come to me with similar stories to Dianna's. One said a tall, gangly North American was present during his torture. Another man, who was with the security forces and was present at torture sessions, said it was not unusual for a North American to come in, not to participate, but to see how things were going and to talk. We need to know the extent of what went on. I need to know where my husband is. Dianna deserves to get an answer. Every day that goes by is another injury."

"I don't know if you can accept this, but we're on the same side of the table," Harrington said. "The CIA, the DOJ, the IOB don't know everything. Our exercise is for the president, but for the same goals that you have in mind."

Their "exercise." I didn't like the word, and neither did Jennifer, if I was reading her look right. And did he really expect us to believe that the CIA didn't have any clue who those Americans were who were talking with torturers? No, the IOB members weren't on our side of the table. They were on the other side, as surely as they were seated on the other side of a conference table at that very moment. I had heard Jennifer say it before, and I would hear her say it again: "Be careful, Dianna. They're the other side." My problem was that I kept forgetting. My family must have brought me up very patriotically. In spite of the conditioning of the torture, in spite of losing my memory and being reborn, in a sense, and taught to mistrust all authority, I had a deep need to believe in and trust the government of the United States.

Harrington went on to say that if we had any complaints about anything in the IOB's domain, or even not in its domain, perhaps the board could help.

Lisel, in spite of her shyness, took him up on his invitation. "My father was killed in 1983," she began. "I was twelve, and I couldn't speak out on his behalf." Tears started to slide from Lisel's aqua-colored eyes down over her sculpted cheekbones. "He was a human rights worker who worked with the poor in Guatemala. He wrote to congressmen, urging them to change foreign policy. He was very active — not shy about his views. He was bludgeoned to death on the beach. Nothing was stolen from my father, but the State Department has always said it was a common crime." Lisel wiped her hands over her face.

Harrington reached into his breast pocket and handed her a monogrammed handkerchief. While Lisel composed herself, Jennifer pointed out that without information, there could be no healing, and the 1984 cutoff date for the IOB investigation left a lot of people with no recourse to information.

Father Steve Judd spoke of Father William Woods, whose plane was shot down in 1976 with Ann Kerndt aboard, as well as three other Americans. Quite a few Americans were left out by the date restrictions put on the IOB investigation, Father Judd noted.

In addition to the cases of all Americans, Jennifer asked, couldn't information related to the cases of the two hundred thousand Guatemalans who had been killed be declassified?

Harrington said he hoped the board could contribute to righting some of the wrongs that had occurred in Guatemala. Nothing would completely right what had happened, he said. "But we hope to help. None of the board members would be involved in a process designed to hide. Of course, there are national security considerations. But we're hoping to move forward, toward disclosure, not back, toward national security."

He said more, but by then my mind was wandering. They had no news for us. Nothing was going to happen. I'd been so nervous I'd spent most of the morning going up to the Hilton again. And the meeting was pointless.

The only worthwhile part of it was the way it ended. Lisel remembered to return to Anthony Harrington the handkerchief he'd lent her. "Here, Mr. Harrington," she said. "Thank you." It looked nothing like it had when he'd given it to her. She'd tried to refold it, but it oozed with her tears and nose blow.

Harrington recoiled. "Keep it," he said, "as a souvenir."

LISEL BURST OUT LAUGHING as we clattered down the stairs. "Men of my generation don't pull out cloth hankies. I had no idea what I was supposed to do with it."

The trees were glistening, and outside our feet left no ghost of sound.

"But now I know. I should have said, 'No, you keep it, Mr. Harrington, as a souvenir of my feelings.' Then I should have stuffed it back in his pocket."

A second meeting took place later that day with just Harrington, Frank Fountain, Nancy, me, and Michele. Once again, I was hopeful. The tone of the meeting was more businesslike. Maybe the IOB actually had information about my case or about declassification.

Harrington told me the IOB report would be out no earlier than June 30. The status of my Freedom of Information Act (FOIA) request was something the IOB had no control over; and the Department of Justice was due to finish its investigation by the end of April.

I sighed and felt my shoulders drop. None of this news was good.

Frank added that one reason the IOB report was delayed was that the IOB was waiting for the DOJ to finish its investigation. The DOJ, meanwhile, was investigating certain leads in my case and waiting to interview me.

I was frustrated, and the physical toll of the vigil was affecting my perceptions. What I heard Frank say was that I was the problem. I was the reason the DOJ wasn't finishing its investigation and one of the reasons, therefore, that the IOB report wasn't getting out.

Doubt began gnawing at me. Maybe I had made a mistake with the vigil. But I had never heard before that I was holding up the investigations because I hadn't been interviewed yet. Suddenly, I sit in front of the White House for one day and the DOJ and IOB can't get their jobs done.

I didn't think of logical comebacks. I felt the hair on my neck stiffen. And even though I was clearly in over my head, talking with people much more knowledgeable and sophisticated than myself, I had to be true to what I knew. The vigil was not a decision I had made overnight. A lot of reflection and prayer had gone into it, and I was guided by my circle of friends. I had to trust them, and I had to trust myself. I went back out to the park and sat down.

Lafayette Park has long since been declared off limits to homeless people, for security reasons, but at the time of my vigil, a number of homeless people were living in the park, more than twenty, I'd say. They lived there for security reasons. With the Secret Service nearby, the park was one of the safest places to sleep out.

Many park residents had gathered around on Palm Sunday to hear the speeches and watch our ceremonies. By the second night of the vigil, they were beginning to linger near us, especially when people brought out guitars. Carlos Salinas, of Amnesty International, not only brought his guitar at night but announced that he had begun a hunger strike to support me during the two weeks of my vigil.

"Um, Carlos," Lisel informed him quietly. "Dianna's vigil isn't going to last two weeks. It's indefinite."

Carlos couldn't fast indefinitely — he wasn't a big guy to begin with — but he did go the whole two weeks without eating or drinking anything but water. Meanwhile, he made trips around Congress, explaining his fast and why he felt so strongly about the issue of declassification.

My friends explained to the homeless folks that I was afraid of the police and didn't want them near me. So if they were going to be loud and cause the police to come, could they do it far away? Also, my friends told them, I was afraid of cigarette smoke and couldn't handle anyone smoking near me.

A Native American man, who said we could call him Chief, although his real name was Tony, took it on himself to explain the situation to the others in the park.

TUESDAY MORNING brought with it a nice surprise. Mary McGrory's column in the *Washington Post* was very positive, my friends said. She was calling on the White House to do something to help me. I couldn't read it. Reading articles about myself brought pain and shame, no matter how positive they were.

I didn't expect what happened next, at least not on a conscious level. But maybe part of the reason I was uncomfortable, even with favorable articles, was that I expected repercussions.

Lisel, Patricia, Jennifer, and I were sitting on the grass. It was midmorning, sunny. People were passing before us in suits, on their way to work. Suddenly a man was standing on the sidewalk in front of me. He had short, blond hair, was wearing a suit and tie, and was tall and seemed in good shape. He was also wearing dark glasses.

"Sister Ortiz, I just want to tell you that at least one American doesn't believe you!"

"Who do you work for?" Jennifer asked.

He ignored her. "You're just trying to bring down those people in there" — he waved toward the White House — "and disrupt the work of our agencies abroad. And not everyone is lucky enough to have Fenton Communications working for them."

Fenton Communications was a small PR firm Jennifer had used during her hunger strikes. I wasn't using any PR firm — Jennifer had broken the freeze on Guatemala — but I was surprised that this man knew about Fenton at all. I just stared at him because I couldn't answer. I was floating off to a safe place. He was becoming smaller and smaller, and I was no longer able to hear him.

When the rest of the conversation was recounted to me later, I realized that the man knew Jennifer's case down to the smallest detail.

"What's your name?" Jennifer asked him.

"None of your business!" he answered. "As for you, you're no more married to that guerrilla than I am!"

The Guatemalan government was always attacking the validity of Jennifer's marriage to Everardo. Jennifer and Everardo had married in front of friends in a backyard ceremony, but with no judge present. When Everardo disappeared, Jennifer had to get a judge to rule the marriage valid so that she could fight for his life as his spouse.

"A declaratory judgment is no kind of marriage," the blond man continued angrily. He knew the intricacies of Jennifer's case. He wasn't just "one American" coming to the park to tell me he didn't believe me.

After a few more exchanges with Jennifer, the man huffed off. Jennifer and Patricia followed him to see if he would turn into one of the neighboring buildings. He got into a Volkswagen with Virginia plates that was parked a block away, never turning around to see if he was being followed. He didn't know Jennifer *that* well.

Lisel referred to him as "the Rush Limbaugh guy" because of his tone. We guessed he was with the CIA, given his short hair, dark glasses, and detailed knowledge of Jennifer's case. Either he didn't believe what I was saying about Alejandro and truly was indignant, or he knew that what I was saying was true, and he was carrying out a tactic to break my morale. Whoever he worked for wasn't issuing press statements about his meeting with me, so his motives would remain a mystery.

THE WHITE HOUSE was different. From White House statements passed along by a journalist friend we were able to learn a bit more about the odd IOB meetings of the previous day. Pointless meetings had a purpose, it seemed.

WHITE HOUSE REPORT, TUESDAY, APRIL 2
— NEWS BRIEFING —
Press Secretary Mike McCurry covered these topics:

NUN OFFERED SUPPORT

[Mike McCurry] said the Ursuline nun tortured and raped by the Guatemalan military met twice with Nancy Soderberg, President Clinton's deputy assistant for national security affairs. McCurry said the White House again pledged to provide the public all available information about her case and those of Michael DeVine and Efraín Bámaca.

According to news reports, Sister Dianna Ortiz, 37, is holding a 21-hour vigil in Lafayette Park seeking information about U.S. knowledge of her 1989 kidnapping, torture, and gang rape by Guatemalan death squads. Ortiz, an American citizen, says a man speaking American English and broken Spanish supervised the episode.

"We are her advocates," Mr. McCurry said. "We are on her side." He noted the administration "is dealing with the actions of a prior administration." Clinton has assigned the Intelligence Oversight Board (IOB) to examine the three cases. McCurry said its final report is expected in the first half of the year.

He said that Ortiz met April 1 with board members as well as Ms. Soderberg, who also conferred with Sister Ortiz in Lafayette Park. "We've made it very clear to her that we are on her side," McCurry said, adding that additional meetings with the nun are to take place this week. "The president," McCurry said, "is determined to get to the bottom of her case," as well as those of DeVine, an American citizen executed by the Guatemalan military, and Bámaca, whose widow, Jennifer Harbury, staged a series of hunger strikes to gain information about his death.

Asked why the nun apparently does not believe the assurances, McCurry said, "I don't know that she doesn't believe. She wants to make sure that those responsible for what she alleges occurred to her are brought to justice. Her presence in Lafayette Park is testimony to the strength of her conviction that justice needs to be pursued and the president shares that conviction."

How was I supposed to believe their assurances after what the White House did to Everardo, letting him be tortured, and to Jennifer, assuring her that they would help her, then doing nothing? The headline and the first sentence told everything. I was "offered support" because White House officials had "met" with me. Excuse me, but they had to do more than meet with me. I wanted my documents. I wanted the truth for myself and for all the Guatemalans.

TONY CAME OVER to me that night, holding a plastic bag, and asked if he could light the sage I kept in a bowl Alice's nephew had made. He knelt on the ground next to my candle, and as he lit the sage, he said, "I am grateful to you, Sister Dianna, for what you are doing." His long hair swung around his shoulders when he sat back on his heels to open the bag. Out of it he drew a wool poncho, woven of different colors, in Native American patterns.

I ran my fingertips over the wool, wondering how he had kept the poncho so spotless, so perfect, amid the rain and mud in the park.

"Your presence here is on behalf of many suffering people," he said, "mine among them." Smoke curled above him and disappeared in the darkness. His face shone in the glow of the candlelight.

I had wondered briefly when I'd first met him why people called Tony "Chief." Now I understood. From his dignity and presence it was clear. He probably really was a chief.

Cloaked in Tony's generosity, warmth filled me, not hunger; I didn't need to eat. Someone brought me a dish of warm lasagna and I sent it over to Tony, to be shared as bread broken among friends.

IN THE MORNING, Frank Fountain came by. "How are you doing, Dianna?"

I nodded, since I wasn't talking.

"I just wanted to pass along the message that Hillary Clinton wants to meet with you tomorrow afternoon."

Four days of diarrhea and sleeplessness had left me fuzzy-brained. But Frank was smiling, so I smiled back, although I felt nothing. I was stunned, I guess, or too afraid to hope.

Anna and Michele, when I told them about the meeting, were jubilant. Jennifer congratulated me, telling me she thought the fact that I had gotten a meeting with Hillary Clinton was really great. I just wondered if I would get information.

Anna and Michele and I had a planning session in a corner of the park. They said I would have to focus on my case alone — no bringing up other Coalition Missing members, no pleading for information about any other cases. "She's meeting with you, Dianna," Anna explained. "This meeting has to be about your case. It has to be focused."

"I can't talk about why I'm out here, what I'm asking for?" I scribbled quickly.

"Talk about the Alejandro part and about finding out who he is and say you want your documents and a full investigation."

"It's better to limit the subject of the conversation to one case for now," Michele added.

I didn't like it. I wasn't sitting out in front of the White House day and night just for information about my case. My request was for declassification of all information related to human rights in Guatemala since 1954. What was I supposed to do if the First Lady gave me significant information on my case? Suppose she handed me a folder or even a box full of declassified documents answering all the questions I had. Was I supposed to be satisfied then and end my vigil, forgetting about all the

Guatemalans? I remembered the words Alejandro had said as he took me out of that building: *Don't concern yourself with them.*

Why was Hillary Clinton meeting with me instead of Concepción, who had been in the park for twenty years, protesting nuclear weapons? Why was she meeting with me instead of Lisel, who wouldn't have the satisfaction of any kind of government investigation into her father's death? Why was she meeting with me when Jennifer's only access to her had been as Martin Sheen's date to a celebrity dinner — when Everardo's life had been at stake? Why was I getting a special privilege? Shame was beginning to take hold of me.

Kerry Kennedy Cuomo came by the park that afternoon and explained how the meeting had come about. Kerry, who had founded the Robert F. Kennedy Memorial Center for Human Rights, kept up with human rights issues in Guatemala and elsewhere. She'd had dinner with Mrs. Clinton the night before. Mrs. Clinton hadn't heard anything about me or my vigil and hadn't read Mary McGrory's column, so Kerry explained my case and told her the purpose of the vigil. It happened to be pouring, and Kerry said she was worried about me, out there in the rain. How glad I was that she spoke up for me! Apparently, Mrs. Clinton made the decision that night that she would talk with me.

Knowing how the meeting had transpired, I felt less guilty about it. And as hard as it was for me to focus on my case alone, I began to hope that Mrs. Clinton, as a result, would Fed Ex me a box of documents and hand me a critically important file to read in the meantime. I just wanted to go home. I'm a creature of comfort. I like my warm bed and my soft pillows. Already I was getting bruises from the ground.

As the sun was going down, I had my headphones on and my eyes closed. I was thinking about that box of documents the First Lady would give me and how I would soak in the bathtub before bed once I had it. I savored best-possible-outcome scenarios, and morning finally came, after a night of daydreams and sudden trips to the Hilton.

I'm sitting on a bench, only a foot or so from Mrs. Clinton. There's a tapestry behind us, an ornate carpet at our feet, but I'm focused on Mrs. Clinton, not the splendor of the room. I intend to give the First Lady a brief summary of my case, looking at notes in my lap so that I don't get lost in an adrenaline haze. But even telling about what happened to me in the barest terms, I smell the torturers' bodies, feel their hands, smell their cigarettes, hear their laughter. Tears start out of my eyes. Then shame and anger overtake me, and I put my head in my hands. I have to take a break and recompose myself before I can go on.

"I will follow through on this," Mrs. Clinton tells me when I return from the bathroom. "There is no effort to hold anything back. Agencies are working in good faith. A lot is at stake here to do this right, to get you everything you are entitled to have. I will push on the Justice Department task force in trying to identify Alejandro."

"I understand the need for a thorough investigation," I answer, "but I've waited six years to find out why I was targeted, and not until President Clinton ordered the review did any U.S. government investigation take place. And the IOB investigation has dragged on for over a year now."

"We have no excuse for why the previous administration did not investigate — no excuse," Mrs. Clinton answers. "You will have everything we have. This has been pushed ahead and given personal attention. There will be information available within sixty to ninety days. We don't want you to give up or be discouraged now. I will personally make sure that you will get everything you are entitled to. I hope you will have the documents in your hand by June, but June's a long way away. We don't want you to . . ."

"Another concern — I have continued to receive threats." I tell her about the envelope on the back stairs. "I don't know if that was from someone in the U.S. government, Alejandro . . ."

"No one in any position of authority in this government today wants anything but full information. We want to keep pressure on to keep all the people out there working as hard as they are with a deadline. . . ."

"I am a survivor. My control was taken away during the torture. Everyone else has control over and information about what happened except me. I'm only sitting out in front of the White House to get that control."

"Your sitting in front of the White house gives eloquent testimony to your strength and commitment. It can't move the process any faster along. The President and I and people in this White House are doing everything we know to do to get the information for you as soon as possible. I know it's hard for you, but the process is being expedited — it has gone much more quickly because of the pressure. I can't promise I will have all of it tomorrow morning, but we will give you everything we can in June, and between now and then . . ."

"I want to believe, but I also have in my memory how my government has betrayed me."

"I can't excuse that, but I give you my word that we will give you everything we can as soon as possible. I will work personally, and Milan

Above: *Jennifer speaking at the LASA conference in Washington, while Ambassador Strook (at far right) listens.*

Below: *Vigil in front of the White House* (Photo: Rick Reinhard)

SILENT VIGIL FOR TRUTH
DIANNA ORTIZ

Above:
Fr. Joe Nangle and supporters of the vigil.

Right:
Bishop Gumbleton is among those arrested
for praying in front of the White House.

Below:
Meeting with Hillary Clinton in the
White House.

will," she added, referring to her personal secretary, "to make everything available to you."

PERHAPS ALL Mrs. Clinton's assurances were meant to make the vigil unnecessary. But I wasn't stopping for promises because I had seen the very same administration offer Jennifer a meeting. I had seen Jennifer go into the meeting and come out of it, still somewhat hopeful, and I'd watched her hope die as the months passed and she realized the White House meeting had only been a way for administration officials to lure her out of the plaza in Guatemala City. Hillary Clinton inspired more trust than the National Security Council officials Jennifer had dealt with. But who knew what kinds of forces Hillary Clinton was up against? If she was fighting an old boys' network of secrecy, publicity and public pressure could only help her. I wasn't leaving my spot.

WE HAD AN EASTER MASS at the vigil site three days later. Alice had brought flowers and a table to put them and the bread and wine on, and John played the guitar. But what I remember is how awkward I felt. I had invited people to come and celebrate the Eucharist with me, to come and break bread. And yet when the plate was passed around, I took none. Everyone noticed that I wasn't taking Communion. Everyone stared or tried not to.

I had taken it before, of course, but acknowledging the Woman publicly made what I had done to her all the more real. I had too much blood on my hands — hers, the child's. I felt the weight of my sin.

People magazine was covering the Mass. Being photographed was some-thing I had to get used to. The press had covered the vigil from the start, and after my meeting with Hillary Clinton, the press coverage doubled; the meeting, in the media's eyes, had conferred legitimacy on me.

ALONG WITH NEW MEDIA AND SUPPORTERS, new protesters appeared in the park. A man and a woman wandered around in ankle-length white robes, carrying Bibles, yelling, "Abortion is murder! Baby killers! People who have abortions are baby killers!" They came to the park every day. The park was big, but they always stayed close to our group. I wrote a note to Tony, asking if he'd ever seen them before. Never, he said. He checked with the others in the park. This was the couple's first appearance.

The DOJ was talking to the sisters at the Mount, I knew, and trying to talk with nurses and doctors at Our Lady of Peace. I had refused to sign a release of my medical records there, but I asked myself if the investigators somehow had found out through other means about the choice I had made. Had Dr. Snodgrass talked again? Or one of the sisters? Or someone at Su Casa or Kovler? Those were the only people who knew, and the DOJ was making the rounds to question all those people. Who could have talked?

I told myself to get a grip. Just because a couple of protesters show up in the park, you don't have to think your friends have betrayed you. To think that these protesters are fakes, planted by the U.S. government to whittle away your morale, is just a wee bit paranoid, no? Anyway, I reasoned, who could have talked? Dr. Snodgrass would be risking his career, and the sisters who know about the choice — the former council members, for example — are trustworthy. As for Mary, Antonio, Pat, and Juanita, they would never reveal anything confidential.

I WAS RELIEVED when the *Today Show* asked to interview me. I could get out of the park and away from the protesting couple. So off I went to New York. Patricia went with me. We stayed in an elegant hotel on Central Park, courtesy of NBC, luxuriated in the enormous bathtub, and ordered a room service dinner.

We rode in an NBC limousine to the studio the next morning. I was still having culture shock. This was a far cry from my tarp and Alice's wheezing buggy. In a room where we waited for what seemed like forever, a TV monitor relayed the show as it was being filmed in the studio next door. A stately blond woman with long, wavy hair was talking about her sketch of the Unabomber, which she'd made from talking to witnesses about the split-second glimpses they'd managed to get. "People remember a lot more than you might think, a lot more even than they think. If you elicit the information from them in the right way, you can really reconstruct a face, and it can help in finding the criminal. Memory is evidence."

I had a vague feeling that I should be paying attention. Her words nudged at something in my mind. But my interview was coming up, and I was thinking about the questions Katie Couric would ask me. I wanted to be sure I was prepared. The interview went fine. I didn't even cry, although my eyes filled up once. Katie Couric was understanding and gentle, and I was relieved when it was all over and I could go back to the waiting room to collect my stuff and get a hug from Patricia.

The blond sketch artist was sitting in one of the chairs by then. She introduced herself as Jeanne Boylan and said she had seen my interview. "Listen, if I can help you in any way, let me know." She gave me her card.

"If you want to work together to make sketches of the American and your torturers, I can help you. Give me a call."

FLYING BACK, resting my head on the window, I knew that meeting the sketch artist was the most important part of the trip. I would call her. That would be the next step, part of it. I had soaked in a bathtub and slept in a bed. I had eaten good food. And my brain was ticking away like a watch that had just been wound. I was two weeks into the vigil. I had met with Hillary Clinton and gotten a lot of press. Mrs. Clinton would try to get me some documents — or all the information I was entitled to — as soon as possible.

But she'd said it could take sixty to ninety days, and I couldn't stay in front of the White House for two to three more months. Even if she got me my documents by June, I'd have to last another month and a half, and I couldn't. Besides, I didn't want declassification to be limited to my own case. I wanted broad declassification, and I wanted documents in the hands of the public well before the IOB and DOJ finished investigating. The investigations, that way, might have to be more honest, more thorough.

I had to find a way to increase the pressure.

The motor hummed, I nibbled at my peanuts, and the clouds rose in ghostly shapes around me. I already had my answer by the time we dipped over the Pentagon: a hunger strike.

ALICE DIDN'T LIKE IT. Neither did Marie, Vianney, Jennifer, or anyone else. But I had a less extreme version of the plan ready that I thought they would support: a fast of bread and water. I could last for a while eating a slice of bread a day, giving whatever pressure the fast might generate time to build. The traditional food of prisoners seemed just right, since I was being stonewalled and kept in the dark.

I decided to begin the fast the third week of my vigil. Meanwhile I bolstered my morale with the faxes and clippings Alice brought me. Carmelite Sisters in Chile wrote, "From our Sisters in Washington, we have learned of the battle you have undertaken for justice, truth, and the liberation of so many people oppressed, tortured, and marginalized by the abuses of power of those who consider themselves the owners of everything." They were praying for me. I was so glad they understood that I was fighting for many people, not just for myself. I had heard that a new GHRC board member had misunderstood my vigil horribly, making some remark about how I got to "be the star out there," but what good was it really doing for

Guatemala? In El Salvador people held a vigil outside the U.S. embassy, carrying signs asking, "Who is Alejandro?" and calling on the United States to release information about human rights abuses involving themselves, their friends, and relatives. There was a vigil in Honduras, too. If my vigil was striking a chord in people outside U.S. borders, encouraging them to step forward and ask for information, so much the better. No matter what happened inside the White House or with my case, at least my efforts were sparking others.

PEOPLE WHO VISITED the vigil site sometimes wrote messages in my notebook. One woman who wrote was teaching religion in an inner-city school. Many of her students came from broken homes, with one or both parents serving time for minor or serious crimes. A lot of the children carried anger inside, and they resented how their lives were turning out. Her class discussed the issue of forgiveness and decided that forgiveness wasn't possible. "You, as a Catholic nun," she insisted, "have the responsibility to set a good example by forgiving your torturers. If my students knew that you were able to forgive the people who hurt you, maybe they would learn from you."

She waited while I read her message.

I didn't respond. I just covered my anger and guilt with a noncommittal little smile.

I respect and appreciate her and all the people who took the time and energy to visit with me and share their ideas. Having had time now to ponder the question, I would answer her by explaining that I don't hate my torturers. I only despise their actions. While I'm not forgetting the torture, I am getting on with my life. I'm not doing what I was trained to do — I'm not working with children — but I suppose I am working for children, trying to ensure that they have a future that doesn't involve torture. Holocaust survivor Elie Wiesel said, "To forget would be an absolute injustice. To forget would be the enemy's triumph. The enemy kills, tortures, and disappears twice, the second time in trying to obliterate the traces of his crime." By refusing to forget, I hope I am keeping the memory of the dead alive. As to forgiveness, I would say this: get my government to tell me who my torturers were and who Alejandro is. Bring them to Washington, D.C. Get my government to bring to the table those who formulated the policies that resulted in my torture and those in the U.S. government who for years covered it up. And then we will all sit down and discuss the question of forgiveness together.

LUCY MURPHY, a Washington activist who was part Nicaraguan and part African American, came to sing for me in the park one Sunday. She needed no instrument but her voice, which was strong and full. Hardly anyone was with me, and the sun coming through new-grown leaves gave a green light to the afternoon. Lucy sat back on her heels, and began. The song was not a song of protest. It was "Gracias a la Vida," a song written by Violeta Jara, whose brother Victor Jara was brutally executed by the Chilean army during the 1973 coup. I listened to the beauty of Lucy's voice and watched her face as she sang, more than I listened to the words. But toward the end of the song, some of the words sank in: "Gracias a la vida, que me ha dado tanto, que me ha dado la risa, que me ha dado el llanto." Tears began to slide down Lucy's face and then followed down mine: "Thanks to life, which has given me so much, which has given me laughter, which has given me mourning. These are the two materials from which I make my song. And my song is your song and is the song of everyone."

I'm not sure why we were crying. Sometimes you brush against a truth, feeling it before you can say it, and instead of theories or conclusions, tears are the evidence it leaves.

FROM SU CASA, Pat and Juanita came to visit me. Mary Fabri had come for a few days at the beginning of the vigil but had to leave. She told Marie to call her when it was time to come again. Marie called her and explained my plans for the fast. "It's time to come again," she said. This time, Mary brought her husband, David, the doctor, and their young son, Josh. Adriana Bartow, whose daughters had disappeared after the army raided her house in Guatemala, also came with Mary. I knew what she wanted more than anything in the world was information, and the intensity of her desire to know what had happened to her daughters gave me strength. If I could help her I would, no matter what that took.

From the Mount my old best friends Alicia and Mary came, as well as the first Ursuline I ever knew, Sister Elizabeth Ann; I'd called her in eleventh grade to get information on becoming a nun. Some of my newer friends came, too: Luisa and Kim were among the sisters who made the ten-hour trip by car, along with Marietta, Gia, Mary Irene, and Mary Lois. It meant so much to me to have them there. Some of them even slept out with me on the cold grass and shivered beside me at dawn as we rolled up our blankets. Darleen flew in from California, and Ottie, Mimi's sister, came up from Kentucky.

In the midst of the visits and interviews, Michele told me the Inter-

American Commission on Human Rights had ruled on my case, and the commissioner wanted to meet with me to tell me the commission's findings. Michele, Jose, and I walked down to the OAS building, just a block away from the White House. The Inter-American Commission had been investigating my case for five years. I knew the commission was fair and unbiased. If the Inter-American Commission of the OAS didn't believe me, no investigative body ever would.

But I hardly dared to hope. The Senate Sub-Committee on Intelligence had shut down its investigation suddenly, after conversations with someone like Stroock or the Guatemalan government's investigator Carl West, I suppose. Was the OAS commission really sophisticated enough to recognize the damage control and cover-up efforts of the U.S. and Guatemalan governments? And if so, was the commission strong enough to denounce them?

No small talk preceded the announcement. The commissioner invited us to sit down and then, beaming, got right to the point: The Inter-American Commission was going to recommend that my case be forwarded to the Inter-American Court. The commission only recommended that very strong cases be forwarded to the court, he said.

The commission believed me, not the Guatemalan government. And the commission was giving me a chance to sue the Guatemalan government in international court.

I WANTED TO SHOUT the ruling out to everyone I saw as we walked the two blocks back. I wanted to shout it out as we passed the Old Executive Office Building. But I had to keep the ruling secret until the Guatemalan government responded. Still, what a delicious secret. The OAS commission believed *me*, and that meant the Policeman was wrong. His prediction wasn't a prophecy or a curse. *No one will ever believe you.*

Ha. You wish. Tell it to the judge.

THE OAS RULING gave me a new kind of strength. At the beginning of the third week, I held a press conference at the National Press Club to announce my fast, inviting everyone on our press list and new friends, such as Kerry Kennedy Cuomo and her mother, Ethel Kennedy. I was angry enough not to mince words:

> For the past three weeks, I have spent my days and nights in front of the White House, holding a silent vigil for truth — the truth about my case and the truth about all those Guatemalans who have suf-

fered and died at the hands of the officially sponsored death squads, for years supported with U.S. dollars. While some U.S. officials may have been moved by my vigil, others have stated to me that I seem comfortable in the park.

That was a reference to Frank Fountain. Maybe it was unfair of me to mention his remark, but it made me so angry! He was coming out of his office late one night. Both he and Anthony Lake had made a point of saying hello when they were coming out of their offices around midnight. Maybe they wanted to let me know how hard they were working. I wish Alice had been around to ask them if they'd been doing it for two decades straight and on weekends, too. Anyway, he peered into my makeshift tent of blankets and said, "Looks comfortable in there."

"No!"

"What?"

"It's not!" He was going home to a soft, warm bed. I was going to spend the night shivering and bruise my hips on the ground.

Others, still, have relegated my vigil to the category of irrational whim. One official remarked, "Declassification will happen. It's too bad that Dianna feels like she has to sit in front of the White House in the meantime. It's her choice."

But is it my choice? I have listened patiently to explanations for six years. For six years, I've been told to wait. I've attended meeting after meeting. Each month I have expected the results of the Intelligence Oversight Board's inquiry, which was supposed to be concluded last July. I have filed a FOIA [Freedom of Information Act] request. I still do not have my documents. If I am in the park, it is because I need the truth, and my options have gradually been eliminated.

I appreciate the White House officials who have taken time to meet with me. I especially appreciate the willingness of Hillary Rodham Clinton to speak with me on April 4. I believe Mrs. Clinton is in good faith trying her best to help me. I know the documents I seek do not belong to her, but to the CIA, the Department of State, the Department of Defense, and other government agencies. Yet our government could choose to order the declassification of information for victims and survivors of human rights abuses in Guatemala.

Since January, twenty-seven people have been tortured in Guatemala. Eighty-one have been murdered for political reasons. The hundreds of thousands of people in Guatemala who have lost loved ones to torture and murder, who are struggling to recover from heinous forms of torture, who are desperately trying to prosecute human rights violations and break the cycle of impunity that allows the atrocities to continue need the information.

The release of documents does not necessarily mean that the truth will be allowed to surface. When documents are eventually declassified by the U.S. government, they are oftentimes blacked out almost in their entirety, and the paragraphs that we are allowed to read are usually the most meaningless of paragraphs. I want the truth, not just documents. I want to know who Alejandro is. I want to know why our government has protected him. I want to know why a U.S. citizen had the authority to supervise and give orders to my torturers. Until I receive this information, I cannot heal.

In recent weeks, with so much fear, I opened the lid of my Pandora's box and shared with the world what I experienced and witnessed at the hands of the Guatemalan security forces and Alejandro, the U.S. citizen. You may think this strange, but even at this moment, I can sense the presence of my torturers.... I can see them blessing me with the blood of the Woman. Will this end?

Jean Améry, an Austrian philosopher tortured by the Gestapo, said, "Anyone who has been tortured remains tortured. Anyone who has suffered torture never again will be at ease in the world.... Faith in humanity, already cracked by the first slap in the face, then demolished by torture, is never acquired again."

It is with great horror that I repeat those words. Améry took his life in 1978.

I want so desperately to live. I want so desperately to believe in humanity again, to be free of Alejandro and all my Guatemalan torturers. Thousands of Guatemalans who have been tortured by the security forces also want to live and to believe in humanity again. Only the truth will set us free.

Because I am still barred from knowing the truth, because I am still in a prison of silence, because U.S. government agencies deny me access to the documents that could allow me to recover my life, I will now begin a fast of bread and water, continuing my silent vigil in front of the White House and daring to place my life in the hands of the U.S. government.

Weathering the heavy rains, harsh sun, blustery winds, and cold temperatures has not been easy.... When I go home at 5:00 in the morning for my hour of rest in a bed, my body is so sore from the ground that I have to pile pillows on top of the mattress. Although loving and concerned people bring me all sorts of food, I have lost ten pounds in the twenty-two days of my vigil. And as my weight drops, the ground gets harder.

The dark I live in ten hours a day reminds me of that cell where I waited for my torturers' hands, the blindfold that kept my eyes from their faces. But whether I am in the park or out of the park, the darkness of the blindfold is with me. This time, it is not my torturers who conceal their identity from me. It is the U.S. government.

Whether I am in or out of the park, I am still in a clandestine cell, in the dark, waiting, wondering what will happen. My hands are tied. . . . It is the U.S. government who keeps me with the Policeman, bound hand and foot, in the dark, with the rats. It is the U.S. government who controls the information about the event that haunts me, who could ensure that Alejandro and my Guatemalan torturers will *never* torture again, and that no one else in Guatemala will ever have to live this hell.

Saint Augustine said, "Hope has two daughters — anger and courage: anger at the way things are and the courage to work to make things other than they are."

I say, enough is enough! I demand that the U.S. government stop playing games and stop toying with the lives of people. Give me and the people of Guatemala the TRUTH! We have a right to know the truth.

Kerry Kennedy Cuomo took the mike and said a few words extemporaneously, supporting me and calling for declassification, and her mother told some journalists who interviewed her after the press conference that she was ashamed of what the United States government had done in my case. I was so pleased to have their friendship, support, and help.

EVERY DAY Marie brought me bread she had baked. She put all sorts of nutritious things in it — she wouldn't even tell me what, sometimes, in case I objected and wouldn't eat it; I was strict about my fast. Often I split the bread with whoever was sitting beside me. My friends protested, thinking I needed that other half a slice. But the communion, the sharing, gave me more sustenance than those few extra calories.

From Jennifer's fasts, I knew to drink a lot of water, and it stopped the hunger pangs for a while. I also drank Pedialite, a hideous liquid given to dehydrated babies, containing all the essential electrolytes. With no food in my stomach, liquids went right through me. I spent more time walking up to the Hilton bathroom than I did sitting. At least I got out of the sun from time to time. The sun was hot during the day, and my face had started to peel.

NOT EVERYTHING was so grim. Some Latino poets were reading at the Library of Congress, and knowing that I liked poetry and could use a lift to my spirits, Patricia contacted them and asked if they would give me a private reading in the park. Demetria Martínez, a poet from New Mexico, wrote for the *National Catholic Reporter* and knew my story well. She convinced the poets' agent that she and the others should accept the offer, so the agent squeezed it into their schedule.

It was a damp, blustery, bone-cold night, but the poets drew a crowd of people — not a literary crowd, but a crowd of activists. Alicia Partnoy, a local D.C. resident and a survivor of torture in Argentina, was the first to read. She asked to be introduced as one of Argentina's former disappeared. She didn't stand at the podium that had been set up but walked back and forth, using as a prop a white handkerchief, like the Mothers of the Plaza de Mayo used. When she spoke in the voice of a mother she put it over her head. When she spoke in the voice of a survivor she put it over her eyes. The poem began, "No me hables de las puertas del infierno. Yo he estado allí" (Don't speak to me of the gates of hell. I've been there). She read the poem first in Spanish, then in English. She listened respectfully to the others read, but I heard that later she was behind a tree trunk, sobbing. When I think of what it took for her to read that poem, I am doubly grateful to her for standing before me on that dark, cold night, letting me know something of her experience of hell so I could feel connected to her and less alone. I wish I had known how badly she was hurting. I wish I could have comforted her.

Claribel Alegría, a survivor of political violence in El Salvador, was present, too. She and Martín Espada and Luis Rodríguez and Demetria read beautiful, moving poems and endured the weather to share their work with me. Afterward, Tony suggested that we close with an Our Father. We all joined hands. Everyone knew the words. Everyone said the prayer. And in that communal recitation was a moment of closeness and healing.

I GOT MANY SPECIAL VISITS. Keith, one of the men who was sleeping in the park, spent a lot of time with me. He was a sweet, youngish man who was trying to help me speak. He must have thought the people around me lacked compassion and understanding; they told him I could speak if I wanted to, but I was choosing not to. I wrote him notes to the same effect. He just looked at me with sympathy and said gently, "Start with the consonants. The vowels will follow." Then he would sit facing me and encourage me to watch his lips as he formed words. I couldn't help smiling, no matter how low my spirits were to start with. Keith told me about his own recovery from a speech problem, and he shared his faith with me. "Be patient. Pray to God. God will answer your prayers, and one day you will be able to speak again."

Two brothers also lived in the park. One was schizophrenic. The other was homeless to accompany his brother. Both visited me, talked to me, told me stories about their lives, and gave their opinions on politics. Several weeks into the vigil, they brought me a potted rose bush with tiny pink buds that were just starting to open. To think that they, who had nothing, had spent money on me, buying me a plant when they couldn't afford a night at a cheap motel and when they could have used the money for a good meal — well, it reminded me of something about the human heart that I had forgotten or quit believing. Later, they gave me a locket shaped like a heart, with a small cross inside.

I left Lafayette Park at five o'clock in the morning. It was still dark, although two hours earlier the first bird had started its lone, loud calls. I wondered if the birds could somehow smell the sun-warmed air coming in off the Atlantic. How else could they start singing in the dark?

Instead of relief, I felt fear as I climbed into the car. In a few hours I would be reconstructing the torturers, seeing them and describing them to Jeanne, the sketch artist I'd met on the *Today Show.* She was coming to Washington for a few days to work with me. But I was so exhausted, and I was afraid that, remembering their faces in detail, I would be sucked under like a shell in the pull of the ebb tide. I would feel the burns and blows. And I wouldn't be able to go on. Once again the torturers would win. They would mock me. And they would stay inside me forever. I would be alone with the dark, penetrating eyes of the Policeman, the cratered skin of his face. The Guate-man's stern, arrogant stare. José's droopy eye, his dirty teeth. For years I had heard their footsteps, their laughter, their voices, smelled their hands, their armpits, their breaths. Felt them. But I had tried my best not to see them.

In dreams I saw them, every inch of them. When I was awake, too, and unguarded, they hovered before me. But I always tried to banish them.

Today I would have to will them to appear and hold them there, studying them, describing them.

I sat in the center of my bed and held one of the feather pillows tightly on my lap, checking Jeanne's face for any sign of impatience. I had gathered up all the candles in the house, making Jeanne and Mary wait. I had told Jeanne we would work in the living room, and she had pulled her materials out and gotten herself settled. People kept coming and going, though, so after a few minutes I had asked Jeanne to move up to my room. She had packed her sketch pad and pencils back up and I had packed up all the candles.

But she didn't look miffed. At the corner of her mouth was the same hint of tenderness I'd seen when she first walked into the house. Mary, who was sitting near me on the edge of the bed, gave me an encouraging smile when I looked her way. They were willing to wait all day.

The air was thick with the scent of candle wax. It was all I could smell. That's the way I wanted it and, I hoped, the way it would remain. I didn't want to smell anything else when the work began. Although the candles made the room warmer and sweat glistened on Mary's upper lip and on Jeanne's forehead, I was cold.

Jeanne and Mary were waiting for me. I might as well begin. "Let's start with Alejandro." My voice didn't sound strong and decisive, as I'd hoped. It cracked, betraying my fear. Although he didn't inflict physical pain on me, Alejandro was the one who frightened me the most. He was the most powerful. He represented the U.S. government and what it was capable of doing and denying. Watching my torturers obey him, hearing him tell me not to concern myself with the other prisoners there, hearing him tell me to forgive the torturers and then threaten me when I didn't had shaken my trust in the U.S. government. For years I'd been told I'd imagined that he was an American. I wanted to reveal his face, to show to the world the absolute, undeniable gringoness of his features.

I half-expected the usual questions — Alejandro's height and weight, his build, his clothing. But Jeanne asked different ones: "Tell me about his face. Was it round? Square? Long and narrow? What was his skin like? Was it lined? Tell me about the texture of his hair."

His face was starting to appear, and I was fighting it, covering my eyes, shaking it out of my head. But I knew I couldn't turn back. I had to choose to see him if I wanted to use what I knew of him as evidence. I took hold of Mary's hand, hoping that as I called up his memory, her touch would keep me in the present.

I closed my eyes.

Immediately I saw him. The dark glasses he used to hide his eyes. His hair, bushy and dark, unnatural and wig-like. His mustache and his beard, which were lighter than his hair. He was pressing his lips together, as if he were going to say, "Forget what you saw here, forgive your torturers. Don't talk about any of this. If you do, the photographs and the video . . ."

People already know about the Woman. I told them. You're too late. You no longer control me. And he knew nothing about the other secret, the choice I had made. That dark secret was well hidden. He and the others had nothing on me. Right?

I was floating, looking down, watching Mary watching the curled up woman, who was crying, clinging to a pillow.

It didn't last long. A voice inside me said, "Go to her. Together stand up to Alejandro." And I was on the bed again, clutching the pillow, hearing myself describe him and Jeanne's pencil whispering on the paper and the side of her hand brushing against it.

Her voice was soothing, narcotic, and it lulled me into a peaceful place where I could search my memory without too much fear. "Tell me about his eyes. Are they oval, or more like globes?"

"He's wearing sunglasses."

"So he's wearing sunglasses. Did you notice anything around the area of his eyes?" She draws the sentences out, trying to be gentle.

How easy to answer no and block the memory. But the lines that branched from the corners of his eyes have already swum into my view, so I tell Jeanne about them. I tell her about his eyebrows, too, which are lighter than his hair.

WE WORKED ON THE SKETCH for about an hour, maybe less, but to me it seemed like an eternity. I eventually asked to stop for the day, and we agreed to resume the next evening, at Jeanne's hotel, which would be more comfortable for both of us.

WHAT IT WAS LIKE to see the sketch, once Jeanne was finished, is something I don't remember much about. Jeanne told a reporter who questioned her for an article, "At first it took her an hour to look at Alejandro. She hyperventilated and then passed out. [Later] she curled up in a ball on her bed weeping."[1]

The pain and stress involved in working with Jeanne were worthwhile. By Thursday, after working together for a few hours in the evenings, we had finished the sketches, and they looked as accurate as photographs.

Jeanne, in a chapter of her book, entitled *Portraits of Guilt,* says I asked to see the sketches all at once, side by side, when the last one was finished. She was afraid I would be overwhelmed, but she reluctantly laid the sketches down.

I knew I was ready to confront the torturers. I'd been seeing them in my mind's eye day after day. Now I wanted to see them where they belonged — outside of me.

Jeanne says I inhaled, then moved my eyes along the line of faces, pausing at each one. According to Jeanne, instead of reacting as I had to the sketch of Alejandro, I was calm, strong, and dry-eyed.

"That's them — all of them — exactly as they were," I said, wrapping my arms around my body. Jeanne says she noticed a shift in my posture. For the first time since she'd met me, I was standing tall and upright.[2]

DURING THE DAY my friends were getting arrested. Standing still on the sidewalk for any extended amount of time was against the law. You had to keep moving. But people were choosing to stand and kneel in front of the White House, singing and praying and holding signs calling for the truth, even though it meant they would soon be cuffed and led away to the waiting paddy wagons. Joe Nangle carried a huge cross and wore his brown Franciscan robe. He and Vianney led the daily protest marches that ended with the civil disobedience.

Civil disobedience was new to some of my friends, old hat to others. Ann, who lived at the Assisi community and worked at the Ecumenical Program on Central America and the Caribbean (EPICA), organized the actions and gave instructions and advice to people who had never done civil disobedience before. Ann had invited her mother, Ruth, to come up for the vigil. Ruth was the dean of students at Berea College in Kentucky — a wise, thoughtful, dignified woman who had a wild sense of humor but a serious respect for careers and futures. In a phone conversation with Ann the week before, she had told Ann that getting arrested wasn't such a good idea. The arrest would be on her record forever, she wouldn't always get a chance to explain the idealistic reasons for it, and it could limit her options for the future. Ann went ahead and got arrested on the first day of the protests, along with eleven other people, and every day after that, too.

Ruth arrived at the park, and after watching the civil disobedience for a few minutes, she crossed Pennsylvania Avenue, stood with the protesters, and got arrested, too. From Ruth, I learned that, although we might desperately want to protect our reputations and those of others, at times we need to let go of that security and stand up for what we believe in.

I HATED WATCHING the arrests. My only experience with jail was the Politécnica, so I couldn't see people being handled by the police without wincing. But Ann and the others came back and said they weren't treated harshly — the Park Police knew they were doing civil disobedience because they believed in a cause. And when they came back, those who had been arrested seemed pleased with themselves. They took pride in what they had done, and they said it felt good to have stood up for what they believed in. Listening to them, I realized that I could see my experience in Guatemala in the same light. Instead of feeling ashamed — that senseless feeling of shame that so many torture survivors have and that torture is designed to provoke — maybe I could feel pride, too, pride that I stayed in Guatemala and stood up for my convictions and risked prison and the consequences that went with it. Maybe I, like my friends coming back from jail, could hold my head high.

The number of people protesting grew steadily. By the end of the ten-day period of civil disobedience, 125 people had been arrested. I noticed a new pin Jennifer was wearing on her jacket lapel, identical to the dolphin on her ring, gracefully arched, only bigger, with a long, sharp, weapon of a nose. No more Mr. Nice Guy. I guess that's what the swordfish meant. Members of the local Amnesty International group got arrested, too, along with members of Jonah House, Sojourners, and other local Guatemalan solidarity and religious groups. Harold Nelson, a sociology professor at the University of Texas Pan American, read an article about the vigil, packed up his life, and moved to Washington to work as a volunteer doing whatever he could to help with my case and with the cause of ending torture. His first step was to get arrested again and again. He wore a baseball cap, like my dad often did, and he was around my dad's age, too, I think. Like my dad, Harold lived his beliefs. He would give me comfort, solace, and wisdom in the days, months, and years that followed and teach me by his example.

Daniel Ellsberg, Phillip Berrigan, and Father Jim Flynn, of Louisville, also participated in the actions. Sisters from my order broke the law, too, as well as two Erie Benedictine sisters and a Sister of Loretto, several Franciscans, Dominicans, Sisters of Mercy, and School Sisters of Notre Dame. On the last day of the actions, Bishop Thomas Gumbleton, the auxiliary bishop of Detroit who had gone to Guatemala to support Jennifer on her hunger strike, got handcuffed and pushed into the paddy wagon with the rest of the demonstrators.

I RECOGNIZED BARBARA from afar because her whole body moves when she walks. Her hips sway, her hair bounces, her hands move uncontrollably when she talks — and she was talking — and her head moves with her hands. My mom was crying. I saw tears shining on her face. I dragged myself up and ran to meet them, or tried to. I staggered down the brick sidewalk as far as I could, they walked as fast as they could, and I fell into their arms. My mom was talking a lot as we walked back to the candle and signs, telling me all about my dad, my little brother Josh, my brother Pilar, and my nieces and nephews. Then she wanted to know all about how I was doing. Alice had given her and Barbara an update, so they knew the basics, but as we settled ourselves on the grass she kept asking questions. I kept writing, Mom, I'm on a silent vigil, I can't talk. She wanted to know about my intake of water, if I was eating my bread and drinking my Pedialite. She was good. She didn't talk about how thin I was. The last thing I needed to do was worry about my mom worrying about me. She took my hand, massaged it, put it close to her face, kissed my cheek, and said, "I love you. And your daddy loves you, too."

Barbara spent the night once. A lump in a sleeping bag was all I saw most of the night — headless, and at times, sprouting hair. The gel she had used wasn't meant for Washington weather. The night was damp and chilly, or cold and rainy, to be more accurate. Freezing, in Barbara's opinion. By the time she got back to New Mexico, she'd lost her voice.

Mom stayed at Assisi. On Thursday, she was waking up just as I was getting in to take a shower and rest before going back to the park. She wanted to talk.

"Mom, I'm tired," I whispered.

Her voice was so soft and soothing that even though she kept talking, I started to yawn. Those few hours in bed, having heard her voice and knowing she was there, I was able to really sleep.

"She's fine. She's among friends and people who believe in her and support her," I heard her say to my dad as I awoke. She called him every day to keep him updated. That's when I knew my mom was fine, too.

MICHELE, ANNA, AND JOSE, who technically was Jennifer's lawyer but who had been brought in to help with the vigil and to lend advice on the OAS case, were arguing about the sketches. We were off in a corner of the park, sitting in the grass, each in the tangle of our own thoughts. I wanted to release the sketches publicly. Jose supported me. But Anna and Michele thought I should give them to the DOJ team and do nothing more with them than that, at least for a while. They thought it was disrespectful not to give DOJ investigators time to act on the information the sketches provided before releasing them publicly; and the investigators otherwise might claim that the public release of the information had harmed the case.

Between my thumb and finger I stroked a blade of grass. The Guatemalan government had done nothing with the sketches the police artist had made, and I was afraid the DOJ would do nothing with Jeanne's. I thought of the Woman. I owed it to her to get the Policeman's face out before the public. And after so much pain and work, I owed it to myself, too. I wanted them out in the light of day, where people could see them and where someone might recognize and identify Alejandro or the Guate-man or even José. So I put my foot down. I said I wasn't coming off the fast unless I could release the sketches. In the end, we came to a compromise. I said I would at least give them to the DOJ and the IOB an hour or two before I presented them at a press conference.

Thanks to the efforts of Jennifer, who relentlessly pounded the halls of Congress, and of Carlos Salinas, at Amnesty International, who had been starving himself and meeting with people on the Hill, I was presented on Thursday afternoon with a letter signed by an unprecedented number of congressional representatives calling for declassification.

The year before, our tried and true friends in Congress had signed a letter on declassification. Aides as well as other human rights groups had encouraged Coalition Missing, which put the letter together, to select fifty prominent human rights cases and ask for the declassification of material related to those cases and no others. Narrowing down our request would give us a better chance of success, they told us. We didn't like those restrictions — selecting particular cases implied that not all cases were equal, that some people had more of a right than others to information. Twelve signatures were on that letter.

But the new letter was signed by a hundred and three members of Congress. They were asking President Clinton to issue an executive order that would quickly declassify all U.S. government information related to all human rights abuses in Guatemala. It was a huge victory.

Congress was aboard. If I can't make it on this vigil as long as I have to, Congress can take over the fight for declassification, I realized. Congress, in any case, is stronger than I am.

LATER, I GOT A MESSAGE that the IOB wanted to meet with me. We assumed they must have news, since I had made it clear that I wouldn't meet with IOB members unless they had something important to tell me. My lawyers and I showed up as requested in the greenish room and settled ourselves across the table from Anthony Harrington and Frank Fountain. "Sister Dianna," Harrington said, "tomorrow you'll be receiving more than two thousand pages of declassified documents on your case."

Chapter Nineteen

WHITEWASH

THE DOCUMENTS ARRIVED the next day at Michele's office in several big boxes. Michele, Anna, Jose, and a few other friends and I tore open the boxes, divided the documents into stacks, and began to read. Already we had learned from a reporter friend that the State Department spokesperson, Nicholas Burns, had said none of the documents indicated "that an American official was present when [I] was abused." He had tried to be careful with his wording, correcting himself several times, and we noticed that the wording he'd settled on left open several possibilities. We might find a document that indicated that an American was present — just not a U.S. official. Or we might find one that indicated that an American or an American official was present, not as I was being abused, but afterward.

We had also been warned that the documents would contain information upsetting to me. If I remember correctly, someone in the State Department had asked Frank Fountain to pass that message along, and he had. So we began scanning the pages with that warning in mind. I was terrified that the State Department or embassy had found out about the choice I had made and had put that information in a document, which, now declassified, would be available to the public.

For hours and hours we read. We didn't find anything about me that was new or different. The embassy and State Department were tossing around the usual calumnies. The difference was that they were now in black and white.

Each person pulled out the important pages, sometimes reading parts of them aloud to the group. Patricia said, "Wow. It sounds like the political affairs officer threatened to discredit you unless you kept quiet about the American. That was before you'd even left Guatemala."

Anna said, "Dianna didn't mention the American until she left Guatemala."

I agreed with Anna. I didn't have any memory of what I'd told Darleen in those first hours following my escape. I assumed I had always kept quiet about the American until I was safely in the United States. I knew I hadn't authorized my affidavit to be released until then.

383

"Well, you must have mentioned him to Darleen and she must have mentioned him to Lew Anselem because listen to this: 'PAO pointed out Nov 3 to a nun that any charge that U.S. embassy personnel tortured Diana would damage the credibility of her story.' "[1]

I'VE SINCE CONFIRMED that Father Dan Jensen and Darleen both remember that I mentioned the American with the embassy connection while I was still in Guatemala.

ON THE SAME CABLE, signed by Ambassador Stroock, we found this conclusion:

> Her refusal to speak to U.S. government representatives, either here or in the U.S., and the insistence by those around her on maximum publicity via press releases and phone conversations with congressional staff and religious groups in the U.S. leads us to question the motives and timing behind the story: apparently a debate is scheduled in Congress this week on aid to Guatemala.

Stroock added, "Given the potential damage to U.S. interests resulting from this case, if the incident is a hoax, that, too, should be revealed."

I had expected to find in the documents true but secret information that could be used against me — what I had done to the Woman and the child. Instead, I was finding the dry tinder of government lies. And anger was burning through me.

A LOT OF PAGES, paragraphs, and words were blacked out. Many of the pages that government censors had left untouched were newspaper articles, letters I or my friends had sent to government officials, replies they had sent to us, and human rights reports that had never been classified in the first place.

Finally, it was dark outside. No more papers were in the box, and only a few remained on the table. We hadn't learned anything about Alejandro or the Guatemalan torturers. My head hurt. Marie reached into the small pile remaining and after a moment began reading the 1991 memo from Deborah McCarthy to a colleague: "VERY IMPORTANT: We need to close the loop on the issue of the 'North American' named by Ortiz as being involved in the case.... The EMBASSY IS VERY SENSITIVE ON THIS ISSUE, but it is an issue we will have to respond to publicly."

That was all we learned about Alejandro.

I GOT A GLASS OF WATER. On Monday I would call a press conference. I had several things to announce. The release was entirely inadequate. I had expected as much. Why would the State Department voluntarily release anything useful? Michele explained to me that when an agency makes a "voluntary" release, as the State Department did, no one had the right to appeal anything that was blacked out. If the State Department had released the documents in response to my Freedom of Information Act (FOIA) request, we could have appealed the redactions.

Well, it wasn't too late. At the press conference, I would announce that I was filing a FOIA lawsuit against the State Department, the CIA, the FBI, the Department of Defense, the National Security Agency, and the Defense Intelligence Agency. I wanted every document I was legally entitled to have. I was down to eighty-five pounds. Congress had promised to take up the fight for a presidential executive order to declassify all documents on Guatemala related to human rights violations since 1954. I had done what I could. I had to let Congress and a FOIA judge do the rest.

I SPENT THE WEEKEND in the park, still fasting. I wouldn't call the vigil off until Monday. Fewer people than usual were around. Jeanne was at Kinko's, making copies of the sketches. I would reveal them at the press conference, where I would announce the FOIA lawsuit. Alice was faxing out a press release. Jennifer had been subpoenaed to court in Guatemala in relation to her case against Colonel Alpírez. Mom, Barbara, and Suzanne, as well as the folks who lived in the park and a few other friends, kept me company.

I was arguing gently with Mom and Barbara during the period I could talk, and then arguing on paper. I didn't want them at the press conference. Already they had to imagine the twenty-four hours I was in that secret prison and what had been done to me. I had given them those images, revealing to them over the years what had happened. I had spared them the faces. But now they would have the whole picture, the heads to go with the uniform, with the hands, with the bodies, with the voices. They would have the torturers with them, as surely as I had had them with me all these years.

And it wasn't just Barbara and Mom. Everyone in the room and everyone who saw the sketches in whatever photos might be taken, in whatever television footage might air, would have those images. Before I had believed that my body could transmit the torturers' evil — it could seep through my skin into whoever touched me. Isolating myself was easy

enough, keeping myself untouched. But if evil had stamped itself into
the contours of their features, the landscapes of their faces, and I brought
those images before the world, I was again an arm of the torturers, a carrier of their evil. And if I put those images before the world, I would be
responsible for whatever damage ensued. I could try to prove my honesty.
I could fulfill that selfish desire and risk hurting other people. Or I could
keep the torturers safely imprisoned within me. But was it selfishness if I
unveiled the sketches? Didn't I have a moral obligation to reveal what I
knew and search for the truth so that they couldn't continue to torture?
I felt trapped: I could try to free myself and risk hurting other people;
or I could play it safe, do nothing — and other people would get hurt
because I'd done nothing. It was a trap my brain always set up for me,
one I've learned now to predict. But back then I hadn't learned my own
patterns. I had to rely on hard evidence. I had shown the torturers' faces
to Jeanne and Mary, and they hadn't been hurt by them. It would probably be fine to show the sketches to the world. But I knew my mom and
Barbara shouldn't see them.

I get my stubborn streak from my mom. She said, over and over, "No,
Nana. I'm going. I'm going to be there with you."

I LEFT A MESSAGE for Frank Fountain to come by the vigil site on Monday
morning, and he showed up and came over to stand beside me. I was too
weak to stand. It was my silent period, so I wrote in my notebook that I
had met Jeanne and we had worked together on some sketches. I would
be unveiling the sketches at a press conference later that day, I wrote, but
out of courtesy to the IOB and the District Attorney's Office, I was giving
the sketches to them first.

Frank looked surprised when I handed him the manila folder, but he
didn't take the sketches out.

I wrote, "These are the *Real* things!"

"How sure are you?" he asked.

My handwriting got big and I underlined my answer twice: "<u>100%</u>."

THE PRESS CONFERENCE was in a hotel downtown. It was hot, and I was
hiding in the bathroom while journalists gathered, reading through my
press statement time and again and running cold water over my wrists.
Mary was with me. The sketches were in the room already, laid down
near the podium and covered with a blue and white shawl a Guatemalan
woman had given me. I was using it to cover the torturers' faces. They

would stay there on the floor until the end of my statement, when I was ready to lift them up.

Patricia kept peeking into the bathroom, telling me the press was getting restless because I was so late. She finally coaxed and badgered me out.

The room was packed. I had to thread my way through sixteen TV cameras and all the cameramen and wires. Photographers were squatting against the wall, and journalists were standing in the back.

In the second row, pale and stiff, sat Mom and Barbara. I had asked friends to sit nearby to support them, but Barbara was next to a reporter. It couldn't be helped. At least she and Mom had each other.

I began to read my statement, dread drying my mouth as I glanced down at the sketches. I tried to concentrate, meanwhile, on what I was saying. Since I'd begun my vigil, ten people had been tortured in Guatemala. Thirty more had been assassinated. Impunity allowed the cycle of violence to continue, and the U.S. government needed to break that cycle by declassifying all documents on human rights violations in Guatemala since 1954. In my case, the documents revealed that Ambassador Stroock had only abetted the impunity granted to the security forces. "He did not ever intend to undertake a serious, impartial investigation. I left almost immediately for the United States, and within a week of my abduction and escape, before any serious investigation had been conducted and before I had submitted any formal testimony, Ambassador Stroock had drawn conclusions about what he referred to as my 'alleged disappearance and subsequent reappearance.'" I mentioned his suggestion to the State Department that I had staged my abduction as a plot to get aid cut off. I also cited Sue Patterson's letter to U.S. embassy Consul General Rudi Boone in Belize, in which she asked for information about Sister Clare McGowan. Patterson wrote the letter "informally" in an attempt to leave no paper trail in case the embassy might "be accused of being partial or disbelieving" in my case.

"The U.S. embassy," I said, "was inconsistent and, in fact, deceptive, paying lip service to the need to find the truth in my case and secretly undercutting me, slandering me, and trying to prevent the truth from emerging." I noted that the embassy had never seriously investigated the involvement of an American but had engaged instead in intimidation. I referred to Lew Anselem's warning that the mention of an American's involvement would hurt my credibility. I also told how my testimony about the involvement of an American with ties to the embassy was, in Stroock's view, "an insult to every mission employee" and how he had accused me of bearing false witness against my neighbor. I finally had some proof of the embassy's double dealing and cover-up, and it felt good revealing that proof to the world.

But I was getting closer to the time when I was going to disclose the sketches, and I was very conscious of my mom. I just wanted her to close her eyes.

I could see Jose, our lawyer, following along on a copy of the press statement I'd given him. He would be ready to help me when I needed him.

"I am leaving the park, but my vigil continues. I hope the candle I lit on March 31, which has burned day and night in the park as a reminder to President Clinton of the hundreds of thousands of us who have suffered in Guatemala, now burns with you. We must all ask together, 'Who is Alejandro?'

"That question has gone for so long unanswered. But there is always hope. By chance, when I appeared on the *Today Show,* I met forensic artist Jeanne Boylan. She offered to help me, and for the past four days I have had the opportunity to work with her to produce these four sketches. I would like to unveil the three Guatemalans first."

Jose came to the podium to help me lift the sketches up. They were still neatly draped with my shawl, and Jeanne had attached them to a long pole. Jose held one end of it. I held the other. All I had to do was pull off my shawl. But I sensed the presence of the torturers. "You'll be sorry," I could hear them hissing. I was trembling. What kind of retribution would there be? What instrument of doom was I? Looking out into the room I saw familiar faces — Mary, Patricia, Alice, Marie, Harold. I had my legal team with me, and Jeanne was there. Which would be stronger, my torturers or my friends? The present or the past?

I pulled the scarf off. The Guate-man, the Policeman, José. Lightning struck. I was blinded.

Screams began — the Woman's, mine, those of the other people in that building?

I was being sucked back, I was starting into a flashback.

I heard the Woman. "Sea fuerte, Dianna."

Then I was aware that the torturers hadn't appeared. The flashes were cameras, not lightning or cosmic rifts. It was Mom and Barbara who had wailed. Now they had quieted. And triumph swelled inside me.

No one can tell me that these men do not exist. That's what I was thinking. And I pulled the last bit of shawl off the pole.

"This is Alejandro, the man whom my torturers referred to as their boss — the man who gave explicit orders to my torturers, the man who had access to a clandestine prison: the Escuela Politécnica, or Old Military School, in Guatemala City.

"This is Alejandro. He is not a figment of my imagination. He is real."

THE CAMERAS were flashing and rolling, but they were my instruments now. I imagined the torturers watching TV, saying, "Oh, my God, we've got to hide." I could see them calling plastic surgeons. They never expected me to have in my memory every bump, mole, and line on their faces. They never expected me to find someone who could help me retrieve the horror of their faces and who could get down on paper, as accurately as a photograph, every inch of my memory. You couldn't stymie me with your pathetic police artist. You can't hide. Nice try, Alejandro. But you couldn't keep me silent.

I asked anyone who recognized any of the torturers to contact Michele or the Guatemala Human Rights Commission. "I want to ask all of you for help," I said, "for myself and for the people of Guatemala — for the innocent students, church workers, journalists, human rights advocates, and others typically targeted for disappearance, torture, and murder because they are working for truth and justice in a society characterized by inequality and oppression."

I WAS FREE. The Guate-man, the Policeman, José, and Alejandro were out of me. So many times before, I'd stuffed and locked them deep in the recesses of my mind. Riding the Metro in downtown D.C. or maybe crossing a street, I'd often seen someone who sparked a memory. *They're here. They've found me.* I would start to recall the torturers' faces, to make a comparison and evaluate the danger. But before I could even recall their faces, I would tell myself — "Dianna, you're being paranoid. This is Washington, D.C. This is not Guatemala. You're not going to see the torturers here." And I would stuff the memory of their faces back in.

Guatemalans who were known to be torturers were in and out of Washington, D.C. I could easily have seen one of my torturers on the Metro or on the street. But if I acknowledged that much, I would have to remember them. And, remembering their faces, as I did in working with Jeanne, meant admitting that I couldn't protect myself from the torturers — they were more than memories, and I couldn't control them by locking them in a corner of my mind. They were real.

I HAD BEEN HIDING the truth from myself, the truth of what I knew and how completely I knew it. Working with Jeanne was one level of admission.

Revealing the sketches publicly was the next. I was inviting the world to bear witness to the torturers' existence. As I removed the scarf from their faces, I was taking another blindfold from my own. The torturers existed, and they could appear, even on the Metro in D.C. That was the insecurity I would have to deal with. They existed, and however uncomfortable it was for me and my government, they were responding to orders from an American. I couldn't hide from the responsibility, and I was asking everyone to help me. I had asked the question before, but now I understood that I couldn't stop asking it: How many Alejandros are out there, supervising torture?

WHEN THE PRESS CONFERENCE ENDED I explained to my friends that we were having some time for silent prayer in the park. It was also a time for purification and celebration. Purification by fire. Jeanne brought some extra copies of the sketches. Rose Berger, of *Sojourners*, somehow managed to get hold of a yellow balloon. She stood near me on one side. Jeanne knelt beside me on the other. I lit sage in the bowl Alice's nephew had made and let the smoke rise into the blue afternoon. Then Jeanne handed me the sketch of José and I lit a corner. The white space curled, fell to ash, then his neck, his chin, his mouth, nose, eyes, forehead, and hair, and then there was nothing left, he disappeared, and the ash rose into the sky with the smoke and fell into the bowl with the sage and littered the grass in front of the White House. Then the Guate-man, the Policeman, and Alejandro slowly curled under the flame. I was asking God to purify me, to tame my heart. I carried so much hatred inside me. I was asking God to show me the way to be less angry. I managed to pray for them, too, to pray that they could realize what they'd been doing. If they are caught up in greed, deceit, and confusion, free them. Nudge them on the right path. Because we were burning them with sage, the sketches as they burned had a sweet smell. I had expected a smell of rot, a stench, a testament, somehow, to their evil. Who was I to judge? Maybe they weren't wholly evil.

Rose let go of the balloon as the last of the ashes rose up, and the balloon kept climbing, so high we couldn't see it. With it I felt I'd released the torturers, not only my own but Otto's, Eloisa's, Julio's — the torturers of each person I'd known. I imagined the Woman and my friends of the circle, dancing. I'd broken one more form of silence that the torturers — all of them — had counted on. I had shown that survivors know what our perpetrators look like, and those images don't leave our minds. So if any of them think they've gotten away with torture, they haven't. They're at risk of being found out. Let them live with the fear, or let it prompt them to come forward, confess, and be at peace.

My mom called my dad on Jose's cell phone, and Jose passed the phone on to me. It was so great to talk to my dad after all those weeks of the silent vigil when I would listen to him, just listen, and couldn't respond. "The Man Upstairs will take care of you." That's what he would say. Now I could tell him I was doing fine. Now I could thank him and tell him I loved him.

When we got home, the community was about to have Mass. I was so glad that my mom and Barb would have that way to feel nurtured. The press conference had been hard for them. Barb had fallen into the reporter next to her. The reporter grabbed her arm and held on to her. Seeing the torturers' faces and realizing they were human beings — that humans had done all that to me, that they could have been our neighbors, the man at the store, the man down the street — had taken a toll on both Mom and Barb. But standing with the members of the community, holding hands, saying the Lord's Prayer, and singing together would help them, as it was helping me. We sang "The River Will Rise," a song that, for some reason, moved us all. Assisi community members still talk about that Mass and singing that song and the moment of communion we had — whether it was the words or the melody, no one knows. The song defines God as our light, greater than grieving, more than our death, and says we can hear a nameless voice, crying within our hearts. And God is that nameless voice, and God is the name of the nameless voice, the name that no one calls alone, which the world will hear, deep in the night, when the river will rise. Peace will flow like a river and the river will rise.

I took Communion at that Mass. The weight had lifted from me, as the faces of my torturers had vanished to ash.

We were doubling up, now that I was no longer in the park, and Mom lay down next to me in my bed. She massaged my head, ran her fingers through my hair. For the first time I could remember, I was absolutely sure that no harm would come to me in the night. And for the first time, I really slept.

After the press conference, a man who used to work for the G-2 got in touch with Anna. He told her he recognized the Guate-man: his name was Captain Guillermo Fuentes Aragón, he said. He even knew his G-2 code name, Aníbal, and said a nickname the officers had for him was Popeye. Fuentes, a naval officer, was in charge of counterintelligence, and worked at the National Palace and at the Politécnica. The witness had also seen him in Antigua. He first saw him in 1987, and he was still working during the time period of my abduction and torture. Anna passed the information, including the witness' contact number, along to the DOJ.

ALTHOUGH I DIDN'T USUALLY read the articles that were sent to us, I always gathered up and filed everything. I felt more in control of the information that way. If my life was an open book I wanted all the pages, and I wanted them in order. Reading the articles about the press conference now, I realize that most of them were well done. "Nun Blasts U.S. over Past Ordeal," read the headline in the *Bangkok Post.* "Nun Sues U.S. for Secret Documents," was the UPI headline. The Reuters story was entitled, "Nun Shows Sketches of Four Alleged Torturers." The *Washington Post* article, published May 7, was the only negative one. The reporter, R. Jeffrey Smith, focused on the embassy's treatment of me and put it down to disbelief rather than intentional cover-up. Although he quoted my assertion that the embassy was "slandering me and trying to prevent the truth from emerging," the headline read, "U.S. Documents Confirm Skepticism on Nun's Rape; Embassy Had Cited Gaps, Inconsistencies in 1989 Account of Torture in Guatemala."

Smith interviewed Stroock for the article. "I haven't got a clue what happened," Stroock said. But "it wasn't for lack of interest," Smith argued. "[Stroock] said Ortiz had clearly been 'traumatized' but blamed her for 'rebuffing us at every turn' when the embassy attempted to obtain details.

"'I would have given half my salary to have had the sketch [released yesterday] then and there,' Stroock said."

Smith cited the November 1989 cable to the State Department in which Stroock expressed his theory about the motives behind the "story," noting that a congressional debate on aid to Guatemala was scheduled for the coming week. Smith ended the article recounting Stroock's wonderment at my escape from Alejandro, given the physical abuse I had endured.

What Smith didn't mention was that Stroock said in that cable that I jumped out of a moving vehicle, although Stroock had my affidavit, which clearly said the jeep was stopped. Stroock resorted to other distortions in the same cable: he said I had suffered "deep shock" rendering me "incapable of talking," and therefore it was odd that I seemed to have little difficulty asking Guatemalans for protection and then placing telephone calls to a retreat in Antigua that I "had visited once."

STROOCK KNEW I WAS CAPABLE of talking — he had spoken to me himself. He noted in a cable dated November 3, 1989, "Ortiz barely spoke, indicating only that she had talked with her parents, although she did not inform them of her exact whereabouts. Ambassador did not try to elicit any information about her ordeal from Ortiz, who appears traumatized."[2] Furthermore, he knew that I had not visited the retreat center only once. In a November 4 cable to the State Department he reported that I had been staying at the retreat center for a week and a half.[3]

These distortions began to appear in cables Stroock sent out after receiving my affidavit on November 6, which repeated my assertion that the man who got me out of the clandestine prison spoke heavily accented Spanish, understood English, and said he was taking me to a friend of his at the U.S. embassy.

The embassy's attempts to discredit me continued. In February 1990, according to an embassy chronology, embassy consul Phyllis Speck and a legal attaché interviewed the dermatologist who had treated my wounds at the Vatican embassy.[4] But almost a year later, Stroock asked the State Department to delete a line about my case from its 1991 human rights report on Guatemala: "Delete: and a physician confirmed that she had been burned; note: we don't know if that is true; her lawyers say it is but we have no independent confirmation."[5]

THESE WERE THE KINDS OF DETAILS we noticed only after examining the documents very carefully, which we couldn't do in the weekend before the press conference. In fact, it would be years before I had the time, stamina, and heart to devote myself to the enterprise. But at least one reporter spent enough time with the documents to understand that a cover-up had taken place. Larry Rother, of the *New York Times*, wrote, "[T]he papers made public indicate that Thomas F. Stroock, a Wyoming businessman who was the Bush Administration's envoy here, . . . mounted a wide-ranging public relations effort to distance American officials from the incident." Rother quoted Human Rights Procurator Julio Arango, who had received and examined a box of documents on my case which had been sent to Guatemala. " 'These are not declassified documents,' he said, waving a sheaf of papers in the air. 'They are censored documents.' " Vicente Cano Ponce, a member of the procurator's special investigative team, added, "You can clearly see the concern of the American Embassy regarding the management of the Ortiz case. That seems to be their principal consideration."

In 1996, Stroock was still "managing" my case — speaking about it dishonestly. A photographer friend of ours, Mark Bowman, had sent Stroock some photos from the LASA conference. In a letter dated January 25, 1996, Stroock responded, "Regarding Diana Ortiz — her statements were untrue and her attitude of open antagonism was very difficult to bear in view of the major efforts that the undersigned, personally, made to rescue her from whatever happened, protect her, get her out of the country, secure the cooperation of the Guatemalan government, and hunt down whoever perpetrated whatever happened." Stroock had never before mentioned the "major efforts" he had made "to rescue" me. Could those have involved sending out a CIA officer to hunt me down?

The following spring, Anna received this letter from a human rights lawyer named Lee Tucker:

> During the summer of 1990 I worked in Guatemala as a Harvard Human Rights Fellow. On July 23, 1990, I interviewed Ambassador Stroock at his office in the U.S. Embassy in Guatemala City. Regarding the case of Sister Dianna Ortiz, Ambassador Stroock made the following comments to me at that time:
>
> 1. Sister Ortiz presented "a phony situation."
>
> 2. "She wasn't raped, that never happened."
>
> 3. "[Monsignor Próspero] Penados isn't telling the truth; he didn't see that [cigarette burns, other physical evidence]."
>
> 4. "From the time she came into Guatemala City until the time she left, she refused medical attention."
>
> 5. "I don't even know if she really is or was a nun."
>
> 6. "What didn't happen is what she said happened."
>
> These are actual quotes taken from my contemporaneous notes of the interview.

Stroock had seen for himself that on November 3, 1989, I couldn't sit back against the chair, as he would swear under oath before the Guatemalan court. The burns had been well established by other embassy officials for their own records through officials' conversation with the dermatologist months before Stroock and Lee Tucker met. Yet Stroock was willing to accuse Archbishop Penados of lying about the burns, and he was willing to tell Lee Tucker that I had received no medical attention, when he knew for a fact that I had. Stroock desperately wanted to cover up what had happened to me. We passed Lee Tucker's note on to investigators at the DOJ.

At the end of my first vigil-free week, Frank Fountain called a meeting with me and Michele. Some CIA documents had been released, he said, and he wanted to discuss them with us. Frank and Roland de Marcellus, a thin young assistant "on loan from the State Department," met us at Michele's office.[6]

Frank said the IOB had found ten intelligence documents in its review of my case. The IOB had planned to release the documents when it released its report in June, but, concerned about my welfare on the vigil, the IOB had pressed the CIA to make them available sooner. So here they were. Frank handed me a manila folder.

I pulled out the documents.

Frank called our attention to the first one, saying it was written sometime before October 15, 1991. "This document was never sent forward as a formal cable," he said. "It's still in draft form."

I scanned the document quickly. Little handwritten notes were in the margins and above some of the sentences — corrections someone had made. I could see the document was a draft that was supposed to undergo revision before being sent to the CIA headquarters in Langley, Virginia.

The first paragraph indicated that the document was a human rights report:

> Over the past year, Station has been receiving increasingly disturbing reports of alleged human rights violations involving the [censored] service, the Guatemalan army or other components of the Guatemalan security services. We have taken all such reports seriously and have attempted to obtain information to confirm or disprove them. Of course, this has not been easy; there is seldom sufficient evidence to warrant intelligence dissemination. [Three censored lines follow.]
>
> In the past few weeks reports received [censored] have created what we believe are reasonable grounds for believing that certain specific accusations and other, more general, accusations may be true. We have arrived at this conclusion, not just from reporting on individual incidents, but also from supporting reporting that has provided the "atmospherics" surrounding the cases. We stress that in

all of these cases further investigation is warranted, but we present the following information in detail to provide to HQ the content of some recent revelations. Needless to say, the Station has made the further investigation of all of these incidents a top priority.[7]

I flipped through the pages and saw reports on Michael DeVine's and Myrna Mack's murders. Then I saw my case. Michele and Frank were discussing the document, and I knew I should listen, but I couldn't resist scanning the paragraph beneath my name.

Dianna Ortiz is a U.S. citizen and Roman Catholic nun who claims to have been kidnapped and released more than a year ago by Guatemalan security forces. Until now, Station (and the embassy) has been inclined to regard her story with suspicion because of the tactics commonly used by leftist propagandists in Guatemala (false kidnapping, etc.) and the unconvincing content of her story. [Censored] told station, however, that she was in fact kidnapped as she claimed, probably by the S-2 office of military Zone 302, with headquarters in Chimaltenango, Chimaltenango Department [she was kidnapped in Antigua, Guatemala, which is in MZ 302].

"Frank, why was this document left in draft form?" Michele was asking.
"Some information in the document *was* sent forward in a formal cable," Frank said. "But the information on Dianna's case wasn't. And also some other information in the document wasn't because it wasn't adequately sourced."

I couldn't take notes. The story was already too complicated. The entire document was left in draft form, as Frank had said at first? Or the part about my case, as he'd said next? Or the part about my case, as well as "other information"?

I went back to reading and left Michele to sort the questions out.

Station must stress that [the source] has simply said that he knows she was kidnapped, but has not provided any specific information surrounding the kidnapping. In view of the extreme sensitivity of this case, this is a crucial point. As HQs may be aware, the case has received extensive news coverage in the U.S., including a story on the 20/20 news show.

"So the part about Dianna was never sent on at all — even in draft form?" Michele asked.
Frank nodded.

"Why wasn't it sent on?"

"The information on Dianna's case wasn't adequately sourced," Frank said. "There wasn't enough information."

AT THE END OF THE PAGE a sentence caught my attention: "[The source] added that Ortiz was in contact with leftist guerrillas, which led to her arrest."

Blood burned in my cheeks. My torturers told me I deserved all they were doing to me because I was guerrilla. It couldn't be true. Although I had hardly any memory of my time in San Miguel, I was sure I wouldn't have been working with the guerrillas. I had never supported violence.

But then I remembered what Mimi once told me: we might have been in contact with guerrillas without knowing it. It wasn't as if they were all wearing uniforms and carrying guns. The Guatemalan National Revolutionary Unity (URNG) involved civilian structures, and the people in those were undercover, unidentifiable to everyone but their own and, at times, the army. The people in our youth groups, people I was friends with . . . who knew? They might have been guerrillas.

I FORCED MY MIND back to the meeting. Roland was saying he had found the draft document in the files at the U.S. embassy during his trip there the previous summer, and it was "readily retraceable."

Sometimes, when I'm having trouble concentrating, I build a mental image of what is being said or translate the words into simpler language.

I pictured Roland tracking down the people involved with the document: finding out whose hands it had passed through, who had made the little corrections and notes in the margin, who had read it, and who had written it in the first place.

Roland went on to explain his method: he had retraced the document "by interviewing all the people who might know" about it. He had even learned the name of the source who provided the information.

"We can't reveal the source," he said. "The source's credibility is highly questionable. He has no credibility. There is no indication of how he came to know this information."

I looked again at the document. In the margin, next to the information the source gave about the probable involvement of the Chimaltenango S-2, was a handwritten note: *personal knowledge*. An editor's note, to be included in the final version. What else could it be? It looked like all the other notes. The source had told the CIA that he had personal knowledge of my abduction. Whoever was correcting the draft wanted to include those words — "personal knowledge." But the IOB was faulting the source for giving no indication of how he had learned the information. Saying that he knew for a fact, or even that he had personal knowledge, wasn't enough. He was supposed to outline the steps he'd taken to acquire that knowledge. But what if he, too, needed to protect his sources?

"The IOB hasn't excluded the possibility that the source was telling the truth," Frank said, "and we are continuing to check it out." Then he put the draft document under the stack and moved on to the next one.

Michele and I moved on, too. These, after all, were the first CIA documents we'd ever seen on my case — and, according to the IOB, the only ones that existed, the only ones we were ever likely to see. Absorbed in reading, we let questions about the draft document slip away before they could form completely. Although Roland didn't contribute much to the rest of the meeting, we didn't ask ourselves if he'd come along just to explain the circumstances around that one document — the process by which he'd retraced those involved in it and learned about the source's unreliability. We didn't ask ourselves why Frank hadn't sent the documents by mail before meeting with us to explain them. We didn't ask if the IOB wanted us to hear Roland's explanation of the draft document immediately, before we had time to read, raise questions, talk to the press.

We were in a trusting mode. Frank and Roland said they had looked at the other cables carefully and had found nothing else of any significance regarding my case. They said they didn't think I was helping the guerrillas, but the "other side" may have, and that might account for my abduction. Michele passed on Lee Strickland's notes of her interview with Stroock, and Frank didn't seem surprised. He said he thought she wasn't aware of what the IOB already had.

Anna talked to Frank by phone about the document that had been withheld, and when she gave me a copy of her notes, I put them in a file and thought no more about them until much later, when I would compare her and Michele's notes with the explanations of the document in the IOB and DOJ reports and find some striking differences.

IF ONLY I had made a habit of reading, instead of simply filing everything. I knew what had happened to me — that was my attitude. Why read someone else's opinion of it? I had been hurt so many times by disbelief. I filed the *Time* magazine article that began, "A nun raped and tortured in Guatemala demands answers on alleged U.S. involvement in the crime." If I had read on, I would have been surprised. "The Justice Department has launched its own investigation but has been frustrated by Guatemalan stonewalling, both in this case and in the murders of two men allegedly involving a Guatemalan army colonel in the pay of the CIA."

Guatemalan stonewalling wasn't something that I or my lawyers had heard about. I kept hearing about my own lack of cooperation.

The article quoted State Department Spokesman Nicholas Burns: "There has been a cover-up in the past. Officials in the Guatemalan government have repeatedly tried to cover up for Guatemalan military officials who, we believe, are implicated in some of these murders and in the torture of Dianna Ortiz."[8]

If I'd had the courage to read the articles I was filing, I could have asked Nicholas Burns who the State Department believed those military officials were who were implicated in my torture — and who the Guatemalan government officials were who had repeatedly tried to cover up for them.

Chapter Twenty

THE INNER VIEW

THIS WAS A DAY Michael Tubach had been waiting for. I was going to be interviewed. He sat at the head of the table, alongside Pat Riley, chief of the Sex Offense Section of the Department of Justice. He was trying to make the interview process easier for me, he said, by giving me the opportunity to have Ms. Riley there.

She had a kind face, I thought, surveying her.

Noticing my eyes on her, she gave me a soft smile.

I smiled back. I pictured her acting as my advocate, rephrasing questions, telling Michael when to stop, when I might need a break, when a particular question might be too difficult.

FBI agent Xanthie Magnum was also present, to take notes. I realized Tubach was making an effort by having Xanthie there, instead of a male FBI agent.

The interview went on for about four hours. I told Tubach all I knew about my family, my decision to become a nun, my academic career, and my decision to undertake missionary work. I answered everything I could about my life in San Miguel. Most of the information I had reconstructed over the years through conversations with Mimi, but I also had a few memories left. Certain names that they mentioned to me I remembered. The threatening notes I had some memories of. The first letter was slipped under my door.

Michael Tubach wanted to know what it said. The investigators, of course, had copies of the original letters in their file. But Tubach wanted me to say the words.

My heart sped up. I started shaking. "Be careful..." I said. *We tried to warn you, but you didn't take the notes seriously. If anyone's to blame for what happened it's you.*

ACCORDING TO DECLASSIFIED FBI notes of the interview, "Ortiz could not state the rest of the phrase."

A DECISION WAS MADE to suspend the process for nearly two weeks. I was too exhausted to be interviewed intensively.

When we began again, the interviews were in earnest. From May 29 to June 7, I gave over forty hours of testimony.

THE MAY 29 INTERVIEW must have lasted all day. The FBI later released to me thirteen pages of single-spaced, typed notes summarizing that one interview. The FBI notes of the interviews afford not so much an accurate picture of what happened during those hours as a glimpse into the interviewers' attitudes and methods:

5-29

On the morning of November 2, 1989, Ortiz did not want breakfast.... Ortiz stated that she was wearing her watch, a ring (gift from her parents when she made her final vows), blue jeans, tennis shoes, a light blue/pink shirt and royal blue sweatshirt, a gift given to her by her nephews.

Ortiz went to the garden by asking someone to unlock the gate. She could not recall who opened the gate. Ortiz was asked what type of underwear she was wearing on that day but was unable to answer the question without the assistance of her attorney, Michelle Arrington [sic]. Arrington stated that Ortiz wore a t-shirt, brassiere, and underpants.

. . .

When asked who took her shirt off, Ortiz did not respond.

. . .

Ortiz initially stated that while the photographs were being shown to her the burning of her back with cigarettes had not started. Later she stated that the Guate-man showed her photographs from the front while the police officer was burning her back with cigarettes.

If I initially stated that the burning with cigarettes had not started while the photographs were shown to me, the FBI's handwritten notes, taken during the interview, show no record of that statement. At the top of each set of typed notes is the phrase "date of transcription" — as if the documents were typed up from tapes or from the handwritten notes, as if each page were a record of what I said, contemporaneously recorded. But these documents are summaries or commentaries, not transcriptions. Assertions are made out of the blue that are false. For example, the FBI notes state that I said the indigenous man I was shown a picture of was holding a rifle in his left hand, but that later I said he was holding it in his right hand. Later when? Nowhere in the handwritten FBI notes is there any record of my stating that he held the rifle in his right hand. The typed notes also say that at one point I stated that the ceiling of the garage was high and at another I said it was low. The handwritten notes show no record of my ever saying the ceiling was low. I don't trust the summaries at all as a record of what I said.

But as a cross-reference they're useful. They help me know what I imagined about the interviews, as far as the tactics and motives of the investigators, and what was real.

5-30-96

The police officer began grabbing Ortiz.

"Where did he grab you?" Michael Tubach asked.

When asked where she was grabbed Ortiz used a stick figure drawing to illustrate.

"What were you wearing? Were you naked at that point? Were you on the floor? Was the policeman beside you, behind you, or in front of you?"

Ortiz stated that she was still wearing her brassiere, underwear, t-shirt, pants, and shoes. Ortiz was still in the chair. The police officer was standing in front of her and faced her. He began touching under her t-shirt and began touching her breasts.

"How did you respond?"

Ortiz stated that she tried to fight him off and to protect herself so that she could be strong but she began to cry. The Guate-man told the policeman they could get to that later.

Continuing the Guate-man and the police officer started asking Ortiz questions. The policeman began to touch Ortiz's upper body only.

"Had he taken your brassiere off yet?"

She stated that her brassiere was still on. While the Guate-man was still asking questions the police officer remained close by. Ortiz stated that the police officer was sitting on the desk and she could see his legs swinging. Ortiz stated that the Guate-man was standing in front of her and then walked behind her and began to burn her back with a cigarette.

Ortiz stated that the first burn was in the front near her breasts. Ortiz could smell the smoke and feel the burn of the cigarette even though the cigarette was not left on her body long. Ortiz stated that the burns started in the front and then they went to the back. Ortiz stated that she never told anyone that she was burned in the front first because she was ashamed to show her chest.

"Did they burn your nipples?"
Everyone stares. I feel their eyes on my chest.

THE HEAT OF THE CIGARETTE, nearing my skin. Their eyes on my chest. The Policeman's. The Guate-man's. Don't feel. Each time the cigarette and my body meet, a scream shoots up my nerves, pain so real and at the same time so foreign slams against the back of my head.

Please God. Make them stop.

MY LAWYER IS SILENT. She, like God, has abandoned me.

I look at Pat Riley. She sits back from the table. As if she would like to help, right? — but can't, because her hands are tied, like José's were. She wants to help me, she's on my side, but she can't. Or as if she's resigned to this form of questioning, disgusted, but resigned.

BUT SHE, TOO, STARES, waiting for me to answer.

Xanthie has her pen poised over her notebook.

I lower my head. I won't let anyone see that it hurts.

I close my eyes and am in another world, a glass fish tank, where I swish and float and breathe bubbles, not words, where every breath is silent and nothing can be heard. I am drowning.

Ortiz did not recall any burns in the nipple area.

The next day, the investigators wanted to know about the room where the Woman was. Where the light was coming from, whether I was naked, where in the room I was sitting, and how I was sitting. What I saw. What I heard. What I smelled.

That the door opened into the room and seemed to be made of metal could be important. They might need to know that the walls were made of cement, and that I knew this because I could see them and they felt scratchy against my back. But they wanted to know what covered the Woman, what the cot looked like that she was lying on, whether I could see the legs of it. Was the sheet over her a fitted bed sheet or a loose sheet? They wanted to know that the room smelled of human waste and body rot. And they wanted to know what sensations and thoughts I was having as I observed the Woman.

MARIE CAME WITH ME to the next meeting. She started out by explaining her presence to Michael. "I'm concerned about the interview process and the consequences of it on Dianna. I'm afraid it may destroy the achievements she's made in these years of recovery."

"In any rape case, there's a need to speak about the rape," Michael answered.

Anna, who was representing me that day, suggested that we stick to physical descriptions. She was afraid I would shut down and be unable to continue the process otherwise.

Michael said that he understood. "But I need to try to get as much information as possible. But if Dianna can't go on, she can't."

Marie explained to Michael that one of my fears was that if I stopped the interview, the investigation would stop.

"If I stop and can't go on," I added, "does that mean I'm not cooperating? That's a heavy burden. Also, I don't know anything about the investigation. All the memories are coming back.... I want to die...." I fought to keep my voice steady. I didn't want Michael to see my weakness. "I know this is part of the process, but I don't feel like I have control of what's happening. I understand your need to investigate...."

"Talking in the third person makes things easier," Michael said, "and talking about the periphery of the events. Whatever you say will be included in the investigation. Now, I don't want to be in the position of causing you to commit suicide. If you talk and that's going to be the result, I don't want you to keep talking."

Anna said, "We want to be clear that if Dianna can't go forward, it's not that she's not cooperating. As an attorney and a person that cares for her, I'll advise her to stop if she feels she can't go forward."

Pat Riley leaned forward on one elbow and gave me a sugary look. "Dianna, you speak to all our humanity. I understand you. It's hard to watch you go through the pain. But the more you talk, the more we can use the information to investigate. We would never risk a victim for our investigation. If that's a choice we have to make, we have to choose your mental health. But the more you give us, the more we can work with."

I felt like a wild animal being lured into a trap. How sincere were they? I asked for information about how the rest of the investigation was going.

Michael said he had interviewed the former G-2 agent Anna had talked to after my press conference. He was the one who had identified the Guate-man on the basis of my sketch as a G-2 officer, a lieutenant named Federico Fuentes Aragón, with the code name Aníbal.

Anna's eyes sharpened and she flipped to a clean sheet of paper. She was going to get down every word Michael told her about that interview.

"The man who approached you struck the investigators as credible," Michael told Anna. "But the man he mentioned wasn't in Guatemala at the time. He was in the States."

So much for that lead.

"Everything you tell us about the details of the place you were detained is very helpful to me," Michael added. "It's possible that it wasn't the Politécnica. It's important for me to find the building."

"I feel like I'm crumbling inside. Could we have two-hour sessions at a time?" I knew a break in the middle would help me, instead of doing four hours of solid interviews.

Pat Riley agreed that we could have a two-hour session in the morning and a two-hour session in the afternoon.

I added that I would need flexibility to be able to move to a different topic if whatever they were asking me about was too difficult.

No one voiced opposition. At least I had set some limits and won some space for myself. But I still didn't know whether I could handle going forward.

At that interview, we didn't just stick to physical descriptions, as Anna had suggested. But more emphasis may have been placed on such details.

"What did the Policeman's teeth look like?"

Dirty, with yellow stains. His nails, dirty and bitten. His upper arms, heavy and flabby. His neck, blemished, acne-scarred.

The Guate man had clean, straight, even teeth, with no gaps. His eyes were a mixture of black and brown. He had no moles or scars on his face. He wore a pendant around his neck on a heavy, dark, gold chain. It was a square horoscope pendant, and it had holes in it.

"And the cigarette butts on the floor, were they two-toned? Did they have a filter?"

That afternoon, I asked Anna and Michele and Joe and Marie to meet Alice and Patricia and me at the commission to help me talk through whether I should continue the interview.

Anna was the first to speak up. She said it was clear that I had cooperated. She said her concern now was about the cost of the interview to me. She pointed out that the investigation wouldn't stop even if I couldn't continue to be interviewed. She also said I didn't have to make any decision now about my participation in any future trials. If the DOJ were to indict someone, I would have to testify before a jury. If the case were sent to trial, I would have to testify and be cross-examined by the defense attorney. It would be hard. If the OAS sent my case to the Inter-American Court in Costa Rica, the process could take years. That, too, could be hard, but I wouldn't have to make a decision just yet.

Michele told me that the additional details I had given the DOJ investigators had been helpful and had clarified a lot. "To give more at such a great cost to yourself may not be so important," she said. "I would be comfortable if you stopped now or said you would have one wrap-up session with a limited number of questions."

"If I stop now, will it undo all I've done so far?"

"No," Anna and Michele said together.

"As lawyers we can help with a witness list. They may ask you a few bits and pieces," Anna said.

"The OAS would be much the same," Michele added. "We can help set up a list of witnesses and do things to make it easier for you."

"It's their work now," Anna argued. "You've given them a huge amount of identifying information. Now other sources have to come into play. The investigation will continue. And you don't have to make any long-term decisions now."

"It's so important to me to hear that from other people," I said. "This is not just my journey. I'm connected with so many others . . . the people of Guatemala. . . . "

"You've given what you can," Alice told me, putting her hand on my shoulder. "I support your decision. I'm with you a hundred percent."

"There's a part of me that still believes that the Woman is alive. If so, will I help her by giving them more information? If I discontinue, will I abandon her?"

"What you have given her is enough," Michele said. "They can go on with what they have to find out something like that — to be able to find her, to be able to help her. You've done that. And you've built a better relationship with the U.S. Attorney's Office and made them more sensitive. I hope you have a sense now that they are serious."

"A lot of this has to do with the voices that are in me," I admitted. "The voices of the torturers."

Patricia spoke up, reminding me, "The torturers are liars. Don't let those voices impact your decision. You should feel confident that everyone who has worked in support of your efforts will support you."

"It's OK, Dianna," Anna told me. "You are stubborn as a mule! I'll call

Michael Tubach tomorrow and tell him we'll take a break — you may not want to continue. You're thinking about it."

"It means a lot to me that you accept my decision," I said. But I was the one who couldn't accept it.

A couple of days later, I was back in front of Michael Tubach, continuing the interview. Part of the discussion was about my medical records. The investigators were being particularly nice. Michele wrote in her notes, "They will not get those records without talking with Dianna first and trying to get her permission. They will respect her privacy. They will not try to get records that she doesn't want disclosed."

Michael explained that they wanted as much information as they could get about how various places where I'd sought help worked and didn't work in order to help them understand how or why my story had expanded or become more detailed. "That may be the most cogent explanation as to why the whole story didn't come out in the beginning; it may not be so much a failure of memory as that you couldn't talk about things."

Pat Riley added, "We will *not* sacrifice the victim to this case. We will *not* seek a court order. If we do find the persons and a prosecution ensues, then we can't necessarily control that.... But that's a different issue, a different time."

EVEN AS Michael Tubach and Pat Riley were reassuring me that they would obtain my permission before seeking medical records, two other DOJ investigators were in Kentucky at Our Lady of Peace, asking for my medical records. The staff at the hospital refused to release them. Bob Chaney (a large, round man who reminded me of Tubach) and FBI agent Tim O'Neill (the one with the cowboy boots) were "very intimidating," according to Father Jim Flynn's sister, who worked at the hospital. But the staff was tougher than they were. "We'll be back," the investigators threatened.

It would be a couple of days before Father Jim Flynn called Anna to pass this information along. On I went, meanwhile, answering questions.

After the lunch break we spoke more about my trip up the long hallway to the room where the Woman was. I explained that coming out of the first room, we turned right into the hall. I remembered that José had removed my blindfold in the hallway and I had seen several men standing around. One was wearing a military uniform, dark green camouflage with shiny black boots.

I described the encounter with Alejandro, my conversation with him, the left turn we took to walk down the hallway, the stairs with the two landings, the garage.

The garage was spacious. It could fit about fifteen cars. The roof was flat.

Alejandro's jeep was very clean and neat. A rabbit's foot hung from the rear-view mirror. A black radio, like a CB or walkie-talkie, was in the jeep, attached to the front. Alejandro didn't use it, but I could hear static and muffled voices in Spanish coming through on it.

The seats were soft, a combination of fabric and leather. The jeep was a stick-shift.

THE NEXT DAY, I gave more details: I could hear dogs barking as I got into the jeep. I didn't hear any gunshots, helicopters, or planes at that point, but I had heard them at other times.

After he began driving, we seemed to go through two gates. The gates must have been open, because Alejandro didn't push any buttons or talk to anyone or show any pass card, but I thought I heard them clash behind me. I didn't look back. We seemed to be in some sort of compound, between the gates.

Once through the second gate, we turned right onto the road. I remembered a mixture of tall and short buildings. In the rearview mirror I could see a black stripe, like a wave, on my side of the car, where the door was. There was almost no traffic, and it seemed to take about five minutes before we reached the point where I saw the sign for Zone 5.

Michael asked about the identity of the indigenous woman who helped me after I escaped from Alejandro.

I told him that I didn't remember her name or any specifics about where she lived.

He continued to insist that I give him an answer.

I told him again that I couldn't remember; I wouldn't allow myself to remember.

"Don't lie to me!" he shouted.

Silence hung in the air. Then I heard a rasping, like fingernails being filed. It was my breath, I realized. I was back there, in the Politécnica. Or were the torturers before me, disguised as Michael Tubach, Pat Riley, and Xanthie Magnum? It's no coincidence that there are three of them. And I have been telling them my most private feelings, my most intimate reactions to everything they did to me.

I walk to the door, but I'm trapped. I'm back there. The knob gives, finally, and I make it down the hall, into the bathroom, where I run cold water over my hands and face.

Michele is waiting for me in the hallway when I come out.

"I want to go home." Those are the only words I get out before the sobs come. "Michele, I won't allow myself to remember the woman. I won't put another person's life in danger. I can't. I won't."

I could tell from Michele's eyes that she understood me and believed me.

"I have to leave." I couldn't face Michael. I was so afraid that if I looked at him again, I would see the faces of the torturers. Looking at photographs, sometimes you can get lost in the reality they represent, until images get superimposed, until there's a flaw. I had seen that flaw, that split-second superimposition, and I couldn't trust that Michael was simply a DOJ lawyer. A slip had given him away.

"Tell him what you're feeling," Michele said. "He needs to hear it from you. I'll be in there with you."

Tell the Devil what you're feeling. Tell the torturers what you're feeling. Right.

I looked at Michele. Her face was full of understanding. "I can tell him, if you want," Michele said. "I can tell him your reasons for not remembering anything about that woman who helped you. But I think he needs to hear from you what his words did to you. I think he needs to hear how upset you are." Anger flashed through Michele's eyes as she spoke.

I knew she was on my side. I would go back and face him with her beside me. I would pull myself out of this demi-flashback, and I would make him confront how his abusive words had affected me.

I COULD HARDLY BREATHE. I could barely lift my feet as I walked to the door and opened it. I didn't look at him. I pulled my chair closer to the door, and farther away from Michael. With my forehead pressed against my hand and my elbow against my knee I could keep my hand from shaking as it covered my eyes. Even so, my voice cracked. But I forced each word out. I explained once again why I wouldn't allow myself to remember the woman who assisted me. I can't recall if Michael or anyone else said anything in response.

The next thing I remember is being in the elevator. I have this vague memory of Michael being in the elevator, too. My vision was slightly distorted. Things seemed to gape and bend at the corners.

Outside the building, I left Michael and Michele and went to rest on a cement bench that surrounded a scrawny tree. My body was numb, except for my cheek — it was throbbing.

When I looked up, Michele and Michael had finished chatting and were coming toward me. Michael stopped in front of me while Michele hung back.

"I'm sorry," Michael said. He had taken off his jacket and his tie dangled and lifted on the breeze. "I just got frustrated. Well . . . see you next week."

I watched him walk away. What was I supposed to have said? I forgive you? It's OK? Forget about it? I could have said all that. But it wasn't OK. And he could forget about it, but I couldn't. The torturers would return that night. I could smell them, just as I had smelled them in that room. How was I going to protect myself from them? Did he think his apology could erase or undo what had happened? It might ease his conscience to apologize, and he might be able to go home and forget that he had yelled "Don't lie to me!" But I couldn't. His words had destroyed a world within me.

MICHELE AND I went to Anna's office to tell her about what had happened with Michael. Michele recounted the incident and praised me for having the courage to return to the room and talk with Michael. Anna must not have gotten the call from Father Jim Flynn yet because she didn't tell me anything about it that afternoon. I don't remember when or if she ever told me. I found the information in the files years later. Maybe she thought it would just upset me to know the DOJ investigators had broken their word.

Once we finished talking about Michael, Anna and Michele pulled out their appointment books and started talking about who would accompany me to which interview in the coming week.

I was stunned. They expected me to go on — not only to face Michael Tubach yet again, but to continue answering his questions, opening myself up to him, as if I hadn't just seen through him. They weren't defending me. They weren't standing up for me. And they didn't understand what had just happened.

Part of me wished that Anna and Michele would say, "Dianna, this is too much for you. This is abusive. We're not putting you through this process any more." It was up to me, really, to make that call. But as I thought about it, I realized there was no way out. I couldn't discontinue. I had called on my government to investigate my case. Six years later, the government was investigating. If I walked away now, I would be accused of not cooperating. Anna and Michele could tell me that wouldn't happen, but I knew how things worked. That's exactly what would happen.

WHEN I GOT HOME, I went to my room, lit all the candles, burned sage, and played a tape Jennifer had shared with me, Everardo's favorite piece of music, "Hymne Sauvage." Several phone calls came in for me, but I didn't take them. I wanted to be unreachable. Finally, I fell asleep.

I'M CLUTCHING THE WALL for support in my dream. I allow the floor to hold me up. But the floor opens up and swallows me. I am falling into the abyss — into hell. Hands, faces, come out of the wall....

MONDAY CAME, and I met Michele outside the Department of Justice to continue the interview. I didn't really look her in the eye, and I walked very slowly to the glass door. Tubach would be asking me questions about the size of the room, the height of the ceiling. Who cares about the height of a ceiling when one is being raped, tortured? I recall when the Policeman first raped me the ceiling seemed so beyond my reach that I tried to lift my arm — thinking maybe that the ceiling would open up and an arm from above would grasp my hand and pull me away from them. That didn't happen. Instead, it seemed like the entire room — the walls, the ceiling — were all closing in on me and I couldn't breathe. But how could I tell the investigators that? Would they understand me?

I can picture now how the FBI agent would have typed it up if I had tried to explain to her that the height of the ceiling and the size of the room were the last things on my mind — that I just wanted out. That I was praying. That I was thinking about whether God existed. I imagine the agent writing:

> Ortiz stated that she envisioned the walls and ceiling of room #1 closing on her during the rape. Ortiz stated that the room seemed to become smaller at that point. She stated that she thought she might be rescued by someone accessing the room from above. Asked if the ceiling had any visible hatches or if she heard any noises, such as footsteps, on the ceiling, Ortiz stated she did not. She was unable to explain why she thought that she might be rescued by someone accessing the room by way of the ceiling.

I suppose for purposes of an investigation, the size of the room, the type of door, and the height of the ceiling were important technicalities. I guess I should have paid more attention to my surroundings and been more observant — maybe I should have taken notes and asked for a tape measurer.

I knew there was no use lingering on the sidewalk with the cars snarling by. I went on in the building, to face Michael Tubach and answer his questions. He had encouraged me to speak in the third person when I needed to. Although it had made the process somewhat easier, I was going back into that building, not as another person, but as Dianna Ortiz. I was going home every day and having nightmares as Dianna Ortiz. I was having the flashbacks in the first person — I was feeling the pain, not "she." And Pat Riley wasn't doing anything but sitting there, watching me be revictimized by Michael Tubach's questions and accusations. I guess I went back on in because I wanted to prove how strong I was. I had fallen into the old trap, pledging to myself that I wouldn't let Michael Tubach know how much he'd hurt me, staying on my feet, even if that meant he could swing at me again. My show of strength had just enraged the Policeman and made him rougher. But I didn't want to give in. And I didn't want to believe that the whole interview process had been for nothing. Anna and Michele didn't seem to think what Michael had done was such a big deal. Michael had made a mistake, that was all.

But I'd seen who he was. He was no different from the Policeman, the Guate-man, Alejandro. He was trying to break me. And I wouldn't let him.

I went on, sharing my secrets, telling myself not to be paranoid — the investigators were not the torturers, and if they were, I would be strong, I wouldn't break, the truth would set me free....

I continued to tell them very personal things:

> In regard to the events at the Maryknoll House and the papal nuncio's, Ortiz was asked who looked at her back and what was [censored] reaction. Ortiz stated that she did not know and that she did not want to hear [censored] reaction. Ortiz stated that she felt dirty and marked for life. Ortiz was asked if she looked at herself and she stated that when she was at the papal nuncio's bathing, she could not look down at her body. Ortiz stated that she only looked at her face to apply ointment that was given to her for the burns. Ortiz stated that she applied the ointment to her chest area and not to her back. Ortiz stated that her body was in shock when people were around her, but at the papal nuncio's, when she took a bath, the water would sting her body.

My body in those days was wise. It knew to go numb, to play dead around strangers. But by the time of the DOJ interviews, I had "recovered," I had learned to trust, and day after day I was willingly having flashbacks, putting my body back in each phase of the torture to answer these strangers' questions. The irony was that, unlike the typical torture scenario, I was the one who wanted the truth.

I knew that, on some level. But I went on because I was stubborn, and stubbornly optimistic, stubbornly hopeful. If I could have peered over Xanthie's shoulder at her notes I would have walked out and never gone back. The investigators asked about my stays at Our Lady of Peace, and I told them that returning to the Mount after my first stay in the hospital was difficult because, by speaking of the rape at the hospital, I had opened a can of worms. At the Mount I had no one to talk to that I could process all the emotions with. And the worms, meanwhile, were escaping: I started having flashbacks. Xanthie rendered my testimony this way:

> Ortiz was able to make some progress at the hospital and stated that for the first time she felt as if she could breathe and a lot of the psychological garbage had been let out.
>
> Ortiz stated that while at Maple Mount there were no activities such as those at the hospital. There was nothing to really keep her occupied and she spent a lot of time alone. These events caused her to have flashbacks in which she envisioned her head as a can of worms.

Was she so hopelessly unskilled in understanding metaphor, or did she make a conscious effort to paint me as a lunatic? The flashbacks, obviously, were flashbacks of my torture, not flashbacks of my head as a can of worms.

IT WOULD TAKE ANOTHER BETRAYAL — much more serious than the abusive questioning and Michael Tubach's outburst — to break through the denial and stubbornness that kept me going back.

WE ONLY HAD one more meeting with Michael Tubach, where I was supposed to identify photographs and answer any lingering questions. I assumed the investigators were getting the photos and their final questions ready, reading through the testimony I had already given. They were probably going to bring up the issue of a medical exam — Tubach had mentioned once to Michele that, when my trust was stronger, it would be a good idea to arrange for a doctor to examine my back. I was prepared for that question. I would agree to the exam. After all these interviews and all this pain, it was one more small thing, by comparison.

Meanwhile, I was getting a break. I couldn't stand to be alone, though. Footsteps, screams — even the shrieks of children playing in the street — terrified me. And silence was even worse.

I went to the office to avoid being alone in the house. I was getting my desk cleaned up when Alice told me Mary was on the line.

Mary always worried about me. I would be glad to talk to her and tell her what a poor decision I'd made by agreeing to do the interview. But I had to hold on. And Mary would support me. She had a way of helping me see that I was strong enough to do whatever I needed to do.

Mary's voice was flat and she took big breaths between her words. I knew the signs. She was tense. This wasn't a call to see how I was doing. This was what I had feared so often — she was calling to tell me that a friend from Su Casa had committed suicide.

"Listen, Dianna ... I wanted to tell you ... "

"What? What happened?"

"That I talked with the DOJ investigators."

I let my lip escape the grasp of my teeth. Big deal. Everyone was talking to the DOJ investigators. They'd been interviewing the sisters in Kentucky off and on for months.

"Bob Chaney and this other guy who said he was new — a young guy, kind of good-looking — came to my house very late at night. The young guy's name was Tim O'Neill. They were supposed to meet me at my office and then they wanted to go to Su Casa before they talked with me, and they asked if they could come by my house later, and they complained that if I said no they would have to make another trip to Chicago because they had a flight out the next morning." She stopped to get her breath.

My breath, meanwhile, was getting harder to draw.

"Anyway, they didn't leave til about 11:00 o'clock at night. And — I don't know, they harassed me. Bob Chaney, it was like he was playing the bad cop, the other guy was playing the good cop. Anyway, Dianna ... The thing is, they *know*."

"They know about what?"

"They know about the choice. I wasn't the one who told them. They knew before they talked to me. They told me they just wanted to know if I knew about it. They wanted to know if you had told me about it."

"What did you say?" I didn't really have to ask. I knew the answer. Mary's voice was so tense because she had told them yes.

I remembered each day turning the chairs a little more until I faced her that first summer in Chicago. She was the first person I had told everything to — the Woman, the life I took. The torturers' prophecy burned through my mind. *No one will care.* If she had cared about me, she would have said, "I am not at liberty to answer that." She would have been silent. How easy it would have been. Mary. The only person in the world I thought I could trust without question. She held me up in Guatemala behind the Posada de Belén, she wiped my face. How could she have told them?

She told, just like Dr. Snodgrass.

"Dianna, they knew before they came," she repeated.

All that meant to me was that someone at the Mount, too, had betrayed me. So instead of listening to her explanations, I typed into the computer before me a sentence that stopped the pain, that opened the door to another place.

I WANT TO DIE.

BUT I WASN'T GOING TO ACT on that desire. I was going to be responsible. I called Anna and explained that Mary had confirmed to the investigators the "choice" I had made.

"Do you know what I'm talking about, Anna?"

"Yes. I know what you mean."

I tried to ask Anna what we should do next, but I could only sob.

"Everything will be OK, Dianna. It's OK."

Everything would not be OK. The DOJ was trying to break me. And now it was in the investigators' power to let everyone know that I was a murderer — first the Woman and then whatever it was that was growing inside me. My mom and dad, the sisters in the community would all know. My family are devout Catholics and are prolife. The members of the Assisi community would find out. I had heard some of their views on such issues. They might ask me to leave. And the Assisi community was where I felt safest. And the sisters — what would they say? Would they demand that I leave the Ursuline community? Who ever heard of a Catholic, a nun at that, having that procedure?

"Anna..."

"It's OK, it'll be OK." She was starting to sound exasperated, as if she were talking to a thick-headed child. "I'll talk to Michele, and I'll talk to Michael. We'll take care of it."

Who took off your shirt? My last piece of clothing was off. I was naked. And Mary had helped. So how could the lawyers take care of it? How could they make the world a different one, one in which there were people I could trust?

"Dianna? Don't overreact."

I couldn't talk. I managed not to slam the phone down.

I WANTED TO TALK to Jennifer, but Jennifer was away. Alice gave me a ride home. She knew that I was upset. She'd seen the note on the computer screen. But how could I tell her what it was about without revealing that I was a monster, that I was just like the torturers: evil, destructive, defiled?

I WENT TO MY ROOM and threw myself on my bed. I thought about ending my life, but my thoughts never materialized into actions. I had left my razor blade in New Mexico. I had thrown away all my dangerous pills.

Why would one of my own sisters hurt me in this way? What reason could she have had? Was she punishing me? Had I hurt her? Was I a bad influence on the Ursulines? Did I deserve to be punished?

She had handed a weapon to the very people who were trying to destroy me.

I tried to convince myself that whoever had provided the information must have had good intentions. She must have thought she was helping my case by providing evidence of the rapes. Still, she had betrayed me. She had betrayed a confidence. She had no right.

Mary called. I wouldn't talk to her. Alice, Patricia, and the lawyers called. I wouldn't talk to them, either. I couldn't even call my community to ask for their prayers. I didn't know who had told. I didn't know who had betrayed me.

I wanted to be alone. I wished I had never talked to anyone about anything. I wished I had never lived through the torture.

Message after message was slipped under my door. Message after message from Mary. Finally I decided to talk to her. Maybe my Woman Friend was speaking to me, telling me not to let the investigators break me, telling me to keep a small part of my heart open. And underneath the debris and wreckage of the investigation and the hurt and the hardness that had set in, I could still feel that Mary was someone I could trust. So I listened.

She acknowledged that she had made a mistake, and she said she'd allowed herself to be manipulated. Also, she wanted to pass on something Bob Chaney had said to her during their meeting that night: he would be willing to speak with me directly. "I told him that it might be helpful and that I would talk to you about it," Mary said. She must have had the impression that Bob Chaney might be able to help me understand what was going on in the investigation. He had also told her that the investigators needed to understand the "inconsistencies" in my account, not because they didn't believe me, but because if the case ever went to court, they would have to explain them. Chaney had explained to Mary that he was the "investigator in the field" and Michael Tubach was the one conducting the interviews of me, so maybe Mary thought he didn't have enough personal contact with me to understand my story. Maybe Mary hoped that, by talking directly with me, Chaney would come to believe me.

Anyway, with Mary's encouragement, I called Chaney to set up a meeting. Mary had said he could help me understand where the investigation stood. I'd met with him once before; he'd told me and my lawyers that, along with Dan Seikaly, he was the chief investigator. I remembered him as a big man who seemed used to being in charge. By meeting with him, I would be going right over Tubach's head, straight to the top. Chaney knew about the "choice" I had made. My lawyers, apparently, didn't share my concern about his acquisition of that knowledge. They said they would straighten things out with Tubach. But here was Chaney, offering to meet with me. So let them talk to Tubach and tell him I was "upset," "overreacting." I would meet with Chaney myself.

HE PICKED ME UP at the office, and we drove over to an outdoor café facing the Potomac. Chaney was even whiter in the sun, and his suit in the light, etched with a delicate pattern, seemed to shimmer. He had a generous paunch, and his white hair thinned to nothing at the top of his head. But he wasn't self-conscious. He seemed to have spent a lifetime in charge.

He ordered soup and a salad. I ordered a salad. And we sat there, moving our water glasses around, looking out at the blinding river. Jennifer once told me, "The other side doesn't invite you to lunch unless they want you to pick up the tab in some way." Was he the "good" torturer — was he going to pretend to befriend me, like José, and then try to convince me to strike a deal? José wanted me to "forgive" him for massacring people. He wanted me to condone atrocities. What could Bob Chaney want?

I kept alive a senseless hope that he was going to give me information about Alejandro.

Chaney made small talk between bites, and I made small talk back, pushing the salad around. My stomach was gurgling nervously. I couldn't even pretend to eat. After a while, he mercifully was through with his own food and he called for the check and paid the bill. He glanced at my salad bowl, still full, and told the waitress, "We'll just take that to go." I didn't want the salad. I didn't want to carry any remnant of that lunch back with me. But I dutifully tucked the bag under my arm.

WALKING OUT TO THE PARKING LOT I wondered what I was doing with this salad I didn't want. Why couldn't I have said, "No, thank you," if not to him, then to the waitress? He didn't have a gun to my head. Like in the garden — why didn't I resist? I've always told myself that if I were in that situation again, I would resist and take my chances on being shot.

But here I was, unable to say no in a simple situation involving a salad. Did it mean that I hadn't changed, that I was still a sheep that could be led to slaughter, or did it mean that Chaney, though not armed, was one of those people who could get others to do what he wanted? He was scary. The situation was scary, walking into the deserted parking lot.

That was when he began explaining why he wanted to meet with me. "There are a number of inconsistencies in your case," he said. "One inconsistency is the T-shirt. The T-shirt was clean. There were no signs of blood and skin. However, there was a trace of body oil."

When the FBI documents on the investigation were declassified to me, I would see that he was lying: the lab report said there was no trace of blood or other tissue. No mention is made of finding any trace of body oil. But nothing had been declassified yet. I couldn't answer him.

"Another inconsistency is the burns. According to some people, the burns on your back were in a pattern, up and down. But the cigarette burns on the T-shirt are random.

"Then there is the question of the location where you were taken. A military conference was being held at the Old Polytechnical School — the Politécnica — in 1989, around the time of your abduction, and the military installation was being renovated, which makes it very unlikely that that would have been the location of your detention.

"Other questions that have been raised: How did the men know you would be in the garden on that particular morning? Why were you targeted and not one of the other nuns, who was more outspoken?"

I just stared out him. I couldn't speak. I didn't know if I was supposed to try to answer. He sounded as if his mind were made up — as if he didn't want answers.

I felt betrayed, frustrated, and isolated, as I had in the first year after my torture. He didn't believe me.

The tears were coming. I couldn't stop them. They rolled hot down my face.

Mr. Chaney scowled and handed me his handkerchief.

I sat down on a cement rise at the end of the empty parking spot.

He put his foot on the edge of it. "Sister Dianna, what I'm telling you is that there are a lot of inconsistencies in your story. And I believe you may be aware from Mary Fabri that in the process of our investigation we have also learned about the abortion you had."

"I will neither confirm nor deny that."

"I just want you to know about the information we've uncovered. And I want you to know the direction the investigation is headed in. Now if you've gotten yourself into something, if people that you now live around and work with have influenced you, you don't have to feel that there's no way out. You don't have to feel stuck."

I was trying to take in what he was saying. I knew he didn't believe me or didn't want to believe me. He was going to offer me some kind of alternate story, I guessed. A false confession I could sign if I wanted the choice I'd made to remain private. This was the Devil's bargain. Through my tight throat I could barely speak. "All I know is that what I have shared with the DOJ is the truth."

MARY CLARIFIED SOME THINGS in the weeks and years that followed. The night after the interview at her house, Chaney had called her and said, "I feel like I need to let you know this information. Did you know that Sister Dianna was having an affair with a medical student? We have witnesses. We have informants. You know she's not the first nun who's gotten pregnant," he added.

"The next evening Bob Chaney called me at home again," Mary told me. "Both evenings he called me after 10:00 p.m. He said he wanted me to have his telephone numbers for the weekend, so that if anything came up and I needed to reach him, I could. He said again that it was important that the truth be known. He said that if you had been having an affair with this man, he would find out. He asked me what I thought about this information he had: you had a telephone conversation with Sr. Mary Mathias the Saturday before you were abducted about how you were having doubts about your faith and your calling.

"After the weekend Bob Chaney called me again at home. This time he again told me that it was crucial that you tell him the truth and that if there was any information you had not yet disclosed, he would be willing to talk to you again. He said he would help you get out of this if that was needed. He said he felt like you were in a position now where you might not feel you could back down, but that he could assure you that he could help you if that was needed.

"I think he was trying to plant the seed that there was a lot more information that you had never shared with me and you were playing me as a dupe. He was really trying to destroy my trust. He was calling me sometimes two times a week or four times and dropping these little bombshells — always in the evening. He was trying to break your support system."

It didn't take Mary long to figure out what was going on. Two weeks after Chaney interviewed her, I took these notes from a phone call with her:

Reminder from Mary —

> Remember you are dealing with powerful people.
> Assume they are trying to break you.
> Assume they are trying to break your support system.
> Assume they are covering up for someone.

Mary was going on instinct. She didn't know how many falsehoods Chaney had told her. Mathias never told Chaney I was having doubts about my religious calling. That's not in the FBI's notes of that interview. The notes say Mathias asked me whether I still thought I could be effective in Guatemala, given the fear I was experiencing. And Mathias has told me — and perhaps she told Chaney and the FBI this too, and they didn't bother recording it — that I answered that I had always learned from the retreats she had directed that one had to take up one's cross and persevere in spite of fear and other hardships.

No FBI notes from any interviews in Guatemala mention any affair with a medical student. And Chaney told my former lawyer Paul Soreff a different story. Paul brought up a lieutenant who asked me to dance my first week in San Miguel and suggested that my refusal to dance with him might have made him angry and gotten me put on a local watch list.

"Would it surprise you to learn that Sister Dianna saw the lieutenant again?" Chaney asked.

"No," Paul answered, "she might have seen him on the street."

"Would it surprise you to learn that she had a romantic relationship with him?"

EVENTUALLY, I told Michele that I had met with Chaney. She was upset with me, but she hid her anger. She knew I had been feeling alienated and misunderstood, so her anger with Chaney was all she revealed to me. She didn't think he should be trying to meet with me alone and going through Mary to arrange that.

Michele called Chaney to clarify what he had said to me, and she took these notes of the conversation: Chaney said he had "wanted to present information to Dianna that could put her at rest and make this whole thing go away." He explained to Michele, "She's now caught up in a whole new lifestyle. I didn't want her to think that she was boxed in. I wanted her to understand that and to know about some of the information we had and were looking into. I wanted her to understand what we knew, what we had found out. More and more people are giving us information now," he told Michele, "not people in Guatemala — people with associations with Dianna. I thought I could help her understand where the investigation was going, and it might be helpful to have an informal channel of communication. She needed to know the ramifications of it all," he said. When Michele expressed concern that he had gone behind the lawyers' backs, he told her that he'd never had a case where he'd had to go through a lawyer in dealing with a complainant. "I think Sister Dianna needs help," he concluded. "I think she got caught up in something."

"A pawn?" Michele asked.

"Basically." Chaney said he thought at some point in time someone from the U.S. Attorney's Office would be prepared to sit down and talk with Michele and explain it all from A to Z. He said he thought that something had happened to me but that the story had grown from what had actually happened and that I may have been pressured by others, used. And he needed me to know what other information they had, in order to help me make a decision.

MICHELE TOLD TUBACH about her conversation with Chaney.

"I've told Bob to run with this," Tubach responded. "I know Bob has his own thoughts on the case." He went on to say something that would have crushed me if Michele had passed it on at the time: "The interviews with Dianna were not all that useful or productive."

I DIDN'T NEED TO HEAR THAT to know that I was dealing with people who were investigating me, not the torturers, and who, if anything, were on the torturers' side. I had heard enough already. I wrote a letter to the U.S. District Attorney's Office, informing the team that I would no longer participate in the investigative process:

> I appreciate the resources and countless hours you have devoted to finding the truth in my case. You have taken more steps than necessary to learn to speak the language of a torture survivor and tried approaches to make the interview process less painful and less reminiscent of interrogation.
>
> I, too, have dared to learn to speak your language. Learning to speak the language of people whom I once perceived as the ENEMY has not been an easy undertaking. Unfortunately, there have been many moments when I have felt that some of the remarks made during the interview process and actions taken during the investigation

were a continuation of the torture. Walking out the door and refusing to continue the interview would have been the easiest thing to
do. But because I wanted to believe that you were not the enemy,
I pushed aside these differences and tried to work with you so that
we could find out together the truth of what happened.

You may have doubts about what happened to me. The fact is,
I was abducted from the Posada de Belén; and to the best of my
knowledge, I was taken to the Politécnica. I was interrogated, gang-
raped, lowered into an open pit filled with human bodies and forced
to participate in the torture of another woman. You claim that a case
similar to mine is unheard of. Have you stopped to ask yourselves
how many people in Guatemala have survived torture? There are an
estimated 47,000 disappeared in Guatemala and 150,000 killed in the
past thirty years alone. Can they come forward and tell you they were
raped, tortured, thrown into pits, urinated on, forced to witness the
torture of others, and that dogs were present in the torture chamber?
Those of us in contact with other torture survivors hear more details
than will ever be reported. In spite of your attempts to facilitate the
interview process for me, it seems that, regardless, in the end the
burden of proof rests on me.

As to the issue of the identity of the woman, you may call me
a liar if you wish. You may not believe me when I say that I have
no memory of the woman in Guatemala City who assisted me after
I escaped. I WILL NOT allow myself to remember. I WILL NOT allow
myself to jeopardize the life of another person. Also, you claim that
I gave the woman's name to someone. I have no recollection of
relaying the woman's name to anyone. Again, let me say, I WILL NOT
allow myself to jeopardize the life of another individual.

This repressed memory stems from my participation in the torture
of the woman. I've been told that I am not responsible for what
happened to the woman. I'm not too sure that's true. If I had resisted
harder, if I had "played" my torturers' game maybe the woman would
be alive today. If I had confided in people sooner about the woman
and the other people in the pit, maybe some of them would be alive
today. If I had opted not to live with Miguel and Rosa Pu, perhaps
he (Miguel) would not be disappeared today. Former Ambassador
Stroock was right, some lives could have been saved.

Now I learn from Mary Fabri and Anna Gallagher that you have
knowledge of something that supposedly happened as a result of the

torture. As I told Bob Chaney, I will neither confirm nor deny the claim. . . .

More than you, I want to learn the truth about what happened to me on November 2 and put this nightmare to rest. I want to know why I was targeted. I want to know why Alejandro, a North American, had the authority to give explicit orders to my Guatemalan torturers. I want to know why Alejandro had access to a clandestine prison. I want to know what role my government played in my abduction and torture. But the price for truth is too high. The criminal investigation has touched an area of my life that has once again left me feeling raw — suffused with guilt, anger, betrayal, and hopelessness. How often I have heard people say, "Once you remove all the garbage that's in you, you'll be better off." I don't believe this to be true. All along the way, people have counseled me to talk about what happened. I trustingly heeded their advice and where has it gotten me? Am I any freer than I was six years and seven months ago? Am I any closer to learning the identity of Alejandro and my Guatemalan torturers? Have the memories, the nightmares, the flashbacks, the betrayals, and the feelings of guilt vanished?

Before my very eyes, I have seen history repeat itself. I stand powerless as I watch people invade my privacy. Decisions about my life are being made as if I don't exist. People are providing you with personal information about my life without my consent. My life is an open book that many people have access to and page through at will. The few people whom I thought I could trust . . . have all betrayed me. My renewed faith in humanity has perished, as did my belief that someday, I would be FREE to live a normal life.

I suppose it is likely you could perceive my inability to provide you with more information as dishonesty and an unwillingness to cooperate. I have tried to help you understand how the invasion of my privacy has led to renewed feelings of betrayal and hopelessness. God knows, I have relinquished more details to you than I have to anyone else. I have tried to the best of my ability to provide you with more information. I have few memories of my past. The memories that I have are [of the events related] to my abduction and torture, up to the present. You're asking me to expose the little life that I can claim as my own to the world. I'm an open book as it is. I have nothing else to give.

Intellectually, I understand your position. You have a job to do. You have to gather all the evidence that you can to build a strong case. I understand that you need me to divulge everything that happened before and after November 2, 1989. But, given all that I have shared with you, it pains me to admit that I can no longer carry the torch for truth. It is impossible for me to continue to participate in any investigation. In addition, I realize I cannot and will not participate in any possible prosecution. I need this process to stop if I'm to move forward with my life.

Also, I have considered it carefully and have realized that I cannot risk disclosure of my medical records. Therefore, under no circumstances will I waive my right to the confidentiality of my personnel and medical records.

Based on what you assured me and my lawyers of in previous conversations, you will respect my decision on the issue of the waiver. You will not seek to compel the production of those confidential materials by court order.

I know that I cannot turn the clock back and correct my past mistakes; but I can make one good choice by stopping the death clock and fighting to stay alive.

Finally, I was simply going to walk out of the secret prison. Just walk out, of my own accord.

I met Michele outside the DOJ for my supposed "interview" and gave her a copy of the statement.

She was surprised. But she supported me without argument, and we rode quietly up to the meeting room.

We sat down, and Anna joined us. I glanced at Pat Riley, Xanthie, and Michael. This was the last time I would ever have to look at them, the last time their flat, expressionless eyes would ever meet mine, the last time they would ever give me a lukewarm simper that masqueraded as a smile. And never again would I answer a single question. I was not the interrogee anymore. I was in control now. I was setting the limits and the terms. Then I was leaving.

Michael began the meeting, bringing up immediately the issue of the "choice." It seemed he had a statement, too, prepared. "We need to pursue the evidence. This — discovery — we've made is quite likely the most significant piece of evidence we have. We have no choice but to push for as much information as possible. I wanted to ask of you — I hope we can minimize — if you can give us direct information so that we can go directly to the source. If you don't share that, we're in the awkward position of getting that information from somewhere else."

He wanted the name of the doctor. He wanted the medical records. He would never get anything from me.

"We have no intention of telling anyone else about it; but we want verification. What goes into the report is classified. A select number of people will see it."

Michael paused and looked at Michele, who cleared her throat. Michele told Michael I had prepared a statement.

I read the statement, and had to stop myself, out of politeness, from gathering up my things. As far as I was concerned, the "interview" was over.

Michael wasn't giving up so easily. "There are a couple of different issues," he said, after a moment. "If you'll give us help on the corroboration of evidence, I've tried to lay out why I think it's better for you to do so. At this point, it's not a matter of confirming or denying the abortion. It's more a matter of getting the medical records.

"The other issue is your role in the investigation. The investigation can't stop. We have prepared today pictures of people to see if you can recognize them. I'm ultimately not going to force you to look at pictures or give any information. You're free to do what you want. You should understand that we need to do what we need to do.

"When we last talked about the medical records, we didn't know about the abortion. The issue was the psychological records, which were important to establish the progression of your treatment. We had no idea that the records would contain this corroborating information. Quite frankly, I don't know what decision we're going to make regarding the medical records of the abortion. I wanted your cooperation so we don't have to go on a fishing expedition to find people to confirm it. I think it's in your best interests to cooperate.

"I'm the one that has to prove something happened to those who ordered this investigation. It's not because we're shifting the burden to you to talk about something so private. That's not so. The burden is on me. There's only one thing I'm interested in and that is the truth. I don't perceive us as enemies at all. I perceive you as the person who can help me do my job. Whatever you decide to do, you decide to do. What I planned to do today was talk about this issue first, find out where you stand, and then show you the pictures. But I won't make you stay. You say you can't participate in any prosecution, and that's something you've needed to decide. We need to figure out how it fits in with our plan. But given how far we've come, I don't think we can shut it down. So I'm asking you to stay."

He was quiet, finally.

"If you expect me to put aside all that has happened, to trust you and to trust other people, no."

"You couldn't think that we'd do an investigation of this length and this intensity and not find this out."

Michael and I stared at each other. I thought the investigation was going to be focused on those who tortured me, I wanted to say, not on me and my life.

Michele finally told Michael, "Dianna can't participate in any aspect of the investigation. It's swallowed her up and thrown her back six years. You've seen some of this. This is doing serious damage to her. I'm very concerned for her own mental health. This is something she can't move past. I understand your position. You're disappointed. She has a lot of information. I understand your statement that it's less invasive if she provides you with the information up front. But that's not going to happen. Our concern is that we figure out a way that your search for information if it exists not broaden the web of people who know. I want you to talk about a way you're going to go about this search that is the least intrusive possible."

"If Dianna doesn't want to tell us, she can tell you and you can tell us. Mimi will be here next week. Darleen could be called to testify before the grand jury. Rosa Pu, Bill Hammer in Kentucky. I could go on and on with the list of people.

"Regarding Our Lady of Peace, no decision has been made on whether we'll go to court for the records. The equation has changed. The new information is perhaps the most significant."

He wasn't answering Michele's question. He wasn't going to tell us about how he could get the information in the least intrusive way possible. He was telling us the most intrusive way — calling my friends before a grand jury; issuing a subpoena for the court records. To me, it sounded like a threat. I gathered up my things and we left.

Chapter Twenty-One

WALKING OUT THROUGH
THE THIRD DOOR

A FEW DAYS LATER, I gave the keynote address at Amnesty International's annual general meeting, just a block away from the hotel where the LASA fiasco had taken place nine months earlier. I told the crowd that their solidarity had given me hope, in spite of the betrayals I had experienced, and that they had kept me going in my search for truth.

Despair hadn't grabbed hold of me this time. I was angry. The anger was leading me to look beyond my case and beyond Guatemala and to call for more than I would normally dare. "We must demand an accounting of U.S. actions in *all* of Latin America," I said.

Everyone rose to their feet, applauding wildly. They wanted it, too. They all wanted the full truth.

Reggae played on a boom box as I was gathering up my papers to leave. "Get up, stand up, stand up for your rights," Bob Marley sang. "Get up, stand up. Don't give up the fight." The whole crowd sang along.

I needed the lift. Once the DOJ interviews were over and I was back to my routine at the office, I learned that in previous weeks a reporter had been calling GHRC to ask about the "inconsistencies" in my testimony. He said the holes in the T-shirt I'd been wearing didn't match the burns on my back, which were in a pattern. He also said something about my Bible being found high up in a tree.

Patricia, who took his calls, said, "So? What would that prove?"

He didn't follow the argument out, but clearly he had been led to believe I was telling lies. And, clearly, he had been talking to investigators at the DOJ.

He admitted as much. He wouldn't say who, specifically, was leaking information, but he did say he had inside sources. He had written a few good articles during the vigil, but the investigators had turned his head. Were they trying to demonstrate their power? Did they want me to know how easy it was for them to change public opinion? Michael Tubach had always told me he couldn't share information about the investigation with me because I or "others around me" might leak it to the press. "We don't want details about the investigation to show up in the press," Tubach had said. "It's our policy not to talk about ongoing investigations." But their real policy was not to investigate, apparently, but to discredit me, and the press was useful for that.

I TALKED TO MIMI on the phone when I got a chance and told her all the news — including the fact that one of the sisters had told about the choice. She listened and sympathized, but she also reminded me that only one sister had been involved in giving the DOJ the information, not the entire community.

"Think of Luisa, Kim, Gracie," she said. "I could go on and on. There are good, good people in the community."

It didn't matter. The fact that only a few sisters knew about the choice I had made didn't matter, either. I couldn't get rid of the feeling that any one of the sisters might have betrayed me or might be waiting to betray me in the future.

Now THAT I HAD TIME to think and feel, I found that my thoughts were all bitter ones, my feelings all gradations of anger. At the Assisi community, in the office, and on the sidewalk, I would look down at my hands to find them curled into tight fists. I couldn't stop my teeth from pressing together or my eyes from sliding around to study everyone. Anyone could be the next person to hurt me. My body was preparing to protect me: my jaws and my fists would be strong. I couldn't stop myself. I hoped I would only act in self-defense, but I was starting to feel I had no control, the anger was building, I would explode like a bomb and injure everyone near me.

I couldn't let that happen.

I WOULD LEAVE THE URSULINES — leave for good, theirs and my own. With time and distance, the anger that coursed through my veins would diminish. I would no longer be subject to betrayal. I would no longer risk anything. And they wouldn't have to be ashamed of me if the word got out further about what I had done — and I couldn't guarantee it wouldn't. I would rather leave with a shred of dignity than be asked to leave later, under humiliating circumstances.

For the same reason, I was contemplating leaving Assisi. I would start over somewhere where nobody knew me.

I got out a box and started putting away everything that had to do with my religious life. *The Ursuline Way of Life* was the first item I put in the box. Mathias had given it to me to help me understand again what being an Ursuline was about. I put the *Ursuline Directory* in next, a book with numbers at the Mount and all the sisters' numbers. These would be in the bottom of the box. I wouldn't be able to learn how to live as an Ursuline or be able to reach anyone who was — Kim; Luisa; Fran. I blinked tears away and kept my hands moving. The dream catcher was next. One was given to each sister in the community. In the Native American tradition, we were supposed to hang the feathery web above our beds so that we could remember our dreams. I buried it and whatever dreams it had caught.

Then I came to a book Mathias had loaned me about Angela Merici. On the cover, Angela was holding a basket with four loaves of bread, tipped outward, as if in offering. She was barefoot, dark-skinned, young, and alone, but radiant and confident. "A Woman Faced with Two Alternatives, She Saw and Chose the Third."

The words below the picture tugged at my mind. What if Angela was telling me to wait, to look for another alternative? She was walking, moving forward as I so often prayed I could do. The third alternative must be somewhere between leaving the community and staying in it to be betrayed again and again — remaining angry, resentful, bitter, and constantly at risk of further hurt. Was there any other attitude I could have if I stayed?

This was the smaller version of the question I'd been trying to answer since November 2, 1989. Could I stay in the human community without feeling like bait for the next betrayer, without being consumed by fear, bitterness, anger? Could I see the world as a loving place?

I left the box half-packed in my closet.

I WOULD HAVE TO LEAVE religious and philosophical questions for more leisurely times; at the end of June the IOB report was released.

All of us whose cases the board investigated received the report personally, from the hands of the IOB members, several hours before it was released publicly.

Anna, Michele, Jose, and my friend Patricia and I walked into the pale green room with the long, shiny table and molded ceiling. Anthony Harrington and Frank Fountain greeted us with tense smiles. My team of people sat across the table from Harrington. Frank Fountain sat at the end of the table, between us, as if he were neutral.

Harrington began the meeting with an announcement: the inspector generals of the various government agencies that the IOB's review had incorporated would do a follow-up within a year to review the IOB's recommendations.

None of us knew what the IOB's recommendations were; Harrington hadn't explained them yet. He seemed to be talking out of order, starting at the end of his speech and working his way forward. Maybe he didn't have a speech. Or maybe he was saying anything at all to avoid talking about my case.

He continued, "The allegations that Colonel Alpírez had killed Michael DeVine were incorrect. But Alpírez *was* involved in a cover-up. The report is largely the same as the one the president received," Harrington went on, "but the president received some limited classified information."

I didn't care. I just wanted them to tell me what they had found out about my case. I looked at Jose. He glanced back out of the corner of his eye. We were both thinking the same thing: Why is he stalling?

"In regards to the Bámaca case, we don't know who killed him. But some CIA contacts or assets probably knew of his interrogation and death."

Anger was building up in my chest. I had seen the declassified documents that said Alpírez had ordered Everardo killed. Santiago said Alpírez was bending over the torture table, interrogating him.

And why weren't they telling me about my case? I began to flip impatiently through the report until I found my name. Under "IOB Conclusions" were the following two sentences: "Based on our inquiry to date, the IOB believes that Sister Ortiz was subjected to horrific abuse on November 2, 1989, but U.S. intelligence reports provide little insight into the details of her plight. Because the Department of Justice is still conducting an extensive reinvestigation of the incident, we do not draw any conclusions at this time."[1]

I had waited more than a year for this report. Three times we had been told it would be released, and three times we had been disappointed. Now I had it in my hands, and the IOB had no conclusions for me, except that I was "subjected to horrific abuse."

"What exactly is 'horrific abuse'?" I asked.

"The board believes you were subject to abuse," Harrington answered. "We intended this term to be broad enough to encompass torture and other things that happened to you. The case is still open."

"And these?" I asked, running my finger over a couple of pages of summarized intelligence reports. "Significant Intelligence Bearing on the Case of Sister Ortiz" was the heading. Even at a glance, I could tell that most of the reports suggested that my testimony was fabricated.

"The report just *describes* the intelligence regarding your case," Harrington said. "We're not crediting it or passing judgment on any of it."

"Did you find out anything about Alejandro?"

"There just isn't a paper trail. There's nothing substantive in the documents. The DOJ, as you know, is continuing to investigate. And we will not make our final report until the DOJ investigation is done."

I saw the IOB clearly now — they weren't really any different from the DOJ team. Jennifer was right. They were the other side.

"This is a cover-up!" I cried. I knew it with every bone in my body. I stood up and walked out.

LATER, I READ through the full report and my intuition was confirmed. Generally, throughout the report, the IOB seems bent on justifying the U.S. relationship with the Guatemalan death squads. One method the IOB employs is to invoke a false comparison with the FBI's use of informants:

> [T]he IOB believes that U.S. national interests, with respect to Guatemala and elsewhere, can in some cases justify relationships with assets and institutions with sordid or even criminal backgrounds. We believe that a careful balance must be struck on a case-by-case basis between the value and uniqueness of contributions from the relationship, on the one hand, and the seriousness and credibility of the allegations of abuse, on the other. We note that in carrying out law enforcement activities in the United States, the FBI, police, and other authorities regularly weigh such considerations in establishing informant relationships with persons having criminal backgrounds.[2]

How stupid does the IOB think the American people are? I had to keep asking myself that. The "unsavory" informants that the FBI uses are in the organizations the FBI is trying to shut down. The FBI has informants in drug rings and the Mafia to be able to arrest other members and break up those organizations. The CIA's relationship with the Guatemalan security forces would be more analogous to the FBI paying Ku Klux Klan members as informants, not for information about other Klan members who were breaking the law, but for information about blacks who were organizing politically. The FBI and the Klan would share a common goal and a common foe, as the CIA and the Guatemalan security forces did. And if the FBI regularly paid Klan members for information on black leaders and their plans, knowing that the KKK derived that information by torturing blacks and then murdering them — well, to get information, our law enforcement agencies have to associate with people who do some unsavory things. This scenario, of course, describes nothing other than torture and murder by proxy — quite different from having a member of a drug ring turn on his friends and hand them over to the law.

In respect to my case, the IOB did publish one interesting bit of intelligence: President Serrano dismissed his defense minister, in part for blocking the investigation of my case. But the IOB omitted at least two intelligence reports I have found that support my case and included mainly reports aimed at discrediting me — and even distorted and reworded them for greater effect. Two out of the ten intelligence reports that the IOB included state that I could not have been held at the Politécnica because the D-2 (the Directorate of Intelligence, which gave orders to the rest of the G-2) had moved out of the Politécnica in the mid-1980s. "The [CIA] station commented that this inconsistency in Sister Ortiz's story was viewed by Guatemalans as proof that her claims were fabricated," the IOB wrote.[3]

First, my identification of the Politécnica as the place where I was held is not an "inconsistency in my story." Second, the CIA never claimed that it was an "inconsistency in my story" — those are the IOB's words. The Guatemalan intelligence source argued that my claim to have been kept at the Politécnica was incongruent with the realities of military torture at the time. But even that is contradicted by other intelligence which the IOB omitted.

An intelligence document that the IOB chose not to include in its report, dated February 1990, states, "The Minister of Defense, General Héctor Alejandro Gramajo Morales, has recently established a new intelligence analysis cell located at the Antigua Politécnica and not formally associated with the D-2. For this reason, there is once again a small intelligence related activity at the Antigua Politécnica."[4] An "intelligence analysis cell," according to people who have studied such things, is a euphemism for an interrogation and torture center. The information about the establishment of this new center should have come out, not only in DIA reports, but in CIA reports, as well, since Gramajo, who established the cell, was on the CIA payroll. The only question is why the IOB didn't include this intelligence report among its summaries.

The IOB also left out any reference to this document: Ambassador McAfee asked her human rights officer to look into other cases of detentions at the Politécnica. The human rights officer visited the Archbishop's Human Rights Office and found that Dr. Carmen Valenzuela, too, had reported being detained and tortured at the Politécnica — in 1990.

The document reveals more information: the human rights officer learned that when GAM leader Nineth Montenegro's husband, Fernando Garcia, was abducted in 1984, he was taken to the Politécnica, along with GAM cofounder Carlos Ernesto Cuevas and Gustavo Adolfo López. Nineth learned her husband's whereabouts from a U.S. embassy official, who did nothing to rescue him or the others. The IOB had access to information about a parallel to my testimony — another instance in which someone connected to the U.S. embassy knew the location of a person being secretly detained. The parallel with Carmen Valenzuela's case is more salient. For all the protestations that I couldn't have been kept at the Politécnica because of the late date, here is a report of someone being detained and tortured there in 1990. Perhaps because the IOB claimed to publish "intelligence" on my case — not any relevant information gleaned from any documents examined — State Department material was out of bounds. But the IOB in its own report acknowledged the problem with the CIA's reporting: "the CIA created a misleading impression of the status of human rights by focusing on positive contributions without mentioning ongoing abuses by the services with which the station had a liaison relationship."

ACCORDING TO THE IOB REPORT, station personnel didn't remember seeing at the time the October 1991 draft document saying I was definitely abducted. But in our meeting, Roland told us that he had retraced the document, and it was "readily retraceable." Station personnel must have remembered seeing it. I had never paid much attention to the midsection of that document because the source seemed to have information only about my abduction, not my torture. The source, in fact, implied that I had made up the story of my rape; normally, women who are mistreated physically, he said, are killed, not released:

> In the opinion of [censored], she was probably not raped or otherwise mistreated as she claimed, however. [Censored] said that women are not normally sexually molested, and if there had been any physical mistreatment by her captors, she would have been killed rather than released. [Censored] said that, according to what he knows of such affairs, women who are not released are usually stabbed and left at a public bus terminal so they will be found and the death reported as an ordinary criminal incident. Those released unharmed are sometimes drugged and then released. When they come to they are disoriented and often unable to give an account of what happened to them.

The IOB summarizes the above as follows: "The source, however, said that he did not believe that Ortiz had been raped because women prisoners were not normally sexually molested. Instead, he said, women were usually either stabbed to death to make it look like an ordinary criminal incident, or drugged and released in a disoriented state." The IOB omitted a crucial fact: women who are physically mistreated (and perhaps by this term the source meant raped) are stabbed to death and left at a public bus terminal. "Physical mistreatment," according to the source, does occur during abduction. The IOB insists in its summary that it doesn't. *Instead,* the IOB says, women are stabbed to death or drugged and released. The IOB, in this case, has distorted an intelligence report on my case, not summarized it.

THE INTELLIGENCE ON MY CASE that the IOB neglected to summarize is almost more telling than what it included. Buried in the general section of its report is a reference to an important intelligence document: "In May 1993, the Guatemala Chief of Station initiated a review of many of his assets 'to ensure that no station unilateral asset is or has been involved in human rights violations.' The station started by questioning some of its assets and planned to polygraph them. No station personnel recall, however, what prompted this review or why it was apparently never completed."[5] The quote is from a report by the CIA station chief on the results of an interview with a CIA asset he thought might have been involved in my abduction and torture.[6]

The station chief began questioning his assets a month after I stated publicly that I was detained at the Politécnica. The declassified document quoted above pertains to an asset he questioned about my case and the cases of Michael DeVine, Myrna Mack Chang, and Maritza Urrutia. Those other three cases, according to the evidence that has surfaced in court testimonies and declassified documents, involved members of the D-2; and in DeVine's and Myrna Mack's cases, the evidence pointed to CIA assets.[7] The station chief, Frederick Brugger, must have had reason to suspect that CIA assets were involved in my case, as well. Somehow, the IOB didn't consider the station chief's concern about CIA assets' involvement in my case to be significant.

IN SPITE OF THE SHORTCOMINGS of the report, the IOB did make some honest criticisms of the CIA. The IOB acknowledged that reports that criticized the D-2 and were of questionable credibility were not always sent beyond the CIA headquarters in Langley, Virginia, while equally dubious reports that were favorable to the D-2 were sent on to other agencies more often:

> Concern for how negative allegations against the Guatemalan security services would be received...appears in a few instances to have affected how these allegations were reported. Although intelligence reports with clearly credible allegations seem generally to have been disseminated appropriately, those of questionable credibility that were favorable to the liaison services appear to have been disseminated beyond the D.O. [Directorate of Operations] more often than similarly dubious unfavorable ones.[8]

Credibility standards, then, were applied unfairly; the CIA used the "credibility" issue as an excuse to justify not sending beyond headquarters reports that implicated the D-2 in human rights abuses.

The CIA also used the credibility issue to justify not sending politically inconvenient reports to CIA headquarters in Langley, Virginia. This information, however, which posed no political inconvenience, *was* sent to Langley, and the IOB included it as an item of "significant intelligence" bearing on my case: "In early 1994, a source told the station about a foreign journalist who reportedly stated during one of Ortiz's later visits to Guatemala that he had learned from a URNG source that the Ortiz story was fabricated and had been intended to provoke an end to U.S. funding for the Guatemalan security services. The source could remember no details concerning the journalist's identity, however."

More than the journalist's name escaped the source. The source couldn't remember the location of the meeting, the date of the meeting, or the journalist's nationality. The document, released to me in our May meeting with Frank Fountain and Roland, states, "[Censored] said he could not remember the name or nationality of the foreign journalist, or recall when or where the meeting between the journalist and [censored] took place."[9]

The IOB comments, "The station added that it too had doubts about the Ortiz story, but it did not disseminate this report beyond D.O. headquarters."

Langley, Virginia, the D.O. headquarters, is where this document came to rest — it was not stuck in draft form in a file at the U.S. embassy because the source could not tell clearly how he knew what he knew.

SOMEONE ON THE IOB TEAM had learned the art of the final sentence. The IOB summary of my case ends, "Sister Ortiz departed Guatemala on

The Blindfold's Eyes

November 5, 1989, and was treated for more than 100 apparent cigarette burns on her back. No suspects have ever been identified or charged." Given that the DOJ team had identified at least one suspect and were working on identifying more, the IOB could have written, "No suspects have yet been charged." But the writer of the report, apparently, was intent on portraying my case in the most negative light possible. Years would go by before I learned that the board member who wrote most of the report was none other than the only person I'd ever trusted in the U.S. government, Frank Fountain. He wasn't simply the counsel for the IOB. As I would learn from reviewing Michele's notes years later, he was the chief investigator. And he was not only a lawyer. He was a military officer.[10]

THE IOB'S FINDINGS weren't easy for other Coalition Missing members to accept. For Jennifer, the IOB's findings were shocking and terrifying. The IOB found that "substantial evidence contradicts the allegation that Alpírez directed or was present at the presumed death of Bámaca."

Jennifer had seen the declassified documents herself, pointing to Alpírez as the one who ordered Everardo's death. But aside from that, Jennifer was horrified to hear the word "presumed." Was the IOB suggesting that Everardo wasn't dead — that, after all, he might be alive and still under torture? But if his death was only "presumed" to have occurred, the IOB could have no "substantial evidence" regarding any aspect of it, including Alpírez's absence during it. Substantial evidence of Alpírez's absence during Everardo's death was substantial evidence of his death. The IOB was apparently trying to avoid questions. If they said they knew he was dead, people might ask how they knew, who was present, and who was responsible. It was much easier to say they knew Alpírez wasn't present at Everardo's death, and they presumed Everardo was dead.

The IOB argues that no CIA officers knew of Everardo's illegal detention, interrogation, and torture while they were occurring. Assets were probably involved, the report says, but no CIA officers were aware of this link at the time. The $44,000 that Alpírez received in June 1992, when he was seen bending over Everardo, torturing him, was supposedly backlogged severance pay — he'd been removed from the asset list already, the story goes.

But within days of Everardo's capture, the White House and the State Department, courtesy of the CIA, were receiving information Everardo was telling Alpírez and the other officers gathered around his torture table. If no CIA officers were aware of Everardo's illegal detention and torture, and if no CIA officers were aware that assets were interrogating him, how did the CIA manage to write up those long paragraphs of information that Everardo was giving under torture? Who was recording the information and passing it along, if not their assets? The source of the information seems to have been in the room where the interrogation was taking place. The document reads, "Everardo told [censored] that he has a card from a Mexican government social welfare agency...."[11] CIA officials can't claim they got the information second- or third-hand — that their assets weren't actually in the torture chamber. If that were the case, they would have had to leave this document in draft form, in embassy files, along with the information about my case, because nowhere does the source explain how he came to learn this information. There's no chain of information explaining how the source claimed to have this knowledge. So, if it wasn't acquired first-hand, the intelligence is "inadequately sourced."

While the CIA obviously had assets interrogating Everardo and reporting that information to their handlers, a declaration from Alpírez to that effect would be more powerful, and no doubt he could tell stories. He could, perhaps, identify the tall, blond man seen by a witness Jennifer interviewed who was in the helicopter that was taking Everardo to another detention center in the capital. Alpírez could probably tell a lot about CIA activities in Guatemala.

Alpírez was let off: the documents implicating him in both Michael DeVine's murder and Everardo's murder were said to be unreliable.

According to the *New York Times* (May 7, 1996), the United States government seemed to be making an effort to protect Alpírez. Classified State Department documents released only to Congress gave "a more damning depiction of Colonel Julio Alpírez's role in the killings" than the documents released to the public. A U.S. government official, who insisted on anonymity, read to a reporter from the classified documents, pointing out a "disconnect between what's classified and what's public." Among the documents released to Congress was a cable from the U.S. embassy in Guatemala to the State Department, dated March 24, 1995. The cable said Alpírez "may very well be guilty of DeVine's murder," but cautioned against "naming Alpírez" as a suspect in the killing, since that could lead to legal challenges of the convictions of low-level Guatemalan officers already in jail for the murder. A January 1995 intelligence report released only to Congress says Alpírez was guilty of human rights abuses and "has more wealth than can be explained.... There are persistent rumors of Alpírez's involvement in drug trafficking."

While documents released to the public say it is possible that Alpírez

murdered Bámaca, a classified March 23, 1995, memorandum from the
State Department's Bureau of Intelligence and Research links the colonel
directly to his murder: "It was known within the senior ranks of the army"
in Guatemala that Alpírez killed Bámaca, the memo says, and that a
senior Guatemalan military officer confirmed this in 1995. The memo
cited information provided by a "consistently reliable cooperative source
with excellent access" to the Guatemalan military. The State Department
provided the documents to Congress on May 3, 1996. Citing "national
security" concerns and the secrecy demanded by the intelligence services,
the State Department omitted these documents from the thousands of
pages released to the public three days later.

CAROL DEVINE'S LAWYER read a statement at a press conference a few days
later expressing disappointment that the IOB had agreed with the Justice
Department, which had accepted the Guatemalan government's version of
events: Michael DeVine was interrogated, tortured, and nearly decapitated
by a group of low-ranking G-2 officers who decided to murder him because
they thought he had stolen a rifle. Even Colonel Otto Noack, who was
the director of international intelligence for the Guatemalan military, said
"sending a commission of four to six soldiers to search for missing rifles is
uncommon — no, it is unheard of."
    Although Carol DeVine's lawyer, Monica Shurtman, had sent a letter to
the IOB outlining the flaws in the DOJ's conclusions, the IOB issued the
same findings. Shurtman mentioned several problems with the DOJ investigation. Hearing them, I began to worry. In the DeVine case, the DOJ
had failed to interview several key witnesses, and a number of witnesses
who were interviewed expressed frustration over what they perceived to
be the DOJ's intimidating attitude and lack of familiarity with the case.
"DOJ personnel instructed Carol DeVine to withhold information from
her lawyers," Shurtman said, "a serious interference with the attorney-
client relationship that raises serious questions about the integrity of the
DOJ's investigations."
    So I wasn't the only one the DOJ investigators had played that game
with. They had also gotten between Carol DeVine and her lawyers for a
private chat or two.
    Shurtman continued, "Documents released by the State Department
show that, in the months after DeVine's murder, Ambassador Thomas
Stroock expressed concerns to the State Department that Defense Minister Bolanos might himself be engaged in the cover-up. Despite these
concerns and recommendations to the contrary, Stroock regularly up-

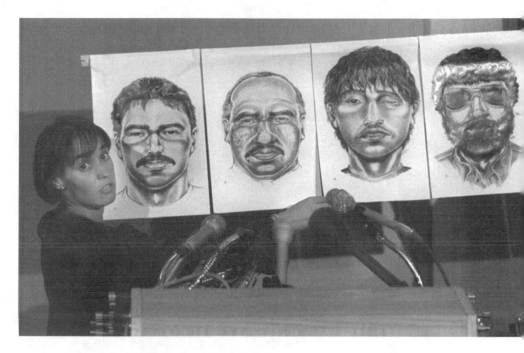

Above: *At press conference, unveiling the portraits of the Guate-man, the Policeman, José, and Alejandro.* (AP/Wide World Photos)

Below: *Meredith Larson displays a censored document from the IOB report in 1996.*

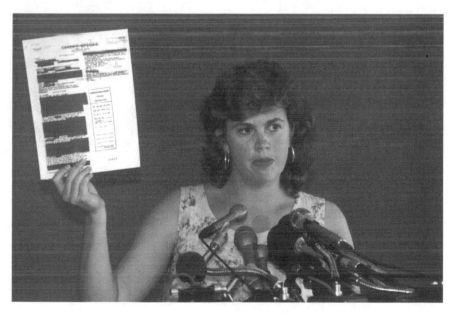

WHO IS
ALEJANDRO ?

(Photo: Rick Reinh

dated Bolanos on the specifics of the investigation, including the names of witnesses with key information. Several of these witnesses and members of their families were subsequently subjected to harassment, threats, and physical harm."

A cold shudder ran across my shoulders. If I hadn't been so traumatized and if I had been a little more naive, I, too, might have talked to Stroock. What if I had talked to him about the indigenous woman who helped me? What if I hadn't willed myself to forget?

JENNIFER SPOKE on behalf of Coalition Missing:

> We are pleased with the finding that the CIA officials have long used Guatemalan "assets," despite their full knowledge that such assets were involved in serious human rights abuses, including torture, kidnapping, and murder. We are also pleased with the recommendation that such assets be screened for human rights abuses in the future. We note the clear finding that the CIA has failed to accurately report the truth about the ongoing human rights situation to the United States government and the recognition that State Department officers have failed to properly inform family members about their own cases. . . . We feel that the scope of certain recommendations should include all Guatemalan cases, and not just those of US citizens, and that the report should include a strong recommendation for full declassification of all human rights files for Guatemala since the CIA-sponsored invasion of 1954. We strongly urge that the recommendations for reforms include stronger measures for congressional supervision and for severe penalties for any violations. Two hundred thousand deaths are enough. . . .
>
> We believe that the United States government has carried out a pattern and practice of intentionally refusing to investigate and act on certain cases for reasons of political convenience. We also believe that in many instances, the truth about certain sensitive cases was well known and that U.S. official statements to the families and the public were intentionally deceptive.
>
> Our question today is, Who gave the order to withhold and conceal the truth in those cases, and why did they give such an order?

I didn't have much to say. I couldn't speak about the IOB's conclusions, and documents I was supposed to have received the weekend before the press conference, which was on a Monday, never arrived. But I did note that, for the first time, the U.S. government had publicly acknowledged my suffering:

> I was not simply suffering from a case of bad nerves, as former Defense Minister Héctor Gramajo would have it. I did not stage my own kidnapping for political reasons, as U.S. Ambassador Stroock has implied. I was not involved in some kinky lesbian sexual relationship where sadomasochism was involved, as U.S. State Department official Lew Anselem suggested. The IOB concedes that I suffered "horrific abuse." This is progress. I am grateful to the IOB for beginning to investigate my case and for making this preliminary finding. "Horrific" is a very strong adjective.
>
> But it does not depict what I experienced — secret detention, interrogations, gang-rape, and torture by members of the Guatemalan security forces: the CIA's "partner" in a war fought with US funding but without the knowledge or consent of the American people. The majority of the victims of this war, like myself, have been civilians. The IOB notes that instructors at the School of the Americas and Southern Command, while training Guatemalan officers, used instruction materials that apparently condoned extrajudicial executions of guerrillas, extortion, physical abuse, coercion, and false imprisonment — some of the things I suffered. Former Guatemalan defense minister General Héctor Gramajo, incidentally, trained at the School of the Americas. It was under his command that I and thousands of other civilians were abducted and tortured.
>
> But who is ultimately responsible? Even after his reign as minister of defense, in which nearly two thousand civilians were murdered by death squads and approximately five hundred more were "disappeared," the United States Agency for International Development granted him a scholarship to study at Harvard.
>
> I find it ironic that "the station officers assigned to Guatemala and the CIA headquarters officials the IOB interviewed believe the CIA's contact with the Guatemalan services helped improve attitudes toward human rights." What the CIA's contact did was allow millions of dollars a year to reach the Guatemalan security forces after US military funding was officially suspended. It enabled them to abduct, torture, and assassinate civilians, a major part of their counter-insurgency strategy. From 1990 to 1995, 2,161 civilians were assassinated. That was done with our tax dollars, with the knowledge of U.S. policy makers.

Little of the truth has emerged in my case. Nonetheless, thanks to the IOB, we at last have in writing what the US government has denied for years: we have been fighting the dirty war in Guatemala. I am one of the victims of that war. I know what few U.S. citizens know. I know what it is to be an innocent civilian, and to be accused, interrogated, and tortured. I know what it is to have my own government eschew my claims for justice because they cause political problems. I know what it is to wait in the dark for torture, and what it is to wait in the dark for truth. I am still waiting.

A few days later I met with representatives of the OAS and found out that on that front, too, a major hurdle stood in the way: the Guatemalan government had requested to interview me. Supposedly, the newly elected administration in Guatemala wanted to respond to the OAS's recommendation that my case be sent up to the Inter-American Court in Costa Rica. Before the government could do that, Guatemalan government officials "needed" to interview me. I knew what such an interview would involve: more abuse.

I had a few weeks to make a decision about whether to comply with the Guatemalan government's request and be interviewed or say I wasn't going forward and wanted the case closed instead of sent up to the court. Patricia had invited me to go to Italy when she learned that I had been planning to go with the Ursulines but the DOJ investigation had interfered. She and I had arranged with Alice to take a week and a half off at the end of the month. That would give me time to think. At the top of my calendar for July, I wrote, IS IT POSSIBLE TO TRUST PEOPLE??

BEFORE I LEFT for Italy, Mimi came to Washington to be interviewed by the DOJ. She remarked afterward that Michael Tubach really had a gift for putting a person right back in the place and circumstances. For her, his tactics were useful — she was able to remember more details. For me, they caused flashbacks. A survivor of torture should never be asked to walk back into the torture chamber. Mimi said Michael was pleasant to her, and she found the interview cathartic. She finally got to say everything she had been wanting to say for years. If anyone was accusatory, it was probably Mimi. When he asked her about my clothes and she told him they were washed at the papal nuncio's, he said, "If only we had been there."

She said, "Why weren't you?"

He asked several times about the choice I had made, but Mimi just kept repeating, "I will not betray Dianna. Dianna is my friend, and I will not betray her." She had the benefit of knowing in advance that he would ask her about the issue, and she checked with Michele to find out what she had to tell him.

"We can force you to talk, you know," Michael said. "We can put you before a grand jury."

"I know you can, but I hope you won't."

In the end, they didn't, and Mimi got to go home. Her loyalty sealed my faith in our friendship. It was possible to trust at least one person.

THE EXPERIENCE WITH THE DOJ had severed all my deep connections with everyone else. I could see it happening but I couldn't do anything about it. I kept telling myself that I had to keep going for the Guatemalan people. I couldn't let anyone down because if I did, people would see what I was — nothing, just empty space. Just a body occupying empty space.

But I was excited about going to Italy. I was hoping that being on the ground that Saint Angela, the founder of the Ursuline order, had walked would connect me more deeply to her and maybe more deeply to God. One thing I knew about Angela was that she reached out to orphans, and I felt I was an orphan. I didn't belong anywhere. Between the experience in Guatemala, the DOJ interview, and the revelation of the choice I had made, I was stripped. Maybe I have been in the community to prove something to the torturers and to prove something to Tubach — who kept calling me Dianna in person and Ms. Ortiz in writing. Maybe it was my way of gaining a little respect. Maybe it was my way of not acknowledging that I didn't have an identity. Maybe it was my way, too, of not acknowledging the rapes. I had to look deep within to find out whether I had a vocation or even a God and what all that was.

WE LANDED IN MILAN and traveled to Brescia by train. I talked a lot to Angela during that train ride, as I would during the entire trip. It was easier. With God I was so angry — God had betrayed me, once again. Rationally, I knew God wasn't responsible for what people chose to do, and I knew God didn't abandon people. But I heard the Policeman's words: Your God is dead.

I felt God had died again.

AND I KNEW that I'd made another big mistake. A survivor of torture I had met a year earlier at a talk I had given had called me during the week that I was shut in my room. The message was slipped under my door with all the others. I'd eventually called her back, and we usually talked about once a month. Sometimes we wrote. But then I was busy with the DOJ investigation: my life was in turmoil; and for a time I didn't call her. I planned to get back to her. I finally called her from a public phone so we could talk without any fear of our conversation being monitored. The person who answered told me tersely, "She's dead. She committed suicide."

ONCE WE'D FOUND a place to stay in Brescia, we set off to find the church and abbey where the Ursuline order began and where Angela's body was kept. The hours were strange, though, and the first day we made the long walk up to the end of the street and found everything closed. The next day, although it should have been open, the church was closed again.

We stood there, talking about what to do, when a woman suddenly opened the door to sweep the dust out. She let us into the little chapel where Angela's preserved remains were encased in glass. How her remains were preserved from the fifteenth century is a mystery to me. But Angela's body was intact, and she appeared to be smiling slightly. I felt her embrace me and all the darkness I was carrying. And from then on I felt she was with me on my journey. I felt an aura of light around me.

We prayed in the chapel, and then the woman who had opened the door led us to the mother superior of the order. Patricia explained to her that I was with the Ursulines in Kentucky, who had recently visited, and that I was a nun.

"You mean she's studying to be a nun," the mother superior said, looking at my toenails and fingernails, which were painted bright red, and at my double-pierced ears and dangling earrings.

"No, she is a nun."

"You mean she's studying to be a nun."

Finally the mother superior told us they had no rooms, we couldn't stay there, and she turned on her heel and left.

The woman who had opened the door watched the whole exchange and felt bad about the way we were treated. She asked us if we would like some coffee and took us to a café next door. She was from Slovenia and her name was Aura. As far as I was concerned, she was an angel. By chance, she had opened the door, and I had been able to see Angela. She insisted on paying for the coffee. Her kindness was the first act that began restoring my faith.

Venice was noisy and crowded — some kind of festival was going on — so we moved on to Assisi. On the way, we passed vast fields of sunflowers, bright yellow, alive. I remembered how those flowers followed the light. And as the hour grew later we passed field after field faithfully bent to the sun's new angle. Like the young Angela, offering her basket of bread, they tilted their pockets of seeds toward the sun, having found a means to move, a third door to turn through, somehow, though they were rooted in the earth.

WE STAYED AT A HOMEY PLACE with several windows that had wooden shutters and no screens. The nights were cool and lace curtains breathed quietly in front of the windows. Patricia and I had to share a bed. It was a big bed, but I hung over the edge, as far away from her as I could get. I felt I was carrying evil.

I was also carrying fear that the secret would spread still further. And selfishness. I wanted to think about myself first, not the people of Guatemala. I never wanted to go before any other court. I just wanted to rest.

WE EXPLORED ASSISI for several days. The bushes behind the basilica spelled out PAX. I found comfort in their message. Peace. The bushes — or someone, a gardener — wished me peace, as though I deserved it. Walking down the main road, we passed a bookshop where I saw displayed in the window a book Joe and Marie had written on Saint Francis. I felt it was another message. They were telling me they were with me. And I felt connected again to the Assisi community.

The warmth, the fields, the light — nature itself was a healing source. For me, the beauty was a sign that God had not died, that God was there. I took photograph after photograph, capturing the beauty, turning the camera into my tool, my means of proving the Policeman wrong.

SOMEHOW ON THAT TRIP I was able to see the light within myself. I was able to see that I do have the right to live and to recapture the feeling I had just after I attempted to take my life — to realize I was being given another chance.

I WANTED TO GO somewhere restful for the last week, so we skipped Rome and Florence and spent the last five days in a seaside village, near a monastery where Irish monks had first landed in the fourth century to begin spreading the Gospel. It was a beautiful place, right on the sea and at the base of a verdant mountain. Unlike most monasteries, it had no encircling wall, no defense. Windows large enough to stand in opened right onto the water. The monks had already been driven out of Ireland by violence, and the monastery had been attacked again and again. I wondered why some people never learned to defend themselves. They were turning the other cheek, maybe. Come on in. Take all our stuff. Kill us.

I was done with that. I had a right to live and a right to defend myself.

WHEN WE WERE winding through the Alps on our way up to Zurich to get our flight home, the scenery was remarkable, but we kept going through tunnels and the train compartment would suddenly darken. I pulled a flashlight out of my suitcase and asked Patricia to shine it on her face and talk to me. After a few tunnels, the older German-speaking couple in our compartment understood that I was afraid of the dark, and they got up and searched the train (unsuccessfully) to find me a compartment with a light that worked. I thought back to the vigil and remembered how people understood my needs, even when I said nothing or used a few gestures, and how people who owed me nothing, people who were total strangers, gave from their hearts.

Chapter Twenty-Two

THE LENGTH OF THE LIGHT

WHEN I GOT BACK TO WASHINGTON, I told Anna and Michele about my decision. I was going to say no to the OAS case. If they were disappointed, they didn't say so. No one did. At one point they had both told me that if I continued with the DOJ case, viewing the photos and testifying before a jury, they couldn't continue to be my lawyers — it was too difficult to watch me suffer. Maybe with my OAS decision, they were relieved. But I would come to regret my decision as the years passed and as I realized the OAS was not the same as the DOJ. The proceedings would have been much fairer, much less intense, and much less abusive. But at that time, I couldn't handle the idea of any more judicial proceedings, and I couldn't face an interview with the Guatemalan government. So I told the Inter-American Commission not to send my case up to the Inter-American Court. I asked the OAS commission to issue its findings in writing, if possible, and to explain that I had chosen not to have the case sent on.

Before the OAS commission could do that, the Guatemalan government swung into action. Eduardo Stein, the Guatemalan minister of foreign affairs, told the Guatemalan press that the OAS had decided to close my case after finding that in Guatemala I had had full cooperation and access to all legal remedies to resolve my case. He failed to mention that the OAS had recommended that my case be sent up to the Inter-American Court precisely because of the inadequacy of legal remedies in Guatemala and that I was the one who had declined. He added that the documents recently declassified by the State Department had not provided relevant information to allow "the untangling of the intricate odyssey of what Ortiz experienced."[1]

"Sometimes I feel like I am a voodoo doll," I wrote in my journal, "and government officials from both Guatemala and the U.S. take pleasure in pricking me with one insult after another. All I know is that these attacks hurt, and immediately I think that I have to defend myself. I spoke with Michele. Her composure calmed me and before long I was able to think rationally. I sent a copy of the article both to Michele and the OAS. What

I need to do is take a deep breath and not allow myself to get caught in this web of feeling attacked and defeated."

I was threatened, too, that month, by a death squad. My name appeared on a death list, along with the names of seventeen other civilians, Guatemalan president Alvaro Arzu, and fifty-seven high-ranking military officers. The communiqué, dated August 1996, was signed by a group calling itself "For the Re-vindication of the Army of Guatemala" (PREGUA), which was believed to be a clandestine group within the Guatemalan army. Jennifer was also on the list, along with GAM leader Nineth Montenegro, Nobel Peace Prize winner Rigoberta Menchu, and a collection of Guatemalan officials, journalists, and military officers whose attitude toward the peace negotiations was viewed by PREGUA as too soft. According to the group, the leaders of the country were turning over the control and the direction of the country to the "frustrated and defeated communists of the URNG."[2]

Someone at GHRC faxed the article about the death threat to Michele, who sent it on to the DOJ. Luckily, no one told me about the death threat. I was at the Mount, blissfully ignorant of the Guatemalan army's attempt to intimidate or silence me.

THE VISIT TO THE MOUNT was a blessing in that respect, and it was easier than I expected it to be. Luisa was a bridge. She, too, was different from everyone else in the community, having lived in Chile for so many years. She was a free spirit. On her days off in Kentucky, she would go down to the river and lie in the sun in her bathing suit, unconcerned about what others in the small town might think about a sunbathing nun.

She picked me up at the airport, and we stopped by her house before going on to the Mount. I felt so at home in her tiny clapboard house in the middle of the countryside. She loved living in total simplicity. Her house reminded me of Chile. There was warmth there. She had a wood burning stove, and even though it wasn't on in the summer, the house always smelled a little bit like burned wood and warm winter nights. Luisa brought out a picture album to show me photos of the sisters' trip to Italy, the one I had missed. I listened to her accounts of the trip. She talked about the places I never got to, Florence, for example. She finally got to see a work of art she had loved from afar, Michaelangelo's *David*. What she had never realized until she was full upon it was that David was stark naked. She was so shocked she had to leave the museum to catch her breath. Luisa's smile suddenly reminded me of Angela's and I felt Angela's embrace.

I HAD REQUESTED SOMEONE to take instruction from about the history and ideals of the Ursuline order, and Rose Marita, the new superior of the community, suggested that I work with Sister Annalita. The first time I met with Annalita, I expected her to be professorial and formal — I thought we would work from a book. Instead, Annalita talked about the first five Ursuline sisters who established the Mount, making their way from Germany to work in this rural part of western Kentucky. She showed me where they had shared their first meal together under a maple tree, before they had begun to build the convent, and then we went to look at photos of the sisters who had served in leadership positions since the mother house was formed. Annalita told me each of their personal stories. I saw that there was room for individualism, diversity, and a wide range of talents and work, even in the years when the order was more traditional. Annalita obviously saw my human rights work not as "Dianna's ministry," but as part of the ministry of the Ursuline community; and she helped me to see it that way, too.

At times I asked Annalita her opinion about decisions I had to make. I worried about making decisions because I knew all of my actions had an impact on the community. I also questioned whether I could make decisions that were healthy for myself. My decision to return to Guatemala in the fall of 1989, my decision to cooperate with the DOJ investigation, my decision to trust a number of the people I had trusted — Dr. Snodgrass, Frank Fountain — they all made me question my judgment.

Annalita answered, "You can't worry about all the sisters' responses; if you do, you'll be paralyzed. You have to be true to what you believe you're called to do. And you have our support."

By trusting me that way, and supporting me in advance, she gave me the courage to make decisions on my own and take full responsibility for them. "Never lose hope," she said, "no matter how things turn out. And remember, there's someone who loves you always, no matter what."

I knew she meant God. In the past I would have thought, "A fat lot of good it's done me, that kind of love from that supposed, so-called God, who leaves us to be tortured, deaf to our prayers, who leaves people to be killed." But I was alive, wasn't I? How could I complain? I had prayed to live. I had also prayed to God to let me die, there in the secret prison — I had prayed that the torturers would just go ahead and shoot me. God had other plans, I guess. Maybe God had other plans, too, for the thousands who must have prayed for their lives but ended up in the pit or in the ravines and common graves of Guatemala. I don't know. But I believe that even in the darkness God was with me: the fly came to visit. The Woman reached out to me. And ever since that day God has been with me in the goodness and love of people who have come into my life.

WHEN I GOT BACK to Washington, a surprise was waiting for me on my desk: a stack of declassified FBI documents which Michele had photo-copied and sent to me. They were notes of the interviews the FBI agents had conducted. I noticed, flipping through, that no notes of any interviews with Guatemalan military officers were included. I couldn't help wonder-ing if any had really been interviewed. And no notes of any interviews with CIA or DEA employees were in the stack. The notes were records of interviews with the sisters at the Mount, people at Su Casa, Mary and Antonio, and other friends. I read for only a few minutes before I real-ized that the documents contained information about the choice I had made. Mary, Antonio, Pat, Juanita — I saw mentions of it just glancing through. The documents had been on my desk since late July: they had been declassified, in the public domain, for over a month.

I called Michele, panic-stricken. She acted quickly to have the doc-uments sealed so that they would no longer be available to the public. I was relieved, but I felt I'd been warned. I now understood the power of the DOJ to leak the documents or accidentally declassify something compromising.

THEN I CALLED Rose Marita and told her I would like to talk with her and Annalita about a very important matter. They drove to Washington, and I told them about the choice. I told them, too, that someone in the community had provided the information about the choice to the DOJ. They were just so accepting. I felt, once again, as I had in Angela's presence.

THE DOJ, a short while later, offered me a last chance to identify photos. At first I agreed, after Frank Fountain assured me that viewing the pho-tos didn't imply that I would be continuing in any other sense with the investigation. When I learned that his information was mistaken and that looking at the photos would in fact commit me to further involvement in the investigation, I once again declined to participate.

Ambassador Stroock seemed to be taking precautions — perhaps he had heard that I was going to view the photos; perhaps he, like the journalist, had an inside source. At any rate, although four months had passed since the vigil and no other event made my case current news, in September, an article came out in the *Wyoming Catholic Register*. It was entirely devoted to Stroock's point of view. The article began, "Former Wyoming State Senator Tom Stroock said that the case of an American Ursuline nun was 'easily the most frustrating human rights matter that we handled during the three-and-a-half years I served in Guatemala.'" Stroock's version of what happened to me was identical to the IOB's: "... Stroock said he does not doubt that Sister Ortiz ... suffered a terribly traumatic experience while in Guatemala, but that because 'not a single piece of corroborating evidence or testimony has come to light,' her account of the incident could not be verified." Stroock claimed that he was "shocked and surprised to be met with hostility and a total lack of cooperation" from me and from Church officials when he visited the papal nuncio's home. "For eighteen months following the November 1989 incident, Stroock said he was told Sister Ortiz was too traumatized to talk to him, although she gave several interviews to the news media during this time.... Most disturbing, Stroock said, was that Sister Ortiz refused to help investigators locate the place where she had been abducted, even though she claimed to have heard at least two other persons being tortured at the same location."[3]

In light of the documents that have been declassified, this accusation of Stroock's irks me the most. He knew very well himself how to help investigators find clandestine prisons. An embassy chronology states that on the night of November 2 at the Maryknoll House, "[Consul General Phyllis] Speck offers to begin calling hospitals and morgues; the offer is accepted."[4] But a declassified document shows handwritten notes taken by an embassy official, probably Speck, on the same night: "We — D-2, hospitals."[5] They called the D-2, known for its death squad activities, to get information about where I was kept. Another declassified document points out the ties the embassy had with members of a death squad. Stroock, in a 1991 cable to the secretary of state, refers to "numerous contacts we have made over the past few years, including with members of a 'death squad.'"[6] He goes on to relate that death squads are made up of members of the security forces, often from military intelligence (D-2), but also others from presidential security, zone commands, and occasionally the civilian police forces. They don't report for duty to official installations, Stroock notes, and members' names might not appear on the official rosters of the security forces. They wait at home for orders, usually via phone, or are picked up without prior notice to perform a job. They operate in cells so that tracing orders up the hierarchy is difficult. And an abduction that occurs in the city and involves a car and a "safe house" implies a more senior level of organization. "Safe house" here is the euphemism Stroock uses for what he refers to in his letter to Paul as "this place of illegal incarcera-

tion and torture" that I had to help them shut down. If their death squad
contacts were willing to tell officials at the embassy so much about their
operations, surely they would be willing to reveal where people were being
tortured, if anyone bothered to ask.

IN THE *Wyoming Catholic Register* article, Stroock went on to say that I
had added to my initial report a later account of being lowered into a pit
"where rats gnawed at my wounds."

That was a new one.

"Stroock said that the only medical examination of Sister Ortiz was by
a dermatologist. It revealed no evidence that she had been bitten.

"Stroock emphasized he was not accusing Sister Ortiz of a falsehood —
'She may be telling the truth,' he said — but that he objected vigorously
to Sister Ortiz' accusing the American embassy of inaction on her case
when they had offered her a wide variety of assistance.... Embassy officers
pursued every possible lead, exhausted all legal and practical remedies, and
conducted as thorough an investigation as was possible, he said."

He expressed outrage that I thought Alejandro might be a CIA officer — it was a "slander and a slur on the reputations of the many people
who served in Guatemala and worked so hard to try and discover the
truth of whatever happened.

" 'It is not a simple case,' Stroock said. 'Your heart goes out to Dianna
Ortiz. Something very upsetting happened to her. I have no way to know
what that was. I hope the truth comes out as fully and as quickly as
possible.... I was hoping we would find out in seven days, and then seven
weeks and then seven months and now it's seven years. The trail grows
colder all the time.' "

NOT AS COLD as Stroock might have liked. Jennifer went to a conference
in Dallas that fall, where she heard Celerino Castillo speak. He mentioned
a CIA official who used the code name "Alex" and who often visited the
U.S. embassy. "Alex" did not at all match my sketch of Alejandro, though,
and Jennifer dismissed him from her mind. But later, during Celerino's
slide presentation, she sat up in her chair.

"This one is of me," he had said, "with CIA agent Randy Capister."

"I focused on the image on the screen and felt a tremendous jolt of
recognition," Jennifer recalls. "The man in the photo had light hair that
was receding, and did not wear sunglasses. So the top portion of his face
did not match the sketch, of course. But the lower half of his face was
identical to Dianna's sketch of Alejandro. The cheekbones formed the

widest part of his face, narrowing into a long, pointed chin, and the lips were thin. The nose, too, was long and narrow and straight, and the beard was short and light. More than anything, it was the way the features fit together and the expression on the face that was so startlingly like the sketch."

Jennifer didn't let the opportunity pass. She asked Celerino for the photograph of Randy Capister. He sent it to her, and she had an artist draw the dark, curly wig and sunglasses depicted in the sketch onto tracing paper to form an overlay. After placing the wig and sunglasses on the image, Jennifer was even more certain that the photograph and the sketch were a perfect match. She told me what she had discovered. But I just couldn't face Alejandro. Not yet. Not in the dark of winter. A few months later, in the spring, when I was ready to look at the photograph and the overlay, we went to Amnesty International and sat in the big conference room with Carlos Salinas and Stephen Rickard, the director of the Amnesty International Washington office. As a lawyer, Jennifer knew it was important for someone impartial to see how I reacted to the photograph. She passed me the photograph, and let me look at it as it was. I had to remember that Alejandro — if this were he — would not be wearing the wig and the glasses in the photo. I had to look at his nose, the shape of his face, his ears, his teeth, his forehead, his neck, his cheeks.

I looked, and I felt my breath coming faster. Then Jennifer lay the transparency with the glasses and wig over the photo.

I looked again. Two words drummed inside me until I spoke them: "It's him."

I didn't want to cry, but I felt myself being pulled back into that November day, and the sobs came.

We learned that the DOJ had finished its investigation when the reporter with the inside DOJ source called for my comment on the results. It was February 1997. He sent us the brief article about the investigation's conclusion that he published in the *Atlanta Constitution:* "A U.S. Justice Department investigation has ended without identifying any suspects in the alleged kidnapping and torture of an American nun in Guatemala in 1989, and investigators still aren't certain that a crime occurred. A 282–page classified report corroborates some details of Sister Dianna Ortiz's description of being abducted and brutally tortured by Guatemalan security forces, but it casts doubt on other aspects of her account."[7]

Finding out that the report was classified was both good news and bad news. No one else would have to know about the choice I had made. But because the report was classified, not even I could see it.

THE INTELLIGENCE OVERSIGHT BOARD didn't disagree with the Department of Justice's conclusions, I was told, and wouldn't look into my case any further. I didn't understand. The IOB said I had "suffered horrific abuse." How could I have "suffered horrific abuse" if no crime had been committed? Isn't the infliction of horrific abuse a crime? Were the IOB and the DOJ both suggesting that the horrific abuse may have been self-inflicted?

I wouldn't know until I got the report. Going back day after day to answer Tubach's invasive questions had almost taken away my will to live. I kept going, thinking I wouldn't let him break me, thinking I wouldn't let it be said that I didn't cooperate, thinking I would learn a little more about the event that completely changed my life. And the DOJ had the audacity to classify the report so that I couldn't see it and not even tell me they were finished investigating. On top of it all, when we met with Seikaly and I asked why the report was classified, Seikaly told me it was to protect, not only national security, but my privacy. Only four copies of the report existed, he said, and they would be kept under lock and key.

But they weren't. A reporter friend of mine called Stroock to get Stroock's comment for an article she was writing. Stroock made sure she knew he had read the report. Stroock said he had gotten it from a State Department official, who had also seen it. Apparently, it had been passed around to a number of officials in the State Department. A senator from Wyoming admitted in writing to having read the report. He wrote a letter petitioning the Justice Department to declassify it because he believed, after reading it, that it would help his constituent Thomas Stroock rehabilitate his reputation, which I had damaged. No one at the Justice Department has ever been able to explain how the senator from Wyoming, Stroock, or State Department officials got the report. Seikaly at first said Stroock couldn't possibly have gotten the report. He later admitted that Stroock had gotten it from a State Department official. Seikaly's final word on the matter was that Stroock might have seen the parts of the report that pertained to him.

MICHELE, MARIE, AND I met with Seikaly to get some understanding of the DOJ's conclusions and the possibilities of getting a copy of the report. Seikaly told us that if I filed a FOIA to get the report declassified, even if I tried to have it declassified only to me, chances were that it would end up being declassified generally. It would be in the public domain then.

Everyone would know about the choice I had made. I tried to content myself with what Seikaly could tell us about the report, then and there, in the meeting.

First, he said, there was no way to stop the leaks. I have Marie's notes of the meeting to remind me that he made that statement, straight out, then went on to the next point: if the DOJ "had credible evidence, we'd go forward with the prosecution, even against Dianna's will." But on the basis of my testimony alone, with no witnesses or solid evidence to corroborate it, they simply couldn't prosecute.

I asked if the report focused on the issue of my credibility. Seikaly said not as such, but oddities in my testimony were noted. The issue of the T-shirt came up. Seikaly said that if the burns on my back were in rows, as some people, he said, contended, then they didn't match the random pattern of burn holes in the T-shirt. But that was not necessarily an inconsistency, Seikaly had said, because more burns may have been inflicted after the T-shirt was removed — as I had testified. He went on to claim that the Guatemalan doctor who had examined me and Dr. Gutiérrez's nurse recalled that the burns on my back were in a pattern. Seikaly also claimed that the dermatologist in Guatemala who had examined my back had "drawn a clear pattern of rows," consisting of 112 burns.

If I had been thinking clearly instead of feeling accused and overwhelmed, I would have told him that was impossible; the dermatologist had originally said I had 75 burns. He couldn't have come up with that number and at the same time have drawn a pattern of rows of 112 burns. As I would learn later, a declassified cable signed by Stroock says that the Guatemalan doctor's certificate "made circumstantial reference to the burns, concentrating on the more visible blows to the face."[8] That description precludes a detailed sketch or diagram of the burns on my back.

Stroock's claim may be suspect, however. According to the FBI's notes, there was no "certificate" — the doctor had kept no record of his visit to me. And we certainly never had a "certificate" for our files.

The Guatemalan dermatologist was kind enough to share with me recently what he remembered about the examination of my back. Regarding a "symmetrical pattern," he said, "The burns were symmetrical; they were all the same diameter." He remembered nothing about the burns being in a pattern of lines or rows. He remembered nothing about drawing any supposed pattern the burns made.

Dr. Gutiérrez's numbers are different from the Guatemalan doctor's because Dr. Gutiérrez determined that some of the wounds on my back actually consisted of two burns. But Dr. Gutiérrez never said anything to me or Fran about "a pattern of rows." The FBI's notes of the interview with Gutiérrez and his nurse don't mention anything about a memory either of them had that the burns were in a pattern of rows. In the final DOJ report, none of the individuals who supposedly saw this pattern are named; the DOJ says "some of the witnesses" saw the burns in rows.

Seikaly said they had noted in the report that I would not consent to an independent physician's examining my back. "We did not consider this to be an inconsistency," he remarked, "merely an anomaly."

The fact is, no one had ever directly asked me to have my back examined. Tubach had mentioned the issue once, but he said he wanted to wait until more trust was built up between us.

I asked for the return of the T-shirt, the death threat letters, and other items of evidence. Seikaly said that because there was the remote possibility that something might happen in the case, he wouldn't return them until the statute of limitations expired, eight years after the abduction, in November 1997. What I would learn eventually from the DOJ report was this: "Ortiz turned over some notes that she said were the original notes she had received. The DOJ Team gave these notes to the FBI for analysis. When a check was made to determine the results of the FBI analysis, the FBI informed the DOJ Team that it had lost the notes."

I asked why the U.S. embassy had launched a campaign of defamation against me.

Seikaly responded that the embassy did not think that they had launched an attack on me, Stroock especially. The investigators also spoke with Consul General Sue Patterson and Political Affairs Officer Lew Anselem. The view of these people was that they received information about my abduction and attempted to be helpful, but I did not want help, and they recognized that. They attempted to follow up, including making demands on the Guatemalan government for information. The Guatemalan government made defamatory remarks which Anselem passed on without saying whether those remarks were true or not. He just passed them on as information received. "The position of the embassy," Seikaly told me, "is that they did not support the allegations made by the Guatemalan government. The Guatemalan government was the one doing the defaming. Several embassy officers doubted the accuracy of your story," Seikaly said, "but we don't feel they defamed you. The cables were harsh, but they were internal, never public."

I asked what the report said about the allegations that I had left the garden of the Posada de Belén of my own accord. Seikaly answered that there was credible testimony that a person had let me into the garden. He said this man's report to the police said that he saw me walking toward a hole in the wall, but when the investigators talked to him, he said that he just saw me walking toward the back of the garden, and they found that statement credible. Seikaly stated that Bob Chaney for a while was working on a hypothesis that I left the garden of my own accord and was picked up outside the garden. However, there was no corroborating evidence of this, and the hypothesis was dropped.

"We were not able to identify the place you were detained," Seikaly added. "We found several locations with some characteristics you described but not all. One was near the airport."

He must have been referring to the fact that I heard helicopters. But what about the gunshots?

He mentioned that the blueprints of the Politécnica offered by the Guatemalan government didn't coincide with my testimony. In those blueprints, the Politécnica has no basement. "The Politécnica," Seikaly added, "has no underground parking. It may have been filled in."

I was too stunned to stop him. I had never said anything about underground parking. The parking garage was upstairs from the basement prison. A cursory reading of my affidavit would have provided him with that information.

Seikaly said all of this suggested to him that the Politécnica was probably a mistaken identification, but he said he wasn't certain of that. From 1985 on, he said, the Politécnica was a school, and the use of that building was inconsistent with the type of torture that I alleged. I mentioned Carmen Valenzuela, who was tortured at the same location in 1990. He said they didn't look into torture at the Politécnica after 1989.

Seikaly said that there was a fair amount of evidence that I had received threats over time. He stated that they considered it an anomaly (but not an inconsistency) that the other nuns did not receive such threats, so they looked for reasons for that anomaly.

Seikaly said that former Defense Minister Gramajo was not interviewed, nor was former President Vinicio Cerezo — although, while living abroad after his term in office, he had told the Mexican press agency CERIGUA that I was abducted and tortured by members of the Guatemalan security forces.[9] Seikaly said "a number" of former and current high-ranking military officials were interviewed, including some who were in command in 1989.[10]

Seikaly said that no one in San Miguel admitted to having been a member of the civil patrol. No one there could identify the officer who asked me to dance, and he wasn't located.

I asked if anyone who talked with them was transferred, disappeared, or mysteriously killed.

Seikaly said they did receive a call from another component of the DOJ who said that they had a person in jail who said he had information about my case. They spoke to the person in jail, who told them a long story of sitting in a police car near Antigua at the time of my abduction, as part of an operation in which someone was being abducted. He identified an officer in charge of the group. The officer, Seikaly said, was a lieutenant who had died in 1993 or 1994 in an accident. The DOJ investigated, Seikaly said, and found out that the lieutenant had been in the United States at the time of my abduction, attending the School of the Americas. Seikaly said that the story of the guy in jail didn't pan out for other reasons, as well.

Only one officer died in an accident in 1993 or 1994, according to the Guatemalan government's weekly paper, *Diario Centroamérica*. His name was Carlos Enrique Cardenas Sagastume. He was a major, not a lieutenant, and, according to records available from the National Security Archives and SOA Watch, he was not at the School of the Americas in November 1989. Either Seikaly's information was wrong or he was purposely lying.

SEIKALY ADMITTED that there was some stonewalling on the part of the Guatemalan government during the investigation, but he said that eventually the investigators were able to interview everyone they wanted. However, Seikaly said the Guatemalan government "may not have told the truth."

I asked whether the investigators looked into the death squad that threatened me in August 1996. Seikaly said that letter was not part of their investigation — they were not aware of it.

I asked what they had found out about the excrement left on my doorstep in March 1996. Seikaly said nothing about that incident was passed on to him. He said that he would ask the FBI investigators about it.

Seikaly stated that all CIA personnel were interviewed. Two were given lie detector tests.

"Was Randy Capister interviewed?" I asked

"Everyone."

I asked whether CIA files were subpoenaed. Seikaly said they were not subpoenaed, but they were obtained and looked at by investigators. He said they learned some new things and followed up on them. As a result, they submitted one agent to a lie detector test. "We are fairly confident he lied about other things," Seikaly said, "but not about this."

The declassified FBI documents, which I would eventually examine in detail, reveal information about one polygraph exam, given to a person whose name is blacked out. He was asked only two questions: "Are you or were you ever Alejandro?" and "Did you ever place Dianna Ortiz in your vehicle?" I would like to have asked the DOJ team whether two questions were adequate to determine someone's veracity on a polygraph exam — and shouldn't they try different phrasings of the questions? What if the vehicle belonged to the embassy, not to him? What if he led me to it and told me to get in but didn't "place" me in it? And what if, once again, I was wrong about assigning the name "Alejandro" to him when I heard it, blindfolded, then heard him speak?

IN RESPONSE TO MY QUESTION about Jeanne Boylan's sketches, Seikaly said that she was considered credible. They did interview her. The drawings were shown in Guatemala to embassy personnel, and they compared them to photos of every male embassy employee between the ages of eighteen and fifty, including DEA agents and others who were in Guatemala between 1989 and 1990. Seikaly said that they had a photo array based on this to show me. However, there was nothing they thought was an absolute match. Seikaly said the photos they were going to show me were of embassy employees, but they did not include any Guatemalans. He said that the DOJ was mainly interested in identifying Alejandro, and, at any rate, the DOJ had not succeeded in coming up with a good photo group of Guatemalans.

Seikaly said that former DEA agent Celerino Castillo, in his testimony before the grand jury, swore that, on two separate occasions, Capister (whose name, as we learned years later, is in CIA records as Kapasar)[11] had implicated himself in my case in conversations he'd had with Castillo. Seikaly went on to say that Capister swore under oath that at least one of those conversations had never taken place. Capister's photo was in the array they planned to show me, Seikaly said. He added that they didn't think he was Alejandro, but he was the right age to fit my description, he was in a position to have such contacts at the time, and he was "in the arca" at the time.

I WANTED SEIKALY to write up a statement saying that the investigation was finished and prosecution had been denied. But he said he didn't know how he could provide me with anything more than what he had already said to me orally in the meeting without running the risk that it would be viewed as a final decision, which meant that others would be clamoring for the reasons for their official decision.

I could read between the lines — others might ask why they didn't prosecute and he would have to tell them I hadn't wanted to go forward, and if he were asked why not, certain difficult issues might come up....

WE HAD GOTTEN a quick rundown, but the report itself obviously was being leaked to the key players, who were talking to the press. Seikaly had admitted as much. I needed the report to be able to defend myself. And I deserved to know how the DOJ reached its conclusions. It was my right.

But I was afraid to push for anything. I was afraid the DOJ would leak the information about the choice. Seikaly had put it this way in a conversation with Michele: "The interviews with Dianna and others described in the report are not classified and therefore would be available to those requesting the report if I can't keep them confidential under privacy concerns. We're trying to keep the entire report withheld on those grounds. If Dianna files a FOIA request, perhaps we could be forced to disclose portions of the report regarding her interviews and statements, but then other requesters might have access to that information also. There is a risk that some disclosure to Dianna would result in disclosure to others."

I was paralyzed for a year. I tried to forget about the information I had in my hands — the information about Randy Capister — and about the information the DOJ had in its hands.

MEANWHILE, my life got better and I got stronger. The Inter-American Commission of the OAS put its findings in writing: "Sister Ortiz was placed under surveillance and threatened, then kidnapped and tortured," and "agents of the Government of Guatemala were responsible for those crimes against Sister Ortiz." The commission found that the State of Guatemala violated my rights to "humane treatment, personal liberty, a fair trial, privacy, freedom of conscience and religion, and freedom of association and judicial protection."

"Sister Ortiz is a credible witness," the commission wrote, "and her consistent statements support a finding that she was kidnapped and taken to a clandestine detention center where she was tortured."[12]

I WROTE A CHAPTER about treatment of torture survivors from the survivor's perspective for the National Institute for Mental Health. The NIMH was sponsoring a series of panel discussions which would end in a book, *The Mental Health Consequences of Torture and Related Trauma*.

Meredith, Carmen Valenzuela, Adriana Bartow, and I attended, and the NIMH panel opened the door to us. I ended up interviewing dozens of survivors of torture from around the world, transcribing what they said about their torture and what had helped and hurt them as they tried to heal. The panel gave me as much space as we needed in the book. And, during the process, I realized torture survivors needed a group like Coalition Missing that would provide mutual support and come together for lobbying and public education efforts. So, with a few other survivors, I formed the Torture Abolition and Survivors Support Coalition International (TASSC). Alice allowed TASSC to be a project of GHRC, lending us her staff, machines, and advice, and she allowed me to run the organization out of her office.

WE WERE GETTING READY for our first big event, a commemoration of June 26, which the UN had designated as the first annual International Day to Commemorate Torture Victims and Survivors. As I was inviting survivors from several different continents to come to Washington for a vigil and to meet with U.S. officials to push for changes in policies that could affect them, I realized I could no longer remain silent about the choice I had made. In March, I wrote a letter to my sisters, Barbara and Michelle. First I apologized for not telling them in person:

> Being with you all during the holidays was an experience that made me glad to be a member of the family. At that moment, I could honestly say that I was glad to be alive. This is a feeling that I haven't felt in such a very long time. Perhaps it was selfish of me to want to cling to that moment...nor did I want to lose that feeling of belonging to a family.
>
> I think it would be fair to say that fear and shame also prevented me from turning to you for advice. As in the past, the voices of my torturers returned, telling me that no one, not even my family, would believe me if I were to share with them something more about my experience in Guatemala.... Why, after all these years, do their words still haunt me? Perhaps their words are true — and that's what I fear most.
>
> Shell and Barb, I don't know where to begin. I'm sure there is a better way of saying all this — but I don't know how. Please bear with me. You need to know that certain circumstances have put me in an uncomfortable position — forcing me to deal with a private matter on a public level. What I am going to share with you is something

that a few people know. It's something that Mary Fabri, Mimi, and a few of the sisters have known from the beginning. It's something that even to this day I am unable to talk about without breaking down in tears. My greatest fear is that it will be leaked to the press and/or the public. And for my own sanity, I need to confront head on a dark secret. And once you know my dark secret I hope that you will not despise me or think of me as a monster. I hope and pray that you will still allow me to be your sister — but if you don't — I'll respect your decision.

When I returned to the States after leaving Guatemala, I was unable to tell anyone that I had been raped. I didn't recognize anyone and I was afraid that no one would believe me. I thought it was my fault because I couldn't defend myself — and in the end, I didn't resist. Everything that happened in Guatemala was my fault. That is what the torturers drummed into my head. And I believed them. But I was also convinced that no one would ever have to know what happened and that I could forget that horrible nightmare.

I almost succeeded in doing that. Then something happened — something that to this day I cannot forget. My body began to undergo some changes. I don't think I have to tell you what I mean by that. I didn't know what to do. I didn't know to whom to turn. People around me were strangers. I didn't recognize anyone. What was real to me at that moment was that something was growing inside me — something that came from the seed of one of my torturers — perhaps all of them. At that time, I was bleeding off and on, and I prayed like never before that I would discharge whatever it was that was growing inside me. I tried to understand what was happening. Was God punishing me because I had participated in the torture of another human being? What was growing inside me? Was it human? I had so many questions but no answers. All I knew was that something was growing inside me — and to me it was a monster, a product of the men who had raped me. I could not bring something into this world that came from evil — it had to be destroyed or it would have destroyed me. To make a long story short, I turned to someone for assistance (someone whose identity and whereabouts remain unknown to everyone except me). I destroyed that something that was growing inside me.

But I was reminded each day of how much I was like the torturers. First I had participated in the torture of another woman and then I destroyed what could have been an innocent life. How could a

Catholic nun commit such acts? Shame and guilt gnawed at me day and night.

Someone at the Mount disclosed my dark secret to DOJ investigators. They tried to convince me that this information was crucial to the investigation and they wanted me to provide them with the name of the doctor who assisted me and copies of the medical records (at least I was smart enough to make certain that no records existed). As far as I was concerned, this was a private matter that was irrelevant to the case. I told them I would no longer participate in the investigation. By this point, I had already given my complete testimony and government officials could not say, as in the past, that I had not cooperated.

Barb and Shell, I hated them so much. God forgive me — but I even wished they would be tortured for one minute. I can't believe I would wish torture on anyone. I thought that, like the people of Guatemala, I had the right to know the truth. But the consequences were much more than I could handle. I walked away feeling psychologically tortured and betrayed by everyone — and feeling like a coward. I let the people of Guatemala down, especially those who were in the clandestine prison. The U.S. government found something that would silence me. And I allowed them to — all because I was afraid of what my family, my community, and my friends would think of me. I felt like I had sold my soul to the Devil. Today, Alejandro and people like him are free and are being protected by our government.

After all this happened, I tried to put my life back together. As long as I kept quiet, I was safe. That's what I thought.

Shortly after, I started to receive phone calls from reporters saying that the Justice Department had completed its report and it was not favorable. From the very beginning, their goal was to discredit me. I was called a liar. It was said that I was emotionally unstable and hallucinating — horrible things like people being thrown into open pits or being forced to participate in the torture of others just don't happen in Guatemala, I was told. They went so far as to say that they didn't think I was a lesbian. They decided that I was having an affair with a medical student in Guatemala City so that meant I was bisexual (before long, they're going to say that I'm a transvestite). For the record, I did not have an affair with a medical student nor am I a lesbian.

When I found out the report would remain classified, a part of me was relieved, while another part of me was filled with guilt and anger. Why was I helping the U.S. government protect people who possibly participated in the torture and killing of innocent civilians? I saw myself like the U.S. government, an accomplice — in my silence I was saying, "It's OK to disappear, to assassinate, to massacre or to torture anyone."

Now, each time the phone rings, I take a deep breath and pray to God, "Please don't let it be a reporter — please don't let them ask questions about..." Sometimes I just want to hide under a rock or move far away where no one knows me.

But it is impossible to run away from the past. Mary has been instrumental in helping me stay focused and has helped me understand that what happened to me is not unique. Rape is a form of torture that is used by governments to punish women who may be viewed as a threat. In many instances women find themselves carrying the offspring of their torturers and like me they are forced to make a decision that haunts them for life. I have mustered the courage to talk with a priest about this matter, and he assures me that I am not to blame for anything that has happened. What brings me some peace and consolation is hearing him say that I do not need to be forgiven by God for what happened or by anyone else, for that matter. Sometimes I believe his words but then someone like Stroock says something to the press and the feelings of guilt and shame return.

I know that there are people who would disapprove of my decision. And I'm sure they would say it was not my right to decide if this human or nonhuman should live or die. All I can say is that I did what I had to do. I hate the choice I was forced to make. You may find this a bit odd — as horrible as this experience has been, I'm a much better person. I am more sensitive to people. I care for those who are oppressed, and for those who commit crimes against humanity. And I do not judge people — I leave that to God. I have a deeper understanding of the fragility of humanity and the evil that dwells in our midst.

I used to think that God made an error in allowing me to survive — but I no longer believe that to be the case. God, for some reason unknown to me, gave me the courage to stay alive. Believe me — survival is more painful than the actual torture itself. I don't know how to put this into words — but I understand what happens to those who survive the horrors of torture. For far too long, their suffering, whether it is physical, psychological, or spiritual, has been misunderstood and has gone unnoticed. God, I believe, has united our voices. As one voice, we are calling for justice and truth — calling for an end to torture. When I left Guatemala in 1989 I made a promise to the people who I left behind in the clandestine prison — that I would do whatever I could to prevent something as horrible as what happened to us from happening to anyone else.

As I look back and try to understand everything that has happened, it all seems like a nightmare that will never end. It will end, I am told, once I can free myself of this dark secret. I have started to share this dark secret by confiding in you. There's no turning back.

Now I have to find the right way to tell Daddy and Mom, and the rest of the family. How do I tell them? I worry so much about Mom and Dad's health. I don't want to cause them or anyone in the family more grief or embarrassment. I keep telling myself that I should just forget about it and not say anything. I fear that someone in the government is going to leak it to the press and/or the public. I can feel it coming. Stroock, I think, already knows. They have to hear it from me — not someone in the government or the press. Shell and Barb, I turn to you for "big sister" and "baby sister" advice.

Would it be better if someone like Mary or Father Joe Nangle told them? (Of course I would be present.) Would it be better if I wrote them a letter? Would it be better if I told them directly? Would it be better left unsaid?

I'm going to end this note now — please let me hear from you as soon as possible. Now that you know the truth about me, I hope and pray that you still consider me to be your sister. As I said earlier, if you choose to have nothing to do with me, I will respect your decision. For what it's worth — I'll love you always.

Michelle and Barbara called as soon as they had gotten the letter. They didn't judge me but were loving and supportive. They said they would take on the task of telling Mom and Dad about the choice I had made.

With my secret partially in the light, I decided to go ahead and file a FOIA for the DOJ report. I would make the announcement that I was filing the FOIA during the week of June 26, when we had some public events scheduled. I thought about holding up the photo of Capister and my sketch at the same time and inviting the press to compare them and investigate. But I was afraid the DOJ would reopen its investigation and force me to testify. Everyone acknowledged that, although not likely, it was possible. I didn't want to get dragged back into a DOJ investigation. I couldn't survive another, and I knew the DOJ would never investigate seriously anyway.

When I announced the FOIA lawsuit for the DOJ report, I would reveal my dark secret. That was terrifying enough. But I would have a supportive group of people around me: torture survivors, new and old friends. The congressional briefing we had organized for survivors seemed the best place to make the revelation.

THE OTHER SURVIVORS let me speak first. I couldn't stand waiting. I got my papers in order and glanced at Representative Lantos. He gave me a gentle smile. Rose Marita was in the crowd, waiting to support me when I finished. She had flown up just to attend the briefing. If I had to pinpoint a single moment when I decided to remain with the Ursulines, seeing her at that briefing might have been it.

Mary McGrory was in the front row. I knew that at least she would do a balanced story. Jennifer and Patricia were sitting in the front row beside her. Alice was standing against the wall. I felt like she was holding the whole building up. My old friends were there — Carlos Salinas, of Amnesty International, was in the audience, and Craig Powers, Representative Connie Morella's aide, had come to be supportive as well. Hans Hofgren, Lantos's aide, nodded to me, encouraging me to go on.

I grabbed the little silver dolphin around my neck, the one Mary had given me. It was warm in my hand. I got about half way through my statement, to the most essential part — I said I was unable to carry what the torturers had left inside me, what I could only view as a monster, and I turned to someone for assistance and destroyed that life. Then I left the room.

I tried to piece myself together in the hall. I was ashamed because of the choice I had made and because people had seen me break down — again. Craig Powers came out into the hall and cupped my shoulder in his hand. Then he gave me a hug. We stood there wordlessly, then Alice and several others joined us. Patricia was finishing my statement. I was glad the door was thick and I couldn't hear it. But I knew it by heart. I wondered if she would repeat the same sentence I had just finished, the one that had caused me to break down. "Am I proud of what I did? No. But if I had it to do over again, I would probably make the same choice."

I hated it, but it was true. In the garden I didn't fight hard enough. I didn't defend myself because the Guate-man said he would hurt my friends if I screamed. On the bus I didn't try to escape. The Guate-man told me innocent people would die. So I let the torturers remake me. And I had had enough of it. I wasn't going to let their seed grow in me and come into the world through me. I was carrying enough of their evil.

I GOT CALLS AND LETTERS from female survivors after the briefing. Many had also been raped and had made the same choice when they found themselves pregnant. Many told me I was the first person they had ever revealed their choice to. One was Catholic and had confessed her choice to a priest, hoping the priest would be understanding. The priest said, "You have committed a mortal sin." She had nothing to do with the Church after that. I wonder if that priest knows how much damage he did to her. Sharing my secret, I opened a door to other survivors. We could understand each other. Many of us were put in positions where we had to make horrible choices. And no one has a right to judge us. If the Church is so concerned that what we did was a mortal sin, the Church leaders had better take a position and say, "You don't torture and rape women." They'd better get off their behinds and not only say "We don't support torture and rape" but also do something about it. It's so easy for the male authority figures of the Church to condemn women for making these choices. They can't understand the domestic violence, the political violence, the abuse. I'm not advocating that women make the choice that I and other survivors have made, but I'm saying each woman has to do what she thinks is right. And it's between that woman and God.

A few days later Rose Marita sent this statement from the Leadership Council to the GHRC office:

> Statement of the Leadership Team of the Mount Saint Joseph Ursuline Community regarding the disclosure of Dianna Ortiz, OSU, that she terminated the life which was conceived as a result of gang rape experienced during her abduction.
>
> *We cannot and will not judge Dianna but will respond to her with compassion and we will call the Mount Saint Joseph Ursuline Community to prayer and action for the creation of a torture-free world.* Furthermore, upon hearing this disclosure, we find ourselves experiencing wonderment and gratitude. Despite insurmountable odds and paralyzing fear, Dianna was able to find the spiritual, emotional, and physical courage to conquer the demons that held her captive all these eight long years. Her revelation of the abortion disarms her enemies and frees her to pursue unafraid and unchained the agenda of justice and truth.

Her Ursuline sisters will continue to walk with her to the very end, knowing that ultimately truth and love prevail; knowing, also, that at this very moment, even in the midst of unspeakable corruption and evil, GOD is ever present to all who seek mercy and work for justice.

I knew that statement had come from the whole community, not just Rose Marita, Annalita, or the sisters who I knew supported me. The community had welcomed me back, knowing my worst secret. Whatever shame I had put my community through and whatever anguish, turmoil, expense, and grief I had caused over the years had been forgiven, at least by the great majority of the sisters. It's taken me years to dare to believe that — to dare to walk forward and believe they're beside me, and will be until the very end.

WITH THE SUPPORT of my family and the Ursuline community and no more secrets that could be used against me, I filed my FOIA. A year later, I got the response: the DOJ report was denied in full. I filed a lawsuit, and another year later, in September 2000, I finally received the DOJ report.

It was a poorly argued, poorly written, desperate attempt to discredit me. Seikaly, in his 1997 meeting with us, had said Bob Chancy's theory that I'd left the garden alone had been discarded, since the DOJ could find no corroboration for it. But in the report the DOJ insists, "[T]he DOJ Team found evidence that the kidnapping did not take place as Ortiz has claimed. One witness, a gardener at the retreat center, told the DOJ Team that he saw Ortiz walking alone in the garden just prior to her abduction." The gardener told DOJ investigators he saw me walking toward the main garden path with my Bible, corroborating exactly what I wrote in my affidavit: I went out to the garden alone to pray. The investigators admit this nearly a hundred pages later. But the DOJ tries to use the gardener's testimony to imply that, because he saw me alone in the garden with my Bible, I wasn't abducted. The gardener, however, never said he saw me leave the garden, alone or accompanied.

The next "witness" the report cites is the petty thief and vagrant who saw me only from behind. He gave a description of me that investigators admit was "suspiciously similar to the description of Ortiz that the religious workers gave the police when they first reported her missing, raising the considerable possibility that the local police gave him the description of the person they were looking for and told him what to say."

The DOJ team doesn't ask the logical questions: Why would the police give "the witness" the description of me and tell him what to say? Doesn't that suggest that the police were covering something up, that he wasn't a *real* witness? If so, can it be because the security forces were involved — and the abduction took place exactly as I claim?

This witness, according to the DOJ, was interviewed on numerous occasions by the police and participated in a videotaped reconstruction of what he had seen (with his back to the camera). The DOJ notes, "He explained that he had given a false name at the time of these interviews because he was afraid to be identified by those involved in Ortiz' abduction." The witness told the DOJ, then, that I was abducted and that he was afraid to be identified by those involved, and that, therefore, he gave a false name to the police. But the DOJ in its report still tries to claim him as a witness against me.

The DOJ, out of witnesses, turns to strange arguments. The DOJ team acknowledges that no one they talked to saw my Bible in a tree. But, citing the National Police's claim that "students" at the retreat center found my Bible in a tree on November 4, the DOJ states, "If in fact Ortiz' bible was found in a tree, this would cast serious doubt on her claim that she was abducted from the garden. It is difficult to imagine why they [the torturers] would have climbed a tree during the abduction to stash Ortiz' bible in a place where it would have been discovered eventually anyway."

It is also difficult to imagine why I might have climbed a tree to stash my Bible in a place where it would have been found eventually anyway. The DOJ team conjectures that I hid it there because I wanted to leave the garden but did not want to take it with me. But I could have simply left my Bible in my room. If I planned to sneak off, I planned very badly, carrying my Bible and my Walkman to the garden with me. If my decision to leave the garden was, supposedly, a last-minute one, the DOJ doesn't address what prevented me from hiding my Bible as well as I apparently hid my Walkman, which was never found.

The investigators speculate that I hid my Bible in a tree so that it would be kept "out of view temporarily." That is how they explain that no one saw the Bible in the tree, although numerous people were searching the garden for me on the day of my disappearance. Somehow the tree was keeping the Bible temporarily invisible. But the next day, the tree supposedly allowed the Bible to be seen.

The DOJ notes that my broken watch was found under the tree. Instead of considering that a sign of a struggle — I had told investigators that the band snapped when the Guate-man grabbed my wrist — they argue that perhaps I broke it on a branch when I was climbing the tree to hide my

Bible. "In order to hide the bible in the branch of the tree, Ortiz would have had to climb onto the branch." At this point the investigators might ask themselves, Yes, so why would she go to all that trouble when it would have been so much easier to leave her Bible inside? And, if she was trying to sneak off, why be so careful to hide her Bible, then carelessly leave her watch under the tree in plain view? And this is the point where they're supposed to ask, Was the Bible *really* found in a tree? And why did the police claim in their first report that they'd found no evidence at the site, then tell the press that a Bible, shawl, and watch were planted there the next day to make the abduction seem more real, retract that statement when they learned Darleen had already reported to the embassy that she'd found my shawl on November 2, and claim in a later report that "students" at the retreat house had found the Bible in a tree, making the abduction seem less real? Who is scrambling to hide things badly?

THE DOJ TEAM had focused so much on whether the burn wounds on my back were in a pattern of rows because they wanted to make an argument beyond the one involving the T-shirt and the fact that the burn marks on it were not in a pattern. "[S]ome of the witnesses indicated that Ortiz' burns were arranged in a pattern on her back — suggesting that perhaps her back came in contact with a hot metal grate of some kind." The DOJ has no theories about what, exactly, this "grate" might be or why it might make burns the exact size and shape of cigarette butts. If the DOJ team could have found such a grate and proved that it existed in Guatemala in 1989, they might have compared the pattern of wounds that "some of the witnesses" supposedly said they saw on my back with the pattern of burns such a grate could have made. But the DOJ has not been able to specify what kind of a grate this might be or whether it has ever existed, let alone in Guatemala in 1989.

REGARDING THE CIA DRAFT DOCUMENT that was kept in embassy files — the document in which a source with "personal knowledge" says I was definitely abducted — the DOJ team insists, "The document stated only that a CIA source, [censored], had stated that Ortiz had been kidnapped as she claimed but probably not raped."

The document actually says that I was probably abducted by the S-2 in Chimaltenango — regional military intelligence operatives. The DOJ reportedly interviewed the source of this information and also interviewed the CIA agent who worked with him (his "handler"). Frank Fountain and Roland had said the report was "readily retraceable." It would seem, then, that, in speaking to Roland, whoever wrote the report must have admitted to it. But in the DOJ's version, the CIA agent who dealt with the source named in the document denied ever receiving any information from him about my case. The DOJ doesn't address how the document did get written, then, and by whom and who is lying and why.

The source's assertion of the motive for my abduction is another piece of information investigators omit. Instead of including the source's suggestion that I was in "contact with leftist guerrillas," which led to my abduction, the DOJ suggests there was no motive for my abduction at all, devoting a whole section of the report to "The Search for a Motive."

From the DOJ report, bad as it was, I learned several important things. The DOJ followed up on the information the former G-2 officer had given about the Guate-man, identifying him as Guillermo Fuentes Aragón. "The DOJ Team obtained a photograph of the navy officer, and the officer does bear a strong resemblance to one of the sketches of Ortiz' abductors." Later, the DOJ repeats, "In fact, Fuentes does bear a strong resemblance to the sketch of Suspect #2 released to the press by Ortiz in May 1996. However, the DOJ Team was able to determine that at the time of the abduction, the officer in question was attending a DEA-sponsored counter-narcotics course in Virginia."

The DOJ claims that the Office of the Inspector General of the DEA reported that Fuentes attended an international Narcotics Enforcement Management Seminar (INEMS) at the DEA offices in Virginia from October 16, 1989, until November 10, 1989 — "but that virtually all official records of the seminar had been destroyed after three years.

"According to the graduation program and the DEA's International Alumni Directory, INEMS class number 65 was held in Arlington, Virginia, from October 16 to November 10, 1989. The graduation program and the class roster contain the names of thirty students, including 'Capitan Federico Gmo. Aragón' from Guatemala. The class photograph, which according to the class instructor, was taken during an excursion to the University of Virginia, depicts the thirty attendees, including Fuentes, as well as a DEA agent and an interpreter."

While the DOJ says the names of those pictured were written on the back of the photograph, one obvious omission is the date. If the photograph wasn't taken on November 2, the photograph is no proof that Fuentes was not in Guatemala on that date. The fact that Fuentes's name appears in the graduation program is not proof that he was at graduation, and even if he were at a graduation ceremony in mid-November, that is no proof that he couldn't have traveled back to Guatemala before then.

"Given . . . the reliability of the information confirming that Fuentes was in Virginia on November 2 and 3, 1989, Fuentes can safely be ruled out as a suspect in the Ortiz case," the DOJ concludes, completely illogically. The DOJ team does not even report asking the class instructor whether Fuentes was there during the entire duration of the course, nor does the DOJ report asking when the group photograph was taken.

With a simple trip to the Library of Congress the DOJ could have learned that Fuentes was in all probability in Guatemala, not in Virginia, on October 30, 1989. *Diario Centroamérica,* the official publication of the Guatemalan government, listed Fuentes Aragón as one of the men who received an award from the Guatemalan military in Guatemala on that date. Under Guatemalan army regulations, recipients of awards must appear in person at ceremonies to claim their awards. Either Fuentes disobeyed military regulations, missing a chance to receive a prestigious award, the course in Virginia was over, Fuentes cut out early, or he was home for a long holiday weekend — a four-day weekend, perhaps. According to CIA information, cited in the DOJ report, the course was over; Fuentes attended a month-long course in Virginia that took place in October.

In addition to the former G-2 officer who spoke to my lawyer Anna after the press conference in 1996, another former G-2 collaborator has identified the Guate-man as Fuentes. He worked closely with Fuentes for over a year and a half and identified him on the basis on my sketch.

AFTER EXAMINING the DOJ report, I had to think carefully about the agency's vested interests. In the margin of a declassified memo referring to the delay in the letters rogatory — the formal request by the Guatemalan government that I present my testimony before a U.S. court — a State Department official wrote, "The DOJ sat on this for other reason." The letters rogatory had taken nearly a year and a half to reach me. I had to wonder what "other reason" the Justice Department would have for sitting on the letters rogatory? Did the Department of Justice purposely delay my case in the Guatemalan court so that investigators could claim the trail had grown cold? If Fuentes was working for the DEA (he is listed in Guatemalan army records as the G-2's liaison with the DEA) and if Fuentes was also involved in my torture, it would make sense that the DOJ initially hindered the investigation of my case in Guatemala and investigated so sloppily years later. Since the DEA is part of the DOJ, the DOJ would have had the embarrassing task of investigating one of its own wayward employees.

A FOIA REQUEST I FILED with the DEA in 1996 yielded a twenty-two-page document about a DEA program known as Central American Drug Enforcement (CADENCE). The document, which seems to contain instructions for DEA agents participating in the operation, mentions which captains to contact within D-2 intelligence (their names are blacked out). Several other large sections are blacked out in the document as well. Somewhere my name must be mentioned because that's how declassification works: you get documents with your name on them. But the section with my name must be blacked out.

I HAVE FILED a FOIA request for the appendices to the DOJ report, which contain the photograph of Fuentes. The complete version of the report — including the unredacted interviews of CIA officials and the appendices — is mysteriously missing. The DOJ official in charge of processing FOIA requests says they are "doing a massive search for the report in its entirety." Typically, such a report in its entirety would be sent to the DOJ's executive office, he said. But due to the level of secrecy, he assumed, certain sections of the report were held back. Where, no one knows. He says it is not typical not to be able to find a report. He has interviewed several people, all of whom are "in the dark." He's trying to interview Dan Seikaly.

OFFICIALS CAN STALL AND LIE, but the truth will eventually come out. A few years ago, Paul and I begged the Guatemalan government for the names of the military base commander in Huehuetenango from 1987 through 1989, for the person in charge of the Politécnica in November 1989, for the commander of the military base in Chimaltenango. I now know all those names. All that information is available now from non-profit organizations in the United States, such as the National Security Archives and School of Americas Watch.

IN GUATEMALA, human rights organizations and individuals are attempting to bring to justice the army officers who have massacred and tortured and assassinated so many people. Even though a peace agreement was signed in 1996, the offices of these organizations have been raided, and files and computers related to the lawsuits have been stolen. The Catholic Church compiled a four-volume analysis of the human rights violations during the years of the war and attributed 89.7 percent of the violations to the army and security forces. In April 1998, two days after the report was released, Bishop Juan Gerardi, who had presented it to the public, was bludgeoned to death with a concrete block in his garage. Two high-ranking members of the D-2 were finally convicted. The 360 captured guerrillas secretly imprisoned and tortured were never turned over by the army. Presumably they, like Everardo, were murdered. Meanwhile, assassinations, abductions, and threats continue, and impunity is still virtually guaranteed. In the summer of 2001, an American nun, Bobbie Ford, was shot to death in broad daylight in Guatemala City, where she had gone to purchase supplies for the rural indigenous community she was working with. The Guatemalan government and U.S. embassy attributed the killing to common crime, saying the murderers wanted to steal her truck. But her truck was abandoned a few blocks away, in front of the police headquarters. The death squads are still operating, and the violence against unionists, human rights workers, campesino and youth leaders, educators, religious workers, exhumation teams, political leaders, and academics has reached levels not seen since the 1980s. And now, with the peace talks long over and the world's attention turned away, impunity seems guaranteed.

But I believe that, just as I am obtaining more information about who harmed me, information about the atrocities in Guatemala will surface. It's inevitable. We have the records of which officers served where and when. Some people have reached places of safety where they can speak out. Eventually, Guatemala will be like Argentina. Even if no one is convicted for past crimes, their photographs can be plastered on billboards with the dates and details of what they did, and the names of their victims. And, as in Argentina, those responsible won't dare go out for a cup of coffee for fear of being confronted.

If only we in the United States would hold our officials responsible as well. President Clinton made front-page headlines in 1999 saying, "What we did in Guatemala was wrong." Are a few words all we owe when we created and maintained an army that slaughtered hundreds of thousands? With that sort of impunity, what will keep us from doing it over and over again?

EPILOGUE

DURING THE WEEK OF JUNE 26, 2000, I went with eighteen other survivors of torture to speak with an official of the National Security Council. We calculated that each of us would have about three minutes to tell what had happened to us and what changes we would like to see in U.S. policy.

We were escorted to the pale green room in the Old Executive Office Building. The official spent twenty minutes giving us the architectural history of the room, pointing out details such as the molding around the ceiling.

We shortened our talks accordingly. Survivors from the Philippines, Latin America, East Timor, and various African countries pleaded for an end to the funding and training of torturers. All but one of us had been tortured by security forces that had been trained or funded by the U.S. government.

The official's pen was busy on his notepad as each survivor talked. He appeared to be taking notes.

But he was drawing.

I LOOK FOR ANSWERS, still, in the Bible. I reread the Miracle of the Loaves and Fishes not long ago, just by chance, letting the Bible fall open where it would. I no longer felt angry and confused, as I had in Chicago when the Bible kept opening to that parable.

At last I understood. Jesus asks Phillip how they could feed all the people gathered on the hillside. Phillip is a man who can do the math. He does the calculations and knows exactly how many silver coins feeding the crowd will take. What he has — what they all have together — will never be enough.

Back at Su Casa, when I thought about putting my life back together and asked God for help, I knew it would take a miracle: nothing and no one would ever be able to give me back what I had lost. The same went for the other survivors. And there was nothing I could do to heal Dolores, after her husband died; to bring Raúl's wife, father, or sister back; to make Julio normal again. I couldn't undo their pasts. All I was left with was anger. I could offer a hug, maybe, or a smile. But their lives were changed

474

forever. If those of us at Su Casa had been like Phillip — entirely logical — we might have killed ourselves.

What I had to learn, though, is that math is not enough. You have to take into account the unexpected. As Graham Greene said, "Life is absurd. Therefore, there is always hope."

Jesus accepted what there was: five loaves of bread and two fishes offered by a boy. He didn't complain or despair. He gave thanks to God for them, however insufficient they seemed, and he started passing them out.

Take what you have, in an attitude of thankfulness, and give what you have, in an attitude of faith, and it will be enough. It will be more than enough.

That was what God was trying to tell me in Chicago.

I have forgiven God for not working some dramatic miracle. I've learned that God was working a quiet miracle all along, healing me through other people. I still have the horrible past with me — I carry it in my memory and in my skin and I always will — but laid over it, like new skin over a wound, is a newer past, a past of caring and love.

I still have nightmares sometimes, but every now and then I have a good dream. A couple of years ago I dreamed I was riding in a car with Sister Rita. We were on our way to help someone who was very sick. The road was icy and we were sliding all over. I was talking to the sick person on a cell phone. We were driving toward a mountain that rose up in the distance. "Hold on," I told the person who was sick. "Just hold on. The mountain is beautiful."

As I IMPROVE, I have faith and hope and trust again, on my good days. But even on my good days, the smell of cigarette smoke reminds me of the burns the torturers inflicted on me. The sight of a man in uniform reminds me of the Policeman. I jump if someone runs up behind me, and if someone stands too close or stares at me, I back away. I sleep with the light on. I ask people not to smoke, not to stare, not to talk about torture tactics in front of me, and not to invite me to movies that are violent. Some people, because I make these requests, have accused me of having "an ungodly need to control." That's the way it is, and I imagine that's the way it will always be. I've learned to avoid situations that bring back the pain — on my good days, when I'm feeling assertive.

On my bad days I still say I should have died back in that prison, before I had to be used to inflict pain, before I had to make a choice about another human being's life or death. I still wish I had died.

Not everyone reacts to torture like I did. As my college English teacher has told me, I was a "fragile" person to start with, an artistic type who would write poems on my exams and sit on the hillside writing songs with my guitar. Not everyone is like me.

But no one ever fully recovers — not the one who is tortured, and not the one who tortures. Every time he tortures, the torturer reinforces the idea that we cannot trust one another, and that we cannot trust the world we live in. I'm sure the Policeman doesn't believe in God or in his own goodness.

In Guatemala now, years after the war has ended, torture is accepted as part of society. Many people who have tortured others are working as soldiers and police officers still. And torture continues, although the guerrillas no longer exist. Torture is used to oppress and terrorize people into conforming with the government's agenda. That's the risk of allowing torture to be used, ever, for any reason. It doesn't go away.

As I write this, attorneys and journalists are advocating the legalization of torture in the United States. Over a thousand people are being secretly detained, the majority on visa violations. The damage torture does can never be undone. If I survived for any reason, it is to say that.

According to Amnesty International's statistics for 2001, more than 150 governments engage in torture or ill-treatment. The number in 1999 was 114.

I guess if I were entirely logical, I would despair. But the lessons of my torture didn't stick; I was supposed to have learned that I am powerless, that nothing I say or do can stop the torture. I was supposed to have learned despair. But I can't help hoping. I have faith in the unexpected, the miraculous, the power of people working together and of God working through us. I have to offer all I have and believe and hope it's enough.

And I do.

THE PRESENT Clarissa gave me — my razor blade — made one more appearance with me at a conference. I had been invited to speak at Amnesty International's national annual meeting in Nashville, Tennessee, in April 2001. I showed the audience the razor blade, explaining that I used to carry it with me in my backpack and sleep with it under my pillow because that way, no matter what happened, I would never be captive to anyone again.

"My razor blade is here with me today for the last time," I announced to the audience. "After today, I will give it to a friend who will dispose of it for me. I have dared to begin to trust other people instead of a piece of metal — to trust life instead of death. Looking out at your faces, I know

I will have the strength to go on, because the world will not be the way it's always been, or even the way it is now. It will change because you are in it."

I gave the razor blade to Meredith, and she buried it. I don't even know what city it's in.

I DREAMED the other night, as I often do, about the Woman and the people who were in the pit. They were crying. I didn't know why they were crying. We were in the woods. Light-green buds were on the trees, and I could hear birds singing. I could hear the Woman and the other people who had been in the pit sniffling. They were looking at the base of a tree. I smelled lilacs, and I realized they had them in their hands. They began placing them at the base of a tree, where my razor blade was buried. They were marking the grave. They were weeping with joy because she was no longer with me.

NOTES

Preface

1. Adrienne Rich, "North American Time," in *Adrienne Rich's Poetry and Prose*, Norton Critical Edition, ed. Barbara Charlesworth Gelpi and Albert Gelpi (New York: W. W. Norton, 1993).

Chapter Three: The American

1. *Guatemala Memory of Silence: Report of the Commission of Historical Clarification: Conclusions and Recommendations* (Guatemala City: Litoprint, 1999), 20.

2. As the Commission of Historical Clarification CEH) would note: "The army's perception of Mayan communities as natural allies of the guerrillas contributed to increasing and aggravating the human rights violations perpetrated against them, demonstrating an aggressive racist component of extreme cruelty that led to the extermination, en masse, of defenseless Mayan communities purportedly linked to the guerrillas — including children, women, and the elderly — through methods whose cruelty has outraged the moral conscience of the civilized world. . . . The army destroyed ceremonial centers, sacred places, and cultural symbols. . . . Through the militarization of the communities, . . . the legitimate authority structure of the communities was broken; the use of their own norms and procedures to regulate social life and resolve conflicts was prevented; the exercise of Mayan spirituality and the Catholic religion was obstructed, prevented, or repressed; and the maintenance and development of the indigenous peoples' way of life and their system of social organization was upset" (ibid., 30).

3. F2016, May 1991. This and subsequent references to government documents refer to the identification number on declassified documents available in the National Security Archives or the State Department Reading Room.

4. Mimi and I didn't know that the government's wiretapping capability had increased notably during the Cerezo administration, as the Catholic Church's report, *Guatemala: Never Again*, makes clear. See Recovery of Historical Memory Project, the Official Report of the Human Rights Office, Archdiocese of Guatemala, *Guatemala: Never Again* (Maryknoll, N.Y.: Orbis Books, 1999), 112.

5. *Owensboro Messenger-Inquirer*, December 5, 1989.

Chapter Four: The Rules of the Game

1. *El Gráfico* (Guatemala City), March 14, 1990. The Guatemalan press and U.S. officials misspelled my name for years. State Department and embassy officials had been provided a copy of my passport when I disappeared. My name on my passport was spelled incorrectly, with one *n*. A State Department officer, according to a declassified memo, asked my lawyer Paul Soreff about the discrepancy between the way Paul and I spelled my

---

In the interests of privacy, certain names have been changed.

name and the spelling on my passport. Paul mistakenly told him that the official spelling of my name was with one *n* but that I preferred spelling it with two.

2. The Americas Watch Committee, *Messengers of Death: Human Rights in Guatemala, 11/88–2/90* (March 1990).

3. E1223, January 29, 1989.

4. Ibid.

5. E1126, November 1989.

6. *La Hora* (Guatemala City), November 13, 1989.

7. E1113, November 1989.

8. *El Gráfico* (Guatemala City), March 12, 1990. The article was classified and then declassified by the State Department (E1281).

9. *Los Angeles Times*, April 14, 1990.

10. E400.

11. E1344, April 1990.

Chapter Five: Our Lady of Peace

1. I remember bits and pieces of my conversations with Dr. Snodgrass, but my memory is not exact. Based on his assessments of me, described in the medical records, and based on what I do remember, I have imagined how our conversations might have unfolded.

Conversations with government officials, on the other hand, I have rarely had to imagine. My lawyers took nearly verbatim notes, and the dialogue is constructed from those notes.

Chapter Six: The Second Abduction

1. E1309, March 27, 1990.

2. E1304, March 1990.

Chapter Eight: Breaking Out

1. E1584, September 24, 1990.

2. E1754, November 1990.

3. E1763, November 1990.

4. E1762, November 1990.

5. E1658, November 1990.

6. E2953, January 1991.

7. E1883A.

8. E1933, March 8, 1991.

Chapter Nine: Su Casa

1. E1294, March 19, 1990.

2. *Prime Time Live*, June 6, 1991.

Chapter Ten: Back to the Garden

1. *Siglo Veintiuno* (Guatemala City), April 3, 1992, and *Pensa Libre* (Guatemala City), March 14, 1992.

2. Reuters, March 10, 1992. Also E2455A.

3. E2401, February 1992.

4. E2872, March 1992.
5. E2153, April 13, 1992.
6. *New York Times*, April 9, 1992.

Chapter Eleven: The Embassy's Cross

1. E2507, April 1992.
2. *CNN Presents* interview with Thomas Stroock, Caspar, Wyoming, August 8, 1996.
3. E2513, April 3, 1992.
4. E2516, May 1992.
5. E2517, May 1992.
6. E2524, May 1992.
7. E2536, June 1992.
8. E2772A, June 1992.
9. E2536, June 1992.
10. E2596.
11. E2576, July 1992.

Chapter Twelve: Into the Otherworld

1. E2648.
2. *Siglo Veintiuno* (Guatemala City), March 22, 1993.
3. State Department document E3290, May 21, 1993.

Chapter Thirteen: A Leave of Absence

1. E3228, May 1993.
2. *Siglo Veintiuno* (Guatemala City), January 27, 1994.
3. A former G-2 collaborator who I interviewed told me the stairs leading down to the basement from the garage at the Brigada de Honor are not visible; the entrance is hidden in the back wall of a shed where tools to repair cars are kept. One must walk fully into this closet or shed to see the metal door. Behind the door are the stairs down. I asked him what the stairs were like. He remembered a landing in the middle of the stairwell, just as I did. I asked him what the hallway floor was like. He remembered the details just as I had: the floor was made of cement and was smooth at first and became rough as one went farther down the long hallway. He remembered a humid smell. He counted four rooms, all with closed doors, and a fifth room, which contained munitions and bunk beds. He added that in 1989 people were definitely detained as prisoners and interrogated in the Politécnica.

   The basement has two entrances, he said: the long hallway I remember is actually a tunnel connecting the Brigada de Honor and the Politécnica. One stairwell leads down from in a garage at the Brigada de Honor. Another stairwell leads up to the Politécnica. The former G-2 person I interviewed had entered the basement from the garage at the Brigada de Honor. The garage matches the description of the garage I gave. As he described it, it has a high ceiling and holds fifteen to twenty cars. Carmen Valenzuela, who was detained in the Politécnica/Brigada de Honor complex in 1990, was kept for a short time in a garage and describes it the same way.

   A different former G-2 agent interviewed by a friend in 1995 said my description of where I was tortured reminded him of the Politécnica. He, too, mentioned a "hidden door" leading to the place where those tortured were kept. He also mentioned the room where munitions were stored, and he specified that the floor was rough.

Chapter Fourteen: Everardo

1. Angela delli Sante, *Nightmare or Reality: Guatemala in the 1980s* (Amsterdam: Thela Publishers, 1996), 118–19.

Chapter Fifteen: Starving Next to the Palace

1. Cuestas was helpful to me, even though I found the meeting with him excruciating. He said the evidence that I had been abducted and tortured was very strong, and the problem with my case was that there had been a lack of political will on the part of the military to investigate thoroughly and determine whether military personnel were involved.
2. DOS 002557, November 30, 1994.

Chapter Sixteen: Torn Secrets, Torn Skin

1. *Washington Post,* March 30, 1995.
2. *New York Times,* April 2, 1995.
3. E5755.
4. Cited in Dennis Bernstein, *San Francisco Bay Guardian,* August 1991.
5. Noam Chomsky, *Z Magazine* (March 1992): 9; based on an interview given by Gramajo to the *Harvard International Review.*
6. 003515, R1119372, April 1994.
7. E2305, November 1991.
8. *The Nation,* April 17, 1995.
9. *Miami Herald,* April 30, 1995.
10. *The Nation,* June 5, 1995.
11. E2489.
12. CIA document Z-055.
13. *Washington Post,* June 22, 1995.
14. *New York Times,* July 26, 1995.
15. *Boston Globe,* July 27, 1995.
16. *New York Times,* August 21, 1995.
17. CIA document 000167.
18. E3610.
19. P 2006472, January 1990.
20. Allan Nairn, in *The Nation,* May 29, 1995.

Chapter Eighteen: The Vigil

1. Frank Smyth, *Washington Post,* May 12, 1996.
2. Jeanne Boylan, *Portraits of Guilt* (New York: Pocket Books, 2000), 275.

Chapter Nineteen: Whitewash

1. E1053, November 1989.
2. E1003.
3. E1017.
4. E2132A.
5. E1875.
6. Frank left out Roland's full title in the introductions: Major Roland de Marcellus.
7. Unnumbered CIA draft document.
8. *Time,* May 20, 1996, 33.

Chapter Twenty-One: Walking Out through the Third Door

1. Intelligence Oversight Board, *Report on the Guatemala Review* (June 28, 1996), 44.
2. Ibid., 4.
3. Ibid., 44.
4. Defense Intelligence Agency document, February 1990.
5. IOB, *Report on the Guatemala Review*, 21–22.
6. Z077, May 1993.
7. The intelligence reports referring to Alpírez's involvement in Michael DeVine's murder are explained in the text of this chapter. General Edgar Godoy Gaítan, a former G-2 chief who was on the CIA payroll, has been accused in court by Myrna Mack's family of being one of the intellectual authors of her murder. The CIA reported the D-2's involvement in Maritza Urrutia's abduction, according to the IOB report (34).
8. IOB, *Report on the Guatemala Review*, 7.
9. CIA document Z-114, November 1994.
10. Conversation between Patricia Davis and Frank Fountain, June 2001.
11. 000167, March 18, 1992.

Chapter Twenty-Two: The Length of the Light

1. *Prensa Libre* (Guatemala City), September 12, 1996.
2. *Noticias de Guatemala* (Guatemala City), August 13, 1996.
3. Scott Farris, "Puzzle of Nun's Ordeal Missing," *Wyoming Catholic Register*, November 15, 1996, 11–12.
4. E2132A.
5. E9738.
6. E2016, May 1991.
7. Jim O'Connell, article in the *Atlanta Constitution*, February 11, 1997.
8. E114.
9. *Siglo Veintiuno* (Guatemala City), July 21, 1994.
10. Those interviewed should have included the following:

> S-2 officer in Military Zone 19 (Huehuetenango) between June 1986 and June 1988: Ángel Leonel Estuardez Baidez Paz. He was then transferred to Military Zone 302, in Chimaltenango, where he was an S-3 officer (in charge of operations)
>
> Commanding officer in charge of Military Zone 302, Chimaltenango: José Luis Quilo Ayuso
>
> San Miguel civil patrol chief in 1989: Miguel Pascual Head of military commissioners in San Miguel 1989: Jesús Alonzo
>
> Chief of the Estado Mayor Presidencial from March 1, 1988, to January 14, 1991: Edgar Augusto Godoy Gaitán
>
> D-2 director, June 26, 1987, to April 30, 1990: Luis Francisco Ortega Menaldo
>
> Base commander of Military Zone 19 (Huehuetenango) between January 1988 and January 1989: Julio César Ruano
>
> Base commander of Military Zone 19 (Huehuetenango) until May 1990: Enrique Roberto Mata Gálvez
>
> Head of Brigada de Honor from July 1987 until at least October 1989: Juan José Marroquín
>
> Head of Politécnica from January 1988 to January 1990: Mario René Enríquez Morales

Head of Archivo from January 1989 to January 1991: Juan Valencia Osorio
Guillermo Federico Fuentes Aragón, along with Edgar Alfredo Trujillo Salguero and
    Edgar Ricardo Bustamante Figueroa, who both worked with the D-2 in 1989,
    reportedly in contraintelligence, like Fuentes and reportedly were involved in
    planning and ordering my abduction and torture.

11. Central Intelligence Agency, *Allegations of Connections between the CIA and the Contras in Cocaine Trafficking to the United States,* volume 2: *The Contra Story* (96-0143-IG). Randy Kapasar is referred to on 1031 and 1063.

12. Inter-American Commission on Human Rights, *Annual Report of the Organization of American States* (Washington, D.C., 1997), report number 31/96.